ISAIAH II
יֶשַׁעְיָה ב

AUGUST PIEPER

Translator, ERWIN E. KOWALKE

An Exposition of Isaiah 40-66

NORTHWESTERN PUBLISHING HOUSE
Milwaukee, Wisconsin

This translation was carried out
under the auspices of
the Commission on Christian Literature,
Wisconsin Evangelical Lutheran Synod

Library of Congress Catalog Card Number 79-87532
Northwestern Publishing House
3624 W. North Ave., Milwaukee, Wis. 53208
©1979 by Northwestern Publishing House. All rights reserved
Published 1979
Printed in the United States of America

ISBN 0-8100-0109-8

CONTENTS

TRANSLATOR'S FOREWORD

This translation of Professor August Pieper's *Isaiah II* was undertaken at the instance of the Commission on Christian Literature of the Wisconsin Evangelical Lutheran Synod.

Even in 1919, when Professor Pieper's commentary was published, the dominance of German as the language of the pulpit and of the college and seminary classrooms of our Synod was coming to an end. German was fast becoming a foreign language in the homes from which our students came. The transition from German to English would have become complete even if there had been no World War I, although the change would, in that case, have proceeded at a slower pace.

In the years that *Isaiah II* was in the making, Professor Pieper could not have foreseen that his book would have few purchasers, and be read by even fewer, simply because it was written in German. Forty years after its publication this valuable contribution to the understanding of the Gospel of the Servant of the Lord lay almost forgotten on the shelves of the few who owned a copy. If the book were to be saved from oblivion, a translation had to be made.

Isaiah II is a compendium of the Gospel of Salvation. The author ranges over the Old and the New Testaments, from Genesis to the Revelation of St. John, and shows how God's plan of salvation dominates all of history, not only the history of Israel, but the history of all mankind. Professor Pieper testifies to the inestimable benefit to his own knowledge of the Gospel that he derived from the study of this Evangelist of the Old Testament. I can with all my heart second that statement. The translation was merely a matter of walking a path that the author had hewn and leveled through a forest of difficulties, but the effect of the prophet's inspired preaching has been the same. The reader of *Isaiah II* who makes a study of the book cannot fail to have his understanding of the Gospel enriched, his faith strengthened, and his joy greatly increased in the salvation prepared for him through God's chosen Servant, Christ our Lord.

The grammar to which reference is made is the Second English Edition of Gesenius' *Hebrew Grammar* as edited and enlarged by the late E. Kautzsch and translated by A. E. Cowley, 1910, published by the Oxford Press.

I feel deeply indebted to Mrs. Werner Franzmann, Mrs. Carl Lawrenz, and Mrs. Terrance Ganyo, who relieved me of much of the chore of preparing copies of my manuscript for the printer and for the seminary library. Thanks are also due to Professor Heinrich Vogel, Professor Wilbert Gawrisch, and Pastor Harold Wicke for reading the manuscript and suggesting changes and corrections.

In conclusion, I express the hope that this translation will be of some help in bringing to the readers of Professor Pieper's *Isaiah II* that blessing which he had hoped to share with them.

Erwin E. Kowalke

Watertown, Wisconsin, August 26, 1970.

ABOUT THE AUTHOR

When this volume first appeared in 1919 in the original German of *Jesaias II*, it was introduced to the readers by such scholarly reviewers as Ludwig Fuehrbringer in *Lehre und Wehre* and J. Michael Reu in *Kirchliche Zeitschrift*. They pointed to and praised the exegetical excellence of the commentary. In some technical issues they disagreed, but they appreciated the Gospel message and tone and the skilled treatment of Chapters 40-66 of the Hebrew prophet of prophets.

The writer of this introduction brings no such scholarly qualifications to his assignment. It is a mere accident of chronology that makes him suitable for this writing task. Back in the school year 1939-40 he was a member of the last Wisconsin Lutheran Seminary class to hear Professor August Pieper lecture on Isaiah II. As such he regards it a privilege and a labor of love to introduce the English version of *Jesaias II* to a new generation of Wisconsin Lutheran Seminary graduates and students and in the process to pay tribute to the author.

Professor August Pieper was born on September 24, 1857, in Carwitz, Pomerania, the fifth son in a family of six sons and two daughters. Four of the sons became Synodical Conference pastors. Reinhold went from Wisconsin Synod pastorates in Wrightstown and Manitowoc to head the Missouri Synod's Concordia Seminary, Springfield, from 1891 to 1914. Franz, who also served the Manitowoc congregation, became Dr. Walther's successor as head of Concordia Seminary, St. Louis, in 1887 and from 1899 to 1911 was also Synodical President. Anton was a Wisconsin Synod pastor, serving most of his years at Newton.

In an autobiographical sketch preserved in the vertical file of the Wisconsin Lutheran Seminary library, August Pieper refers to his "unionistic father" and his "strictly Lutheran mother," Bertha nee Lohff. It was the mother who brought her four younger sons to America in 1870 to join Reinhold and a brother who had crossed the ocean earlier. She settled in Watertown because a relative, Julius Voss, was teaching there and became stewardess at Northwestern College where the four ministerial students did their pre-seminary studying.

Because the Wisconsin Synod transferred its seminary program to St. Louis during the years 1870-1878, August Pieper studied there after his Northwestern graduation in 1876. How much he enjoyed his Concordia years is evident from his unwillingness to transfer to his Synod's Milwaukee seminary when the opportunity came. When President Bading asked him to do this, the seminarian, as he himself tells it, replied, "For two years I have studied under Walther and his colleagues, Schaller, Guenther, Lange, Brohm, each one a model in his particular field, and now my brother Franz. I should trade all this for a few teachers and leaders of whom I know nothing? You cannot ask this of me."

That this decision was motivated by genuine liking for studies and teachers and not by any disloyalty to his own Synod is clearly indicated by August Pieper's reaction when Dr. Walther asked him through his brother Franz whether he too would accept a call into the Missouri Synod. "I let him know," August writes, "that in the past God through my mother had led me into the Wisconsin Synod. I therefore felt an obligation to show my gratitude to this Synod to serve it." He accepted assignment to the Kewaunee congregation.

Several episodes of the Concordia years are highlighted in the autobiographical sketch previously mentioned. After pitching on a hot St. Louis afternoon, August drank some rainwater and became very ill with typhoid fever. Near death he barely heard the kneeling Professor Schaller say, "Be of good cheer. You shall not die, but live, and declare the works of the Lord." From that moment on he began to improve.

An assignment fondly recalled was reading proof for Dr. Walther when his edition of Baier's *Compendium Theologiae Positivae* was being readied for publication. The task was to check the correctness of the Latin, Greek and Hebrew quotations. Describing this exacting "but very gratifying" work, August Pieper comments, "I owed my knowledge of Hebrew to Dr. Notz in Watertown; he had spared no effort to give me a thorough understanding of this language."

August Pieper served as a Wisconsin Synod pastor for twenty-two years. The Kewaunee years were 1879-1885. Then came six years at Menomonie, Wisconsin, interrupted by a Texas visit to recuperate from a throat ailment. In 1891 the call to St. Marcus of Milwaukee came. He remained there until he assumed a seminary professorship in 1902. At this post he remained a pastor at heart, as all who heard his Pastoral Theology lectures will testify. An energetic and faithful minister in all respects, August Pieper distinguished himself as an effective preacher, frequently as *Festprediger* at special services. Long after the event, he could recall preaching at the special Synod meeting in 1894, called to cope with problems created by the Watertown fire, and using Isaiah 27:6-9 to encourage disheartened Synod members in the rebuilding task.

The pulpit power remained to the end. At what may have been his last festival speaking assignment, a campus Christmas gathering in 1938 or 1939, Professor Pieper presented an exposition of Psalm 2 that lives in memory after forty years. For those who heard that address, Advent and Christmas took on new meaning and retained it ever after. On another less formal but sadder occasion, the class period that immediately followed the sudden death of a colleague, Professor F. Brenner, August Pieper put aside the assigned task, opened his Hebrew Bible to Psalm 90 and supplied a commentary that must rank with the most effective funeral addresses ever delivered.

As is to be expected in the circumstances, Professor Pieper was frequently assigned the task of presenting doctrinal essays at local conferences, District meetings, and Synod conventions. Numerous instances could be cited. One that stands out, however, is the Western Wisconsin District essay titled *Gottes Zorngericht ueber die Gottlosen nach Roem. 1:18-32* and subsequently distributed throughout the Synod in pamphlet form.

Practical and concerned churchman that he was, Prof. Pieper added to his ringing application of an old message to the contemporary situation a discourse on obduracy, then a burning subject of discussion in the District he was addressing. Prof. Pieper was no "ivory tower" theologian. He showed his concern for everything that concerned his church body, working energetically for Wisconsin Lutheran High School, Children's Friend Society and other similar endeavors. His theology was truly a *habitus practicus*.

Evidence of Professor Pieper's theological and literary abilities abounds in the *Quartalschrift,* the *Wisconsin Lutheran Quarterly* of his day, which he helped inaugurate in 1904. Worthy of special mention is the lengthy *Die Herrlichkeit des Herrn* appearing in Volumes XXIX-XXX and subsequently translated for English publication. This writer's favorite is *Jubilaeumsgedanken,* an extended discussion of the Synodical Conference's golden anniversary appearing in Volumes XX and XXI.

No discussion of Professor Pieper as theologian would be complete without reference to his leadership role in clarifying the Wisconsin Synod's position on church and ministry. "*Meine Amtslehre,*" Professor Pieper would flatly declare and Professor J. P.

Koehler, a colleague, also in this endeavor, writes in his *History of the Wisconsin Synod,* "I can now appreciate Pieper's expression '*meine Amtslehre.*' At the time it was used Schaller was no longer with us and Pieper's articles cover the whole subject in minute detail and provide Synod's source material for the study of the discussion."

The Pieper articles on church and ministry, to which Professor Koehler refers, include: *Menschenherrschaft in der Kirche* in Volume VIII of the *Quartalschrift,* a rebuttal to objectors titled *Die Suspension noch einmal* also in Volume VII, an article on Walther's book *Die Stimme unserer Kirche in der Frage von Kirche und Amt* in Volume IX, a discussion of the marks of the Church titled *Die Lehre von der Kirche und ihren Kennzeichen in Anwendung auf die Synode* in Volume IX, and finally in Volume X an offering aptly titled *Abschluss der Diskussion ueber die Lehren von der Kirche.*

These articles, as Professor Koehler generously acknowledges, are the "source material" for the study of the discussion of church and ministry within our church body and in Synodical Conference circles. Koehler's penetrating exegesis played a large part in laying the foundation and charting the course, but it was Pieper's writing that influenced the church body in appreciating new insights into the Bible's teaching on church and ministry. Together the two, with Professor J. Schaller's help, bequeathed the Wisconsin Synod this outstanding gift of the Wauwatosa Gospel.

Those who heard August Pieper's lectures on Isaiah, and that includes almost two generations of pastors, will think of him first of all as a teacher in the classroom rather than as a churchman or writer. The scholarship he brought to the classroom task is in ample evidence on every page of the Isaiah commentary. Professor Pieper was an effective teacher because, for one thing, he mastered his subject material, using for the task all those gifts a generous Lord had granted.

Professor Pieper, however, was much more than a scholarly teacher. He possessed and demonstrated the ability of getting to his students, motivating them, even inspiring them. Involved was an initiatory humbling experience. Class after class entering the Seminary and the Professor's classroom would soon find themselves wondering how they could ever qualify as candidates for the ministry. In not too long a time, under the Professor's guidance, they would find themselves eagerly looking forward to the day when they could preach the Gospel. Even the bleak prospect of a two-year wait for assignment in the 1930's could not dim that enthusiasm and desire.

By 1940 Professor Pieper was obviously long past the peak of his ability as a teacher. Memory was playing tricks. Diversion from the point at hand came easy. Even then, however, the old powers could be roused. The piercing eyes flashed anger at inept reading or translating of an Isaiah passage. The ringing *naḥamū naḥamū ʿammī* became more than a phrase to render in German; it sounded out like an imperative for Gospel ministry.

Professor Pieper's outstanding teaching effectiveness is best demonstrated by his ability to make *Encyclopaedie und Methodologie der Theologie* an unforgettable classroom experience. When his former students discuss the Professor, they invariably exchange recollections of bits and pieces from this lowliest of theological courses. In Professor Pieper's hands it became a true foundation course.

Professor Pieper would regard with contempt erroneous efforts in our day to read into his title, *Jesaias II*, evidence of an avantgarde historical-critical espousal of the view that more than one Isaiah wrote the book. A glance at the last section of his introduction is enough to indicate what his stand on Isaiah authorship was. His title simply says that he chose to treat in his commentary only the last twenty-seven chapters of the book.

Actually a companion commentary on *Isaiah I* was originally envisioned. As Dr. Fuerbringer recounts in his *Lutheraner* obituary of his old friend, "His Isaiah commentary was actually supposed to be a joint work with Stoeckhardt, as I learned from what both related. Stoeckhardt intended to treat the first section of the book, Chapters 1-39, and Pieper the second section. Unfortunately Stoeckhardt could not carry out his intention because of other tasks and other exegetical works and only published a short commentary on the first twelve chapters."

What would August Pieper say about an English translation of his commentary? For one thing, he recognized the necessity of English preaching and teaching and writing for a Lutheran church body in our land and century. On the other hand, Professor Pieper would not have accepted the English version of *Jesaias II* without some strong objections. He would question why pastors would need a translation. It was his firm conviction that any Lutheran pastor and any Lutheran seminary student, to be worthy of

11

the name, would have to have a reading knowledge of the language of Luther.

If practical realities, however, dictate the need for English theological works, then it is a cause for rejoicing that the long labor of bringing out *Jesaias II* in English has now been completed. Much of the force and flavor of Pieper's picturesque style will have been lost on the way, but the all-important Gospel message of the great Old Testament prophet and the Gospel insights of this great commentator will be transmitted to a new generation of Wisconsin Synod pastors and to many generations to come. Thereby their preaching and teaching and believing will be fortified. Professor Pieper would desire no better outcome. God grant it!

Prof. E. C. Fredrich
Wisconsin Lutheran Seminary
Mequon, Wisconsin

ABOUT THE TRANSLATOR

Probably the nearest Prof. Kowalke came to writing an autobiography was in his WELS history, *You and Your Synod*, published in 1961. In the section devoted to Northwestern College, he told the story of a typical student whom he called John. But he drew on events from his own early life and on traits of his own character to compose the sketch of this fictional boy. Between the lines we are really reading the biography of young Erwin Ernst Kowalke, familiarly called EEK by schoolmates and later by family, colleagues, friends and students. The quoted passages in the next three paragraphs apply as much to Erwin as they do to "John."

Born August, 31, 1887, Erwin was the youngest son in a family of six — four boys and two girls ("John was the youngest in a family of five"). His parents, Ferdinand and Sophia Kowalke, were God-fearing people who had "always wished that one of their sons might enter the service of the church." They were happy to see how readily their youngest son "took to his books as he grew up." He could "spend hours, forgetful of all else, absorbed in an interesting tale." Yet he was a normal boy who "loved fishing, skating, swimming and games of all sorts."

His parents, "by their Christian example, by their reverent attitude toward the Bible, and by the way they always spoke of their own minister, made the office of the ministry seem a sacred thing" in their son's eyes. With such a background, it comes as no surprise that Erwin looked forward to the day in September, 1903, when he "was at last on his way to Watertown to begin a new chapter in his life" by entering the junior class in the Northwestern Preparatory School.

Like his fictional counterpart, Erwin was one of those boys who found almost everything at Northwestern to his liking — the studies, the games, dorm life, the companionship of fellow students, the religious spirit, the discipline, and even the meals, which were "not greatly different from those he had been accustomed to at home, where economy had been a necessity and luxuries appeared only at intervals." The habit of frugality he acquired in the home of his parents — his father was a railroad employee — stayed with him for the rest of his life.

Erwin Kowalke's first love for Northwestern grew as his career became more and more closely linked with the institution. During his five years in the preparatory department and in college, he was a leader among students, distinguishing himself in the classroom and on the athletic field, where he was a star player on both baseball and football teams. After the football season of 1907, a fellow student, writing in *The Black and Red*, the college magazine, commented enthusiastically: "Kowalke was the greatest fullback in the state, a player of remarkable speed and endurance. He has the distinction of not having taken out one minute of time during the four years he participated in collegiate football. He was coach of the team, too."

Graduating in 1908, Kowalke spent the next three years in the study of theology at the Wisconsin Lutheran Seminary, then situated in Wauwatosa. His first pastoral assignment took him to Tomahawk, Wisconsin, where he served a year and a half before receiving a call to his Alma Mater in January, 1913. At Northwestern he taught English and gymnastics and coached all athletic teams.

The following year he also took over the college classes in Hebrew, after a summer of study in that language at the University of Chicago. For the next fifty-three years he trained numerous generations of future pastors in the basics of Hebrew and laid the groundwork for their Old Testament studies at the Seminary under his former mentor, Prof. August Pieper, and Pieper's successors. The present translation of Pieper's German commentary on Isaiah II may be considered Kowalke's crowning achievement in the field of Hebrew and Old Testament.

When President August F. Ernst resigned in 1919, Erwin Kowalke was unanimously chosen to be the fourth president of Northwestern by the Board of Control. In addition to his courses in Hebrew and English, Kowalke now also taught the important senior course in religion. More than any other man he helped to shape the character of those who graduated from Northwestern over the next four decades. In 1959 he resigned from the presidency but continued to teach for another seven years until finally at the end of the second semester in 1966, he entered this brief item in his diary: "Today I met my last class." He often said that in his day he had taught almost every subject offered at Northwestern and sometimes carried a teaching load of thirty hours a week.

During his tenure as president, Northwestern greatly reduced the teaching hours of college professors; added an extra year to the college curriculum, making it a full-fledged college; made the difficult transition from German to English as the medium of instruction in history and the classical languages; weathered the depression of the 1930s and the war years of the 1940s; and witnessed the inauguration of a great building program that changed the physical appearance of its campus.

But Prof. Kowalke's influence reached beyond the Northwestern community. In countless essays that he gave before Synod and District conventions and pastoral conferences, and in his annual commencement addresses, he never tired of defending the traditional classical curriculum of Northwestern and strengthening the confessional stand of the Synod. For many years he also wrote editorials for *The Northwestern Lutheran*.

After Prof. Kowalke retired from the presidency, he devoted much of his spare time to two works for which he may be remembered longest: the history of his Alma Mater, *Centennial Story*, and the translation of Prof. Pieper's *Jesaias II. Centennial Story*, the 320 page history of Northwestern, was commissioned by the College Alumni Society and completed in time for the celebration of the college centennial in 1965. Based on careful research of all available records and documents, it is a definitive work, as interesting as it is authoritative and comprehensive. A reviewer in *The Milwaukee Journal* called it "an inspiring and uplifting story. . . . Any reader, regardless of creed, could gain a surge of spirit by this saga of a vital institution."

Even more impressive is the translation of Pieper's massive opus on Isaiah II. In restoring this "buried treasure," Kowalke was also reaffirming his faith in Pieper's staunchly Lutheran approach to Scripture. He caught the tone and spirit of the German original and in effect recreated the commentary for the benefit of his church and its theological students and pastors.

Erwin Kowalke passed away on April 30, 1973, at the age of 85. In his obituary in *The Black and Red*, a student, James Witt, paid him this tribute as a teacher: "He was an impressive classroom figure, widely read, scholarly, virile . . . getting faithful work and respect from his students without asserting his authority. . . . In his teaching he tried to impart a Christian philosophy and a set of values which reflected his own personal moderation, self-sacrifice and sobriety."

The afore-mentioned traits of "moderation" and "sobriety" gave some students the impression that Prof. Kowalke was aloof. Actually, to those who knew him he was warm-hearted and companiable. He loved children, though he had none of his own, and was deeply concerned about his students. He relished good conversa-

15

tion and once remarked that he considered no committee meeting a complete success unless he brought back from it a good story to tell his friends. This side of his character is revealed in a series of delightfully chatty letters he wrote to Prof. E. H. Wendland, missionary in Zambia, Africa, at the time. Excerpts from the letters are quoted in the chapter titled "E.E.K." in Wendland's booklet *Dear Mister Missionary.*

EEK's hobbies were golf and flower gardening. In the latter he was ably assisted by his wife, the former Miss Gertrude Deebach of St. Paul, whom he married in 1919. She was able to keep their garden at the peak of its summer splendor for several years after his death.

Erwin Kowalke's first love for Northwestern, dating from the time he enrolled in the prep school back in 1903, remained one of the dominant motivations of his career. In 1939 he received a call to be professor at the Seminary, but returned it. Life could afford him no greater privilege than to head a school that transformed boys like his fictional John into educated Christian men. Northwestern laid the foundation for what to him was the highest of vocations: preaching the Gospel of Jesus Christ.

Prof. em. Elmer C. Kiessling
Watertown, Wisconsin

FOREWORD

The following volume is a summation of my exegetical work at Wisconsin Lutheran Theological Seminary. Its appearance is due to wishes expressed by a number of my students and by certain pastors who had heard me preach on texts from Isaiah. A heavy teaching schedule and a consciousness of not being equal to the task would have prevented a decision to publish the work if the requests had not become more numerous and urgent. It was noted that a commentary on Isaiah such as our pastors needed did not exist, with the exception of the commentary by Stoeckhardt on Isaiah 1-12. When I finally decided to publish the work, I first published a prospectus of the book in the *Quartalschrift* (now *Wisconsin Lutheran Quarterly*) and appealed for subscriptions. I wished, for one thing, to learn how much interest in Isaiah there might be in the Synodical Conference, and for another, I hoped to be able to protect our Northwestern Publishing House from suffering a possible financial loss. Certain circumstances, of which no further mention shall be made, made it impossible for me to reach the attention of the pastors of the Synodical Conference through any church publications other than our own *Quartalschrift*, which had comparatively few readers; and I did not feel called upon to make any special effort to have my appeal accepted by other church organs, much less to approach other synods. Nevertheless, the Northwestern Publishing House decided to proceed with publication of the book on the basis of the 300 subscriptions received.

The outbreak of World War I caused such difficulties at our Publishing House, particularly in the matter of setting the Hebrew type, that it seemed that the project would have to be abandoned. Then the Synod decided to assume all costs of publication and to make the book its own. Outside help in setting the Hebrew type had so often disappointed us that we despaired of finding help in that area. When the Publishing House turned to the students at the Seminary for help, a number of them responded and did the work with such industry and skill that it was possible to complete the book in its present form. Many delays and the tremendously increased costs of publication in the meantime made it impossible to offer the book at the advertised price, and it was decided to release subscribers from any obligation to purchase the book. If we nevertheless hope that in the course of time the volume will find its way not only into the hands of the original subscribers, but also into the studies of many other pastors, it is because we assume that it will meet the needs of Lutheran pastors in our country for a reliable commentary on Isaiah.

For the circle of readers whom this book hopes to reach, it is not necessary to dwell on the unique importance of Isaiah, particularly of the second part of his prophecy, in the revelation of God's plan of salvation. The prophet is known to all of us as the "Evangelist of the Old Testament." Isaiah is the evangelical heart of the Old Testament. All the Old Testament writings put together do not reveal to us Christ and the New Testament economy and salvation with such clarity, depth, and fullness as does Isaiah. By way of proof, one needs but to turn to chapters 4, 7, 9, 11, 12, 25, 26, 28, 32 and 35 in the first part; and 40, 42, 49, 50, 53, 55, 61, 62 and 63 in the second part. No writer in the Old Testament is so stirred in spirit by the promise of salvation; none preaches it in such heart-warming language. No one so captivates the heart of the reader seeking salvation, no one teaches and comforts like Isaiah. There is no book in the Old Testament to which one who is familiar with the New Testament so gladly turns, or from which he gathers for himself more benefit, more satisfaction, and more joy of salvation. The glorious hymn of Isaiah II can bring warmth to a heart that has grown cold and lifeless, and can cause it to glow with new enthusiasm for the Gospel of our salvation in Christ. The author of this commentary has gained inestimable profit for his understanding of the Gospel through his study of Isaiah, and has won from it priceless joy of salvation. This book has no other purpose than to offer in a modest way a like strengthening of faith to those who know even less Hebrew than the author and have even less time than he. Through this work I should wish also to serve the Christian people of our church through those who have been called to preach the Gospel to them.

Regarding the confessional point of view from which this book was written, I have expressed myself in the Introduction. While the publication was being delayed, I carefully worked over the manuscript in order to present to my readers the very best of which I am capable. But I am still so conscious of its defects, particularly in the form of presentation, that I should be willing, even today, to jettison it, if that were still possible. However, the work is now finished. May it go forth and see if it can be of some use here and there! Students of Hebrew will find that the book linguistically takes into account all the latest findings of Hebrew scholarship.

I must not neglect to mention that three commentaries have

been especially important to me for an understanding of the prophet: those of Vitringa, Delitzsch, and Drechsler-Hahn. I was familiar with Delitzsch from my student days. As a pastor, I learned to know Vitringa, at first in a German translation and abridgement by Buesching, and then in the Latin original in two large folio volumes graciously presented to me by an old friend, Pastor Ad. Baebenroth of Milwaukee. I learned to know Drechsler-Hahn through Stoeckhardt. Of all other commentaries, from Gesenius (1821) to Duhm (1902) and Marti (1900); from Lowth (1778) to Cheyne (1884, 1894, 1898), Whitehouse (1905), and Box (1908), of which I have consulted dozens in the course of my seventeen years of teaching at our Seminary, none has as appreciably influenced my understanding of the prophet as did the three mentioned at the beginning of this paragraph. Two smaller works have at times served me well, and I should like to call the attention of my readers to them. One of them is Franz Delitzsch's *Schlussbemerkungen* to Hahn's *Commentary on Isaiah II.* The other is Samuel Driver's *Isaiah, his Life and Times, and the Writings which bear his Name* in the "Men of the Bible" series, 2nd edition, 1893, a valuable series which must, however, be read very critically.

When one takes into consideration the stage at which research in the Hebrew language and history had arrived in the early eighteenth century, Vitringa has not been equaled by any of the later commentators for learning, for sound, systematic, thorough treatment and clear arrangement of his material. Unfortunately, his work suffers from allegorizing and from the tendency of his time and his church to interpret the individual prophecies as referring to specific incidents in the New Testament. Delitzsch holds the position of supreme authority on the Hebrew language and related dialects, on the Old Testament, on Biblical archeology and Rabbinic lore. His philological thoroughness, his fine sense of feeling for the many peculiarities of the Hebrew idiom, the grandeur of his grasp of all situations, and above all his deep and sincere Christian feeling, without which no prophet can be understood, place him in a class by himself, even above Cheyne, the greatest of the English Hebrew scholars. The naturalistic exegetes of modern times must still reckon with Delitzsch. And so, it is natural that I worked with Delitzsch ever before me and, whenever necessary, came to terms with him. The beauty about Hahn (Drechsler-Hahn) is his unaffected, cheerful confession of Christian faith, which in no way detracts from his philological soundness. But he also gives voice to many an odd fancy.

I felt that I could spare myself the trouble of preparing a bibliography of Isaiah commentaries, since bibliographies on this subject are readily available.

A few words about the arrangement of this book might not be superfluous. In the exegesis itself I sought to establish the meaning of each verse on the basis of its grammatical construction and to follow the line of thought through to the end without deviation. I spared no pains in the effort to discover at the end of each smaller and larger section the true content, the controlling point of view, and the goal toward which each part of the discourse was moving. Accordingly, each separate portion has been supplied with a summary of contents which shows its logical connection with the next larger portion. The contents of the separate sections and discourses and their relation to each other determined the superscriptions of the discourses and chapters; from these the headings of the separate triads were determined, and finally the headings of the three large divisions of the prophecy. These headings will, I hope, enable the reader to follow the development of the thought and to apprehend the general point of view of each part and of the whole book. The structure of Isaiah II demands such a procedure; and the writer who neglects to follow it does not do justice to the book or to his readers. For an easier overall view of the contents, I have added a separate table of contents.

A feature that is peculiar to this commentary is the printing of the Hebrew text at the head of the discussion of each verse. I am not aware that any commentary before this one has followed that plan. I have always found it to be annoying not to have the Hebrew text conveniently before me, and continually to be forced to turn to the Bible which lay to one side. This unique arrangement might be a welcome suggestion to others. I did not feel it necessary to reproduce in the Hebrew text the full Masoretic interpunctuation, for that would have further retarded the setting of type and increased the cost. If the pointing appears to be essential for the interpretation of the text, reference must be had to the Hebrew Bible. Only Silluq with Soph Pasuq and Athnach have been retained. The text is that of the Kittel Bible. In general, Kittel's divisions into poetic lines have been followed, even where they seem to have been in error.[1]

My original manuscript was so replete with Hebrew words that

---

1. In the English translation the Kittel text is used by permission of the publisher, the Wuerttembergische Bibelanstalt of Stuttgart, Germany, and includes the Masoretic punctuation.

the publishers declared that the cost of printing would be prohibitive. So, *nolens volens*, I had to resort to transliteration of the Hebrew words. I realize how annoying this can be to one who is familiar with the Hebrew alphabet. But there was no way around the difficulty; and the matter is made at least tolerable by the fact that the Hebrew text of each verse is printed separately and completely. I have appended a table showing what German letters and signs were used to represent the Hebrew consonants and vowels.[2]

Apart from the transliteration of Hebrew words, the most burdensome and time-consuming task was the change in citation of grammatical references from the 24th edition of the Gesenius grammar that I had used in my studies, to the 28th edition that my students were using. I could not omit these references because I felt obligated to those of my readers who wished to study this book thoroughly to give them the opportunity to convince themselves of the correctness of my interpretation where a point of grammar was involved. If reference was to be made to a grammar at all, it should be to the latest reliable one that was available, and Gesenius quite rightly is still the grammar being used in our circles.[3]

I have no apology to offer for the fact that this commentary is philological in character, rather than practical or popular. The book grew out of my teaching at the Seminary and is intended to serve those in our circles who are able to approach the study of this great prophet with some knowledge of the Hebrew language. I do hope, however, that others who have no knowledge of Hebrew will be able to garner the exegetical results from the headings, the translation, and the comments on the meaning of the text. The technical language of grammar could not be avoided when a point of grammar had to be discussed, but throughout I have tried to employ a language that will be understood by all who have enjoyed an average education.

Wherever I could do so without doing violence to the sense, I have used the iambic rhythm in the translation.[4] That was done for no other reason than to impress on the reader the fact that in

---

2. The system of transliteration used in the English translation is found on pages 62 and 63.

3. In the English translation all grammatical references are made to the latest edition of *Gesenius' Hebrew Grammar* as edited and enlarged by the late E. Kautzsch, Second English Edition, Oxford, 1910.

4. Professor Kowalke's translation of the Hebrew text is also made into English blank verse.

Isaiah he has before him a prophet who speaks in highly exalted and poetic language. The result does not presume to be great poetic art. The rhythm seemed natural because my native German has, to a great extent, the same iambic-anapestic rise and fall as the Hebrew.

In conclusion, I express my heartfelt thanks to my students, Fred Kolander, Paul Naumann, Gustave Schlegel, Karl Sievert, H. Sprengeler, and Walter Bodamer, who ungrudgingly gave of their time and skill in the setting of the Hebrew type. I am especially grateful to Mr. Bodamer, who with selfless energy and great skill edited and completed the setting of the Hebrew type. Every page of the book attests also to the extraordinary care and technical skill with which the typesetter set up the German text, especially in the case of the transliterated Hebrew words. I also express my appreciation to our Publishing House for putting out this book in such distinguished form.

May our dear Lord Jesus Christ, the exalted "Servant of the Lord," who now sits at the right hand of Power, grant that this humble work, which seeks only to praise His glory revealed in Isaiah, will prove to be a blessing to those into whose hands it may come!

August Pieper

Wauwatosa, Wisconsin, on the Festival of Reformation, 1919.

INTRODUCTION

Not everything that needs to be said for an understanding of the prophet Isaiah properly finds a place in a commentary on Part II. An introduction to Isaiah II must concern itself chiefly with the literary and historical backgrounds on which this unique cycle of prophecies rests, and it must meet the challenge of that theological "science" which denies that the Isaiah of history was the author of this prophecy. A few words will suffice to explain what is necessary to know about the literary form and the arrangement of these prophecies.

The Literary and Historical Background of Isaiah II

That chapters 40 to 66 of Part II form a firmly knit unit and are in some way closely related to chapters 1 to 39 of Part I is generally acknowledged, even by those who ascribe Part II to a Deutero-Isaiah, or a Trito-Isaiah, or to many unknown later authors. Usually this relation is described in a wholly external and superficial way, the first part being designated the book of denunciations, the second the book of comfort. There is also quite general agreement that the historical chapters 36 to 39, whether ascribed to Isaiah himself or to some editor, constitute the link that connects the two parts. Chapters 36 and 37 bring to a close the story of the Assyrian threat, about which the chief prophecies of the first part revolve. Chapters 38 and 39 turn the attention to a new danger threatening out of Babylon. However, the second part of Isaiah is not based solely on the event related in chapter 39 and on the prophecy connected with it relative to the Babylonian captivity; rather, all of the prophecies of the first part constitute the immediate background of the second part. Proceeding from the later prophecies back to the earlier, they are: The fall of Babylon and the rescue of Israel, chapters 13-14:23, and 21:1-10; the coming destruction of Jerusalem, the downfall of the people, and the rescue of the penitent remnant, 1-5; 22:1ff; 28:7ff; 28:23ff; 32:9-20; the hardening of the hearts and the rejection of the people, and of the renewal of those remaining, 1; 6; 28:7ff; 30:9ff; 31:7; 25; 26; 27; 33:5f; 35; likewise the Messianic promises of the renewal of Israel in the future kingdom of peace under Immanuel, the Virgin's Son, the Seed of David and the Prince of Peace, in 7-12; 32:1ff; and in no less degree, all the promises of judgment upon the enemy nations throughout the first part. These promises — and this is not to be overlooked — constitute the background of the second part, which in three deep breaths, as it were, prophesies the deliverance out of Babylon, the deliverance from the guilt of sin and from all evil — and thus prophesies also the perfect salvation and glorification of the ideal united Israel of gentiles and Jews. Part I is the broad and firm pedestal on which Part II is erected as a glorious pillar; it is the church structure standing upon which Part II, like a glorious three-fold spire, points toward heaven.

For that reason Isaiah II cannot be properly understood without a reasonably thorough knowledge of Part I. Attention must be given not only to the contents of each prophecy, but also to the structure of the book. The principle according to which the book was arranged was long misunderstood, and it will forever remain hidden to the modern unbelieving exegetes, so long as they consider the book to be a hodgepodge ("*fliegende Blaetter*," as Ewald called them) of random pieces written by Isaiah or by some pseudo-Isaiah and put together by some later editors. The arrangement of the material is neither strictly chronological nor purely topical. Drechsler must be credited with that discovery. It is a pity that he did not express it more clearly and concretely. He writes: "The book of Isaiah is a closely knit unit, coherently planned and consistently developed. In my opinion, neither the chronological nor the topical principle, as has heretofore been so superficially assumed, can lead to the truth. One must not consider the relation of time nor the similarity of contents to be the primary principle of arrangement. The arrangement of the material in Isaiah is determined by the inner urgency according to which the prophet's mission was taking its course. If chronological sequence and similarity of topic happen to agree beautifully with this inner urgency — as I sincerely believe to be the case, regardless of some seeming contradictions which I have noted above — that is just additional evidence of the marvelous character of Him who spoke through Isaiah" (Introduction to Drechsler's Commentary, page 26).

What Drechsler means is this: Isaiah is the prophet who deals with the hardening of the hearts of Israel (Jerusalem-Judah). Hardening of the hearts of Israel is the mission to which God called him (chapter 6). The Lord has finally become so wearied with this incurably rebellious people (cf. chapter 1, which is an epitome of the whole book) that He has determined its rejection, but at the same time also the preservation of a remnant, out of which He will build the future kingdom of the Messiah. It is Isaiah's mission, by his preaching, to carry out the part assigned to him to bring this plan to fruition. The manner in which this plan of God's is realized in Israel by the preaching of Isaiah and its application to existing historical situations, or to put it more concretely: How the persistent preaching of the prophet more and more hardens the hearts of the house of David and of the people and hastens the coming of the judgment, and how the same preaching detaches a remnant from the rejected mass of the people, and how this remnant is to be saved and become the kernel of the kingdom of God of the future — that is the point of view from which the prophet has arranged his prophecies. This is not the place for a detailed proof that the arrangement of the prophecies is really determined by this point of view. The proof may be found in Drechsler. One may not concur with Drechsler's judgment respecting the relation of this or that smaller piece to the larger whole, but there can be no doubt that he has correctly identified the principle of arrangement and has offered proof that in general it is the dominant one. Drechsler sees Isaiah's activity as revolving about two crucial historical events: the siege of Jerusalem in Ahaz' time by Rezin of Damascus and Pekah of Samaria, which most seriously threatened the continued rule of the house of David (chapter 7), and secondly, the invasion of Sennacherib in the fourteenth year of Hezekiah, which actually devastated all of Judah and threatened the destruction of Jerusalem (chapters 36 and 37).

In the first of these emergencies, the house of David, in the person of Ahaz, decided *against* the help of the Lord, which had been offered and guaranteed by the prophet, and *for* the assistance expected from the world-power Assyria (Tiglath-Pileser). That thereby Ahaz brought about the final rejection of the royal house of David (indirectly also of the people of Judah) is shown by the ensuing prophecy of the Virgin's Son and Immanuel. Ahaz had wearied the Lord (Luther: insulted), had exhausted His compassion with David's house. The immediate calamity was, it is true, turned aside from the Davidic line, but from here on it is rejected for all time. Chapters 2 to 6 serve as a preparation for this act of Ahaz and for the ensuing proclamation concerning the Virgin's Son, which includes both the rejection of the house of David and the future provision of a special Son of David for a new kingdom. "Israel *would not* believe (chapters 2-5); henceforth they *shall not be able* to believe (chapter 6)" (Drechsler). The chapters following Ahaz' act and the accompanying proclamation (chapters 7-27) develop the theme in three phases: chapters 7-12: the establishment of a better kingdom under a descendant of David; chapters 13-23: the judgment of God upon all heathen nations for the purpose of establishing and perfecting the new kingdom of God (all must seek salvation from Israel's God, and thus, from Israel itself; those who do not do so will be destroyed; even the remotest heathen will be gathered for the reestablishment of the new kingdom of Israel); and finally, chapters 24-27, the result: out of the Lord's judgments there shall proceed a blessed community of Israel and many ransomed heathen nations.

"The second focus of the collection of prophecies is provided by chapters 36 and 37" (Drechsler), which report the invasion of Sennacherib and the destruction of his army as predicted by the prophet. About this as a center, chapters 28 to 35 group themselves as a *preparation*, namely, the judgment by means of Sennacherib upon Ephraim and Judah, and upon Sennacherib for the deliverance of Judah, with chapters 34 and 35 a description of the final judgment upon all heathen and the final deliverance of the church. Chapters 38 and 39 are a transition to what follows in 40-66, chapter 38 announcing a respite of grace, and 39 the Babylonian captivity, a renewed judgment. Finally, as the great chief section, chapters 40-66 reveal the lesson to be learned from the recent deliverance out of the hand of Sennacherib and, in advance of the next crisis, the Babylonian, provide the survivors with instruction and guidance. To this we add that these last chapters also reveal the consoling *promise* that there will be a *return* from the Babylonian captivity through a leader already chosen by the Lord; that through a special Servant of the Lord there will be a *remission* of the guilt of sin which was the cause of all of Israel's misery; and that there shall be a *deliverance* from sin's bondage and eternal *glorification* through the Spirit of the Lord and His Gospel (chapter 59:21 and chapter 61). The instruction drawn from the deliverance out of that crisis is: Repent and take hold of the promise of grace by faith. So, the great lesson of Isaiah II is none other than that which the Baptist and the Lord Himself impress upon Israel and all the world: Repent, and believe the Gospel!

It is obvious that a knowledge of the times in which a prophet lived is necessary for an understanding of the prophetic message. In Isaiah the historical situations which need elucidation belong almost exclusively to the first part, whereas the historical background of the second part is very simple. The second part presupposes the Babylonian exile, indicates the imminent appearance of Cyrus, proclaims the fall of Babylon and the release of the captive

Jews to their homeland, which Cyrus will bring about, and records the Lord's command to rebuild Jerusalem and the Temple. Frequent reference is made to Babylonian idol worship and Israel's participation in it, and to the defection, blindness, and impenitence of the mass of the people. That is clearly the historical background of the first section of Part II, chapters 40-48.

In the second section the historical background is even more meager. In chapters 49-57 the Babylonian captivity and the captivity of Israel among all the heathen nations constitute the background against which the deliverance of Jews and gentiles and their union into one congregation by the Servant of the Lord are depicted. In this part the name of Babylon no longer occurs. Just as the Servant of the Lord is introduced in the very beginning at chapter 49 (cf. 42) as the Savior not only of Jews but also of gentile nations, so also are the Children of Israel who are to be redeemed described as coming from afar, "those from the north and from the west, and those from the land of Sinim," that is, from all points of the compass, 49:12. Even at 52:5, where one would as a matter of course expect Babylon to be mentioned along with Egypt and Assyria, there is — obviously this is intentional — no mention of her. The same is true of the closing verses of chapter 52. The Lord reveals His holy arm not just to Babylon, but to *all the nations*, to the ends of the earth, and calls upon His captive people to "go forth from there," not only from Babylon, but from all places, 52:10,11. Compare also the general nature of the phrases "to the king" (*lammelekh*, generic article) and "far off" in 57:9.

In the third section of Part II there is a complete change of scene. The prophet sees Israel in its homeland and in its own city. That vision emerges, although still somewhat dimly, in chapters 58 and 59 (58:12; 59:20). In chapter 60 it comes into clear focus. There the city of Jerusalem is addressed. Jerusalem is the point to which the nations stream from all directions, together with the scattered Children of Israel. Zion is pictured as restored (60:3ff), the worship of the Lord as reinstated (61:6). It is this Zion, which has again been established, which as chapter 62:12 says shall be glorified, "Frequented, the city not forsaken." It is to Zion that the Hero out of Edom makes His way, chapter 63. The prayer in 64:10-12 cannot be cited as contradicting this, even though it points out that all the cities, Jerusalem, and the Temple are still lying in dust and ashes. The preceding chapters, it must not be forgotten, are a prophecy, and they reach out into the future when everything shall be restored. The complaint in chapter 64 describes the actual presence of the one offering the prayer and is it-self proof that all are again at home and that the devastation lies before their very eyes. The idol worship described in chapter 65 should also be understood as taking place at home, since it is being practiced by those "who have forgotten My holy hill" (verse 11), and beginning at verse 17 the prophecy again locates all happi-ness in Jerusalem, verses 18 and 19. Similarly, chapter 66:1 places us into the time when the people who have returned prepare to rebuild the Temple, and in verse 6 the judgment upon the rebel-lious people goes forth from the city, out of the Temple; in fact, to the end of the chapter Jerusalem remains the seat of action (verses 10,23,24). Thus we have before us the historical-geo-graphical background against which Isaiah projects his threefold picture of the future — in the first section, Babylon immediately before and at the beginning of the time of Cyrus; in the second sec-tion, the world of nations and the diaspora of the Jews among them; and in the third section, Jerusalem partly rebuilt, although still lying in ashes.

Of course, one must not attempt to obtain an account of the his-tory of the times of Isaiah entirely from either of the two parts of the book. Where history is related, as in chapters 6; 7; 8; 36-39, it is absolutely reliable. But history as such is only incidental; the real content of the book is prophecy, which often employs illustra-tions and symbols to present the entire picture, especially the de-tails, and that in poetic embellishment besides. Whoever inter-prets these pictures literally will find himself going astray. For ex-amples see 2:2-4; 7:17ff; 11:6-9; 13:20ff; 34; 35; 47; 60; 63, etc. For another striking example, compare Amos 8:8-10. The condition of Israel in its captivity, the circumstances of the destruction of Babylon, the release of the captives, the return to the homeland, the restoration of the city and the land, did not take place pre-cisely as the prophet-poet described them. It is on this point espe-cially that exegetes face the greatest difficulty. On the one hand, naturalistic exegetes who interpret everything in the most natur-alistic way possible erect for themselves an obstacle which totally prevents them from understanding the prophecy and thus con-clude that the prophecy is in error — to their own condemnation. Many believing exegetes, on the other hand, who look upon all physical references as mere pictures, symbols, and allegories, sep-arate the prophecy from its historical basis and draw conclusions that are without any basis in fact. We contend that history is to be gleaned from those passages that intend to be understood as historical, but not from the poetical and richly figurative portrayal of prophecy. For an understanding of Isaiah it is, above all, the historical books of the Old Testament that come into consideration. Indeed, whoever wishes to understand this prophet must at least have a general knowledge of the entire development of the kingdom of God in Israel, beginning with Abraham. He must be acquainted with the history of the royal line of David, but also with the development of the northern kingdom after its separation from Judah-Jerusalem. Isaiah also reaches out beyond the Babylonian exile into the time of the restoration under Zerubbabel, Ezra, and Nehemiah. If one wishes to have firm ground under his feet in the study of Isaiah, one must by all means study the books of the Kings and the Chronicles, Ezra, Nehemiah, Jeremiah, Ezekiel, Zephaniah, and Haggai, and must not ignore the last two, Zechariah and Malachi. From its beginning, the history of Israel is not only closely connected with the history of the surrounding nations, Edom, Moab, Ammon, Philistia, Phoenicia, and Syria, but is also strongly influenced and finally decisively determined by the great powers of that day. First of all, and continuously, by Egypt, and then, beginning in the middle of the eighth century (Menahem in Israel, 2 Kings 15:19 — in the northern kingdom the same danger had threatened a hundred years earlier), by Assyria since Hezekiah's time (Isaiah 39) and after the fall of Nineveh (ca. 607) and the battle of Carchemish in 606, by the Babylonian world-power, and finally by the mighty Persian empire, founded by Cyrus. A knowledge of the history of these three world-powers, from 750 to the end of the rule of Artaxerxes Longimanus (465-425 — the times of Malachi and Nehemiah), is necessary for an understanding of the prophecies of Isaiah, the history of the Persian rule being especially important for Part II. To an understanding of this voluminous history the results of recent cuneiform studies render highly valuable service, added to what is derived from Scripture and from the well-known secular historians, Berosus, Herodotus, Josephus, and a few lesser writers. They all support and amplify the Biblical account. The divergence of the chronological dates before and after 722 (2 Kings 18:9,10) between the Bible, on the one hand, and the Ptolemaic Canon and the Assyrian Eponym Canon, on the other hand, need not disturb us. Up to now, no one knows with any real certainty what principles govern the Biblical chronology of the times of the kings, which clearly is derived from the frequently mentioned annals of both kingdoms, nor how the coregency of such kings as Jotham is to be reckoned. Until that has been established, it is too early for anyone to declare the Biblical accounts to be in error. Only when it has been proved that the Bible and the cuneiform inscriptions reckon their dates according to the same principles, can one speak of error on the part of one or the other. It must be admitted, moreover, that it is just in the dates given in the Bible that errors in copying could easily occur. Sennacherib deliberately falsified the date of the tribute paid him by Hezekiah (2 Kings 18:14) and placed it after his retreat from Jerusalem in order to cover up his defeat. That inscriptions may tell lies, see Schrader's *Keilschriften des Alten Testaments* (Cuneiform Inscriptions of the Old Testament) re 2 Kings 18. With reference to the old chronology of Ussher such works as Schrader's (above), Kamphausen's *The Chronology of the Hebrew Kings*, the works of August Koehler and of Klostermann, and the articles on chronology in the newer encyclopedias might be consulted.*

Again I must call attention to a fact the recognition of which is essential for an understanding of the Prophet Isaiah, particularly of Part II: Isaiah is preaching to an incurably hardened people and to a preserved remnant. It is his mission to harden the incurable ones through his preaching and, also through his preaching, to preserve the remnant. Isaiah lived at that time in the development of the Davidic kingdom when it reached the peak from which it unavoidably plunged into the depths. Meant is not the development of the kingdom's power and temporal glory — that peak was reached during the reign of Solomon — but of the development of its carnal-mindedness, its sin, its disobedience to the Lord, its unbelief under the rule of the Old Testament Law, specifically under the Davidic theocracy. Isaiah's very first strophe (1:2-9) relates the whole story: Except for a small remnant, Judah is like Sodom and Gomorrah. The section 1:27-31 at the end of the chapter foretells the future history, namely, that Zion must be saved through *God's forensic judgment* (the judgment of the Gospel, cf. 42:1ff; 49:5ff; and especially 59:9ff) and that those who repent must be saved through *righteousness*, the righteousness of grace, cf. 62:1ff. The contents of 1:2-9 summarizes Part I (chapters 1-39); 1:27-31 summarizes Part II (chapters 40-66).

For anyone who fails to recognize this, the whole prophecy will remain a closed book and no amount of historical or grammatical

---

*See also Edwin F. Thiele, *The Mysterious Numbers of the Hebrew Kings*, Chicago, 1951.

scholarship will be of any help. Whoever fails to recognize that Isaiah has despaired of the people as such, of the Davidic theocracy, of the Old Testament economy of the Law, and that he knows that he has been called to be God's instrument for the destruction of all these things; or whoever sees in the *mishpāṭ* and the *tsedhā-qāh* of 1:27 nothing more than just another judgment and righteousness of the Law, for him the book of Isaiah will do what Isaiah's preaching did, and was meant to do, for the blinded people of Israel, according to chapter 6.

Isaiah stands on that peak of the development of the kingdom of God in the Old Testament from which he discerns clearly that the Sinaitic pedagogy of the Lord has ended in the complete apostasy of His chosen people, 1:2; 5:2ff, etc., and that any further application of this kind of rearing by the Law is useless, 1:5. There is no longer any possibility of change for the better that might lead to salvation (1:16ff). Only destruction is now in order (1:24ff). The house of Jacob has been rejected (2:6ff; 5:6f, etc.). Therefore a wholly different Royal Child must appear and establish a new kingdom — He who is Wonderful, Counselor, Power, Hero, Everlasting Father, Prince of Peace, who will prepare and establish His kingdom with a judgment and a righteousness of another kind. There is no possibility of mending and patching the old (9:10ff). God's anger is not quieted by such means (9:12,17,21); only grace and Spirit can now be of any help (10:20ff; 11:1ff). What Jeremiah says in blunt words in chapter 31:31-34 concerning the old covenant which is broken and of the new covenant that the Lord must establish, can be taken as a characterization of the contents of the book of Isaiah.

With this thought as a guiding star, it is possible to understand the great ultimatum in 7:9b: "If ye will not believe, surely ye shall not be established," and also all the prophecies of judgment and all the denunciations throughout the book. It will then also be possible to recognize Christ in the prophecy of the Branch of the Lord (4:2ff), in the Virgin's Son Immanuel, in the Child Wonderful, Counselor, Mighty God, in the Rod out of the stem of Jesse, in the raising up of the mountain of the Lord and the feast of fat things thereon; in the Destroyer of the land of the dead; in the Cornerstone of Zion; in short, in all prophecies that treat of the future restoration of the kingdom of Israel. Likewise in Part II, from "O comfort, comfort My people" in chapter 40 to the "Worm" and the "Fire" and the "Abhorring" of the final verse, it will be possible to recognize Christ and His righteousness, His salvation, His reign of

31

grace, His kingdom and eternal government; yes, find in it what St. Paul in Ephesians 1 writes concerning the gathering together into one of all things in Christ. What is it that blinds the eyes of most modern theologians, rationalists like Ewald and naturalists like Duhm, so that they cannot find Christ in Isaiah and see only a renewal of physical glory — not a prophecy in the name of God, but merely a human hope and dream? They do not recognize the one great truth proclaimed in Isaiah and in all of Scripture that all flesh is as grass and that all its goodness is like the flower of the field. The grass is withered and the flower faded because the breath of the Lord has blown upon it, Isaiah 40:6f. They neither recognize the righteousness which is of God, nor do they believe in sin. They ridicule the Law and its terrible earnestness, and the rejection which follows when God's grace is blasphemed. They profess to know that these things are the hallucinations of fevered brains — they believe men to be essentially religious and morally competent, needing no outside help to get along with that "good-natured" God above, who certainly could not be so cruel as to condemn even a single poor fellow to damnation! It is the same old offense and the same foolishness — Christ crucified. Whoever hopes to understand Scripture and to understand Isaiah must have some experience in his own heart both with Law, sin, and condemnation, and also with grace, justification, and life. Comprehension comes in no other way.

The Critics

If one disregards the remarks about Part II that Ibn Ezra made in his Isaiah Commentary in A.D. 1155, then Isaiah's authorship of the entire book, including all of Part II, remained unchallenged for almost 2,500 years. It remained for the rationalists to question Isaiah's authorship, first of the whole of Part II and later also of a number of sections in Part I. They ascribed all of these portions to a so-called Deutero-Isaiah, of whom they assumed that he lived during the last third of the exile. J. B. Koppe was the first to note that chapter 50 clearly presupposes the exile. Thereupon Doederlein in his commentary (1775) expressed strong doubts about whether Isaiah had written any of Part II. The ingenious Koppe, in his addenda and comments to Richerz's translation of Bishop Lowth's commentary, then declared that the second part of Isaiah was a collection of 85 different fragments.

The attack on Part I began with Rosenmueller, who noticed that a long list of passages were related to Part II in subject matter, in spirit, and in language. He ascribed these to a Deutero-Isaiah. whom Ewald benevolently styled "The Great Anonymous," "The Great Unnamed." Although the critics continued to wrangle among themselves about various individual points, still, about the year 1850, they excised some 12 chapters of Part I: 12; 13:1-14,23; 15; 16; 23-27; 33-35, plus a few smaller sections. All of these, together with the entire second part, they declared not to be Isaianic. Eichhorn, de Wette, Gesenius, Vatke, Hitzig, and Ewald were the leaders in this critical undertaking. Since it was an age when unbelief was in full control, defenders of the genuineness of both parts of Isaiah, such as Hengstenberg, Haevernick, Keil, Kleinert, Drechsler, Hahn, Stier, Delitzsch, and others, received no hearing. Even Delitzsch, the greatest master of Hebrew and of Semitic literature in his day, became infected by the spirit of the age and began to doubt the genuineness of Part II and the related portions of Part I. He did, however, vindicate Isaiah's authorship in the sense that these parts, if they were not written by Isaiah himself, must have been written by his pupils, were conceived in his spirit, and were therefore to be combined with the prophecies attributed to Isaiah in one undivided whole. "That is *perhaps* the way it is. To me it seems probable and almost certain that it is that way, but I am not absolutely certain, and to my dying day I shall not be able to overcome this wavering." Thus wrote Delitzsch in the fourth edition of his commentary (1889), which he dedicated to Cheyne and Driver, after his own son, Fritz Delitzsch, the famous Orientalist and cuneiform researcher, had long gone over to the opposition.

Delitzsch was a victim of the naturalistic, rather than the rationalistic spirit. What happened to him was similar to what happened in more virulent form to Cheyne, who in a comparatively short time, under the influence of the new spirit, changed from a positive into a negative critic. The enlightenment and the rationalism that emanated from England about 1700 deserve credit for having given a mighty impetus to historical and scientific studies. Philosophy, as a result, quickly turned from the rationalism of Kant and the idealistic pantheism of Hegel to the evolutionistic naturalism of Spencer. With his scientific philosophy and by his distinction between the *Knowable* and *Unknowable*, and by his keen logical examination of everything scientific from the point of view of evolution, Herbert Spencer drew the entire scientific world into his orbit. German scholarship, which prided itself on being thorough, already wholly dissatisfied with the meager fragments of "godly" religion and morals that rationalism had spared, appropriated the new doctrine and speedily outstripped Spencer, Darwin, Tyndall, Wallace, and Huxley. German scholarship rejected even Spencer's *Unknowable* and thereby rejected also the possibility of the existence of a God who might have brought forth a material world charged with energy and who could in some way govern that world.

The names of Vogt, Buechner, Helmholtz, Haeckel, Wundt, and Ostwald mark the path that this philosophy took in Germany, where it actually ended in monism. The idealism of Eucken was too feeble to prevail against it. European theology, especially that of Germany, which at all costs wanted to be recognized as scientific, readily and quickly followed the English lead when, as a result of Grotefend's discovery, the cuneiform inscriptions found in the Assyrian excavations revealed their secrets to the learned world. Here at last was a historical and real parallel to the Old Testament, *Babel — Bibel!* Now everything was as clear as the light of day. If Israel's religion was not derived from Babylon, it was nevertheless just like Babylon's religion, only here and there somewhat nobler, more idealistic! In their opinion the cuneiform inscriptions had to be a hundred times more reliable than the Bible, convicting the Bible of error in its dates and in almost everything else. For scientific theology the conclusion seemed to be inevitable. Israel's history and religion must have evolved according to exactly the same natural laws that produced the Babylonian and all other religions. Belief in revelation, in miracles, in God's special intervention in the laws of nature and in the life of a people or of an individual — a belief which rationalism had already almost rendered empty — now collapsed entirely. From then on it was a fundamental principle on their part that everything could happen only in accordance with natural laws. Israel's religion, the prophetic gift, Israel's Law and priesthood, all were to be explained naturally. Historically, the Law was to be dated after the prophets and was therefore a forgery. This swing from rationalism to naturalism occurred very shortly after the appearance of Spencer's *First Principles,* the first volume of his *Synthetic Philosophy,* and after Darwin's *Origin of Species* in the 1860s and 1870s. In German theology the movement was signalized by the rise of the Wellhausen school of religious history, which was inaugurated by the publication of his "History of Israel," the second edition of which was translated into English with the title *Prolegomena to the History of Israel.* Wellhausen was already a thoroughgoing naturalist, while Ewald, his mentor, was still a rationalist.

The Wellhausen school had its roots in the historical criticism of de Wette. Its pioneers were Leopold George, Wilhelm Vatke, and Eduard Reusz. Karl Graf of Meissen formulated its principles, and Wellhausen was its brilliant advocate. It became the dominant school of criticism in Germany and gained enthusiastic supporters in England, in other European lands, and also in our own country. Operating from their evolutionistic-naturalistic base, the critics of this school moved to the attack with the assumption that the "original documents" of the Pentateuch (P) were of postexilic authorship, and they soon succeeded in molding all Biblical criticism to conform to their theories. With the exception of Ezekiel, not a single book of the Old Testament was permitted to remain intact. The promoters of this theology were Reusz, Graf, Wellhausen, Kuenen, Smend, Stade, Wildeboer, Cornill, Giese-brecht, Greszmann, Budde, Kautzsch, Benzinger, Baentsch, Steuernagel, Duhm, Marti, Holzinger, Volz, Hackmann, W. R. Smith, Wm. R. Harper, and Charles Briggs. Although men like Dillmann, Koenig, Kittel, Strack, Orelli, Gunkel, Merx, Guthe, Sellin, Cheyne, Driver, Whitehouse, Black, Hastings, Addis, Sanday, Kennett and many others differed in principle with the Wellhausen theory of the development of religion, they were still more or less under the spell of the Wellhausen spirit in the field of literary criticism. Only Klostermann maintained an independent position, similar to that of Franz Delitzsch.

According to Cornill (*Introduction*, page 158), the acknowledged result of the criticism of Isaiah, Part I, is as follows: "Of undoubted authenticity, although declared to be to some extent worked over, are only 1; 2:6 to 4:1; 5; 6; 7:1-8 and 18; 9:7 to 10:4; 10:5-15; 17:1-11; 18; 20; 22; 28 to 31. Acknowledged by some notable critics are also 4:2-4; 8:19 to 9:6; 10:16 to 11:9; 14:24-32; 15; 16; 17:12-14; and chapter 32. Ruled out by almost everyone are 2:2-4; 4:5,6; 11:10-14; 11:23; 19; 21; 23 to 27; 33 to 35, as well as the words attributed to Isaiah in the historical account in chapters 36 to 39." The source of these latter speeches is said to be 2 Kings 18ff.

In opposition to this dictum Sellin, for example, wrote: "The following sections have in the main proved themselves to be genuine, in spite of all the critics: 1 to 12; 14:24 to 20:6; 22; (23:1-14?); 28 to 33." He considers as definitely not genuine 13:1-14 and 23; 21; 24 to 27; 34; 35; 36 to 39. Duhm admits the genuineness of fewer passages than Cornill, and Cheyne fewer than Duhm. Whereas Duhm, for example, rejects only the superscription and verses 27 and 28 in chapter 1, Cheyne rejects not only these verses but in his "Notes" places a question mark after verses 2-4 and assumes that a redactor added verses 29-31 as a different Isaianic prophecy. To add a few more examples: Duhm accepts 9:2-14; Cheyne accepts only 9:8-14 and considers verses 2-7 as not genuine. In chapter 30 Duhm takes verses 27-33 to be genuine; Cheyne labels them postexilic.

As for Part II, already the rationalists held that the entire section from chapter 40 to chapter 66 was not by Isaiah. They placed its author in the middle period of the exile, between either the Eastern conquests of Cyrus (549) or his Western conquests (546) and the destruction of Babylon (538), and gave the author the name Deutero-Isaiah. Gesenius, however, considered the conclusion of the book, chapter 63 to the end, an older composition. It was the opinion of the imaginative Ewald that 56:9 to 57:11a had been borrowed from a contemporary of Ezekiel, and that the conclusion, from the prayer in 63:7 to the end of the book, had been added after the return from exile. Not much attention was paid to his conjecture because he still held to his "Great Anonymous" as the author.

The chief point of contention among the critics was the author's place of residence. Some placed it in Babylon, some in Jerusalem, others in Egypt, and still others somewhere in the north. The critics soon also noticed that, beginning with chapter 49, a tone predominated which was different from that of 40 to 48, since Cyrus and Babylon and also a great part of the earlier theology had disappeared and had given way to a new situation and, to some extent, also to a different thought-cycle. So they decided that a different author must have been at work here, and only chapters 40 to 49 were to be ascribed to Deutero-Isaiah. Kuenen assigned all of chapters 40 to 49 to Deutero-Isaiah, together with 52:1-12, possibly also the following section about the great Sufferer, 52:13-15 and chapter 53. Everything else, according to him, was written after the return to Jerusalem from the exile, while 64:10 to the end perhaps belonged to Nehemiah's time. Thus the critics remained indecisive until Bernhard Duhm in 1892 declared (and, of course, also "proved") that chapters 49 to 55 were indeed written by Deutero-Isaiah, but that chapters 56 to the end were by a Trito-Isaiah of the time of Ezra and Nehemiah. He derived his argument chiefly from the fact that in 56:1-8 the law concerning the Sabbath and the separation from the gentiles was emphasized in a totally legalistic way, which clearly pointed to Ezra 9 and 10 and to

Nehemiah 9,10, and 13. Beginning with 56:9, he said, it was always the Samaritans and the apostate Jews who were the adversaries of the faithful Jews, and 66:1ff was spoken directly against the schismatic Samaritans. From the section attributed to Deutero-Isaiah, Duhm cut a long list of to him unauthentic pieces, and also 42:5-7 and 20-22a. He declared the so-called Servant of the Lord Hymns (42:1-7; 49:1-6; 50:4-9; 52:13 to 53:12) to be the product of another author. Duhm's theory, it seemed for a time, laid to rest the question concerning the composition of Isaiah II. Marti, Count Baudissin, Kittel, Cornill, Budde, and even Cheyne and Whitehouse voiced their assent. But Cheyne, always independent, then went a long step beyond Duhm and claimed that Trito-Isaiah was not the product of an individual but of a composite of various writers in various times. This theory won zealous supporters not only in the persons of Kittel and Budde, but especially among English and American critics. At present (1919) the pupils of Duhm and Cheyne are industriously working at exceeding their masters' work of dissection.*

Though we cannot take time to refute each critic in detail, we do have to come to grips with their chief principles.

In its present form the book of Isaiah has been handed down to us by the Jewish church. Second Chronicles 32:32, in all likelihood, refers to this book. Whether the Chronicler, who wrote after the exile, was acquainted with more than chapters 1 to 39 cannot be ascertained; but that Isaiah II was included as part of the book that Jesus Sirach had before him is clear from the concluding verses of chapter 48 of his book, Ecclesiasticus 48:20-25. Isaiah II is also included in the LXX as part of Isaiah. Even though Jesus Sirach's book did not appear until about 130 B.C., he knew of the Greek translation of the prophets, which was finished about 250 B.C. Masoretic tradition even informs us that there are 1,295 verses in Isaiah, in 26 "chapters," the present chapter 33:21 being the middle verse of the book. In the New Testament, Isaiah is quoted or referred to in more than 50 places as Isaiah, or the Prophet Isaiah, or as the prophet, or the Scriptures. These references begin at 40:3 and continue to 66:24. Chapter 53, together with the verse just preceding, is referred to in eight different places. The church at all times and in all climes has (we admit,

---

*See the remarks on the "History of Tradition" School, Charles Cutler Torrey *The Second Isaiah,* and the work of Karl Elliger in Edward J. Young, *Introduction to the Old Testament,* Eerdmans, 1958, pp. 217-218.

very uncritically) accepted the entire Book of Isaiah as the work of the Prophet Isaiah.

It was the enemies of the church, the old rationalists and the newer naturalists, who first declared all of Part II and much of Part I to be unauthentic, and with their claim of being "scientific" converted many who claim membership in the church to their opinion, so that today there is hardly a scientific theologian left who holds that Isaiah is the author of Part II and the related portions of Part I. Those who do believe in the genuineness of Isaiah are regarded with pity. Such people are said to be ignorant, either not competent to grasp a scientific demonstration or just plain dishonest. Even men like Klostermann and Bredenkamp are considered as hardly belonging among the ranks of scholars.

The writer of the present commentary disclaims any right to be regarded as a scientific theologian. The testimony of the New Testament has wholly convinced me of the Isaianic authorship of the whole book of Isaiah, and particularly also of Part II. I do not indeed maintain that the manner in which the New Testament ascribes the authorship to Isaiah precludes the possibility that earlier materials or, in general, extraneous matter might have been included, perhaps even added at a later time by other hands. For example, I do hold, in spite of all the arguments of the Documentary Source Theory, that Moses was the author of the Pentateuch, although I do not believe that he described the circumstances of his own death, burial, and funeral ceremonies. Neither do I believe that Moses added the closing item of verses 10 to 12 in Deuteronomy 34, nor do I believe that he himself added the list of Edomite kings and tribal heads in Genesis 36:31ff. I believe that there are some post-Mosaica in the Pentateuch as well as some pre-Mosaica. Nevertheless, I consider the Documentary Hypothesis, or Source Theory, to be a monstrous fraud, which in the name of science has insinuated itself into theology. Likewise do I consider Wellhausen's ethnological theories and his hypothesis of literary history to be an indelible blemish on the world of theology. I consider it quite possible, moreover, that there may be in Isaiah not only occasional corruptions of the text but also pieces that were contributed by another hand, whether by Isaiah's pupils, as Delitzsch, Bredenkamp, and Klostermann assume, or by people not connected with Isaiah. The book would not lose its right to the name of Isaiah because of such possible additions or insertions. I consider it possible that another hand added chapters 36 to 39 and that later writers edited the text here and there, or even made small additions. Still, I am convinced that even if such should be the case, then it was done according to God's will by men who were called and inspired by the Holy Ghost, and that the Lord's assurance that "the Scriptures cannot be broken" applies to the entire book. As for the critics of Isaiah, from Doederlein to Duhm and Cheyne, who ascribe Isaiah II to a Deutero-Isaiah who lived between 548 and 538 in Babylon, who assign chapters 56 to 66 to a Trito-Isaiah or to a number of authors of the Ezra-Nehemiah period, or who assert that a second or a hundredth Isaiah must have written those parts of Isaiah I that seem related to those already assigned to Deutero- or Trito-, or Fourth-, or Fortieth-Isaiah — I consider their criticism to be as great a scientific fraud as their criticism of the Pentateuch. Certainly, if they offered scientifically binding proofs, what sensible person would refuse to yield! But where are such proofs?

Let us begin with their principle argument. In order to present it simply and clearly to the ordinary reader, we will present it in the form of a syllogism:

1. The basis of all genuine prophecy is the time in which the prophet lived and that the prophecy is addressed to his contemporaries, that is, to persons of his own time.

2. The basis of Isaiah II is not the time in which Isaiah lived, and his prophecy does not address itself to his contemporaries, but is the time of the exile, between 549 and 538, or the postexilic period, and his prophecy is addressed to the people of the exile or to those who had returned from the exile.

3. Therefore Isaiah II and all sections of Part I that have the same point of view as Part II (13:1-14:23, exilic; 21:1-10, exilic; 24 to 27, postexilic [Delitzsch]; 34 and 35, exilic) were not written by the Prophet Isaiah, who lived 150 to 200 years before that time, but were composed by authors who lived at the time of the exile or after the exile.

If the first two statements are correct, then the conclusion is inevitable. With some restrictions we admit the correctness of the minor premise. But here, as is usually the case with false conclusions, **the major premise is false.**

Since the matter is so important, let us look at the syllogism of the Isaiah critics in a somewhat altered form:

1. The basis of every genuine prophecy of the Prophet Isaiah is his own time.

2. The basis of Isaiah II is not the time of Isaiah.

3. Therefore Isaiah II is not a genuine prophecy of the Prophet Isaiah.

That is as though we should say:

1. Every child of the tailor H. in S. has ten fingers and ten toes.

2. Pastor H. in M., Wisconsin, the alleged child of the tailor H. in S., has eleven toes and ten and one-fourth fingers.

3. Therefore Pastor H. in M., Wisconsin, is not a genuine child of the tailor H. in S.

Or:

1. No light rays can penetrate through a Webster's dictionary six or seven inches thick.

2. Roentgen rays do penetrate through such a dictionary.

3. Therefore Roentgen rays are not light rays.

But I happen to know that Pastor H. in the city of S. is a genuine son of parents with ten fingers and ten toes, and a genuine brother of eleven brothers and sisters, each of whom has ten fingers and ten toes. I have also frequently seen keys, nails, and other objects through a Webster's dictionary. Then what is wrong with the above syllogisms? The major premise in every case is false!

This is also the case with the logic employed by the Isaiah critics. The major premise that *all* prophecy of a prophet must be based in his own times; that Isaiah could prophesy of the future only from the standpoint of the historical conditions of his own time; and furthermore, that he must address his prophecy to the people of his own time; that he could not prophesy from the standpoint of 200 years later, at the time of the exile or after the exile, nor direct his prophecy to the people of that later time — this assertion, which the critics make their major premise, is purely arbitrary. Why? It is obtained through mere analogy. Driver, in his *Introduction*, page 237, writes:

"Judged by the analogy of prophecy, this constitutes the strongest possible presumption that the author (of chapters 40-66) actually lived in the period which he thus describes, and is not merely (as has been supposed) Isaiah immersed in the spirit of the future, and holding converse, as it were, with the generation yet unborn. Such an immersion in the future would be not only without parallel in the Old Testament, it would be contrary to the nature of prophecy. The prophet speaks always, in the first instance, to his own contemporaries; the message which he brings is intimately related with the circumstances of his time. His promises and predictions, however far they reach into the future, nevertheless rest upon the basis of the history of his own age, and correspond to the needs which are then felt. The prophet never abandons his own historical position, but speaks from it. So Jeremiah and Ezekiel, for instance, predict first the exile, then the restoration; both are contemplated by them as still future; both are viewed from the period in which they themselves live. In the present prophecy (Isa. 40-66) there is no prediction of exile: the exile is not announced as something still future: it is presupposed, and only the release from it is predicted. By analogy, therefore, the author will have lived in the situation which he thus presupposed, and to which he constantly alludes."

As Driver says, the major premise of the syllogism was obtained by analogy. Jeremiah and Ezekiel and all the other prophets prophesy from the historical basis of their own time and do that to warn or comfort their own contemporaries. That is what Isaiah usually does also. But here (chapters 40-66; 13; 14; etc.), according to Driver, the prophet's historical point of view is the exile and the postexilic age. It is from that point of view that he admonishes, warns, comforts, and teaches. There is no analogy for that in Scripture. Therefore, it is assumed, Isaiah cannot be the author of these discourses. By analogy, the authors must be persons living in exilic or postexilic times. This, we are told, is what analogy teaches us. What has been so in other cases, what was usually, regularly, and without exception so, that must be so always, everywhere, and in all circumstances. People regularly have ten toes; therefore there are no people with eleven toes. Heretofore twins were always born separately, not joined together; therefore there can be no such phenomenon as Siamese twins. That is "without parallel" in the history of twins; it would be "contrary to the nature" of the birth of twins. X-rays are without parallel, are contrary to the nature of light; therefore there are no X-rays. "Since the fathers fell asleep all things continue as they were from the beginning of the creation," 2 Peter 3:4; therefore there is no future coming of the Lord Jesus Christ for a Day of Judgment. Every novel is written from the point of view either of the past or of the present. *Looking Backward* is written from the point of view of the year 2000; therefore *Looking Backward* was written in the year 2000 or later. Edward Bellamy, however, wrote his novel in 1888.

It is upon such slovenly logic that the entire Isaiah criticism rests, which so apodictically denies to the prophet the authorship of more than half of his prophecies. Yet the critics shrug their shoulders contemptuously at those who do not submit to their "scholarship." But you believing theologians, if you must insist on the absolute binding force of conclusions from analogy, how is it that you gentlemen do not join the unbelieving theologians and the men of science in saying that there simply is no such thing as actual prophecy and supernatural and infallible prediction of the future? You admit that except for Biblical prophecy there is no true prophecy in the whole wide world or in all its history; therefore, according to the principles of analogy, Biblical prophecy cannot be genuine either — which is exactly what all consistent men of science, on the basis of personal experience, have been pointing out all along. About ten years ago I attended a public lecture by Wundt at the University of Leipzig and heard him scoff at the theologians who still believed in something besides natural cause and effect as governed by unassailable laws of nature. Professor Barth expressed the same sentiments in a Spinoza seminar. Wilhelm Ostwald, in all his books, demonstrates that there can be only one single kind of prediction, the prediction of absolutely necessary effects of given causes. That only, he declared, is true science, and for that reason he scoffed at the Kaiser and the Kaiserin because they said grace at meals. These people are just as poor logicians as you are, since their entire system rests on proofs from analogy, but they are much better scientists than you are, because they consistently follow through with their thesis that the laws of nature are the universal and only effective forces. But you believing theologians do not do that. You still believe in a personal God who is free and who has not absolutely tied His hands with the bonds of the laws of nature. You believe in prophecy and inspiration, although you have greatly watered down those concepts. You believe in an inspiration that is not just a shrewd estimate (as Ostwald maintains) of what the natural consequences must be of certain observable causes working together. You believe in an inspiration that is over and beyond all natural human knowledge. Yet . . .

Everywhere, in the entire field of science, we encounter the same logical self-deception, namely, the conclusion that what now exists determines what is possible and what is impossible, what must necessarily be and what cannot possibly be — a conclusion that is drawn from incomplete premises. Since the sun has demonstrably risen and set every morning and evening for some 6,000 years, therefore it must continue to do so for ever and ever. That is what the wise men of 2 Peter 3:4 concluded. There is no analogy for the creation of the world, for the creation of the first human pair, for the Red Sea crossing, for the revelation of the Law, for the talking ass of Balaam, for the sun that stood still on the day of Gibeah and Ajalon. There is no analogy for our Lord Christ, for the Last Day, for the entire Gospel, no analogy for any part of the Gospel or any part of the Apostles' Creed. Ergo, all of that must be crossed out, or it must be classified as superstition. There is no analogy for it. Only that is permitted to stand that can be attributed, according to definite analogies, to the working of a universal law of nature. Or, expressed in a different way and stated plainly, since you believing theologians also believe in absolutely inviolable laws of nature, you leave no room for the unique, for any special intervention of God, for miracles, for supernatural inspiration and revelation, and for the God-Man Christ. You believe only the obvious: two times two is four, three angles of a triangle equal two right angles, two pounds of good beef boiled for four hours with some good seasoning in the right amount of water will produce a pretty good soup.

We who are Bible-believing Christians are not unacquainted with science and its presupposition of the inviolability of the laws of nature, but our philosophy is that of the supranaturalists and we believe miracles to be possible. As Christians we also believe that thousands of miracles have actually happened. As philosophers we do not believe in an absolute regularity of all things and processes, which would really make impossible anything exceptional, any free action, or any irregularity at all. Such a relentless regularity in the functioning of natural laws could only lead to absolute disintegration, to complete nothingness. We rather believe in irregularity within regularity as the highest law of all things. Expressed in the language of the Christian, we believe in a God who rules in nature with a free hand. In all seriousness, we believe in the miracles of creation and preservation, the miracles of Christ, and the miracle of supernatural inspiration and prophecy. Compared with our faith in these mighty miracles, a belief in such insignificant miracles as a talking ass, a floating axhead, a resurrected Tabitha, presents no difficulties. It seems to me that such faith is a result of practice. We have experienced the one very great miracle, the miracle of which Paul speaks in Galatians 1:15f: It pleased God to reveal His Son in me. With that, the objective miracle of Christ, Son of God and Son of Mary, our Savior, became for us something certain and true; likewise also the miracle of the revelation of Christ in the Word, the miracle of Pentecost, the miracle of the inspiration of facts and words (1 Cor. 2:10-13; 2 Peter 1:19-21), also the miracle of the real inspiration of the prophets, including the Prophet Isaiah. And while proceeding by faith from one miracle to the next, we still remained strictly faithful to the scientific method. For when one or two miracles have by the mediation of the Holy Spirit become wholly certain, then the possibility of a thousand miracles is not excluded, even though specific analogies may be missing. Consequently, we believe that the Prophet Isaiah always, everywhere, wherever, whenever he prophesied, did so by supernatural revelation, as appears in chapter 6 of his book. He produced no portion of his book, not one, out of his own human will, deliberation, divination, intuition, or any such faculty; everything was poured into his natural spirit in a supernatural way by God Himself. Even if we suppose that in every other instance he did prophesy from the point of view of the events of his own time, why should the Spirit of God not be able to move him and empower him to prophesy from an as yet future point of view and to address a future generation?

As a matter of fact, Isaiah II does take a position that lies in the future. It was a serious mistake on the part of devout exegetes, with the exception of Delitzsch, to insist that passages like 43:22-28, 66:6 and 20, and some passages in chapter 57 and elsewhere treated of conditions before the destruction of Jerusalem and the exile. It is altogether unlikely that the prophet, once he had adopted a point of view lying in the future, would abandon it and again speak as though from a time preceding the exile. By doing that, he would have made his prophecy confusing and unintelligible. Careful examination reveals that once he had adopted a point of view lying in the future, he never again abandoned it. Modern Isaiah commentators, however, quite arbitrarily fix the historical point of view adopted by Isaiah as lying between Pasargadae (548), or even Sardis (546), and Babylon (538). They base that assumption on the perfects *hēʿîr* and *haʿîrōthî* in 41:2 and 25; 45:13; and on the fact that in 44:28; and 45:1 Cyrus is called by name and the perfects in the account of his calling are there repeated. It is of no importance to us whether Isaiah in his prophecy projects himself a few years earlier or later into the time of the exile; but it is of great importance that we retain a sound basis for our exegesis. It cannot be established that these perfects are historical perfects. They could just as well be present or future perfects. And the following consecutive imperfect, like *wayya' th* in

41:25, would simply be governed by the time-circle of a preceding perfect. Who but a naturalistic exegete would take *nāthattī* in 42:1, or *qerā'thikhā* in 42:6, or *shillahtī* in 43:14, etc., as historical perfects! The actual time of these perfects can be determined only by comparison with other details of the text, and such comparison does not yield any evidence that here the prophet points to Cyrus as having already appeared on the scene, thus becoming factual proof of a fulfillment of earlier predictions of his future appearance. No such earlier predictions about Cyrus are to be found in Isaiah or anywhere else. The prophecies in chapter 41 and in the following chapters up to 48:14-16 are the *only* ones about Cyrus.

The point of dispute in these discourses — and here the opponents always shift the issue — is not whether the gentiles and their idols can produce an example of the *fulfillment* of one of their predictions, but whether they are able to match this prediction now being made about Cyrus with a similar prediction, whose fulfillment they will guarantee — for example, a prediction about a future successful opponent and conqueror of Cyrus. The gentiles and their idols are not able to foretell anything with certainty — that is what the Lord declares throughout all these discourses. The recurrent charge against them is that they do not speak, do not open their mouths, remain silent — not that they had brought no earlier predictions to fulfillment. That's why there is no rejoinder from the gentiles to the challenge in 41:4; there is only dismay, 41:5-7. In the same manner, in verses 21-24, the Lord challenges them to proclaim, to prophesy, to speak, and tells them that they are nothing, because they do not open their mouths, verses 24, 26, and 28. By foretelling future events, the Lord distinguishes Himself from the idol-gods and evidences His Godhead. It is He, not they, who does all things, makes all things come to pass and fulfills all His predictions (41:4,25,27; 42:9; cf. 43:9,12; 44:7ff). The coming of Cyrus here still lies in the future, just as do also the fall of Babylon and the return through the desert (43:14-20). The prophecy about Cyrus has as the guarantee of its reliability those great deeds of God that lie in the past (43:16-20). He who *said* to the deep: "Be dry," He says to Cyrus: "Build the city and the Temple." Thus He *confirms* the prediction of His prophets (44:26-28). Chapter 45 also, especially verse 13, is, like 46:11, not a reference to a Cyrus who has already appeared, but is a prediction of a Cyrus who is yet to come.

In order to support their contention that according to 41:2-7 and 21-29; 44:27ff; 45:1 and 13; 46:11; 48:14ff Cyrus has already ap-

45

peared, the naturalistic exegetes, whom the conservatives simply follow, point out that Cyrus is here actually called by his name. That, they say, is not only proof that Cyrus has already appeared, but also that Isaiah II was written by a man who lived at the time of Cyrus. If one asks why they say that, the answer is always that there is no analogy for this kind of prediction. Since we have already discussed at length the value of proof by analogy, it is not necessary again to disprove the validity of that form of argument. Basically this kind of talk is unbelief — naturalism, which cannot comprehend how a prophet can have knowledge beforehand of the victorious career and the name of a hero. The assertion that prophecy must always be rooted in history that is contemporary with the prophet really says nothing else than that the prophet prophesies by calculating the future from present events by the exercise of his exceptional, though still merely natural, gifts. To find that expressed, one needs but read the rationalist Ewald (*The Prophets of the Old Testament*, I, Introduction, page 2ff), or the rationalistic Wellhausen (*Prolegomena*, 6th edition, page 398: "In a prophet the mysterious accord that exists between Godhead and the man manifests itself as energy") and Cornill (*The Israelitic Prophetism*, page 35f: "The prophet has, namely, the ability to recognize God in history. When a catastrophe is in the air he senses it. In this sense, and only in this sense, does the prophet of Israel foretell the future"). In short, these theological gentlemen do not believe in real prophecy at all. Naturally, we cannot come to terms with such persons. What a pity that the modern theologians who still profess faith are to such a great degree under the spell of this unbelief and believe that they must follow the naturalists! Science, dominating everything at the German universities, has charmed them. The scientific method is the god that the German scholar worships. That explains everything. Not to go along would mean to be labeled unscientific, and that is something that no German theologian, not even a believing theologian, can endure. Thus the unbelieving theologians have robbed the poor German people of their faith in the Bible and the Gospel and have completely destroyed the morale of the people, and in the final analysis, have brought about the present political collapse (1919). And believing theologians have assisted in doing this. Moreover, they fail to perceive that when they profess faith in any miracle, especially faith in Christ as their God and Savior in the sense of St. Paul's epistles, they are actually being unscientific. For that reason the unbelieving naturalistic theologians ridicule the believing theologians, and the professors of philosophy and natural science on their part ridicule the naturalistic theologians. Does not this strongly remind one of the second Psalm?

In the second part of his book Isaiah, through the Holy Spirit, adopts a point of view not only in the time of the exile, but in chapter 42 and from 49 onward, in the time of Christ. In chapters 42 and 49 God presents His true Servant, His Son, "His salvation unto the end of the earth"; and in chapter 49 the Servant Himself addresses the isles and the far distant gentiles *of His own time*, not of the time of Isaiah. The Lord promises an influx from the gentile world into Zion. In chapter 50 the prophet again speaks as from out of the midst of the exile, and in verse 4 the revealed New Testament Servant speaks again. In chapters 51 and 52 no certain historical point of view can be determined unless it is that of the New Testament, for these chapters address the devout diaspora throughout the whole world, and the Zion that is addressed is already the ideal Zion, to which the physically ruined Zion only lends its color. And where is there an exilic or an immediate post-exilic historical foundation for chapter 53, in which even Duhm finds an individual portrayed, and in which all believing theologians recognize the portrayal of our Lord Jesus Christ? It is clear that here the prophet is standing at the foot of the cross, as Delitzsch has correctly said. But according to the law of analogy the chapter must have been written by a contemporary of the apostles. Beginning with chapter 56, the Lord's House of Prayer is still standing — or standing again — which? If one agrees with Duhm, Marti, Cheyne, and Whitehouse, one must say standing *again*. It is Zion, prostrate in its misery. It is the city — and not the people still languishing in Babylon — which, according to chapters 59 to 62, is to be rebuilt and glorified. Without any reference to contemporary history, the Servant of the Lord in chapter 61 reappears with His proclamation of the year of grace. And unless one is a naturalistic theologian, what are the historical roots for chapter 63:1-6? But enough of this historical point of view!

The Holy Spirit of God, the Spirit of revelation, had revealed to the Prophet Isaiah, whose activity ceased about 700 B.C., that God had rejected the physical Israel and that the people were to be banished to the prison house of Babylon. The Spirit also revealed to him that a remnant would be preserved in Babylon and later return to the homeland, that within this remnant another remnant should remain faithful to the Lord throughout all times, and that from out of this remnant the Servant of the Lord would in due

47

time arise. He would save from sin a spiritual Israel from among Jews and gentiles, while the old rebellious Israel would be wholly destroyed. Through the Gospel He would choose from among Jews and gentiles in the whole world a new Zion, which He would sanctify and eternally glorify in spite of all the powers of the ungodly world. The prophet is to preach and write this so that by his preaching and writing the Lord's plan might be set in motion, that is, that those who were beyond all help might be hardened and bring down judgment upon themselves, while the remnant would be saved through the preaching of chastisement, comfort, and admonition up to the time of the exile, through the exile, and beyond the exile. To accomplish this the prophet was to admonish his generation unceasingly and to put down in writing the substance of his sermons. In the second part of his book he was to present a beautiful, poetic, coherent prophecy in three parts treating of the deliverance from Babylon, from the guilt of sin, and finally from all evil. The point of view from which he would write this was that of the exile, the time after the exile, or the time of the revealed Savior, always as he would be inspired by the Spirit. The purpose would be that all hopelessly irredeemable unbelievers in all the world might take offense at his book and fall just as the two houses of Israel stumbled over this stone of offense, while a preserved remnant, gathered from all nations, would be sanctified and eternally glorified. This is the attitude that simple faith takes toward the Book of Isaiah, as opposed to the ravings of the modern critics. At the same time this faith is convinced that it has in no point betrayed even a single aspect of the true scientific method.

We can just as readily dispose of the second premise on which the critics base all their remaining arguments to the effect that Isaiah was not the author of Part II. The objection is that Part II displays a different spirit and employs a wholly different language.

It is true that the author of Part II employs words, illustrations, and phrases different from those in Part I. His style is now flowing, while that of Isaiah I is concise and heavy. The rhetoric of Isaiah II is warm, impassionate, whereas the author of Part I is grave and restrained. In Isaiah II we have pathos; in Isaiah I, majesty. The illustrations in Isaiah II are taken from life, especially from the sphere of human emotions, as is demonstrated by the many personifications. Even heaven and earth are exhorted to rejoice. Similarly, the author of Part II shows a preference for dramatic presentation. His theology, too, is more fully developed than that of Isaiah I. Isaiah I dwells on the majesty of God; the author of Part II describes the infinity of God as Creator, Sustainer, Giver of Life and Author of all history, as the First and the Last, the Incomparable One.

"This is a real difference," says Driver, from whose *Introduction*, page 238 and following, we have taken these statements. Driver says furthermore that what in Part I is a matter of assertion, appears here as a matter of reflection. And secondly, the remnant, which there plays such an important part, has almost wholly disappeared here. Israel's relation to the Lord is presented in different terms. Similarly, the Messianic King has disappeared, and the "Servant of the Lord" has taken His place, the Sufferer, not indeed as a continuation of the King, but as a parallel to Him. God's plan for the nation is now more fully developed. "In a word, the prophet moves in a different region of thought from Isaiah's" (*Introduction*, page 243).

We have given so much space to Driver on both counts in order that full justice might be done to the opponents. But, at the same time, this amounts also to their refutation, for almost every one of their assertions is exaggerated. Look, for example, at the very first chapter of Isaiah. Isaiah II is said to be the one dealing in personifications. He even personifies nature, says Driver on page 241: "He bids heaven and earth shout at the restoration of God's people" (44:23; 49:13; 52:9; 55:12). But we have always thought that Isaiah I began with a personification of heaven and earth: "Hear, O heavens, and give ear, O earth" (1:2). It is said to be a peculiarity of Isaiah II to call out as he does in 44:23: "Rejoice, ye heavens, for the Lord has done it; ye depths of the earth, shout aloud!" On the contrary, every ordinary man would conclude from the similarity of these literary figures that the authors were identical. But perhaps that would not be scientific!

Driver (page 240f) says: "Isaiah's rhetoric is grave and restrained, but the rhetoric of chapters 40-66, by contrast, is warm and impassionate." But, we ask, can anything be more impassionate than the language of the first chapter as expressed in its three strophes? "Ah, sinful people!" "Hear the word of the Lord, rulers of Sodom — people of Gomorrah." "How is the faithful city become a harlot!" Is it also not self-evident that the fervency of joy in the description of the promised glory of Zion in chapter 62 should pour forth more smoothly than the vehemence of anger and sorrow in the description of the incurability of the people? Wherein is the "grandeur" of the first part distinguished from the "pathos" of the second part? O you critics, you can hear the grass grow and the lettuce sprout! As for "the real difference" supposedly found in the theology of the two parts: Where is there a theological difference between the concept of the *majesty* of the first part and the *infinity* of God in the second part? For ordinary people, does not the majesty of God lie precisely in His "infinitude," which Driver describes in these terms: "He is the Creator, the Sustainer of the universe, the Life-Giver, the Author of history (41:4), the First and the Last, the Incomparable One"? To choose but one example from the first chapter, is the *'abhīr yisrā 'el* of 1:24 less infinite than the *'abhīr ya'aqōbh* of 49:26 and 60:16, and is the latter less majestic than the former? Is it not self-evident that the Isaiah of Part I with his threats and denunciations is emphasizing the moral majesty of the infinitely powerful God, and that the Isaiah of Part II with his promises of salvation is emphasizing the infinite power of the majestic God? Such playing around with manufactured abstract concepts can deceive only those who have given up their ability to think concretely.

"Again, the doctrine of the preservation from judgment of a faithful remnant is characteristic of Isaiah. It appears both in his first prophecy and in his last (6:13; 37:31f); in chapters 40-66, if it is present once or twice by implication (59:20; 65:8f), it is no distinctive element in the author's teaching; it is not expressed in Isaiah's terminology, and it is not more prominent than in the writings of many other prophets." Therefore Isaiah cannot be the author of Part II! But this is just a new bit of deception. In Part I Isaiah refers expressly to the remnant seven or eight times: 6:13; 10:20-23; 11:11-16; 24:13f; 28:5,23-29; 37:31f. Almost all critics assume that 11:11-16 is not genuine; they say that Deutero-Isaiah is the author and that it belongs to the other part of the book. Some critics also deny the genuineness of 37:31. That, however, would leave five passages for Part I against two implicitly and one expressly assigned to Part II. What reasonable person would therefore conclude that a different author wrote Part II? And why should Isaiah II expressly have to *say* that a remnant should be saved, since he *addresses* all of his discourses to this remnant itself and promises it deliverance, redemption, and salvation, from 40:1 all the way through 66:24? In their search for differences between Isaiah I and Isaiah II the critics have become mere mechanics. It is really quite marvelous! First they take a number of chapters out of Isaiah I, assign them to Deutero-Isaiah for purely naturalistic reasons, and then call attention to the differences in phraseology and theology between Part I and Part II. Again, if it serves their purpose, they may restore those same passages to Part I and say: Don't you see the difference? If that is scientific, then it is possible by that same method to prove that a sphere is a cube!

Again, in the first part we have a Messianic King, in the second part a preaching and suffering Servant of the Lord — proof, they say, of separate authorship! But what would a preaching and suffering Servant be doing in the first part where Isaiah is proclaiming the rejection and judgment of an incurably hardened royal family and sovereign people? Under such circumstances a different kind of king and a different regime were needed as God's emissary. A Sufferer would have experienced nothing but derision. By the same token, how could the prophet approach the faithful remnant, to which he addresses himself in Part II, with the idea of a new king and a new kingdom without awakening in them the false expectation of an earthly king and new worldly grandeur? Here only a meek, powerless Prophet and a vicarious Sufferer are in order. In Part I, the Messianic King; in Part II, the Prophet and High Priest — what could be more natural, more fitting, more glorious, provided one does not, like the naturalistic theologians, ascribe only materialistic thoughts to the prophet, but rather believes that the Holy Spirit intended through Isaiah to reveal Christ, the true Messiah and Savior of sinners! Therein lies the premise of all negative criticism of Scripture, including that of the Book of Isaiah. Between the critics and us a gulf is fixed that makes it impossible for them to cross over to us and for us to cross over to them. Our faith lets us see Christ everywhere in the Old Testament, even as He saw Himself there. The negative critics, however, are unbelievers, naturalistic philosophers who consider the Scriptures a deliberate fraud, or at the least a book full of superstition. Isaiah is pictured by them as a naturalistic dreamer and fanatic materialist, who in pure enthusiasm dreamed up and prophesied a fools' paradise for the Israel of the future, and thus of course deceived both himself and others.

Is it still worth our while to spend time discussing the differences in command of language, vocabulary, and phraseology between the two parts? It has become the universal custom of those who deny Isaiah's authorship of Part II to say that Isaiah wrote Part I in the days of his youth and in his mature days in the midst of the turmoil in the life of his people, while Part II is marked by the serenity and detachment of old age. But where are the proofs and what is the purpose of such an assertion? It seems to me that the reverse would be more reasonable. Part II may well be the revelation of his youth, and Part I contain primarily the discourses of his mature years and of advanced age, and finally it may well be that in his old age he joined the two parts into a unit by means of the connecting chapters 36-39. If I were a modern scientific theologian, I dare say that I could prove that point more cogently — and that on the basis of psychology and the strictest observance of the rules of logic — than any negative critic of Isaiah has ever proved a single one of his points. In time of youth hopes blossom forth as in the springtime flowers blossom in the meadows. In autumn there are only a few late bloomers, and all green things — including those of the heart — change to gray. In old age the heart realizes the seriousness of life. Experience teaches one not only wisdom, but moral strength too, a firm judgment and a sense of pessimism. The youthful writings of every great man resemble the spirit of Isaiah II; what they produce in old age resembles Isaiah I. Think of Luther and compare "Of the Freedom of a Christian Man" with "Against the Papacy at Rome, Founded by the Devil." Because of the difference in tone, in vocabulary, in phraseology between these two works of Luther, it would be much easier to arrive at the conclusion that they were written by two entirely different persons, than it is for the Isaiah critics to assign the prophet's book to two, three, four, or even 40 different authors. But to make such a statement about Luther's work would be a psychological-naturalistic explanation of a literary phenomenon, and, on principle, I would not offer such an explanation, because even in the area of the natural life of the spirit such a critical method turns out to be dead, mechanical, and of necessity false. If Isaiah possessed no more inspiration than Luther, he could still, all scholastic psychology notwithstanding, have written both parts of his book as certainly as Luther wrote his two dissertations.

The vocabulary and the diction that I employ, the theology or other knowledge that I develop, the tone that prevails in my writings, all of that, provided I am possessed of some geniality of spirit and some mental capability, will depend on external circumstances and on the impression that these circumstances make on my mind and spirit. One and the same man will write an objective exegesis, a lecture intended for scholars, or a popular sermon, all on the same general subject, but so different in vocabulary, diction, theology and anthropology, in spirit and in fluency, that a psychologist employing the methods of the modern Isaiah critics might easily assume that some three different authors had been at work. Present Isaiah criticism was produced in the critics' study and was not developed by people in contact with real life. It has the stench of the oil lamp about it! How can one expect from them a true appreciation of an inspired book which refuses to permit itself to be shackled by any laws of psychology, no matter how much the Holy Spirit accommodates Himself to the peculiarities of His human agents? Although it seems, humanly speaking, quite likely that Isaiah wrote Part II in his youth and Part I in his old age, this is something I cannot prove, nor do I want to try to do so. I should have to tell myself that I was guilty of employing the same kind of "scientific" fraud which the Isaiah critics of our day and of days past employed. The book of the prophet Isaiah has an even greater witness to its unity than that of John — cf. John 5:36.*

---

*Criticism of Isaiah to the Present Time

In the twentieth century Hermann Gunkel and Hugo Grossmann developed the school of form-criticism, which assumes that Hebrew literature falls into types (*Gattungen*) which can be clearly distinguished by certain characteristics. Gunkel acknowledges that Duhm had exhibited deep insight into the inner life of the prophets, but adds that the more careful study of comparative religion has also exerted an influence, and that there is also the method of investigation known as literary-historical criticism.

In 1928 Charles Cutler Torrey in his *The Second Isaiah* concluded that the two passages that call Cyrus by name and three other passages which speak of a flight from Babylon and Chaldea are the only passages in Isaiah II which seem to point to Babylonia as the place of composition of this part of the book. He considered all five of these passages as interpolations on the basis of metrical considerations. In the same year Karl Elliger endeavored to show in the first work in a series entitled *Die Einheit des Tritojesaia* (the unity of Trito-Isaiah) that chapters 56-66 were written largely by one author toward the close of the sixth century B.C., but that it has been edited by an unknown redactor who lived in the fifth century.

In 1931 Sigmund Mowinckel wrote an article on the composition of Isaiah 40-55 in which he calls attention to the importance of *Gattungsforschung,* and concludes that this prophecy cannot be regarded as one unified composition with a logical and planned construction. The following year Paul Volz of Tuebingen in his

The Literary Form of the Book

In spite of the modern critics, I still hold that the book is uniformly arranged in the form of a trilogy. Its contents prove that. There are three compact units: 40-48; 49-57; 58-66. The refrain at the end of 48 and 57 is an external mark of this division. Modern criticism with its characteristic willful blindness either ignores or denies this obvious fact. The proof of the pudding is in the eating thereof. The mincing-knife of the critics has made it impossible for them to recognize the contents and the continuity of thought in Isaiah II, and therefore they are unable to see the glorious organic structure of the book. We refer our readers to the outline of the contents that appears in a following section, and that demonstrates, as nothing else can, the unity of the book.

Isaiah II consists of three times nine sections. These collections of discourses, or chapters, as we shall call them, are in substantial agreement with the chapter divisions that Rabbi Isaak Nathan used in preparing the Hebrew Concordance. He adopted the division of chapters that Hugo St. Cher († 1262) had devised for the Latin Vulgate. Jakob ben Hayyim later used that same division in his four-volume edition of the Hebrew Bible that was printed in

---

Jesaias II criticized Elliger's work and expressed the belief that in chapters 56-66 there are a number of unconnected pieces which come from different times and different authors. In his Schweich Lectures for 1940 Sidney Smith called attention to historical material which he believed illustrated Isaiah 40-55.

Two commentaries on chapters 40-55 appeared in the next two decades, Christopher R. North published *Isaiah 40-55, The Suffering Servant of God* in 1952, followed by *The Second Isaiah*, a commentary on these chapters in 1964. In 1965 George A. F. Knight published a commentary on these chapters entitled *Deutero-Isaiah*. In the same year James D. Smart produced a commentary on Isaiah 40-66 and 35 entitled *History and Theology in Second Isaiah*. In the following year Claus Westermann published a commentary on Isaiah 40-66 in German, which was translated and published in English in 1969. All these commentaries follow the majority view of contemporary scholarship concerning the date and authorship of the second half of the book of Isaiah, that Deutero-Isaiah wrote chapters 40-55 about 550 B.C. and that chapters 56-66 were produced by a disciple of Deutero-Isaiah at a later date.

Robert Bomberg's printing establishment (1525). This chapter division is the one used in this commentary.

It is perhaps not an accident that chapter 53, the main chapter of the book, occupies the exact center between the thirteen preceding and the thirteen following chapters. The Servant of the Lord, who rises to supreme glory through His substitutionary, atoning sacrifice for a guilt not His own, but ours, is the actual and main subject of the entire book. Everything that precedes is introductory to this chapter and its central figure; everything that follows is an unfolding and development. Just as chapters 52 and 54 are firmly tied together with chapter 53 to form a smaller unit, so throughout the book each group of three chapters or discourses forms a smaller complete unit. We refer again to the outline of the book. The sum of three times three of these triads forms a section, or one-third of the book. The basic literary unit is the discourse, designated as chapter in our Bibles. Within each discourse the division varies greatly. Chapter 63 is expressed in one breath, without a break; chapter 61 has two parts, one long one, verses 1-9, and one short one, verses 10-11; chapter 62 has three parts, verses 1-5, 6-9, 10-12. Some other chapters have four short sections. Chapter 53 has been divided into five, but such minute division can be overdone. To the larger division of each chapter or discourse we have given the name of strophe, or major strophe. The real basis of division or composition is, however, the minor strophe. This is similar to the verse of a hymn and consists of one, two, three, four, or more lines, which together constitute a shorter or a longer unit of thought.

Several good commentaries on Isaiah have appeared in these same years which do not share these modern views of date and authorship. In 1936 F. C. Jennings published *Studies in Isaiah*, in which he established with convincing evidence that it is the writing of one man, the prophet Isaiah, inspired of God. More recently Herbert C. Leupold published a two-volume commentary entitled *Exposition of Isaiah* (1968-1971) and Edward J. Young completed a three-volume commentary before his death entitled *The Book of Isaiah* in the New International Commentary on the Old Testament (1965-1972). Both of these commentaries are also written by scholars who believe that Isaiah is the author of the entire book which bears his name and take a dim view of modern criticism which would project the writing of portions of this book into the time of the Exile or beyond.

This brings us to the very important matter of the literary form, which deserves more than mere passing notice. Isaiah II is written in the form of Hebrew poetry, both as to the outer form and the inner spirit. The outer form, the mechanics or technique, is governed by two laws. One law, long recognized, and given the designation of parallelism of members by Robert Lowth, an English bishop, is that corresponding members of a statement are placed alongside each other in one verse, or that corresponding thoughts are expressed in two or more lines of verse. For example, the Hebrew poet is not satisfied to express the nothingness of the nations of the world by the simple statement:

The nations, all are as nothing before Him,

and to continue:

To whom then would you liken God?

Rather, he takes up each of these two thoughts once more, or perhaps even several times, and expresses them in a slightly different way. Thus the first sentence becomes a two-line verse or strophe:

The nations, all are as nothing before Him,
As nothing and as a void are they reckoned before Him.

The second sentence becomes a double line:

To whom then would you liken God,
And what likeness place beside Him? (Isa. 40:17,18).

This parallelism may contain two, three, or more members. For example, Psalm 1:1 has three members; Isaiah 40:12 has four or five members. The above examples are cases of synonymous parallelism in which the thoughts are almost identical in content. The second member may, however, also be opposite in meaning to the first, as in Psalm 1:6: "For the Lord knows the way of the righteous; but the way of the ungodly shall perish." This is known as antithetical parallelism. The second member may also express a progression of thought, as in Isaiah 44:8:

Do not be afraid, nor be disquieted!
Have I not let you hear it from of old,
And have I not proclaimed it — are you not My witnesses?
Is there yet a God beside Me?
But there is no Rock; I know of none.

While the last two members are synonymous, the first three express a progression of thought. This is called a synthetic or progressive parallelism. These three types of parallelism follow in no regular order but are used whenever it pleases the speaker or the poet to employ them. It is not only single lines that are set down in this parallel relation to each other; but pairs of lines, groups of lines, verses, strophes, or even whole sections of discourses may be so arranged. A striking example of the use of the three types of parallelism in lines, pairs of lines, minor strophes, and major strophes appears in chapter 62. The reader may examine the chapter in the light of this formula. The "Hymn of Scorn" about Babylon in chapter 47 is another example, although this chapter contains a special peculiarity that must be noted.

Parallelism is seldom perfectly regular. It is so when the thought expressed in the second member corresponds to the first in all details, in subject, predicate, and object with its modifiers:

> *For like a garment the moth will devour them,*
> *And like wool the worm will devour them.* (51:8a)

The immediately following lines of this minor strophe, which are in antithetical relationship to one another, are irregular, since in the second member the predicate is missing, which has to be supplied out of the first:

> *But My salvation will stand forever,*
> *And My redemption to all generations.* (51:8b)

This is true of most parallelisms. For example, in the very next verse the missing element in one member must be supplied out of the other:

> *Awake, awake, clothe Yourself in power — , O arm of the*
>   *Lord,*
> *Awake, — as in the days of old, in generations of long ago!*

In the first verse the designation of time (*now, again*) is to be supplied out of the second line; and the second line must borrow from the first its predicate "clothe Yourself in power" and also the address, "O arm of the Lord." This point, which is true of all parallelism, can be very important for the exegesis of a passage, as for example in the explanation of 60:9.

A much rarer form than the parallel arrangement of the members is the chiasmus (so named from the form of the Greek letter Chi), in which the second line begins with the concluding thought of the first line and ends with the initial member of the first line:

> *Truly, the nations — like a drop are they in a bucket,*
> *And like a kernel of grain in a scale are they counted.*
>
>   (Isa. 40:15)

A careful examination of 43:1-7 reveals that the chiasmus may also be extended to cover longer portions. Verse 4 corresponds to 3; 5 and 6 with 2; 7 with 1, the only difference being that in this case the correspondence is looser than it is in the minor strophe. A chiasmus of this kind is so rare that it is easily overlooked. At 59:8 there is a verse in which the two interior members correspond to the two exterior members.

When several lines are combined they form a verse, that is, a strophe, or minor strophe, which is similar to a verse of a hymn, except that the verses are not regularly made up of the same number of lines. A verse may contain one, two, three, four, or more lines. The Masoretic division of verses frequently, but not regularly, corresponds to the poetic verse, especially in the prophets. The combination of several verses or minor strophes into one larger group of thoughts constitutes a major strophe or part of a discourse. Several such parts finally combine into a complete well-rounded discourse.

Regarding the rhythm of Hebrew poetry, the dictum that we learned in school that Hebrew poetry has neither meter nor rhyme needs to be corrected. Hebrew poetry does not have rhyme, but does have a kind of meter, although not in the sense of the measured rise and fall of a certain number of syllables as in poetry written in the dactyl, anapest, iambic, and trochee measures. The Hebrew counts only the stressed syllable in a word. It allows any number of unstressed syllables, except that every word, whether it be short or long, has but one stressed syllable. Words combined by the Maqqeph count as a single word. Thus the little word *hēn* (behold) represents one full stress, and the word *wetse'etsā'eyhem* (their offspring) has also just one stress. The usual line has three, four, or sometimes more stresses. The longer the line, and consequently the greater the number of stresses, the more closely does the line approach prose diction, as we can observe occasionally, especially toward the end of the book where the matter becomes less poetic and the poet seems to be growing technically weary.

It follows that in this kind of poetry no distinction can be made between naturally long and naturally short syllables. For example, 42:1 has four lines, each containing three words and three stresses; the second verse in the chapter has four stresses in the first line and three in the second; the third verse has four stresses in each of the first two lines and three in the last line. When a line has more than four or five separate words and stresses, one may consider dividing that line into two parts.

This leads us to the consideration of a special kind of line, the Qinah line, which is frequently used in Isaiah II. Budde gave the line this name because it is peculiar not only to the first four chapters of Lamentations (the fifth chapter has the ordinary rhythm), but also to other elegiac chapters of the Old Testament. The Qinah is a long line which is usually divided by a caesura into a longer first part and a shorter second part. To illustrate:

> *How doth the city sit solitary — that was full of people!*
> *How is she become as a widow — she that was great among the nations,*
> *And princess among the provinces — how is she become tributary!*

The caesura is as easily located in the Hebrew as in the translation; but the count of stresses before and after the caesura does not always follow a regular pattern. It varies. The rule seems to be three stresses before the pause, two after it. Such lines have received various names, such as five-stress line, pentameter, limping line, or echo line. Isaiah II begins with a pair of lines in this rhythm:

> *O comfort, comfort My people — says your God.*
> *Speak comfortably to Jerusalem — and say to her*
> *That her servitude is at an end — that her debt has been paid,*
> *That she shall receive double at the hand of the Lord — for all her sins.*

The number of stresses in the two members is seldom the same. All studies that have so far been made of Hebrew prosody have still not penetrated to the heart of the system, unless it be that Hebrew poetic art did not permit itself in such external matters to be bound by any hard and fast rules. The Hebrew is like Heine in that respect, or rather Heine is like the Hebrew. In fact, the prophets, and Isaiah in particular, observe the external poetic technique much less exactly than the lyricist. In the Psalms it is a wholly irresponsible undertaking to make "meter" a criterion for the genuineness of the text; still less is such a procedure in place with a prophet, for he is more than a poet. It is noticeable even in the writings of the Apostle Paul how he strives to find words to express thoughts given to him by the Spirit — and he was writing in prose! Poetic forms can on occasion act as a shackle. In such cases the Holy Spirit simply departs from such forms and speaks as He chooses.

This leads us to a discussion of the inner poetic form. It consists in that intuitive clarity with which a poetic spirit grasps the fundamental truths of the world and of life, truths which the everyday person either does not recognize at all or else arrives at by uncertain calculations and combinations. The poetic spirit, on the other hand, by virtue of his imaginative powers gets to see truths in their ideal perfection and then expresses them in their simplest and noblest form, portraying them in a way that is vivid and gripping. If the poet is at the same time to a high degree a master of language and poetic technique, then his word of wisdom and his speech become sheer music. In the case of the poet-prophet, supernatural inspiration takes the place of natural intuition. It has to do not with natural truths but with God's hidden counsels, which concern not just the simple future but the salvation promised in Christ and the measures that will be taken to bring that salvation to pass, measures that will include also judgment upon individuals and upon entire nations. In place of human certainty regarding truths of nature there is a divine certainty regarding those matters revealed to him. As these are etched into his very soul, they excite his imaginative powers to portray their realization in the most splendid and daring pictures and in the most exalted language at his command. Such a man was Isaiah.

By divine revelation Isaiah knew of the ignominious fall of arrogant and idolatrous Babylon; his poetic imagination pictures it to his mind and, in chapter 47, he sings of it. God revealed to him the future glory of the church and set his heart aglow with the highest rapture. In poetic ecstasy he envisions the glory of the church and, in the most exalted pictures his genius is capable of, he commits this vision to writing in chapter 62. In like manner he describes the Sufferer in chapter 53 and portrays the victorious Hero in chapter 63. This is the divinely revealed truth of our salvation in poetic form. It is not only the external form of line and verse and stanza and strophe that is poetic, but the inner character of the diction as a whole is poetic and meant to be understood as poetry, just as one understands metaphor, metonymy, synecdoche, and hyperbole in prose to be figures of speech. Just as these figures of speech are purely human, so also is the external poetic form, and therefore to be distinguished from the divine truths which the figures express. The Spirit of God has clothed Himself with them as with a human garment. They, however, remain poetry and do not become literal reality, since they were meant to be understood poetically and not literally. One of the most striking examples of such poetic description is chapter 60, which describes the throngs of gentile nations streaming toward Zion. The entire book is written on that level, although not always to the same degree. What is true of the Book of Isaiah, is true of all prophecy which is clothed in poetic form. The poetic form and the rhetorical figures of speech are hulls or shells from which one must extract the more or less abstract or concrete truth lying within; otherwise one will lose the intended meaning. All of this is, of course, quite self-evident, but I felt mentioning it might not be superfluous.

The real difficulty faced in offering an exegesis of Isaiah is distinguishing between the contents and its poetic expression, particularly the highly imaginative Oriental forms that are characteristic of Old Testament ideas. For example, chapter 53 employs comparatively little poetic imagination. Almost everything in that chapter is to be understood literally. The opposite is true of chapter 63. But what is reality and what is poetic adornment in, for example, 60:13ff or 61:4-6? It should hardly be necessary to mention that this fact does not contradict the doctrine of divine inspiration.

TRANSLITERATION OF THE HEBREW

TABLE

Consonants

Aleph	א	’
Beth	בּ ב	bh,b
Gimel	גּ ג	gh,g
Daleth	דּ ד	dh,d
He	הּ ה	h
Waw	ו	w
Zayin	ז	z
Heth	ח	ḥ
Teth	ט	ṭ
Yod	י	y
Kaph	כּ כ ך	kh,k
Lamed	ל	l
Mem	מ ם	m
Nun	נ ן	n
Samekh	ס	s
Ayin	ע	‘
Pe	פּ פ ף	ph,p
Tsade	צ ץ	ts
Qoph	ק	q
Resh	ר	r
Sin	שׂ	s
Shin	שׁ	sh
Taw	תּ ת	th,t

Long Vowels

Qamets	בָ	$\bar{a}$
Tsere	בֵ	$\bar{e}$
Hireq	בִי	$\bar{i}$
Holem	בוֹ בֹ	$\bar{o}$
Shureq	בוּ	$\bar{u}$

Short Vowels

Pathaḥ	בַ	a
Segol	בֶ	e
Hireq	בִ	i
Holem	בָ	o
Qibbuts	בֻ	u

Hatephs

(Compound Shewas)

Hateph Pathaḥ	בֲ	a
Hateph Segol	בֱ	e
Hateph Qamets	בֳ	o
Vocal Shewa	בְ	e
Silent Shewa	בְ	*no special indication*
Dagesh forte	בּ	*the consonant is doubled*

ILLUSTRATION
Transliteration of Isaiah 40:1-2

	Hebrew	**Transliteration**
Verse 1	נַחֲמוּ	*naḥamū*
	נַחֲמוּ	*naḥamū*
	עַמִּי	*'ammī*
	יֹאמַר	*yō'mar*
	אֱלֹהֵיכֶם	*'elohēykhem*
Verse 2	דַּבְּרוּ	*dabberū*
	עַל־לֵב	*'al lēbh*
	יְרוּשָׁלַם	*yerūshālayim*
	וְקִרְאוּ אֵלֶיהָ	*weqir'ū 'eleyhā*
	כִּי מָלְאָה	*kī māle'ah*
	צְבָאָהּ	*tsebhā'āh*
	כִּי נִרְצָה	*kī nirtsāh*
	עֲוֹנָהּ	*'awōnāh*
	כִּי לָקְחָה	*kī lāqeḥāh*
	מִיַּד יְהוָֹה	*miyyadh YHWH*
	כִּפְלַיִם	*kiphlayim*
	בְּכָל	*bekhol*
	חַטֹּאתֶיהָ	*ḥaṭṭo'theyhā*

63

SUMMARY OF ISAIAH 40-66
The Future Glorification of the Church
Part I: Chapters 40-48
The Deliverance of God's People out of Babylon

First Triad: Chapters 40-42: *The Glory of God's Power Is the Guarantee of Israel's Deliverance.*

First Discourse: Chapter 40. The Lord will come in unequalled power to deliver and glorify Israel.

Second Discourse: Chapter 41. The Lord establishes His eminence above the gentiles and their gods by providing a victorious champion, through whom they are put to shame and proved to be   nothing; through him Israel, however, destroys her enemies, and herself is gloriously restored.

Third Discourse: Chapter 42. The Lord reveals His glory by sending forth and upholding His true Servant, who brings the Gospel to Jews and gentiles; also by exercising His judgment of destruction against the ungodly and His chastising judgment against the hitherto unprofitable servant Israel.

Second Triad: Chapters 43-45: *The Majesty and Grace of the Lord as Guarantee for the Deliverance of Israel.*

First Discourse: Chapter 43. The faithful love of Him who alone is true God delivers His people by grace alone.

Second Discourse: Chapter 44:1-23. The faithful love of Him who alone is true God creates for His faithful people a period of renewal through the outpouring of His Spirit and the forgiveness of their sins.

Third Discourse: Chapters 44:24-45:25. Israel's deliverance and glorification accomplished by Cyrus is a summons to all the world to seek salvation in the Lord who alone is true God.

Third Triad: Chapters 46-48: *A Preaching of Judgment and a Call to Repentance.*

First Discourse: Chapter 46. A preaching of judgment against the rebellious people of Israel.

Second Discourse: Chapter 47. A preaching of judgment upon arrogant Babylon.

Third Discourse: Chapter 48. A final appeal to the house of Jacob in view of the impending deliverance: a testimony against those whose hearts are hardened and a fervent invitation to those who might still be converted.

Part II: Chapters 49-57

The Redemption from the Guilt of Sin

First Triad: Chapters 49-51: *The Faithfulness of the Lord Accomplishes the Salvation of Israel.*

First Discourse: Chapter 49. The faithfulness of the Lord equips His Servant to be an effective Savior, and with His mighty arm He restores her children to Zion.

Second Discourse: Chapter 50. Through the perfect obedience of His Servant, the Lord in His faithfulness makes amends for the misery that His people have brought upon themselves through their sin and guilt.

Third Discourse: Chapter 51. All flesh is grass; but God's Promise of Salvation to His people stands firm forever (40:6-8).

Second Triad: Chapters 52-54: *The Lord's Zealous Love Leads His Servant Safely through His Vicarious Suffering and together with Him His Afflicted Congregation to Sublime Glory.*

First Discourse: Chapter 52:1-12. Because of the triumphant howling of the tyrannical enemies, and because of their blasphemies against His holy Name, the Lord will glorify the newly sanctified Jerusalem and reveal His holy arm by redeeming His people and leading them safely home.

Second Discourse: Chapters 52:13-53:12. The Lord exalts to divine glory the Servant who had been sent to humble Himself and take upon Himself the guilt of all as their substitute.

Third Discourse: Chapter 54. The glorification of the afflicted congregation.

Third Triad: Chapters 55-57: *An Appealing Invitation to Accept the Lord's Salvation; Renunciation of Those Who Despise the Call.*

First Discourse: Chapter 55. Invitation and call to repentance.

Second Discourse: Chapter 56:1-8. Whosoever repents with his whole heart shall receive grace abounding and shall be glorified, even though he is physically cut off from association with the people of God.

Third Discourse: Chapters 56:9-57:21. Renunciation of hardened apostates and the promise of healing extended to those who repent.

Part III: Chapters 58-66
The Spiritual, Eternal Deliverance

First Triad: Chapters 58-60: *Only if the House of Jacob Repents fully and sincerely, can the Glory of God's Grace Rise upon it for its Outward and Inward, its Temporal and its Eternal Glorification.*

First Discourse: Chapter 58. If Israel will turn from its shamelessly hypocritical show of repentance to true godliness, it can again enter into its inheritance in renewed strength.

Second Discourse: Chapter 59. The Lord's people, the house of Jacob (58:1), is so completely ensnared in apostasy and sin that no one by himself can come to the rescue of the people. Therefore the Lord Himself, with His own arm, must intervene to wreak vengeance on His irredeemable enemies and to save those who repent.

Third Discourse: Chapter 60. The glorification of Israel is realized, as the "Glory of the Lord" descends upon it.

Second Triad: Chapters 61-63:6: *The Glorification of Zion in its Highest Perfection and the Destruction of All Her Enemies.*

First Discourse: Chapter 61. The Year of Grace proclaimed by the Servant of the Lord brings freedom and happiness to the church and leads her back to a rightful priesthood with a two-fold inheritance in the newly rebuilt city.

Second Discourse: Chapter 62. Jerusalem in glorious array as the bride of the Lord.

Third Discourse: Chapter 63:1-6. The Lord's judgment of annihilation against the enemies, and the complete deliverance of those who are His own.

Third Triad: Chapters 63:7-66: *The New Order in Its Final State: the Rejection of Israel and the Adoption of the Gentiles.*

First Discourse: Chapters 63:7-64:12. The final, ardent prayer of faithful Israel for grace toward all Israel and for deliverance of the people.

Second Discourse: Chapter 65. The final rejection of apostate Israel and the preservation of the faithful remnant for a blessed new order of things.

Third Discourse: Chapter 66. The end of the old congregation and the beginning of the new church.

PART I

The Deliverance of God's People Out of Babylon

Chapters 40-48

PART I

Chapters 40-48

The Deliverance of God's People Out of Babylon

The theme of Part I (chapters 40-48) is announced in 40:2b: *Jerusalem's affliction, her captivity, is at an end.* In 40:3-5 the prophet announces how he intends to carry out this theme. As the herald of the promised Lord he has the assignment to call upon the people to prepare the way for their God, that is, to *repent*, because the *Glory of the Lord is to be revealed* for the deliverance of His people. In the actual execution of his commission (40:12 — 48:22) the prophet reverses the order of these two subjects: in the first six chapters he speaks of the *Revelation of the Glory of the Lord* and then in the last three chapters (46-48) continues with his *Admonition to Repent.* The first three chapters (40:12 through chapter 42) differ from the next three chapters (43-45) in that the former group treats of the Glory of God's *Power,* while the latter group treats of the Glory of God's *Grace.*

FIRST TRIAD
Chapters 40-42

*The Glory of God's Power
is the Guarantee
of Israel's Deliverance.*

First Discourse: Chapter 40

The Lord will come in unequaled power to deliver and glorify Israel.

The first discourse is divided into two sections or major strophes: verses 1-11 and 12-31. The first section is a complete sermon on the *imminent coming of the Lord to deliver His captive, suffering people;* the second part presents the Lord's *unequaled power and wisdom* as guaranteeing the deliverance and renewal of His faithful people.

First Section: verses 1-11: *The Lord will come to deliver His afflicted people.*

This section is constructed with a dramatic artistry that is unusual for Isaiah. It consists of four minor strophes, each of which unfolds a separate picture. In the first strophe, verses 1-2, the prophet presents God Himself, delivering as out of a cloud from heaven a command to comfort His people. The second strophe, verses 3-5, directs our attention to a voice preaching repentance and proclaiming the revelation of the glory of the grace of God. The third strophe, verses 6-8, is a dialog in which the voice of God speaks and the prophet answers. The voice directs the prophet to preach that all flesh, including God's people, is as grass, but that the promise of the grace of "our God" stands firm forever. In the last strophe, verses 9-11, the Lord turns to Jerusalem with the admonition to proclaim to the cities of Judah the advent of the Lord and the faithful shepherding of their gracious God.

This superbly constructed section is not only a complete discourse in itself, proceeding forward in rapid, powerful thoughts, but it also serves as a prologue and finally presents a program or outline of the entire book (cf. the Table of Contents in the Introduction).

72

First Strophe: verses 1-2: *Jerusalem's God issues a proclamation of comfort.*

1   *O comfort, comfort My people,*
    says your God.
2   *Speak comfortably to Jerusalem,*
    And say to her
      That her servitude is at an end,
    That her debt has been paid,
    That she shall receive double at the hand of the Lord
      for all her sins.

נַחֲמוּ נַחֲמוּ עַמִּי יֹאמַר אֱלֹהֵיכֶם: ¹

This strophe, as well as the entire section, with the exception of verses 5-8, employs the Qinah rhythm (cf. the Introduction). It is a striking peculiarity of the prophet that he has no introduction, but with the very first words plunges into the middle of things. Thus here, at the very beginning, without any preliminaries, we hear his proclamation: *"Comfort, comfort My people,"* and it is only the following parenthesis that names the Author of the call: *"Says your God."* The suffixes in *'ammī* and *'elōhēykhem* correspond to each other — *My* people, *your* God. In the second line the parallel to "My people" is "Jerusalem." Clearly, it is the God of the inhabitants of Jerusalem who is introduced as the speaker. Wherever *'elōhīm* appears with a pronominal suffix, the *gracious* Lord is indicated. It is the God of Grace who in the following discourse earnestly desires that His people be comforted. The repetition of *nahamū* emphasizes God's earnestness. On the one hand, it points to the people's great need of comfort and, on the other hand, to the Lord's ardent desire to extend the needed comfort. The communication of this comfort is to equal in its intensity both the people's great need and the warmth of the Lord's desire. The following discourse shows that comfort is available in greatest abundance.

Even the better exegetes write a great deal of but little consequence about the imperfect form of *yō'mar* in the parenthetical phrase "says your God." Klostermann and von Hofmann explain it as a pure future, as though a command were here referred to which the Lord would address to the prophet at a future time. According to Delitzsch, the imperfect expresses duration, action both present and continuing. Both explanations are incorrect. By far the most frequent form of this phrase in Isaiah II is an introductory *kōh 'āmar YHWH* (42:5; 43:1,14,16; 44:2, 6, 24; 45:1,11,14,18;

48:17; 49:7,8,22,25; 50:1; 51:22; 52:3,4; 56:1,4; 57:15; 65:8,13; 66:1,12). Twice *kōh 'āmar* is preceded by *we'attāh* "but now" (43:1; 49:5). Placed parenthetically, or at the end, *'āmar* appears in 48:22; 54:6,8,10; 57:19,21; 65:7,25; 66:9,20,21,23. *ne'um YHWH* "Oracle of the Lord," appears parenthetically in 41:14; 43:12; 52:5; 55:8; 59:20; 66:22, and at the beginning of the verse in 56:8. A careful comparison of these passages shows that when the phrase is expressed in the form of the perfect it does not have a temporal connotation, nor does it emphasize the termination of the act of speaking. The perfect is purely abstract and connotes nothing but the action itself. In German it is to be expressed, as Luther does, with the simple present. The same is true of the imperfect *yō'mar*. It occurs eight times in Isaiah in this same phrase: 1:11; 1:18; 33:10; 40:1; 40:25; 41:21; and twice in 66:9. In no case is there a reference to time or to the completion of an action. The noun-construct *ne'um* (really a Qal passive participle) could in every case take the place of simple *'āmar* or *yō'mar* without the least change in meaning. However, the phrase does take on various rhetorical shades of meaning according to its syntactical position at the beginning, in the middle, at the end, or as an addition. In each form of the phrase and in each position it lends emphasis to the speech by indicating the identity of the speaker.

The phrase receives special emphasis at the beginning when it is preceded by *kōh,* "thus." In that case it always appears as *kōh 'āmar*, never as *kōh yō'mar*, and of course not as *kōh ne'um*. Plain *yō'mar* or *'āmar* do not occur at the beginning. In 43:1 and 49:5 the opening *'āmar* is preceded by *we'attāh*. Both *'āmar* and *yō'mar* are restricted to second or third place in a sentence, while *ne'um* introduces a sentence only once (56:8) and otherwise is in second or third place. Thus *yō'mar YHWH, yō'mar 'elōhēykhem* etc., when occupying a secondary place, have no particular significance beyond the characteristic difference between imperfect and perfect. Whereas the perfect is the mode of objectivity, the imperfect rather expresses the emotions of the speaker, or else introduces a *new action* that lies in the immediate present and links that action with an existing situation. Consequently, the phrase as used in Isaiah always appears near the beginning, never at the conclusion of a discourse, whereas the parenthetical *'āmar YHWH* always comes at the close of a sentence. Insofar as the phrase refers to a present situation, it acquires a certain literary-critical importance in this passage. It is a clear proof, if not of Isaiah's authorship, then at least of an intentional and inseparable connection of thought between Isaiah I and Isaiah II. With this parenthetical *yō'mar 'elōhēykhem* at the head of the discourse, whoever it was that wrote the second part of Isaiah directs attention to a situation just described, with which he now establishes a connection by introducing a new thought. The situation just described in Book I is the judgment that has been passed on Judah-Jerusalem because of its hardness of heart: all that belonged to Judah-Jerusalem would be taken to Babylon (39:6-8). But this "word of the Lord Sabaoth" (39:5) is not the final word that He has for His people. He has another word, another sermon, a great sermon of comfort to reveal, and that sermon is introduced by *yō'mar 'elōhēykhem,* which at the same time refers back to the preceding book.

If some Deutero-Isaiah had wanted to write a second book wholly independent of Book I, he would have had to use an introductory *kōh 'āmar* instead of the parenthetical *yō'mar.* It might be added that the antithetical character of the contents of Books I and II (message of judgment, message of salvation) gives *yō'mar 'elōhēykhem* an adversative shading that could be expressed with: "and now says your God."

As for the imperative in the twofold *naḥamū,* it is quite generally assumed that the Lord is thus formally and directly addressing the official messengers of God, the prophets. The LXX inserted ἱερεῖς at this point. But that implies a misunderstanding of the poetic-rhetorical form of prophetic speech and of the relation of this sentence to the rest of the prophet's book. Isaiah II is prophecy in poetic, often dramatic, form, which frequently employs the imperative plural in very general exhortations, such as, Hallelujah, or "Give thanks unto the Lord," "Sing unto the Lord a new song," and similar phrases at the beginning of numerous Psalms. This dramatic imperative occurs again and again in Isaiah II, for example, in 41:1; 45:8; 46:3,12; 47:1, etc. In this sentence the *naḥamū* simply expresses in poetic form God's will that His people be comforted. Moreover, the author of the book testifies with these words concerning his own mission. He gives notice, at the very beginning, of his own calling, as he does also in verses 6-8. He thus emphasizes the divine authority of the entire following sermon.

In this book the prophet appears as God's own messenger of comfort. The very first strophe abounds in comfort. Every word is literally a word of comfort. Following upon the double "comfort, comfort" immediately follow the Lord's words "*My* people" and the prophet's corresponding phrase, "*your* God." Israel captive in

Babylon, overwhelmed with disaster ever since the destruction of its holy city (54:11), devoid of all comfort, complaining that the Lord had forsaken and forgotten it (40:27; 49:14), is to be assured beforehand, on the authority of God Himself, that in spite of all the sufferings with which God has visited it, it still has not been rejected conclusively. It is still *His* people, the chosen, peculiar people of the Lord, and the Lord is still its gracious God who, in spite of all its disobedience, has kept the covenant to which by His oath He had bound Himself.

The second verse develops the promised comfort by means of concrete statements. To begin with, there is a strong parallel to verse 1:

$$\text{2 דַּבְּר֞וּ עַל־לֵ֤ב יְרֽוּשָׁלִַ֙ם֙ וְקִרְא֣וּ אֵלֶ֔יהָ}$$
$$\text{כִּ֤י מָֽלְאָה֙ צְבָאָ֔הּ כִּ֥י נִרְצָ֖ה עֲוֺנָ֑הּ}$$
$$\text{כִּ֤י לָקְחָה֙ מִיַּ֣ד יְהוָ֔ה כִּפְלַ֖יִם בְּכָל־חַטֹּאתֶֽיהָ׃}$$

dibbēr 'al lēbh, literally "to speak to the heart," always means to speak to someone cordially, lovingly, in a manner that is friendly, that awakens confidence and gives comfort. Thus Genesis 34:3; 50:21; Ruth 2:13; 2 Samuel 19:8(7); 2 Chronicles 30:22; 32:6; Hosea 2:14 (16). So also in this passage. It is really a poetic paraphrase of the *nahamū* of the first verse in accordance with the principle of parallelism of members, the basic rule of Hebrew poetry (cf. the Introduction). As *dabberū 'al lēbh* is the parallel to *nahamū,* so *yerūshālayim* parallels *'ammī* of the first verse. The object of the consolation is thus concretely expressed. "My people" and "Jerusalem" are equivalent in meaning. Jerusalem was God's city, the Lord's dwelling on earth (Ps. 46:5,6(4,5); 132:13,14). Jerusalem's inhabitants, together with those of the whole land whose center of worship was in Jerusalem, were His people. Now the city lay in ruins and her inhabitants languished far away from those ruins, in the Babylonian captivity. Outwardly the loving relationship between God and the city and its inhabitants had been terminated. But now the Lord again calls the rejected people *His* people and refers to them by the name of His City and their City. Thus "Jerusalem," with its parallel "My people," becomes a name of endearment, an honored name, with which the Lord wants to remind exiled Israel that the former relationship of grace and love between Him and them still continues unbroken with all its inherent promises.

weqir'ū 'eleyhā corresponds technically (poetically) to *yō'mar*

76

'elōhēykhem. we is *Waw explicativum* (Ges. K. Gram., 28th ed., 154a and Note b, page 484), and may be translated "namely." *qir'ū 'eleyhā* means "call to her," or "preach to her," as Luther translated.

The next three clauses express the contents of the proclamation of comfort. Each is introduced by *kī*, "that." Luther translated the first *kī* with "that" and the next two with "for." In his notes to Isaiah he explains that the second clause gives the reason for the first, and that the third clause contains the reason for the first two. Except for a few modern theologians who follow the LXX in striking the second *kī* and who take the third to be a particle expressing cause, it is generally agreed that in all three cases *kī* introduces an object-clause and is to be translated with "that." There is no reason why the second and the third should be translated differently from the first. The three clauses are the grammatical object of *qir'ū 'eleyhā*.

The first message of comfort that is to be proclaimed to the Lord's people is "that the affliction of Jerusalem and of the people is at an end." The basic meaning of *tsābhā'* is "host" or "army" as in *YHWH tsebhā'ōth*, Lord of Hosts, then also "warfare, military service." Thus the word came to designate figuratively the trouble and affliction of human life. It is so used in Job 7:1ff and 14:14. Here it is the designation of all of Israel's suffering that followed the destruction of Jerusalem and the exile to Babylon — the misery of prisoners of war. Now this trouble is *māle'āh*, that is, completed, fulfilled, at an end, past. The verb, like those in the two following sentences, is in the perfect. It is hardly necessary to say that the three perfects, each preceded by a governing *kī*, are all of the same type. The question is only, of what type? The question will have to be answered at some length in connection with the controversial last phrase. At this point it suffices to note that the three perfects are all prophetic perfects, perfects denoting confidence, presenting the facts as already accomplished in the thought of the speaker, although the actual completion still lies in the future. (See Par. 106 in Ges. Gram. 28th Ed. This grammar will from now on be referred to as G. K. Gr. or simply as Gr.) In prophetic speech this meaning of the perfect proceeds from the fact that the prophet sees future facts as already accomplished and so expresses them. In the sentence before us God Himself is speaking. With Him, saying and doing, foretelling and fulfilling, are one and the same, just as past, present, and future are one. In point of time the situation of the speaker is antecedent to what is being prophesied, in this case, the end of the exile. His speech is a prediction and the perfects announce the future as an already accomplished fact. Before God, Jerusalem's trouble is already ended, by virtue of God's all-powerful counsel; therefore its termination in time is also assured. That is the first great comfort that is to be proclaimed to God's people.

The second clause reads: *That her debt has been paid.* The word *ʿāwōn* means "sin," "sin as guilt or debt." That it has that meaning here is indicated by its predicate *nirtsāh,* which means "paid, discharged, removed." The verb *rātsāh* usually has the meaning "to delight in," and in the Niphal "to be made agreeable." But the word is also used transitively, especially in connection with *ʿāwōn,* and then it means "to pay a debt, to atone for"; in the Niphal "to be atoned for, to be made good." Its use in Leviticus 26:41-43 is decisive for this meaning of the word. What is meant here is not what modernistic exegetes, including Delitzsch, understand on the basis of the passage in Leviticus, namely, that Israel has itself by its suffering in the exile atoned for its guilt. Isaiah is here speaking of that vicarious Sufferer for sins, *the* Servant of the Lord, of whom he writes in the 53rd chapter: "Surely, He hath borne our griefs."

The threat in Leviticus 26 and elsewhere (cf. Deut. 28), according to which Israel will have to bear its own guilt, is the voice of the Law. In our passage we have a promise of the Gospel, namely, that the Lord has cast upon HIM the iniquity of us all (Isa. 53:6). It is the removal of the guilt of sin through Christ which is to be preached to this people as their great comfort and which is also the underlying reason for the termination of the affliction of the people. The people themselves were completely unable to atone for their own debt of sin, as is stated in verses 6-8 and carried out fully in chapters 49-57. Not only is all flesh in general as grass, but just *this* people in particular is as grass. But "the Word of our God" (v. 8), the old, old promise concerning the Bearer of our sins, still stands firm and will forever remain so. Because of this Word, the removal of the guilt of Israel's sin was in God's mind already an accomplished fact, and this fact was to be proclaimed as the reason why Israel's warfare was at an end.

Modern historical-critical exegesis is afflicted with the curse of not being able to find Christ anywhere in the Old Testament, in spite of such passages as John 5:46; Luke 24:26f, 44-47; Acts 3:18-24; 10:43. It is unable to find Christ even in those passages where He is portrayed in the brightest of colors. As for the book of

Isaiah, modern exegesis has sunk to the level of the Jewish-rabbinical interpretation, which sees in the "Servant of the Lord," who with His own blood is to save Jews and gentiles from their guilt and punishment and lead them to glory, none other than the people of Israel, deaf and blind and of hardened heart, upon whom the Lord has poured out the fury of His wrath. In this passage, as elsewhere in Isaiah II, especially in chapter 53, they do not see Christ, *the* Servant of the Lord, in whom His soul delights and upon whom He poured out His Spirit (42:1ff; 61:1; Matt. 12:18ff; Luke 4:18). In their opinion the Lord's Servant is the hardened and rejected people of Israel, in its more ideal portion, that is to be the vicarious sufferer for sin and the savior of itself and the rest of the world. There is nothing we can do about that kind of exegesis; its point of reference is essentially different from ours. Exegesis that is still essentially believing and Christian sees in the *nirtsāh 'awōnāh* the atonement for sin by the promised Redeemer, the Servant of the Lord in the highest sense of the term, namely, Christ. Thus also the entire New Testament.

Concerning the last clause — *that she shall receive double at the hands of the Lord for all her sins* — Delitzsch has this to say: "Gesenius, Hitzig, Ewald, Umbreit, Stier, and Hahn are inconsistent when they take *lāqehāh* to be a prophetic perfect expressing certainty of a future event, which it cannot be, since it is linked with two regular perfects, and then explain *kiphlayim* as double *grace* (like *mishneh* 61:7 and, perhaps borrowing from Isaiah, Zech. 9:12) which Jerusalem is to receive, instead of the double *punishment* which she has already endured (like *mishneh* in Jer. 16:18)." But on both points Delitzsch is in the wrong as compared with the commentators previously named. *lāqehāh* is not linked with two "regular" perfects. A regular perfect is one that expresses an act that is actually of the past, definitely finished. (See G.K. Gr. 106b, page 309.) But what is expressed in these three clauses is not in the past, not even according to those commentators who place the author of chapters 40-48 in the last third of the exile. They too understand these clauses to be at least a mantic prediction of the future, namely, of the overthrow of Babylon and of the release of the Jews by Cyrus, events which had not yet taken place. These perfects are and will continue to be prophetic perfects. Only one who assumes that the author was writing after the events described happened could call these "regular perfects," and such an assumption would stamp the author as a fraud.

This settles the meaning of *kiphlayim*, "double, twofold." If this word is taken to mean the punishment of the exile, one is forced to agree with Delitzsch who says: "The third clause repeats in a loftier and more resounding tone the contents of the second." That reduces the contents of the three clauses to the mere historical statement that Jerusalem's past captivity came to an end, because by it the city fully atoned for her guilt before God. Thus the prophet is made to appear as a divinely commissioned interpreter of an exile that lay in the past, who now *post factum* explains to the people that the exile was God's punishment for Israel's sin and that God permitted the exile to come to an end because by the exile Israel had made ample atonement for its guilt. Such an explanation cuts the very heart out of the prophet's message of comfort and makes the message of the rest of the book altogether purposeless. But the commentators do not seem to have noticed that. No, as surely as these words are prophecy, even if written, as the modernistic exegetes assume, only five years before the fall of Babylon, the prophet is writing of the future in all three clauses, including the clause *lāqeḥāh kiphlayim miyyadh YHWH.* This therefore cannot refer to punishment and must denote grace and favor. The reference to *mishneh* in 61:7, "For your shame ye shall have double," is in place. For it is just this twofold, abundant grace which shall be the allotment of the people who are to be saved from the exile that forms the subject matter of the third part of the book (chapters 58-66). Just as atonement by the Messiah for their guilt is the subject of the second part (chapters 49-57), and the release under Cyrus is the theme of the first part (chapters 40-48).

What about *bekhol ḥaṭṭō'theyhā?* We can state without fear of being refuted that *ḥaṭṭā'th,* at least in Isaiah 5:18; Zechariah 14:19; Numbers 32:23; and Proverbs 10:16, means punishment for sin, chastisement. That the word has this meaning in these passages is generally conceded. "She has received twofold for all her chastisement." In the elaboration of this clause in chapters 58-66 the future glorification of Jerusalem is consistently and emphatically referred to not only as requital but even as double requital for earlier chastisement. Cp. 60:15ff; 61:7; 62:8ff; 66:12; with 65:8ff. Just that is also the meaning of this passage.

This sermon of comfort applies particularly to the God-fearing portion of Israel, which though not without sin, still was not the real object of the Lord's punishment. That punishment was meant for the impenitent, callous people; but the God-fearing portion had to share the punishment of the exile on account of their godless brethren. That suffering, however, shall be made up to them by a twofold recompense based on the vicarious suffering endured in payment of their debt by the promised Redeemer. Even if *ḥaṭṭā'th* is taken in the sense of sin or liability and the *Beth* as *Beth pretii* (at, for, as remuneration for), the sense remains essentially the same. It is not at all a foolish thought that God repays sin with grace and favor. It is, in fact, the foolishness of the Gospel that God repays the sin of His chosen people with forgiveness and exaltation. The *Beth* connected with *khol ḥaṭṭō'theyhā* is broad enough in meaning to permit rendering it with *in, at, with,* or *in spite of.* If we proceed from the unassailable assumption that *lāqeḥāh* is a prophetic perfect, *Beth* will of itself take on a correct meaning.

Thus we have in the first strophe an expression of the gracious will of the Lord to the effect that His people, languishing in the Babylonian captivity, shall be comforted with the threefold message that its trouble is at an end, that its debt has been paid by the promised Savior, and that all suffering shall receive double compensation. Logically and theologically, clause number 2 contains the inner reason for 1 and 3, and number 2 is an amplification of clause 1. At the same time this strophe serves as the outline for the entire following book.

In the next three strophes, verses 3-5, 6-8, 9-11, the prophet shows in three vivid pictures how his threefold message is to be fulfilled, or, rather how he intends to present their fulfillment in the following three great sections of the book.

Second Strophe: verses 3-5: *The Voice in the wilderness preaching repentance and the revelation of the glory of the Lord.*

3 *A Voice, preaching: "In the wilderness*
  prepare the way of the Lord,
 Make straight in the desert
  a highway for our God.
4 *Let every valley be raised up*
  and every mountain and hill brought low,
 Rough places be made a plain
  and the ridges a low valley.
5 *So shall the glory of the Lord be revealed,*
 And all flesh shall see it together,
 For the mouth of the Lord has spoken."

The strophe consists of seven lines, of which the first four are written in Qinah rhythm. The remaining three lines, which form the conclusion, are in the usual rhythm of three stresses. Duhm and Cheyne therefore simply assume that the last three are an interpolation. This arbitrary judgment, which makes mere rhythm (of which, to this day, we still know so very little) a measure of the genuineness of the text is rejected even by other members of the same school of modernistic exegetes. Certainly the prophet Isaiah has as much right to vary the rhythm as Schiller, for example, in his *Die Glocke.*

$$^3\ \text{קוֹל קוֹרֵא}$$
$$\text{בַּמִּדְבָּר פַּנּוּ דֶּרֶךְ יְהוָה}$$
$$\text{יַשְּׁרוּ בָּעֲרָבָה מְסִלָּה לֵאלֹהֵינוּ:}$$
$$^4\ \text{כָּל־גֶּיא יִנָּשֵׂא וְכָל־הַר וְגִבְעָה יִשְׁפָּלוּ}$$
$$\text{וְהָיָה הֶעָקֹב לְמִישׁוֹר וְהָרְכָסִים לְבִקְעָה:}$$

This entire strophe is presented in highly dramatic form. *qōl qōre*, meaning "Voice of one speaking," identifies what follows as a scene in the drama. In spirit the prophet already hears the sermon that in due time will be proclaimed in Israel. With the very first words he directs the reader's attention to it. Concerning the use of *qōl* as an interjection, cf. G.K. Gr. 146,b, p. 467; Genesis 4:10; Isaiah 13:4; 52:8; 66:6; Jeremiah 10:22; Song of Songs 2:8; Micah 6:9.

The sermon is an unusual one. "In the wilderness prepare the way of the Lord, make straight in the desert a highway for our God." The two sentences, constructed strictly according to the poetic device of the parallelism of members, say essentially the same thing. There is a question whether *bammidhbār*, "in the desert," belongs to *qōre*'or to *pannū derekh.* In the New Testament (Matt. 3, Mark 1, Luke 3, John 1), in agreement with the LXX, the ἐν τῇ ἐρήμῳ is attached to βοῶντος *(qōre'):* "the voice of one crying in the wilderness." In the Hebrew text *bammidhbār* is attached grammatically and technically to what follows. The Hebrew accentuation could lead the beginner in Hebrew astray. *qōre*'has the small Zaqeph, *bammidhbār* has the great Zaqeph. But in this case, says Delitzsch, "Zaqeph qaton divides more sharply than Zaqeph gadol, as in Deuteronomy 26:14; 28:8; 2 Kings 1:6; Zephaniah 1:7," although the force of the two is usually the same. Consider also the parallelism of the two lines: in the wilderness prepare — make straight in the desert. In the second line "in the desert" is an adverbial modifier of "make straight"; so also "in the wilderness" is to be understood as modifying "prepare." Perhaps the problem is to be solved by thinking of *bammidhbār* as occuring twice, but to be read only once. Since it is a desert highway that is to be prepared, the herald of this command is to be thought of as appearing in the desert. And after all, the Masoretic pointing is later than the LXX, the Targums, and the Gospels and is not *per se* definitive. Finally, the principle of parallelism is flexible enough to permit *bammidhbār* to be attached to *qōrē'* rather than to *pannū derekh.*

The highway that is to be prepared is not the way "upon which the exiles will return home, which is called the highway of Jehovah, because this is His counsel and His work and He journeys with them and at their head (v. 9-11)" (Budde in Kautzsch's *Great Bible*). Rather, it is the way that the Lord will come as Savior of His people. The *lē'lōhēynū,* "for our God," makes this interpretation certain, if *derekh YHWH* does not already settle the matter. The thought is that as the Lord once came through the desert of Paran and from Sinai to deliver His people out of Egypt (Deut. 33:2; Judges 5:4; Hab. 3:3), so He will now come from Jerusalem by way of the Arabian desert that lies between the Jewish homeland and Babylon in order to save His people. That is why the herald's voice admonishes that the trackless way of the desert be made into a highway, lest the coming of the Lord be delayed. This, of course, is figurative, poetic language; neither the prophet nor the people had such a naive and gross conception of God as to imagine that something physical was meant here. The picture derives from the custom of Oriental potentates who, when on a journey, sent emissaries ahead of them to warn dwellers along the road to make a highway smooth and level. Cf. Psalm 68:5(4), where Luther mistakenly translated "gentle" for "through the desert."

What the prophet has here presented in a picture, he puts into the form of a discourse in the last three chapters of the first part of the book — cf. especially 45:22ff; 46:12,13; 48:1ff. The rough and uneven desert highway is a representation of the condition of the heart of the people, of their indifference, of their false sense of security, their carnal attitude and self-righteousness, in short, their impenitence. But one goes too far if one tries to put a special spiritual significance into each separate figurative expression, such as, valley, mountain, hill, etc. These are all poetic, pictorial representations for but one thing: obstacles to the coming of the

Lord — impenitence. The admonition has but one meaning: Repent! That was the burden of John the Baptist's preaching.

This prophecy was fulfilled in a very special sense in John the Baptist, as the Scriptures clearly testify, Malachi 3:1; 4:5; Matthew 3:1ff; 11:10ff; Mark 1:2ff; Luke 1:76; 3:2ff; John 1:23. Matthew says plainly: "For this is he that was spoken of by the prophet Esaias, saying, etc." This is testimony to the effect that in those words of Isaiah God had John the Baptist in mind. Whether or not the prophet was conscious of that when he received the words and wrote them is of no importance, cp. 1 Peter 1:10ff. This prophecy, let it be said, concerns not only John the Baptist but also all other preachers who have a similar calling, whether they lived before John or later than he. Prophecy frequently has a way of locating future events of the same general kind in the same level of time, regardless of the actual date of their occurrence. The most familiar example is found in Matthew 24, where the judgment upon Jerusalem and the Day of Judgment are combined in a single picture, since the lesser event is in its characteristic features a faithful picture of the greater event, and therefore foretells and gives positive assurance of its subsequent occurrence. In the same way, in the very first triad of discourses, Cyrus, who delivered Israel out of the Babylonian exile (ch. 41), and Christ, the Savior of gentiles and Jews, appear side by side (42:1-9), since Cyrus is an exact type of Christ. Similarly, 42:10-25 is a description of the zeal of the Lord, both when He judges the hypocrites on the Last Day and when He judges the hardened and impenitent Israel of the exile.

The same relationship holds true throughout the book. Immediately after Part I (ch. 40-48), which treats predominantly of the deliverance of Israel out of Babylon, we find in Part II (ch. 49-57) salvation through Christ portrayed on the background of the Old Testament conditions of the exile. In the same manner the prophecies in Part III (ch. 58-66) pertaining to the physical restitution of the exiled people are constantly intertwined with those pertaining to the spiritual renewal of the New Testament Church. The two prophecies are, in fact, a part of each other. This is so, because God and man, grace and sin, the Gospel of salvation and the rage of the devil do not change, but remain the same throughout all times. There is really nothing new under the sun. History keeps on repeating itself till the Last Day. As in the realm of nature seedtime and harvest, cold and heat, summer and winter, day and night constantly follow one another so long as the earth shall stand (Gen. 8), so also God, who says of Himself: "I Am that I Am" (Exod. 3:14), does not cease to be "the Lord, the Lord God, merciful and gracious, long-suffering and abundant in goodness and truth, keeping mercy for thousands, forgiving iniquity and transgression and sin, and that will by no means clear the guilty; visiting the iniquity of the fathers upon the children and upon the children's children, unto the third and to the fourth generation" (Exod. 34:6,7). Until the Last Day every imagination of the thoughts of the human heart will be evil continually (Gen. 6:5). Therefore the history of man will produce only sin and grace, unbelief and judgment. The saints alone will escape the general doom, although they share in all the experiences common to humanity. Human history reaches its climax in the cross of Christ and comes to its final conclusion on the great Day of Judgment. Until then the history of mankind is a constant repetition of the offer of grace and the call to repentance, of the rejection of grace and of judgment. Only the historical, geographical, ethnic conditions, the external and individual peculiarities vary; the essence of what takes place is always the same.

Since Christ crucified is the culmination of every demonstration of grace, every prophecy of grace must terminate in Him; and since Christ on the Last Day is the culmination of every act of judgment, therefore every prophecy of judgment also terminates in Him. Both kinds of prophecy, whether of grace or of judgment, are alike in that they culminate in the person of Christ. The prophecies may treat the earlier historical events as being contemporary with the final Day of Judgment, or they may treat the earlier occurrences separately, without, however, severing their inner connection with the great climactic event. The earliest of the holy prophets, Obadiah, for example, combines the imminent judgment upon Edom with the Lord's judgment upon all gentiles (verse 15) and with the final Day of Judgment (verse 21). That combination becomes routine in the prophets after Obadiah. Indeed, since salvation and judgment are both an expression of the identical zeal of our gracious God, the day of grace and the day of judgment are often presented as one thing, occurring simultaneously, cf. 42:1-9; 42:10-17; Joel 3(2:28-32); Malachi 3:1ff; 4:1-6.

This manner of presentation is especially characteristic of Isaiah. Throughout the second part of his book he links together Old Testament manifestations of grace with New Testament grace, and Old Testament acts of judgment with the Last Judgment. Likewise there appears a juxtaposition of Cyrus and Christ, of Israel, the servant of the Lord, and of Christ, the Servant of the Lord, so that the reader must always carefully note of what and of whom the prophet is speaking. Hence, the various Old Testament elements in the prophecy are almost always figures and types of New Testament spiritual realities. Zion-Jerusalem, Israel, Jacob, My people, etc., are designations of the church of all times, particularly of the New Testament Church. Compare Galatians 4:26ff where Paul explains Isaiah 54:1 as referring to the New Testament Church. In the New Testament, Babylon became so much a type and representation of godless world power that the name was used by New Testament writers as a synonym for all powers hostile to God, as in 1 Peter 5:13; Revelation 14; 16; 17; 18. The hardened and impenitent among the Jews are counterparts of the hypocrites of the New Testament Church; the Babylonian exile is a faithful picture of the grievous captivity of Christendom under the power of sin, the Law, the world, and the devil; the deliverance out of Babylon is a picture of the final deliverance of the church from all evil, the restoration of Israel, a picture of the spiritual renewal of the Christians through the Word and the Spirit — even in their wretchedness. Christ and the kingdom of God are thus the heart and soul of the Old Testament, and whatever the prophet may be preaching — it all points to Him.

Unless this fact is kept in mind, one will not be able to understand any prophet, least of all, Isaiah, who in all three parts of his book, even in Part I (chap.40-48), really is prophesying of Christ and of the New Testament and the eternal kingdom of God, even though his view is directed first of all to the deliverance of the Old Testament people from Babylonian despotism. The glad tidings: Comfort, comfort My people, etc., with its threefold basis certainly applies first of all, but in a restricted sense, to the exiled people of Israel. In its fullest sense it applies to the New Testament people of God — to us poor, wretched Christians today. So also the voice in the desert. The prophet Isaiah himself was this voice, specifically in this book. In these verses and in verses 6-8 he tells how he was called to carry out this office. Jeremiah, Ezekiel, and others were also this voice calling out to Israel. But all these were the voice only in a restricted sense, insofar as it was meant for the Jewish people languishing in Babylon or the same people being so pitiably rehabilitated later. Perfect fulfillment did not come until John the Baptist appeared, to be followed immediately by the Angel of the Covenant, the Lord Himself, who came to reveal the glory of His grace and His judgment for the salvation and the judgment of all the peoples of the world. As Isaiah, Jeremiah, Ezekiel, and the later prophets were preachers of repentance for the spiritually devastated Israel of their own time, so John was the preacher of repentance, κατ' ἐξοχήν, who came at the time when Israel's ruin had reached its climax. He was the true and real voice that prepared the way before the Lord who appeared in the midst of Israel, but was not recognized by them. Whoever is called to preach the Gospel since the appearance of John and the Lord should be aware that he too is included in this passage and that he too has been called to prepare the way before the Lord by preaching repentance and proclaiming to believing hearts the abounding comfort of God, which rests firmly in the revealed glory of the Lord, so that in them too the glory of the Lord may be richly revealed.

The separate words and phrases in verse 4 are clear enough. *gey'*, usually written with Tsere or with Patach (in the latter case with Shewa under *Yod* and most frequently without the final *Aleph*), means a deep valley, a gorge, a mountain cleft. *biqʿāh* is a broad, open, flat valley. It is a question whether *heʿāqōbh* might not mean a winding road and *mīshōr* a straight road. Luke translated καὶ ἔσται τὰ σκολιὰ εἰς εὐθεῖαν No one really knows what *rekhāsīm* are. The most probable meaning is mountain ridges, from *rākhas*, to bind together, like *jugum* from *jungere*, yoke, mountain yoke. The verse contains only individual features of the general thought expressed poetically in verse 3, and the words must not be pressed.

5 וְנִגְלָה כְּבוֹד יְהוָה וְרָאוּ כָל־בָּשָׂר יַחְדָּו כִּי פִּי יְהוָה
דִּבֵּר:

The *Waw* in *wenighlāh* introduces an apodosis. In verse 4 there is a *Waw* consecutive perfect in *wehayāh* which continues the line of jussive imperfects that precede it and that sets forth the conditions for the revelation of the Glory of the Lord proclaimed in this verse (cf. G.K. Gr. 112, kk, p. 337). The results of research into the use of *Waw* being still incomplete, (cf. loc. cit. pp, p. 338), no definite conclusion can be drawn from the grammatical construction. The *Waw* may connect the apodosis with the participle *qōre'* at the beginning of verse 3 (G.K. Gr. 112, oo, p. 337f and 116, w, p. 361); it will then yield this meaning: The revelation of the Glory of the Lord will come after the appearance of the preacher of repentance. This interpretation really is the only one that accords with the fulfillment. The revelation of the Lord depends on the coming of the preacher of repentance, not on the repentance of the people. Others simply take the *Waw* in a causal sense, introducing the effect of the call to repentance. One cannot object to that interpretation, for the call to repent and the repentance itself are meaningless apart from the appearance of the Lord of grace and of judgment. Cf. Matthew 3:2: "Repent, *for* . . ., etc." Cf. also Acts 17:30ff, and Peter's call to repentance in Acts 2:36 and 38. The *Waw* in *werā'u* is one of the same kind as the *Waw* in *wenighlāh*.

The term *kebhōdh YHWH* must not be passed over lightly. It is true that it is here an abstract expression, but the abstract term does not attain its full dignity unless it is viewed in connection with that concrete physical manifestation that bears the name "glory of the Lord" as a *terminus technicus* and that symbolizes that glory. Maimonides correctly describes it as *"splendor quidam creatus, quem Deus quasi prodigii vel miraculi loco ad magnificentiam suam ostendendam alicubi habitare fecit,"* although that description does not present it in its full form. Scripture sometimes presents it briefly, and then again in great detail. All the references to it in Scripture that I am aware of are here noted: Exodus 3:2ff; 16:7,10; 24:16f; 33:22; 40:34ff; Leviticus 9:23f; Numbers 14:10; 16:19,42; 20:6; 2 Chronicles 5:14; 7:1ff; 1 Kings 8:11; Isaiah 6 (cf. John 12:41); Ezekiel 1; 3:23; 8:4; 9:3; 10; 11; 43:2,4,5; 44:4; Luke 2:9; 9:28ff (cf 2 Peter 1:16f); Acts 7:55; Romans 9:4; Revelation 4; 15:8; 21:11,23. Compare also Psalm 18:8ff and 50:1ff. Ezekiel 1 has the most complete description. The Revelation of St. John differs in details, possibly because it changed the form somewhat. Its basic feature was the flame of fire ("like devouring fire," Exodus 24:17), canopied by the blue vault of heaven, wherein God in human form sat enthroned on a throne borne by four winged cherubim. Its outer frame was a rainbow. In its complete form it was a symbol of all God's perfections.

In this connection we call particular attention to a few details. The rainbow stands for the goodness and grace of God, Genesis 9:12-17; Revelation 10:1. The blue vault of heaven, in which the throne is set, represents His royal majesty. That He is enthroned above the cherubim expresses His actual rule over all creatures, Isaiah 37:16; Psalm 99:1. The bright inner flame of fire that burns between the cherubim and lights up the blue of heaven as it emanates from the form of God represents the purity, holiness, and unapproachableness of God (cf. especially Deuteronomy 4 and 5.)

The overall meaning of this manifestation might be expressed in the word *qādhōsh,* holy. Compare the "holy, holy, holy" in Isaiah 6.

Whenever this vision appears, it first creates fear and terror, because it signifies the presence and the intervention of the great and holy God. But — and this is important — the meaning of *kebhōdh YHWH* is not fully expressed by "holiness of the Lord." The Lord, the Holy One, who is a devouring fire, is seated in His majesty on His kingly throne, surrounded by the bow of grace which spans the heavens, is rooted in the earth, and encompasses His universal governance. This vision thus becomes a symbol of the grace of the Holy One, who is in Himself a devouring fire. Encompassed by grace, clothed in grace, He, the Holy One, draws near to the sinners to bless, to succor, and to save them. In history, too, this vision from its first manifestation in the burning bush till it appears in the fields of Bethlehem is both mark and symbol of the grace of God, whose will it is to save His people. It is in this very grace that God is holy, unapproachable, unassailable, and a devouring fire for all who wantonly spurn His grace. It is the *gracious* God who is not to be mocked, Galatians 6:7; Exodus 20:5; 34:7; Numbers 14:10; 16:19,42. The *kebhōdh YHWH* is the gracious holiness of the holy grace of the Lord, a symbol of the Gospel, which the Lord has summed up in these words: He that believeth and is baptized shall be saved, but he that believeth not shall be damned, Mark 16:16. Yes, it is a symbol of the Lord Christ Himself, the Savior of the lost, the Judge of the unbelieving world. It is thus that John describes Him; it is thus that Christ speaks of Himself, as do also His disciples. Christ it is in whom this word of Isaiah's about the revelation of the glory of the Lord is really to be fulfilled, John 1:14-18.

The prophet sees this glory first of all as it is revealed in the deliverance of Israel out of the Babylonian exile and, as is clear from the description in 40:12-31; 41; 42, he views it at first as the unequalled majesty, power, and wisdom, and then in chapters 43,44,45 as the abounding grace, love, forgiveness, mercy, and faithfulness of the Lord. But always it is the one great Holy Thing that must be treated with greatest reverence, which brings faith, salvation, and exaltation to those who repent and believe, but ruin and destruction to those who despise and reject it. The instrument for this manifestation of the glory of the Lord is Cyrus, (chapters 41,44,45,46,48). In chapter 42 it is Christ Himself who, after being revealed in the flesh to Jew and gentile alike, manifests it through His preaching.

"And all flesh shall see (it)." *rā'ū, constructio ad sensum,* is a plural. As often happens in Hebrew, especially in emphatic discourse, the verb has no formally expressed object. Its object is the *kebhōdh YHWH* of the preceding sentence and not, as Luther thought, the following clause introduced by *kī* (cf. Luke 3:6). What the sentence says, first of all, is that the deliverance from Babylon by Cyrus will make manifest to all the world the glory of the Lord, revealing His power over all nations and His faithfulness to His people Israel. And all flesh together (*yaḥdāw*) shall see it, all flesh as one mass. "*yaḥdāw* is a favorite expression with Isaiah, who uses it ten times in Isaiah I and seventeen times in Isaiah II" (Hahn). In its wider sense the prophecy reaches forth to the manifestation of Christ in the flesh and the accompanying preaching of the Gospel in all the world. Cf. 42:4-6; 49:6,26; 52:10,15; Luke 3; John 1:9,14. The *kī* in the concluding clause is causal, as always in this stereotyped phrase of Isaiah's (cf. 1:20; 21:17; 58:14, and the Isaianic sentence, Micah 4:4). This construction lends emphasis; it confirms what has just been said, Numbers 23:19; Psalm 33:4.

Third Strophe: verses 6-8: *A dialogue between a voice from heaven and the voice of the prophet about the proclamation to be made asserting the vanity of all flesh over against the unchangeable promise of salvation.*

6   *"Hark!" one saying, "Call out!"*
       And he says: "What shall I call out?"
      "All flesh is grass,
       And all its goodness like the flower of the field.
7   *The grass is withered and the flower faded;*
       For the breath of the Lord has blown upon it;
      Truly, the people (too) is grass.
8   *The grass is withered, the flower faded;*
       But the Word of our God shall stand forever."

A new scene vividly expressed, a dialogue between two voices, in which the solemn and somber trochaic meter, or the iambic, alternates with the fluid anapest. Our translation does not attempt to reproduce the rhythm of the Hebrew verse.

6 קוֹל אֹמֵר קְרָא וְאָמַר מָה אֶקְרָא

כָּל־הַבָּשָׂר חָצִיר וְכָל־חַסְדּוֹ כְּצִיץ הַשָּׂדֶה:

The construction of *qōl 'ōmēr* is exactly like that of *qōl qōrē'* in the third verse and is to be translated in the same way: "a voice preaching." The portrayal is impersonal, which is the case also with the perfect *we 'āmar*, "and someone answers." The reader will have to decide for himself to whom the voices belong. Obviously, the first voice is that of God or of an angel, His emissary. Only the Lord issues the call to preach. Instead of the impersonal *we 'amar* the LXX has *wā 'ōmar*, I answered, which the modern critics are mistaken in accepting, for it is plainly an interpretation. Luther correctly adhered to the Masoretic text. First of all, of course, the prophet himself is meant; he is describing the call that he has received to write this book, and so this passage is the counterpart to chapter 6 in the first book. But the drama of the situation requires the impersonal presentation, which leaves it to the spectator to recognize the speakers even though they are not named.

The first voice calls out *qerā'*, Preach! without specifying what should be preached. The second voice asks: *māh 'eqrā'*, What shall I preach? — with the accent on the interrogative pronoun. What follows is the first voice giving the answer. In this case the prophet shows that he is not speaking in his own name, but only as the Lord Himself has revealed and commanded. Two things have been commanded. The first is contained in verses 6 and 7 and the first half of 8: All flesh is grass, etc. The basic meaning of *bāsār* is flesh in the physical sense (Gen. 2:21), and by synecdoche it may refer to all bodily creatures that possess the breath of life, Genesis 6:17, 19; 7:15, and elsewhere. Particularly, it refers to mankind corrupted by sin, Genesis 6:3 Isaiah 31:3. The ethical sense of flesh, as St. Paul so often uses the word, is not yet present in this passage. Here the word signifies all mankind as corrupted by sin in all its powers, acts, and faculties. Only in this passage and in Genesis 7:15 does the word have the article and a preceding *kol*. Cf. G.K. Gr. 127,b,c, p. 411. Not flesh of every kind — *kol bāsār* — but the sum of all flesh, that is, all of humanity in its entirety, is grass. Grass is the picture of nothingness, impotence, lack of all power of endurance; it stands for the infirmity of the human family, Isaiah 37:27; 51:12; Job 8:12; 14:2; Psalm 37:2 90:5,6; 102:12(11); 103:15ff; 129:6; 1 Peter 1:24,25; James 1:10,11. Occasionally it refers to the sum total of human individuals, Isaiah 40:15,17; Psalm 39:6(5),12(11); 62:10(9).

The following sentence, "And all its goodness like the flower of the field," is a poetic embellishment, in the form of subject and predicate, of the preceding sentence. 1 Peter 1:24f translates *ḥesedh* with δόξα , as does also the LXX. Luther translates with *Guete,* the King James Bible with *goodliness*. Since *ḥesedh* otherwise always signifies an emotion or feeling, the translation here is not an easy one. Some translate with *charm, loveliness, winsomeness;* while others are quick to emend the text and substitute *hōdh, hādhār,* or *ḥosen* for *ḥesedh*. But our lack of acquaintance with this use of *ḥesedh* surely does not justify changing the text to suit our occidental ideas and opinions. If δόξα is the correct Greek rendition, then goodliness or glory is a correct English translation. In any case, *ḥesedh* must bear the same relation to *bāsār* as flower bears to grass: the most beautiful and best that grass can produce. The word is intended to represent the finest knowledge and ability, the highest aspirations and achievements of sinful mankind, and especially its *virtue,* which in the opinion of mankind appears to be the only thing of permanent value. Solomon's glory and splendor, his power, wisdom, riches, his good fortune and his honor are an example of *ḥesedh*. All human eminence and greatness of whatever kind, however grand it may appear, is still no more than the glory and goodliness of the flower which today blossoms and tomorrow is cast into the fire, Matthew 6:29f. "Vanity of vanities, saith the Preacher, vanity of vanities, all is vanity" (Eccles. 1:2). — In *tsīts hassādheh (tsīts* is a collective and therefore indefinite or generic, in spite of the construct state) the prophet, like the Lord in Matthew 6:28, no doubt refers to the wealth of blossoms in the plains of Sharon and Jezreel, where the anemone because of its profusion and the lily, (*shūshan, shōshan-nāh,*τὸ κρίνον) because of its regal form and splendor were particularly prominent. But the searing east wind often blasted all their glory in a single day.

7 יָבֵשׁ חָצִיר נָבֵל צִיץ כִּי רוּחַ יְהוָה נָשְׁבָה בּוֹ אָכֵן חָצִיר
הָעָם :

"The grass is withered and the flower faded, for the breath of the Lord has blown upon it."

The verbs *yābhēsh* and *nābhēl* are in the perfect. This is not, as Delitzsch supposes, a perfect like the Greek *aoristus gnomicus,* and therefore a perfect equivalent to the gnomic imperfect (Ps. 37:2), for in that case the following *nāshebhāh bō* would have to be similarly construed and the preceding *kī* translated with *when* or *as often as, as soon as,* as in Psalm 103:16: When the wind passeth over it, it is gone. Delitzsch would not have wanted that. The voice is describing a state or condition and pictures the grass and the flowers as actually lying there faded and withered because the breath of the Lord has blown upon them. *nāshebhāh* is a perfect action in its simplest sense (G.K. Gr. 106, b, a, p. 310), and *yābhēsh* and *nābhēl* belong to the group discussed in 106, g, a, page 311 and are best translated with adjectives: The grass is withered, the flower faded. *rūaḥ YHWH* in the present figurative description is to be understood here and in the parallel passages as referring first to the purely physical breath of God, to a wind which He generates by blowing with His lips (Ps. 33:6; Isa. 11:4). Without doubt, in the picture before us, the notorious wind of the month of May is meant, the parching east wind, the *rūaḥ midhbār* or *rūaḥ qādhīm* (Jer. 13:24; Job 15:30; Ezek. 42:16; cf. Isa. 59:19; LXX καύσων — on Mt. Lebanon called *semum,* in Syria and Arabia called *sharkiya,* whence our *sirocco*), a wind that in a few hours completely destroys growing grass and blooming flowers.

All of this is predicated of the totality of all flesh, of mankind corrupted by sin. That is what is shriveled and wilted, faded and completely dried up. The *rūaḥ YHWH,* before which mankind has shriveled and withered, is of course not physical, but is the breath of the Spirit of the Lord. What that means is expressed in Psalm 90:7ff: "For we are consumed by Your *anger* . . . You have set our iniquities before Yourself, our secret sins in the light of Your countenance." The *kebhōdh YHWH* was in its essence "like a consuming fire" (Exod. 24), representing the unapproachable, consuming holiness of the Lord. The Lord is the Holy One, Isaiah 6. Holiness is the real basis of His moral being. And this Lord dwells in the blue of the heavens, is the absolute and all-governing Majesty. All creation, all the activity of His creatures, including also all morally responsible beings, all thoughts and desires of men, lie open before Him. He sees and clearly discerns all things, Psalm 14:2; 33:13,14; 139. Job in 7:20 calls the Lord *nōtsēr hā'ādhām,* the Observer, the Watcher of men (Luther: *Menschenhueter*). His holiness, "the light of His countenance," penetrates, measures and judges all that we are and all that we do. The holiness of the Lord is not passive, intransitive, or inactive, but is an attribute of God that is ceaselessly active and effectively in operation. Without pause it pierces all things with its light, blows upon, judges and thus sears, burns and consumes everything sinful, unclean, and unholy. This holiness was revealed through the spoken Word: "Thou shalt; thou shalt not." "On the day that thou eatest thereof thou shalt surely die." "What is this that thou hast done?"

"Cursed is the ground for thy sake . . . till thou return unto the ground, for out of it wast thou taken" (Gen. 3). That is the blowing of the Holy Spirit of God upon all flesh and its glory. That is the word of the Law which was revealed in connection with the first sin, and again, with thunder and lightning proclaimed on Sinai as the *kebhōdh YHWH,* a consuming fire that unceasingly blows upon all flesh, judges and consumes it, as the *rūaḥ qādhīm* carries away the grass and the flowers.

Note, however, that the operation of the breath of God on the grass and the flowers does not bring about an absolute and total annihilation, but is described as causing no more than a withering and fading. The threat of death pronounced over Adam and Eve was unlimited and promised immediate and total death. The execution of this threat, however, brought on death gradually within a certain span of time, because grace had intervened, which was designed to rescue men for eternity during that span of time when they were plunging toward their death. Still, because of the activity of God's holiness, man's whole life is cut off from its root and source and is become powerless and helpless, a vain and futile thing, just as mown grass and a plucked blossom at first wither and dry up and finally die completely. Whatever of all flesh on earth is laid hold of by this grace receives new strength from above (40:31), grows up in the midst of the vanity of this life into a "tree of righteousness" (61:3), and is saved from the judgment of the Last Day for life eternal. Those who resist the grace of Christ during this time of forbearance, who are already cut down by the breath of the holiness of God, being already withered and dried up, powerless and helpless, will become the prey not only of bodily death but of eternal death at the Last Judgment. The entire visible creation, which was formed to be man's domicile, lies under the uninterrupted, actively destroying curse of God because of man's sin. Creation is now in fact nothing more than dry grass and a faded flower. Mankind and its doings still have the appearance of strength and beauty. But it is actually only the freshness and glory of grass that has already been cut and of the blossom already plucked, which soon vanish altogether.

This truth of Scripture needs to be emphasized in our sermons today. We are living in a time of Naturalism, which has dethroned God and has declared lifeless matter to be eternal and indestructible, and its inert power to be eternal and omnipotent. According to immutable, eternal laws, inert matter is said to have brought forth all the forms of life that we see. The rise and fall, the life and death of all things are no more than the working out of eternal, immutable laws. The Πάντα χωρεῖ of Heraclitus is made the sum and substance of all knowledge. The only binding moral precept is that you accommodate yourself to the eternal flow of all things. That is the view of the world and of life held by modern Monism. In opposition to that view of life it is necessary today to emphasize as strongly as possible that wasting away and dying, the constant strife in nature, the inward and outward disruption of man's life, his trouble, pain, and death, in brief, the entire "warfare" of man (Isa. 40:2; Job 7 and 14) together with the groaning of creation (Rom. 8), are not the original nor the eternal shape of things, but are the consequence and punishment of sin. The wages of sin is death (Rom. 6:23; Ps. 90). The strength of sin is the Law (1 Cor. 15:56), namely, the breath of God's holiness, which has smitten sinful flesh and because of man's sin has condemned to futility and destruction all visible creation (Gen. 5:29). This truth comprises one aspect of Christian teaching; the other is the Gospel of deliverance from the curse, and from misery and death, through our Lord Jesus Christ (1 Cor. 15:55,57).

Our call also requires that we confront human arrogance with this truth. In these days of intellectual progress in technology and the fine arts, in culture and materialistic living, the unbelieving world bows down in worship before its own power and achievements. What mastery has not the human spirit achieved over the forces of nature! How deeply have we penetrated into the secrets of nature! In his knowledge and achievements man has become a little god. Finally, the spirit of man will have solved the last riddles of nature and have made the forces of nature his plaything! It is our duty to oppose this megalomania with the preachment that all flesh is as grass and all its glory like the blossoms of the field. The grass is withered, the flower faded, for the breath of the Lord has blown upon it. In and behind nature there stands the Almighty, the infinite and unsearchable God, whom no finite spirit can search out nor any human power cast from His throne. However far human skill and knowledge may progress, before the secret workings of God it will not only be ignorant and powerless, but is condemned to confuse and destroy itself, because the breath of the Holy God not only darkens the organs of man's perception and cripples his mental powers but has also *disturbed* the original perfect order of nature and condemned it to self-destruction. The curse that God pronounced upon this world because of sin has left nothing intact. Death lurks at the heart of creation and will unfailingly do its deadly work. All wisdom and philosophy, all power and all achievements of man, are but dry grass and faded blossoms.

The same is true of man's morality. The world has much to say in praise of ideals and lofty aims, of virtue, and of the nobility and beauty of the human soul, of truth and faithfulness, of purity and chastity, of love and self-denial, as though these qualities were the natural and inborn characteristics of mankind. But it is just man's "noble" virtues that God has set before the light of His countenance and has weighed and found wanting. This too is but dry grass and faded blossoms before the breath of His holiness; it too rests under the curse and is given over to condemnation. There is none that doeth good, no, not one (Ps. 14:3; Rom.3). Even the moral virtue of all flesh is still nothing but flesh; it is an earthly, unspiritual, ungodly cast of mind (Gen. 6:3; John 3:6; Rom. 8:5ff). The moral beauty and nobility of the human spirit, even when it has attained its highest development, as in the persons of Socrates, Cato, Scipio Africanus, Penelope, Cornelia and her sons, since it lacks a divine source and root is, like the physical strength and beauty of youth, nothing but dry grass and faded blossoms. The great World Wars have shown how hollow and hypocritical human morality is. Under a thin cultural veneer there lay hidden the brutal and satanic nature of the human heart, unbounded greed, unheard-of mendacity, and an insatiable lust to kill. The wars brought these qualities to light in their most horrible form. No article of Christian doctrine is more clearly attested by the history of human development than this doctrine of the moral depravity of the human heart. Truly, the virtues of the heathen are but vices disguised. Through Adam's fall all human life and nature was corrupted and therefore lost. Unless this truth is preached in all its severity the Gospel cannot exert its regenerative and saving power.

In the words under discussion God declares all flesh and its glory, that is, all mankind with its knowledge, talents, and virtues, together with its achievements in every field, to be worthless and impotent, condemned and devoted to destruction. This appraisal of the flesh stands here in relation to and in contrast with what God is and does and with "the Word of our God." Standing alone, this statement would be irrelevant. But within a vain and corrupt creation which is devoted to destruction the Word still stands and God governs and works His will in accordance with it. Over against God and this Word all flesh and its splendor is as nothing. His

Word prevails against all the opposition of men and nations. They are altogether powerless to hinder His counsel, Psalms 2 and 46.

The Lord now continues with these words: *ʾakhēn ḥatsīr hāʿām*, truly, the people (too) is grass. Liberal exegetes simply omit these words, since they think that they disturb the rhythm and appear to be "a weak homiletical addition" (Cheyne). Here we have an example of liberal scientific criticism. Instead of simply accepting the irregularity of the Isaianic rhythm, they force upon the prophet an assumed systematic rhythm and then declare everything to be spurious that does not fit into the system. Rejection of the phrase is due partly to a false exegesis, which takes "the people" to be the same as "all flesh." That explanation makes the phrase appear to be an interpolated gloss which is intended to explain to the uninformed reader that the preceding words about the perishability of grass and blossoms really refer to people and that the collective term "the people" here designates the people of the whole earth, all mankind. But there is no evidence to support such an interpretation of the singular noun in the absolute state, with the attached article. Isaiah 42:5 does not apply, because there *ʿāleyhā* (on it, on the earth) is added as a modifier. In Job 34:30 the article is missing. Ever since the calling of Israel, "the people," in its absolute state, even when the context does not clearly fix its meaning, can mean only "this people," Israel (Exod. 3:21), which in the historical books is self-evidently designated simply as "the people" countless times. Compare Exodus 4:16,21,30,31 and Exodus 5:6,7,10,12, etc. See also, for example, Psalm 72:3; Isaiah 9:12(13),18(19); 62:10. And so here too "the people" can refer only to Israel — the people to whom 40:1,2ff applies, the people that every reader recognizes as the people of God in a very special sense, the chosen people. If that is established, then the conjecture collapses that we have in this phrase nothing but a pedantic exegetical or homiletical gloss. This is not a mere tautological explanation of "all flesh." The phrase specifically emphasizes that even the people of God, the people of the eternal covenant, which might therefore be thought to be exempt from the curse and the consuming breath of the Holy God, is still only dry grass and a wilted blossom. Such a surprising statement must be the revelation of God or of one inspired by Him; it could not have occurred to a mere writer of glosses.

ʾakhēn also supports this interpretation. The word lends emphasis to something unusual, something unlikely and otherwise unbelievable. What no one in Israel would have thought possible is actually a fact; despite the unbreakable covenant, even the people of the covenant of God is only grass, like all common flesh. That *hā ʿam* refers to Israel is furthermore confirmed in verses 6 to 8 and in every chapter from 49 to 57. The worthlessness of all flesh in contrast to the eternal grace and the eternal Word of grace as expressed in these verses, is again emphatically stated in the second part (cf. especially 51:6-8). Not only that, but the contrast between the worthlessness of all flesh and even of the people of God, on the one hand, and the omnipotence and eternity of the grace of God, on the other hand, completely dominates the contents of the chapters referred to above. Compare the worthlessness of God's people as contrasted with the saving grace and Word of God in 49:14ff; 50:1ff; 51:18ff; 53:6; 54:1ff, and 11ff; 55:8ff; 56:8ff; 57. Indeed, just this people of God, despite the grace promised to it, is in its very being, also in its Old Testament form, nothing but flesh on earth. The people has broken the covenant and refused to hear, 50:1ff, and thus has nullified for itself the old covenant, and the Spirit of God has cut it down. In its own midst there is no one to deliver it from its misery, 51:18ff; and therefore there is left to it only despair and inability to believe, on the one hand, 49:14, and self-righteousness, stubbornness, and apostasy, on the other hand, 57:3ff.

8 יָבֵ֥שׁ חָצִ֖יר נָ֣בֵֽל צִ֑יץ וּדְבַר־אֱלֹהֵ֖ינוּ יָק֥וּם לְעוֹלָֽם׃

In verse 8 the Lord repeats what He has said about the withering of the grass and the fading of the blossom. This is dramatic emphasis. Yes, it is indeed so — all flesh, even God's own people, is cut down and now withers away toward destruction, struck down by the breath of the holiness of God. This repetition also strongly emphasizes the great contrast with the declaration that "the Word of God shall stand forever." *dābhār* can refer to any spoken word, and *debhar 'elōhīm* can refer to any Word of God. But the Word of *"our"* God (the Voice here associates itself with the faithful people of God) is the Word of the gracious God, the Word of grace. It is not some separate, isolated word of grace, but the comprehensive promise first given to this people in its fathers (Rom. 15:8) and then constantly repeated and confirmed, Genesis 12:2,3,7; 17:2-8; 18:18; 22:18; etc., etc. It is the promise on which the prophet bases his glowing description of the Messianic glorification of faithful Israel (in Book I: chapters 7, 9, 11, 12, 25, 26, 27:6-9, 28, 33, 34, 35, and in all of Book II). It contained the assurance of the deliverance of faithful Israel from all affliction, especially from the Babylonian exile, and also promised an Old Testament restoration, modest and humble though it was to be. In the fifth verse, "and the glory of the Lord shall be revealed," namely, for the deliverance and glorification of Israel, this *Word* is proclaimed again in its full scope by the Voice in the wilderness. The second Voice says that in contrast to the nothingness of all flesh this Word "shall stand forever." This contrast suggests that all flesh with all its power opposes the fulfillment of the Word of promise, meaning in the first place Babylon, the world-power of the time, which had devastated Israel's inheritance and held God's people captive. In chapters 49 to 57, where this theme is carried out, Babylon no longer appears by name and only represents the hostile unbelieving world, behind which, as the actual leader, Satan stands as a strong man armed and holds God's people captive. (Cf. 49:24; Matt. 12:29; Luke 11:22; Rev. 12:7.) In 51:9 and 10, Egypt is adduced by way of comparison, and in 52:4, Egypt and Assyria. Compare also the description of the conquest of the enemy in 54:15ff and 57:13 with 49:24ff. The total power of all flesh on earth is impotent before this promise of deliverance and will not be able to hinder its fulfillment. The people itself, Israel, can contribute nothing to this fulfillment but lies helpless in the bonds of its oppressors, 49:26; 51:23. The promise of Israel's deliverance and glorification will be fulfilled despite the raging of the heathen and without Israel's assistance. (Cf. 59:14ff and Ps. 33:10f.)

Fourth Strophe: verses 9-11: *The glad tidings of Zion to the cities of Judah that their God has returned home in triumph with the liberated and will care for them as a shepherd cares for his sheep.*

9 *Get you up upon high mountains,*
    O Zion, herald of good news;
  Lift up your voice with strength,
    O Jerusalem, herald of good news;
  Lift it up, be not afraid!
  Say to the cities of Judah:
    "Behold your God!"!
10 *See, the Lord God*
      Is coming with might,
    His arm having won Him a Kingdom;
    And see, His reward is with Him,
      And His recompense goes before Him.

11 *Like a shepherd He tends His flock,*
In His arms He gathers the lambs
And carries them in His bosom.
Carefully He leads those who are giving suck.

The prosody of the modernists forces this entire strophe into the pattern of the Qinah rhythm. It assumes that after the third and fifth lines there have been omissions, and it rearranges words arbitrarily, even making deletions at the expense of the sense of the passage. That is arbitrary. In reality Qinah lines alternate with regular lines.

The picture that the prophet presents to our eyes in the fourth strophe is widely misunderstood. Zion and Jerusalem here are not, as in verses 1 and 2, the captive people in Babylon, but are a personification of the old Holy City itself which lies in ruins, inhabited by small remnants of the people. This sense is established by the fact that she is called to be a herald to the other cities of the land, as a mother to her daughters. That picture could not possibly fit the people in exile. Zion is, to be sure, not pictured as already restored, but she does see the Lord returning over the hills in triumph at the head of the liberated captives and bringing along rich booty. Out of His mouth (for it is the Lord who speaks in this strophe also) Zion receives the commission as the Lord's herald of old forcefully to announce His arrival and its importance to her daughters, the other cities. What is here described is the fulfillment of the promise expressed in 52:7-12; 57:14; and clearly set forth in 62:10-12, the climax of Part III. The complete and final fulfillment is the coming of Christ, as is evidenced by the almost identical prophecies of Zephaniah 3:14-20; Zechariah 9:9; 13:1, and the New Testament citations Matthew 21:5 and John 12:15.

⁹ עַל הַר־גָּבֹהַ עֲלִי־לָךְ֙ מְבַשֶּׂרֶת צִיּוֹן

הָרִימִי בַכֹּחַ֙ קוֹלֵךְ מְבַשֶּׂרֶת יְרוּשָׁלָ͏ִם הָרִימִי֙ אַל־תִּירָ֫אִי

אִמְרִי֙ לְעָרֵי יְהוּדָה הִנֵּה אֱלֹהֵיכֶם׃

The city is addressed in the familiar terms of honor and endearment — Zion and Jerusalem. Both names are of uncertain origin. *tsīyyōn* is most likely derived from *tsāwāh*, to be firm, and means a fastness or fortress, a citadel. It was the name of the citadel of the Jebusites which David captured (2 Sam. 5:6ff; 1 Chron. 11:5) and occupied as his own palace. Later he brought the ark of the covenant there, and on the northern part of this hill, on ancient

Moriah, in the southeast corner of Jerusalem, Solomon built his temple. Since that time, Zion was called the holy mount of God, the place where He dwelt in the midst of Israel, whence He bestowed His grace, governed and protected His people (Ps. 46). The name was extended to include the city and its inhabitants and eventually also the whole people, so that Zion became the designation used to describe people and city as beloved of God.

In the case of Jerusalem (*yerūshālayim* is a *Qeri perpetuum*) the question is whether the first half of the word is derived from *yārash* or *yārāh* (*yārash,* to acquire, possess; *yārāh,* to cast, establish). In the first case the letter *Shin* ought to have a *Dagesh forte,* and the word would then mean possession of peace, that is, an undisturbed, peaceful possession. In the second case, the first part of the word would be a passive participle Qal, meaning founded, an establishment, and therefore a secure, impregnable, peaceful establishment (2 Sam. 5:6). In either case the meaning is about the same. The Arabic grammarian and translator of the Bible, Saadiah (ben Joseph) Gaon, translates it "dwelling of peace." In Abraham's time the city was called only Salem (Gen. 14:18), a name that is used poetically in Psalm 76:3(2). Jerusalem is the name of a place, but here when used as a parallel to Zion, as is often the case, it shares with Zion the meaning of God's dwelling among His people. In poetry and in the prophets, in the New Testament and in Christian poetry, Zion and Jerusalem frequently have the meaning of "church."

The genitive relation expressed by the two constructs: *mebhassereth tsiyyon* and *mebhassereth yerūshālayim* is that of apposition, as is usually the case with proper nouns (G.K. Gr. 128, 2, kff, p. 436), and designates Zion-Jerusalem as a herald. So also *bethūlath bath bābhel* (Isa. 47:1) is not the virgin, the daughter of Babel, but the virgin daughter Babel. Likewise *bethūlath yisrā'el* (Amos 5:2 and *bath tsūyyon* (Isa. 52:2) are not the virgin of Israel, daughter of Zion, but the virgin called Israel and the daughter called Zion. Israel and the city are thus characterized as being virgin, unconquered, unravished. Some modern commentators take the relation expressed by the construct state to be the subjective genitive and translate "herald of Zion, herald of Jerusalem," and explain the herald as referring to a choir of jubilee singers made up of young women organized for the purpose of celebrating victories or other joyous occasions, such as David's victory over Goliath, 1 Samuel 18:6,7. (Cf. Ps. 68:12(11), which should be translated "of jubilee maidens there is a great band" instead of

Luther's "with great throngs of evangelists.") The singular *mebhassereth* cannot be translated with band or throng, since it does not occur anywhere else in that sense; whereas its use in apposition is usual.

The verb *bissar* is a Piel form of an unused Qal stem. Its literal meaning (cf. *bāsār*, flesh, something skinned or made smooth) is to make the face or heart smooth (cf. the English glad, gladden, German *glaetten*, to make smooth), and usually means to bring glad tidings, and then also in general to announce. The New Testament words εὐαγγελίζεσθαι, εὐαγγέλιον, εὐαγγελιστής are based on this meaning. The LXX already has εὐαγγελιζό-μενος Σιών, Ἰερουσαλήμ. The expression does not occur in Isaiah I, but the prophet uses it here and in 41:27; 52:7; 60:6; 61:1, always in the sense of good tidings. The participle in our passage gives the meaning special point. It is not a onetime act (King James Version: O Zion, that bringest good tidings) but an uninterruptedly continuing exercise and therefore a customary, a natural, professional activity. (G.K. Gr. 116, a, p. 355f). It is really a noun. Luther's *Predigerin* is the only correct translation. Zion, the church, God's congregation, is a preacher by birth, by calling and profession, called and endowed by God to be a herald of salvation (43:21; 51:16; 54:13; 59:21; 1 Peter 2:9), to preach the Gospel, that great message of the comfort of God, whose chief exponent in the Old Testament is the prophet Isaiah. This message is placed at the very head of Book II and is then carried out in varied form throughout the rest of the book. It is the proclamation of this message of joy that makes Zion-Jerusalem the "Servant of the Lord" who carries out God's gracious will toward the whole world, 43:21; 35:4ff. Preaching the Gospel is the one specific mission of the church, Mark 16, Matthew 28.

The reference here is to the evangelization of the daughters of Jerusalem, that is, the cities of Judah. "Get you up upon high mountains — lift up your voice with strength." The singular *har*, mountain, is to be taken as a collective. For the dative interest in *'alī lākh* (Gen. 12:1; 22:2; Deut. 2:13, etc.) see G.K. Gr. 119, s, 2, p. 381. It emphasizes the action expressed in the verb. It cannot be exactly expressed in English, not even by "get you up," which tends to obscure the action of rising. The relation of the two sentences is that of progressive parallelism. They graphically express in concrete terms the vigor with which Jerusalem will deliver its joyful message of the victorious return of the Lord. It shall be heard in the most remote cities of the land, its sound carrying from the tops of the hills to the farthest corners. Zion is to put power in her voice so as to be sure to be heard. It is assumed that the herald of such a message would of herself cry out with all her strength out of boundless, uncontrollable joy. In that spirit of great joy the church ought always to proclaim the Gospel. Compare Luke 6:45; 19:40 Acts 4:20; 1 Corinthians 9:16ff; 15:9,10; Romans 1:11-16; 2 Corinthians 12:15.

"Lift up, be not afraid." The speaker is in such a state of strong emotion that his speech breaks through the rhythm of the line and the words gush forth without close connection or grammatical relationship. The object of "lift up" is "your voice." "Be not afraid" does not refer to enemies, but presupposes Jerusalem's timidity, which arises from the unexpectedness of these overwhelming tidings of great joy which she hardly dares to credit and therefore cannot at once summon the courage to proclaim. The words encourage her to carry out her mission with bold rejoicing.

"Say to the cities of Judah: 'Behold your God!' " As daughters of Jerusalem they had gone through the same woes as their mother; their God had turned away from them, they had been wrecked, and their inhabitants carried away to Babylon. Since then they had lain in ruins and eyed the future with despair. The Lord's judgment upon them seemed to be final. This despair is the subject of 49:14; 50:1,2; 54:6ff; 59:2; 60:10,15; 61:4; 62:4; 64:10ff. It is against such thoughts that the message to the cities of Judah is directed. God, who had once turned His back upon them, has now in His wonted love returned to renew the old covenant relation.

But Jerusalem sees yet more and has more to proclaim than just the return of the gracious Lord to His people.

$$^{10} \text{הִנֵּה אֲדֹנָי יְהוִה בְּחָזָק יָבוֹא וּזְרֹעוֹ מֹשְׁלָה לוֹ}$$
$$\text{הִנֵּה שְׂכָרוֹ אִתּוֹ וּפְעֻלָּתוֹ לְפָנָיו:}$$

Out of fear of profaning the holy name (Lev. 24:16), the tetragrammaton *YHWH* was to be pronounced *'adhōnāy* and was written with the vowels of *'adhōnāy*. However, when *YHWH* and *'adhōnāy* appeared side by side, then *YHWH* would be written with the vowels of *'elōhīm* and would be pronounced *'elōhīm*. Hence: *'adhōnāy 'elōhīm*. The form of *'adhōnāy* is from *'ādhōn*, a ruler (*dūn*, to govern), with the addition of the plural suffix of the first person singular and with the lengthening of the "a" vowel. But, as often happens, the meaning of the suffix has been lost (cf. *mon* in

103

monsieur and in *monsignore*) and it merely gives emphasis to the plural idea, like *'elōhīm* from the singular *'elōah*. Hence' *adhōnāy* means Lord, Ruler of all. In connection with *YHWH* the word has become the *nomen proprium* of God. Here God's almighty power is to be set before the eyes of the cities of Judah as their strong comfort and the foundation of their joy. Jehovah, the Lord of all, is coming *behāzāq*. *hāzāq* is an adjective meaning strong. The *Beth* is the so-called *Beth essentiae* and the phrase means "with the characteristics of a strong one." Our translation "with great might" is like Luther's *"gewaltiglich"* except that our phrase comes somewhat closer to the Hebrew meaning. *ūzerō'ō moshelāh lō* is an emphasizing parallel to *behāzāq yābhō*.

māshal means to rule, and the participle is used to establish this rule as continuing without interruption. The time is determined by the time of the verb *yābhō*. *yābhō* is present in time and not, as some have thought, future. Luther too seems to have meant his *kommt* to be understood as a future, since he translated *moshelāh* as a future. At the end of verse 9 "Behold your God" refers to something that is taking place in the present. The *hinnēh* in verse 10 falls in line with *hinnēh* in verse 9 and only points out something special in the same picture, namely, the demonstration of power in which the Lord returns home in triumph. Behold your God! See, with what power He approaches! *moshelāh* should then also be translated with the present. The dative of interest in *lō* strengthens the verbal idea. His arm rules completely. The Lord is pictured as returning victorious from a battle of the nations. He has crushed them and is now sole ruler. That is carried out more fully in 63:1-6. Compare 59:16ff; 64:1ff; 65:1-16; 66:15ff. Now He returns in triumph to His residence among the people, and Jerusalem is to carry the good news to the kingdom, so that all the people might receive Him with jubiliation and rejoice in the captured booty, for He does not return empty-handed, but has won very precious prizes.

"And see, His reward is with Him, and His recompense (goes) before Him." The second half of this sentence is usually misunderstood. Luther too translated *pe'ullāh* with *Vergeltung* and related it to the punishment reserved for the enemies, while *sākhār*, reward, was meant for His own people. That is not correct. *sākhār* is never reward in the evil sense of that word, and *pe'ullāh* in an evil sense occurs only in 65:7 and Psalm 109:20, where the context supplies the meaning. *sākhār* refers to something determined, marked off, agreed upon and then gets the meaning of reward in a good sense. *pe'ullāh* derived from *pā'al*, to work, means something acquired through work, effort, struggle, suffering, pain. So we translate it simply with *recompense*. It has to do with the booty that the Lord has won in battle with His enemies. The parallel relation of the two words indicates that both are used in the same sense. This is true also of 62:11, where the phrase occurs again.

"Is with Him" and "is before Him" are just poetic variations of the same idea. Reward and recompense are not presented as something that the people would have to wait for, but as something the Lord brings with Him for immediate distribution. But what is this booty that the Lord has won and brings with Him? It does *not* consist, as some assume, on the basis of 49:4f; 53:10-12; 49:24f, primarily in the glory of the Victor and the liberated captives who fall to Him as His prize, a prize which Zion-Jerusalem and the cities of Judah then share as their reward. Rather, *their* happiness is the whole purpose of the joyous message. The reward and the booty that the Victor brings with Him are indeed a reward for His labor, and the booty properly belongs to Him, but the passage does not speak of His glory, but rather of the glory of the cities to which He is returning. It is for them that He brings back a reward and a rich prize, which includes not only the liberated captives (Jer. 31:16) but more importantly the "riches of the gentiles" to be divided among them for their enjoyment, their glory, and their restoration. Their misfortune, ruin, and years of shame, their pain and tears which the Lord had visited upon them as chastisement for their sins are to be doubly recompensed to them with the prizes that the Victor has wrested from their enemies. Verses 9 to 11 hark back to the words in verse 2: "she shall receive double at the hand of the Lord for all her sins," i.e., punishment, chastisement for sins. And here "double" is explained as being a reward and recompense given to His afflicted people. The third part of this book, chapters 58-66, explains at length what constitutes this "double" recompense, this booty. Each chapter there treats of it with a wide variety of poetic pictures. The description begins in 58:8 and closes with the next to the last verse in chapter 66. The climax is reached in chapters 61, 62, and 63. The theme in 58:8 sums it up as being the restoration, the gracious guidance, and finally the perfect glorification of Israel.

In the very next verse, however, the picture changes and we see how the Lord dispenses His acquired riches among His people.

כְּרֹעֶה֙ עֶדְר֣וֹ יִרְעֶ֔ה בִּזְרֹעוֹ֙ יְקַבֵּ֣ץ 11
טְלָאִ֔ים וּבְחֵיק֖וֹ יִשָּׂ֑א עָל֖וֹת יְנַהֵֽל׃

Rhythm and contents sharply set this verse apart from the preceding verses. As the picture changes, the returning Conqueror becomes a Shepherd. It is important for the proper understanding of the verse to note that we are here confronted with an entirely new situation. The action here does not lie in the present and is not restricted to the liberated captives. The four imperfects are pure futures and point to future time. The Voice proclaims how the booty-laden Victor will return to His people and make them sharers in His great victory. The Warrior, so fearsome in battle (63:1-6), becomes a gentle, faithful Shepherd of His people. The sheep are first of all the liberated captives whom He brings back with Him to join their impoverished countrymen. They are returning to a land and its cities that are like pastures and sheepfolds (65:9,10) that the Good Shepherd will gloriously restore and in which He will tend His flock with loving tender care. There are no grammatical difficulties in the verse. The purpose of the speaker is to present to the unhappy people, in simple and comprehensive phrases, a most winsome and impressive picture of the blessed work of the Good Shepherd.

The first clause is general; the next two are specific. *rō'eh* as a *species pro genere* expresses not only the act of providing food and drink but also every other activity of a shepherd — leading, directing, caring for, sheltering, and protecting the flock (cf. Ps. 23; John 10). In Christ's own words, the shepherd becomes the embodiment of all His work as Savior in His office of Prophet, High Priest, and King. The picture of a shepherd and his flock is the most winsome, the most comprehensive and frequent representation of the relation of the Lord to His people. (Cf. Jer. 31:10; Ezek. 34; Zech. 13:7; Ps. 23; Ps. 80; Matt. 9:36; 25:32; 26:31; John 10; 1 Peter 2:25; Heb. 13:20.) The office of public preaching is consequently often referred to in both Testaments as the office of a shepherd — a notable mark of distinction!

The *telā'īm* are what in German would be called *Laemmlein*. A *tāleh* (65:25) is a very young, delicate lamb that is as yet hardly able to walk. A good shepherd takes such lambs on his arm and carries them in his bosom. The moderns connect *bizrō'ō yeqabbēts* (he gathers in his arm) with *'edhrō* (his flock), which presents an impossible picture. They also violate the sense by deleting the *ū* before *ḥēyqō* in order to create a perfect verse in the Qinah rhythm. A *ḥēyq* is a lap, that part of the human body lying between the hips; the word also frequently means breast or bosom. Here it refers to the pouch that is formed by the shepherd's cloak above the girdle, where newborn or ailing lambs are carried, supported by the shepherd's left arm — a picture of the tender care of the weak (40:29-31; Matt. 11:28). *ʿālōth* in the final clause is Qal participle plural feminine of *ʿūl*, to suckle. In the Old Testament it always appears in this form, of cattle in Genesis 33:13 and 1 Samuel 6:7,10; of sheep here and in Psalm 78:71. For the Piel *yenahēl* see Psalm 23:2; 31:4(3); Isaiah 49:10; 51:18. Ewes that are giving suck must not be driven hard. The shepherd spares them, leads them gently — a picture of the gentle and loving patience of the Good Shepherd toward the sinful weaknesses that are common to us all. See 42:3. How comforting for us poor sinners!

With the fourth scene the first major strophe, verses 1-11, comes to a close. It is dramatic throughout, constructed with great artistic skill. As for the dramatic *form,* the Lord Himself is really the speaker in all four scenes, although each time in a different likeness. In the first scene He appears manifestly as "your God"; in the second, as speaking through the Voice in the wilderness; in the third, in dialog with the prophet; in the fourth, He is calling on Zion herself to be the herald of His message. The contents of the four scenes are similarly varied and progressive. The whole is a sermon about the imminent *Coming of the Lord* to save and glorify His afflicted people — an Advent sermon. The first strophe states the theme — Comfort — and presents it in threefold concrete form. The second strophe contains an exhortation to repent and prepare to receive the Savior, who reveals Himself in great glory. The third strophe emphasizes the certainty of the coming salvation despite the power of the enemies and the impotence of the people — because the Lord has promised it. The fourth proclaims the accomplished victory of the Lord and the glorification of the liberated people which shall follow their deliverance.

It is well to be reminded that this first section contains an outline of all of Book II. The first strophe, verses 1 and 2, announces the theme and parts; the second, the contents of 40-48; the third, of 49-57; the fourth, of 58-66. These three larger parts, outwardly separated by the refrain, "There is no peace for the wicked" (48:22 and 57:21), carry out the themes expressed in the introductory tableaus in highly detailed, poetically artistic, uniquely arranged form. Only by keeping this outline in mind can one arrive at a somewhat accurate and thorough understanding of the book. This point is emphasized because it serves to prove that the book is a unit, and upsets the theories of modern unbelieving Isaiah critics, especially the hypothesis proposed by Duhm and now so generally accepted, that a Trito-Isaiah wrote the part beginning with chapter 56. It also exposes the aberrations of those scholars who feed their vanity by offering to show that the book is only a patchwork of literary scraps gathered from many sources and many different periods of time. The leaders of this school of thought have deliberately ignored this point and dismissed it as unscientific, since it does not fit into their naturalistic theory of prophecy. Their followers have hardly even heard of this point and conceive it to be their duty to verify the theories of their masters by seeking for more scraps. A careful study of the book will show how clear and how exact the above outline is. A thorough test will provide the proof.

Second Section: verses 12-31: *The majesty of the Lord as opposed to every other eminence is certain assurance of the deliverance and restoration of the believers.*

This discourse is divided into three rather long strophes, which are separated, and at the same time connected, by the refrain in verses 18 and 25: "To whom then will ye liken God (Me)?" With respect to contents the refrain is the application of what has just been said, while at the same time it provides the point of view from which it was spoken — the incomparableness of the Lord. The last strophe, verses 26-31, after pointing again to the unequalled greatness of the Lord, makes the application of the whole to the people who are so slow to believe.

First Strophe: verses 12-18: *The preeminence of the spirit of the Lord over the spirit of man.*

The strophe has two parts, clearly separate as to contents. In 12-14 the Lord confronts the spirit of man as such, as *genus*; in 15-17 He speaks to men in masses, to the nations. Verse 18 contains the application. Rhetorically the two halves differ in that the first is composed of questions only, while the second contains only declarations.

12 *Who measures the waters in the palm of His hand,*
    And marks off the heavens with a span
    And encloses with a measure the dust of the earth
    And weighs the mountains with a scale
    And the hills with a balance?

13 *Who measures the spirit of the Lord*
    And as His counselor instructs Him?
14 *With whom does He take counsel that he enlighten Him?*
    That he teach Him the way of right,
    And teach Him knowledge,
    And show Him the way of understanding?

Up to this point the section is made up entirely of questions introduced by a threefold *mī,* Who? In verses 12 and 13 the question beginning with Who? is followed by several grammatically similar modifiers introduced by *Waw* conjunctive. The question in verse 14, however, is followed by clauses introduced by *Waw* consecutive. Whenever *mī* is repeated, the thought proceeds to a new subject, while the clauses introduced by *Waw* merely add a new shading to the main question. All of the questions are rhetorical questions, that is, questions that neither expect nor require an answer. They take the place of positive statements, and their purpose is to impart to the thought expressed greater pathos, emphasis, and dignity. For this reason the rhetorical question, a device common to poetry and prophecy, is a special favorite of our prophet.

מִי־מָדַד בְּשָׁעֳלוֹ מַיִם וְשָׁמַיִם בַּזֶּרֶת תִּכֵּן 12
וְכָל בַּשָּׁלִשׁ עֲפַר הָאָרֶץ וְשָׁקַל בַּפֶּלֶס הָרִים
וּגְבָעוֹת בְּמֹאזְנָיִם:

The twelfth verse lists the mighty works of creation — the waters, the heavens, the dust of the earth, the hills, and the mountains, and asks who has encompassed them or taken their measure. The force of the questions lies in the predicates. They are all verbs that denote measuring, and each is supplied with a suitable object and an adverbial modifier naming a kind of measuring device.

The first question asks who measured the waters. The word for waters occurs only in a plural form derived from an unused singular *may* and here refers to all the waters of the earth — the seas, the lakes, and all the streams. Most prominent in the prophet's imagery are, no doubt, the trackless seas, which have always so strongly suggested boundlessness to the human mind. There is no justification for substituting *yammīm* (oceans) for *mayim,* as some have done, because for them *mayim* did not seem adequate. *mayim* is, however, more adequate than the suggested substitute, because it includes more.* The prophet may well have chosen *mayim*

---

*The Dead Sea Scrolls read *mēy yām.*

because of the assonance with *shāmayim* in the next clause. In the Hebrew none of the objects has the article, whereas in English it would be required because the objects are definite. That is a matter of poetic license. Cf. G.K. Gr. 126, h, p. 405.

In the first sentence the predicate is *mādhadh.* This is the most general word for measuring, most commonly used, as in this case, in connection with materials that can be measured with a scoop or bucket. It should be noted that the verbs used here to denote measuring — *mādhadh,* to measure out, *tikkēn,* to determine; *kūl,* to encompass; *shāqal,* to weigh — are naturally ambiguous in meaning. They may mean "to set a limit," or simply "to ascertain the limits or weight of something." Some commentators understand the verbs in the first sense, others prefer the second. In the one case, the answer to the question Who? would be "God," that is, God set the limits. In the other case, the answer would be "no man," that is, no man can ascertain the limits or the weight. We shall prove that the latter interpretation is correct and that the verbs are to be taken in the sense of to estimate, grasp, or measure.

The first sentence asks who measures the waters. The means of measuring is in this case the *shō'al.* The word is rare in the Old Testament, occurring only here and in 1 Kings 20:10 and Ezekiel 13:19. Luther translated it with *Faust.* But that word today always suggests a balled fist and would not be readily understood. Modern Jews translate it with shovel, a word that sounds something like the Hebrew *shō'al.* The word refers to the hand formed into a scoop or cup — a very tiny vessel with which to measure the waters of the earth! If our assumption that *mādhadh* means to measure in the sense of ascertaining the volume of the waters is correct, then the sentence: Who has measured the waters with his cupped hand? anticipates the answer: No one. The prophet asks: Who has ever measured out the waters with his cupped hand as a scoop? Who accomplishes that? This interpretation compels a consideration of the meaning of the perfect in Hebrew. We have here the abstract perfect, which is best translated, as Luther does, with the present tense. The other perfects should then also be translated with the present. See G.K. Gr. 106, b, a, p. 320.

The next question, with the insertion of the interrogative after the copula, asks: And who marks off the heavens with a span? *shāmayim* also occurs only in the plural, like *mayim.* It is the word for the vault which the eye sees stretched above the earth like a canopy in which the stars seem to be placed. Genesis 1:8 calls it the *rāqīaʿ*, the firmament, expanse. Cf. verse 14: "firmament of the heavens." The verb used here for measuring is *tikkēn*, the intensive Piel of *tākhan*, developed from the root *kūn*, to stand upright. The Piel regularly expresses the meaning of the verb as "to establish," both in the concrete sense of setting something down firmly and fixing its limits, as also in the more subjective sense of determining something for one's own mind, to count, to take the measure of. As in the case of measuring the waters with the cupped hand, so here the hand is used as a unit of measuring, the *zereth* being a span, the spread of the hand from thumb to little finger. It is one-half of the Hebrew cubit, which is the distance from the elbow to the tip of the middle finger. Luther translated *zereth* as the width of the hand in Exodus 28:16; 39:9; 1 Samuel 17:4. The span as the unit of measurement for the heavens is just as unsuitable as the cupped hand for measuring the waters. The prophet stresses this contrast in all of the clauses. Of the dust of the earth he asks: Who encloses it with a one-third measure? The verb *kūl* occurs only here in the form *kāl*. This Hebrew syllable is the expression for anything round, spherical, or full. With a variety of endings it is the base form for a long list of words, all reflecting this fundamental idea. Especially common is *kōl*, or *kol* with Maqqeph, meaning fullness, the whole, all. The verb-form means to comprise, encompass, fill up. *shālīsh* from *shālōsh*, three, means one-third. In the sense of a one-third measure it occurs only here and in Psalm 80:6(5). It was very likely one-third of a *bath* or of an *ephah*, the equivalent of our peck. In this passage it is used as a measuring unit for the *ʿaphar haʾarets*, the dust of the earth. This is a poetic designation of the earth itself, which the Hebrews thought of as being composed of dust, just as in our speech earth may refer to the earth as a body and also to soil. Luther showed his feeling for good German when he did not translate *ʿaphar* at all, but expressed the phrase with one word, *Erde*. The last sentence mentions mountains and hills. The verb is *shāqal*, to weigh, and the reference is to weight rather than extent. This is a poetic variation of thought. The means of measuring are *peles* and *mōʾzenayim. peles*, occurring only here and in Proverbs 16:11, is a scale; the second word, a dual, is an apothecary's balance, the kind of scale often seen in representations of the goddess of justice. Note how the poet's choice of instrument is determined by the weight of material to be measured. His purpose here is again to emphasize the vast disparity of the means of measuring and the works of God that are to be measured.

The question whether the verbs are to be understood as expressing the action of seeking to discover the size or weight of an object, or of fixing a limit and determining what the size is to be, must be settled by the circumstances visualized in the text. Everything speaks for the first interpretation. First, the general scope of the text. The ultimate purpose of this section (verses 12-31), like that of the whole chapter, is to comfort this people of weak faith, who are in danger of falling from faith entirely (verses 19-21; 27-31; cf. 40:1). The immediate purpose of section 12-31 is, as must be emphasized, not only to praise the greatness of God, but as is clearly shown in the refrain of verses 18 and 25, to stress the *incomparable greatness* of the Lord above every other eminence. In each of the three minor strophes the Lord is contrasted with other "great ones." In the third He is the Eternal, Infinite, Perfect One as opposed to temporal, limited, imperfect human beings. In the second He is the true God and absolute Ruler over against idols and earthly pretenders. In the first He is the absolute and all-powerful God over against the impotent masses of men (15-17), and the God of absolute wisdom over against the ignorance of men (12-14).

If one takes the Who? in the questions in verses 12 to 14 to refer to God (Who but Jehovah? — Cheyne) and translates: Who has measured out the waters, etc.?, then the strong contrast between God and man evaporates and this semistrophe no longer falls within the scope of the whole section and of its other half, but relates only to the more general idea of describing the greatness of God. That would make the prophet guilty of loose thinking. But tightly knit unity and coherence of thought and firm logic of thought-structure are precisely what distinguishes Isaiah among the prophets. He does not use one word too many; the choice of every word is calculated. He never loses track of the thought — which here is the vast difference between the incomparable greatness of God and every other eminence. Every sentence, every word is related to that one thought. That applies also to verses 12 to 14. The primary thought there is the incomparable greatness of the mind and wisdom of God as compared with the wisdom of men. That appears clearly in verses 13 and 14. In verse 12 it is somewhat veiled, but still unmistakable. The chief emphasis in the sentences does not lie in the objects (the great *works* of God), but in the verbs, in the measuring, and in man's skill and ability in measuring the works of creation. In verse 12 the prophet intends to show how infinitely superior the spirit of God is over the limited spirit of man. That superiority is evidenced by these mighty works, whose greatness man is not even able to measure. The contrast is between God's Spirit and the mind of man. Therefore: What man has ever measured or been able to measure the waters, the heavens, etc.?

The more immediate context supports this interpretation. Verses 13 and 14 begin with the same interrogative as verse 12 — Who? All refer to the same person. Even the predicate following the Who? of verse 13 is the same as in the second clause of verse 12 — *tikkēn*. The Who? in verse 12 must refer to the same person as the Who? and With whom? in verses 13 and 14. *tikkēn* in verse 12 must have the same meaning as *tikkēn* in verse 13; otherwise the writer would just be confusing the reader. St. Paul, who also knew Hebrew translated the *tikkēn* of verse 13 with ἔγνω , meaning "hath known," that is, has estimated or grasped. The passage is Romans 11:33-36, where Paul uses the meaning of this very verb to prove that God's judgments are unsearchable and past finding out. Paul certainly did not take Who? as referring to God. That would have assumed that the prophet was saying: Don't you know that the Lord has known the mind of the Lord? The same is true of the following sentences. Not: God is God's counselor; but: No man is God's counselor. Not: God does not take counsel with God; but: God does not take counsel with any man. If our investigation justifies the assertion that by analogy the Who? in all three verses requires the same answer and also that *tikkēn* must in both cases have the same meaning or else only cause confusion, then it follows that the prophet must have expected the answer "No man," and the verbs must be understood to mean taking the measure of something, calculating or estimating the weight of something. When Delitzsch takes Who? to refer to God and explains the verbs as to fix the limits of something, basing his opinion on Proverbs 30:4, it must be said that he erred. Proverbs 30:4 does not require the answer "God," but rather "No man." Cheyne (*The Prophecies of Isaiah,* 5th Ed. p. 247) bases his opinion on Job 38:5. But that passage proves nothing, because the entire context there makes it abundantly clear that God is being described as laying down the measurements.

Finally, the adverbial modifiers (with a cupped hand, with a span, with the one-third measure, with the scale and the balance) all support our interpretation. These are all human measuring instruments, and not one of them occurs in Scripture as used by God as a means of setting a measure, not even the *shālīsh* in Psalm

80:6(5). The scales in God's hand in Job 31:6 are used as a means of ascertaining, not of setting a measurement. We have no objection to anthropomorphisms as such, but in this passage of Isaiah there are none.

For good measure we return to the structure of our strophe. The Lord enters into a comparison of Himself with man. In the second half, it is His power against men in concrete groups called nations; in the first part, it is His spirit compared with man as a genus. He shows that He, *'ēl* (verse 18), is incomparably above man in wisdom and power (Isa. 31:3; Ezek. 28:2; Hos. 11:9). His superiority is evident from man's inability to measure or comprehend His mighty works. What measure has he for gauging the waters? His hollow hand! For the heavens? The span of his hand! For the mass of the earth? A peck measure! For the hills and mountains? A scale and an apothecary's balance!

In these verses we have the Lord's clear statement that already in the works of creation His spirit infinitely transcends all human knowledge and intellect. That is a truth to which Scripture frequently testifies (Ps. 19; 104; 139; Rom. 11:32ff). The rhetorical questions here emphasize that fact in order to provide God's despairing people in exile with firm comfort, verses 1 and 27-31. The people are unable to see how they can possibly escape from proud and powerful Babylon (14:13). But Israel's God is wiser than men (31:3) and mightier than the sum of all nations.

13 מִי־תִכֵּן אֶת־רוּחַ יְהוָה וְאִישׁ עֲצָתוֹ יוֹדִיעֶנּוּ:

In his presentation of the great works of God, the prophet did not explicitly mention God's mind or spirit, although those works are a revelation of His Spirit, and that was Isaiah's main concern. In the 13th verse he now turns to a discussion of this, his main topic. "Who measures the spirit of the Lord and as His counselor instructs Him?" *tikkēn* has already been explained. Despite Paul's interpretation, Delitzsch and Cheyne here retain the sense of setting a limit and Cheyne translates: "Who hath regulated the Spirit of Jehovah?" That translation falls under the weight of its own unreasonableness. *rūaḥ YHWH* in this case is *not* the third person of the Godhead, is *not*, as Delitzsch says, "the Spirit that moved upon the face of the waters at the creation of the world." As the context (verse 14) and Paul's translation in Romans 11:34 and 1 Corinthians 2:16 show, the *rūaḥ* is here the νοῦς κυρίου that is, the mind or the thinking of the Lord, not, merely the intrinsic nature of His thinking, but God's *thinking activity*, His thoughts and feelings, and His will. Luther translates Paul's quotation with *Sinn*, which refers to God's designs and plans, His counsel, of which Isaiah speaks in the next verse. So, we translate: Who has ever measured God's mind? Who has ever known God's thoughts? The perfect here might be better rendered with the present tense, like the perfects in verse 12.

The next clause, *we'ish 'atsāthō yōdhī'ennū*, is a construction peculiar to Hebrew and strange to our idiom. *'ish 'atsāthō*, literally, "man of His counsel," that is, His counselor. The same construction occurs in Psalm 119:24, *'anshēy 'atsāthī*, men of my counsel, my counsellors. Cf. G.K. Gr. 135, n, p. 440. There is a threefold abbreviation here. Between *Waw* and *'ish*, *mī* has quite naturally been dropped. After *mī* the copula must be supplied: Who *is* His counselor? And finally, *yōdhī'ennū* is an abbreviated relative clause before which *'asher* is understood. It is really an adverbial clause of a kind very common in Isaiah. Cf. G.K. Gr. 155, f, p. 486f. It is the kind of clause we have in English with the omitted relative: The rose I picked. Therefore: Who is His counselor who instructs Him? Since such an act is impossible, we say that *yōdhī'ennū* is a subjunctive and translate: Who is His counselor that he instruct Him? Luther translated *tikkēn* in the first clause with "instruct," thus going beyond Romans 11. But that translation produces a tautology with the next verse — something that does not happen in Isaiah. An accurate translation recognizes the synthetic-progressive parallelism, in which the second clause expresses an advance of the thought beyond the first: Knows God's thoughts — instructs God's mind. The entire second verse is in a progressive relation to the first, and the third is in the same relation to the second.

¹⁴ אֶת־מִי נוֹעָץ וַיְבִינֵהוּ וַיְלַמְּדֵהוּ בְּאֹרַח מִשְׁפָּט
וַיְלַמְּדֵהוּ דַעַת וְדֶרֶךְ תְּבוּנוֹת יוֹדִיעֶנּוּ׃

It is characteristic of our prophet that he will use the last thought of one verse as the theme of the next, or even of the entire following strophe. So here he takes up the last thought of verse 13 and follows with a detailed development of it in verse 14.

The *'eth* before *mī* is the preposition, not the sign of the accusative. *nō'āts*, a Niphal perfect of *yā'ats* to counsel, is to be translated as a reflexive: With whom does He take counsel? *'eth mī nō'āts* is the only independent clause in the verse. The rest are all consecutive clauses introduced by *Waw* consecutive imperfect, and even

115

the last one is consecutive, since it is coordinated with the preceding clause by the *Waw* copulative in *wedherekh*. With whom does He take counsel, so that . . . ? The verbs of discerning, understanding, and teaching (*bīn, hēbhīn; lāmadh, limmēdh; yādha', hōdhīa'*) and the nouns (*da'ath* and *tebhūnōth*) are not always clearly distinguished in meaning. According to its etymology *bīn* means to distinguish one thing from another, or simply to be between. It is related to the preposition *bēyn*, between. In the Hiphil it means to bring about a distinction. *lāmadh* is the usual word for learning, *limmēdh* for teaching. *yādha'* is related to the Greek ἰδεῖν, εἶδον, the Latin *videre*, German *wissen*, English *to wit*. Its original meaning is to grasp or take hold of, also to grasp with the understanding, and in some situations to choose, to love, or even to cohabit. The most common meaning is to grasp with the understanding, and its noun, *da'ath* (an infinitive Qal), denotes either the ability to discern, the understanding, or even objective knowledge. In this verse its meaning is the *ability* to understand. The Hiphil of the verb means to impart understanding, but because it here has the pleonastic object *tebhūnōth* (understanding), the verb serves only as a carrier of the object. *da'ath* denotes simply an apprehension with the mind; *tebhūnōth* goes farther and signifies discernment of a situation to its last and deepest elements. The plural denotes a strengthening of the root idea. We therefore translate *wayebhīnēhū:* that he impart to Him discernment, that is, enlighten Him. The next clause would be translated literally: "that he instruct Him in the path of right." *'ōrah* is the poetic equivalent of *derekh*, way, or path. The first meaning of *mishpāṭ* (from *shāphaṭ*, to judge) is the act of judging or making a decision, and then the result of decision , or objective right. Here it has the meaning of judgment. God's way of judging and His daily decisions regarding the acts of men, His way of disposing, ruling, and governing is what the word means here. *'ōrah mishpāṭ* is the course that God's rule takes. That is expressed in the translation: And instruct Him how He must rule. *wayelammedhēhū da'ath* could be translated: And teach Him to know, to comprehend, to understand. *derekh tebhūnōth* is parallel to *'ōrah mishpāṭ* — the way of deep insight, which knows how to choose the right means to the ultimate goal and understands the way of wisdom. The prophet is not speaking of a way of attaining insight. One ought not to charge the prophet with using unnecessary words. The verse is very skillfully constructed, and in each sentence and clause something new is expressed, which richly rewards the searcher who discovers it. To demonstrate that, we repeat the translation as literally as possible:

With whom has He taken counsel,
That he impart to Him understanding
* And instruct Him in the path of judgment*
And teach Him to understand,
* And cause Him to perceive the way of insight?*

The dependent clauses are here arranged in pairs, the first clause being paired with the third, the second with the fourth. To cause someone to be understanding and to teach him to understand are nearly identical in meaning. Both speak of imparting that understanding the possession of which supplies the insight needed for carrying out what is mentioned in the second and fourth clauses. In the latter two clauses the path that right decision must follow and the road that perfect and complete understanding must choose are nearly identical. The difference lies in the contrast between the possession of the ability to understand as expressed in clauses one and three, and the practical application of that ability as expressed in clauses two and four. Stripped of poetic adornment the thought is simply: Who gives Him the ability to have right judgment? and in the second pair: Who gives Him the understanding to rule with wisdom? The first pair speaks of the theoretical understanding, the second pair of the practical application of it. According to the system of parallelism of members, that would be the arrangement of a simple pair. How the two halves, each made up of two clauses, differ in meaning is clear if one recalls the analysis of the meaning of the words given above. It does seem strange, however, that the poet uses the same word, *yelammedhēhū*, twice in close succession. The critics considered that to be awkward and unpoetic. Some even delete the whole clause *wayelammedhēhū da'ath* as an interpolation. But the word is necessary. The poet is interested in mustering all his poetic technique to extol the unsearchable sovereign counsel of God, and to do that he varies the usual parallel arrangement of a pair and weaves into the description a chiasmus (so named from the two crossed lines of the Greek letter *chi*). He not only repeats the idea of teaching and giving understanding in each of the two pairs of dependent clauses, but places the *yelammedhēhū* twice in the sentence, close together, to make the cross arrangement clear to the eye. He arranges the four phrases in such a way that the two center phrases are parallel in meaning, and the two outer, or ex-

117

treme, ones are also parallel to each other. For example, Isaiah 49:14 literally translated reads: Forsaken me has the Lord; the Lord has forgotten me. In the passage under discussion, the outside members are *wayebhīnēhū* at the beginning, and *tebhūnōth yōdhī'ennū* at the end, while the two inner clauses begin with the same word, *wayelammedhēhū*, so that the order is: Give understanding, instruct — instruct, give insight. It is obvious that the critics are on the wrong track if they consider the repetition of *wayelammedhēhū* to be clumsy and therefore delete it together with its object *da'ath* because the LXX does not have it. Could an interpolation succeed in creating such an artistic example of chiasmus? When the critics delete *wayelammedhēhū da'ath*, they destroy the chiasmus but let three-fourths of it remain as a mutilated torso. In their search after corruptions of text and in their eagerness to discover a poetic meter they ignore the real principles of Hebrew poetry and pronounce a judgment upon themselves.

The thought in verse 14 now moves beyond that in verse 13b. Verse 13b says: Who is His counselor that he instruct Him? But verse 14 says: Of whom does He *ask* counsel? The latter question is stronger. It lays special emphasis on the Lord's independence and absolute sovereignty. He neither needs nor seeks an instructor, neither a philosopher to improve His perception (clauses one and three), nor a practical counselor to give Him directions how to deal with each case that may come up (clauses two and four). He allows no one to meddle in the principles and practice of His world sovereignty. The Lord is above everything called human. He is absolute in His power and knowledge (verse 12); in his knowledge and in what He would add to His knowledge (verse 13); in what He would add to His knowledge and in His deeds (verse 14).

Thus the way is prepared for the discussion in the second half of the strophe of the Lord's eminence over mankind *in the mass.*

15   *Truly, the nations —*
       like a drop are they in a bucket,
     And like a kernel of grain in a scale are they counted;
     Truly, the isles are like a bit of dust that is raised;
16   *All of Lebanon is not sufficient for burning*
     Nor all its beasts sufficient for a burnt offering;
17   *The nations, all are as nothing before Him,*
     As nothing and as a void are they reckoned before Him.

118

15 הֵן גּוֹיִם֙ כְּמַ֣ר מִדְּלִ֔י וּכְשַׁ֤חַק מֹאזְנַ֙יִם֙ נֶחְשָׁ֔בוּ
הֵ֥ן אִיִּ֖ים כַּדַּ֥ק יִטּֽוֹל ׃

hēn, a common word in Hebrew, introduces a new thought. It
may point forward, or it may confirm what has already been said.
Here it confirms: "Truly." *gōyim* are men as a group with a common origin, peoples, nations. Even without the article, which in
poetry is frequently omitted, the word denotes the gentile nations
as contrasted with Israel. The same may be said of *īyyīm* in the
next clause. This is a *terminus technicus* for the islands and shores
of the Mediterranean. The word is frequently written without the
article. It is a figurative designation of the inhabitants of the isles
and shores, who, as the most prominent of the gentiles, are often
mentioned in connection with *gōyim*. The gentiles are *kemar mid-
delī*, like a drop left in a bucket. (The Hebrew says from a bucket,
whereas we say in a bucket.) *shaḥaq*, derived directly from a verb-
stem meaning to pulverize, means anything ground or pulverized.
Cf. Exodus 30:36. Here the word refers to a single tiny particle left
in the pan of a balance. *neḥshābhū*, the pausal form of *neḥshebhū*,
is the Niphal perfect of *ḥāshabh*. One may take it to be the predicate of all three clauses, or one may treat clauses one and three as
independent, by supplying the copula. *hēn*, repeated before *īyyīm*,
singles out the island people as eminent above the *gōyim* and at
the same time lends emphasis to *kaddaq yiṭṭōl*. *daq* is a stronger
expression than *shaḥaq*. It denotes something ground to a fine
dust. *yiṭṭōl* is a normal imperfect form of *nāṭal*, to lift up. But the
prophet's well-known preference for abbreviated relative clauses
has suggested the possibility that it really is a Niphal form of *ṭūl*
expressed by a substitute form of *nāṭal*. The meaning in that case
would be: a bit of dust that is lifted up, that is stirred up by the foot
or by a breath of wind. However, the translation: "The isles He
lifts up like a puff of dust" — think of an earthquake! — is perfectly justified.

16 וּלְבָנ֕וֹן אֵ֥ין דֵּ֖י בָּעֵ֑ר וְחַיָּת֔וֹ אֵ֥ין דֵּ֖י עוֹלָֽה ׃

Lebanon is a poetic name for the forests of Lebanon. The
reference is to the luxuriance and the excellence of its cedars. The
Zaqeph gadol that the Masoretes supplied sets this word apart
from the rest and emphasizes it. The translation of the conjunction with a simple "and" is therefore not adequate. Luther expressed the emphasis by using the definite article. We say : "All of
Lebanon." *ēyn* and *dēy* are construct forms of original nouns,

119

meaning nothingness and sufficiency. *bāʿer* is a Piel infinitive used as a noun. All Lebanon is not sufficient for burning, that is, for an altar fire. The next sentence: *wehayyāthō ʾen dē ʿōlāh,* "and its beasts are not sufficient for a burnt offering," is similar in construction.

כָּל־הַגּוֹיִם כְּאַיִן נֶגְדּוֹ מֵאֶפֶס וָתֹהוּ נֶחְשְׁבוּ־לוֹ: 17

kol haggōyim gathers together into one great mass all the heathen nations including the isles — all heathen nations taken together. *ʾephes* means the end, nothing. *mē* is partitive, from or of nothing, and then, abstractly, of the nature of nothing. (See the lexicon and Gr. 119, v, and Note 1, p. 382.) *thōhū* is absolute emptiness. The *Waw* (with Qamets), as in Genesis 1:1, combines the two expressions into a single pair. *neḥshebhū,* connected by Maqqeph with *lō,* corresponds to *negdō* of the first line: before Him. (Cf. Ps. 39:6(5),12(11); 62:10(9).

The second half of the strophe, verses 15-17, is as skillfully constructed as the first half. *gōyim, ʾiyyīm, haggōyim* form a climax. *gōyim* without an article is indefinite and refers to heathen nations, however great and mighty they may be. *ʾiyyīm,* however, is by its meaning, definite: the most powerful and prominent among the nations. *kol haggōyim* combines them all into one great mass. The objects with which they are compared are arranged in descending order: drop, particle, bit of dust, nothing — the last being expressed three times. The terms denoting the nothingness of the nations are so like one another that if they had been arranged without an interval, the effect would have been awkward, and so the thought of the burnt offering of Lebanon is introduced, with the forceful terms for nothingness following. Logically, verse 16 should follow verse 17, since it is the ethical consequence of verse 15 and verse 17. The comparisons are drastically expressive. The Lebanon sentence is beautiful. It should be understood as being potential in mood, for it suggests something impossible of accomplishment. If one should gather together all the precious trees of Lebanon and all its beasts and heaped them upon a giant altar to be burned, that would still be as nothing compared with the expression of honor due the majesty of the Lord. The chiasmus appears again in the arrangement of *neḥshābhū ʾeyn dēy — ʾeyn dēy neḥshebhū.* In verse 17 the comparison between the Lord and the heathen world is brought to a climax and to its ultimate truth. The nations are a cipher, the Lord is all, Psalm 62:10(9).

18   *To whom then would you liken God,*
      And what likeness place beside Him?

18   וְאֶל־מִי תְּדַמְּיוּן אֵל   וּמַה־דְּמוּת תַּעַרְכוּ־לוֹ:

This verse is really an intermediate strophe, its first half
directed backward and its second half forward. It contains a
pastoral application. The paragogic *Nun* in *tedhammeyūn* is purely
euphonic (Gr. 47, 4, m, p. 135). The *Waw* at the beginning introduces a conclusion: To whom *then* . . . ? The use of *'el* lends
extraordinary emphasis to the reproach. Whatever root one may
suggest for the word *'el,* it nevertheless is clear that it is the root
from which *'elōah* and *'elōhīm* are formed and that it denotes the
essence of God as distinguished from all creatures. It is the exact
equivalent of our *God.* Here it is an appellative which underscores
the genus God over against the genus man. To whom then would
you liken Him who is God? By this time, however, *'el* has also
become *nomen proprium* for the one true God, as in Psalm 16:1;
19:1, and elsewhere. It is the Hebrew word for the mysterious, in-
comprehensible, infinitely mighty, wise and holy Being of Him
whom Creation and Revelation praise as the eternal Creator and
Ruler of all things. But the name *'el* does not contain any suggestion of those close relationships that inhere in the names *'elōhīm*
and *YHWH. 'el* means God, nothing more. In this section it stands
as a counterpart to *qādhosh* in verse 25. It denotes what might be
called the "physical" and intellectual nature of God, while
qādhosh describes the moral nature of God. The strophe just completed described the infinite preeminence of the wisdom and
power of the Lord over against the power and wisdom of men. The
Lord is all, men are nothing. The application sums this up in one
word: To whom then would you liken God?

There is a reproach in the words. Even the faithful in Israel
hardly dared to believe in a deliverance from Babylon. The long
years of captivity seemed to argue that their God *YHWH* was not
able to break the power of Babylon and set His people free. They
compared God's wisdom and power with the might and power of
Babylon and its gods. Babylon's boastful self-glorification and the
homage paid its idols were not without their effect on God's people.
They were beginning to doubt God's supremacy and were in
danger of falling away entirely. The prophet battles against this
spirit by portraying the supremacy of the Lord as above all human
might and wisdom. His purpose is to awaken trust in the Lord in

121

their hearts, to strengthen the weak and to preserve them from falling away.

Résumé: Verse 12: The spirit of man cannot comprehend the Lord in the great works of His spirit. *Verse 13:* Still less does he understand, let alone set limits for, the spirit of God. *Verse 14:* Independent of man, the spirit of God determines His way of governing the world.

Verses 15-17: The power and wisdom of the whole gentile world are before Him a negligible quantity. No sacrifice of Lebanon is worthy to honor His might and wisdom. *Verse 18a:* How foolish then is it to compare Him, who is God, with men! This was summarized in our heading: *The preeminence of the spirit of the Lord over the spirit of man.*

The closing half-verse points forward. The *ū* before *mah* is best rendered with "or." Although the clause is parallel to the preceding one, it does contain a new element. The personal objects of the prepositions appear in reversed order: *To whom* would you liken? What image *beside Him?* The last object is *demūth*, likeness, image, copy, as in Genesis 1:26, where one ought to translate: "Like an image of us," not "like our image." Here the reference in *demūth* is to the idols which are the subject of the next strophe.

Second Strophe: verses 19-25: *The preeminence of the Lord over everything called god in the world.*

The first half of the strophe, verses 19-21, proclaims the supremacy of the Lord over the *idols*; the second half, verses 22-25, His supremacy over the *princes of the world.* The critics consider this to be a corrupt text. Some say that verses 19 and 20 were interpolated by someone who misinterpreted *demūth* and took it to mean an image of Jehovah. And as though enough insertions had not already been made, others insert 41:6 and 7 between these two verses, with the excuse that these verses do not fit in chapter 41 but do fit very well at this spot. Both sides are sure that their emendation is scientifically correct. The reasonable procedure would be to try to understand the passage in its context.

First Half: verses 19-21:

19   *An idol, the master-workman casts it;*
     The goldsmith overlays it with gold,
     And chains of silver he pours upon it.

20 *The idol-priest chooses a tree that will not rot,*
He seeks out for himself a wise craftsman
To set up an idol that will not move.
21 *Have you not known? Have you not heard?*
Has it not been told you from the beginning?
Have you not understood from the foundations of the earth?

19 הַפֶּ֫סֶל נָסַ֣ךְ חָרָ֔שׁ וְצֹרֵ֖ף בַּזָּהָ֣ב יְרַקְּעֶ֑נּוּ
וּרְתֻק֥וֹת כֶּ֖סֶף צוֹרֵֽף :

Verses 19 and 20 are close to being prose. They ridicule the manufacturer of idols. That quite naturally destroys the poetic effect. *pesel* is a carved or sculptured image. One would have expected *nesekh*, a molten image, here to go with the verb *nāsakh*. The word is used as a *species pro genere* in order to avoid the clash of sound in *hannesekh nāsakh*. The article indicates the genus. *pesel,* in the lead position, does not state the theme, but emphasizes the mockery. *ḥārāsh* is the word for any kind of master workman, in this instance a molder or foundryman. *tsōrēph,* a participle Qal, is here a pure noun, as in 41:7; 46:6, and is the word for a gold- or silversmith. At the end of the verse *tsōrēph* is a pure verb. *yeraqqe'ennū,* a Piel imperfect with suffix and *Nun energicum,* is not derived directly from *rāqa',* which can mean only to stretch out or beat into a sheet. It is rather a denominative from *riqqua'* (Num.17:3) meaning tin, or something beaten into a sheet, and means here "to cover with foil, to sheathe." The goldsmith sheathes the idol in foil of gold. *rethuqōth,* perhaps a construct plural of *rattōq,* is a very doubtful form, both as to pointing and to meaning. The singular occurs only in Ezekiel 7:23, the plural in 1 Kings 6:21. (See Qeri and Kethib.) The verb occurs only in the Qeri of Ecclesiastes 12:6 and in Nahum 3:10. In the latter passage it has the meaning of chains. So, perhaps the word means chains, or possibly a hedge, a fence, or pendants. Thus, chains or pendants of silver he hangs on or around them. The participle *tsōrēph* stands isolated, without reference, not an infrequent construction in Hebrew. It is obviously incorrect to refer it to *keseph (ba),* as in Gr. 119, 5, hh, p. 384. The sequence of forms, *nāsakh* (perfect), *yeraqqe'ennū* (imperfect), *tsōrēph* (participle), is common in descriptive writings. Concerning the omission of a personal pronoun to go with the second *tsōrēph,* see Gr. 116, s, p. 360. The verse describes the moment of the construction of the idol, in which the molder has completed his part (perfect) while the gold- or silversmith is still occupied with his (imperfect and participle).

123

²⁰ הַמְסֻכָּן תְּרוּמָה עֵץ לֹא־יִרְקַב יִבְחָר
חָרָשׁ חָכָם יְבַקֶּשׁ־לוֹ לְהָכִין פֶּסֶל לֹא יִמּוֹט:

Verse 20 describes the fabrication of the sculptured image. Three explanations of *hammesukkān,* all incorrect, are current. The form is a Pual participle of *sākhan,* which means to care for, to provide or manage, to busy oneself with something. All occurrences of the word may be thus explained, including Proverbs 10:9, where Luther falsely translates "injured" instead of "provided." (Cf. Lex. and the related verb *sāghan*). On the authority of David Kimchi and by analogy of *miskēn* (the neglected one), the word has been translated as the destitute or impoverished man, and *terūmāh* as votive offering or sacrifice, either as an inner accusative (destitute of an offering), or attached to the following predicate (the destitute man chooses as votive offering a block of wood). This interpretation has, however, not been found satisfactory, for how can the passive Pual form *mesukkān* have the same meaning as the clearly intransitive or even active form *miskēn*? A later explanation derived it from *sāghan,* supposedly meaning to care for, and translated it as the careful person. But that is clearly an incorrect translation. Finally, Duhm, the critic by profession, cut the Gordian knot by substituting *hammaskīn temūnāh* (he who carves an image, the god-carver), fabricating a denominative from *sakkīn* (Prov. 23:2), Aramaic: *sakkīnā*? Since the text is perplexing and this explanation fits nicely into the context, therefore . . . .

The case is however really quite simple. If *sākhan* means to care for or to provide, then the Pual participle can only refer to the person cared for or supplied with something. The *mesukkān terūmāh* (an accusative with a passive participle, Gr. 116, 4, p. 358f) is then the one who has been supplied with votive offerings (singular collective), that is, the priest (cf. Lev. 7:32; 22:12), the idol-priest. The prophet of the true God (verse 18) and of the Holy One (verse 25), respectively the Holy One Himself, is unwilling in this mocking description to use the lofty title of *kohēn,* but contemptuously describes him as a belly-server, who is concerned only about the food as he serves his idol with pretended zeal. Such a priest would be seriously interested in adorning his idol with worthy and durable materials and would make certain that it was fixed on a firm base. As a professional in idol worship and as a responsible servant of his master, he would have the first word in the choice of materials, manufacture and erection of the idol. The priest takes second

place, next to his idol. Verse 19, the idol; verse 20, the idol-priest —
par nobile fratrum!

Before *lō' yirqabh* and *lō' yimmōṭ* (Niphal imperfect) supply
'asher. These are relative clauses. A block that will not rot is sound
and durable; the *ḥārāsh ḥakhām* is an experienced workman, one
who knows his craft. *hēkhīn*, a Hiphil, does not mean to produce or
to construct, but to set up firmly, a meaning that follows from the
immediately preceding *lō' yimmōṭ*. (*lō' yimmōṭ* may also be construed as a clause of purpose, Gr. 165, a, p. 503.) In the suggestion
that the idol might possibly tumble from its base, the irony
reaches its height.

21 הֲלוֹא תֵדְעוּ הֲלוֹא תִשְׁמָעוּ הֲלוֹא הֻגַּד מֵרֹאשׁ לָכֶם
הֲלוֹא הֲבִינֹתֶם מוֹסְדוֹת הָאָרֶץ׃

The biting irony with which the construction of the idol was described is now followed by a description of the absolute nothingness of the idols before the Lord. They deserve nothing but the
mockery that occurs over and over: 41:5-7; 44:9-20; 46:5-7; see
also Jeremiah 10:2-5; Psalm 115:4ff; 135:15ff.

The tone changes abruptly to one of deep seriousness and anger,
which is expressed in four blunt, reproachful questions without
any connecting link. The first two verbs are imperfects, because
they could and should have known (Gr. 107, m, n, r, p. 316ff):
Could you not and *should* you not know and understand? The next
two verbs are perfects because they express historical facts. It has
been proclaimed to them (*huggadh*) by the Lord's revealed Word,
and they have actually been inwardly convinced (*habhīnōthem*) by
the "foundations" of the world. *mōsedhōth* nowhere occurs as an
abstract plural in the sense of *founding*, but always has the same
meaning elsewhere as in this passage: foundations, pillars, upon
which the poet's imagination sees the heavens and the earth resting (Isa. 24:18; 2 Sam. 22:8; Job 38:6). It is the equivalent of the
New Testament τὰ θεμέλια , 2 Timothy 2:19; Hebrews 6:1. The
term is in contrast to the hanging of chains about the idol (verse
19) in order to keep it from toppling (verse 20). Luther missed the
point here. "Who laid them" is to be supplied; not "What they
teach" (Isa. 48:13). *thēdheū* corresponds to *habhīnōthem*, know
and be persuaded; and *thishmāū* corresponds to *huggadh*, hear
and attend — has been proclaimed. The members are arranged in
a chiasmus. "From the beginning" refers to the history of Israel.
But as for these idols, so highly honored in Babylon, they first had
to be fabricated by human hands. Belly-serving priests selected

the raw materials with great care and sought out master workmen who with much care and great skill decorated the image and furnished it with chains to keep it from toppling over. Surely, the people to whom the Word had been revealed and proclaimed from the beginning should know that these dead lumps of brass and blocks of wood could have no place alongside the Lord, who is the true God who created the whole world and set it upon unshakable foundations.

It is an inexcusable mistake on the part of many commentators that they have seen in this passage a rebuke directed at the persons addressed because they constructed and worshiped idols. That is not what the passage says. What constitutes their guilt is what is expressed in verses 18 and 25, namely, that they liken God to human beings and that they place idols and images of gods alongside the true God, in their minds, that is, not physically. As verse 18 also suggests, they seemed to fear that after all there might be some divine power in these idols, from whom their own God might not be able to deliver them. The cult of idols was very highly developed and organized in Babylon. The worship of Bel, Nebo, Gad, and Meni dominated the entire life of the people (65:3-7; 65:11f; 66:17). All the world served them. Was it not possible that it was they that had made Babylon mistress of the world? That was the fear that troubled the people. By entertaining that fear in their hearts they were in effect setting up the idols beside the Lord and consequently were in danger of falling away from the Lord, who had seemingly forsaken and forgotten them (verse 27). It is against that fear that the first half of this strophe is directed. It ridicules the idols in order to preserve the faithful people from falling away and to recall them to a firm trust in the Lord. The passage is *not*, like 41:5-7 and 44:9f, directed against worshipers of idols, whether Babylonian or Jewish. The human mind (verses 12-14), nations (verses 15-17), idols (verses 19-21) and princes (verses 22-24) appear in the entire section as powers against which the people, believing indeed, but of small faith, were in need of comfort. It is because they were so afraid of the Babylonian gods that they are here so earnestly rebuked.

Second Half: verses 22-25:

The second half of the strophe, verses 22-25, pictures the preeminence of the Lord over the *princes of the world*.

22   *He who sits throned above the circle of the earth —*
     And those who live upon it are but as straws —

He who stretched out the heavens like gauze
And spread them out like a tent for habitation,

23 *He who makes the princes to be as nothing,*
Who makes the mighty of the earth a cipher!

24 *Hardly are they planted, hardly are they set,*
Hardly has their stem taken root in the ground
When He blows upon them and they wither,
Like chaff that the stormwind carries away.

25 *To whom then would you liken Me, that I should be like him?*
Says the Holy One.

22 הַיֹּשֵׁב֙ עַל־ח֣וּג הָאָ֔רֶץ וְיֹשְׁבֶ֖יהָ כַּחֲגָבִ֑ים
הַנּוֹטֶ֤ה כַדֹּק֙ שָׁמַ֔יִם וַיִּמְתָּחֵ֥ם כָּאֹ֖הֶל לָשָֽׁבֶת׃

The name of the Lord has not been expressly mentioned since the 13th verse, except as *'el* in verse 18. In verse 21 His name is to be supplied in the answer to the question: Who laid the foundations of the earth? To Him also the participles with the definite article refer: *hayyōshēbh, hannōteh,* and *hannōthēn.* Because of the article they are to be understood as demonstratives, another way of expressing a *hinnēh* or *hēn* with a finite verb, except that here the action is durative. (Cf. Gr. 126, b, p. 404 and 116, f, 3, p. 357.) *ḥūgh hā'arets* is not the vault of the sky. That is expressed by *ḥūgh shāmayim,* Job 22:14. In Proverbs 8:27 *ḥūgh* is the circle that God drew around the deep (Job 26:10). This is the only passage where *ḥūgh hā'arets* occurs, and by analogy with the two passages mentioned the phrase can mean only the "circle about the earth." It is the apparently circular plane of the earth's surface, bounded by the horizon. The LXX has γῦρος. The picture is that of the Lord throned in the *ḥūgh shāmayim,* but above the earth-circle, which is His footstool (66:1; Acts 7:49; Matt. 5:34f). This represents in a figure His unapproachable preeminence and sovereignty over all creatures, especially over *yōshebheyhā,* that is, the world's inhabitants, who in their littleness are as grasshoppers before Him who governs the world and all its puny people. The next sentence contains a variation of the same thought. He who is enthroned in heaven above the circle of the world is now described as He who stretched out the heavens like a sheet of gauze. (*dōq* is something pounded or stretched out flat, from *dāqaq.*) The second part of the sentence changes the picture from the inhabitants to the habitation or canopy that the Lord has spread out over them. *lāshābheth* (a pausal form of *lāshebheth,* infinitive of *yāshabh*), for a habitation for them; not, of course, for Himself.

127

²³ הַנּוֹתֵן רוֹזְנִים לְאָיִן   שֹׁפְטֵי אֶרֶץ כַּתֹּהוּ עָשָׂה׃

Verse 22 compared the Lord with all the inhabitants of the world; the next verse places Him as Sovereign in contrast with the rulers of the world. *rōzenīm,* a word which occurs only in poetry and as a plural, usually as a synonym of *melākhīm,* may be translated, as in the Arabic, with dignitaries, that is, princes, majesties, gods (Ps. 82:1 and 6, and often elsewhere). The *shōphetēy 'erets* are not judges in the ordinary sense, but, *species pro genere,* governors in the world. *'asāh,* coupled with the participle *hannōthēn,* is a frequentative perfect, which has dropped its *Waw* consecutive (cf. Gr. 112, 3 a, b, p. 331f and 143, d, 2, p. 458). *rōzenīm* and *'ayin, shōphetīm* and *thōhū* are complete opposites. People who are somebody are consigned to nothingness; those who preside over order are committed to chaos. This rule of the Lord refers, of course, to actual cases. (See Gr. 116, f, p. 357 and 106, k, p. 312.)

²⁴ אַף בַּל־נִטָּעוּ אַף בַּל־זֹרָעוּ אַף בַּל־שֹׁרֵשׁ בָּאָרֶץ גִּזְעָם
וְגַם־נָשַׁף בָּהֶם וַיִּבָשׁוּ וּסְעָרָה כַּקַּשׁ תִּשָּׂאֵם׃

Verse 24 describes in a vivid picture how majestically this rule of the Lord of heaven and earth is carried out in its dealings with the dignitaries of this world. He hurls them suddenly from their thrones. *'aph,* an assertive particle, is repeated three times. Together with the negative *bal* it has the meaning of not yet, barely, hardly. The three following perfects (for even *shōrēsh* is a perfect Polel, not a Qal active participle, Gr. 55, 1, p. 159) express what has actually happened. *zōrā'ū* is commonly, but inaccurately, translated "are sown." That translation breaks down the climactic arrangement and also destroys the unity of the picture. The picture is that of a *geza',* a stem, a little branch. Planting and taking root fit that picture, but sowing does not. Sowing presupposes a seed, which would not only introduce a different picture but would also be an unsuitable picture for the installation of a prince. Who ever *sows* a prince? But the subject of *zōrā'ū* is certainly *gēza',* which is also the subject of *nittā'ū* and *shōrēsh.* Therefore *zōrā'ū* must be translated with some verb other than "was sown." In Isaiah 17:10 this verb is used of the setting out of the slips of the grapevine, and consequently the verb has another meaning besides sowing, strewing, scattering. It may also mean "to set," and in this sense it is a real synonym of *nāṭa',* to plant. Since the setting out of slips of grape branches requires great care, there

128

emerges a climax: plant, set, take root. So we have: Hardly are
they planted, hardly set out, etc. — *wegham* then introduces the
apodosis: Already they are . . .

nāshaph is a stronger word than *nāshabh* (verse 7) and is used
here to express God's sudden, violent, angry intervention. The
Waw consecutive imperfect with *yibhāshū* expresses the result of
the blowing, and the verb *tissā'em* is attracted into the same construction by means of the *ū* attached to *se'ārāh:* "so that they
wither, and a stormwind blows them away like chaff." The mighty
ones of the earth are as nothing before Him who sits enthroned
over the circle of the earth.

$$\text{25 וְאֶל־מִי תְדַמְּיוּנִי וְאֶשְׁוֶה יֹאמַר קָדוֹשׁ:}$$

Like a refrain, verse 25 repeats verse 18, with a slight but significant change of form. The *Waw* again recapitulates. *'eshweh,* an
imperfect Qal of *shāwāh,* is an emphasizing pleonasm. In place of
the *tedhammeyūn 'el* of verse 18, we now have *thedhammeyūnī
yo'mar qādhōsh. qādhōsh* is a proper name, stronger than, but corresponding to *'el* of verse 18. Israel should not place men and nations, even with all their might and wisdom, on the same level with
the Lord, who is Infinite Power and Infinite Wisdom. Idols and
princes, human dignitaries, are not to be placed alongside Him, for
He is *qādhōsh!* Ordinarily this word signifies anything that has
been set apart from common use, especially something that has
been set apart for God and devoted to Him. By virtue of its dedication to a higher use, the thing so set apart acquires an aura of mystery, of the unknown, of the supernatural, and is therefore to be
approached with reverence and awe. The concept is thus not one
applied at first to God, but contrariwise the holiness passes from
God to the thing set apart. The knowledge and awareness of God
naturally precede the feeling of obligation to serve Him and to
dedicate something to Him. So also the commandment to be holy is
grounded in God's holiness, Leviticus 11:44f; 19:2, etc. *The sepa-
rateness of God from everything else that is not God, the uniqueness
of His Being and His Nature* are the basis for the meaning of
qādhōsh. And yet, this is but a formal definition of the word.

Wherein does the uniqueness of God consist? In His absolute perfection in every respect. Outside of Him there is nothing perfect in
heaven or on earth. He alone is complete, infinitely exalted above
everything apart from Him. Therefore everything that is not perfect is bound to honor, adore, and fear Him. Still, although the concept embraces all of God's perfections, including His absolute

power and wisdom, that is not yet the real reason why He is called Holy. *qādhōsh* is an ethical concept. It signifies God's moral perfection in contrast to all moral imperfection, in every conceivable respect. God is light as opposed to all darkness. Nor is this a static kind of attribute existing in and for itself, but energy and action against what is sinful, unclean and dark. The light shines in the darkness and swallows it up, at the same time creating life and happiness. God's holiness is that attribute by which He does away with sinfulness, uncleanness, and darkness, which is unhappiness and ruin. In their place He creates new life and salvation. For that reason His holiness expresses itself on the one hand as wrath, punishment, and judgment, working unhappiness, death, and damnation; and on the other hand as mercy, deliverance, and salvation, working reconciliation, union with God, holiness, and a life of rejoicing.

God's holiness is not merely that moral quality that hates sin and condemns the sinner to death and destruction. It is just as truly the principle of all goodness, love, kindness, blessing and salvation. That is shown in Isaiah 6, and a hundred other passages. In Isaiah 6, *qādhōsh* is repeated three times. The same holiness terrifies the sinful prophet to the point of perishing and at the same time takes away his iniquity and reconciles him with God. The calling of Peter offers a similar example. In the same ship with him is the "Holy One of God." He fills Peter with terror but at the same time makes him His servant whose sin is pardoned and who is filled with the Holy Spirit. The holiness of God is the same as the *kebhōdh YHWH,* but with this difference that the glory of the Lord is the visible representation of His holiness. The calling of Moses out of the burning bush in Exodus 3 clearly indicates the *noli me tangere,* and just as clearly assures the deliverance of Israel. In Exodus 34: 6 and 7 the Lord proclaims His own name, that is, His glory, which is infinite grace, but also devouring wrath. It is His honor, which He will give to none other (Isaiah 42:8), that He does not break the bruised reed, verse 3, and still cries out like a woman in travail and lays everything waste in His anger. (Cf. 57:15; Luke 1:49-55.) It is from this that the concept of the Holy One of Israel in the Old Testament (30 times in Isaiah), and the Holy One of God in the New Testament (Mark 1:24; Luke 4:34) derive their true meaning. Holiness is the expression for all of God's morality, His "virtue," and thus is the principle underlying all of His work, His creation and government of the world, and particularly His work of redemption. Whatever, outside

of Scripture, is called holy, is holy only because it somehow is related to the holy God. The Lord is *qādhōsh*, the One great Holy
Being and Person, who in absolute and steadfast faithfulness
toward His people and in unquenchable hatred of His own and
Israel's enemies infallibly works Israel's deliverance and the
downfall of its enemies by virtue of His preeminent wisdom and
power. How then can Israel, in doubt and fear, for one moment
dare to compare men, nations, and gods, and all earthly dignitaries with Him?

Résumé of verses 19-21: The idols that men fabricate and decor-
ate can be made to stand up only by means of devices of belly-serving priests, whereas you know Me as the One who revealed Himself as the Creator of the world. *Verses 22-25:* The Lord is
enthroned as Ruler above the circle of the earth and lets its puny
inhabitants dwell safely under the heavens as under a canopy, but
He suddenly, at will, casts down the proud potentates, so that their
place knows them no more. With whom then would you compare
Me, the Holy One?

Third Strophe: verses 26-31: *The power, wisdom, and holiness
of the Lord are the certain guarantee for the preservation and
restoration of His faithful people.*

The concluding strophe is divided into three parts: verses 26,
27-28, and 29-31. Verse 26 directs our attention once again to the
starry heavens, convincing proof of the boundless power of the
Lord. Verses 27 and 28 apply what was said in verse 26 to Israel's
littleness of faith, with first a concrete and then an abstract assertion of His limitless power and His unfathomable wisdom. Verses
29-31 contain the promise that the Holy One of Israel will employ
His power and wisdom to the glorious preservation and restoration
of those who believe Him.

This concluding strophe offers an example of the great care
with which Isaiah constructed his discourses. It takes up in order
the main thoughts of the two preceding strophes and makes the
application to Israel. God's power in the heavens in verse 26 takes
up the thought contained in verse 12 that no man can take the
measure of the heavens. Israel's denial of the omniscience of the
Lord echoes verses 13 and 14. Verse 28 repeats what was said of *ēl*
in verse 18. What is said of the creation of the ends of the world
restates what was said of the foundations of the world in verse 21.
That He does not tire or grow weary is the equivalent of His unin-

131

terrupted government of the world (verses 22-24). His profound
understanding (verse 26) repeats the thoughts of verses 13 and
14. Finally, in verses 29-31 he develops the *qādhōsh* concept of
verse 25, with verse 26 in mind. The reference of verse 26 to verse
12, and the refrain appearing in verses 18 and 25 constitute a
proof that our division of the strophe is the one intended by the
prophet, even though verse 26 itself is not yet an application of the
preceding strophe.

26 *Lift your eyes up into the height:*
    And behold! Who created these?
    He who leads out their host by number,
    Who calls them all by name —
    So great is His strength and so mighty His power
    That not one of them is missing.

27 *Why then do you say, Jacob,*
    And do you speak, Israel:
    Hidden is my lot from the Lord
    And my just cause departs from my God?

28 *Do you not know, or have you not heard?*
    The eternal God — the Lord who called into being
        the ends of the world —
    He neither tires nor grows weary;
    There is no comprehending His understanding.

29 *He gives strength to the weary,*
    And to those of no strength He increases power.

30 *Young men may tire and grow weary,*
    Young soldiers may stumble and fall,

31 *But they that trust in the Lord shall have new strength,*
    Like eagles they shall lift up their wings,
    They run and never tire,
    They journey and do not grow weary.

26 שְׂאוּ־מָרֹום עֵינֵיכֶם   וּרְאוּ מִי־בָרָא אֵלֶּה
הַמּוֹצִיא בְמִסְפָּר צְבָאָם   לְכֻלָּם בְּשֵׁם יִקְרָא
מֵרֹב אוֹנִים וְאַמִּיץ כֹּחַ   אִישׁ לֹא נֶעְדָּר׃

marōm, a height, the height of heaven, an accusative of direction, is a favorite word in Isaiah, cf. 24:18; 32:15; 37:23; 57:15;
58:4. The meaning goes somewhat beyond lifting up on high. That
meaning already lies in the verb *re'u*. Here the sense is: Lift up
into the heights, namely, into the skies, into the canopy of the
stars. *re'u*, being without an object, is intensive: behold, contemplate, observe! In place of stars, the expected object, the prophet

sets an emphatic rhetorical question: Who created *these (up there)?* The pronoun is emphatic and its reference is self-evident.

hammōtsī', a Hiphil participle of *yātsā'*, is not an answer to the preceding question, which is rhetorical and asks for no answer. Here the participle takes the place of a finite verb and in combination with *hinnēh* it introduces a new thought, like the participles in verses 23 and 24. (Cf. Gr. 116, 5, u-x; and especially 7, p. 361f.) In all sentences that begin with a participle, with or without the article, and that close with a finite verb, with or without *Waw*, the sense is: "Behold, while," or, "as often as." Therefore the sense here is: As often as He leads their full number forth, He calls them all by name. Grammarians call this construction the *casus pendens.*

A *tsābhā'* is an organized group, an army, or a host. *bemispār*, in number, or according to number, has the emphatic meaning of "in their full number." Behold! He leads forth their host in full number, complete. The following sentence, "He calls them all by name," is a vivid poetic development of *bemispār* and makes the counting of the stars a matter of the heart. The last clause: "From the multitude of strength and strong of power," is simply unintelligible in this literal translation. To clarify the clause, the critics resort to emendation and harmonize the two elements of the clause by changing *rōbh* into the adjective *rabh* and then translate the resulting *mērabh*: from Him who is great in powers and mighty in strength. What unbelievable foolishness that is! That such a use of the preposition *min* occurs nowhere in Scripture does not seem to trouble them. Others apply their changes to *'ammits kōaḥ*. But all such changes are without authority. The construction as it stands is good Hebrew, as Psalm 63:2(1) shows. The preposition *mē* before *rōbh* is causal and means "in consequence of," or possibly explanatory in the sense of "because, by reason of." (Cf. Gr. 119, z, p. 383.) *'ōnīm*, a plural of *'ōn*, is emphatic and means ability or power. Like *kōaḥ* it has no suffix, since the meaning is clear without a suffix: Because of the multitude or mass of His strength, and mighty of power. (*kōaḥ* is an accusative of reference.) *'īsh*, anyone, when connected with *lō'*, means "not one, not even one." *ne'dār*, Niphal of *'ādhar*, to follow (cf. *'ēdher*, a herd), to be left behind, to be overlooked, to be missing. The Niphal has the same meaning as the Qal.

Before the prophet, or the Lord, for it is really the Lord Himself speaking in the entire chapter, makes his application, he once more underscores the omnipotence and the wisdom of the Lord, by means of a charming picture. In verse 21 he had referred to the foundations of the earth, and in verse 22 to the earth itself with its outstretched canopy of stars as evidence of the Lord's unequaled power. In verse 26 he directs the reader's eyes to the uncounted host of the stars in the heavens. What a magnificent spectacle! The incalculable host of stars in the quiet nocturnal sky preaches even more impressively of the glory of the Lord, of the *kebhōdh 'el* (Ps. 19), and of the γνωστὸν τοῦ θεοῦ (Rom. 1), than do the restless stir and noise of daytime.

Who is it that created these? The question directs our attention in two directions. First, who leads them forth each night — that is what is meant — in their full number to their place in the heavens?

The uncounted host of the heavenly bodies, fixed in their place in unimaginable depths or wandering through the heavens, is pictured as the really overwhelming wonder. Nothing preaches so impressively as this about the Lord's creative might. Secondly, the question introduces an exceedingly charming picture. The Lord is pictured as a shepherd who each night leads this uncounted host of stars like a flock of young sheep out of the fold into the pasture, calling them each by name and leading them in perfect order to their proper place. Not one is missing of all the great multitude. All of this puts into relief God's infinite strength and His effective might and power. But the expressions at the same time are chosen so as to throw a strong light on God's *wisdom* and understanding. The infinite multitude of the stars is counted exactly. The Lord knows each single one. The words also preach of God's loving care. The picture of the shepherd and the other details do that. The counting is not a cold intellectual operation. He Himself has given each its name and He calls them all by name. He knows the individual (John 10:14) and concerns Himself directly about each one; He sees to it that not a one is forgotten or left behind. Such is the faithfulness of God's heart. In His infinite power and wisdom, by His word, He has not only called into being the separate things whose countless number cannot even be imagined, but in His faithfulness and goodness also cares for each one. Not one of His works, not even the tiniest particle of one, is excluded from His concern.

This hymn of praise is based on Psalm 147:4. But with what creative power has not Isaiah developed that text! Both passages are designed to give comfort to the intimidated children of God on earth, the *'anwēy 'erets* (Zeph. 2:3; Ps. 76:10(9), in Isaiah (chapters

41, 49, 51, 54) and elsewhere called *'aniyyīm,* the poor and miserable people, the miserable, stormbeaten, comfortless city (Isa. 54:11). Our passage teaches the faithful but almost despairing little body of believers languishing in exile that the same God who nightly demonstrates His power, care, and wisdom by marshalling the countless host of stars is surely wise and strong and faithful enough to lead the people whom He has chosen and made His own out of the Babylonian prison back to their own home, and that not one of them will be forgotten.

This passage echoes in many a Christian hymn and poem and sermon. " *Weisst du wieviel Sternlein stehen?* " ("Can you count the stars above you?"), the precious gem composed by Wilhelm Heys, used to be sung in every Christian home and schoolroom, conveying healing balm to many a wounded breast. Nothing is more sorely needed by pious children of God in the misery of their sin and their thousand afflictions on earth than the comforting assurance that every single circumstance, be it ever so insignificant, is still the object of God's faithful and omnipotent concern. Even the hairs of our heads are numbered (Matt. 10:30). The pastor who does not give due emphasis to this truth of the Gospel in his preaching is neglecting something very precious. New Year's Eve, New Year's Day, the Fifteenth Sunday after Trinity, birthdays, weddings, funerals, etc., are occasions for which this truth is especially appropriate.

27 לָמָּה תֹאמַר יַעֲקֹב וּתְדַבֵּר יִשְׂרָאֵל

נִסְתְּרָה דַרְכִּי מֵיְהֹוָה וּמֵאֱלֹהַי מִשְׁפָּטִי יַעֲבוֹר:

The formal application of this truth begins with a rhetorical question containing a reproach. The *Waw* consecutive of verses 18 and 25 is missing here. *lāmmāh,* accented on the first syllable, as always except when followed by a gutteral or *YHWH,* as in Psalm 22:2, was developed from *le māh,* for what, to what purpose, and means: With what justification? — since matters stand as they do. The imperfects *thō'mar* and *thedhabbēr* express continuing saying and speaking. The Piel *dibbēr* is intensive and iterative and is stronger than *'āmar.* Modern Yiddish jargon uses *dibbern* to express endless gabbing. The names Jacob and Israel are terms of endearment for the *faithful* people. Jacob was the son beloved of God and chosen in preference to Esau (Mal. 1:2f; Rom. 9:12f). Israel refers to the man of faith, tested and proved, Jacob reborn in the Spirit, Genesis 32:27ff. The Lord's heart is with His beloved spiritual people living in exile. These titles themselves already

135

show how unjustified their murmuring complaint is. They complained that their way was hidden from God and that their just rights were being passed over by the Lord. *derekh*, here and in Job 3:23, Psalm 37:5, and elsewhere, means lot or destiny, the way of life. The exile is meant in this instance. *nisterāh* is placed emphatically at the head of the sentence in contrast with what had been proclaimed of God's all-wise and all-powerful care. The preposition *min* is always written *mē* before *YHWH*, since *'adhōnāy*, beginning with the guttural *Aleph* is to be read. *nishpāt* is right or justice in the objective sense and refers to the right by grace to childhood in God's family, the right of the firstborn among the nations (Exodus 4:22), possessing the promise of the Messiah (cf. Rom. 9:4; Gen. 12; 18; 22:17; Deut. 7:14, etc.). Israel did indeed look upon this right as a right by grace (Deut. 7), but the Israel κατὰ σάρκα over and over again perverted it into something carnal (Matt. 3:9; John 8:33, 39ff), and in the present instance even the pious people, to some extent beguiled by seemingly endless misery, complain that their right passes by and escapes (*ya'abhōr*) their God, be it that the Lord has forgotten them or deliberately ignores them. The first sentence is, by the way, arranged in the common synonymous parallelism, the second in a forceful chiasmus.

הֲלוֹא יָדַעְתָּ אִם־לֹא שָׁמַעְתָּ 28

אֱלֹהֵי עוֹלָם ׀ יְהוָה בּוֹרֵא קְצוֹת הָאָרֶץ

לֹא יִיעַף וְלֹא יִיגָע אֵין חֵקֶר לִתְבוּנָתוֹ :

The question in verse 28 adds force to the reproach directed against the people. Israel ought to know, because ever and again it has heard it preached. A colon should be placed after "Have you not heard?" because the two clauses that follow are direct objects of the verb. *'elōhēy 'ōlām* is not, as has been sometimes explained, a predicate following *YHWH*: An eternal God is Jehovah, who, etc.; but *'elōhēy 'ōlām* is the subject of the entire following sentence and *YHWH bōrē'* is an appositive: the eternal God, namely Jehovah. The pointing of the Masoretes supports this interpretation, because they separated *'elōhēy 'ōlām* from the next phrase by a Legarmeh (Munach plus Paseq, the curb). The verbal ideas *lō' yī'aph* and *lō' yīghā'* are inseparably based in *'elōhēy 'ōlām*, the eternal God — because He is eternal God, therefore He neither tires nor grows weary, and because He is God His understanding is unsearchable. The apposition *YHWH bōrē'* identifies the eternal

God as the covenant God of Israel. The participle attribute adds the idea of omnipotence, for it is by the creation of the ends of the earth that God reveals Himself as the eternal God. The Almighty is also the Eternal One.

qetsōth hā'ārets is the equivalent of *ḥūgh hā'ārets* of verse 22. The ends of the earth are the earth from one end to the other, together with everything that lies within their circuit. The eternal God, the Creator Jehovah, Israel's almighty Covenant-God, neither tires nor grows weary. *yīghāʿ* is a stronger term than *yīʿaph*. Tiring is the beginning, becoming weary or exhausted is the end of the process of waning strength. To the eternity and omnipotence of the Lord the final clause adds His *tebhūnāh*, His perception of all things in their profoundest depths. *ʾeyn ḥeqer* or *lōʾ ḥeqer* — there is no searching — occurs also in Job 5:9; 9:10; 36:26; Psalm 145:3, and Proverbs 25:3. Here it occurs with *le,* the sign of the indirect object (Gr. 119, s, l, p. 381), where we should employ a genitive. There is no searching *of* His perception, it is beyond finding out. For that reason God is not at a loss for ways and means to deliver His people.

²⁹ נֹתֵן לַיָּעֵף כֹּחַ וּלְאֵין אוֹנִים עָצְמָה יַרְבֶּה:

Since the almighty and all-wise God is Jehovah, Israel's Covenant-God and faithful Shepherd, it follows that when God deals with His people He gives strength to the weary and increase of power to those of no strength. Luther's translation of this passage is unsurpassed. The participle *nōthēn* expresses repeated, conventional, customary action. So often as and whenever one grows weary, He gives strength. (Gr. 116, f, 3, Note p. 357.) *leʾeyn ʾōnīm* (to whom there is no strength) does not explain *yāʿeph;* it rather strengthens it. The one has lost his strength, the other lacks it altogether. But the Lord makes his strength great. *yarbeh* is an imperfect Hiphil of *rābhāh,* to be many, to be great. *ʾotsmāh,* occurring only here and in 47:9, is from *ʾōtsem,* strength.

³⁰ וְיִעֲפוּ נְעָרִים וְיִגָעוּ וּבַחוּרִים כָּשׁוֹל יִכָּשֵׁלוּ:

³¹ וְקוֹיֵ יְהוָה יַחֲלִיפוּ כֹחַ יַעֲלוּ אֵבֶר כַּנְּשָׁרִים יָרוּצוּ וְלֹא יִיגָעוּ יֵלְכוּ וְלֹא יִיעָפוּ:

Verses 30 and 31 form a single sentence, a protasis and an apodosis, joined by two *Waw*'s. The first *Waw* is concessive: even though; the second is adversative: still, nevertheless. *neʿārīm* and *baḥūrīm* are very similar in meaning. Both signify strong, agile young men or young soldiers. *na'ar* may also be used of very young lads, while *baḥurīm* are always mature young men and, often, soldiers. *baḥur* is actually a passive participle of *bāḥar,* to select, and means one who has been selected. There have been other explanations of the form, although there is agreement as to the meaning of the word. As the next clause shows, the important words are the two abstract terms, strength and renewal of strength. *kashōl yikkāshēlu* is the infinitive absolute with a finite verb, a common construction that is used to give emphasis to the verbal idea. (Gr. 113, 3, 1, n, etc., p. 342ff. See also w, p. 344 for the use of Qal infinitive with other conjugations than Qal.) Here the construction emphasizes the completeness, the thoroughness of the falling. *qōwēy YHWH* a construct plural of *qōweh,* a Qal participle, with a following objective genitive, they who wait upon the Lord. *qāwāh* is somewhat stronger than *bāṭaḥ,* to believe or trust, and means to trust unswervingly, *finaliter credere.* Luther uses the verb *harren.* Luther also struck the right note when he translated *yahalīphū kōaḥ* with "they get new strength." There is no general agreement over the meaning of *ḥalaph.* Perhaps the root meaning is "to be smooth." It is generally agreed that the Hiphil means "to exchange, to substitute." In the verse before us it derives its meaning from the contrast with growing weary and becoming exhausted. Young men may well lose their natural strength, but those who trust in the Lord will constantly gain more spiritual strength and renew their youth from day to day.

'ebher in the next verse refers to a large wing or pinion. The singular is a collective. Luther and others take *ya'alū* to be a Qal imperfect and translate it: "they rise up." *'ebher* then has to be interpreted as an adverbial accusative. But that is going to unneccessary trouble. *ya'alū* is a Hiphil and *'ebher* its direct object: "they lift up the wings." As in Psalm 103:5, eagles are a symbol of strength. The whole clause, in a picture, lends emphasis to the idea expressed in *yahalīphū khōaḥ.* In the last two clauses life is pictured as a career or course. Thus St. Paul too in 2 Timothy 4:7: τὸν δρόμον τετέληκα . The stronger expressions: run and become exhausted, come first; the weaker ones: walk and grow weary, follow. They form the conclusion of the whole discourse, which ought not end in a climax.

Résumé of verses 26-31: Who is it that by the stars so clearly demonstrates His almighty power, His wisdom, and His faithfulness as a Shepherd? Why then do My beloved people complain that I have neglected them? Am I not the eternal, almighty God, the eternally powerful and the unsearchably wise God? I daily renew the strength of all that is weary and without strength. Even though the powerful lose their strength and break down, those who rest their trust in Me daily get new strength and end their life's journey in victory.

Résumé of the entire section: verses 12-31: The wisdom and the power of the Lord are infinitely superior to all wisdom and power of the race of men, of all nations, all gods and princes. He is, in addition, a faithful, wise, and almighty Shepherd of His flock. As such a Shepherd He will manifest Himself to those who trust in Him.

Second Discourse: Chapter 41

The Lord establishes His eminence above the heathen and their gods by providing a victorious Champion, through whom they are put to shame and proved to be nothing; through him Israel, however, destroys her enemies, and herself is gloriously restored.

This discourse is by some divided into two almost equal parts, verses 1-16 and 17-29, each part again being divided into two strophes: 1-7, 8-16 and 17-20, 21-29. This results in a chiasmus: the Champion appears as a terror to the heathen, but as Israel's comfort; for Israel's restoration, but for the discomfiture of the gentiles. We prefer a division into three parts, combining the two middle sections into one. I, verses 1-7: The Lord's glory and the nothingness of the gentiles demonstrated by the manifestation of the famous Champion; II, verses 8-20: The comforting of Israel through the coming triumph over her enemies and her bountiful restoration; III, verses 21-29: The nothingness of the gentile gods and the glory of the Lord demonstrated by the sending forth of the Champion. The third strophe is not essentially different from the first. Both have the same semidramatic form. In the first the Lord steps forth and challenges the gentiles, and in the third He challenges the gentile gods to a judicial contest in which it shall be determined who it is that is capable of accomplishing something. Who is God, they or He? The middle strophe in its first three parts (8-10, 11-13, 14-16) takes the form of direct comfort, while the fourth part (17-20) that of objective promise, with Israel in the third person.

First Strophe: verses 1-7:   *The Lord challenges the gentiles to a judicial contest to determine who it is that sent the famous Champion against them as a scourge.*

As to contents, the strophe falls into three parts: verse 1, the summons to the contest; verses 2-4, the question at issue and its answer; verses 5-7, the resulting discomfiture of the gentiles.

First Half: verses 1-4:

1 *Be silent before Me, O Isles,*
   And let the nations summon new strength,
   Let them approach, then let them speak,
   And together let us draw near for judgment.
2 *Who calls one up out of the East,*
   Whom righteousness summons to her service,
   Giving up nations before him,
   Letting him trample upon kings,
   Making them as dust before his sword,
   Like swirling chaff before his bow?
3 *He drives them into flight and passes safely along*
   On paths that never before his feet had trodden.
4 *Who begins this work and carries it out?*
   He who from the beginning called forth the generations,
   I, the Lord, I am the first, and with the last
   I am He.

1 הַחֲרִישׁוּ אֵלַי אִיִּים   וּלְאֻמִּים יַחֲלִיפוּ כֹחַ

יִגְּשׁוּ אָז יְדַבֵּרוּ   יַחְדָּו לַמִּשְׁפָּט נִקְרָבָה:

This verse is a model of Hebrew poetic form. Each of its four sections advances the thought of the preceding section a little nearer to the goal. The progress of the thought also determines the choice of the verbs and nouns. The change in persons, which to our taste is disturbing, is intentional, a bit of rhetorical art that is common in Isaiah. For purposes of euphony, there is also a very liberal use of gutturals and sibilants which is not pleasing to our ears. These alternate with liquids and with the bright, clear i, a, and e vowels, and only occasionally with the more somber o's and u's.

As in the preceding chapter, the speaker is the Lord Himself. In fact, this is true of the entire book with the exception of 53:1-10; 59; 61:10f; 63:1f; and 63:7-64:12. The *'iyyīm* and the *le'ummīm* are being addressed. For *'iyyīm* see 40:15. *le'ōm* refers to the ethnic unit resulting from common ancestry, therefore, a nation. The *'iyyīm* as the leaders and the *le'ummīm* as their gentile followers, both as the enemies of the Lord, are being summoned by Him to judgment. *ḥārash* means to be rigid, motionless, struck by terror, dumb, deaf, and stupefied. The Hiphil strengthens the idea. The

141

Lord calls the teeming heathen nations who ceaselessly rage against Him (Ps. 2:1) to come to order and attention — *'elay*, toward me — an idea for which we have no exact equivalent. Perhaps the closest parallel would be the military command "Attention!" or the "Silence!" of the classroom. *yaḥaliphū khōaḥ* (40:31) is jussive. The gentile nations, declared in 40:15-17 to be as nothing, are to marshal all their strength and gather all their arguments (verse 21) in order, if that were possible, to triumph over the Lord in the debate. *yiggeshū, 'az yedhabbērū*—they are to draw near, to hear first of all the Lord's announcement, and *then*, *afterwards*, they are to speak and present their case. *'az*, usually used of the past, here points to the future, as in 35:5; Psalm 96:12; Micah 3:4; Zephaniah 3:9. The last phrase expresses the purpose of the Lord's summons: Together let us draw near for judgment. *yaḥdāw*, often purely temporal, in this instance is connected with *niqrābhāh* (1. person plural impf. Qal in pause with *He* cohortative, Gr. 48, c, d, p. 130) and unites the two parties. *mishpāṭ* is the judicial proceedings. The Lord does not summon His enemies before His court, but before an unspecified one that is to hand down an objective decision regarding the actions of the two parties to the contest. — In the following verses the Lord first presents His case in one long question and one shorter one, and concludes with an answer to both.

מִי הֵעִיר מִמִּזְרָח צֶדֶק יִקְרָאֵהוּ לְרַגְלוֹ ²

יִתֵּן לְפָנָיו גּוֹיִם וּמְלָכִים יַרְדְּ

יִתֵּן כֶּעָפָר חַרְבּוֹ כְּקַשׁ נִדָּף קַשְׁתּוֹ :

The grammatical construction of this passage is perhaps the most difficult in the whole book. There are as many different translations as there are commentators, and the critics embrace this opportunity to offer emendations of the text. The sentence treats of the One, at first not named, who has been called to take part in the debate, namely, the famous Champion later identified as Cyrus (44:28). The first clause is clear enough: Who calls one up out of the East? The next clause is the subject of much contention. Luther, led astray by the LXX, takes *tsedheq* to be the subject of *hē'ir*, and then changes the abstract *righteousness* into concrete form, the righteous one. We shall give no space to the many different translations, but translate as literally as possible. *tsedheq yiqrā'ehū leraghlō* is a relative clause, before which *'eth 'asher* has been omitted (Gr. 155, 3, n, p. 488), "whom righteousness calls to her foot." In Isaiah, as also in the Psalms, Jeremiah, and elsewhere, *tsedheq,* when used of the Lord, is His covenant-faith toward Israel, according to which He will accomplish salvation for Israel and destruction for her enemies — as will be carried out in the tenth verse. In 42:6 it is said of the Servant of the Lord, and in 45:13 of Cyrus, "I, the Lord, have called him *betsedheq.*" Here, however, *tsedheq* is a personification. The same is true of 58:8, where *tsedheq* forms the vanguard for Israel, and *kebhōdh YHWH* the rearguard, just as in 52:12 the Lord Himself is both. So, *tsedheq* is the personified covenant-faith which calls forth the Champion. *Calls,* not *called forth,* since the imperfect in a dependent clause is not a consecutive imperfect following *hēʿir,* but is really *final* in meaning (cf. Gr. 107,q,3,p.318). But no one can be faulted who construes *tsedheq* as an adverbial accusative, the equivalent of *betsedeq* (Cf. Gr. 118,q,p.375). The sense remains the same. She calls him to her foot. That pictures her as a queen on her throne calling him into her service. But *reghel* denotes not only a *foot,* but also a step, pace, or footprint. *bereghel* regularly means on the track of, behind someone. *lereghel,* in a single instance, means at the pace of (Gen. 33:14); otherwise it can mean *on the track of* (Gen. 30:30; Hab. 3:5; 1 Sam. 25:42); or somewhat more expressively, *step for step* (Job 18:11), where it is a synonym for *sābhībh,* round about. The meaning, therefore, is: Whom Righteousness calls to her trail, that is, to follow while she leads and prepares the way (cf. 45:2). The expression conveys the idea of obedience and service. The Champion has been called to serve the covenant-faith of God toward Israel. There is, therefore, no reason to spell *qaraʾ* with final *He* instead of *Aleph.*

The next two clauses are simpler. *mī* is to be supplied before *yittēn* (equivalent to Gr. ἔδωκεν in John 3:16, *deliver*). Since this is description, the imperfect expresses present time (cf. Gr. 107,f,2,p.315). *yard* is Hiphil apoc. imperfect of *rādhāh:* He lets trample. *melākhīm* is the object. Therefore: Who delivers the heathen before him and lets him trample kings?

The last two clauses are difficult but not incapable of solution. *mī* is again to be supplied before *yittēn,* which in this vivid description follows *yard* directly without grammatical connection; but it refers to *melākhīm* and *gōyim* as its objects and, if fully expressed, would take the form of *yittenēm:* Who gives them, that is, makes them, like dust? *ḥarbō* and *qashtō* are accusatives of means or cause, and are equivalent to *beḥarbō* and *beqashtō* (cf. Gr. 117,s,3,p.367 and 118,1,4,p.374). Who, with his sword, makes them

143

as dust; as driven chaff with his bow? This explanation does no violence to the text, which all the other translations, the LXX included, do. The LXX changes *ḥarbō* into a collective, *ḥarbām,* and relates the suffix to the kings and the heathen — *their swords.* If *ḥarbō* and *qashtō* are taken as subjects of *yittēn,* the rhetoric of the passage is destroyed, which clearly intended a threefold question with a single subject. *niddāph* is a Niphal participle of *nādhaph.* (Cf. also 45:1ff.)

³ יִרְדְּפֵם יַעֲבוֹר שָׁלוֹם אֹרַח בְּרַגְלָיו לֹא יָבוֹא:

Of the two verbs set asyndetically alongside each other, the second contains the main idea, and the first is subordinate (Gr. 120,g,h,p.386f): In pursuit of them he advances. *shālōm* is an adverbial accusative (Gr. 118,q,p.375): *in peace,* that is, unmolested and secure, like the *shālēm* in Genesis 33:18. Changing the noun *'orah* into a participle *'orēah* is completely arbitrary. *'orah* is the object of *ya'abhōr.* He walks a path. The next words are a shortened relative clause — which he had never trodden with his feet. *yābhō'* may be construed as impersonal, which then would just emphasize the thought (cf. 45:2). The Conqueror here spoken of, in pursuit of his enemies, advances on a pathless way across streams and unknown, untrodden heights, overleaping walls, unlocking dungeons, unhindered, unmolested (cf. 37:24f; 45:1-3).

⁴ מִי־פָעַל וְעָשָׂה קֹרֵא הַדֹּרוֹת מֵרֹאשׁ

אֲנִי יְהוָה רִאשׁוֹן וְאֶת־אַחֲרֹנִים אֲנִי־הוּא:

mī pha'al we'asāh is a summarizing and concluding question which refers to what precedes, not to what follows. *pā'al* refers to the beginning of a work, *'asāh* to its completion. This distinction is, however, often not observed. The answer to the question appears in the clause beginning with *qorē'.* He alone who has called into existence out of nothing all generations of men from the first to those now living awakens this conqueror and delivers nations and kings of past and present ages into his hand. Only one who can create men out of nothing can consign them to another as his plunder. Only He who controls the being and the fate of the generations of men is able to determine the lot of present generations and provide the instruments of His will. The present generation is, as regards its achievements, its weal and its woe, largely the product of preceding generations. But generations upon generations do not come into existence and develop according to inanimate laws of nature. They are the work of *'anī YHWH rī'shōn we'eth 'aḥarōnīm 'anī hū'*. The Lord is the First, that is, before the first of all generations (Col. 1:17). He called the first generation into being and determined its destiny; and in every generation, till the very last, He is the same as He was when He called the first into being — the Eternal One, calling forth the generations and determining their destiny. So, too, He has called this man into His service and furnished him to be His instrument to do His will upon the nations (44:28). The phrase beginning *'anī YHWH* is a rhetorical amplification of the more common *'anī rī'shōn wa'anī 'aḥarōn*, 44:6; 48:12, etc. Compare Revelation 2:8. The phrase is really an interpretation of the *YHWH* (Exodus 3:14) and designates Israel's God as the eternal and only One, before whom, beside whom, and after whom there can be no other God. In Him all things have their source, including the triumphant career of the conqueror of the nations here spoken of.

What the Lord here declares to the nations is meant for the instruction, the encouragement, and the comfort of us Christians. The great convulsions on earth, usually set in motion by a strong personality, such as Cyrus, Alexander, Attila, Mohammed, Genghis Khan, Charlemagne, Napoleon, or Moses, David, Isaiah, Paul, Luther, and others, do not just happen as the normal unfolding of the laws of nature, nor as something determined by human will and counsel. They are the special dispensation of God, who at the proper time calls forth His instrument to carry out His will. The world does not recognize this, nor does modern-day Christianity rightly appreciate it. But Scripture is full of instances of this truth, and the Old Testament especially has many expressions that show how clearly the believers saw the hand of the Lord directly involved in governing the world. Compare the *'alīlōth, ma'alālīm* (Ps. 77:12f[11f]; 103:7); the *niphlā'ōth* (Ps. 9:2; 136:4); the *nōrā'ōth* of God (Ps. 65:6[5]; Isa. 64:2[3]). Pastors and preachers have the special duty to reestablish this knowledge among the Christians of our day. It is not some one man, but the LORD who brought the World Wars upon those nations that had rejected the Gospel and devoted themselves to self-deification and to the service of mammon and the flesh. Out of the deceitful glamor of modern culture, which He has weighed and found wanting, God creates something new — for the well-being of His saints on earth. Oh, that we might put Isaiah 30:15 into practice and learn to observe what the hands of the Lord are doing!

The Lord has spoken. Now it is the turn of the nations who have been summoned to present their case. But they are unable to answer (verses 26 and 28). In place of the answer that is not forthcoming, we now have, in the second strophe, a description of the effect that the appearance of the Champion (or, respectively, the Lord's discourse) has upon the nations.

Second Half: verses 5-7:

5   *The Isles behold it and are afraid,*
    The ends of the earth tremble,
    They draw near and flock together.
6   *Each desires to help the other*
    And says to him, "Have courage!"
7   *The molder cheers on the goldsmith,*
    He who wields the hammer him that strikes the anvil,
    Saying of the soldering, "It is good!"
    He fastens it firmly with nails,
    So that it cannot totter.

Since this section is descriptive, the present, not the historical tenses are employed. The imperfects, either standing alone or connected by a simple copulative *Waw*, show that. The two perfects, *rā'u* and *qārebhū* and the participle *'ōmēr* in the seventh verse are subordinated as antecedents to the following imperfects. Understandably, the passage is not very poetic, but it still is vividly descriptive.

$$\text{רָאוּ אִיִּים וְיִירָאוּ} \quad \text{קְצוֹת הָאָרֶץ יֶחֱרָדוּ} \quad \text{קָרְבוּ וַיֶּאֱתָיוּן :}^5$$

'iyyīm refers back to the first verse. *rā'u*, without a connective, heads the sentence, not to lend emphasis, but to make the description vivid. *weyīrā'u*, in pausal form, echoes the sound of *rā'u*, an effect that cannot be reproduced in English. *rā'āh* means only to see or observe; *yārē'* means to be afraid. When they become aware of the invincibility of the Conqueror, they are afraid. *yeḥerādhū* of the following clause heightens the fear to trembling, quaking with fear. The form *ye'ethāyūn*, for *ye'ethū*, is third person plural imperfect Qal of *'āthāh*, to approach, to come walking along. The form is constructed by restoring the *Yod (He)*, which in the Lamed-He verbs is usually elided before vowel afformatives, and by opening the penultimate syllable (Gr. 75, 3, h, and Note 4, p. 209 and 212). This is usual in pausal forms. The final *Nun* is euphonic. *qārebhū* and *waye'ethāyūn* form a hendiadys, the second term being the

146

more important of the two. "They approached each other and came advancing" — they came thronging, crowding together.

$$\text{אִישׁ אֶת־רֵעֵהוּ יַעְזֹרוּ וּלְאָחִיו יֹאמַר חֲזָק:}^6$$

For combining *'ish* with *rēa'* and *'āḥ,* or with the feminines of these nouns, by means of various prepositions to mean the one — the other, see Gr. 139,b,1, and c,p.447f. Before *le'āḥīw, 'ish* is to be supplied. The predicate is plural in the first member, singular in the second. *ya'zorū,* the pausal form for *ya'zerū,* is inchoative: They seek to help each other with their work. *ḥazāq,* an imperative in pausal form, gives moral support: Be strong, stand firm. Cf. Deuteronomy 31:7,23; 2 Samuel 10:12. Each seeks to allay his own fears by encouraging the other.

$$\text{וַיְחַזֵּק חָרָשׁ אֶת־צֹרֵף מַחֲלִיק פַּטִּישׁ אֶת־הוֹלֶם פָּעַם}^7$$
$$\text{אֹמֵר לַדֶּבֶק טוֹב הוּא וַיְחַזְּקֵהוּ בְמַסְמְרִים לֹא יִמּוֹט:}$$

ḥārāsh and *tsōrēph* have already been discussed in 40:19f. The present passage and also the ones in chapter 40 and 44:9-20 treat of the manufacture of idols, not of weapons, as the phrase *lō'yimmōṭ* here and in chapter 40 makes clear. *yeḥazzēq* refers to the strength of mind or purpose. *maḥalīq,* a Hiphil participle of *ḥālaq,* to be smooth, is one who makes smooth, a skillful smith, a gold- or silversmith. *paṭṭīsh,* a hammer, is here an instrumental accusative. In the other two passages in which the word occurs, Jeremiah 23:29 and 50:23, it refers to a heavy hammer, here to a light hammer. He who beats the metal smooth with a hammer strengthens the *hōlem pā'am,* him who smites the anvil, that is, the silversmith encourages the blacksmith. The words are arranged in the form of a chiasmus: pourer, smelter; silversmith, blacksmith; the fine metalworkers in the means, the heavy smiths in the extremes. Some exegetes recognize only two different kinds of workers in the picture, rather than four, taking the second member to be a repetition of the first in slightly different terms. They may be right; but it is more likely that four are meant — two workers in precious metals, two in gross metals. The whole passage is to suggest a milling crowd. In *hōlem,* a Qal participle, the accent has been drawn back to the first syllable to avoid having two strong accents side by side, and the sound-effect is of the clang of a great hammer. The subject of *'ōmēr* is most likely the silversmith who completes the soldering. He says that it will hold but decides to make certainty doubly sure and fastens the idol to its base with nails, lest it topple over — "a fatal omen for its worshipers" (Kay-Cheyne, p. 255). Compare the remarks on 40:20. Some critics consider verse 7, or both verses 6 and 7, to be meaningless here and therefore interpolated. But the lack of good sense is perhaps to be sought elsewhere.

Résumé. The Lord challenges the gentiles to a debate before judges on the question who it is that leads forth the victorious Conqueror and causes him to crush the nations under his irresistible advance. Instead of answering, they tremble before the Conqueror who has been sent against them. They seek to strengthen one another and arm themselves by constructing new and more reliable idols.

The question of the identity of the historical personage here described has in the course of the years received widely differing answers. The ancient church fathers thought that Christ Himself was here being allegorically pictured, and this view has to this day still a few advocates. Jewish tradition and the Isaiah Targum applied the passage to Abraham and his victory over the kings of the East (Gen. 14). Luther expresses the same view in his Scholia. Sixteenth and seventeenth century exegesis vacillates between Christ and Abraham. Cocceius proposed Paul, but found no supporters. Ibn Ezra already rejected the reference to Abraham. Following the lead of Hugo Grotius, Vitringa pioneered the view that Cyrus is meant. Since then this view has been almost universally accepted, correctly so. A comparison of this passage with similar passages, in some of which Cyrus is mentioned by name, establishes the correctness of this interpretation beyond contradiction. In fact, with the exception of the directly Messianic forty-second chapter, this entire section, chapters 40-48, treats of Cyrus the Champion, the special servant of the Lord (46:11), who carries out the Lord's judgment against Babylon and delivers His people — in his role as a prototype of Christ.

Second Strophe: verses 8—20: *Faithful Israel is comforted through the covenant-faithfulness of the Lord with the promise of help, of the destruction of her enemies, and of abundant restoration.*

This major strophe is divided into four smaller sections arranged in order of climax. The first section, verses 8-10, assures Israel of the faithfulness and the effective help of God for her *preservation.* The second section, verses 11-13, foretells the total *destruction of her enemies* by the might of the Lord. The third, verses 14-16, says, more specifically, that *Israel herself* shall by the hand of God destroy her enemies. The last section, verses 17-20, tells of the *eventual restoration* of God's people, who had been exhausted by prolonged suffering. At the same time, in the first three sections, Israel's helplessness is pictured, and in the last, her suffering and despondency. The argument for climactic arrangement is at the same time also an argument for grouping verses 8-20 into a single unified strophe.

First Minor Strophe: verses 8-10: *Israel should not be afraid, because the faithful hand of the Lord upholds her.*

8 *But you, O Israel, My servant, Jacob, whom I have chosen,*
   Seed of My friend Abraham,
9 *Whom I have brought from the ends of the earth,*
   Called out from its farthest corners,
   And said to you: My servant you are,
   Whom I have called and have not spurned —
10 *Do not fear, for I will be with you;*
    Be not afraid, for I am your God;
    I will strengthen you, yes, and help you;
    Yes, I will uphold you with My true right hand.

8 וְאַתָּה֙ יִשְׂרָאֵל֙ עַבְדִּ֔י יַעֲקֹ֖ב אֲשֶׁ֣ר בְּחַרְתִּ֑יךָ
זֶ֖רַע אַבְרָהָ֥ם אֹהֲבִֽי׃

9 אֲשֶׁ֤ר הֶחֱזַקְתִּ֙יךָ֙ מִקְצ֣וֹת הָאָ֔רֶץ וּמֵאֲצִילֶ֖יהָ קְרָאתִ֑יךָ
וָאֹ֤מַר לְךָ֙ עַבְדִּי־אַ֔תָּה בְּחַרְתִּ֖יךָ וְלֹ֥א מְאַסְתִּֽיךָ׃

The Lord's words to His enemies were overpowering, commanding and threatening. Since they remained mute in their defeat, and in their dismay only turned to new idols for protection, the Lord turns away from them in vexation and contempt, and with loving words full of power to comfort turns to His own people, who were consumed by great fear. The *we* before *'attāh* is adversative: But you, O Israel. *'abhdī* is an emphatic apposition, like the adjuncts to Jacob and Abraham. The names Israel, Jacob, and Abraham's Seed are here, as elsewhere, terms of endearment and honor, through which the Lord at the very outset wishes to give assurance of His love and of His faithfulness to His covenant. The appositions and attributive adjuncts express characteristics of the substantives. *Israel* is the spiritualized Jacob who prevailed over

149

God and man (Gen. 32:28); he is *'abhdī,* My servant, the servant of
the Lord who has a spiritual mission to carry out on earth in God's
name, namely, the same mission that the Servant of the Lord κατ᾽
ἐξοχήν actually carries out (chapter 42): To bring the Gospel to
the gentile world (cf. 43:10,21). Since he is the servant of the Lord,
he is *eo ipso* certain of the Lord's protection and preservation until
he has accomplished his mission (cf. 42:1,4). To assure the people
of their preservation is the ultimate purpose of this portion of the
discourse. The tenth verse ends with that assurance. Jacob is the
man, that is, the people, of God's *choice,* "whom I have chosen" —
rather than the hated Esau, Malachi 1:2-4 — because I loved him
and have bound Myself to him with an unshakable love to be his
God (Gen. 28:14f) through time and eternity. That is expressed by
'asher beḥartīkhā.

The term "Seed of My bosom friend Abraham" combines the
two elements of servanthood and of being chosen into a single expression. *'ohabhī* (Qal participle with suffix) in its original sense
means simply my lover; but in the course of time it became an
epitheton ornans for Abraham, a *terminus technicus* meaning
beloved of God; and finally the meaning became fixed in the sense
of an intimate, a friend, a special friend, a bosom friend (LXX: ὅν
ἠγάπησα , James 2:23, "the friend of God," on the basis of this
passage and 2 Chron. 20:7). The expression embraces the entire
relation of intimacy, the bosom friendship into which God had entered with Abraham, with all the promises and revelations included in that relationship (cf. Gen. 12:1-3, 6; 13:15f; 15; 17;
18:17-19; 22:16-18). This is developed in the clauses that follow.
The Lord had brought Abraham, and in him his Seed, the people to
whom the Lord is now speaking, from the ends and the far corners
of the world and made him to be His servant in that He chose him
and did not spurn him. All this lies in the term *'ohabhī.* Therefore
there is no more glorious and comforting a name for this people
than *Abraham's Seed.* The people knew very well what this name
meant, but they degraded it into something fleshly (Matt. 3:9;
John 8:33ff; Rom. 11:1; 2 Cor. 11:22; Gal. 3:29). — The relative
'asher before *beḥartīkhā* and *heḥezaqtīkhā* does not refer to the
subject of these verbs: I who chose thee; but rather to the suffix
khā: You whom I have chosen (Gr. 138d,p.445). The first meaning
of the Hiphil of *ḥāzaq* is, no doubt, to make firm, or to strengthen;
but it may also mean to grasp, or to take hold of. The exact sense
in this case is: To take hold of and fetch (cf. Gen. 21:18).
qerā'thīkhā has a synonymous meaning. Luther misses the mean-

ing of *mē'atsīleyhā,* and σχοπιά of the LXX is also inexact. *'atsīl* or *'etsel* is a side, or rim, the outer border; here a synonym of *qetsōth hā'ārets.* Our suggestion is nook or corner. What is meant is that Abraham's home in Ur of the Chaldees, which for an inhabitant of Canaan lay at an immeasurable distance beyond the impassable Arabian Desert, was at a far corner of the earth. There — that is the point here — the Lord took hold of Abraham, and in him of Abraham's Seed, and brought him to Himself through His call. It is strange that Genesis tells us nothing of Abraham in Chaldea. Genesis obviously presupposes such a calling.

'ōmar lekhā 'abhdī 'attāh is explanatory to *qerā'thīkhā:* I called you to be My servant. It is a vivid and simple way of saying, I appointed you as My servant. Before *behartīkhā welō' me'astīkhā,* after verses 8 and 9, *'asher* is to be supplied. The sentence is still dependent on *'ōmar lekhā* and lends emphasis to the phrase. The same purpose is served by the addition of the negative *lō' me'astīkha,* which means to disdain, to pass something by as worthless — the very opposite of *bāhar,* to prize, to cherish and take to oneself.

אַל־תִּירָא כִּי עִמְּךָ־אָנִי אַל־תִּשְׁתָּע כִּי־אֲנִי אֱלֹהֶיךָ 10
אִמַּצְתִּיךָ אַף־עֲזַרְתִּיךָ אַף־תְּמַכְתִּיךָ בִּימִין צִדְקִי׃

Verses 8 and 9 are introductory to the formal consolation in verse 10. The heartening encouragement of *'al tīrā',* be not afraid, finds strong support in the assurance that "I am with you," now and forevermore. *'im* means something more than just to be with someone, at his side. It means that God is united with Israel as an ally and comrade in arms (cf. Ps. 46:8(7); 1 Chron. 12:21; Gen. 21:22; 26:3,28). *'al tishtā'* is stronger than *'al tīrā'. shā'ah,* to look, means in the Hithpael to look around, in this case in fear and apprehension. This is an apocopated form of the verb. As in the terms of encouragement, so also in the reason given, the order of climax is observed: "I am your God" is more than "I am with you." "I am your God" does not just place God's omnipotence in Israel's service for a fixed short time, but endows him with God's love and grace, and ultimate salvation. The three following promises reveal *how* the alliance of the Lord with Israel is put into practice: *'immēts, 'āzar, tāmakh,* strengthen, help, preserve, a climax which is also indicated by the repetition of *'aph,* also, besides, even. *tāmakh* or *sāmakh* means to establish one so firmly that nothing can overthrow or defeat him, enabling him to stand unsubdued. The promises refer to the physical deliverance of God's defeated and enslaved people. *bīmīn tsidhkī* is an adverbial modifier of all three verbs, not only of the last one.

What is the meaning of *bīmīn tsidhkī?* *yāmīn* is the right hand, the familiar symbol of power. The genitive in the phrase "in the right hand of My righteousness" is the epexegetical genitive and, like the genitive in *har qodhshī* (My holy mountain), is to be translated as an attributive modifier — My righteous right hand, as though the reading were *bīmīnī hatstsaddīq* (Gr. 128,p,p.417 and 135,n,p.440). Examples of similar genitives are to be found in verses 11 and 12. But what does *tsedheq* mean? That is one of the weightiest questions faced in interpreting Isaiah or indeed all of Scripture. *tsedheq, tsedhāqāh* is one of the important, really the most important, terms in the history of salvation in both the Old and the New Testaments. Isaiah did not invent the term; it is as old as revelation. It was the daily food of the faithful people of the covenant. The word is extremely common in the Psalms. Jeremiah and other prophets use the word more sparingly. Isaiah treats it like a costly pearl, letting light shine upon it from every side. Paul built up the entire theology of the New Testament on this term. Without a proper understanding of this term no one can understand the Bible, least of all Isaiah. So it will be necessary at this point, where the term now occurs for the second time, to investigate it rather thoroughly, although it is not possible to exhaust the subject. Whole books have been written about it.

Comparative philology has not succeeded in finding a concrete meaning of the root *tsdhq*. It seems to be one of the few *a priori* abstract word-forms in the Hebrew language. In ordinary usage it is simply a simple conventional expression like our *right, proper;* basically it expresses nothing more than the *right* relation of a person, thing, action, or attribute to another person, etc. Its primary meaning is equivalent to our proper, right, correct, fitting, due, appropriate — constituted as the circumstances may require. Since the word can be applied to all manner of circumstances of persons and things, of actions and conditions, it is not surprising that it has acquired such a wide variety of meanings. It would lead us too far afield if we were to examine its use in an area unrelated to the present subject. Of primary interest to us is the religious meaning of the word. Among the people to whom God revealed Himself, religion was the one matter of greatest importance, which governed every act, circumstance, and situation in life. To proceed directly to the heart of the matter: In every religion there are three essential elements: the God who is being served, the service that is being rendered to Him; and the servants who by this service serve their God. If such a religion seeks to be taken seriously, then everything about it must be *tsaddīq,* appropriate to the service and its purpose, namely, the glorification of God and the blessedness of the worshipers. The God who is worshiped is considered a true God, and all His being and His every act are right, proper, fitting, correct. Furthermore, if the service that is rendered to Him has been enjoined by that God Himself, then it is right and proper. If those who serve Him are honest and faithful in their service, then they too are right and fitting; and the purposes and consequences of this relationship are right and fitting; both as to God and to God's servants. One need only apply this pattern to Israel's religion to perceive the meaning of rightness as used here.

It was Israel's firm conviction that its God was the *right,* the true God. He was *YHWH* (see the explanation of this name in 41:4). What He does is *eo ipso* right. Jehovah had revealed Himself to Israel in preference to all the gentile nations (Ps. 147: 19 and 20). And this revelation is, of course, right, correct. What was it that Jehovah revealed? Israel was persuaded, by revelation, of the tremendous fact that overshadowed everything else, namely, that Israel was *chosen to be the Lord's peculiar people.* Its election in Abraham is what the Lord in His opening address in verses 8 and 9 so impressively proclaims to this people. When for the second time the Lord's world lay in spiritual ruins, He plucked Abraham, a worshiper of idols, a man no better than anyone else in this corrupt generation, out from the *massa perdita;* out of pure grace He did not reckon his sin unto him and made him His *'ohēbh,* φίλος , His bosom friend and servant for time and eternity, and concluded a covenant with him and his seed (Gen. 15) with a promise of life in this world and in eternity. We know that Christ is the very heart and essence of this covenant and that His salvation was meant for "everyone that believeth, to the Jew first, and also to the Greek." The preparation, execution, realization, and fulfillment of the covenant is the subject matter of all Scripture, of both Testaments — yes, of all history. Though everything that pertains to this covenant of grace and that at the same time is in accordance with its origin, its substance, its nature, and its purpose, may indeed be described in other terms, it first of all is *tsaddīq, tsedheq, tsedhākāh,* whether reference is being made to God, to men, to objects, or to circumstances. This is, of course, a *special* use of the concept which does not preclude its application to circumstances other than those that have to do with the covenant. Insofar as God establishes this covenant, carries it out and preserves it, He is *tsaddīq* in His thought, word, and deed. Objectively, this covenant is *righteousness* for Abraham and his seed in what it promises, gives, and accomplishes. Abraham and his seed are *righteous* insofar as they are included in this covenant by faith, continue in it, and walk in accordance with it. Everything that is contrary to this covenant is in every sense *lō' tsedheq*. What the covenant purposes and accomplishes is deliverance from destruction, salvation, happiness, and blessedness. This is the starting point from which all words formed from the *tsdhq* root (and their synonyms) must be examined — from the first *mishpāt* in 1:17 to the last *kebhōdī* in 66:19 — in order to determine the specific meaning of each word according to the special circumstances prevailing in each passage where the word occurs. If this is done, one may occasionally fail to hit the bull's-eye, but one will hardly miss the whole target.

The word *tsedheq* occurs, for example, in verse 2. *tsedheq* there summons Cyrus into her service. If one follows the above guidelines, one might be undecided, whether the Lord's gracious faithfulness, His subjective gracious intention toward Israel, is being personified, or whether it is the objective salvation by grace that the Lord has extended to Israel. But there cannot be any doubt whatsoever that the Lord's gracious relation to Israel is meant. There can be no thought of taking the righteousness of God to mean the retributive righteousness with which God dispenses justice among heathen nations. If one then also observes from Psalm 132:9 and 16, or Psalm 71:15, that *tsedheq* and *yēsha'*, righteousness and salvation, are one and the same, then one will never interpret God's righteousness in Psalm 31:2(1) (Deliver me in Your righteousness); Psalm 119:40 (Quicken me in Your righteousness); or Psalm 17:15; 5:9(8), and many other similar passages, as referring to God's righteousness judging according to the Law, but rather as the righteousness of the covenant, which forgives sins and works salvation. From that it should also be clear what is meant by "My judgment" in 40:27. The meaning of *bīmīn tsidhqī* in our passage follows the same line. The right hand of My righteousness, or My righteous right hand, can only be that hand or act that effects Israel's preservation, either by virtue of the purpose of God's covenant, or by virtue of its content (that is, grace itself); or because of its objective, namely, deliverance and salvation. One would have to translate: My faithful right hand, or: My gracious, redeeming, saving, right hand. Here, without a doubt, the expression emphasizes God's faithfulness to the promises of His covenant, since everything that precedes has the purpose of quieting Israel's anxious fears by the assurances of God's love, and those fears arose from Israel's idea that God had forsaken and forgotten His people (40:27; 49:14). If anyone objects that this makes too fine a distinction, let him translate: By My gracious right hand, or: By the right hand of My covenant.

We recall Luther's experience with the concept *tsedheq* or *tsidhqath YHWH*—the righteousness of God. In the New Testament he translated it: *Die Gerechtigkeit, die vor Gott gilt.* That is satisfactory for all practical uses, but is still not quite exact. In our passage the term occurs in its *objective* sense. It has already occurred in the Psalms and now appears very frequently, especially in this part of Isaiah, as a synonym of *yēsha', yeshū'ah, teshū'ah,* etc. Its real meaning is the salvation that proceeds from the covenant-grace, the righteousness that the Lord *prepared* for the believers in Christ. Thus also the *YHWH tsidhqēnū* of Jeremiah 23 and 33 is not to be understood as our righteousness *before* the Lord but as our righteousness received *from* the Lord. By effecting our salvation, the Lord has become our Salvation.

Second Minor Strophe: verses 11-13:   *Israel's enemies shall be completely destroyed.*

11   *Behold, all shall be put to shame and confounded*
        who are incensed against you,
     They shall be as nothing and shall perish,
        who are your adversaries,
12   *You will search for and not find those who strive with you,*
        Those who fight against you shall be as a nothing and as a cipher.
13   *For I, the Lord, your God am I, who strengthens your right hand,*
        Who says to you: Be not afraid, it is I who helps you.

הֵן יֵבֹשׁוּ וְיִכָּלְמוּ כֹּל הַנֶּחֱרִים בָּךְ 11

יִהְיוּ כְאַיִן וְיֹאבְדוּ אַנְשֵׁי רִיבֶךָ׃

This section employs the Qinah rhythm. Up to this point the subject of the prophecy has been Israel's deliverance from its enemies; now the Lord promises complete destruction of those enemies. *hēn* is an emphatic particle. *kālam,* occurring only in the Niphal and Hiphil, is stronger than *bōsh;* the two together promise that the enemies shall be put to shame and confounded. *neherim,* a Niphal participle of *ḥārah,* was rendered by Luther with *gram sein*

155

(to be angry with), and in 45:24 with *widerstehen* (to withstand). The verb does not occur in the Old Testament in its physical sense of burning or glowing. It is commonly used as the expression of an emotion, especially in the impersonal phrase *ḥarāh le,* to become angry (cf. Gen. 4:5). The Niphal participle *hanneherīm* describes the enemies, with emphasis on their rage. The enmity of the world against God's people is truly a deadly hostility, which has its basis in the offense and foolishness of the Gospel in the judgment of natural reason (1 Cor. 1:23ff). The claim of the Jews that they were God's own chosen people has always made them hated and despised everywhere in the world. Parallel to *hanneherīm bākh* is *'anshēy ribhekhā,* men of your strife, men who strive against you (objective genitive). The same construction occurs twice in the next verse (Gr. 128,t,p.417). Being put to shame and confounded becomes concrete in becoming as nothing and perishing.

¹² תְּבַקְשֵׁם֙ וְלֹ֣א תִמְצָאֵ֔ם אַנְשֵׁ֖י מַצֻּתֶ֑ךָ

יִהְי֥וּ כְאַ֛יִן וּכְאֶ֖פֶס אַנְשֵׁ֥י מִלְחַמְתֶּֽךָ׃

Outwardly the two verbs at the beginning of this verse are simply coordinated, but in reality the first is subordinate to the second: You would not find them if you were to seek them (Gr. 107,m,r,x,p.316). The three nouns, *ribh, matstsūth, milḥemeth* form a climax: *strife, fight, battle. ke'ephes,* "like an end," is an intensification of *ke'ayin.* The expression is the equivalent of our "to be at an end, to be done for." The accumulation of synonyms in verses 11 and 12 emphasizes the completeness of the destruction of the enemies.

¹³ כִּ֗י אֲנִ֛י יְהוָ֥ה אֱלֹהֶ֖יךָ מַחֲזִ֣יק יְמִינֶ֑ךָ

הָאֹמֵ֥ר לְךָ֛ אַל־תִּירָ֖א אֲנִ֥י עֲזַרְתִּֽיךָ׃

Verse 13 offers substantiation for what was just proclaimed. It lies in the very first clause: I am the Lord your God. He it is who makes the hand of Israel strong for battle (*maḥazīq*). The object of *hā'omēr lekhā* is not only *'al tīrā'* but also *'anī 'azartīkhā,* although the second phrase contains the reason for the first. The reason given is twofold: the strength imparted to the right hand, and the Lord's personal support. *'omēr lekhā* indicates the form in which the comfort will be proffered.

Third Minor Strophe: verses 14-16: *Israel itself, assured of victory by the Lord, shall bring about the destruction of the enemies.*

14   *Be not afraid, you worm Jacob, O feeble folk of Israel;*
      I help you, that is the Lord's word,
      And the Holy One of Israel is your Redeemer.
15   *Truly, I will make you a sharp, new threshing-sledge*
      With a double row of teeth;
      You shall thresh and grind the mountains
      And reduce the hills to chaff;
16   *You shall winnow them, and the wind will scatter them,*
      And the stormwind will blow them away;
      But you will rejoice in the Lord
      And glory in the Holy One of Israel.

14 אַל־תִּירְאִי תּוֹלַעַת יַעֲקֹב מְתֵי יִשְׂרָאֵל

אֲנִי עֲזַרְתִּיךְ נְאֻם־יְהוָֹה וְגֹאֲלֵךְ קְדוֹשׁ יִשְׂרָאֵל:

This third strophe, like the first two, develops the theme of comfort: Be not afraid. In the first section (verses 8-10), this formula appears in the middle; in the second (verses 11-13), it is at the end; and in this section (verses 14-16), it comes at the beginning. Such externals are also characteristic of Hebrew poetic art. Unique are the two forms of address, *tōlaʿath yaʿaqōbh* and *methēy yisrāʾel*. The meaning of "You worm Jacob" is clear. Since *methēy* in its primary meaning of *men* does not fit with its companion expression, "worm Jacob," the critics have assumed that the text is corrupt. There are two occurrences in the Old Testament of *rimmāh* with *tōleʿah*, Job 25:6 and Isaiah 14:11. In the Job passage *rimmāh* is used in the transferred sense, as *tōleʿah* is used here; so, that word would fit perfectly here: You worm Jacob, you grub (or maggot) Israel. Ergo: Read *rimmāh* instead of *methēy!* The LXX seems to have used a different text and has ὀλιγοστός (a tiny portion or thing) before the name of Israel. All critics who use the Masoretic text give *methēy* a meaning similar to that of *tōlaʿath* and translate: "O tiny folk of Israel" (German: *Voelkchen*). Thus, Vitringa, Gesenius, and others. Delitzsch, Kautzsch, and others: *Du Haeuflein.* It is true that in a few cases *methīm* is coupled with *meʿaṭ* (a little), or with *mispār* (number), and the meaning then is "men, few in number"; hence, Israel, a pitiful little band. "They are no longer the compact mass of a nation; the bond of community of existence has been torn, they have shrunken to a few individuals scattered here and there" (Delitzsch). So, these are the *nidhhēy yisrāʾel*, the scattered people of Israel, Isaiah 56:8; 11:12; Psalm 147:2. It is not to be understood as though the Lord has in mind all the scattered persons in Babylon; He is speaking of Israel

157

κατὰ πνεῦμα. The appellations at the beginning of the strophe and all the promises of this section are first of all to be understood spiritually, although they are also fulfilled externally by the deliverance through Cyrus. But verses 15 and 16 cannot have an external meaning only. The prophet's "O worm Jacob" finds its echo in the Lord's "Fear not, little flock" (Luke 12:32).

Finally, we cannot altogether rule out the possibility that *methīm* here, as often in other passages (Isa. 3:25; Deut. 33:6, etc.), is used in the sense of heroes or warriors, particularly since it is used in connection with *Israel*, the spiritual contender with God. Thus, *methīm* would not be synonymous with *tōla'ath* but would stand in contrast to it. Those who in the eyes of men appear as a futile little worm are, in the eyes of the Lord, His spiritual battle heroes. The difficulty with the interpretation of *methīm* as a feeble little band is that it assumes an ellipsis.

The two genitives, *ya'aqōbh* and *yisrā'el*, are epexegetical (Gr. 128,k,p.416). "I help you" is the material reason why Israel should not be afraid, *ne'um YHWH* is the formal reason. *ne'um* is the construct state of *nā'ūm*, a Qal passive participle of *nā'am*, to proclaim an oracle of God. Literally: "Proclaimed as an oracle of God." The phrase occurs often in Isaiah and, except in Isaiah 56:8, it is parenthetical. It is a stronger term than *'āmar*. It designates something as unshakably firm, and in this instance strongly emphasizes the words of comfort.

The last clause, *wegō'alēkh qedhōsh yisrā'el*, is not to be understood as in apposition to the preceding *'anī*. The particle *we* precludes that. *we* coordinates this clause with the one preceding. *gō'alēkh* is the predicate of *qedhōsh yisrā'el*. It has a feminine suffix because *tōla'ath* and *yisrā'el* are still in the fore: "And the Holy One of Israel is your Redeemer." *gō'el* deserves special attention. *gā'al* means to redeem, to repurchase. It was used primarily of the repurchase of that which had been devoted to the Lord and was therefore holy. See Leviticus 27:13ff. The participle *gō'el* designates the nearest relative, on whom the obligation lay to repurchase a lost piece of land; to redeem the person of a blood relative who had been sold into slavery; to be the "revenger of blood" if his nearest relative had been slain; or also to take to wife the childless widow of his brother (the levirate). From that custom the word derives its meaning of savior, helper, avenger, as referring to men of power, but especially to God, the helper and avenger of His people. In this use the term retains its special meaning of avenging and redeeming. The presupposition is that Israel, through God's free election of grace, belongs to God as His peculiar people, who cannot be lost. The enemies therefore attack Israel or rule over it unjustly. They are murderers and tyrants. If God gives Israel into the hands of her enemies to chastise her, He has not thereby divorced her (Isa. 50:1) and given the enemies a right to possess her; they are still robbers, murderers, and tyrants. As Israel's *gō'ēl*, Redeemer, the Lord forcibly frees His people from the hands of their enemies, restores them to their rightful position as His peculiar possession, and at the same time takes vengeance on the persecutors. This term in Isaiah and the still more common *mōshĭa'*, helper, are the basis for the New Testament term σωτήρ.

qedhōsh yisrā'ēl, the Holy One of Israel, is the subject; *gō'alēkh* is the predicate. He, the Holy One, is Israel's Redeemer and Avenger. This is the first occurrence of the phrase *qedhōsh yisrā'ēl* in Isaiah II. The phrase occurs twice in the Psalms (78:41; 89:19[18]) and a few times in the prophets following Isaiah (Jer. 50:29; 51:5 Ezek. 39:7; Hos. 11:9[?]), but in both parts of Isaiah it is a favorite expression and in this second part alone occurs some 30 times, besides the passages where *qādhōsh* occurs alone. In this chapter it occurs three times in quick succession, in verses 16 and 20. That it is an evangelical expression, that is, one that denotes God's grace towards Israel, is evidenced by the frequency of its occurrence in this chapter and elsewhere as a parallel to Jehovah, Jehovah *'elōheykhā*, Jehovah *tsebhā'ōth*, or together with *gō'ēl*, *mōshĭa'*, *melekh*, *bōrē'*, *yōtsēr*, *bōḥēr* of Israel. *qādhōsh* as a proper name of the Lord was explained in 40:25. The combination of Israel and *qādhōsh* adds the concept that this Holy One has joined Himself to this people, once and for all, for its temporal and its eternal salvation — in spite of all its enemies. The Lord is the *qedhōsh yisrā'ēl* because of His zeal for Israel against all enemies, within and without: 1:4; 10:17,20; 12:6; 17:7; 29:19,23; 30:11,12, 15; 31:1; 37:23, and so on in almost all of Isaiah II. It denotes the zeal of the Lord's love and the zeal of His wrath. To cleave to the Holy One of Israel is salvation; to blaspheme the Holy One of Israel is the *non plus ultra* of sinfulness and inevitable perdition. So, to say that the Holy One of Israel is her Redeemer is to say that her God, who cannot forsake Israel, and who suffers no enemy to mock her, is the surety for her redemption. The sentence contains the supreme assurance of God's care for His chosen people.

159

15 הִנֵּה שַׂמְתִּיךְ לְמוֹרַג חָרוּץ חָדָשׁ בַּעַל פִּיפִיּוֹת
תָּדוּשׁ הָרִים וְתָדֹק וּגְבָעוֹת כַּמֹּץ תָּשִׂים:

Verse 15 tells by what means God will destroy the enemies. It shall be done by Israel's own hand. *'immatstīkhā* in verse 10 and *maḥazīq yemīnekhā* will now become reality. The Lord will make of His weak and fearful people an irresistible and effective threshing-sledge to grind the powerful enemies into shreds. *mōragh* is the threshing-sledge used in the Orient. There were two forms of it. The one referred to here consisted of two skids or runners joined at the front and at the rear by crosspieces. Between the runners was a row of rollers fitted either with sharp, disk-shaped, metal plates or with rings of iron teeth called *pīphīyoth*. *ba'al pīphīyoth*, lord of the double blades, is idiomatic Hebrew for "possessor of double cutting edges," that is, equipped with double blades. Oxen drew this sledge over the grain spread out on the hard ground, and the blades cut the straw to shreds and threshed out the kernels. With threshing shovels this shredded mass was then tossed into the wind, which separated the shredded straw from the kernels of grain. This threshing-sledge was also employed as an instrument to execute especially reprehensible prisoners of war, Amos 1:3; 2 Kings 13:7; 2 Samuel 12:31(?). Into such a threshing-sledge, sharp and new, the Lord will transform His impotent and defenseless people. *ḥadhāsh* does not merely repeat the idea of *ḥarūts*, but adds that the sledge is both new and strong, so that it will not break down in use, but remain sharp, new, and effective. Mountains and hills are obviously figurative expressions for the great and seemingly invincible world powers. Babylon and its satellites are meant. *thādhōq*, from *dāqaq*, means to pulverize; it intensifies *thādhush*, from *dūsh*, to thresh.

16 תִּזְרֵם וְרוּחַ תִּשָּׂאֵם וּסְעָרָה תָּפִיץ אוֹתָם
וְאַתָּה תָּגִיל בַּיהוָה בִּקְדוֹשׁ יִשְׂרָאֵל תִּתְהַלָּל:

zārāh, to strew, related to *zara'*, is the technical term for winnowing (Ruth 3:2; Jer. 4:11), as the latter is for scattering (sowing) the seed. The picture is very vivid. The object of the verb is the enemy, already cut into small shreds by the sledge. Israel now casts them high into the air and the wind carries them away. *ūse'ārāh tāphīts 'othām* is in each of its components stronger than *rūaḥ tissā'em*. *hēphīts*, Hiphil of *pūts*, means to scatter violently.

When that has been done, then Israel will rejoice *over* the Lord and will glory in her Holy One.

Fourth Minor Strophe: verses 17-20: *Weak and despondent Israel shall be gloriously revived.*

17 *The miserable and the poor seek water, and there is none,*
Their tongue is parched with thirst;
I, the Lord, will hear them,
I, the God of Israel, will not forsake them.
18 *On the bald heights I will open streams,*
And springs of water in the midst of the valleys;
I will make the desert into a sheet of water
And the parched land into gushing fountains.
19 *In the wilderness I will plant cedar and acacia,*
*   yes, myrtle and olive trees,*
And in arid land the cypress, the plane tree, and the box.
20 *So that men shall see, and know, and take to heart, and also*
*   understand*
That the hand of the Lord has done this and that the Holy One
*   of Israel created it.*

With verse 17 there is a shift in the direction of the thought. No longer is Israel described as engaged in battle with her enemies, but as consumed by thirst in a dry and burning desert. That, however, is not a reason for linking this section with the one following, with which it has nothing in common, whereas it shares with the preceding section the thought of a despondent Israel and of the promise of hope. The picture is throughout one of the spiritual condition of the exiled people. Israel in Babylon did not have to suffer any exceptional hunger or thirst of the body. Obviously, the discourse is directed to the spiritual Israel, which felt its exile as a spiritual distress. Its spiritual relation to the Lord seemed to have been broken. The Lord — so Israel thought — had divorced His youthful bride, rejected her because of her infidelity and delivered her to be violated by a world power (cf. 49:14ff; 50:1ff; 51:17ff; 54:4ff; 57:3ff). The spiritual distress that is expressed in the long prayer of 63:7 and 64 is here figuratively described. Even though the carnal mass of the people did not feel such spiritual misery, it nevertheless gnawed at the very heart of the spiritual remnant and awakened a burning thirst for the gracious countenance of their God, like David when he was thrust from his throne and banished from the Holy Place, Psalm 42. Compare also Psalm 137. Nor was there any helper or comforter to be found (42:22; 51:18,19). This section offers comfort to Israel in its spiritual distress. There is in it an echo of Matthew 5:3.

הָעֲנִיִּים וְהָאֶבְיוֹנִים מְבַקְשִׁים מַיִם וָאַיִן לְשׁוֹנָם בַּצָּמָא נָשָׁתָּה ¹⁷
אֲנִי יְהוָה אֶעֱנֵם אֱלֹהֵי יִשְׂרָאֵל לֹא אֶעֶזְבֵם:

'*anī* and '*ebhyōn* often appear together in Scripture. This combination is primarily descriptive of physical need, as in Proverbs
31:9, Jeremiah 22:16, and Ezekiel 18:12; but frequently also of
both physical and spiritual need, which commonly occur together,
as in the case of the faithful exiles, Psalm 70:6(5); 86:1. Here,
however, as in Psalm 40:18(17), the spiritual distress is especially
meant. The Piel participle *mebhaqeshīm* (Dages forte is often
dropped over a Shewa mobile) expresses the uninterrupted continuation of the action. In the *wā* before '*ayin* there lies the idea of
contrast, as is often the case also with our English *and*. The
simplest explanation of *nashattāh* (with Dages forte affectuosum
after a pause — Gr. 20, i, p. 73) is that it is a Qal form of *nāshath,*
to dry up, to shrivel. The verb adds emphasis to the condition
being described — like an exclamation mark. '*anī* before *YHWH*
belongs also to the parallel words '*elōhēy yisrā'el. lō' 'e'ezbhēm* is a
litotes, an understatement that emphasizes *e'enēm*. The poor and
miserable people seek water, the spiritual water of comfort. Their
tongues, that is, their hearts, are shriveled because of spiritual
thirst caused by deep tribulation. In the ears of the Lord this is a
cry for help — perhaps unuttered — (cf. Exod. 14:15), which He
must hear and answer. He cannot desert them, but must come to
their aid and quench their thirst.

אֶפְתַּח עַל־שְׁפָיִים נְהָרוֹת וּבְתוֹךְ בְּקָעוֹת מַעְיָנוֹת ¹⁸
אָשִׂים מִדְבָּר לַאֲגַם־מַיִם וְאֶרֶץ צִיָּה לְמוֹצָאֵי מָיִם:

In "I will open streams" we have a zeugma, a transfer from one
object to another. It is the *shephāyīm* that shall be opened, the
bald, dry rocks; they shall split apart and open the way for
streams to burst forth. *biq'āh* is a broad valley. *ma'yān,* a stronger
word than '*ayin,* means not one but many springs, the prefix *mem*
in such words corresponding to the Greek *syn,* the Latin *con,* and
the German *ge. mōtsā'ey māyim* are outlets or sources,
headsprings of waters. The people are pictured as being in a
waterless desert. But the Lord will transform this arid waste into a
richly watered landscape, all of this being a figurative description
of Israel's spiritual need and of the comfort with which the Lord
will fill their desponding hearts — Matthew 11:28.

¹⁹ אֶתֵּן בַּמִּדְבָּר אֶרֶז שִׁטָּה וַהֲדַס וְעֵץ שָׁמֶן
אָשִׂים בָּעֲרָבָה בְּרוֹשׁ תִּדְהָר וּתְאַשּׁוּר יַחְדָּו:

Of the trees and shrubs named in this verse, the cedar, the acacia, myrtle, and cypress are familiar. *'ets shemen* is not the cultivated *zayith*, but the wild olive, oleaster. Though its oil was of little value, the tree was prized as an ornamental tree, and as such it is to be considered here. *tidhhār* is thought to be the plane tree, or perhaps the yew. *te'ashshūr* is the box, or kind of cedar. The LXX names only five trees in this verse. Delitzsch saw a symbolism in the number seven: "Seven represents the divine element in the variety of display." By His creative power the Lord transforms the desert into a spiritual paradise. All of this is to be understood figuratively, of a spiritual resuscitation.

²⁰ לְמַעַן יִרְאוּ וְיֵדְעוּ וְיָשִׂימוּ וְיַשְׂכִּילוּ יַחְדָּו
כִּי יַד־יְהֹוָה עָשְׂתָה זֹּאת וּקְדוֹשׁ יִשְׂרָאֵל בְּרָאָהּ:

The strophe closes with a clause of purpose. The ultimate purpose of the gracious and miraculous deliverance and restoration of the chosen people is the glorification of the grace and deep love of God for His people. That same purpose may be observed in all of Scripture. That too is the unending occupation of the blessed, Revelation 11:15; 19:1. A necessary prerequisite, however, is an unshaken conviction that it is the hand of God, the effective power of the Lord, the God of grace and the Holy One of Israel, which has brought about the deliverance and restoration of those who are His own. The repetition of synonyms of "to know" together with *yaḥdāw* heightens the idea of the fullness of this knowledge.

And so, the closing emphasis and thought of this entire strophe, verses 8-20, is the glorification of the Lord, the revelation of the *kebhōdh YHWH*, 40:5, as contrasted with the confounding of the heathen idols described in strophes 1 and 3.

Résumé: Israel should not be afraid, for the Lord upholds and strengthens her, verses 8—10; by those same acts of the Lord the enemies shall be totally destroyed, verses 11-13; in His zeal for Israel the Almighty will make the weak and infirm worm Jacob into a grinding threshing-sledge against his powerful enemies, so that every vestige of them shall be blown away, verses 14-16; and those who now languish in misery shall be restored with richest comfort, to the glory of the Lord, verses 17-20.

Third Strophe: verses 21-29:   *The infinite greatness of the Lord
above all the gentile gods is made manifest by His proclamation of
the future beforehand, whereby the gentile gods are revealed as
less than nothing, the Lord, however, as the Mighty God.*

This strophe has two parts. Verses 21-24 set forth the inability
of the gentile gods to foretell future events; verses 25-29 contrast
the Godhead of the Lord with the nothingness of the gentile idols.

First Half: Verses 21-24:   *The gentile gods know nothing of the
future and are therefore themselves nothing, and worship of them
is an abomination.*

21   *Present your case, thus says the Lord,
      Set forth your arguments, says Jacob's King.*
22   *Let them bring forward and show us
      What is yet to come to pass;
      The next things to happen, proclaim to us what they are,
      So that we may lay them to heart and know their outcome;
      Or what is yet to come, let us hear it.*
23   *Tell us what is coming hereafter,
      So that we may recognize that you are gods;
      Yes, do good or do evil — anything —
      That we may be fearful, too, and dismayed.*
24   *Behold, you are nothing, and what you do is nothing;
      An abomination is he who chooses you.*

The critics make a shambles of this section. Sometimes they
follow the LXX; sometimes they ignore it or delete a portion, or
they add something or make a change, as they deem the sense or
the rhythm requires.

²¹ קָרְבוּ רִיבְכֶם יֹאמַר יְהוָה הַגִּישׁוּ עֲצֻמוֹתֵיכֶם יֹאמַר
מֶלֶךְ יַעֲקֹב׃

In the first strophe (verses 1-7) the Lord had required of the
gentiles that they say who it was that called forth that Conqueror,
and their discomfiture is described; in verses 8-20 the Lord promised His people victory and comfort; in this section, verses 21-24,
He demands of the idol-gods themselves that they present proofs
of their divinity by foretelling future events. They are thus
revealed as being less than nothing. *qārebhū* is a Piel imperative.
rībh is a *cause*, a case to be decided by a court or judge. For *yōʼmar*,
see 40:1. The LXX has *hāʼel* before Jehovah and translates:
κύριος ὁ θεός. *ʼatstsumōth* (some texts have an unexplainable

Dagesh in the *Tsade*) is the plural of an adjective and means strong ones, a concrete term for spiritual bulwarks, reasons, or proofs. It is not an abstract plural meaning "strengths." In *melekh ya'aqōbh* the Lord identifies Himself as the people's King, the supreme advocate and defender of Israel against the gods of all other nations.

22 יַגִּ֫ישׁוּ֙ וְיַגִּ֣ידוּ לָ֔נוּ אֵ֖ת אֲשֶׁ֣ר תִּקְרֶ֑ינָה

הָרִֽאשֹׁנ֣וֹת ׀ מָ֣ה הֵ֗נָּה הַגִּ֔ידוּ וְנָשִׂ֥ימָה לִבֵּ֖נוּ

ᵇוְנֵֽדְעָ֣ה אַחֲרִיתָ֔ן א֥וֹ הַבָּא֖וֹת הַשְׁמִיעֻֽנוּ׃

'asher tiqreynāh, a Qal imperfect of *qārāh*, to befall, to come to pass, is the most inclusive word for introducing future events. The meaning of this verse depends entirely on the interpretation of *hārī'shōnōth* — the first things — and *'aharīthān* — what succeeds or follows after them, their outcome. Consult the lexicon for *'ahar* and its derivatives. An erroneous interpretation will certainly result if one does not treat *hārī'shōnōth* and *'aharīthān* as correlatives which require one another. Cf. 41:4; 44:6; 48:12, etc: the first — the last; the earlier — the later; beginning — end; early ages — succeeding ages, etc. It is necessary in each case to give careful consideration to the relation of the terms as to time. Both may refer to past time, or both may refer to future time. Only the context can determine that. A considerable number of commentators refer both terms in this instance to past time. They translate: The early events, what they were, tell us . . . ! According to that interpretation the idol-gods are being called upon to say what had happened in the past. But that is nonsense, because that is not foretelling events *'asher tiqreynāh*, which shall come to pass. So also they take *rī'shōnōth* to refer to what had been proclaimed in the past, namely, concerning Cyrus (41:2-4), and they quote 42:9 in support. Thus Calvin, Gesenius, Hitzig, Ewald, Knobel, and also Hengstenberg and Bredenkamp. But that is clearly a wrong interpretation. Reference to 42:9, as we shall show later, is not justified. Furthermore, since when does *hārī'shōnōth* mean something foretold in time past? Then *'aharīthān*, its correlative, would have to mean something that was foretold at a later time, since it is a pendant to *rī'shōnōth. Qualia illa, talia haec!* But the advocates of this interpretation do not want to draw such a conclusion. Every explanation that places *rī'shōnōth* in the past does violence to the immediate context. What is here required of the idols is that they foretell the future, not that they tell what had been foretold in times past. *higgīdh*, of course, does not mean anything more

than to declare, to announce; but its object is *'asher tiqreynāh,* and this means nothing else than "what *will* take place," not "what *has* taken place." The idols are required to prove their godhead by revealing *'asher tiqreynāh.*

Isaiah often makes a general statement in an opening sentence or clause and then develops it in those that follow. So here he separates the *'asher tiqreynāh* into two elements: the *rī'shōnōth* with the pendant *'aharīth,* and the *bā'ōth.* (In the next verse the *bā'ōth* are explained as *hā'ōthiyōth le'ahōr.*) Thus the *bā'ōth* are designated as occurring in a more distant future, while the *ri'shōnōth* lie in a nearer future. Vitringa, Delitzsch, Hahn, Stier, Cheyne, and others thus correctly interpret. The idols are to tell *'asher tiqreynāh.* First, and that is the simpler part, they are to foretell things that lie in the immediate future, what will happen tomorrow. Let them tell *māh hēnnāh,* what and of what nature these things are, and then we shall be able to recognize and acknowledge what their *'aharīth,* their realization or fulfillment, the consequence and the outcome of the prophecy is. (*'aharīth* is not just the following time, as Hahn says, but it is the outcome.) *yādha'* here is a *nosse cum affectu,* and means to acknowledge, that is, to know and accept as fulfillment of the prophecy.

The phrase *sīm lēbh* is not identical with *sīm 'al lēbh,* to take to heart, although that would fit very well here. The complete phrase is *sīm lēbh 'al,* to apply the heart to something, to direct the understanding to something, to observe closely and put to proof. Tell us what the very next events are going to be, and we will carefully observe their outcome and acknowledge their fulfillment. That is the meaning of the text. With *'ō* the prophet introduces a new thought: Or something that is yet to come, let us hear it. This stands counter to *rī'shōnōth;* in what way, the following verse will show.

23 הַגִּ֣ידוּ הָאֹתִיּוֹת֮ לְאָחוֹר֒ וְנֵ֣דְעָ֔ה כִּ֥י אֱלֹהִ֖ים אַתֶּ֑ם

אַף־תֵּיטִ֥יבוּ וְתָרֵ֖עוּ וְנִשְׁתָּעָ֥ה וְנִרְאֶ֖ה יַחְדָּֽו׃

With *hā'ōthīyōth* the prophet picks up the *bā'ōth* of the preceding verse and identifies them as the later, ensuing, final things, as distinguished from the *rī'shōnōth.* *'ōthīyōth* is a Qal feminine plural participle of *'āthāh,* to step, to go, to come, and is a synonym of *bā'ōth.* If the idols can predict these, then the Lord promises that He will acknowledge them to be gods. (*yādha'* is again used in the intensive sense.) As here, *'elōhīm* is often construed as a plural.

With *'aph* the Lord ironically adds His last and most trivial demand. About *hēyṭībh* and *hēra'* (both here in the imperfect) much has been written that is beside the point. The *we* between the two verbs may be translated with *and* or with *or*. The verbs can be translated "to do good or do evil," or "to make something good or make it evil." But the verse does not speak of a good or of a bad prognostication, or of a prophecy of good or of evil things. Here we have to do with a phrase that is no longer to be understood literally and that simply means: Do anything at all, of whatsoever nature it may be. Cf. Zephaniah 1:12; Jeremiah 10:5. Mockingly, the Lord reduces His demands to the very minimum — if they but do something, anything; if they but stir a finger, just open their mouths, the Lord will acknowledge them. The irony continues. In the next verse there is no suggestion of acknowledgment, but *wenishtā'ah wenir'e yaḥdāw*. There has been a great deal of dispute about these verbs. *nishtā'ah* is a Hithpael imperfect, first person plural of *shā'ah, to look,* with apocopation of the final syllable, addition of the cohortative ending, and a pausal lengthening of the penultimate syllable. Literally: We will look about us in alarm, we will be afraid, 41:10. It is to be noted that the Hithpael of this verb occurs only here and in 41:10. Most of the commentators take the phrase to mean: We will confront each other, face each other in a contest, with reference to 2 Kings 14:8 and 11 and 2 Chronicles 25: 17 and 21 (Amaziah's self-assurance over against Joash). That interpretation is unjustified, for in those passages we do not have *nishtā'ah,* but *nithrā'eh* (Hithpael of *rā'ah*), *pānīm,* that is, "we will look one another in the face" (2 Kings 14:11). That the Hithpael of *shā'ah* ever occurs together with *pānīm* and has that meaning is pure assumption. Besides, it would also be necessary to assume that *pānīm* has somehow been dropped from the text. Moreover, the Hithpael of *rā'ah* without an accompanying *pānīm* never occurs in that sense. That translation, accordingly, has no foundation. It does violence to the text. On the basis of 41:10 our translation is the only justifiable one. The Lord addresses the idol-gods in deepest irony: Do anything at all, and we will then show fear, as such who have approached you with hostility and provoked your vengeance.

The case of the verb *wenir'e* is similar. The Masoretes put *wenir'eh* (Qal imperfect, first person plural) in the margin. That reading ("And we shall see") would fit nicely with the translation that we have rejected: "We'll face each other, fight it out, God against god; and we'll see." It would also suit our translation: "We will show fear and see," that is, we will wait and see what you can do to us. But the expression "We shall see" is a more recent colloquialism, and we are hardly justified in assuming that it is also an Orientalism. It is safest, often even in dissent from the Masoretes, to stick to the written consonants in the text. The consonants here are *nr'* and when supplied with vowel points that can only be *nirā'*. That is a defective writing of *nīrā'*, a Qal imperfect, first person plural, of *yārē'*, to fear, and must be translated: "We shall be afraid." Taken together with *nishtāʿah* the sense is: Do anything at all and we will then be afraid and show fear besides. That is genuine Hebrew, and Isaiah's style. It also suits the general context, for it heightens the irony and provides a strong ending to the discourse, while the other translations present us with ideas that do not otherwise occur in Scripture.

24 הֵן־אַתֶּם מֵאַיִן וּפָעָלְכֶם מֵאָפַע תּוֹעֵבָה יִבְחַר בָּכֶם׃

Verse 24 contains a summing up of the proceedings. The idols have returned no answer, either to the Lord's challenge or to His mockery. He therefore pronounces His final verdict upon them: You are nothing! There is no good reason to understand *min* before *'ayin* and *'epha'* as being a condensed comparative, as in Psalm 62:10(9) (as if preceded by *me'aṭ*), as Vitringa and others suggest (cf. Gr. 133, e, p. 430). It is much more likely that it is to be taken in the partitive sense, as in 40:17. Concerning *'epha'* (the Qamets is pausal), a word that occurs only here, Delitzsch says: "*me'āpha'* is not a copyist's mistake for *me'āphes*, but *'epha'* from *'ph'* is the same as *pāh*, *pāʿah*, 42:14, *hiare,* to gape, breathe with open mouth, and the word appears here as synonymous with *'awen, hebhel, rūah.*" To which we would remark that even though the verb *'ph'* does not appear in the Hebrew Scriptures and *p'h* (42:14) occurs only once, in the first person of the Qal imperfect, it still is true that verbs that begin with *ph* and end with a guttural (*ph-h, ph-g, ph-kh*) are imitative of blowing. (Cf. *'eph'eh,* the adder, the spitter or hisser, in the noun form of that verb, 59:5.) Consult the lexicon and also *p'h* in Deuteronomy 32:26. And so, here, *'ph'* quite likely means breath, wind, nothing, and *me'epha'* is then "of nothing." It is fully synonymous with *'ephes* and *me'ephes,* both common in Isaiah. (Cf. 40:17; 41:12; 52:4.) Luther hit the correct meaning. The last verse in the strophe includes the idol worshipers, heretofore not mentioned, in the condemnation pronounced upon the idols. Cf. Deuteronomy 7:26; 32:16; 2 Kings 21:2. — Before *yibhhar* supply *'asher.*

Second Half: verses 25-29:   *The omnipotence and omniscience of the Lord contrasted with the dumb ignorance of the idol-gods.*

25   I arouse one out of the north, that he comes,
     From the east, one who proclaims My name,
     And he will tread upon princes as upon mortar,
     Like a potter who tramples his clay.
26   Who ever revealed this from the beginning, that we must
          needs acknowledge it?
     And beforehand so that we had to say, "Right!"
     Oh, there is no prophet, there is no preacher,
     No one, who ever heard a word from you.
27   To Zion I give the first one who said: "See, there it is!"
     And I sent messengers of joy to Jerusalem.
28   But when I look toward them, there is no one,
     And among them, no prophet is there,
     And when I ask them — do they give an answer?
29   Truly, all of them — a naught are they, a nothing are
          all their works,
     A breath, an empty waste, their images.

In this section the Lord's challenge to the idols reaches its climax in the sharp accentuation of the differences between the Lord and the idol-gods. In verse 25 the prophet sets forth the Lord's great act of arousing Cyrus (verses 1-7) as proof of His Godhead in contrast to the total inability of the idols to proclaim anything in advance. In verse 26 the ability to foretell the future is set up as the decisive consideration, and it is at once asserted that the idols are incapable of that. Verse 27 emphasizes the fact that Zion-Jerusalem was the first to receive the revelation of the deeds of Cyrus as a message of joy from the Lord. Verses 28 and 29 bring the section to a conclusion with the devastating verdict that all idol worshipers are nothing and all their works worthless.

25 הַעִירֹ֤ותִי מִצָּפֹון֙ וַיַּ֔את מִמִּזְרַח־שֶׁ֖מֶשׁ יִקְרָ֣א בִשְׁמִ֑י
וְיָבֹ֤א סְגָנִים֙ כְּמֹו־חֹ֔מֶר וּכְמֹ֥ו יֹוצֵ֖ר יִרְמָס־טִֽיט׃

At this point it would be in place to consider the question whether the perfect in *ha'irothī*, followed by the imperfect *wayya'th*, and also the perfect in *he'īr* (verse 2) are historical perfects or perfects of another type. If they are taken to be historical perfects, then this section, and in fact all of Isaiah II, was written after the appearance of Cyrus in history, and after the conquest of Croesus and the Lydian empire, that is, after 546, but before the

169

fall of Babylon in 538; or else the prophet was transported in spirit
into that period of time by the Holy Spirit. Let it be said at once
that the decision does not rest with the grammar of the passage.
An intelligent answer is possible only after one has taken into consideration everything that Isaiah II has to say about Cyrus. For
that reason we will postpone discussion of the matter till after
chapter 48, where in verse 14 Cyrus is mentioned for the last time.

In chapter 41 Luther translates verses 2,3,5,6, and 7 as referring to past history, not for grammatical reasons, since they were
not involved, but because he understood those verses to refer to
Abraham; but here in verse 25 Luther employs the futuristic present and retains it to the end of the chapter. Naturally, nearly all
modern critics declare that to be a false translation. In spite of
that opinion, we also employ the present tense because we hold
that to be the only choice we can be certain of. In justification of
that choice we refer in regard to the perfect tense to Gr. 106, 2 and
3, p. 311 and 312, and in regard to *wayya'th* to 111, 4, p. 328f. So we
translate: "I arouse one that he come." The clause "That he come"
to our Western mind seems to be a superfluous addition, and since
the LXX does not have it, many modern critics strike it and say
that it came from a *wa'anī* which had been introduced from some
other passage (Budde). Very plausible! If only we could be sure!

Coupled with *mimmizraḥ shemesh* (cf. verse 2) we have
mitstsāphōn, out of the north. Compare especially Jeremiah 50:
3,9,41 and 51:11,25,28. Cyrus came from Persia, from the east in
respect to Babylon. He was the son and successor of Cambyses,
king of Persia. After the overthrow of the Median king Astyages
at Pasargadae in 558, he became king of Media, which lay north of
Babylon: out of the east he advanced against Asia Minor, out of
the north against Babylon.

Before *yiqrā',* as previously in the case of *wayy'ath,* we should
supply either *wa* or *'asher. qārā' bheshēm* does not necessarily
mean to call upon the name of the Lord, but may also mean to call
out in the name of the Lord, that is, to proclaim Him, to preach, as
in Exodus 33:19; 34:5ff. That is what is here being said of Cyrus.
By publishing and carrying out his edict releasing the Jews (2
Chron. 36:23; Ezra 1:1,2) Cyrus, stirred to this act by the Holy
Spirit, confessed Israel's God and glorified His name before all the
world, although he did not become an open proselyte to Judaism.
But the Holy Spirit did His work through him, as through Balaam
(Num. 22-24); Nebuchadnezzar (Dan. 4:31-34[34-37]); and Darius

(Dan. 6:26f). — The *seghānīm* in Ezra and Nehemiah and in Jeremiah 51 and Ezekiel 23 are Persian satraps. The word is said to be derived from the Babylonian *saknu*. In this passage it is most likely used in a wider sense. *sōkhēn* is derived from the same stem and in Isaiah 22:15 is a title of the steward Shebna. In 1 Kings 1:2 and 4, Abishag of Shunem is called David's *sōkheneth*, his serving-maid or nurse. Luther perhaps struck the right meaning with *die Gewaltigen*. Since the usual *'al, 'el,* or *be* does not follow *yābhō',* in this case, but rather the comparison "like mortar," the critics have substituted *yābhūs* for *yābhō',* as suggested by 14:25 and 63:6. That is a probability, but no more than that. Between this clause and the next (*yirmos tīt,* etc. — he treads) we have the same climax as in Nahum 3:14: To go into the clay and tread upon it. The only distinction between *ḥōmer* and *tīt* is that the latter term is more expressive of contempt. The point of comparison is really the contemptibility of the opponents.

מִי־הִגִּיד מֵרֹאשׁ וְנֵדָ֫עָה וּמִלְּפָנִים וְנֹאמַר צַדִּיק ²⁶
אַף אֵין־מַגִּיד אַף אֵין מַשְׁמִיעַ אַף אֵין־שֹׁמֵעַ אִמְרֵיכֶם׃

What kind of perfect is *higgīdh*? Is it historical, or merely an abstract perfect? Does *higgīdh* refer to the contents of verse 25 as its object, in the sense of: Who has foretold this, namely, the victorious progress of Cyrus? Or is *higgīdh* totally without reference, without a specific object, merely asking a question: Who foretells? Luther inclined to the latter interpretation and took the perfect to be abstract. The matter cannot be settled grammatically. In 49:21 we have a purely historical perfect; in 66:8 an abstract question. But verses 27ff clearly refer to the prediction of the coming of Cyrus. So too the mission of Cyrus with all its consequences is throughout Part I the object of the same recurring question (43:9,12; 44:8; 45:21; 48:3, 5ff, 14, 15, 16). Therefore, in this passage also, the reference is in all likelihood to Cyrus, and the perfect is historical. However, in the chapters cited, there also occur wholly general questions of this kind, without specific reference to Cyrus, for example, in 44:7 and 46:10. There is therefore no clear and conclusive refutation of the interpretation favored by Luther and those who support him.

mērō'sh and *millephānīm* are not absolute terms but are to be understood relatively: "Before this was done"; or, if *higgīdh* is understood as abstract: "Before it happens." Concerning *nēdhā'ah* with attached *Waw*, a final or consecutive cohortative, see Gr. 165

and 166, p. 503f. It will then be translated: "Then we will acknowledge" or "So that we may acknowledge." This form of the verb, instead of *nēdhā'ah*, is probably influenced by the pausal position (cf 5:19). *'attāh* is perhaps to be supplied after *tsaddīq* — "just you are" — namely, in your predictions, although this translation does not bring out the formal meaning of "right," "correct." It really is the same as "You are right." The threefold repetition of *'aph 'ēyn,* each time with a participle, is a strong negation of the existence of a thing — there simply does not exist any foreteller, any announcer, any herald or prophet. An inversion of the thought in the final phrase — "anyone who hears your utterances" — gives still more emphasis to the negation. Some editions have the letter *Ayin* instead of *Aleph* in *'imrēykhem,* a typographical error.

27 רִאשׁוֹן לְצִיּוֹן הִנֵּה הִנָּם   וְלִירוּשָׁלַ͏ִם מְבַשֵּׂר אֶתֵּן׃

Commentators cause themselves unnecessary difficulty with the first part of this sentence. It is evident that *'ōmēr,* or its equivalent, must be supplied before the direct address of *hinnēh hinnām*: See, there it is. (The ending *ām* is neuter.) Cf. 14:8. Some commentators, including Delitzsch, now add *'anī* before *rī'shōn,* or supply *'āmartī* instead of *'omer,* and translate, as Luther does: "I am the first who says to Zion: Behold, there it is." They feel that the contrast with verse 26 makes it necessary to make the Lord the subject and *rī'shōn* the predicate. No one is there (verse 26); but here am I as the first herald of these things (verse 27). That is very plausible. But the addition of *'anī* is unnecessary, unless one insists that *rī'shōn* must refer to the Lord as the subject. It is possible, however, to go along with the text as it stands. The whole sentence has but one subject and one predicate, *'ettēn,* which serves both parts of the sentence. One needs but to place *'ettēn* at the head and take *rī'shōn letsīyōn 'ōmēr* as its object, and everything falls neatly into place: "I give the first one who says to Zion: See, there it is; and to Jerusalem, a herald of joy." Or else: "I give Zion the first one who says . . . " Such economy in the arrangement of subject and predicate is common in poetry. This construction also preserves the perfect parallelism of the two members, nothing unnecessary has to be supplied, and the contrast with verse 26 is preserved. The contrast is also preserved by the second member, in which the Lord is joined in a common cause with Zion-Jerusalem. The sense is: The idols have not foretold these things concerning Cyrus; Zion-Jerusalem was the first to receive that announcement, which was a message of joy, from My own messengers, whereby My Godhead is proved. Cheyne also takes *rī'shōn* to be the object but allows Luzatto to lead him into taking it to be an independent object in the sense of a forerunner, which merely increases the difficulty.

וָאֵרֶא וְאֵין אִישׁ וּמֵאֵלֶּה וְאֵין יוֹעֵץ וְאֶשְׁאָלֵם וְיָשִׁיבוּ דָבָר: 28

Once more the Lord turns His attention to the idols, and with their condemnation the discourse reaches its conclusion. The *we* at the beginning is adversative. *'ēre'* is the protasis, *we'ēyn 'īsh* the apodosis: "If I look (namely, to the other side, to the gentiles and their idols), then ...." Now it is no longer the idols themselves, but as the conclusion shows, their worshipers who are considered the opponents. Concerning the apocopated jussive form *'ēre'*, see Gr. 48, h, p. 131 and 109, h, p. 323. *mē'ēlleh* must be supplied to *'ēre'*, and in the next member *'ēre'* must be supplied to *mē'ēlleh*. Each word is used only once, but each serves a double purpose, like *'ettēn* in the preceding verse. The *mē* before *'elleh* ought to cause no difficulty. Compare *miqqedem* and *miyyām*, eastward, westward. *yō'ēts* is usually rendered as *counselor*, and the next two verbs with the consecutive *Waw* are taken to be dependent on *we'ēyn yō'ēts:* So that I may ask them and they return an answer. Since this construction is awkward and disturbs the parallelism, one feels constrained to seek a different explanation. The parallelism suggests a meaning similar to that of the first member: "And if I ask them, they return no answer." But this rendering requires a *lō'* which is missing in the text. Such an important omission can hardly be assumed. But, how does the LXX arrive at οὐ μὴ ἀποκριθῶσί μοι At this point, where the LXX may very well be right, the critics refuse to follow it. We take the second member to be a question: And if I ask them, do they return an answer? (Cf. Gr. 150,1,p.473.) The interrogative particle as a rule leaves the answer undecided; not so the interrogative sentence without the *ha*. That is what is meant here. (Cf. Gr. 150,d,p.474.) — And now that *we'esh'ālēm* has been separated from *yō'ēts*, we do not translate "counselor," but, what here seems more natural, "prophet, prognosticator," as *yā'ats* is used in Numbers 24:14 (Balaam) and Jeremiah 38:15. Therefore: "If I look toward them, there is no prophet."

173

29 הֵן כֻּלָּם אָוֶן אֶפֶס מַעֲשֵׂיהֶם רוּחַ וָתֹהוּ נִסְכֵּיהֶם:

The suffixes in *niskēyhem* (*nesekh*, from *nāsakh*, to pour, is a molten image) and *maʿaseyhem* show that not the idols themselves but their worshipers are now the subject under discussion. According to Delitzsch the asyndeton in *ʾawen ʾephes* is an expression of strong feeling. This sentence contains the final verdict upon the idols and the idol worshipers. They are nothing! Cf. Jeremiah 51:17f.

Résumé of verses 21-24: The idols of the gentiles, challenged by Israel's King to a judicial contest, are required to furnish proof that they are able to foretell the future. If they can do so, the Lord will acknowledge their Godhead. Yes, if they are able to do anything at all, the Lord will admit to a fear of them. But they are nothing and therefore whoever has anything to do with them is an abomination. *Verses 25-29:* The Lord proves His eternal power and His Godhead by sending Cyrus against the world powers. Had the idols foretold that, then they should have received recognition, but among them and their adherents there was none to prophesy the future. Jerusalem heard it first from the Lord as a message of joy. Among the idols and their worshipers not a syllable of this was heard. The idol worshipers are nothing, and their idols are nothing but what they have made with their own hands.

Third Discourse: Chapter 42

The Lord reveals His glory by sending forth and upholding His true Servant, who brings the Gospel to Jews and gentiles; also by exercising His judgment of destruction against the ungodly and His chastising judgment against the hitherto unprofitable servant Israel.

The chapter is clearly divided into three parts: verses 1-9: The true Servant of the Lord and His mission to Israel and the gentiles; verses 10-17: The judgment of destruction against the ungodly; verses 18-25: The former servant of the Lord, the people, is incurably hardened, and the Lord has therefore poured out His wrath upon him.

First Strophe: verses 1-9: *The true Servant of the Lord in His mission as Savior to Israel and the gentiles.*

This strophe has two equal parts: verses 1-4 and 5-8, the ninth verse serving as a transition to the following strophe. The beginning of the second half is indicated by the phrase *kōh 'āmar hā'ēl.* The first half introduces the Servant in His relation to the Lord, in regard to His endowments and His mission. The latter is described in verses 2 and 3 as being the deliverance of the people from their miserable state through revelation of the *mishpat,* that is, the Gospel. The fourth verse says that He will surely accomplish His mission.

First Half: verses 1-4:

1   *Behold, My Servant, whom I uphold,*
    My Chosen One, in whom I delight!
    Upon Him have I laid My Spirit,
    He shall bring forth Justice to the gentiles.

2 *He shall not cry nor lift up*
  Nor cause His voice to be heard in the street.
3 *A bruised reed will He not break,*
  A smoldering wick not quench,
  Truly, He shall bring forth the Right.
4 *He shall neither flicker nor break*
  Till He have established the Right in the earth
  And the isles trust in His Word.

As in every preceding section, so also in the three strophes of this chapter, the dominant point of view is the glory of the Lord. In the first strophe this glorification is found in the preparation of the Servant for the accomplishment of His mission, as the eighth verse expressly states. The second strophe calls on the whole world to glorify the Lord because of the judgment that He carries out on it, and in the third the Lord's glory appears in the judgment visited upon His reprobate servant Israel.

הֵן עַבְדִּי אֶתְמָךְ־בֹּו בְּחִירִי רָצְתָה נַפְשִׁי ¹
נָתַתִּי רוּחִי עָלָיו מִשְׁפָּט לַגּוֹיִם יוֹצִיא׃

Once before, in 41:8f, the Servant of the Lord was mentioned as *'abhdī*, My Servant. In that passage faithful Israel was meant. There the Lord lavished terms of tenderness on His people and promised not only to strengthen, help, and preserve them in battle, but also assured them of triumph over all their enemies and glorious deliverance from their misery. In chapter 42 the Servant of the Lord is presented in twofold form. In the first strophe He appears as a servant who victoriously carries out the gracious will of the Lord for the enlightenment of the gentiles and as the Mediator of the covenant with His people Israel. In the third strophe he appears as the servant of the Lord who is so blind and hardened that no revelation of the Word, however abundant, is sufficient to open his eyes. Nor does chastisement cause him to understand. — Those are three distinct forms of the same person, who in succeeding chapters will appear again and again with the same distinctive characteristics, often designated as servant, still more often without that express designation. The first form in which he appears is clearly that of *faithful* Israel, as in 43:1-7; 44:1,21,26; 45:4; 48:20, and elsewhere. The third is reprobate Israel, as in 43:8; 48:12, and other passages. The second appears again in 49:3,5; 50:4,10; 52:13ff; 53:11; 55:4; 61:1ff. Who is this? Already the Aramaic Targum translates the opening words of this chapter as "Behold,

My Servant, the Messiah." The LXX adds "Jacob" to the first clause and "Israel" to the second. In this and the other passages the New Testament recognizes the Christ: Matthew 12:18 (differing from the LXX); Luke 4:18ff, referring to Isaiah 61:1; cf. Matthew 8:17; Mark 9:12; 15:28; Luke 2:32; 22:27; John 12:38; Acts 8:30ff; 13:47; Romans 10:16; 15:21; 1 Peter 2:22; Revelation 1:16. The later naturalistic and unbelieving commentators, in agreement with the Jewish-Rabbinic exegetes, explain these passages as referring only to the people of Israel. Budde's remarks to 42:1 are characteristic: "The servant of Jahwe is, according to 41:8, Israel." Probably that was also expressly stated in this passage, since the LXX has *ya'akōbh* before *'abhdī* and *yisrā'el* before *beḥiri.* Therefore: "Behold, My servant Jacob, etc.; and, My chosen one Israel, etc." For all Christian exegetes the Messianic interpretation is *a priori* the correct one because of the precedent set by the New Testament writers.

What can be determined in this connection by purely exegetical methods? It cannot be denied that Delitzsch was right when he stated: "The term *'ebhed YHWH* is, figuratively expressed, a pyramid. The base is the whole of Israel; the middle section, the people who are Israel not only κατὰ σάρκα but also κατὰ πνεῦμα the apex is the person of the Mediator of salvation who came forth out of Israel. He is (1) the very core and center of the kingdom of the promise — the second David; he is (2) the very core and center of the people of salvation— the true Israel; he is (3) the very core and center of the human family — the second Adam." — In this connection we would refer to the parallel of the Seed of Abraham in Scripture (cf. 41:8). That term too has a threefold scope: (1) Abraham's seed κατὰ σάρκα, Genesis 12:7, etc.; (2) Abraham's seed κατὰ πνεῦμα, Galatians 3:7; Romans 4; John 8; and (3) the Christ, Galatians 3:16. The same is true of the term *Israel.* Externally, Israel is the people; in truth and reality, however, only the believers; and in its innermost sense, the Christ, Isaiah 49:3. The middle term is the one out of which the other two concepts develop, the one downward, the other upward. What really characterizes Abraham is faith, Genesis 15:6; John 8:39ff. Abraham's seed, therefore, in a strict sense, are the believers. In applying the term to the physical seed of Abraham, the term has actually been debased to include those who should have been believers but were not, still were descended from Abraham and thus could still be called his seed. In that case the designation *seed* is almost a misuse of the term. In the upward development the term is raised to the ideal and designates the Believer, and therefore the Just One, the Chosen One, in the fullest and highest sense, a designation that fits only the Christ. If the naturalistic exegetes could have entertained this interpretation of Scripture, they would not have crucified the Lord of Glory in Isaiah II. Moreover, it can be established from the exegesis of this chapter in connection with chapter 49, which is almost identical in content, that verses 1-8 do not refer to the spiritual Israel (not to mention Israel according to the flesh), but to Israel, respectively, Abraham's Seed, in the ideal sense, as the (one true) Servant of the Lord (the Christ.)

With *hēn 'abhdī,* as is customary in Isaiah's manner of presentation, the Lord without any preamble dramatically states the theme and subject of His discourse and then describes it in the following clauses so fully that the following verses of the strophe merely serve to develop it. *'abhdī* is the primary theme. Everything is comprised in the one term "My Servant." He is the Lord's. The Lord chose Him to be His Servant to carry out a special mission, made Him to be His own, and equipped Him for this mission. He is the Lord's Representative and Ambassador, His Master Builder and His Emissary for a certain designated work. The Lord's first pronouncement about Him is *'ethmokh bō.* One may add *'asher* and construe this as a relative clause or take it as an independent clause; either is grammatically permissible. But what is the meaning of *tāmakh* in this connection? Matthew translates it ὅν ἡρέτισα, whom I have taken hold of, chosen. The Hebrew word is even stronger than that: whom I have grasped firmly, hold firmly, establish and uphold with strength — all that in the one expression (cf. *sāmakh*). The Lord has taken hold of this Servant, placed Him in the world and sustains Him so firmly that no power can overthrow Him, as if to say: Here is My Servant, let us see who is able to stand against Him.

Verses 4 and 6 develop this thought. *behīrī,* asyndetically connected with *rātsethāh naphshī,* selects from *tāmakh* the single element of choosing and adds (*'asher* again to be supplied): "In whom I am well pleased," Matthew 3:17; 17:5, etc. Son in the New Testament and Servant here are one and the same, as also in Psalm 2:7 and several other passages (cf. Acts 13:33). The pleasure of the Lord rests upon Him with wholehearted, joyous sincerity. There is in Him nothing that might displease the Lord. Therefore the New Testament calls Him ὁ ἀγαπητός, Matthew 3:17; Luke 9:35; 2 Peter 1:17. The sixth verse carries this out further: I have called You *bhetsedheq,* etc. In the two preceding clauses the inner relation of the Servant to the Lord was described; the next, *nāthattī rūḥī 'ālayw,* describes the power with which He is invested. The Lord has placed His Spirit upon Him. This Spirit was not His originally, but He requires it for the accomplishment of the task assigned to Him. The nature of that Spirit is explained in 11:2-5. How the endowment with the Spirit was carried out is told in Matthew 3:16f; Mark 1:10f; Luke 3:22, etc. As for the measure in which this Spirit was given, see John 3:34. That is His entire equipment. For the assigned task He needs nothing further, no external powers, as is at once carried out in verses 2 and 3. The assigned task is mentioned at the end: *mishpāṭ laggōyim yōtsī':* right, or judgment, He will bring forth to the gentiles. The all-important word here is *mishpāṭ,* for in the entire strophe this is the object of all the Servant's acts.

That the word is used here in its objective sense of *right,* of that which is the consequence of an act of judgment, or as the content of a judicial pronouncement, is evidenced by its predicates *yōtsī'* and *yāsīm* and by its synonym *tōrāthō* (verses 3 and 4). Matthew's use of κρίσις in quoting this passage need not perplex us, since that is a literal translation, having the same objective meaning. The same is true of ἐκβάλῃ εἰς νῖκος τὴν κρίσιν, at the end of the quotation (Matt. 12:20). The circumstances of the establishment of this judgment or right make it altogether certain that the Law of Sinai, the Law of moral right and judgment, is not meant here. The Servant does not establish this judgment with force (verse 2), but rather with gentleness toward those who are bruised (verse 3); the gentiles (isles) put their trust in it; the Servant establishes it in His character as the personification of the covenant made with the people; through this judgment He becomes the Light of the gentiles and employs it to open their eyes and to lead them out of their dark prison. For substantiation, see chapter 49. This right or justice is the righteousness of the New Testament, of the covenant with Abraham, of the Gospel of grace in Christ, which Jeremiah describes in 31:31-34, in contrast to the Law of Sinai, as being the law that God will put into the bosoms of the believers and write in their hearts, through which He will impart knowledge of the Lord and confer forgiveness of sins. It is the Messianic salvation, of which Isaiah in Parts I and II and all the rest of Scripture in both Testaments are the clear echo. The Gospel is here called *mishpāṭ,* a judicial pronouncement, a judge's verdict, a right or judgment, since it does proceed from a real and actual judicial proceeding. The world, found guilty according to the

179

justice of the Law, is condemned to death before the tribunal of God; also standing before the same tribunal is the innocent Servant of the Lord. To the former, God does not impute its sin; the latter, He makes to be sin for us, reconciling the world unto Himself (2 Cor. 5:19-21; Isa. 53). That is the judgment of God, the right or justice which, according to the covenant with Abraham, is to be the norm in the kingdom of God, and which shall be decisive in matters of life and death, salvation and damnation, namely, grace, forgiveness of sin, sometimes also called the *tsedheq* or *tsidhqath YHWH,* or also *YHWH tsidhqēnū.* To bring forth this judgment to the gentiles, to non-Israelites, is the mission of the Servant of the Lord. *yōtsī',* He shall bring it forth out of Zion, which is its dwelling place. There the Lord dwells in the *kebhōdh YHWH,* the Holy of Holies, the tabernacle, the temple in Israel, Psalm 132:14; Isaiah 2:3; John 4:22; Luke 24:47. The ultimate source is the Lord Himself, 51:4.

² לֹא יִצְעַק וְלֹא יִשָּׂא וְלֹא־יַשְׁמִיעַ בַּחוּץ קוֹלוֹ:

The second verse tells how this Servant will carry out His mission to bring forth judgment to the gentiles. This sentence is a litotes, as is also the first half of the third verse. The negative, minimizing statement is meant to convey the opposite idea in an emphatic manner. What is meant is the *'anī* of Zechariah 9:9 and the πραΰς of Matthew 21:5 — humble and gentle. Thus the Servant of the Lord is set in contrast to the one whom chapter 41 revealed as the Lord's instrument to subdue the gentile nations, namely Cyrus, who carries out his mission by means of physical force. The various expressions — to cry out, to lift up the voice, cause the voice to be heard, in the street or marketplace — are intended to describe poetically the manner in which a worldly conqueror performs his deeds. These expressions should not be pressed. The predicates *yissā'* and *yashmīa'* both have *qōlō* as their object. Or, one may construe *yissā'* as an abbreviation of *yissā' qōlō* and as an independent statement, as in verse 11. The result will then be a reverse climax (so necessary in a litotes) — cry out, shout, make his voice heard.

³ קָנֶה רָצוּץ לֹא יִשְׁבּוֹר וּפִשְׁתָּה כֵהָה לֹא יְכַבֶּנָּה
לֶאֱמֶת יוֹצִיא מִשְׁפָּט:

His gentleness is observed in His treatment of those to whom He brings forth judgment. The figures of a bruised reed and of a weak

or weakly glimmering wick are very striking. They refer to the
'anawīm, or *'aniyyīm,* of the world, the *'anwēy 'erets,* the *'aniyyīm
we'ebhyōnīm* (41:17; 49:13; Ps. 76:10(9); Zeph. 2:3, etc.); not of the
people of Israel alone, but of all men, Matthew 11:5,28ff: John
6:37. *qāneh* is a reed (Isa. 19:6; 1 Kings 14:15), or also a stalk of
grain (Gen. 41:5,22). In Isaiah 36:6 Egypt is referred to as a
bruised or broken reed. *pishtāh,* flax, occurs also in 43:17 in the
sense of a wick of braided flax. The adjective *kēhāh,* feminine of
kēheh, means weak, dim, smoldering. The verb *yekabbennah,* from
kābhāh, to go out, expire, echoes the sound of *kēhāh.* In Isaiah
43:17 and 66:24 this verb occurs in the Qal as an intransitive; here
and in 1:31 it is a Piel and transitive. *le'emeth* is the same as
be'emeth and its meaning is "in deed and in truth" (1 John 3:18),
that is, "with real success." That meaning is verified by the next
verse, which, as so often in Isaiah, is a further development of the
thought in this sentence. Luther's *wahrhaftig* is correct. His *halten
lehren* also expresses the sense well. The meaning of the sentence
is that the Servant will effectually plant His judgment, His Gospel,
in the hearts of the broken-hearted, so that they possess it as their
own, in faith.

4 לֹא יִכְהֶה וְלֹא יָרוּץ

עַד־יָשִׂים בָּאָרֶץ מִשְׁפָּט וּלְתוֹרָתוֹ אִיִּים יְיַחֵלוּ׃

yikhheh and *yārūts* correspond to *rātsūts* and *kēhāh* of the third
sentence. For *yārūts,* a *Qal* imperfect of *rūts,* to run, the prophet-
codex of the year 916, based on Ben Naphthali, has the reading
yeרūts, with Babylonian pointing. But *yārūts* is not a copyist's error. The long *ū* in the second syllable is a broadening of *ō.* The
regular form would be *yārōts* or *yērōts,* a Qal imperfect of *rātsats,*
to break. (Like *yāsōbh* and *yissōbh* from *sābhabh,* Gr. 67,q, p. 180.)
— Just as the Servant will not break the bruised reed or ex-
tinguish the smoldering wick, so He will neither be broken nor
subdued — the picture has been retained — until He shall have accomplished His mission to set up and firmly establish (*yāsīm*) judgment upon the earth. The imperfect has the force of the *futurum
exactum,* Gr. 107, 1, p. 316. It is presupposed that hostile powers
will assail Him and strive to destroy His work — Satan with his
hosts and the powers of the world with the hosts of the ungodly.
Cf. Matthew 4:1ff; Luke 22:53; John 14:30, etc. Since He is not,
like Cyrus, equipped with *worldly* power, but solely with the Spirit
of God, and since He walks in gentleness and humility, man's
judgment could only expect that He would go down in defeat with-

181

out having accomplished His assigned task (cf. 49:4). Nevertheless, He will accomplish His mission *be'emeth*, in deed and in truth. Matthew says that He will successfully carry out His judgment, 12:20. Chapter 53 tells us how He will do it.

Whether one understands the final clause of the fourth verse as independent, or dependent on *'adh*, is grammatically a matter of indifference; nor does the Masoretic Athnach in *mishpāṭ* decide the matter. The only question is, which interpretation best fits into the context. This clause gives concrete expression to what was stated in abstract form in the preceding words. Judgment is *de facto* established upon the earth when the isles, that is, the heathen nations, with an enduring trust, place their hope in the Lord's Torah, which is His instruction, His Word. Some exegetes, notably Delitzsch, extract from the term *yeyaḥēlū* the concept of a deeply felt hunger for the Torah of the Lord, a yearning among the heathen, of which they might be wholly unaware, produced by the *gratia praeparans*. For evidence they cite 2:3 and 51:5. We answer: It is indeed a teaching of Scripture, corroborated by experience, that all mankind, yes, all creation, longs for a release from the troubles of this life into a condition of happiness (Rom. 8). Every worm writhes when it is stepped on. Consider how the unbelieving world cursed God, groaned and complained under the terrible burden of suffering during the World War. But that was not a yearning for the Gospel, for the Torah of the grace of Christ Jesus. This the world hated and resisted more than ever. It was at best a longing for worldly, carnal ease and pleasure, or for a kind of nirvana or painless condition after all the woes of life. The warring nations and their governments were not concerned about setting up a kingdom of God by continued war; rather, each wanted to establish its own economic and cultural supremacy. The deeply felt desires of the human breast, whether of the highly cultured man or of the almost subhuman savage, are always the "wine, women, and song" of the poet Heine and the acquisition of wealth, power, and fame. That is the "all that is in the world" of 1 John 2:16. Christ and His Torah were, and always will be, to the Jews an offense and to the Greeks foolishness, 1 Corinthians 1:23.

Still, it is true that Isaiah and all prophecy speak of an expectation and yearning of the heathen world for a Messianic salvation. The chief passages are Isaiah 2:3; 42:4; 51:5; 60:9; 65:1; (Rom. 10:20). But if these passages are to be taken literally — read 2:3 again — then the gentiles are filled with not only an unconscious, but with a conscious, truly believing, spiritual longing for God's teaching and sovereignty — a *contradictio in adjecto.* The matter is, however, quite simple. Isaiah is a poet, an Oriental poet at that. As such he endows lifeless things with emotions and even with spiritual responses. Even the ships of Tarshish (60:9) wait with longing for the time when they shall carry Israel's children back to Zion from afar and glorify the name of the Lord. If this is poetic fancy, why should it not be the same in this and other similar passages where — besides the ships in 60:9 — the isles, whether they be taken literally as islands or as masses of people, are pictured as being endowed with an expectation and a longing for the Torah of Christ. In Isaiah every hill and valley, the desert and the streams, praise the Lord and rejoice in faith, etc. Even the camels and dromedaries proclaim the praise of the Lord, and the lion and the adder become pious. Certainly it is poetic fancy that endows everything with life, imparts emotions to everything, and here even gives it *spiritual* life. The yearning of the gentiles in Scripture for the salvation of Christ is also poetic fancy. He who knows that can without hesitation translate: "And the isles trust in His Word," long for His teaching. He will thereby no more be attributing faith to the isles than to the ships of Tarshish. Our translation of verse 4 thus appears as the more natural one, and *yiḥēl* is then to be translated not as waiting and hoping for something in the future, but as trusting, relying on, believing in something present. That the word can be taken in this sense as well as in the other is borne out by such passages as Psalm 31:25(24); 33:18,22; 119:43,- 49,74,114; 130:7; 131:3; 147:11. Finally, that is also Matthew's understanding, even though he translates it in his own way with

καὶ ἐν τῷ ὀνόματι αὐτοῦ ἔθνη ἐλπιοῦσιν.

In verses 1-4 we have the proclamation that the elected and beloved Servant of the Lord, by virtue of His anointing with the Spirit of the Lord, will bring the Gospel to the spiritually destitute gentile peoples, and by the conversion of the gentiles will firmly establish the Word of grace upon earth. The same thought is repeated in a different way in the next half of the strophe.

Second Half: verses 5-8.

5   *Thus says the true God, the Lord,*
    Who created the heavens and spread them out wide,
    Who laid down the earth and what it produces,
    Who gave its inhabitants their breath
    And spirit to those who walk upon it:

6   *I am the Lord; as I called You in righteousness,*
        so do I grasp Your hand,
      And will keep You and make You a Covenant of the
        people and the Light of the gentiles,
7   *To open eyes that are blind,*
      To lead prisoners forth from prison,
      Out of the prisonhouse, those who dwell in darkness.
8   *I am the Lord, that is My name,*
      And I will give My honor to none other
      Nor My glory to the idols.

A Transitional Verse:

9   *As for the first, it has come to pass,*
      And a new thing do I proclaim;
      Before it springs into being, I let it be heard.

5 כֹּה־אָמַ֞ר הָאֵ֣ל ׀ יְהוָ֗ה

בּוֹרֵ֤א הַשָּׁמַ֙יִם֙ וְנ֣וֹטֵיהֶ֔ם רֹקַ֥ע הָאָ֖רֶץ וְצֶאֱצָאֶ֑יהָ

נֹתֵ֤ן נְשָׁמָה֙ לָעָ֣ם עָלֶ֔יהָ וְר֖וּחַ לַהֹלְכִ֥ים בָּֽהּ׃

The phrase *kōh 'amar* with which the fifth verse begins occurs
here for the first time in Isaiah II but is common in succeeding
chapters, sometimes introducing whole sections. Compare the
remarks about *yō'mar*, 40:1. The perfect here is neither the
historical nor the prophetic perfect. It is purely abstract and
represents the act of speaking as being finished, nothing more
than that being implied. An acceptable explanation may be found
in Gr. 106, i, (b), p. 311, or m, (a), p. 312. It is a set expression that
marks what follows as something momentous and true.

The subject in this sentence is *hā'el YHWH.* Regarding *'el,* see
40:18. The word appears here with the article and, like *hā'elohīm,*
it is not a proper noun but an abstract designation of the Godhead
with the special emphasis that justifies our translating it as "the
true God." Thus speaks He who is God according to His being and
according to His nature. The apposition *YHWH* tells who this true
God is, namely, the God of Israel. This particular combination of
the names of God occurs in only one other passage, Psalm 85:9.
The terms are carefully chosen. *ha 'el* especially emphasizes the
power and wisdom of God. The Servant is to have the assurance
that the power and wisdom of God will make certain His preservation and the success of His mission. — Isaiah's description of creation is vivid and beautiful. The Lord has unfurled the heavens and

spread out the earth with all that grows on it as a dwelling place for His creatures whom He has endowed with a reasoning spirit. See 40:22 and 45:12 for the same thoughts with a different application. The endowment of the inhabitants of the earth with *neshāmāh* and *rūah* is not only a demonstration of the Creator's might and wisdom, but it is a counterpart, although a weak one, to the endowment of the Servant with the Spirit of God (verse 1). Delitzsch's comments on the distinction between *neshāmāh* and *rūah* do not apply here. The poet uses the two terms without distinction and does not always observe the difference between them. *rūah* in this instance, as is often the case, is the rational spirit that distinguishes a creature as a human being.

אֲנִ֣י יְהוָה֩ קְרָאתִ֨יךָ בְצֶ֜דֶק וְאַחְזֵ֣ק בְּיָדֶ֗ךָ 6
וְאֶצָּרְךָ֙ וְאֶתֶּנְךָ֔ לִבְרִ֥ית עָ֖ם לְא֥וֹר גּוֹיִֽם:

Verse 6 begins the presentation of the subject introduced by *kōh ʾamar*. *ʾanī YHWH* occupies the position of emphasis: I am the Lord, the covenant God of Israel, the worker of Israel's salvation. The burden of the thought is concentrated in *bhetsedheq*. The specific meaning of *betsedheq* was explained at 41:10. Not only this Servant of the Lord, but Cyrus as well, was called *betsedheq*, 45:13. The context here and in 45 shows that the *tsedheq* of the Lord is the source and origin of the call which works Israel's deliverance and will also provide salvation for the gentiles. *tsedheq* is the source from which the acts of the Lord flow concerning the Servant — taking Him by the hand, watching over Him, making Him to be a covenant for the people, and the Light of the gentiles. Thus *tsedheq* can be nothing other than the Lord's will to save, His zeal for the salvation of Israel (cf. *qādhōsh*, 40:25), "the tender mercy of our God, whereby the dayspring from on high hath visited us," Luke 1:78. Compare also Zacharias' hymn of praise, in which the Holy Spirit Himself has brought together all the prophecies of Christ contained in Moses and the prophets. It is difficult, perhaps impossible, to express with one English word all that *tsedheq* conveys; for while the word here and elsewhere denotes especially the Lord's purpose to save, it also includes the objective salvation itself together with its preparation and ultimate goal. We have translated it "in righteousness," meaning to say: In faithful purpose to be the salvation of My people Israel. *ʾahzēq* (Hiphil jussive) is not another preterite linked to *qerāʾthīkhā*, but is a concluding clause following the introductory *qerāʾthīkhā* (Gr. 109, k, p. 323) in the sense: Having called You, so will I also uphold You, etc. It is to

185

be translated as a future, or as a present with the force of a future. *'etstsorkhā* and *'ettenkhā* also are future in meaning. *'etstsorkhā* is a form of *nātsar*, to preserve, not of *yātsar*, to form — in contrast to 44:21 and 49:5, where *yātsar* is clearly indicated by the perfect form or by modifiers.

The words *'ettenkhā libhrīth 'am* in this sentence determine exegetically that the Servant in question cannot be the people, but must be some other Servant of the Lord. In 41:8ff the servant of the Lord is clearly the *spiritual* Israel. In 42:19ff the servant is that part of Israel that is blind, deaf, rejected — Israel according to the flesh. It is worthy of note that this is the only instance where Israel after the flesh is actually called the Lord's servant. The Lord often speaks to this people and reprimands it (46:12; 48:1ff; 50:1,2; 56:9; 57:13; 58; 59, etc.) but never again as the Lord's Servant, or My Servant. The prophet seems to shrink from applying that name to the deaf and blind portion of the people. Having renounced its calling, the people as a whole has become unworthy of that exalted name. The name Servant for the spiritual Israel, after excluding those passages that conservative exegetes assume to refer to the Christ, occurs frequently: 43:10; 44:1,2,21,26; 45:4; 48:20. Since the Servant of the Lord who is to be made a covenant for the people is referred to in this strophe also as being God-fearing, it is not possible that Israel according to the flesh can be meant. The idea of rabbinical and later believing commentators that *'am* here refers to the whole family of men on earth and that the clause "I will make thee to be a covenant of the people" is synonymous with the following "and the light of the gentiles" is not acceptable, because *'am*, when not so indicated by the grammatical construction, or the express context, never means the people of the world, or all mankind, but always refers to Israel. Reference to verse 5 is not relevant, because in that verse *'aleyhā* modifies *'am* and defines it as referring to all people on earth. The idea of a covenant applying to mankind or of a covenant applying to gentiles is not Scriptural. According to Scripture, God made a covenant only with Abraham and his seed, with the Jewish people, and not with the gentiles. These can only be received into Abraham's covenant as individuals and have part in it only by being added to it by conversion. That, however, is not a separate covenant made with the gentiles, but an entrance on their part into the unique covenant established with Israel. There is only one people of the covenant — Israel. No gentile nation, nor the sum of all gentiles, ever became a people of the covenant. Cf.

Romans 9:4,5; 15:8f; Acts 3:25f; 2:39; Matthew 15:24ff; Romans 11:11ff. It is possible to speak of a covenant of Abraham with the Jews and the converted gentiles only if one disregards the external features of Abraham's covenant and assumes the seed of Abraham to be purely his spiritual seed. It is in this sense that the covenant and the people of the covenant are understood in the sixth verse. The *'am,* of which the Servant of the Lord is to be the *berīth,* is the *ba'al berīth* of the Lord (cf. Gen. 14:13), that is, the other party, with whom the Lord is concluding a covenant. And so surely as this covenant, in its essence, is spiritual and has Christ and His salvation as its content, so surely also the person and the people with whom He concludes the covenant are a spiritual person and a spiritual people. The physical seed of Abraham is only externally, incidentally, in an improper sense, a people of the covenant (John 8:39) and shares only in the external blessings of the covenant. God does not make a covenant with this part of the people. His covenant is entirely with the people κατὰ πνεῦμα . Since the spiritual Israel is the real *ba'al berīth,* the people of the covenant, it should be clear that *berīth 'am,* the covenant established with the people, is not the same as the people of the covenant, because a people cannot be its own mediator in establishing a covenant. *berīth 'am* means mediator of a covenant, nothing else. The expression is an impersonal designation for a person, as in the next clause *light* of the heathen also designates a person, one who enlightens the heathen and is their savior. And so also, *berīth* is really a Covenanter, a Mediator of a covenant with the people, that is, for the benefit of the believing people. See 49:6, "my salvation" for "my Savior"; Micah 5:4 (5), "Peace" for Peacemaker; Ephesians 2:14; 1 John 2:2, etc.

"I will make You to be a covenant of the people" clearly means to say that the Mediator will make the people partakers of the blessings of the covenant, particularly of the spiritual salvation, that is, of real healing for believing broken hearts and of effective salvation, grace, and forgiveness, together with bodily release from the exile for the believers. The same holds for what He will do for the isles (verse 4) and for the gentiles (verses 6 and 7). He leads them out of darkness into light, to knowledge of His salvation, to faith in His Torah. By imparting His Spirit to them He makes *believing* Jews and *believing* gentiles participants of His salvation. If one now reviews all the passages in Isaiah II in which faithful Israel is called the Lord's Servant, one will find several in which the activity just described, that of saving believing Israel from sin and external need and at the same time of converting the gentiles, recurs again and again. These passages must be understood as referring to the Servant of the Lord who is not the spiritual people of God, but rather the ideal and perfect Servant of the Lord — the Messiah, the Christ. The relevant passages are: 42:1-7; 49:1-9; 50:4-9; 52:13 — 53:12; 55:4,5; 61:1-3, and others of essentially identical content, except that the name Servant of the Lord does not occur, as for example, 61:1-3. The passages say something more than what is suggested by the commentators' designation "Ebed-Jahwe Hymns."

The New Testament, as is well known, recognizes Christ in these passages. Compare Matthew 12:18ff; Luke 1:70ff; 2:32; Revelation 1:16; Acts 13:47; Hebrews 9:15; John 12:38-41; Mark 9:12; Matthew 8:17; 1 Peter 2:22-25; Acts 8:32ff; Mark 15:28; Luke 22:37; Revelation 1:5 (with Isa. 55:4); Luke 4:18. — It is hardly necessary to add that the covenant described in this passage, of which the Lord's Servant is to be the Mediator, is not the Sinai covenant, but, as the wholly evangelical content of our strophe (keeping in mind chapter 49) demonstrates, the old Abrahamic covenant of grace, which Jeremiah (31:31-34) calls a new covenant consisting in conversion of the heart and forgiveness of sins. See the closing words of verse 6 and verse 7. For "Light of the gentiles," which corresponds to "Covenant of the people," compare especially Ephesians 3.

7 לִפְקֹחַ עֵינַיִם עִוְרוֹת לְהוֹצִיא מִמַּסְגֵּר אַסִּיר
מִבֵּית כֶּלֶא יֹשְׁבֵי חֹשֶׁךְ:

Verse 7 is an amplification of the concluding words of verse 6. The infinitives may be understood as noun clauses, or as purpose clauses, or as adverbs (Gr. 114,f,g,p.348). As Mediator of the people and Light of the nations, it is the mission of the Servant to set the prisoners free and to open the eyes of the blind. The arrangement of the phrases is chiastic: *liphqoaḥ ʿeynayim* corresponds to *leʾor goyim*, and deliverance from prison to *libhrīth ʿam*. The words following *mibbēyth* are a paraphrase of *lehōtsīʾ*, etc. The Servant proves Himself to be the Light of the nations by opening blind eyes (an abstract expression for eyes of the blind), and the covenant of the people by leading prisoners out of the prisonhouse (*ʾassīr* is generic or collective). This last refers to the people of Israel who are languishing in physical captivity; but it is not physical captivity alone, or even primarily, that is meant. The captivity is the basis for the expression referring to the spiritual bondage of

Israel, just as opening the eyes of the blind gentiles also refers to spiritual enlightenment of the kind that reached fulfillment through the preaching of Paul, Acts 26:18. This people that now suffers bodily imprisonment is also enslaved by the bonds of unbelief and sin through the power of Satan and because of the wrath of God. However, deliverance is to come through the covenant, that is, through the Mediator of the covenant, by way of conversion, exactly as with the gentiles. The remnant of Israel, the God-fearing little flock, is here meant, who now seem to be withering away in ignorance and darkness. *yōshebhēy ḥoshekh* also refers to that condition. This expression is suggested by the darkness of a dungeon, but describes the spiritual darkness in which the people still sit, as is shown by its position at the end of the sentence as counterpart to the phrase "to enlighten blind eyes." The use of such harsh expressions as prison and dungeon should not be taken to imply that the people in Babylon were actually held in such confinement. As in verse 22, this is a hyperbolic way of describing the "warfare" (*tsābhā',* 40:2) of Israel in Babylon, which shall come to an end because of the Mediator of the covenant. This physical deliverance will be the pledge for the complete deliverance from spiritual bondage which the Lord will accomplish.

אֲנִי יְהוָה הוּא שְׁמִי 8

וּכְבוֹדִי לְאַחֵר לֹא־אֶתֵּן   וּתְהִלָּתִי לַפְּסִילִים׃

Verse 8 presents the last of the objective proofs for the promise. It is an inherent part of the Lord's honor that He prove Himself to be what His name signifies. I am Jehovah, that is My name! He gave Himself that name, Exodus 3:14. The name means that He is the one true, eternal God, 41:4; 43:11; 44:6ff; 45:5,14, etc., who is all-powerful, before whom all the world, the nations, and all their princes are as nothing, 40:12-25; 41:1-7, 28, 29. But even before He gave Himself this "official" name, He had already bound Himself by a solemn oath to a covenant with Abraham and his seed that promised eternal grace, eternal blessing and faithfulness (Gen. 15). Over and over He repeated the assurance that He was the God of Abraham and of his seed and Israel's God and Helper, the Holy One of Israel, their Redeemer and their Rock of salvation (Exod. 3:6; Isa. 41:13,14,20; 44:8; 45:21, etc.). This strophe repeats the same promise. His honor as Jehovah, that He is the one true God, depends on the fulfillment of His promises, particularly of the promise to send His Servant as the Mediator of the covenant and the Light of the gentiles. If He does not send Him, if He fails to work salvation through Him for Jews and gentiles, then the God of Abraham and his seed will have forfeited His right to the name Jehovah and will no longer be the true God. Compare especially 2 Samuel 7:22-29. The Lord offers His name and His divine honor as pledge that He will fulfill the promise of this prophecy concerning His Servant. This honor will He give to no other "God," nor will He give this glory, which is His alone, to any of the idols. It is hinted that the heathen would blaspheme Him as a non-God if He failed to keep His vow, 48:11; Psalm 79:10; 42:4(3); 115:2.

The exposition of God's grand design for the sending of the Servant ends with verse 7. The next verse is the Lord's solemn seal on that thought. Verse 9 is the transition to the next strophe.

הָרִאשֹׁנוֹת הִנֵּה־בָאוּ וַחֲדָשׁוֹת אֲנִי מַגִּיד ⁹
בְּטֶרֶם תִּצְמַחְנָה אַשְׁמִיע אֶתְכֶם:

"As for the first (previous, earlier) things, behold, they have come to pass." Nearly all later commentators explain *rī'shōnōth* as referring to Cyrus and thus miss the point. Delitzsch too says that the *rī'shōnōth* refer to Cyrus and the mass migrations that followed his conquests. They then interpret the *ḥadhāshōth* as the coming of the Servant of the Lord, of the restoration of Israel and the conversion of the gentiles. That is especially the opinion of the later commentators. But they are wrong, and they contradict themselves without noticing that they do so. They take the *rī'shōnōth* to be the first of the prophesied events. That almost hits the mark, although the thought (paired with *maggīdh* and *'ashmīa' ḥadhāshōth*) really is: The first, the earliest things that I foretold, they have come to pass. Those earliest things quite obviously lie in the past, in a time previous to the present "proclaiming" and "causing to be heard." Also the foretelling of the *rī'shōnōth* naturally lies in a time previous to the present prophesying of *new* things. But modern exegetes do not admit that there ever was any real foretelling of the triumphant career of Cyrus. They maintain that what is said in 41:1-7, 25-29, about the coming of Cyrus refers to contemporary events. They assert that in those passages Cyrus is presented as already having conquered Croesus and already ruling. Those passages, according to them, only state that the God of Israel called Cyrus and made him a conqueror. The agitation and turmoil of the gentiles in 41:5-7 also are said to be contemporary happenings. The victorious career of Cyrus, they say, was already past history and was the basis for the prediction that he would restore Israel. It is only after Cyrus had won his first victories that Isaiah II, in such passages as 41:7 and 41:8-20, prophesies concerning Cyrus as the future conqueror of Babylon and deliverer of Israel. If that is true, and if before Isaiah II there was no prophecy of Cyrus as deliverer of Israel — as in fact, there was not! — how then can the *rī'shonoth*, the previously prophesied things, now suddenly be interpreted as a prophecy of Israel's deliverance at the hands of Cyrus? According to their exegesis, the deliverance is *only now* being foretold, as something not at all fulfilled. But note that concerning the *rī'shonoth* Isaiah says *hinneh bha'u*, behold they *have* come to pass! — Such modern exegesis is arbitrary, and does not take the context into consideration. It refuses to note that prophecy does not so mechanically separate events lying in the future, some of which are earlier and some later, so that it designates the earlier as *rī'shonoth* and the later as *hadhashoth*, but as a rule weaves the two together and designates both as *hadhashoth*. — 41:22f is an abstract arrangement of thought and does not refute this statement. For example, 42:1-7 combines the physical deliverance of Israel out of Babylon (verse 7) with the conversion of the gentiles and the Jews through the Servant of the Lord. In similar manner, the next strophe, verses 10-17, treats of the destruction of Babylon and also of the Last Judgment; both are hailed by the prophet as *hadhashoth* in his *shir hadhash*. It should be clear that the strophe about Cyrus and his deliverance of Israel out of Babylon refers to *hadhashoth*, and not to *rī'shonoth*, in the same manner as the enlightenment of the Jews and the gentiles by the Servant of the Lord is part of the *hadhashoth*. What is meant by *rī'shonoth* is expressly and clearly stated in the next chapter, 43:14-20. In that chapter the *future* destruction of Babylon and the deliverance of Israel are compared to the *long past destruction of the Egyptians and the rescue of Israel at the Red Sea*. The deliverance of Israel is there called *rī'shonoth*; and the destruction of Babylon *hadhashoth*. Compare 51:9,10,11.

The same is true in this strophe. In verse 8, where the prophet (God) spoke of the name Jehovah and of His defense of His honor and glory, he was reminded of how the Lord had glorified His name in His dealing with Pharaoh — "The horse and his rider hath He thrown into the sea. . . . the Lord is His name" (Exod. 15). That deed is here referred to as *harī'shonoth*, and its counterpart, the new and greater deliverance of Israel out of Babylon, is called the *ḥadhāshōth*, the subject of a song of triumph, a *shīr ḥadhāsh*. Moreover, the prophecy includes the future deliverance of the godly through the destruction of their enemies and also the deliverance wrought by the Servant of the Lord on the Last Day, Matthew 24. Luther, it is to be regretted, did not at this point hit upon the correct interpretation. *bhā'ū* is a historical perfect. The first, or earlier, things, namely, the destruction of Pharaoh's hosts and the deliverance of Israel, did come to pass, just as they had been foretold (Exod. 14). That fulfillment is the guarantee that the new things now being foretold will also surely come to pass.

Resume of verses 1-9: The beloved and chosen Servant of the Lord will, in perfect gentleness toward the broken-hearted and in the strength of the Spirit with which He is endowed, successfully establish the Gospel on the earth by enlightening the gentiles, verses 1-4. The almighty Creator of heaven and earth and of the spirit of man will in complete faithfulness make His Servant the Mediator and Fulfiller of the covenant with Israel and also the Light of the gentiles, in order to set free and enlighten His own, who are as yet blind and imprisoned. For that He pledges His honor as Jehovah, an honor that none shall take from Him. His wonderful deeds of the past, which all came to pass as prophesied, are the guarantee for the fulfillment of the new things which are now being prophesied.

Second Strophe: verses 10-17:   *Let all the world sing a new song unto the Lord, for He will destroy His enemies in a fearful judgment, deliver His afflicted people, and put the worshipers of idols to shame.*

At the end of verse 13 there is a division of the strophe into two parts. The first part is a summons to glorify the Lord with a new song. The second part introduces the Lord Himself proclaiming the coming Judgment.

First Half: verses 10-13:

10   *Sing unto the Lord a new song,*
      His praise to the ends of the earth!
      Those who go down to the sea, and that which fills it,
      The isles and those who inhabit them.
11   *Let the desert shout aloud and its cities,*
      The shepherds' villages that Kedar inhabits;
      Those who dwell among the rocks, let them shout,
      From the mountaintops let them shout for joy.

12 *Let them give honor to the Lord*
    And proclaim His glory, upon the isles proclaim His praise.

13 *The Lord will go forth like a conqueror,*
    Will awaken His zeal like a man of war;
    He will send forth His battle cry, yes, cry out aloud,
    He will show Himself as a Hero to His enemies.

10 שִׁירוּ לַיהוָה שִׁיר חָדָשׁ תְּהִלָּתוֹ מִקְצֵה הָאָרֶץ
   יוֹרְדֵי הַיָּם וּמְלֹאוֹ אִיִּים וְיֹשְׁבֵיהֶם:

It is the prophet speaking here. The new things that the Lord had just announced he accepts in faith as though already accomplished. Therefore he calls upon all the world to sing a song of praise to the Lord. A *new song* is one that sings of a new deed, cf. Psalm 33:3; 40:4(3); 96:1; 98:1; 149:1. *shīr*, the object of *shīrū*, is a song of any kind. *tehillāthō*, a second object of the verb *shīrū*, expresses the content and character of the song. It is to be a song or hymn of praise. — Where the Hebrew says *miqtsēh*, "from the end," we say "unto the end" of the earth. As the earth is to be filled with the *knowledge* of the Lord (11:9; Hab. 2:14), so shall all the earth resound with His praise. Therefore it must be concluded that the admonition contained in *shīrū* is addressed to all the gentiles in the world. In the following words they are designated according to three different regions of the world. The *yōredhēy hayyām*, those who go down to the sea, are the seafaring peoples who inhabit the isles and the coastlands of the Mediterranean Sea, the first and principal recipients of the Gospel. *melō'ō* can only mean "its," that is, "the sea's" fullness. It always refers to the fish and other creatures in the sea, Psalm 96:11; 98:7; 1 Chronicles 16:32 — not to people. The text critics here offer a correction, this time disagreeing with LXX. For *yōredhēy* they substitute *yir'am hayyām* to make this passage agree with those just cited — let the sea *roar* and its fullness. That is an appealing change, but it is not justified. According to the text, the people who sail on the sea and the creatures that live in it are exhorted to praise the Lord. *'iyyīm weyōshebhēyhem*, the isles and their inhabitants, is a parallel clause to *yōredhēy hayyām*. The two are arranged chiastically: seafaring people (rational creatures), fish (not rational); isles (not rational), their inhabitants (rational). This typical arrangement argues for the correctness of the *yōredhēy* reading. But that kind of argument does not appeal to the critics.

193

11 יִשְׂאוּ מִדְבָּר וְעָרָיו חֲצֵרִים תֵּשֵׁב קֵדָר
יָרֹנּוּ יֹשְׁבֵי סֶלַע מֵרֹאשׁ הָרִים יִצְוָחוּ:

qōl is to be supplied as the object of *yis'u* (Jussive). For the omission of Dagesh in *Sin*, see Gr. 20,3,m,p.74. The desert in verse 11 is the great Arabian desert between the Holy Land and Babylon. The prophet's face is now turned to the East. Since there never were any real cities in the desert, *'arayw* may refer to the cities on its western edge: Sela and Bozra in Edom, Kir Hareseth and Ar in Moab, Aroer on the Arnon, Rabbath Ammon, etc., or the word may be a euphemistic designation of the *ḥatsērīm*, the villages inhabited by Kedar. *ḥatsērīm* would then be the concrete designation for the more general *'arīm*. This is quite probable, since *'ir* is a word of wide meaning and may well include the fenced villages of the shepherds. According to Genesis 25:13, Kedar was the second son of Ishmael, and the sons of Kedar dwelt in the Arabian desert. In Jeremiah 49:28f they are called *benēy qedhem*, sons of the East, and are described as tent dwellers and herders of sheep. Cf. Isaiah 21:16f; 60:7; Ezekiel 27:21; Song of Solomon 1:5. In the next clause the prophet turns toward the south, toward Edom. But *sela'* here is not Sela, the chief city of the Edomites, as in 16:1; it is an appellative, as in Jeremiah 49:16, and is to be understood as a generic term. *yōshebhēy sela'* are rock-dwellers, inhabitants of the rocky highlands of Edom, in contrast to the previously mentioned inhabitants of the desert plateau. All are to rejoice and sing forth the praises of the Lord from the hills and from the mountaintops. *rō'sh* is here a collective. *tsāwaḥ* occurs nowhere else as a verb. The verbs in verse 11 form a climax.

12 יָשִׂימוּ לַיהוָה כָּבוֹד וּתְהִלָּתוֹ בָּאִיִּים יַגִּידוּ:

Verse 12 summarizes. Those who have been named shall, as representatives of all gentile peoples, sing praises to the Lord, and shall proclaim to the gentiles on the isles in the west the honor of God, who will certainly fulfill the promises contained in verses 1-7. The prophet's conception seems to be that the dwellers to the east who lived round about Israel would be the first to learn of the fulfillment of the prophecies and should therefore bring the message to the more distant dwellers on the isles in the west.

13 יְהוָה כַּגִּבּוֹר יֵצֵא כְּאִישׁ מִלְחָמוֹת יָעִיר קִנְאָה
יָרִיעַ אַף־יַצְרִיחַ עַל־אֹיְבָיו יִתְגַּבָּר:

This entire strophe and the preceding one also will be wholly misunderstood if one takes verse 13 and the statements in the following half-strophe to be the only basis for the prophet's exhortation to sing praises to the Lord. Certainly these verses contain reasons for praise, but they must not be separated from the promise in verses 1-7, the promise to send the Servant of the Lord for the deliverance of the Jews and the enlightenment of the gentiles. It is this work of redemption that inspires the prophet to rejoice inwardly and to exhort the gentiles to sing a song of praise. In verses 13ff he first sets forth in what way and with what accompanying events the redemption of the Jews and the enlightenment of the gentiles will be accomplished, namely, with a fearful judgment upon the enemies. In verse 16 the work of salvation described in the first strophe again finds expression. Verses 13ff contain an added reason for the song of praise. It is that the Lord will come forth *like a hero* for the redemption and salvation of His own. The next clause adds to the qualities of the Hero by naming Him *'ish milḥāmōth*, a battle-hero, one skilled in warfare and furnished with weapons for the destruction of the enemies. As a hero He stirs up His rage (*yā'ir qin'āh*), or, to use an even more anthropomorphic term, stirs up the *furor martialis*, the fury of battle, in His own breast, the kind of fury a soldier feels when he sees the enemy advancing and his own comrades falling beside him. The Lord goads His own heart to grim wrath. The whole picture is, of course, starkly anthropomorphic. *herīa'* and *hitsrīaḥ* (both Hiphil) are *termini technici* for the utterance of a piercing battle cry. The final clause, *'al 'oyebhāyw yithgabbār*, briefly describes His victory and triumph. Literally, against His enemies will He boast as victor. The picture is of a victor standing proudly over his fallen enemies. The climactic arrangement of thoughts should be noted.

Second Half: verses 14-17:

14   *Long have I kept silence,*
     Was quiet and restrained Myself;
     But like a woman in travail
     I will cry out, will gasp, and pant together.
15   *I will lay waste the hills and mountains*
     And dry up all their greenness;
     I will change the streams into dry places,
     And the pools of water will I dry up.

16   *But the blind will I lead in a way they have not known,*
    Over paths they never knew will I guide them;
    The darkness will I change to light before them,
    And the rough ways make into smooth paths.
    These are things I will do and will not leave undone.

17   *Rejected, altogether put to shame, shall all those be*
    who worship idols,
    Who say to molten images: You are our gods!

14 הֶחֱשֵׁ֙יתִי֙ מֵֽעוֹלָ֔ם   אַחֲרִ֖ישׁ אֶתְאַפָּ֑ק
כַּיּֽוֹלֵדָ֣ה אֶפְעֶ֔ה   אֶשֹּׁ֥ם וְאֶשְׁאַ֖ף יָֽחַד׃

In verses 10-13 the prophet was the speaker; in verse 14 it is the Lord who again speaks. The two halves of the strophe are like a call and its echo. The second half develops what the prophet had briefly announced in verse 13, and *confirms* the promise contained in verses 1-9 and the exhortation to praise in verses 10-13. Note the closing words in verse 16. A prose writer would have started out with these words in order to make the situation clear at once. But a dramatic poet does not immediately explain a situation; he trusts that the hearer or reader will gain understanding from the impression that the speakers make on him.

The second half of the strophe has no external connecting link with the first half. Every verse is constructed with consummate art. In the very first verse the two parts of the sentence are in sharp contrast with each other and all the clauses steadily ascend to a climax.

heheshāh (Hiphil of *hāshāh*) means to be inactive; *heherīsh*, (cf. 41:1), to be quietly active; *hith'appēq*, to restrain oneself forcibly. *mē'olām*, grammatically connected with the first verb only, really modifies all three verbs. It does not in this instance denote an endless duration of time, but merely a long time. On the other hand, to assume that a definite historical period is meant does not give credit to the poetry of the passage. God's infinite patience toward His enemies is meant. In Hebrew poetry the sharpest contrasts are often placed side by side without a connecting link. The Lord's silence, expressed by the perfect *heheshethī* lies in the past, and the following imperfects also denote past time; but the imperfects in the second half of verse 14 bring the action into the present — but now I will, etc. The Lord illustrates His change in attitude with the picture of a *yōledhāh*, a woman in travail. The three verbs expressing heavy breathing describe the breathing of a woman writhing in pain and fear while giving birth to a child. Delitzsch is

196

mistaken when he seeks to determine the different degrees of pain expressed by these verbs, for there is no language in the world that has technical terms to express the degrees of labored breathing of a woman in labor. The verbs work up to a climax, nothing more. The first two, *pā'ah* and *nāsham*, occur only in this passage and are imitative of the sound of heavy breathing. *shā'aph* is more common and denotes quick, sharp breathing. The fact that the meaning of this last word is well established and that *nāsham* has a harsher imitative sound than *pā'ah* indicates that a climax was intended. That ought to be expressed in the translation. We used cry out, gasp, and pant to express it. One arrangement in German is: *keuchen, schnauben, schnaufen*; another, *schreien, aechzen, schnaufen*. Cheyne has groan, pant, gasp. Anyone who thinks he can improve on these efforts is welcome to try. Luther missed the climax.

15 אַחֲרִיב הָרִים וּגְבָעוֹת וְכָל־עֶשְׂבָּם אוֹבִישׁ
וְשַׂמְתִּי נְהָרוֹת לָאִיִּים וַאֲגַמִּים אוֹבִישׁ׃

Verses 13 and 14 described the wrath of the Lord in terms of His angry demeanor; verse 15 tells how He puts His anger into effect. Surprisingly, His anger is not directed against His enemies but is revealed in His destruction of nature. The Lord will make waste the hills and mountains, will dry up the streams and the seas. Here we have a counterpart to 41:18f. There the Lord promises to transform the desert into a paradise, here He makes a waste of the fruitful earth. This is, of course, a poet's figurative language. Chapter 41 depicted Israel's homeland and its homeward journey; here Babylon, the seat of the enemy, is described. There the deliverance of God's people was involved, here the destruction of the Babylonians. The description is purposely not given in precise terms. Here the Lord threatens to visit Babylon with the same judgment that chapter 63 describes as befalling Edom. It is the destined Day of Judgment, which, according to 13:6-9, comes "cruel both with wrath and fierce anger, to lay the land desolate: and He shall destroy the sinners thereof out of it." According to chapter 3:13f and chapter 34, this is not merely a judgment against Babylon and Edom, but the Lord's great Day of Judgment which all the prophets, beginning with Joel, describe as "the Day of the Lord," when the Lord will judge the whole world and destroy it, while delivering His own people from all evil and leading them into His heavenly kingdom. The last chapters of Isaiah's prophecy especially refer to that consummation. The destruction of Babylon

197

is only a brief act in this drama which is being continuously enacted in the world upon those nations that have become incurably hostile to the Gospel and the church. It began with the Deluge and will close with the tremendous finale of the Day of Judgment. Delitzsch errs badly here when he takes the changing of streams into islands and the drying up of the canals to be an act of grace, as though this referred to turning the streams and swamps into dry land in order to remove all obstacles from the path of God's people as they journey homeward from Babylon. That interpretation is weak, because the streams and canals of Babylon in fact were no obstacle to Israel's return; and, besides, such an act of gracious assistance would hardly require such angry warlike breathing on the part of the Lord. Both clauses speak of the destroying judgment of the Lord.

As for the details, lexicographers offer two original meanings for *hārēbh:* to be dry, and to be broken into pieces. Both original meanings then develop the meaning of "to be laid waste." The meaning of "to be dry" is almost certainly the one intended here, because that meaning is repeated in the two identical predicates, *'ōbhīsh* and *'ōbhīsh.* The Lord will carry out His destruction of the hills and mountains by fire, which shall wither all green things (*'esbām*) and dry up the rivers and the seas. Unlike the Hebrew, we employ the definite article here in order to indicate that the Lord is referring to the Day of Judgment and at the same time also to all of Babylon, so that the streams are not streams in general, but *the* streams of Babylon. In prophecy, judgment always denotes total judgment, although in executing the judgment in a specific case the judgment may be tempered by mercy and be only partial destruction. We have rendered *'iyyīm* with "dry places," not because those who manipulate this text replace *'iyyīm* with *tsīyyōth,* but because this rendering is required by the context.

16 וְהוֹלַכְתִּי עִוְרִים בְּדֶרֶךְ לֹא יָדָעוּ בִּנְתִיבוֹת לֹא־יָדְעוּ אַדְרִיכֵם

אָשִׂים מַחְשָׁךְ לִפְנֵיהֶם לָאוֹר וּמַעֲקַשִּׁים לְמִישׁוֹר אֵלֶּה הַדְּבָרִים עֲשִׂיתִם וְלֹא עֲזַבְתִּים:

The Lord now turns to address His own elect. "The day of Jehovah has two sides, a dark and a bright; the stern work of retribution being over, Jehovah's Servant will step forward, and assume His delightful office of winning souls." Cheyne, *The*

Prophecies of Isaiah. — Clearly, the Lord is speaking of His labors for the salvation of His people. The only question is, in what sense His chosen ones are called blind. In verse 7 the blind eyes were mentioned as the object of the Servant's work of enlightenment. Verses 18-25 speak of the incurably blind and hardened servant. In 43:8 the blind people had received sight. The sinful blindness of the watchmen is described in 56:10f. The clearest reference is 50:9ff, where the blindness of the people that are to be saved is described as an unhappy, helpless, and hopeless condition brought on through their own fault by persistent disobedience and refusal to believe God's promises. Because of their disobedience and unbelief the people are unable to find a way out of their hopeless situation. That is what *'iwwēr* denotes. That also describes the condition of that portion of the people that the Lord had preserved as a remnant. They are no better than the rest of the *massa perdita.*

The promises in 29:18ff; 32:15ff; 35:4ff; 42:7 are to be fulfilled when the Lord leads the blind unharmed and safe over ways that their eyes had never seen. The God-fearing blind are meant. If the text critics had had some understanding of the situation and some sense for the poet's imaginative use of language, they would not have so ruthlessly stricken the two *lō' yādheʿu* as meaningless. The monotony of repetition is sufficiently broken by the pausal form of the first of the verbs, and the repetition brings the thought sharply to a point. What with the complete destruction carried out by a Jehovah panting with fury (thus the poet pictures the Lord), with hills and mountains reduced to rubble (so the prophet views the destruction), even seeing persons would not be able to find a way of deliverance. But the Lord finds roads and paths to rescue even the blind who see no possible path. *yādhaʿ* still contains a hint of its original meaning, ἰδεῖν , *videre*, to see. The whole verse is a figurative, poetic description of the actual rescue of *completely helpless people out of the seemingly inescapable woe of the judgment* pronounced upon the enemies of the Lord. The following clauses, "the darkness will I change to light before them," so that they see even without eyes, and "the rough ways make into smooth paths," are two more pictures depicting the *certain deliverance of the helpless elect*. Critics have deleted the final clause, "these are the things, etc.," as a prosaic and poorly constructed verse, but compare our remarks on verse 14 at the end of the first paragraph. The perfects *'asîthim* and *'azabhtîm* are prophetic perfects. The suffixes do not refer to persons, as Luther

199

supposed, but to *debhārīm*. *'asher* must be supplied after *debhārīm*.

נָסֹגוּ אָחוֹר יֵבֹשׁוּ בֹשֶׁת הַבֹּטְחִים בַּפָּסֶל ‎17

הָאֹמְרִים לְמַסֵּכָה אַתֶּם אֱלֹהֵינוּ:

Verse 17 contrasts the happy lot of the God-fearing blind with the downfall of the idol worshipers. The predicates are placed at the head for emphasis. *'ahōr*, modifying the Niphal *nāsōghū*, and *bōsheth*, an adverbial accusative modifying *yēbhōshū*, are pleonastic additions that lend emphasis to the verbs. The first is physical: tumbling backwards; the second, ethical: completely put to shame. The *bōtehīm bappesel* are the subject of the verbs, those who trust in images. The concluding clause, beginning with *'omerīm*, is a concrete paraphrase of the first part of the sentence.

Résumé of verses 10-17: In verses 10-13 the prophet calls upon the heathen world to sing a song of praise for the promise of the sending of the Servant of the Lord to save Jews and gentiles, a promise that is already as good as fulfilled. An added reason for this song is that God, while carrying out His work of salvation, like a Hero in battle, will at the same time destroy His enemies. Verses 14-17 take up this thought, and the Lord speaks, breathing fury and proclaiming execution of the judgment that will lay waste all the earth, but spare the helpless, God-fearing elect, while the idol worshipers perish.

Third Strophe: verses 18-25: *Israel after the flesh as the blind servant of the Lord, afflicted by Him, but to no avail.*

Verse 18 is introductory. The strophe is divided into two parts, verses 19-22 and 23-25, each part beginning with the interrogative *mī.* The first part describes the servant, the second sets forth the reason for his unhappy doom.

First Half: verses 18-22:

18 *Hear, you deaf, and you blind, look up and see!*
19 *Who is still blind, if not My servant,*
  And deaf, like My herald whom I send;
  Who is blind like My trusted one,
  And so blind as the Lord's servant!
20 *Having seen much — yet nothing have you kept!*
  With opened ears — and yet nothing understood!
21 *It pleased the Lord for the sake of His righteousness:*
  He made His instruction great; He made it glorious.

22   *And still it is a wasted and plundered people,*
      All of them fettered together in caves,
      Hidden away in prison houses,
      They have become a prey, and there is none to help,
      A spoil, and there is none to say: Give back!

18 הַחֵרְשִׁים שְׁמָעוּ   וְהַעִוְרִים הַבִּיטוּ לִרְאוֹת:

Isaiah is fond of the dramatic address. Cf. 1:2; 8:9; 29:1; 33:1;
34:1, and most of the chapters in Part II. As a rule the address also
contains the theme of the section that follows. Here the Lord's
purpose is to reprove the spiritual insensibility of the people that
He had once chosen to be His Servant. Therefore He addresses
them as blind and deaf. These two characteristics are repeated
again and again in the strophe, either in the same terms or in
paraphrase. The deaf are directed to open their ears to what the
Lord is about to say, and the blind to turn their eyes to see what
the Lord has to show them. They should become aware of their
blindness and deafness. That is what the Lord charges them with,
and that is now described as total obduracy. With that charge the
prophet calls to mind chapter 6:9ff and the verdict of rejection pronounced against the incurably hardened people in chapters 1-5
and following. It is certain that here only Israel after the flesh is
meant by the term servant of the Lord. This strophe does not even
hint at a possible improvement or rescue. It is purely a lament for
a lost people that has irrecoverably forfeited its calling as servant
of the Lord. Consequently, it is a melancholy counterpart to
strophes 1 and 2, in which the true Servant of the Lord has
replaced the ruined servant and is hailed as the effective Bringer
of salvation to the remnant of the people and to the gentiles. The
first discourse in this chapter is a new proclamation of redemption; the second is a hymn of victory; this third and last section is a
lament.

19 מִי עִוֵּר כִּי אִם־עַבְדִּי   וְחֵרֵשׁ כְּמַלְאָכִי אֶשְׁלָח
   מִי עִוֵּר כִּמְשֻׁלָּם   וְעִוֵּר כְּעֶבֶד יְהוָה:

When *kī 'im* follows *mī,* it has the same meaning as after a negative — except, if not, unless. Cf. Genesis 28:17; 39:9. Who is blind,
if not My servant? If he cannot be called blind, then no one can
ever be so called. Of all the blind, he is most blind. This is the
superlative in the comparison. The *we* with *ḥerēsh* repeats the *mī*
in the usual form of comparison: Who is so deaf as My messenger
whom I send? The verb *'eshlāḥ* does not refer to a time; it serves

201

only to emphasize *mal'ākh* in order to bring out the anomaly in the designation of a deaf herald. The picture is, of course, of a herald with a message that is to be spoken, who must first receive the message from the mouth of the Lord and must therefore have a discerning ear if he is to relay the message effectively. Thus the true Servant of the Lord says of Himself (50:5): "The Lord God has opened My ear, etc." See also Psalm 40:7(6); Hebrews 10:5. — This messenger, this servant, who is to be sent out to deliver a message is stone-deaf, hears and perceives nothing at all of what the Lord imparts to him as a message to the gentiles. The next sentence refers again to the servant's blindness. *mī 'iwwēr* occurs three times, whereas *ḥērēsh* occurs only once. Blindness is the chief element in the servant's inadequacy. He is called both *meshullām* and *'ebhedh*. *meshullām* is a Pual participle of *shālēm*, to be sound, unimpaired. Since this verb covers a very wide range of meanings, there is much dispute about the meaning of *meshullām*. Since the word is here used as a synonym of *mal'ākh* and *'ebhedh*, it very likely has the same meaning as *shōlemī*, my friend, Psalm 7:5(4). Cheyne and those who follow him are clearly in error: "As the surrendered one — one might almost say, 'as the Moslem,' for the prophet's word is closely akin to the Arabic muslim (Moslem), i.e., he that devotes or submits himself (to God)." That translation would require *moshlām*, a Hophal participle. "The trusted one," a more recent translation, has much more justification. To this servant, chosen from all the nations of the world, God had revealed His inmost heart and entrusted His revelation concerning himself and the rest of the world, and had called him to preach His Word to the gentiles. *'ebhedh* refers to his office as preacher, *meshullām* to the trust reposed in him. Verse 20 also supports this meaning. Cf. also Romans 3:2; 9:4f. Since Israel is the Lord's trusted messenger and servant in a very special sense, his blindness is such an anomaly that the Lord again and again shows His displeasure. Verse 20 shows how the servant's blindness and deafness become manifest.

20 רָאִׄית רַבּוֹת וְלֹא תִשְׁמֹר פָּקוֹחַ אָזְנַיִם וְלֹא יִשְׁמָע:

The Masoretes were uncertain about the first word in verse 20. The *Kethibh* read *rā'ūthā*, thou hast seen. But because of the following *pāqōaḥ* (infin. absolute), they suggested the *Qeri rā'ōth* (also inf. abs.), thus making the two verbs similar in form. Since the infinitive absolute can substitute for any other verb form (Gr. 113,f, p.340), the sense remains the same, whichever form is chosen, except that the infinitive emphasizes the action, while the finite verb draws attention to the person. The Masoretic suggestion is perhaps justified.* We use a similar construction in English and could omit mention of the person in *thishmōr* and *yishmā'* and say: Seeing much, observing nothing; open ears and nothing heard! *'oznayim* is the accusative object of *paqōaḥ, rabbōth* is the object of *ra'ōth.* The shift from second person in *thishmōr* to third person in *yishma'* is poetic and is common in Isaiah. The Lord is saying that ever since Israel's deliverance out of Egyptian slavery the people had seen and experienced many great deeds and wonders, but had kept none of them in their memory, that is, did not appreciate them as works of God, but rather despised them. With open ears Israel again and again heard Moses and the prophets proclaim the words of God with thunderous clarity, but they did not take anything to heart, did not perceive anything spiritually — that is the meaning of *shāma'* here. Blind and deaf! And that in spite of what follows in verse 21.

יְהוָה חָפֵץ לְמַעַן צִדְקוֹ יַגְדִּיל תּוֹרָה וְיַאְדִּיר : ²¹

Luther's translation of this line confuses the sense. It is really quite simple: It pleased the Lord (historical perfect) because of His *tsedheq.* He exalted instruction, He made it glorious. Luther's *noch* in the sense of *dennoch* does not express the connection correctly. Luther has: "Even though they heard nothing, still the Lord is pleased to make great, etc." That should be reversed: "Even though it pleased the Lord to make His instruction great and glorious, yet they heard and saw nothing." *tsedheq* here, as in 41:10 and 42:6 is the Lord's will to save, His faithfulness to His covenant of salvation, His grace toward Israel. The Lord's *tsedheq* focuses attention on Israel's blindness and deafness. God's full and glorious revelation was purest grace, and still His trusted servant closed eyes, ears, and heart against it. Compare the later emphasis on "not for your sake, but for My own sake," 43:22ff; 48:8,9,11.

One would have expected *yaghdīl* and *ya'dīr* to be subordinated to *ḥāphets* by means of *le* and the infinitive, instead of being co-ordinated, but see Gr. 120,2,d,(a),p. 386. We use the same kind of construction in English. We can say: "I am willing and will go," instead of "I am willing to go." Thus here: "It pleased the Lord, He made great and glorious," instead of "It pleased the Lord to make

---

*The Dead Sea Scrolls read *ra'īthāh.*

203

great and glorious." *tōrāh* here and in many other passages, such as those in Psalm 119, does not mean the *Law* as we usually understand the word, but is a comprehensive expression for teaching, doctrine, instruction, revelation. It corresponds exactly to our "Word of God." The etymology also points to that meaning: *yārāh*, to throw; Hiphil, *horah*, to indicate with the hand or the finger, to show, teach, instruct. As a proper name for the five Books of Moses, this is the primary meaning of *tōrāh*. The Old Testament conception of the Word was brought into the New Testament in the form of νόμος , the Law. It should be noted that not any revelation in general is meant, but the revelation given through Moses, which ever since his time was written down and preserved. This revelation is called *great* because it governed Israel's whole life; it is *glorious*, because it is God's own Word, and promises Israel both temporal and eternal happiness. Cf. Deuteronomy 33:29; Psalm 147:19.

22 וְהוּא֙ עַם־בָּז֣וּז וְשָׁס֔וּי

הָפֵ֤חַ בַּחוּרִים֙ כֻּלָּ֔ם וּבְבָתֵּ֥י כְלָאִ֖ים הׇחְבָּ֑אוּ

הָי֣וּ לָבַ֗ז וְאֵ֣ין מַצִּ֔יל מְשִׁסָּ֖ה וְאֵין־אֹמֵ֥ר הָשַֽׁב׃

*wehū'*refers to the servant who saw and heard so much and was the object of so much grace. The particle *we* has the force of *nevertheless, in spite of all.* (Gr. 141,e,p.453 and 154, Note on *Waw concomitantiae,* p.484.) The sense is: Although the Lord has done everything to make this servant reliable and to raise him up, he lies there, quite contrary to what might be expected, despoiled and plundered. *hāpheaḥ* is not the Hiphil inf. abs. of *pūaḥ*, to blow, but of the denominative *pāḥah* (*paḥ*, a net), to catch in a net, to hold secure. This is the only occurrence of the verb. *baḥurīm* may well have the meaning of young men, or young soldiers (9:16(17); 31:8; 40:30): The young men are altogether held as prisoners, and in houses of the prisons (*battēy kelā'īm*, both plural) they are kept hidden (Hophal perfect). Usually, however, *ba* is understood as the prefix *be* with the article, and *ḥūrīm* as the plural of *ḥūr*, a hole or cave — they are altogether held bound in caves. The only objection to this is the presence of the article, and some commentators drop the article and read *beḥūrīm*. But the article could be understood as generic, and that would remove this objection. The simplest solution is to read *ḥūrīm* with *be* (in caves), because then *'am* alone is the subject and one is not forced to try to explain why the prophet introduces young soldiers into the picture to describe the miserable situation of the people who ought to be acting as God's servants. But if one prefers to introduce young soldiers into the picture, one is free to do so. The subject of *hāyū* in the next clause is again the people. The nouns (*baz*, plunder, and *meshissāh*, booty) repeat the thoughts expressed by the predicates in the first clause. *ḥashabh* is a pausal form for *ḥashēbh* (Gr. 29,q,p.98). It is a Hiphil imperative — Let return, give back! This entire description is no more to be taken literally than are 41:18f; 42:14f, and similar passages. This is drastic, concrete, poetic language picturing the imprisonment and helplessness of the people. This people, who ought to be enjoying the perfect freedom of the Lord's trusted messenger to the gentiles, are helpless prisoners of the gentiles. This unnatural situation ought to have the effect of opening their eyes. The next section carries out that thought.

Second Half: verses 23-25:

23 *Who among you will give ear to this,*
    Take it to heart and ponder it?
24 *Who delivered Jacob to be plundered and Israel to the*
        spoilers?
    Was it not the Lord, He against whom we have sinned?
    In whose ways they would not walk,
    And to whose instruction they would not hearken?
25 *Therefore He poured out upon him wrath, the heat of His*
        anger, and the fury of war,
    Which raged round about him and he knew it not,
    Which set him ablaze, yet he took it not to heart.

23 מִי בָכֶם יַאֲזִין זֹאת יַקְשֵׁב וְיִשְׁמַע לְאָחוֹר:

wehū' (verse 22) points backward; *zō'th* points forward and therefore refers to verses 24 and 25 (Gr. 136,a, Note 1,p.442). Verses 24 and 25 repeat what was said in verse 22 about Israel's condition, adding only a statement of the causes of Israel's unnatural doom. The question does not require an answer, but is an exclamation that expresses a desire that is never fulfilled (Gr. 151,1,p.476). Compare Absalom's cry: Oh, that I were made a judge in the land, 2 Samuel 15:4. So here too: Oh, that someone among you, etc. — The verbs work up to a climax: *yaqshībh* is stronger than *ya'azīn*, and *yishma' le'āḥōr* stronger than either. Delitzsch translates *yishma' le'āḥōr* with "hear afar off." Cheyne has "and be obedient for the time to come." The Rainbow Bible has "and hear for the time to come." Budde also chose "for the time to come," and Kautzsch has "will consider it in the future." These

205

are very loose translations. It is true that *le'aḥōr* can mean "in the time to come" (41:23); but to translate *shāma' le'aḥōr* "to hear, or listen in the future" makes sense only if one goes along with Cheyne and translates "be obedient in the future." But that translation makes *zō'th* and what follows in verses 24 and 25 the object of *ya'azīn* alone and assumes that the other two verbs with *le'aḥōr* are a mere parenthesis: "Who among you will give ear to what I now say about Israel's sad lot and later be observant and obedient?" Such a parenthesis between the verb *ya'azīn* and its object, verses 24 and 25, would be extremely awkward for such a master of language as the poet Isaiah. One must assume that verses 24 and 25, which explain *zō'th*, are the object of all three verbs, particularly since they are arranged in the form of a climax. In that case, of course, *le'aḥōr* must mean something other than "in the future, later, for the future." It is simply the adverbial *aḥōr*, which occurs frequently (cf. verse 17); and the action is purely physical — listen to the rear, turn the head backward and listen, listen with care to what is being called after you. This physical interpretation of the phrase is the most natural one, and we are forced to abide with it until usage compels a better understanding of it. But that is not likely, since this is the only occurrence of *shāma' le'aḥōr*. If one takes the phrase in its moral sense of weighing mentally, considering thoughtfully, then the three verbs form a perfect climax, and verses 24 and 25 remain the object of all three verbs, as they must.

$$^{24}\text{ מִי־נָתַן לִמְשׁוֹסָה יַעֲקֹב וְיִשְׂרָאֵל לְבֹזְזִים}$$
$$\text{הֲלוֹא יְהוָה זוּ חָטָאנוּ לוֹ}$$
$$\text{וְלֹא־אָבוּ בִדְרָכָיו הָלוֹךְ וְלֹא שָׁמְעוּ בְּתוֹרָתוֹ :}$$

This is what the blind and fettered people are to hear, to take to heart and ponder carefully. How did Israel fall into a condition so contrary to their calling? Who brought this on them and why? The answer is that this is the Lord's doing because of Israel's obdurate wickedness, which aroused God's wrath and brought down His judgment upon the people and so hardened them that they did not even recognize it as a judgment. This is the meaning of verses 24 and 25.

The Kethib *meshussāh* has been corrected by the Qeri *meshissāh* from *shāsas* or *shāsāh*, to plunder (cf. verse 22). *zū* is a poetic variant of *zeh*, usually used as an alternate for the relative *'asher*, like our English *that* for *which*. It is connected with *lō* — against whom we have sinned. With the first person plural the prophet humbly includes himself with the people. In the next clauses he again employs the third person (Gr. 144,p,p.462). — *welo' 'abhu* in Hebrew is much stronger than "they would not." *'abhah* means "to have a strong desire" and is usually coupled with a negative: "It was not their desire," that is, they resisted, they refused. *halokh* is infinitive absolute, "refused walking." The final clause, *welo' shame'u* is by its position included in the resistance expressed by *welo' 'abhu.* These two final clauses develop the *zu hata'nu lo* clause; and the three clauses, separated by the accents Athnach and Zaqeph, correspond to the three verbs in verse 23.

וַיִּשְׁפֹּ֨ךְ עָלָ֤יו חֵמָה֙ אַפּ֔וֹ וֶעֱז֖וּז מִלְחָמָ֑ה ²⁵
וַתְּלַהֲטֵ֤הוּ מִסָּבִיב֙ וְלֹ֣א יָדָ֔ע וַתִּבְעַר־בּ֖וֹ וְלֹא־יָשִׂ֥ים עַל־
לֵֽב׃

Verse 25, connected with verse 24 by a *Waw* consecutive, sets forth the consequences of the stiff-necked refusal of Israel-Jacob — and so He poured out, etc. *hemah* is in the absolute state followed by *'appo* in apposition. Delitzsch supposed that this construction was used instead of the regular construct state in order to preserve the assonance of *hemah* and *milhamah*. But the prophet was more interested in the forcefulness of *hemah 'appo* than in similarity of sound. *'ezuz* is likewise an absolute followed by a word in apposition — war-fury. The terms *Jacob* and *Israel* are here the customary terms of endearment employed for the chosen people. Why should the Lord have so completely rejected His once beloved and spiritual people? The concluding clauses are connected with the first clause by a *Waw* consecutive. The subject of *telahatehu* and *tibh'ar* is *'ezuz milhamah*, although these verbs might also be treated as having an impersonal subject (Gr. 144,b,p.459): "And war raged about him, but he knew it not; and it set him ablaze, but he took it not to heart." What they did not recognize and take to heart is stated in *telahatehu* and *tibh'ar bo.* They saw the flame and fire and the war-fury of the Lord, but even this scourge did not make them see the light.

Resume of verses 18-25: The servant of the Lord is stone-blind and stone-deaf in spite of everything his eyes have seen and his ears heard (verses 19 and 20). In spite of the bountiful and glorious instruction that has so graciously been bestowed, he lies plundered, fettered in hopeless imprisonment (verses 21 and 22). Oh, that they might see and consider that the Lord delivered them to the plunderers because of their stiff-necked disobedience, and that He poured out His anger and the fury of war upon them. But they regarded it not (verses 23-25).

The connection between the three strophes of chapter 42: The true Servant of the Lord will bring salvation to Jews and gentiles through His Gospel. For that, all the world should praise the Lord. The Lord in His power will at the same time come to judgment, to lead the poor blind to safety, but to put the idol worshipers to shame. Israel, however, because of its wanton blindness has forfeited its calling as the servant of the Lord and been rejected.

The theme of the chapter: The glory of the Lord as it is evidenced in the sending and upholding of His true Servant for the deliverance of gentiles and Jews, in the preservation of the God-fearing and the rejection of the wicked in the Last Judgment, and in the judgment upon the reprobate servant. The point of view is clearly expressed in verses 8-12.

Chapter 40: *The glory of the Lord will be revealed in the deliverance of His people.* His unequaled preeminence above all human wisdom and the power of nations, above all idols and princes, and His power over the heavens are the guarantee for the promised deliverance.

Chapter 41: *The preeminence of the Lord over the gentiles and their idols is evidenced by His sending of Cyrus,* by delivering the people, giving them the victory, restoring them, and especially by having proclaimed beforehand that all these things would come to pass.

Chapter 42: *The glorification of the Lord through the sending and upholding of His true Servant* to deliver both Jews and gentiles by destruction of the earth, salvation of the God-fearing, rejection of the wicked, and the judgment upon His reprobate servant Israel.

These thoughts are grouped under three principal themes: the glorification of the Lord, the deliverance of the God-fearing people, and the confounding of the enemies. The first of these is the principal theme. In these first three discourses the glory of the Lord is revealed as a glory of might and divine wisdom. In the next three the emphasis will be on the glory of His Grace. The formal theme of the first Triad of discourses is: *The glory of the power of the Lord is the guarantee for the deliverance of God's faithful people from all enemies.*

SECOND TRIAD
Chapters 43-45

The Majesty and Grace of the Lord
as Guarantee
for the Deliverance of Israel.

First Discourse: Chapter 43

The faithful love of Him who alone is true God delivers His people by grace alone.

This chapter is divided into four almost equal strophes. Verses 1-7: The faithful love of the Lord delivers, protects, and gathers His people. Verses 8-13: Even blind Israel and all the gentiles must bear witness that the Lord alone is the true God. Verses 14-20: By the fall of Babylon and the restoration of His people the Lord will show that He is Israel's Holy One and King. Verses 21-28: Israel's deliverance is not a matter of merit on the part of Israel, but due to God's grace alone.

First Strophe: verses 1-7: *The faithful love of the Lord delivers, protects, and gathers His people.*

1 *But now, thus says the Lord,*
  Who created you, O Jacob, and formed you, O Israel:
  Do not be afraid, for I redeem you,
  I call you by your name, you are Mine!
2 *When you go through waters, I am with you,*
  When through rivers, they shall not overwhelm you;
  When you go through fire, you shall not be scorched,
  Nor shall flame be kindled upon you.
3 *Because I, the Lord, your God —*
  I, the Holy One of Israel, am your Redeemer,
  I deliver Egypt as a ransom for you,
  Cush and Seba in your stead.

4   *Because you are precious in My eyes,*
    Because you are honored and I love you,
    I give up people in your stead,
    And nations instead of your life.
5   *Therefore do not fear, for I am with you;*
    From the East will I bring your seed
    And out of the West will I gather you;
6   *I will say to the North: Give up!*
    And to the South: Do not withhold them!
    Bring My sons from far away,
    And My daughters from the ends of the earth —
7   *Who call themselves by My name, all of them,*
    Whom I created to My honor,
    Whom I formed, yes, perfected.

וְעַתָּה כֹּה־אָמַר יְהוָה בֹּרַאֲךָ יַעֲקֹב וְיֹצֶרְךָ יִשְׂרָאֵל ¹
אַל־תִּירָא כִּי גְאַלְתִּיךָ קָרָאתִי בְשִׁמְךָ לִי־אָתָּה:

we'attāh is separated from the next word by a Rebia (which explains the Dagesh in *kōh*), as though the announcer were taking a
breath before going on. What follows is unexpected. The preceding
discourse ended with the tumult of storm and the violence of God's
judgment. "But now" — the discourse continues in a quiet, gentle,
winsome tone, full of assurances of love. The *we* before *'attāh* is
therefore adversative. Faithful Israel is being addressed. *kōh*
'āmar YHWH is the usual formula announcing a solemn
assurance; Jacob and Israel are the customary, affectionate
names for the faithful people. Every word and phrase breathes a
Father's tender love. *bora'akhā*, your Creator, and *yōtserkhā*, who
formed you, relate to Israel's history and recall how the Lord chose
and built up this people to be God's special people. The terms include all of God's wonderful dealings with His people. This is
therefore a comforting preamble. The words *'al tīrā'* introduce the
comforting assurance: "Be not afraid!" There follows a threefold
reason why they should not fear: For I redeem you; I call you by
name; you are Mine! — These are not historical perfects; they are
perfects that designate all times or no particular time, placing the
emphasis on timeless facts. They correspond to the participles in
the preamble. These three expressions describe the indestructible
relationship of love that once and for all has been established between the Lord and His people, and that necessarily determines
God's dealings with the true people of Israel and shapes their
destiny. The three expressions are extremely rich in content, each

differing from the others, and each more earnest and ardent than
the one before. "I redeem you" includes every act of the Lord for
the salvation of His people. "I call you by name" assures Israel of
the close relationship of friendship between the Lord and the people, indicated by the Lord's use of its name ('ōhēbh, 41:8;
meshullām, 42:19; Jacob, Israel, Abraham's Seed, My servant,
etc.). "You are Mine" states that Israel is the Lord's exclusive
possession, a condition that resulted from the Lord's love, so that
He now looks upon Israel as His greatest treasure and spares no
sacrifice for it.

2 כִּי־תַעֲבֹר בַּמַּיִם אִתְּךָ־אָנִי וּבַנְּהָרוֹת לֹא יִשְׁטְפוּךָ

כִּי־תֵלֵךְ בְּמוֹ־אֵשׁ לֹא תִכָּוֶה וְלֶהָבָה לֹא תִבְעַר־בָּךְ:

The second verse sets forth what this redemption, expressed by
ge'altīkhā, means for Israel. If they must go through fire or water,
through streams or flames, nothing shall harm them, for "I am
with you," namely, as your gō'ēl. No waters shall overwhelm, no
flame consume them. The mention of water and streams should
not immediately suggest that the speaker has in mind a crossing
of the Euphrates. If that were meant, then a physical burning
would also be implied by the mention of fire. Fire and water are
here merely types of great dangers. Cf. Psalm 66:12. Regarding
the poetic form bemō for be see Gr. 103, k, p. 303.

3 כִּי אֲנִי יְהוָה אֱלֹהֶיךָ קְדוֹשׁ יִשְׂרָאֵל מוֹשִׁיעֶךָ

נָתַתִּי כָפְרְךָ מִצְרַיִם כּוּשׁ וּסְבָא תַּחְתֶּיךָ:

The third verse corresponds to the qārā'thī bheshimkhā in verse
1. There the Lord promises to call Israel by its own name as a sign
of an unbreakable bond of intimacy; here He offers Israel His own
names as guarantee of His friendship: The Lord your God, the
Holy One of Israel, your Savior. For an explanation of these
names, see the comments on 40:25 and 41:14, 20, 27. God assumed
these terms as names for Himself in His dealings with Israel. The
first, "the Lord your God," is ancient, having already been
revealed to Moses (Exod. 3:14f; 6:3), and commonly used there-
after, as in Exodus 20:2, etc. "The Holy One of Israel" occurs in the
time of David (Ps. 78:41, Asaph; 89:19(18), Ethan; cf. Job 6:10).
"Israel's Redeemer" also goes back to the time of David (1 Sam.
14:39 — Saul!). Isaiah was the one particularly who popularized
these proper names of God in Israel, so that not only Hosea and
Habakkuk, but also Jeremiah, Ezekiel, and the New Testament

employ them (Acts 3:14; Rev. 3:7). It is worthy of note that these names correspond in reverse order to the three statements in the final clause of verse 1: "The Lord your God" to "You are Mine"; "The Holy One of Israel" to "I call you by your name"; "Your Redeemer" to "I redeem you." The name of God which most clearly corresponds to the proper names of God's people, Jacob and Israel, is "The Holy One of Israel." Jacob is God's Israel, that is, God's holy people, loved and treasured by Him above all things; and the Lord is the Holy One of Israel, to be revered and loved by Israel above all things. To the significance of these three names and to the development of the meaning of *mōshī'ekhā,* your Savior, there is now added as a sequel the concrete promise: I give (*nāthat-tī,* not a historical perfect, but a perfect referring to present or future time) Egypt as a ransom for you, Cush and Seba in your stead. In Proverbs 21:18 the wicked is given as a ransom for the righteous. Cf. also Proverbs 11:8. *kōpher,* from *kāphar,* to cover up, atone for, redeem, is that with which a sin is covered up before the eyes of someone, or that with which a prisoner's freedom is purchased, the *pretium redemptionis,* the λύτρον, ἀντίλυτρον of the New Testament. For releasing Israel Cyrus is to receive Egypt, Cush, and Seba as ransom. Like the former inhabitants of Canaan, these lands are ripe for judgment, because they abused Israel, not only in her early history but later, in fact, to the very end, again and again dealt falsely with her, were to her no more than a "staff made of reed," Ezekiel 29:6, 7. Cf. Isaiah 36:6, and as also referring to this matter, Isaiah 19 and Ezekiel, chapters 29 - 32. This promise was fulfilled under Cambyses. *mitsrayim* is Lower Egypt; Cush is Ethiopia, modern Nubia; Seba is the northeastern part of Nubia, called Meroe by Diodorus Siculus, Strabo, and Josephus; called Sennar in more recent times.

מֵאֲשֶׁר יָקַרְתָּ בְעֵינַי נִכְבַּדְתָּ וַאֲנִי אֲהַבְתִּיךָ 4
וְאֶתֵּן אָדָם תַּחְתֶּיךָ וּלְאֻמִּים תַּחַת נַפְשֶׁךָ:

mē'asher in this instance is causal, like *ya'an 'asher* or *'eqebh 'asher,* Gr. 158, b, p. 492. It can be translated as "since." The concluding clause is introduced by *we,* prefixed to *'ettēn:* "Therefore do I give." *yāqartā,* "you are precious," is made more emphatic by the Niphal *nikhbadhtā,* "you are highly prized." *wa'anī 'ahabhtīkhā,* "and I love you," brings it to its climax. This sentence develops the phrase, "You are Mine," in verse 1. The second half of the sentence repeats in general terms the second half of verse 3.

'adhām is collective. *taḥteykhā* echoes *kophrekhā; le'ummīm* refers to *mitsrayim, kūsh,* and *sebhā'.* Since verse 4 is a repetition, with a different shading, of verse 3; and verses 5-7 correspond to verses 2 and 1, the poet has actually constructed a chiasmus on a large scale, one not so clear as is the case with simple clauses, but one still clearly recognizable.

אַל־תִּירָא כִּי אִתְּךָ־אָנִי ⁵

מִמִּזְרָח אָבִיא זַרְעֶךָ וּמִמַּעֲרָב אֲקַבְּצֶךָ׃

'al tīrā' is a repetition of the *'al tīrā'* in verse 1; *'ittekhā 'anī* also occurs in verse 2. The section from the second half of verse 5 through verse 7 contains the Lord's promise to gather the scattered children of His people together from all quarters of the earth. Those who voluntarily, for business or other reasons, had separated themselves from the people and lived among the gentiles can scarcely be meant here. Israel did not look upon their absence as a loss. Prisoners of war are meant who, according to the universal custom of the time, had been dragged into exile by conquering foes. The prophet sees all of the future in a single composite picture. He is conscious of Deuteronomy 28:64ff, but also Deuteronomy 30:3ff; and in accord with those prophecies he again and again prophesies the gathering together of the scattered people, cf. 11:11f; 27:13; 49:12, 22; 56:8; 66:20. Above all, he must have had in mind not only the deportation of northern Israel, which he had experienced, but also the impending Babylonian exile of Judah and the dispersion of the Jews in the time of the apostles. Still, there is no support here or in similar statements made by the other prophets for a universal conversion of the Jews, or even of a return of all Jews to Jerusalem and Palestine, in the final days of the New Testament age. In physical terms the poet is describing what in reality is to be fulfilled spiritually. He is speaking to the faithful in Israel of the coming of the spiritual kingdom of God. The coming of the kingdom will not restore all Jews and all gentiles, but only some of both, and yet, without exception, all of the true seed of God and Abraham, "the Israel of God," to the "city of God," to Abraham's bosom.

אֹמַר לַצָּפוֹן תֵּנִי וּלְתֵימָן אַל־תִּכְלָאִי ⁶

הָבִיאִי בָנַי מֵרָחוֹק וּבְנוֹתַי מִקְצֵה הָאָרֶץ׃

tēymān is not the section of Edom thus named, but is a common noun meaning "that which lies at the right hand" (from *yāmīn, yā-*

man), that is, the south, since it was customary to face the east when indicating direction. *'al tikhlā'ī,* "do not detain," is a negative way of expressing a strong positive: "set free willingly." There is no need to change *hābhi'ī* to the plural *hābhi'u,* because the form of the verb is influenced by the point of the compass last mentioned, although the sense certainly includes all quarters of the heavens. Cheyne assumes the earth to be addressed in *hābhi'ī,* but that is not necessary. Daughters are mentioned along with sons, not as "respectful mention of the female sex in Messianic descriptions" (Cheyne), but as indicating totality, as the next verse shows.

7 כֹּל הַנִּקְרָא בִשְׁמִי וְלִכְבוֹדִי בְּרָאתִיו יְצַרְתִּיו אַף־עֲשִׂיתִיו:

kōl hanniqrā' bishemī corresponds to *qārāthī bheshimkhā* of verse 1, all who are called with My name, that is, called by My name, or known by My name (Jehovah) as a mark of belonging to Me ("You are Mine"). Cf. *'al shēm,* Genesis 48:6 and the preposition *min (mē)* in Isaiah 48:2; also 44:5. *berā'thīw* is not said of physical creation, but is to be taken in the historical sense of God's election and guidance of Israel, as is indicated by the synonyms that follow: whom I formed, that is, whom I reared through the years with the greatest skill and care (cf. verses 1 and 2); yes, perfected, that is, shaped into that which Israel was to be. *'asīthīw* with *'aph* is an emphatic addition. *likhbhōdhī,* "to My honor," applies to each of the three predicates, cf. verse 21. Of the elect of the Lord, whom He has called, sanctified, and perfected in faith, there shall none be missing on the Last Day.

Résumé of verses 1-7: The faithful in Israel should not fear that they could ever be destroyed, for by the same love with which the Lord made Israel His own and by which He treasures them above all things, He will continue His faithful care of them, preserve them in every danger, consider no sacrifice too great for their redemption, and not lose a single soul of them.

Second Strophe: verses 8-13: *Even blind Israel and all the gentiles must bear witness that the Lord alone is the true God.*

8 *Bring forth the people that are blind and yet have eyes,*
   Who are deaf, although they have ears.
9 *Let all the gentiles gather together,*
   And the nations assemble themselves:
   Who is there among them who could foretell this?
   And earlier matters, let us hear them,

215

> Let them bring forward their witnesses that they may prove them
>   right,
> Who shall hear and say: It is true!
> 10 But you, says the Lord, are My witnesses,
>   My servant, whom I have chosen,
>   So that you might know, and believe, and acknowledge
>   That I am He; before Me was never God formed,
>   And after Me there shall be none.
> 11 I — I — I am the Lord, and beside Me there is no Savior.
> 12 I — I foretold and created salvation and made it known,
>   And there was no stranger among you,
>   And you are My witnesses, says the Lord, that I am God.
> 13 And from this time forward I am the same
>   And no one can deliver out of My hand;
>   I perform it, and who is there that will reverse it!

Like 41:1-7 and 21-29, this section treats of judicial proceedings, instituted by the Lord. He summons blind Israel (42:18-25) and all the gentiles to appear before Him, to determine whether He or another is true God. The criterion is to be the ability to proclaim future occurrences before the event. The Lord had just proclaimed in verses 1-7 the deliverance, preservation, and gathering of faithful Israel. That prediction furnishes the occasion for this summons before His tribunal. In the following strophe (verses 14-20), which is closely connected with this section (verses 8-13), the Lord foretells the fall of Babylon and the restoration of His chosen people. Referring to that prediction, He demands of the gentiles whether they are able to foretell such a thing ($\overline{zo}$'th), or whether they can name any past event that they had announced beforehand. Since the gentiles are unable to answer, the Lord turns to His people, who, although possessing eyes and ears, are blind and deaf. He does not ask them *whether,* etc., because as His chosen servant they had always been associated with Him and are in fact eye and ear witnesses of His sole and true Godhead, having themselves experienced His predictions and their fulfillment (verse 12). The force of the argument lies in the fact that the Lord can call as His witnesses a people admittedly blind and deaf spiritually, and possessing nothing more than physical sight and hearing. All the gentiles in the world are unable to produce a single instance of the prediction of a future event to prove the godhead of their idols; on the other hand, even the deaf and blind people of the Lord must bear witness to Jehovah's predictions and the fulfillment of His prophecies — therefore to His true Godhead.

8 הוֹצִיא עַם־עִוֵּר וְעֵינַיִם יֵשׁ וְחֵרְשִׁים וְאָזְנַיִם לָמוֹ:

hōtsī', like *hābhī'* (Jer. 17:18) is an imperative Hiphil, not a perfect. The pointing *hōtsī'*, instead of the regular *hōtse'* of the imperative, is influenced by the following a-vowel (cf. Gr. 74, Note 5,1,p.207). No particular person is addressed. The imperative is impersonal, like *naḥamū* in 40:1. The reference is not, of course, to the deliverance of Israel out of captivity, but to the answer to the summons to appear before the tribunal at which the people are to be witnesses. Most commentators translate *'am 'iwwēr we'ēynayim yēsh* as "the people that is blind although it has eyes" and render the next clause in a similar way. But that is clearly a mistaken translation and distorts the meaning of the entire strophe. The point here is not the blindness of people that have eyes, but rather the fact that although they are blind, they do have eyes. The emphasis is on the eyes, not on the blindness. They are being produced as witnesses to testify to the Godhead of the Lord, namely, that He both prophesies and fulfills His prophecies. As the Lord's servant (42:20f) they have seen and heard much with their physical eyes and ears, and they are now to testify concerning this, although they had taken none of it to heart. In spite of spiritual blindness and deafness these people had nevertheless seen and heard very much (Deut. 7:19; 11:7; 29:2); therefore they are now to come forth from their prisons and dungeons and bear witness to what they had seen and heard. The translations of Gesenius and Delitzsch leave the way open to a correct understanding of the situation, although they do not make the point itself clear. Calvin, Ewald, Stier, and Cheyne understand the eyes and ears of the people to have been spiritually opened, but nevertheless emphasize the real point of the passage. For the testimony that Israel is called upon to give, Israel no more needs spiritual understanding than do the gentiles for presenting their case. The question is merely one of establishing the concrete facts, easily perceived by the physical senses. Budde translated correctly but misunderstood *hōtsī'* and referred the passage to the preceding strophe instead of this one. In the "Rainbow Bible" Cheyne translated: "Ho, ye people with eyes, but blind, and ye with ears, but deaf." At that point he assumes a lacuna in the text, and continues: "Wherefore will ye hold your peace when *YHWH* pleads with the nations? Can ye not even yet see? Can ye not even yet hear? Let us come together to the tribunal." That permits us, says Cheyne, to understand the summons to the nations. But why assume that Isaiah must have

217

gone to the trouble of setting down so many unnecessary words, when Cheyne is able so easily to imagine the alleged omission. A poet, after all, leaves much to the imagination; he does not spell out every detail. All that is necessary here is to imagine the situation without reading anything false between the lines. Cheyne has confused the matter for himself. There is no lacuna in the text. It is easy enough to understand the summons to the gentiles if one simply understands the eighth verse as it reads. The meaning is then so clear that even the simple should not go astray: "Bring forth the people! It is indeed blind and deaf, as I said (42:18-20), because of its own wickedness, but it still has eyes and ears; and, as I said (42:20f), it has seen and heard much, and therefore can and must testify that I have foretold events and have made them come to pass. That proves My Godhead." But this understanding of the passage can result only from a comparison of this verse with verses 10ff. In verse 8 there is only a citation of the people to give testimony before the forthcoming tribunal. Such a citation is meaningless if Israel is pictured here as physically blind and deaf, for such a person can give no testimony before a judge. Yet such a citation is the best possible means of establishing the Godhead of the Lord, if Israel, in spite of its spiritual blindness and deafness, is called upon to witness to the things that it heard and saw with its physical ears and eyes. Cf. 1 John 1:1-3; John 1:14; Acts 4:20.

> כָּל־הַגּוֹיִם נִקְבְּצוּ יַחְדָּו וְיֵאָסְפוּ לְאֻמִּים
>
> מִי בָהֶם יַגִּיד זֹאת וְרִאשֹׁנוֹת יַשְׁמִיעֻנוּ
>
> יִתְּנוּ עֵדֵיהֶם וְיִצְדָּקוּ וְיִשְׁמְעוּ וְיֹאמְרוּ אֱמֶת׃

How is the form *niqbetsū* to be interpreted? Delitzsch takes it to be an abnormal form of the Niphal imperative *hiqqābhetsū*. Driver, Koenig, Green, and Gesenius-Kautzsch protest and express strong doubt that this is the correct explanation. Cf. Gr. 51, o, p. 139. Delitzsch does not prove his case with his reference to Joel 4:11 (3:11), nor with his reference to *nilwū* in Jer. 50:5. Those forms too are clearly perfects. The trouble is that we in our idiom are unfamiliar with the appropriateness of a perfect in a connection such as this. Koenig's translation of Joel 4:11: "And may they gather," is no solution. The explanation is that the lively imagination of the Hebrew poet assumes an actual perfect, a completed action, even though the primary action is still to follow (in Joel 4:11 an imperative, and in Jer. 50:5 a future). That is the case here. "They are gathered" is a secondary action; the primary action

follows in the imperfect with *we* — "And let them assemble themselves." The perfect thus acquires the meaning of a perfect participle — *having gathered.* Cf. 60:4, *kullām niqbetsū bhā'ū lākh,* which
Luther translates: *Diese alle versammelt kommen zu dir.* The
thought is: After all the gentiles are assembled, the nations shall
gather together. This double expression is, however, really not a
tautology. *niqbats* describes the gathering in one place; *yē'asephū*
the gathering into one great mass. The introduction of a new subject, *le'ummīm,* is a poetic addition and is no obstacle to this interpretation. In the English idiom the two predicates have to be
translated as though they were identical grammatical forms, both
jussive: "Let all the gentiles come together and let them assemble
themselves." Luther has that translation, and Gesenius and
others follow him. — The Lord sees gathered before Him on one
side the obdurate people of Israel, blessed however with eyes and
ears; and on the other side, all the gentile nations in one great
multitude. He begins His judicial inquiry with a demand addressed
to the gentiles: "Who among them can foretell such a thing?" The
imperfect, especially in interrogative sentences, often implies
ability — Who can? Cf. Gr. 107, t, p. 318. Luther has: "*Der solches
verkuendigen moege.*" *zō'th,* which usually points forward (Gr.
136,p.442), can on occasion also point backward (ibid. Note 1). In
this instance it refers to what was prophesied in verses 1-7, and at
the same time also to what follows in verses 14ff. Cf. Deuteronomy
32:29. *rī'shōnōth* are events of the past which had come to pass as
foretold, not previously predicted events. The gentiles are
challenged to prophesy as the Lord has prophesied, or to point to
events that came to pass as the result of their prophesying. They
are to produce their witnesses, *weyitsdāqū* (a pausal form), "and
then they shall be declared to be right" — as a self-evident consequence of their proof. The subject in *weyishme'ū* and *yō'merū* is not
the witnesses; rather, it is impersonal: "And so one will hear," etc.
Meant are the Lord and those on His side. — The gentiles cannot
respond to the demand; they remain silent and thus confirm that
their gods are dead idols that know nothing and can do nothing.

אַתֶּם עֵדַי נְאֻם־יְהוָה וְעַבְדִּי אֲשֶׁר בָּחָרְתִּי 10

לְמַעַן תֵּדְעוּ וְתַאֲמִינוּ לִי וְתָבִינוּ כִּי־אֲנִי הוּא

לְפָנַי לֹא־נוֹצַר אֵל וְאַחֲרַי לֹא יִהְיֶה:

Instead of a question, like that put to the gentile nations, there
now follows an assertion by the Lord Himself, addressed to His

people, to the effect that they are witnesses testifying to His deity. *'edhay* and *we'abhdī* ("My servant are you") are the predicate of the sentence. In the particle *we* there is latent a "for" or "because." Witnesses are they because they are My servant. As His servant, Israel was the Lord's *meshullām,* His trusted one (42:19). By word and deed, by revelation and wonderful works, God had made known His deity. *lema'an,* a conjunction expressing purpose or goal, naturally does not belong to "you are My witnesses," but exclusively to "My servant are you, whom I have chosen"; in fact, strictly speaking, only to *bāḥartī.* The Lord chose Israel for this purpose, namely, to be His servant, in order that they might come to the understanding that He alone is the true God. The verbs *yādha', he'emīn, hēbhīn* build a climax. *yādha'* expresses the conviction that comes from visual observation. The object of *yādha'* would be the *rabbōth,* the many wonders of 42:20. *he'emīn lī* is our English "believe me." I chose you to be My servant so that through observation of My many wonders you might come to trust My words and My revelation which foretold those wonders or accompanied them. *hēbhīn* is the result of *yādha'* and *he'emīn:* to be inwardly and thoroughly convinced, to understand perfectly and clearly. This threefold process of understanding was the immediate purpose of the calling of Israel to be the Lord's servant. Israel's understanding of this was the prerequisite for the fulfillment of its prophetic office among the nations. As a people that became spiritually blind, it was finally deprived of this office, not because it had never attained to the intended understanding, but because it had deliberately rejected it and become reprobate, 1:2ff. As long as it was God's people, it possessed this understanding through its fellowship with the Lord. Therefore God can justly say to Israel: "You are — as My onetime servant — witnesses that I am God." Whether they are willing now to testify to that is not the question. They *are* witnesses before their own consciences, because they had experienced all these things. The Lord's argumentation is now directed to them alone, because the gentile nations are viewed as having been removed from the scene. For that reason it is proper to supply a "but" before *'attem.* In contrast to the gentiles, who are unable to produce a witness to testify to the godhead of their idols, God presents His reprobate people as actual witnesses of His deity. *kī 'anī hū'. hū'* always points back; it means *ille,* that one. I am He who foretells and fulfills and who can produce many such examples from the past. The concluding sentence: "Before Me was never a God formed, and after Me there shall be

none," is a poetic way of describing the exclusive deity of the Lord.
Cf. 41:4; 44:6, etc.

11 אָנֹכִ֥י אָנֹכִ֖י יְהוָ֑ה וְאֵ֥ין מִבַּלְעָדַ֖י מוֹשִֽׁיעַ׃

This sentence, by its very isolation, strongly emphasizes and
confirms the preceding one and also serves as a conclusion to the
preceding half-strophe and an introduction to the following. For
that reason the weightier *anōkhī* is used instead of *'anī*, and even
repeated. Before *YHWH* supply the copula. *mibbal'adhay* is not
strictly a preposition. It is really an adverb made up of *min*, the
poetic negative *bal*, *'adh*, "up to," and the first person plural
suffix, literally: from not to me — besides Me. Instead of *'el*
or *'elōhīm* the sentence has *mōshīa'*, a Helper or Savior. This
word, a Hiphil participle of *yāsha'*, has almost become a noun in
Isaiah. It expresses what *'el* and *'elōhīm* mean for us in a very
practical way, and is the equivalent of "my, your, our, etc., God."
Cf. verse 3.

12 אָנֹכִ֞י הִגַּ֤דְתִּי וְהוֹשַׁ֙עְתִּי֙ וְהִשְׁמַ֔עְתִּי וְאֵ֥ין בָּכֶ֖ם זָ֑ר
וְאַתֶּ֥ם עֵדַ֛י נְאֻם־יְהוָ֖ה וַאֲנִי־אֵֽל׃

In his customary way Isaiah now develops the form *mōshīa'*
which he had just used. I — again the weightier form of the pronoun — have foretold, have delivered, have caused to be heard. "I"
with its predicates stands in contrast to "and there was no
stranger among you," namely, no other God. The three predicates,
higgadhtī, hōsha'tī, and *hishma'tī* have caused the critics endless
difficulty. They either delete the middle verb entirely (Cheyne), or
replace it with *hōdha'tī* (Budde). Marti, in the interest of the meter
that he constructs, felt the need of still another verb and added
'asīthī. Others have followed him. The trouble is that they do not
understand the prophet. We noted above that Isaiah is here developing the term *mōshīa'*. *hōsha'tī* is essential to his purpose. It is a
mistake to make *hōsha'tī*, placed as it is between two other perfects, refer to the future, namely, to the deliverance out of Babylon. That confuses the matter altogether. The three perfects are
all historical, all refer to the past. The very next clause proves
that: "And you are My witnesses that I am God." Only on the basis
of past experience can, and must, spiritually blind Israel bear witness to the deity of the Lord; only on the basis of what it had
learned and experienced through God's words and deeds can it do
so. What God had caused them to experience is expressed in these

221

three verbs. He had *foretold,* namely, the deliverance; and after that He had *helped,* had made the prophecy come to pass; and then He had *caused to be heard,* namely, another prophecy. Had Isaiah been writing prose, he might have added some word to express that God had also fulfilled that prophecy. But being a poet, he does not need to add what is obvious. In prose the sentence would perhaps read thus: I, and not some strange god among you, have caused prophecy to follow upon prophecy, and fulfillment to follow upon fulfillment, so that you must bear witness that I am God.

גַּם־מִיּוֹם֙ אֲנִ֣י ה֔וּא   13

וְאֵ֥ין מִיָּדִ֖י מַצִּ֑יל   אֶפְעַ֖ל וּמִ֥י יְשִׁיבֶֽנָּה:

The preceding verse treated of the Lord's works in the past; this verse deals with His works in the future, and serves as a transition to the prophecy in verses 14ff. *miyyōm* never means "from the first day onward," "from the beginning," "from eternity," as most exegetes have assumed. There is not a single example in the Old Testament for that translation. As Delitzsch has remarked, the *miyyōm* in Ezekiel 48:35 clearly means "from that day onward," as though the phrase were *min hayyōm hazzeh,* just as *kayyōm* (Isa. 58:4; 1 Sam. 9:13) means "today." The translation "from the beginning" was suggested by ἔτι ἀπ' ἀρχῆς of the LXX. That the reference here is to the future is also made clear by the two following clauses, which, although couched in general terms, nevertheless refer to the future and would be meaningless if made to refer to the past. *yādh* is the hand of retributive justice, and stands in contrast to *hōsha ʿtī.* The meaning of *pā ʿal* is "to set an action in motion." It is the counterpart to *ʿāsāh,* which means "to complete or bring to an end." *yeshībhennāh* is an imperfect Hiphil of *shūbh,* with feminine suffix construed as neuter, and means "to turn something back, to hinder, frustrate, nullify, rescind, reverse." Cf. Isaiah 14:27; Job 9:12; 11:10; 23:13; Psalm 33:9-11. The most nearly exact translation of *'eph ʿal ūmī* is a conditional clause: If I act, who, etc.?

Résumé of verses 8-13: The Lord has gathered together the blind and deaf people of God — blind and deaf though they have eyes and ears — and has demanded of the assembled gentile nations that they declare and prove by witnesses that they are able to proclaim something beforehand and make it come to pass. They are unable to produce any evidence whatever. Israel, as the chosen servant of the Lord, cannot but testify, out of its own experience in the past, that the Lord alone is God and Savior. As in the past, so also in the future, God will reveal Himself as true God through His exercise of infallible justice and through His irresistible deeds.

Third Strophe: verses 14-20: *By the fall of Babylon and the restoration of His people the Lord will show that He is Israel's Holy One and King.*

14 *Thus says the Lord, your Savior, the Holy One of Israel:*
    For your sakes will I send to Babylon
    And drive down all of them as fugitives,
    Together with the Chaldeans, to the ships they rejoice in.
15 *I am the Lord, your Holy One,*
    The Creator of Israel, your King.
16 *Thus says the Lord, who made a way in the sea,*
    And a path through the great waters,
17 *Who led forth horse and chariot, the powers of war and armed*
        men —
    Prostrate they lie together, and never will they rise,
    They have been extinguished, like a wick they are quenched —
18 *But do not let your mind dwell on former things,*
    And do not meditate over things long past.
19 *Behold, I am doing a new thing,*
    Already it is springing forth, do you not perceive it?
    Yes, I will make highways in the desert
    And streams of waters in the wilderness.
20 *The wild beasts of the desert shall praise Me, the jackals and*
        ostriches,
    For I shall provide water in the desert
    And streams of water in the wilderness,
    To give My people, My chosen ones, water to drink.
21 *The people whom I have formed for Myself shall recount My praise.*

14 כֹּה־אָמַ֧ר יְהוָ֛ה גֹּאַלְכֶ֖ם קְד֣וֹשׁ יִשְׂרָאֵ֑ל

לְמַעַנְכֶ֞ם שִׁלַּ֣חְתִּי בָבֶ֗לָה וְהוֹרַדְתִּ֤י בָרִיחִים֙ כֻּלָּ֔ם

וְכַשְׂדִּ֖ים בָּאֳנִיּ֥וֹת רִנָּתָֽם ׃

Verse 13: "No one can deliver out of My hand; I perform it, and who is there that will reverse it!" expressed in abstract terms what the strophe beginning at verse 14 states in concrete form. What the Lord now promises to perform is the destruction of Babylon and the deliverance of God's people. This promise is based, in verse 15, on the fact that Jehovah is Israel's Holy One and King. The reference to Pharaoh and the judgment upon him

and his host furnishes historical evidence that Jehovah is Lord
and King and supports the reliability of this new promise. Verses
19 and 20 picture in poetic form the new life to be provided for the
people who are delivered out of Babylon. And so God's people have
another reason to praise their God, verse 21.

lema'ankhem (verse 14) is balanced by *lema'anī* in verse 25 of
the following strophe. *lema'ankhem* expresses not only the purpose of the sending to Babylon, namely, to deliver you, but is also a
reminder of the Lord's high regard for Israel, which was described
in verses 1-4. The unnamed object of the sending is Cyrus together
with his armies. Through him as His instrument the Lord will
drive down (into their ships) *kullām,* all of them, i.e., all of the inhabitants. Luther follows the Vulgate in assuming that *bārīḥīm* is
the same as *berīḥīm. berīḥīm* are crossbars, bolts; *bārīḥīm* is an adjective derived from *bārah,* to break, break through, to flee.
Luther translated it in Isaiah 27:1 and Job 26:13 as though it
meant straight or upright; but in both passages the word means
fugitive. In this verse the word is used predicatively: I will drive
them as fugitives. By means of the connecting *Waw* the Chaldeans
are specifically included in the object. It is they, the original inhabitants of Babylon, who are responsible for the idol-worship and
the arrogance of Babylon, and they are to be driven too as fugitives down to the "ships of their rejoicing," that is, the ships that
represented their wealth and power, and of which they were so
very proud. Some commentators take *rinnāthām* to mean cries of
pain, or howls of woe. Cheyne refers to Dr. Weir's remark that *rinnāh* with a suffix never means a cry of joy, but always signifies a
cry of supplication or prayer, and is so used in the Psalms and in
Jeremiah 14:12. The word without a suffix also occurs as a synonym of *tephillāh,* a cry, complaint, or supplication, as in 1 Kings
8:28; 2 Chronicles 6:19; Jeremiah 7:16; 11:14. According to this interpretation the phrase would then read: To the ships of their
pleading or wailing, or cries of fear. But Delitzsch correctly
remarks that the genitive construction prevents this interpretation. What he means is that the genitive expresses a continuing,
not a onetime or momentary relationship. This is naturally true of
cases when the genitive expresses an attribute or purpose. Cf. Gr.
128, p, q, p. 417f. And it is especially true in this case, since *rinnāh*
is made even more definite by the suffix *ām.* Compare this prediction of the fall of Babylon with chapters 13 and 14, and also 21:
1-10. All these prophecies differ in their minute details. But one
would fail to recognize the prophet as a poet if, in the interest of

inspiration, one felt it necessary to believe that each specific detail of the picture would have to be fulfilled literally.

¹⁵ אֲנִי יְהוָה קְדוֹשְׁכֶם בּוֹרֵא יִשְׂרָאֵל מַלְכְּכֶם:

God's special relationship to Israel is the reason why He acts as He does both toward Babylon and toward Israel. Two aspects of that relationship are expressed in this verse, each one characterized by two terms. *YHWH* and *qedhōshkhem* are parallel expressions. Jehovah is the Covenant-God of Israel; *qedhōshkhem* is the God who in the zeal of His love toward Israel (verses 1 and 4) inexorably avenges every injustice committed against His people, because that is a violation of this relationship of love. *bōrē' yisrā'ēl* and *malkekhem* are likewise parallel. The Lord called Israel into being as a people, and established Himself as its Ruler, Provider, and Defender. *qedhōshkhem* looks back to the threat against Babylon, *malkekhem* forward to the good that the Lord has promised to Israel, verses 16-20.

¹⁶ כֹּה אָמַר יְהוָה הַנּוֹתֵן בַּיָּם דָּרֶךְ וּבְמַיִם עַזִּים נְתִיבָה:

Verses 16 and 17 recall God's judgment against Pharaoh in the Red Sea, a judgment by which He rescued His people. Concerning *hannōthēn* and *hammōtsi'* Delitzsch states: "The participles must not be rendered *qui dedit, eduxit;* general attributes are deduced from Jehovah's deeds of old: He who makes a highway in the sea, as He once showed." Gr. 116, 5, o, p. 359 disputes this interpretation. The participle with the article is simply an alternate for a relative clause, with a strong demonstrative emphasis, and the connection in the text determines the tense, which in this case is the past. The grammar cites as examples Genesis 32:10; 12:7; 16:13; 35:1,3; 36:35; 48:16; 2 Samuel 15:31, etc. That the reference here is not to any general attributes of God, but to God's great saving acts in Israel's history, is shown by verse 18, which speaks of them as *rī'shōnōth*, etc. Therefore our translation uses the past tense. On the other hand, it is also clear that with *yaḥdāw* and *yishkebhū* (verse 17) the poet places himself in the midst of that scene and speaks as though he were present. The participles that follow *kōh 'āmar* are attributes of *YHWH,* and the words that *kōh 'āmar* introduces do not appear until verses 18ff: Do not dwell on the former things, etc.

225

17 הַמּוֹצִיא רֶכֶב־וָסוּס חַיִל וְעִזּוּז יַחְדָּו
יִשְׁכְּבוּ בַּל־יָקוּמוּ דָּעֲכוּ כַּפִּשְׁתָּה כָבוּ:

rekhebh and *sūs*, coupled by *Waw* with Qamets, form a natural
pair — a war-chariot with its horses. *ḥayil*, a host, and *ʿizzūz*, a
hero, a man in the heroic sense, here a collective, are joined in the
usual way. Note the similarity in sound of *sūs* and *ʿizzūz*. It was the
Lord Himself who prompted the Egyptians to pursue Israel into
the Red Sea, Exodus 14:4,8. *yishkebhū*, in the description that
follows, is a present tense, *bal* is the poetic negative, *yāqumū* is
future, and *dāʿakhū* and *khābhū* are present perfects. See Gr. 106,
2, g, p. 311.

18 אַל־תִּזְכְּרוּ רִאשֹׁנוֹת וְקַדְמֹנִיּוֹת אַל־תִּתְבֹּנָנוּ:

Verse 18 introduces the second half of the strophe. It contains
the object of *kōh ʾamar* in verse 16. *qadhmōnī* (from *qedhem*, what
lies before) is a synonym of *rīʾshōn*, although a stronger expression. Both are really abstract terms signifying something earlier
or ancient, and they generalize the historical event that was just
mentioned. Like the nouns, the verbs too are arranged in climactic
order. *zākhar* means "to remember," *hithbōnēn* (Hithpolel of *bīn*)
"to consider, to think about." The imperatives are purely rhetorical. The Lord compares the deed that He has in mind for His people with that great act of the past of which He has just spoken. The
intention is not to minimize the earlier deed, but by comparison to
emphasize the greatness of the deed that will be described in the
following verses. Great as were the acts of the Lord in the distant
past, compared with the new thing the Lord is about to do, they are
hardly worth mentioning. Cf. Jeremiah 16:14f; 23:7f.

19 הִנְנִי עֹשֶׂה חֲדָשָׁה עַתָּה תִצְמָח הֲלוֹא תֵדָעוּהָ
אַף אָשִׂים בַּמִּדְבָּר דֶּרֶךְ בִּישִׁמוֹן נְהָרוֹת:
20 תְּכַבְּדֵנִי חַיַּת הַשָּׂדֶה תַּנִּים וּבְנוֹת יַעֲנָה
כִּי־נָתַתִּי בַמִּדְבָּר מַיִם נְהָרוֹת בִּישִׁימֹן
לְהַשְׁקוֹת עַמִּי בְחִירִי:

hinnenī, with its participle, and *ʿattāh*, which is here purely a
particle expressing time, place the action in the present time. The
Lord is carrying out a new thing; it is already springing forth, it

has begun to be a present fact. Therefore *tēdhāʾuhā* is not to be translated with the future tense (Delitzsch and others), but with the present: Do you not perceive it? The deliverance out of Babylon is meant. That is the essence of the *ḥadhāshāh*. In the next clauses this new thing is expressed in terms describing the accompanying conditions, in order to bring out the contrast with the deliverance from Egypt. In that case the Lord had made a highway through the seas and streams, now He will lay roads through the wilderness, and streams in the dry desert. *yeshīmōn* is an intensification of *midhbār*. Before human eyes this is a greater wonder than that of the Red Sea. The complete pathlessness of the Arabian desert and the total lack of water in that great waste were known since time immemorial. To lay highways through this desert and to make streams of water break forth is so contrary to nature that even the desert creatures that suffer under the unceasing, parching drought are moved unconsciously to praise the Lord for this unaccustomed relief. *tan, tannīn*, plural *tannīm, tannīnīm*, usually designates elongated animals of some sort, but at times the word clearly refers to the jackal, as it does in this instance. (See the lexicons.) *benōth yaʿanāh* occurs only in connections like this one, and the meaning has never as yet been satisfactorily explained. Lamentations 4:3 has the Qeri *yeʿēnīm*, a plural of *yāʿēn*, ostriches. Possibly *yaʿanāh* is a feminine of *yāʿēn*, and *bath yaʿanāh* is then a young ostrich. *tekhabbedhēnī* at the beginning of verse 20 need not be understood as expressing a result or consequence. It is independent, though *kī* in the next line could be translated with "when," as well as with "for" or "because." The latter is preferable, however, because of the length of the following clause. The purpose of this new wonder is to furnish water for God's people to drink, who are pictured as journeying through the desert — an impossible feat if the Lord did not provide a highway and streams of water. *beḥīrī* is not an adjective modifying *ʿammī*, but is a noun placed in apposition: My chosen one, that is, My beloved servant Israel.

עַם־זוּ֙ יָצַ֣רְתִּי לִ֔י תְּהִלָּתִ֖י יְסַפֵּֽרוּ׃ 21

Concerning *zū*, see 42:24. *yātsartī* includes everything that God has done to create and form this people. He shaped and formed them (Luther has *zugerichtet*) to the end that they (collective construction) should relate those deeds that proclaim His honor. That they have been thus molded by God makes it possible for them to carry out this calling and also gives them the necessary incentive. Each new act of salvation is a new incentive. Such a new incentive is also the promised guidance through the wilderness and the assurance of water for the thirsty in a waterless waste.

Technically, this verse belongs neither entirely to the preceding nor wholly to the following sentence. It is a transitional sentence like 40:18,25; 43:11; 51:21, etc.

Résumé of verses 14-21: The same Holy One and King of Israel who once led His people through great waters, in which He also overwhelmed the hosts of Pharaoh, will drive the Babylonians as fugitives to the sea, but will lead His own people safely through the great desert and provide them amply with water. This is to serve as a strong incentive for them to praise their Lord, as the fathers were once led to praise Him because of the deliverance out of Egypt.

Fourth Strophe: verses 21-28: *Israel was delivered, not because of its merit and worthiness, but wholly by the grace of the Lord.*

(21   *The people whom I have formed for Myself shall recount My praise.*)
22   *For you, O Jacob, did not call Me,*
     That you should, O Israel, have wearied yourself for Me;
23   *You did not bring Me your lambs for a burnt offering,*
     Nor honor Me with your sacrifices;
     I did not burden you with meat offerings
     Nor weary you with incense.
24   *You have not bought Me sweet cane with your money*
     Nor sated Me with the fat of your burnt offerings;
     You only burdened Me with your sins
     And wearied Me with your iniquities.
25   *I, it is I, who forgives your transgressions for My sake,*
     Who no more remembers your sins.
26   *Call it to My mind, and let us contend together,*
     Relate it yourself, so that you may be justified! —
27   *Your very first forefather sinned,*
     And your mediators have broken faith with Me.
28   *Therefore have I profaned holy princes,*
     Given up Jacob to destruction
     And Israel to calumny.

22 וְלֹא־אֹתִ֥י קָרָ֖אתָ יַעֲקֹ֑ב כִּֽי־יָגַ֥עְתָּ בִּ֖י יִשְׂרָאֵֽל׃

The *Waw* at the beginning of verse 22 introduces a statement of the reasons why Israel should proclaim the Lord's praises. This people should glorify the Lord, because, as the following verses set forth, the position of preference that Israel enjoyed before the Lord did not rest on Israel's merits, but entirely on the Lord's free grace. Most modern commentators understand *qārā'thā* to mean "call upon," because they do not recognize a logical relationship between this word and the following statements. *qārā'*, with God or Jehovah as its object, may mean to call upon, Psalm 14:4; 17:6, etc., but its primary meaning when followed by an accusative is "to call," in the sense of select or choose (cf. 41:9; 49:1), and this sense is to be retained. Luther's *gerufen* (called) is correct. The word embraces in its scope all of the thoughts included in the predicates in verses 23 and 24a. *kī* is consecutive. Gr. 166, b, p. 505. The parallel in the following line shows this. *yāgha'tā bī,* "so that you should weary yourself for Me," is the practical side of this calling and a consequence of the choosing. *qārā'thā* is used here in the same manner as *qerā'anī* in 49:1. In that passage the word is used of the calling of Israel to be the Lord's servant; here it is used of the calling of the Lord to be the God of this people. It is parallel to what the Lord says in John 15:16: "You have not chosen Me, but I have chosen you." Verses 23 and 24a are a development of the thought suggested by *qārā'* and *yāgha'tā bī.* There is no reason for assuming, as Delitzsch does, that *'ōthī* stands in contrast to other gods. Such a contrast would also have to be expressed by a more emphatic placement of *lī* in the following sentence. The contrast in this verse is: Not you Me, but I you, as is made evident in verse 25.

23 לֹא־הֵבֵ֤יאתָ לִּי֙ שֵׂ֣ה עֹלֹתֶ֔יךָ וּזְבָחֶ֖יךָ לֹ֣א כִבַּדְתָּ֑נִי
לֹ֤א הֶעֱבַדְתִּ֙יךָ֙ בְּמִנְחָ֔ה וְלֹ֥א הוֹגַעְתִּ֖יךָ בִּלְבוֹנָֽה׃

Modern archaeologists have expended a vast amount of verbiage — some of it false, most of it unclear — on the various sacrifices and the offerings of incense and sweet cane mentioned here as representing endeavors to please God. There is this to be said about sacrifices: All sacrifices are essentially gifts to God, prompted by the sense of dependence on the power and goodness of God. The bloody sacrifices are at the same time expiatory offerings and presuppose the rift between God and man caused by sin. Unbloody sacrifices are not expiatory. Their purpose, like that of the offerings of incense and sweet cane, is either purification or worship. The burnt offering, the *'ōlāh,* is the chief sacrifice. It signifies the worshiper's dedication of himself to God and the expiation of

229

general sinfulness, or the attainment of a state of favor in God's sight. Sin offerings and guilt offerings served for the expiation of specific sins. The bloody sacrifice, the *zebhaḥ* or *zebhaḥ shelāmīm,* had as its purpose the preservation, the practice of, and the confirmation of the condition of grace and of reconciliation between God and man or between man and his fellows. Meat and drink offerings, incense, etc., served as means of ceremonial purification for persons and utensils, and as a means of worship. Cf. Leviticus 1 - 7; Exodus 29 and 30.

Concerning the pointing of *hēbhēy'thā* (whether with simple *Tsere* or with *Tsere longum*) see the lexicon. Commentators differ widely in their interpretation of these verses. Calvin simply states that the sacrifices that Israel was bringing to God were no real sacrifices, because they were hypocritical dead works. Vitringa agrees, and adds that since the time of Uzziah the worship involving sacrifices had been deteriorating steadily. Most earlier commentators follow their lead. Most modern commentators, however, see a reference to a natural cessation of such sacrifices during the exile. This latter meaning seems more plausible than the other and also agrees well with the Isaianic authorship of Isaiah II. If the prophet is projected by the Spirit into the midst of the exile, then he is also in a situation out of which he can, in God's name, speak to the people about a cessation of sacrifices. But we accept neither of these explanations. Our translation of *qārā'thā* and *yāgha'tā bī* in verse 22 places the time of verse 23 in the period before God's covenant with Israel was made. None of the patriarchs before they were called, nor the people before the deliverance from Egypt, had called upon the Lord; none had troubled themselves about Him or brought Him any offerings. Nor had the Lord required any sacrifices from the patriarchs (the sacrifice of Isaac does not belong in this category). The ordinance concerning sacrifices was not prescribed until after Israel's deliverance from Egypt and after the establishment of the covenant on Sinai. The fact that sacrifices are named according to the modes that were prescribed later does not militate against this explanation. In a presentation such as this, it is natural that the names of sacrifices that came into use later should be employed for the sake of vividness and clarity. The point is that the people, before they were chosen, called, and freed from bondage, had never brought these sacrifices that the Lord ordained later. They had not troubled themselves with such matters. The opinion of modern exegetes that the cessation of the sacrifices during the exile is here meant is unacceptable because a presentation such as appears here would then be irrelevant since such sacrifices not only self-evidently ceased during the exile, but also were impossible, even contrary to God's ordinance. Above all, the course of the argument also controverts that opinion. The argumentation concludes in verses 26 - 28 with the bases for the present state of exile. The Lord has profaned holy princes, removed them from office, delivered Israel to the curse of God — and that, of course, refers to the exile — because its very first forefather had sinned, and its mediators, the priests, had fallen away from God. Since these concluding thoughts of the argument deal with Israel's sins *before* the exile, therefore verse 24b (Israel has wearied the Lord with its sins) cannot refer to sins committed *during*the exile. And if those sins lie in a period before the exile, then the sacrifices mentioned at the beginning of the strophe cannot lie within the time of the exile.

24 לֹא־קָנִיתָ לִּי בַכֶּסֶף קָנֶה וְחֵלֶב זְבָחֶיךָ לֹא הִרְוִיתָנִי
אַךְ הֶעֱבַדְתַּנִי בְּחַטֹּאותֶיךָ הֹוגַעְתַּנִי בַּעֲוֹנֹתֶיךָ:

qāneh, also *qenēh bhōsem* or *besem,* and *qāneh ṭobh* (Jer. 6:20), fragrant sweet cane or calamus, was used (Exod. 30:23ff.) in the preparation of the anointing oil with which the utensils of the temple were anointed. Scripture says nothing definite about any other use of *qāneh* in the temple service. It was imported from Arabia or India at considerable expense, and for that reason buying with money is especially mentioned. The fat of the offerings was the fat from certain parts of the bloody sacrifices (Lev. 3:3ff.) that was burned as a pleasing odor to the Lord. *lō' hirwīthānī* (from *rāwāh,* to drink, in Hiphil: to give to drink; in the transferred sense: to sate, to satisfy) refers also to the sweet cane and the fat offerings. — *'akh* here means "only." Israel did not trouble itself to gain the Lord's favor, and it deserved nothing from the Lord; the Lord had never burdened it with required sacrifices. This, of course, refers to the period before its call and the establishment of the covenant. On the contrary, Israel, after being accepted by the Lord, had only burdened and wearied Him with transgressions of all His laws and ordinances, and grieved Him with the punishment and chastisement made necessary by its guilty behavior. See Ezekiel 20.

231

אָנֹכִ֧י אָנֹכִ֛י ה֥וּא מֹחֶ֖ה פְשָׁעֶ֑יךָ לְמַעֲנִ֔י וְחַטֹּאתֶ֖יךָ לֹ֥א 25
אֶזְכֹּֽר׃

The frequently repeated "Not you" in the first half of this section is balanced in the second half by the emphatic repetition of
the Lord's "I." The climax of the entire chapter is reached in this
verse. In contrast to the conclusion of chapter 42, the Lord
abruptly changes His tone in chapter 43 to one of most cordial and
winning love. He assures Israel of His ardent love and regard
(verse 4). He lavishes upon the people sublime promises, both in
general (verses 1,2,3) and in particular (verses 5,6,7,14-20). Such
favors could tend to make Israel proud and self-righteous, a threat
facing Israel from the beginning and which in spite of many warnings brought about its ruin in the end (Deut. 8 and 9; Matt. 3:9,
etc.). Therefore the Lord confronts Israel with its lack of merit,
with its later disobedience, and with all its culpability. All His love
for Israel, which moved Him constantly to purge the people of guilt
and to remove their transgressions from His memory, He attributes entirely to His free grace — *lema'anī.*

lema'anī, for My sake, is fully explained in 48:4-11. Compare
verse 9 and verse 11. The primary meaning is "for My name's
sake." "For how should My name be polluted? and I will not give
My glory to another" (Isa. 48:11). Cf. also 66:5; 42:8. By His own
free choice the Lord identified Himself with Israel, but Israel by
repeated transgressions abused this grace and brought upon itself
enormous guilt by its defection to other gods. Even in the exile
there was no improvement (chapters 59,65,66), but nothing but
offenses and faithlessness always. The natural consequence would
have been rejection. But that would have exposed the Lord to blasphemy, ridicule, and calumny at the mouths of the enemies (cf.
Ezek. 20:13ff; Num. 14:16; Deut. 9:28; Isa. 52:5). Since it was the
Lord's declared purpose to exalt His name in all the world by the
deliverance, exaltation, and glorification of this people, He had to
have endless patience with them, blot out their faithlessness, and
daily forget their transgressions. He had to keep faith with Israel
— not for Israel's sake, but for His own honor's sake. Not in Israel,
but solely in the Lord Himself is found the reason why He delivers
Israel out of the hand of Babylon. — It may be well to repeat that
the participle *mōheh* expresses uninterrupted continuation of action. *pesha'* is a breach of faith, rebellion against the covenant of
grace; *ḥaṭṭāth* is any deviation from the Law. *lō' zākhar,* not to
remember, to forget.

26 הַזְכִּירֵ֫נִי נִשָּׁפְטָה יָ֑חַד סַפֵּ֥ר אַתָּ֖ה לְמַ֥עַן תִּצְדָּֽק׃

The purpose of verses 26 and 27 is to make Israel's guilt all the more heinous by repetition. The formal summons: "Call it to My mind, and let us contend together," is poetic and rhetorically cere-monious; the next verse likewise. Israel is to remind the Lord of its merits — if there are such — is to count them up, one after the other, is itself (*'attāh*) to report whatever claim it has on God's help. It is assumed that Israel does lay claim to certain rights over against the Lord, that it considers itself innocent, and that it charges the Lord with injustice. The loving tone which the Lord in this passage directs to the faithful in Israel, however, does not per-mit this arrogance to express itself fully. Cf. 40:27; 45:9, 10; 58:2ff.

27 אָבִ֥יךָ הָרִאשׁ֖וֹן חָטָ֑א וּמְלִיצֶ֖יךָ פָּ֥שְׁעוּ בִֽי׃

This verse offers additional strong proof of Israel's sinfulness and culpability. *'ābh* is to be understood in the broader sense, and *'ābhīkhā harī'shōn*, the first forefather of Israel, reaches back to the very beginnings of the people. Not Abraham is meant, and cer-tainly not Adam. It is Jacob. Both Abraham and Jacob are re-ferred to as the people's fathers, even in contrast to God in 63:16. Jacob is called father in 58:14, Abraham in 51:2. But Jacob is more intimately related to the people as father than Abraham. It is true that the people are described as Abraham's seed (also as Is-rael's seed — 45:25), but they are never simply called Abraham, whereas both Israel and Jacob became common designations for the people as early as Genesis 49:7. The reason for this is the rela-tively large number of sons Jacob had, through whom the people originally became a nation, Genesis 46:27. Moreover, the commis-sion of sin (*ḥātā*) is not connected with Abraham as the first father of the people, but is the mark of Jacob, especially because of the means he employed to obtain the blessing of the firstborn. In-deed, the idea of *ḥātā'*has, by God's providence, been preserved in Jacob's name for all time (Gen. 27:36 and 25:26).

It is difficult to determine who is meant by *melītseykhā*. The form is a Hiphil participle of *līts*, which in Qal and in Hiphil means to scoff. In Genesis 42:23 a *melīts*is an interpreter. In 2 Chronicles 32:31 the ambassadors of Merodach Baladan to Hezekiah are called *melītsīm*. They are clearly diplomats. Ecclesiaticus 10:2 has the Greek λειτουργοἱ servants, *Amtleute* in Luther's transla-tion. In Job 33:23 the word is in apposition to *mal'ākh*, a

233

messenger who bears a word from God. Beyond this the word does not occur. Most commentators therefore take the word to mean agents, middlemen, mediators, namely, between God and the people, and identify them as the priests and prophets. Others understand them to be the political and religious heads of the people. Still others take them to be the tribal heads of Israel. But one will hardly go wrong if one adopts the explanation in Jeremiah 32:32ff: "They, their kings, their princes, their priests, and their prophets . . . have turned unto Me the back and not the face." They who had been set as shepherds and guardians of the people and who should have been the faithful bearers of God's word and will, they are the persons whom Jeremiah holds responsible for the ruin and the misery of the people.

28 וַאֲחַלֵּל שָׂרֵי קֹדֶשׁ וְאֶתְּנָה לַחֵרֶם יַעֲקֹב וְיִשְׂרָאֵל לְגִדּוּפִים:

The *sārēy qōdhesh,* in the strict sense of the term, are the high priests, 1 Chronicles 24:5. It was they who bore the *qōdhesh la YHWH* on their foreheads (Exod. 28:36). They had charge of the Urim and Thummim (Exod. 28:30; Lev. 8:8; Num. 27:21, etc.). They brought the sacrifice of the sin-offering before the Lord. It was they who entered the Holy of Holies on the great Day of Atonement (Lev. 4:5,16; chapter 16). They were therefore the real mediators, the *melītsīm,* between God and the people. It seemed impossible that the Lord should profane these "princes of holiness." But the sacred office does not shield its bearers from God's judgment when they become unfaithful. Aaron himself was not exempted, not even Moses, when he failed to sanctify the Lord at the water of Meribah (Num. 20:12), nor Eli and his sons (1 Sam. 2,3,4). Under Ahaz, the high priest Urijah was an unfaithful servant (2 Kings 16:11-16); at the time of Jeremiah it seems that the entire generation of priests and high priests had become apostate (Jer. 2:8; 8:10; 18:18; 20:1ff; 26:8; 29:25ff). And so the Lord rejected the entire priesthood, together with the royal Davidic line, and profaned, cursed, and disgraced the "sacred princes."

wa'ahallēl is a consecutive imperfect following the perfects *ḥātā'* and *pāsheʿū* and is therefore to be translated as a perfect: therefore have I profaned. So also *'ettenāh,* which is coordinated with *'ahallēl* by means of the copula *we.* The *āh,* appended to *'etten,* is purely euphonic. Cf. Gr. 108, g, p. 320, and the examples listed in Gr. 49, e, p. 134. Jacob and Israel are, of course, the people, here designated by names expressing endearment, in order to emphasize the inner contrast between, on the one hand, Jacob, the chosen and beloved people, and Israel, the holy people, and on the other hand, the *ḥērem*, the destructive ban (Deut. 13:15ff) and the mockery of the heathen (51:7; Zeph. 2:8) to which the Lord had doomed them. Far from standing justified before God and being the victims of an unjust exile, they are a people sinful from the very beginning, rebellious in the persons of their highest and best representatives (cf. 1:22f), and thus themselves responsible for all their misery. That the Lord should now redeem them and restore them to honor is purely an act of His grace, Hosea 13:9.

Résumé of verses 21-28: Israel did not trouble itself or labor to win the Lord's favor, neither did the Lord set any burdensome conditions upon them for receiving His grace. Israel caused the Lord only weariness and labor by its transgressions and its guilt. For His own sake alone, the Lord purges Israel's guilt and redeems the people. If Israel is of a mind to contend with the Lord, then the Lord can confront it with the sinfulness of its forefathers and with the apostasy of its best leaders as just cause for its banishment.

Second Discourse: Chapter 44:1-23

The faithful love of Him who alone is true God creates for His faithful people a period of renewal through the outpouring of His Spirit and the forgiveness of their sins.

The chapter has three parts: verses 1-5, the renewal of Israel through the outpouring of the Spirit; verses 6-20, the sole Godhead of the Lord and the nothingness of the idols (foolishness of idol worship); verses 21-23, the forgiveness of sins and consequent salvation.

First Strophe: verses 1-5: *The faithful love of the Lord will pour out His Spirit upon the seed of Israel and cause it to flourish anew.*

1 *But now hear, O My servant Jacob,*
  And Israel whom I have chosen:
2 *Thus says the Lord who made you,*
  Who formed you from the womb, who helps you:
  Be not afraid, O My servant Jacob,
  And Jeshurun whom I have chosen,
3 *For I will pour out water upon the thirsty,*
  And streams of water upon the dry ground;
  I will pour out My Spirit upon your seed,
  And My blessing upon your offspring.
4 *They shall spring up amid the grass,*
  Like poplars beside the streams of water.
5 *This one will say: "The Lord's am I!"*
  Another will praise the name of Jacob,
  That one with his own hand will write: "The Lord's,"
  And give praise to the name of Israel.

¹ וְעַתָּה שְׁמַע יַעֲקֹב עַבְדִּי וְיִשְׂרָאֵל בָּחַרְתִּי בוֹ:

The introductory *we'attāh* either places this strophe in contrast
with the exile described in 43:28 (like 43:1 in contrast with chapter 42), and is then translated "*But* now"; or it introduces the conclusion that must be drawn from the main thought of the entire
preceding section, as expressed in verse 25, and must then be rendered "And *now* hear," as Luther understood it. The attributes,
"My servant" and "whom I have chosen," are attached to the
proper names in an order the reverse of the one in 41:8. This is
purely a poetic variation. As in chapter 43, there is an accumulation of endearing terms in the address to the people.

² כֹּה־אָמַר יְהוָה עֹשֶׂךָ וְיֹצֶרְךָ מִבֶּטֶן יַעְזְרֶךָ
אַל־תִּירָא עַבְדִּי יַעֲקֹב וִישֻׁרוּן בָּחַרְתִּי בוֹ:

The dividing accent in *'ōsekhā* marks the end of the first clause.
It is to be noted that *mibbeṭen* is joined to *weyōtserkhā* by Merkha-
Tiphcha, so that *ya'zerekkā* (with *Nun* energ.!) stands isolated.
The accentuation serves to mark the participles *'ōsekhā* and *yōtserkhā* as perfect concepts over against *ya'zerekkā*, an imperfect
present: not "He who helped you from the womb," but "He who
formed you from the womb (cf. verse 24 and 49:5) and who helps
you" (today and always). *mibbeṭen* does not exclude the time within the womb, but includes it. The creating, and forming, and helping are, of course, to be taken in the historical sense. — Jeshurun
as a name given to Israel occurs only four times, here and in Deut.
32:15; 33:5 and 26. It is derived from *yāshar*, meaning straight,
upright, honest; but the form *yāshūr* is not a Qal passive participle,
"the one made upright." It is a strengthening of an original *qatul*-
form sometimes formed from intransitive verbs to denote an inherent quality, e.g., *'āmūn*, faithful; *'ātsūm*, strong. Cf. Gr. 50,f,p.
136 and 84,m,p. 231. The ending *ūn* is not the diminutive ending,
"a small honest person"; it is an ending that denotes kind, attitude, disposition, like our ending -ly, as in goodly, uprightly. So
Jeshurun is the one of honest, upright disposition, the godly one;
cf. *zebhulūn* (Zebulun) from *yizbelēnī*. According to Ges.-Buhl,
15th edition, *yeshurūn* is according to its meaning the opposite of
"Jacob," the suppressor, the supplanter. It stands then midway
between "Jacob" and "Israel."

Israel is admonished not to be afraid, *'al tīra'*. What Israel's
fears were is indicated by the promises that follow. Jeshurun, the

honest and upright Israel, feared that it might be destroyed in the exile, might die without spiritual offspring. In the exile Israel is spiritually widowed, expelled from her husband's house, rejected, barren, bearing no children, 54:1; cf. 49:14ff. She produces no spiritual offspring. The believers in exile were constantly diminishing in number. Many of the exiles were entering into mixed marriages with idol worshipers and were falling away from the revealed religion; the younger generation, who were living as captives in strange surroundings, could not easily be enthused for the faith of the fathers. The upright ones, the Jeshurun, therefore had reason to fear that God's faithful people might perish from the earth during the exile. Against this fear the following promise is directed, a promise that is already latent in the names and appellations used in verses 1 and 2.

3 כִּי אֶצָּק־מַיִם עַל־צָמֵא וְנֹזְלִים עַל־יַבָּשָׁה
אֶצֹּק רוּחִי עַל־זַרְעֶךָ וּבִרְכָתִי עַל־צֶאֱצָאֶיךָ:

Delitzsch is in error when he understands *tsāmē'* to mean inhabitants of the land thirsting for rain. By way of explanation he continues: "We must not regard 3a, therefore, as a figure, and 3b as the explanation — the heavenly gifts rising, as in the book of Joel, by a gradual ascent from *mayim* and *nōzelīm* to *rūḥī* and *birkhāthī.*" But the situation here is not identical with that in Joel. In Joel, between the account of physical blessings and the promise of the outpouring of the Holy Spirit there is a dividing phrase, *'aḥarēy khēn*, "after all these things." In this passage, however, the outpouring of the Spirit follows immediately after the promise of water. Since it is a common practice of Isaiah to present something in a figure and immediately afterward in plain language, so here we must look upon this as a figure and its interpretation. *mayim* and *nōzelīm* are figurative, *rūḥī* and *birkhāthī* are the interpretation. *tsāmē'*, a masculine collective term, and *yabbāshāh*, a neuter term, are not separate entities; they refer to one and the same thing, one personal, the other neuter. If one takes *tsāmē'* to refer to trees and *yabbāshāh* to the land, then one attributes to the poet the unlikely statement that in order to make the trees grow, it is necessary to water both the trees and the land. In well-watered land trees grow even without rain. No, *tsāmē'*, the thirsty ones, are in the next phrase called dry land, and 3a is simply a figure of 3b. *mayim* and *nōzelīm* are figurative designations of the Spirit, and *tsāmē'* and *yabbāshāh* figuratively describe the seed, the *tse'etsā'īm* of Israel, who amid the godless conditions of the exile are estranged from the Lord and are as lacking in the Spirit as the thirsty ones and the dry land are lacking in water. *Blessing* is a designation of the Spirit, just as dry land designates the thirsty ones. The blessing includes all the good and salutary gifts of God, James 1:17f.

4 וְצָמְחוּ בְּבֵין חָצִיר   כַּעֲרָבִים עַל-יִבְלֵי-מָיִם:

The fourth verse records the fruits of the outpouring of the Spirit. The *we* is therefore rendered with "and so" or with "so that." *tsāmaḥ* means to sprout, and the word can express not only the first sprouting but also the continued growing. In 42:9 it refers to a springing into being; in Exodus 10:5 and Ezekiel 17:6 the word means growing. It is difficult to decide how the word is to be understood here. Perhaps in the first clause it is to be taken in the sense of sprouting, in the second clause in the sense of growing. Verse 5 and, in fact, the whole promise refer to the newly converted.

Later commentators have simply changed *bebhēyn* to *kebhēyn*, in agreement with the LXX, which seems to have used a text which read *kebhēyn mayim ḥatsīr* — as amid waters, grass. That is appealing, but how can one be sure? A compound preposition is nothing unusual (cf. *mibbēyn*, Gen. 49:10), and since the reading *bebhēyn* did not disturb the Masoretes, it is best to accept that reading as correct.* The thought then is: They shall sprout up amid grass, namely, amid grass that grows luxuriantly beside water; they shall sprout like meadow flowers, here, there, everywhere. *'arābh* or *'arābhāh* is not the willow, which has serrated leaves, but is the Euphrates poplar, which has smooth-edged leaves and thrives along the banks of streams. (See Delitzsch's note on this passage.) Cf. Psalm 137:2; Leviticus 23:40; Job 40:22; Isaiah 15:7. Pictured is the vigorous spiritual growth of the newly converted, cf. Psalm 1:3.

5 זֶה יֹאמַר לַיהוָה אָנִי   וְזֶה יִקְרָא בְשֵׁם-יַעֲקֹב
וְזֶה יִכְתֹּב יָדוֹ לַיהוָה   וּבְשֵׁם יִשְׂרָאֵל יְכַנֶּה:

Verse 5 reviews verse 4 in detail. The threefold *zeh* indicates the great number of converts, and the description of each sets forth their zeal to confess the Lord. One says: "The Lord's am I," that is,

---

*The Dead Sea Scrolls read *kebhēyn*.

239

His servant and adorer. The phrase intimates the rejection of any other god. *yiqrā*, the predicate of the second *zeh*, is commonly translated as though the form were *yiqqārē*: "Will call himself by the name of Jacob." But there is no reason to alter the Masoretic pointing. *qārā' beshēm* (so frequent in Genesis: 12:8, etc.) here does not mean "call upon the name," but "to call or cry out" in praise of the name. Luther uses *predigen*, to call out in praise and devoted acknowledgment, to praise the name of Jacob, to hail as glorious the name that before had been despised. The third *zeh* writes with his own hand: "The Lord's," or "To the Lord" (Lamed indicating the dative or genitive). *kāthabh yādhō* cannot mean "upon his hand," as many translators have rendered the phrase, following the LXX, ἐπιγράψει χειρὶ αὐτοῦ . That would require an *'al* before *yādhō* (cf. 49:16). *yādhō* is here an accusative of the organ or means with which he writes (Gr. 117,3,s,p.367). Klostermann and Cheyne believe that the *be* in *beshēm* would necessarily have had to be repeated with *yādhō* and that it had somehow been lost. But even so, *be* would not introduce the object upon which *zeh* wrote, but rather the means with which he wrote. *kāthūbh bō* in Nehemiah 7:5; 8:14; 13:1, which is quoted as justification for that interpretation, means "written *in* the book" and is therefore not an exact parallel with "written upon the hand." The suffix of *yādhō* is intensive — with his own hand. *yekhanneh* in the concluding clause, as pointed in the text, is a Piel of *kānāh*. The root *kn* or *knn* means to cover or cover up. The word occurs also in Isaiah 45:4 and Job 32:21 and 22. In the Job passages the word clearly means to give an honorable title, to flatter, as an intensive of the preceding "to be partial to, to favor." In Isaiah 45:4 it is a stronger synonym of *qārā'* (to name), and means to surname, to name with honor. In this passage we have the same meaning, with the difference that here we have *be* with its object, and there the accusative. As *qārā' beshēm* means to call out about someone or in the name of someone, that is, to preach or praise the name, so also *kinnāh beshēm* can hardly mean anything other than to name a name as a title of honor. Recent translators have not been content to accept the pointing of the Masoretes but change *yekhanneh* (Piel) to *yekhunneh* (Pual) or *yikkānēh* (Niphal) — will be titled or will be surnamed or will surname himself, and they refer to the Arabic *kunya*, a title. But a change from Piel to Pual or Niphal is in no case required. The Masoretes were also Hebrew scholars, and we ought first of all to try to understand *kinnāh beshēm* before we try to force an English construction on the

Hebrew phrase. And so, *beshēm yisrā'el yekhanneh* does not mean that he will call himself by the honorable name of Israel, but that he will give honor to the name of Israel, praise and glorify it.

And now let us compare the first and second *zeh* with the third. Of the third *zeh* the same statement is made, in somewhat different words, that is made of the first and second taken together. The third *zeh writes* with his hand: "To the Lord," just as the first *zeh speaks*: "I am the Lord's." Thus he utters the name of the Lord with reverence and honor, just as the second *zeh* calls out the name of Jacob with praise. Between clauses one and three and two and four there is an intensifying synthetic parallelism. As one and three express an enthusiastic confession of the Lord, so two and four make a similar confession regarding the Lord's people. A more important question is whether the *zeh, zeh,* and *zeh* are descendants of the Jews or converted gentiles. Some modern liberals take the latter view. It will not do to say that it does not make sense to put such professions into the mouths of Jewish converts, because they by nature already belong to the Lord and to Israel. It does make sense, when we recall that a portion of the Jewish people in exile were ashamed of their God and His people. They considered the faithful portion of the people as worthy of banishment because of their loyalty to the name of the Lord (66:5), and they made a mockery of the name of the Lord. Since that was the case, and because the faithful in Israel saw no hope in the future, the Lord promises them that He will pour out His Spirit upon their seed and their offspring. Seed and offspring must be taken in the physical sense so long as the context does not clearly indicate a change to a spiritual meaning. Whoever takes *offspring,* at its first mention, in the spiritual sense, is assuming a prolepsis: Upon the spiritual seed will I pour out My Spirit. No, the Lord here speaks of pouring out His Spirit upon the unspiritual, physical descendants of Jeshurun. That this outpouring is also to extend to all flesh, we learn from Joel, Jeremiah, and other portions of Scripture, and not the least from Isaiah: 42:1ff; 45:23ff; 49; 55:5; 56:3ff; 60:3ff; 61:1ff; 65:1ff; 66. But Isaiah 44:5 speaks only of the physical offspring of Israel.

Résumé: The Lord's faithfulness is the assurance to believing Israel that it need not fear that it will not survive spiritually, for there will be an outpouring of the Spirit upon Israel's offspring, which will inspire them to a joyful confession.

241

Second Strophe: verses 6-20: *That the King and Redeemer of Israel, the only true God, is the hope and comfort of the believers; the makers of idols, however, will be confounded together with their idols that are nothing.*

The strophe has three parts: verses 6-8, the sole Godhead of the Lord as Israel's comfort; verses 9-17, which describes the folly of idol-manufacture, first in abstract terms (9-11), and then concretely (12-17); and verses 18-20, which pictures the blindness of the makers of idols.

First Section: verses 6-8: *The sole Godhead of the Lord as Israel's comfort.*

6 *Thus says the Lord, the King of Israel,*
   His Redeemer, the Lord of Hosts:
   I am the first and I the last,
   And apart from Me there is no God.
7 *For who prophesies like Me —*
   Then let him proclaim it and set it forth to Me! —
   Ever since I founded the people of olden time?
   So let them reveal to themselves the future
      and what is to come!
8 *Do not be afraid, nor be disquieted!*
   Have I not let you hear it from of old,
   And have I not proclaimed it — are you not My witnesses?
   Is there yet a God beside Me?
   But there is no Rock; I know of none.

כֹּה־אָמַ֣ר יְהוָ֤ה מֶֽלֶךְ־יִשְׂרָאֵל֙ וְגֹאֲל֖וֹ יְהוָ֣ה צְבָא֑וֹת 6
אֲנִ֤י רִאשׁוֹן֙ וַאֲנִ֣י אַחֲר֔וֹן וּמִבַּלְעָדַ֖י אֵ֥ין אֱלֹהִֽים׃

The meaningful names given to the Lord should receive primary attention. They establish the point of view from which the exclusive Godhead of the Lord is examined. "King of Israel" describes the relation of God to His people, both in its majesty and in its loving concern. A king is mindful of the welfare of his subjects. "His Redeemer" describes this relationship of love in respect to the one necessary act, the rescue of His charges out of hostile power. "Lord of hosts" reminds the people of His irresistible power. "I am the first, and I am the last," a familiar sentence in Scripture, is a vivid suggestion of the eternity of the Lord and of His exclusivity, which is again referred to at the end of verse 6. For *mibbalʿadhay* see 43:11.

242

7 וּמִי־כָמוֹנִי יִקְרָא וְיַגִּידֶהָ וְיַעְרְכֶהָ לִי

מִשּׂוּמִי עַם־עוֹלָם וְאֹתִיּוֹת וַאֲשֶׁר תָּבֹאנָה יַגִּידוּ לָמוֹ:

Verse 7 proves the nothingness of the idol gods by their inability to prophesy the future (43:9ff; 42:9; 41:4,22ff). The $\bar{u}$ at the beginning of verse 7 is more than a coordinating conjunction; it introduces verse 7 as the reason and grounds for the statement in verse 6. It is therefore to be translated not with *and*, but with *for* or *because*. I alone am God, for none but Me can prophesy. It is not necessary to supply the copula after *mī* nor the sign of the relative after *yiqrā'*. The Maqqeph binds *mī* and *khāmōnī* closely together. *qārā'* here has the pregnant sense of "to preach or prophesy." The next clause is parenthetical, but by means of the *we* it also becomes consecutive — then let him proclaim it and set it forth before Me. *missūmī 'am 'ōlām* is a temporal clause modifying the opening clause: Who, like Me, calls out, prophesies, from the time of My founding, etc.? *'am 'ōlām* is not an eternal people, as Ewald and Naegelsbach understand the phrase, nor does it refer to the founding of Israel, but it is as Delitzsch says, the original people, the original human race. The reason for that interpretation is not to be found in the parallel passages cited by Delitzsch, least of all in 40:7 and 42:5, but lies in the words themselves and in the context. *missūmī* clearly points to the past: Who, like the Lord, has prophesied ever since that time in the past? The idea of a future everlasting existence of Israel does not fit at all into that picture. The reference can only be back to the founding of Israel through Abraham, Jacob, and Moses. But even Israel is not an *'am 'ōlām* of the past, but is of more recent origin, so that *'am 'ōlām* must refer to the original human race. The prophesying of the Lord begins with the beginnings of the human family, and the question which the Lord puts as proof of His exclusive Godhead goes back into past time as far as possible. The reference to 63:11 is also not relevant. In that passage the reference is clearly to the origin of Israel in contrast to Israel's present, while here the reference is to *an* original people, or *the* original people, which Israel obviously is not. Luther is substantially correct with: "*Der ich von der Welt her die Voelker setze.*" — *'ōthīyōth*, a Qal participle plural feminine of *'āthāh*, to come (41:23; 45:11), are things that lie in the future. The word does not mean signs or portents, as Luther has it. The *we* introduces the apodosis and belongs to the verb *yaggīdhū*, which is to be understood as a jussive: "so let them proclaim." *'ōthīyōth* is the future as such, while *'asher tābhō'nāh* (for *tebhō'neynāh*, Qal im-

243

perfect third plural feminine) most likely points to the immediate future, to the *rī'shōnōth*, 41:22. *lāmō*, for themselves, is a dative commodi, like *'alī lākh* in 40:9 (Gr. 119,s,2,p.381). The LXX has *lānū*, to us. As long as the human race has existed, no idol has, like the Lord, ever foretold the future. If they are able to prophesy, as the Lord does, then let them do so now, *lāmō*, to their own advantage.

אַל־תִּפְחֲדוּ וְאַל־תִּרְהוּ   הֲלֹא מֵאָז הִשְׁמַעְתִּיךָ וְהִגַּדְתִּי 8
וְאַתֶּם עֵדָי הֲיֵשׁ אֱלוֹהַּ מִבַּלְעָדַי וְאֵין צוּר בַּל־יָדָעְתִּי:

The form *tirhū* as pointed in our text can only be a Qal imperfect second person plural from *rāhāh*. Since this verb occurs nowhere else, the form has become the object of much guesswork and many attempts at explanation. The LXX has πλανᾶσθε , to become confused, to lose one's way. The parallelism with *tiphḥadhū* requires that *tirhū* have a similar meaning, either intensified or weakened. That ought to satisfy the scholars. What goes beyond that is mere show.* The object of Israel's fears, which thus are presupposed, are, as in Jeremiah 10:5ff, the pagan deities, and not as Delitzsch supposes, the great catastrophe coming upon the nations, of which Cyrus was the instrument. If that were the cause of Israel's fears, what is the purpose of the lengthy mockery of those deities in verses 9-20, and what would be the relevance of this passage about the exclusive Godhead of the Lord? Isaiah 40:18 and passages that follow show that even the faithful in Israel were not wholly convinced that pagan deities were nothing, but were infected with fear of them, and 40:27 shows also that their faith in the exclusive Godhead of the Lord and in His help was being sorely disturbed. For that reason this entire first section strongly emphasizes the exclusive Godhead of the Lord and the nothingness of the idols; and wherever *'al tīrā'* occurs in this connection its purpose is to free Israel from fear of the pagan deities, to whose power the gentiles, and specifically Babylon, attributed their rise. It is also true that Israel's fear was directed to specific things. It feared that it might perish as a people in gentile lands under the influence of the pagan gods. Added to this was the fear that, because of the lack of the Spirit of God among them (verses 21-28), there might be no restoration of their homeland, of the city, and the temple, upon which according to ancient tradition the

---

*The Dead Sea Scrolls read *tīre'ū* from *yāre'*.

hopes of the people of God rested. In other words, they feared that there might be no fulfillment of the promises of their eternal survival as a people, promises which had been given to them by the Lord's prophets. They feared that the Davidic kingdom would come to an end, that there would be no continuance of the greatness and power of Israel, and particularly since the catastrophe of the Babylonian captivity they feared that the promises now being given of deliverance, regeneration, and rehabilitation in their own homes, and the restoration of Israel to glory would never be kept. These fears were rooted partly in Israel's doubt that Jehovah was God alone, and partly in the fear of the power of the deities that had made the gentile people so strong, who also had their astrologers, their portents, and their magicians, verse 25. This fear of Israel's was the soil on which the seed of the comforting promise of Isaiah II was being sown.

mēʿaz is to be taken in its absolute sense of "from of old," rather than in contrast with the present time, as "earlier, before this." The real object of *hishmaʿtīkhā* and *higgadhtī* is not at this point the sending of Cyrus, but, according to the immediate context, the sole Godhead of Jehovah and the nothingness of the gentile deities. God had preached this to His people, not just since yesterday or the day before, but since time immemorial, since the very beginning of Israel. Of that they had been witnesses since the days of the deliverance from Egypt and the giving of the Law on Sinai. The following rhetorical question: "Is there yet a God beside Me?" and the two positive assertions: "There is no Rock; I know of none," are a highly poetic declaration and confirmation of what had just been said. *'elōah*, occurring only in this one instance in Isaiah, is a generic term expressing majesty, while in the Book of Job, where the word is used very often, it is always a proper name. This abstract term is paired in the next clause with *tsūr*, a rock. What is meant by a rock is shown in 17:10, Rock of your strength; in 26:4, everlasting strength; in Psalm 31:4(3); 62:8(7), and other passages. Our passage quite likely rests on Deuteronomy 32:31 and Psalm 18:3(2), 32(31) (2 Sam. 22:32). Help, Strength, and Refuge are meant. That is what God means to those who trust in Him. Apart from Jehovah there is no such God. The omniscient Lord Himself knows of none. With that, the fate of faithful Israel is sealed as well as that of the idol worshiping heathen — for Israel, deliverance and salvation; for the gentiles, destruction. — The emendations of the text proposed by the modern scholars are all unjustified, and they ruin the poetic beauty of the conclusion.

245

Second Section: verses 9-17:   *The futility of idol-worship.*
Part A: verses 9-11:   *The futility of the makers of idols.*

9   *The makers of idols are altogether as nothing,*
    And their treasured works are worthless,
    And they are their witnesses
    That they see nothing and know nothing,
    So that they may be put to shame.
10   *Who ever forms a god or molds an image*
    So that it should — not help?
11   *Behold all his worshipers stand ashamed,*
    And the fabricators themselves are but human beings;
    Let them all assemble and stand together —
    They shall be terrified and put to shame together.

יֹצְרֵי־פֶסֶל כֻּלָּם תֹּהוּ וַחֲמוּדֵיהֶם בַּל־יוֹעִילוּ

וְעֵדֵיהֶם הֵמָּה בַּל־יִרְאוּ וּבַל־יֵדְעוּ לְמַעַן יֵבֹשׁוּ׃

The preceding strophe asserted the exclusive Godhead of Jehovah; this strophe makes the contrary assertion that the pagan deities are a nothing. The form of the contrast is, however, an indirect one, since it is not the idols themselves that are shown to be
nothing, but rather the makers of the idols. That is a bit of poetic
art that should not be overlooked, because by this kind of presentation the prophet achieves his purpose to dispel Israel's fears all
the more surely, since he now can make the nothingness of the
idols concretely vivid by describing how they are being manufactured.

tōhū occurs rather frequently in Isaiah: 40:17,23; 41:29; 45:18,
19; 49:4; 59:4; also in the first part: 24:10; 29:21; 34:11. Outside of
Isaiah the word occurs only nine times. It obviously derives its
meaning from its use in Genesis 1:2 and is really a substantive
meaning a physical waste, a void. In this sense Isaiah uses it only
three times: 24:10; 34:11; 45:18. Otherwise he uses it in its
spiritual sense: vanity, emptiness, nothingness. He even uses it
twice (45:19; 49:4) in the adverbial sense of in vain, uselessly. (See
the synonyms that accompany *tōhū* in 40:17,23,etc.) The manufacturers of idols are here called *tōhū,* naturally insofar as their occupation is concerned. Paired with the makers of idols are the idols
as *hamūdhēyhem* (Qal passive participle of *hāmadh*), their prized
treasures, their cherished possessions, which, however, are worthless, of no help and no use (Hiphil of *yā'al*). The predicates of the
two opening clauses are to be understood as attributes. The mak-

ers of idols are worthless people, and their idols are dead and useless things that do nothing and accomplish nothing.

hēmmāh, in the next clause, is textually uncertain and was so
designated by the Masoretes, perhaps even earlier. If we accept
hēmmāh as the correct reading, then the clause reads: "and their
witnesses are they." The question then is: Who is meant by *they*
and who by *their*? Do the idol makers bear witness about the idols,
or do the idols bear witness about their makers? Since in verse 8
Israel is cited as a witness to the Godhead of the Lord, it would be
most natural here to assume that the makers of idols are witnesses for their own idols. But it is a grammatical anomaly to
make "their witness are they" refer to the nothingness of the
idols. *ʿedhēyhem hēmmāh*, they are their witnesses, is followed by
bal yir'ū as the object: And they (the makers of idols) are their
(the idols') witnesses that they (the idols) see nothing and know
nothing, Gr. 120,p. 385f and 157,p. 491f. The makers of idols testify themselves to the blindness and unconsciousness of their own
idols. *lema'an yēbhōshū*, so that they are put to shame, refers to
worshipers of idols. *lema'an* here expresses a result that is contrary to the intended one (Ges. Buhl under *m'n*, at the end). This
discomfiture is the consequence of the ignorance of the idols and
of the testimony thereto by their makers. Since they themselves
testify that their idols know nothing, they are put to shame, a
result quite contrary to their purpose in making the idols. The following verses tell how they are put to shame.

That is one possible explanation. If, however, one strikes out
hēmmāh altogether, then the suffix of *ʿedhēyhem*, like that of
hamūdhēyhem, refers to the idol makers, and the witnesses are
the idols. We then have the statement that the idols as witnesses
for their makers neither see anything nor know anything, with
the result that the idol makers are put to shame. The idols can be
named their worshipers' witnesses insofar as the worshipers rely
upon these deities as their helpers in need, their miracle-workers,
their diviners, and their prophets, verse 25. This construction
avoids the necessity of identifying the witnesses with the prized
treasures, namely, the idols themselves. The witnesses could be
the initiated servants, the priests, or similar persons. The sense is
very acceptable: The makers of idols are altogether nothing, for
their deities are worthless and their priests see nothing and know
nothing, and thus — contrary to their purpose — they are put to
shame. We have gone into this matter at such length in order to

demonstrate by this example that the positiveness of commentators often rests on nothing more solid than a *sic volo.**

¹⁰ מִי־יָצַר אֵל וּפֶסֶל נָסָךְ לְבִלְתִּי הוֹעִיל:

A well-known universal truth proves the worthlessness of the makers of idols. No one fashions an idol or molds an image with the intention that it shall not help — *nemo fere, nisi insanit.*

¹¹ הֵן כָּל־חֲבֵרָיו יֵבֹשׁוּ וְחָרָשִׁים הֵמָּה מֵאָדָם
יִתְקַבְּצוּ כֻלָּם יַעֲמֹדוּ יִפְחֲדוּ יֵבֹשׁוּ יָחַד:

The suffix of *ḥabhērāyw* is usually taken to refer to *'el* and *pesel*. The *ḥabhērīm* are the devotees, the members of the guild of priests, the followers of the idols; and reference is made to the fellowship that is created between the idol and his worshipers, of which Scripture frequently speaks. "Here the prophet means the worshipers of the idol, who together formed a kind of guild, and by partaking of the sacrificial meals were brought into a mystical union with the god whom they worshiped; cf. Psalm 106:28; Hosea 4:17; 1 Corinthians 10:20; Mark 1:23." (Cheyne, *Isaiah*, p. 286.) The latter statement is certainly true; but it does not therefore follow that *ḥabhērāyw* refers to the worshipers of idols. There is no reason, either in the grammar or in the context, why the suffix of *ḥabhērāyw* should not be taken to refer to the *mī* of verse 10, the makers of the idol, rather than to the idols' devotees, especially since *ḥarāshīm*, fabricators, follows as a parallel in the next clause. The molders of idol images and their helpers shall be put to shame; and the master workmen are themselves but human beings. So, the entire company of idol manufacturers must be put to shame, because they themselves are but human beings and the creatures of a God, and as such are certainly not able to create the God who made them. *yithqabbetsū* and *ya'amōdhū* are both jussives and form a conditional clause, while *yiphḥadhū* and *yēbhōshū* form the independent clause. Luther's translation is correct. After this abstract description of the worthlessness of the makers of idols, there now follows a vivid description of the complete folly of idol manufacture, 12-17.

---

*In the Dead Sea Scrolls the word *hēmmāh* is omitted in the text, but is written in above the line.

Part B: verses 12-17:   *The foolishness of the makers of idols.*

12   One works iron with a chisel,
Makes it glow over coals,
He works it with hammers,
Shapes it with his powerful arm;
He goes hungry till strength deserts him,
He drinks no water and becomes exhausted.

13   Another works with wood, draws a measuring line,
Marks it with a scriber, shaves it with planes,
With compasses he gives it shape
And forms it into the image of a man,
With the beauty of human form — to dwell in a house.

14   To have fine wood of quality to cut
He takes for himself a Tirsah, or he takes an oak,
Nurtures it among the trees of the forest,
Or plants a sycamore and the rain nourishes it.

15   And since it serves man for fire,
He takes of it to warm himself;
And just as he kindles it to bake his bread,
So he also makes of it a god and prays to it;
He makes an idol of it and falls down before it.

16   One half he burns in the fire
And over this half he eats his meat,
He roasts his meat and satisfies his hunger,
Warms himself at the same time and says: "Ha, ha!
I am warm and feel the fire's glow."

17   And the rest he makes into a god, his idol,
Prostrates himself before it, worships it, prays to it,
And says: "Save me, for are you not my god!"

חָרַשׁ בַּרְזֶל מַעֲצָד וּפָעַל בַּפֶּחָם 12
וּבַמַּקָּבוֹת יִצְּרֵהוּ וַיִּפְעָלֵהוּ בִּזְרוֹעַ כֹּחוֹ
גַּם־רָעֵב וְאֵין כֹּחַ לֹא־שָׁתָה מַיִם וַיִּיעָף ׃

ḥārash may of course be the construct state of a noun; then
ḥārash barzel is a worker in iron, a smith; and *ḥārash ʿetsīm*, in
verse 13, a carpenter. That is the usual explanation. Vitringa has
faber ferrarius — faber lignarius; Gesenius: the smith — the carpenter; Knobel adds *maʿatsādh* to the phrase: the metalworker of
blades or swordsmith — the woodworker; Delitzsch: the smith —
the carpenter; Hahn: the master in iron of the ax — the master in
wood; Bredenkamp: the smith — the carpenter; Cheyne: the smith

— the carpenter; Kautzsch: the smith — the wood-carver; Budde: the master in iron — the master in wood; and so on. The LXX has ὥξυνε τέκτων σίδερον, "the smith sharpens an ax"; but it is not clear how the meaning *sharpens* is arrived at. As the words are pointed and punctuated by the Masoretes, they are quite unintelligible. Of *ma'atsādh* no more is known than that it is some kind of cutting tool. But what does "worker of metal a cutting tool" mean? Knobel and Hahn are not to be taken seriously here. Delitzsch believes that in all probability a word has dropped out, and taking his cue from the LXX, he thinks it may have been the Piel *ḥiddēdh*, to sharpen. Cheyne, also following the lead of the LXX and Peshitta, prefers the Hiphil perfect *hēḥēdh* (of *ḥādhadh*). Driver prefers *yaḥadh* (jussive), or the regular Hiphil form *yaḥēdh*. Still others think that *yāḥadh* (altogether) is misplaced at the end of verse 11 and really belongs here and is not an adverb, but is a Hiphil imperfect of *ḥādhadh*. That seems quite likely when one considers the LXX and Peshitta readings, for everything then becomes clear: The smith sharpens the *ma'atsādh*, the cutting tool, and (now no longer following the LXX) he works (it — the idol?) in the glowing coals, etc. If only one could be certain about these conjectures! It is also possible to put aside the *yaḥadh* conjecture and imagine that *ūpā'al* was originally *yiph'al*, a very slight change from *Yod* to *Waw*. That too would make good sense.*

But why not leave the words just as they were pointed by the Masoretes, who also were Hebrew scholars of note, and take *ḥārash*, as Luther did, to be a verb in the simple Qal perfect (the same in verse 13) with an impersonal subject: One works the iron, etc. (Gr. 144,d,p.460). That clears up everything without forcing the text. *ma'atsādh* is then an accusative of means or instrument, even though in this case the condition mentioned in Gr. 117,3,s,p. 367f. is not met. Cf. Gr. 144, 4.1,p. 461. In order to preserve a natural sequence of the processes of manufacture, we would prefer to accept Delitzsch's "cold-chisel" for *ma'atsādh*. One works iron with a chisel, makes it glow in the coals (*pā'al bappeḥām*), forms it with hammers, works (beats) it with his powerful arm; he goes hungry and his strength fails him, he drinks no water and becomes exhausted. This is simple and quite natural. It describes how zealously a worker in metal shapes his material from the beginning to the end. He forgets to eat and to drink, becomes weak and exhausted at his work.

---

*The Dead Sea Scrolls read the last word of verse 11 as *yaḥdāw*.

¹³ חָרַשׁ עֵצִים נָטָה קָו יְתָאֲרֵהוּ בַשֶּׂרֶד

יַעֲשֵׂהוּ בַּמַּקְצֻעוֹת וּבַמְּחוּגָה יְתָאֳרֵהוּ

וַיַּעֲשֵׂהוּ כְּתַבְנִית אִישׁ כְּתִפְאֶרֶת אָדָם לָשֶׁבֶת בָּיִת:

The manufacture of wooden idols is *mutatis mutandis* the same. *ḥārash* is a Qal perfect: "One cuts wood." All the rest is simple. After the carpenter has hewn his wood, he measures the required piece with a measuring line, marks it with a scriber (*sered* is not a red marking chalk, as Kimchi, Luther, Vitringa translate, but a sharp pointed tool); he planes it down to the marked lines, and with a compass marks it off to the desired shape (regarding the *o* vowels in *yetho'orēhū* instead of *a*, as in the first occurrence of this word in verse 13, see Gr. 64,i,p.171), and shapes it into the form of a man, with the beauty of the human form, to live in a house. There is a certain irony in the last clause. There is an allusion to God's creation of man after His own image, and also to the fact that God does not dwell in temples made with hands, 40:22; 66:1. The description is general enough to include large images to dwell in temples and small ones for private homes.

¹⁴ לִכְרָת־לוֹ אֲרָזִים וַיִּקַּח תִּרְזָה וְאַלּוֹן

וַיְאַמֶּץ־לוֹ בַּעֲצֵי־יָעַר נָטַע אֹרֶן וְגֶשֶׁם יְגַדֵּל:

Commentators have had much trouble with the opening infinitive with *le*. Bredenkamp considers this an impossible reading and thinks *yikhroth* would be just as bad. He and Klostermann move the first three words back into verse 13, and Delitzsch thinks that is impossible. Knobel connects *likhroth* with *weya'asēhū* of verse 13, which is altogether impossible. Delitzsch explains the phrase as an *oratio periphrastica,* "caesurus est," but then rejects this reading and substitutes *yikhroth* for *likhroth,* since the periphrastic future seems too artificial. But the difficulty comes from treating *likhroth* as an independent verb instead of subordinating it to the following *yiqqaḥ.* This explanation is generally rejected because of the *wa* with *yiqqaḥ.* But this is a case of a clause of purpose expressed by *le* with an infinitive (Gr. 165,c,p.504) and occupying a lead position (Gr. 114,g,p.348). The independent verb *yiqqaḥ* follows with *Waw apodosis.* This is similar to the so-called *casus pendens* (Gr. 143,d.p.458). It is like our English construction: In order to cut cedars for himself, he takes, etc. Delitzsch's observation about cedars, *'arāzīm,* is valuable: " *'arāzīm,*" he says, "is a

251

generic idea expressed in the plural, and the trees (*tirzāh* and *'allōn*) are understood by the Talmud and Midrash to be species of cedars." But, even so, the fact that *tirzāh* and *'allōn* follow *'arāzīm* as synonyms shows that the words are not used in their specific botanical sense. *'arāzīm* is, so to speak, a concrete expression designating the abstract idea of high-grade durable wood, and *tirzāh* and *'allōn* are examples of such wood. *tirzāh* has of late been identified by some as the stone-oak, but nothing certain is known about this tree. If *'allōn* and *'ēlōn* are one and the same tree, then *'allōn* is the oak, but this too is not certain. And so, the sense is: In order to have a durable specimen of wood to work with, he takes for himself a stone-oak and/or an oak, etc. The description now goes back to an account of the great care with which the idol maker prepares his material. *ye'ammets* can hardly mean, either here or in Psalm 80:16,18(15,17), "to decide, select, determine mentally." In the Psalm the word is a synonym of "to plant and care for." Here it is parallel with *geshem yeghaddēl*, "the rain nourishes it," and so the word would say that he nourishes the tree and strengthens the tree by caring for it among the trees of the forest. *lō* in both occurrences of the word is a dative *commodi*. In the case of *ōren* (written in the Masoretic text with *Nun minusculum*, which Luther mistook for *Zayin* and read *'erez*, a cedar), we can do no more than make a guess, despite the confident assertions of the scholars. *ōren* could possibly be a pine, but probably it is only another word for *'erez*, since *erinu* in Assyrian is said to be a cedar. Parallel with *ye'ammets* of the preceding clause we now have *nāṭa'*, "he plants," and "the rain makes it grow." The sense is that the makers of idols work at manufacturing their gods over a period of years, exercising the greatest of care and making nature their helper, all of which just makes their efforts seem the more foolish.

15 וְהָיָה לְאָדָם לְבָעֵר וַיִּקַּח מֵהֶם וַיָּחָם אַף־יַשִּׂיק וְאָפָה לָחֶם אַף־יִפְעַל־אֵל וַיִּשְׁתָּחוּ עָשָׂהוּ פֶסֶל וַיִּסְגָּד־לָמוֹ:

The subject of *hāyāh* is the species of those trees mentioned in verse 14. Such a tree when felled serves men for burning (Piel inf. cst.), as firewood. The masculine suffix of *mēhem* serves here, as is often the case, as a feminine to express a neuter idea, Gr. 135, Notes 1 and 2,o,p,p. 440f. A man takes of *it* and warms himself. Some critics substitute *yiqdaḥ* (he burns it) for *yiqqaḥ*. *yassīq* is a Hiphil imperfect of a Qal stem *nāsaq*, which besides this form, occurs only as a Niphal (*nisseqāh*) in Psalm 78:21 and as a Hiphil (*hissīqu*) in Ezekiel 39:9. In those two passages the meaning in the Hiphil and the Niphal is clearly "to ignite, to catch fire, to be burned." The word is not used otherwise. *'aph*, followed by another *'aph*, is like our "both — and" or "as — so also." "As he sets fire to it and bakes bread with it, so also he makes a god of it, prays to it, and falls down in worship before it." For an explanation of the form *yishtāḥū*, see Gr. 75,kk,p. 215. *lāmō* is here a singular for *lō*. See Gr. 103, Note 3, p. 302. This is important for the interpretation of *lāmō* in 53:8.

$$\text{16 } \text{חֶצְיוֹ שָׂרַף בְּמוֹ־אֵשׁ עַל־חֶצְיוֹ בָּשָׂר יֹאכֵל יִצְלֶה צָלִי}$$
$$\text{וְיִשְׂבָּע}$$
$$\text{אַף־יָחֹם וְיֹאמַר הֶאָח חַמּוֹתִי רָאִיתִי אוּר׃}$$

ḥetsyō occurs twice in the verse and is not to be translated as "its one half — its other half." The counterpart to *ḥetsyō* is *she'erithō* in verse 17. The second *ḥetsyō* is only a repetition of the first, and both refer to the same half. For *bemō* equaling *be*, consult Gr. 103,k,p. 303. The sense is: One half of it he burns in the fire, and over this half he eats meat, etc. *he'aḥ* is an expression of satisfaction. Delitzsch explains *rā'ah* as a comprehensive term embracing every kind of sensation and perception. Therefore: "I feel the fire." Compare 47:14 (*'ur lāshebheth neghdō*), a fire before which one sits.

$$\text{17 } \text{וּשְׁאֵרִיתוֹ לְאֵל עָשָׂה לְפִסְלוֹ יִסְגּוֹד־לוֹ וְיִשְׁתַּחוּ}$$
$$\text{וְיִתְפַּלֵּל אֵלָיו וְיֹאמַר הַצִּילֵנִי כִּי אֵלִי אָתָּה׃}$$

The Masoretes separated *ushe'erithō* from the rest of the sentence by means of a Zaqeph. The sense then is: As for the rest of it — to a god he makes it, into an idol. *yisgowdh* contains a superfluous *Waw*, which may be ignored. The verbs of adoration are arranged in the form of a climax and reach their height in the last clause: And says, "Save me, for you are my god!"

Résumé of verses 12-17: The purpose and the result of all this activity is that the idol-maker takes the trunk of the tree which, with the help of nature, he had carefully grown and nourished through the years. He uses part of it to cook his food and to warm himself; the rest he shapes with cunning hand into human form, declares it to be his god, and falls down before it, pleading to be saved. — This was also the purpose and object of the bitter labor of the smiths, as described in verse 12.

253

Third Section: verses 18-20: *The blindness of the idol makers.*

18 *They know not, neither do they understand,*
    For their eyes are sealed, so that they cannot see,
    And their heart, so that they cannot perceive.

19 *And he does not let it enter his head,*
    Nor is there any sense or understanding,
        that he should say:
    Half of it I burned in the fire,
    And baked bread with the heat of it —
    I roasted meat and ate it,
    And the rest I made into an abomination,
    Before an image of wood I bow down in worship.

20 *He who tends ashes — a misguided heart has betrayed him,*
    And he shall not save his soul,
    For he will not say: Is there not a lie in my right hand?

18 לֹא יָדְעוּ וְלֹא יָבִינוּ כִּי טַח מֵרְאוֹת עֵינֵיהֶם מֵהַשְׂכִּיל
לִבֹּתָם:

Beginning with verse 18, the description reverts to the abstract
form. The subject is plural in verse 18; in the following verses it is
singular. That is merely poetic variation; the singular subject is to
be understood as generic. The subject of this description, as distinct from that of the two preceding sections, is the incurable
blindness of the idol makers. In verses 9-11 the subject was their
nothingness; in verses 12-17, their foolishness; here it is their
blindness. The main thought is, as so often, expressed at the very
beginning. *yādha'* implies clarity of understanding; *hēbhīn*, depth
of perception. The negative preceding the bare verb expresses a
denial of any activity of mind. "They know not, neither do they understand," says that there is no perception or understanding
whatever in them. The next clause, introduced by *kī,* gives the reason: "For their eyes are sealed, so that they do not see, and their
heart, so that they cannot perceive." *taḥ* is not a form of the transitive verb *tūaḥ,* to seal, but is a Qal perfect of the intransitive
tāhaḥ, to be sealed. Although the verb is in the singular it is the
predicate of the dual *'eynēyhem* and also of the plural *libbōthām,* a
construction that may occur when the verb, for the sake of emphasis, is placed at the head of the sentence. See Gr. 145, o,p. 465. For
min with infinitive *re'ōth* and *haskīl,* see Gr. 119,y,p. 382. *taḥ*
should be repeated before *haskīl;* it is the governing concept of the
whole passage. *lēbh,* or *lēbhābh,* is not only the seat of the emotions, but often also of the understanding, as in this passage and in
the following verse.

254

¹⁹ וְלֹא־יָשִׁיב אֶל־לִבּוֹ וְלֹא דַעַת וְלֹא־תְבוּנָה לֵאמֹר
חֶצְיוֹ שָׂרַפְתִּי בְמוֹ־אֵשׁ וְאַף אָפִיתִי עַל־גֶּחָלָיו לֶחֶם אֶצְלֶה
בָשָׂר וְאֹכֵל
וְיִתְרוֹ לְתוֹעֵבָה אֶעֱשֶׂה לְבוּל עֵץ אֶסְגּוֹד:

hēshĭbh 'el lēbh does not mean to take something to heart, that is, to repent, as Luther understood it; it has to do with the understanding and means to consider, to take thought, as in Deuteronomy 4:39; 30:1; Lamentations 3:21. It is that activity which produces *da'ath* and *tebhūnāh.* Since they do not let it enter their minds, there is no perception or understanding. *gaḥeleth* is the glowing hot coal; *peḥām* (verse 12) is the coal in general. In this verse we have *yether*, the remainder, in the same sense as *she'ērĭth* in verse 17. For the translation of *'e'eseh* as a *potential*, see Gr. 107,r,p. 318, also Note 4. *būl 'ets* is not a block of wood, but is the equivalent of *yebhūl 'ets*, what the tree produces, what is procured from the tree (from *yābhal*, to lead, to bring forth, to bear). The final clause is a reproof of the immorality of manufacturing idols.

²⁰ רֹעֶה אֵפֶר לֵב הוּתַל הִטָּהוּ וְלֹא־יַצִּיל אֶת־נַפְשׁוֹ וְלֹא
יֹאמַר הֲלוֹא שֶׁקֶר בִּימִינִי:

The participle *rō'eh* is not to be translated "he tends or feeds ashes," nor "a tender of ashes is he." The first part of the sentence is a *māshāl*, a proverb, like the proverbs of Solomon, which contains a universal truth. The entire activity of the idol makers is summed up in this proverb and condemned. The translation is therefore: "He who tends ashes, etc." Tending ashes is a picture of utterly useless activity. Cf. feeding or tending the wind, in Hosea 12:2(1); preserving truth or faithfulness (Luther unfortunately: *und naehre dich redlich*), Psalm 37:3; feeding on foolishness, Proverbs 15:14. Before *hūthal* (perfect Hophal of *tālal*, to hang limp, Hiphil, to deceive, Hophal, to be deceived, led astray), supply *'asher* — "a heart that has been led astray." *hiṭṭāhū* is Hiphil of *nāṭāh*, to incline, to lead from the right path. A deceived heart has led him astray. The consequence is that he shall not save his soul from destruction. The *we* that introduces the last clause is explanatory. He shall not save his soul, since he never comes to understand that there is a lie in his hand, and all his idolatry is self-deception. See 1 Timothy 6:5; 2 Timothy 3:8; 2 Peter 2:12.

255

Résumé of verses 6-20:

First Section: verses 6-8: Israel has no reason to be concerned about its future because the Lord, its King and Redeemer, the Lord of hosts, is the only true God. He alone proclaims the future, as He has done from the beginning. To this Israel itself bears witness.

Second Section: verses 9-17: The manufacture of idols is an utterly vain and useless undertaking, and all who participate in it are put to shame. One person wears himself out completely at constructing a metal idol; another, with much skill and labor, shapes a tree trunk into human form, having first given much care to growing a suitable tree. He uses part of it as firewood to cook his food and to warm himself; the rest he makes into a god and worships it.

Third Section: verses 18-20: All this is a blindness that keeps them from ever coming to the understanding that they are engaged in an activity that is altogether vain and an abomination. He who "tends ashes" is lost.

Third Strophe: verses 21-23: *Israel, the Lord's servant, may glory in the forgiveness of its sins and its actual redemption.*

21 *O Jacob, and Israel, remember this — that you are*
  My servant;
  I formed you, you are Mine, a servant to Me.
  O Israel, do not forget Me!
22 *I purge your transgressions like a mist,*
  And your sins like a cloud.
  Return to Me, for I redeem you.
23 *Rejoice, O heavens, for the Lord has done it,*
  Depths of the earth, shout aloud!
  Hills, break forth in rejoicing,
  The forest and every tree in it!
  For the Lord has redeemed Jacob
  And glorified Himself in Israel.

זְכָר־אֵלֶּה יַעֲקֹב וְיִשְׂרָאֵל כִּי עַבְדִּי־אָתָּה 21

יְצַרְתִּיךָ עֶבֶד־לִי אַתָּה יִשְׂרָאֵל לֹא תִנָּשֵׁנִי :

'elleh refers to what follows, not to something previously mentioned, in spite of what Delitzsch and Cheyne maintain (Delitzsch: the foolishness of idol making; Cheyne, who ascribes verses 9-20 to some other author, takes *'elleh* to refer to the sole Godhead of the Lord, as asserted in verses 6-8). Isaiah 46:8 likewise does not

refer back, but forward to verse 9. *ʾelleh* refers back only in exceptional cases; as a rule it refers forward to something new that is yet to be mentioned, Gr. 136,a,b,p. 442. The mistake comes from unconsciously taking *zekhor*, remember, to mean "call to mind," instead of "to keep in mind." Delitzsch understands it as being in contrast to the blindness of verse 18 and paraphrases it thus: "Jacob was to have firmly impressed upon its mind," namely, the thing to which it had been blind. But that is not the point of contrast here. *zekhor* means to recall something that is passed, to call to mind a past event, as in 43:26. But this idol making in Babylon was not something of that nature, for the manufacture of idols was going on every day before Israel's very eyes. What Israel was to remember out of the past was what now follows, namely, Israel's relation to its God, its servant relation, which is so strongly emphasized here. Those who refer *ʾelleh* to the idol making are forced to understand the following *kī* as causal. The repetition of, and the emphasis on, the servant-relation argues against the assumption that Israel is to remember the blindness and the folly of idol making. A single mention of that relation would have sufficed to call to mind the folly of idol-making, which certainly had already been sufficiently exposed in verses 9-20 for every understanding person. The reason for this strong emphasis on Israel's servant relation must be that it is this great fact that Israel is to keep in mind and never forget. The contrast of this short strophe to the preceding long one is briefly this: Idol making is foolishness, since the idols are nothing and can do nothing. Israel's case is quite different. As the Lord's servant, it has the Lord as its God and therewith also has forgiveness of sins and redemption. *kī* before *ʿabhdī ʾattāh* is therefore to be translated with *that*, since it introduces the object of *zekhor*. The three clauses introduced by *kī* express the content and the development of *ʾelleh*. *zekhor* must be repeated either before or after *yisrāʾel* to read: "Remember, O Jacob, and Israel, remember that, etc." Israel's lot is more fortunate than that of the idol makers; it is the Lord's servant. Israel did not form Him (as the idol makers formed their god); God formed Israel (*yetsartīkhā*), and Israel is therefore His servant and is in possession of everything that being formed by the Lord and belonging to Him as His servant implies — forgiveness and salvation.

The concluding clause repeats the opening clause in negative form. *yisrāʾel lōʾ thinnāshēnī* can never mean "Israel, thou shalt remain unforgotten of Me" (Delitzsch) or "Thou canst not be forgotten" (Cheyne). The LXX, Targum, Peshitta, Vulgate, and Luther are right when they translate this Niphal with suffix as though it were a Qal. Orelli and Hitzig are also right when they say that this translation is possible even if the pointing of *thinnāshēnī* as a Niphal is correct. Delitzsch's argument against this does not hold water. If the reflexive nature of the Niphal is such that in Genesis 4:18 *wayyiwwāledh lahanōkh 'eth 'īrādh* can mean "and there begat itself to Enoch Irad" (Irad in the accusative), then certainly this phrase can mean: Israel, do not let yourself become weak in respect to Me — do not forget Me! Since the Masoretes pointed the form as a Niphal (*thinnāshēnī*) without adding any footnote, it is the business of the exegete to project himself into their way of thinking and to translate accordingly. We have no right to make a change in the text or to invert the sense, just because it is difficult for us to think of a reflexive or a passive verb with an accusative object. Cf. Gr. 117,x,p. 369. We repeat: *yisrā'el lō' thinnāshēnī* is an intentional return in negative form to the thought in the opening clause, with only this difference that here we have *Me* instead of *this* as the object. The next verse spells this out.

22 מָחִיתִי כָעָב פְּשָׁעֶיךָ וְכֶעָנָן חַטֹּאותֶיךָ
שׁוּבָה אֵלַי כִּי גְאַלְתִּיךָ׃

The perfects in *māhīthī* and *ge'altīkhā* are prophetic perfects. With God, purging of sin and redemption are accomplished facts, although the act of redemption still lies in the future. *pesha'* is the word for grievous transgression, usually breach of faith or apostasy (cf. 1:2). *hattā'th* is the common word for sin. Accordingly, *'ābh*, a thick cloud, is coupled with *pesha'*; and *'ānān*, the common word for cloud, with the weaker *hattā'th*. The picture is incomplete. The full picture is: "As the sun dispels cloud and mist, so do I purge your transgressions." That is what Israel should bear in mind (*zākhar*) and should not forget about its God, *lō' thinnāsheh*. As the sun dispels the clouds, so the Lord's sin-forgiving grace eagerly, easily, and completely devours Israel's sin, the cause of its exile to Babylon. Redemption is connected inseparably with forgiveness. "Where there is forgiveness of sin, there is also life and salvation." With this promise as a background there now sounds forth the invitation: "Turn back to Me!" Isaiah 53:6a is presupposed.

23 רָנּוּ שָׁמַיִם כִּי־עָשָׂה יְהוָה הָרִיעוּ תַּחְתִּיּוֹת אָרֶץ
פִּצְחוּ הָרִים רִנָּה יַעַר וְכָל־עֵץ בּוֹ
כִּי־גָאַל יְהוָה יַעֲקֹב וּבְיִשְׂרָאֵל יִתְפָּאָר׃

With an admonition that all creation rejoice and sing because of this promise of the Lord, the prophet concludes this prophecy, verses 1-23. Cf. 42:11; 49:13. Not the Lord, but the prophet, as a member of the redeemed congregation, utters this admonition. The promise is presented as already actually fulfilled. *kī ʿāsāh,* that He had done it, accomplished it, is emphatic and absolute. With God, to say and to do are one. The imperfect *yithpā ʾar* (pausal for *yithpā ʾer*), follows the perfect *gā ʾal,* according to the *consecutio temporum* — He *has* redeemed, *has* glorified Himself. The *taḥtīyōth ʾerets* are hardly *she ʾōl,* as Cheyne has maintained referring to many passages, for *she ʾōl* has no mouth of praise, 38:18; Psalm 6:6 (5); 88:13 (12); Ecclesiasticus 17:27,28 (25,26). The *taḥtīyōth,* with their hills and forests, are just the physical counterpart to *shāmayim,* a designation of the earth as lower than the heavens (Isa. 1:2; Gen. 1:1, etc.). It is not necessary to follow the lead of Delitzsch and picture the depths of the earth as referring to the interior with its caverns and its deepest recesses. His reference to Psalm 139:15 is mistaken, for in that passage the expression is merely figurative. Heaven and earth and everything that is in them are to break forth in joyous song over the wonder of grace and salvation.

Résumé of the Discourse: 44:1-23: "The exulting finale is a safe boundary-stone of this fifth prophecy" (Delitzsch). But it began, not with *kōh ʿāmar* in 44:6, but already with *we ʿattāh shemaʿ* in 44:1, that is, with the wholly new promise of the *outpouring of the Spirit* upon Israel's progeny, verses 1-5, which is here mentioned for the first time in Isaiah. This is the real theme of the passage, which then proceeds to confirm the fulfillment of this promise with the fact of the sole Godhead of the Lord (verses 6-8), and continues with the description of the vain and foolish manufacture of impotent idols, which in no way are able to hinder the fulfillment of the Lord's promise (verses 9-20), and concludes in verses 21-23 with a promise of forgiveness of sins and deliverance out of exile as a means to the accomplishment of the greater promise of verses 1-5. In the following discourse *kōh ʿāmar* occurs no fewer than five times — a sufficient proof that this phrase does not always mark the beginning of a new discourse.

Third Discourse: Chapters 44:24-45:25

Israel's deliverance and glorification accomplished by Cyrus is a summons to all the world to seek salvation in the Lord, who alone is true God.

This discourse has two parts. The first part, 44:24-45:13, presents the deliverance of Israel by Cyrus as an exhortation to all the world to recognize the Lord as the only true God, and also as a chastisement of the Lord's people because of their sinful murmuring. The second part, 45:14-25, presents the glorification of delivered Israel as an exhortation to all the world to seek salvation in the Lord as the one true and revealed God.

The first part is divided into three sub-parts: (1) 44:24-28, the Lord, who does and controls all things, calls Cyrus to restore Jerusalem; (2) 45:1-7, the Lord yields Babylon to him for Israel's sake, so that he and all the world shall recognize His sole Godhead; (3) 45:8-13, salvation in fullest measure comes in spite of Israel's disobedient murmuring, because the Lord in His faithful zeal for Israel's salvation makes Cyrus His servant.

Part I: 44:24-45:13: *The deliverance of Israel by Cyrus is an admonition to the gentiles to recognize the Lord as the one true God, and at the same time it is also a reprimand for Israel, because of its disobedient murmuring.*

First Strophe: 44:24-28: *The Lord who alone orders all things appoints Cyrus as the restorer of Jerusalem.*

24 *Thus says the Lord who redeems you*
And who formed you from your mother's womb:
I am the Lord who is the maker of all things,
Who alone stretched out the heavens
And by Himself spread forth the earth,

25 *Who frustrates the signs of the magicians,*
    Who makes their prophets fools,
    Who turns the wise men backward,
    And makes their wisdom foolishness,
26 *Who fulfills the words of His servants*
    And carries out the prophecies of His messengers,
    Who says of Jerusalem: "Be inhabited!"
    And to the cities of Judah: "Be built!"
    And their ruins do I restore.
27 *Who says to the deeps of waters: "Be dried up!"*
    And your streams do I make dry,
28 *Who says to Cyrus: "My shepherd!"*
    All My pleasure shall he carry out,
    That he shall say to Jerusalem: "Be built!"
    And to the temple: "Your foundation shall be laid!"

We have made the concluding verses of chapter 44 (24-28) a part of the third discourse, not so much because of the *kōh ʾamar* as because of the similarity of contents. This passage introduces Cyrus by name, and he remains constantly before our eyes through 45:13. That the entire section, chapters 40 to 48, is the product of one pen, and is skillfully organized, is manifested by the fact that the prophecy becomes steadily more specific as it approaches the conclusion of the section. Chapter 40, with the exception of the outline in verses 1-11, speaks in such general terms that it does not even mention the deliverance out of exile. Chapter 41 promises help in such general terms that here too one could not know what is meant were it not that a hero from the east appears who shall conquer nations and kings. It is not till the last strophe in chapter 42 that it becomes clear that the prophet is speaking of the deliverance of the blind people of Israel from the captivity in which it was being held by conquering robbers. Chapter 43 plainly declares that it is deliverance from Babylon that is meant. Chapter 44 tells how the outpouring of the Spirit causes Israel to flourish anew despite the idol makers and their idols; it contains the promise of forgiveness of sins, and describes the deliverance as an accomplished fact. The next chapter proceeds to name the deliverer and to cite the acts through which deliverance is accomplished. The Lord's shepherd of the nations is Cyrus. He is to rebuild Jerusalem and the temple, verse 28; 45:13; all the gates of the fortified cities and the treasuries of the kings will be opened to him when the Lord subdues them before him, verses 1-3; and he will set the Lord's people free, verse 13. The second half of the section describes the glorification of Israel. Regarding the argument that mentioning Cyrus by name proves that Isaiah could not have been the author of chapters 40-66, see the *Introduction*.

$$^{24}\ \text{כֹּה־אָמַ֤ר יְהוָה֙ גֹּ֣אֲלֶ֔ךָ וְיֹצֶרְךָ֣ מִבָּ֑טֶן}$$

$$\text{אָנֹכִ֤י יְהוָה֙ עֹ֣שֶׂה כֹּ֔ל}$$

$$\text{נֹטֶ֤ה שָׁמַ֙יִם֙ לְבַדִּ֔י רֹקַ֥ע הָאָ֖רֶץ מִ֥י אִתִּֽי ׃}$$

The frequent occurrence of *kōh 'āmar* in this chapter is occasioned by the nature of the content of the promises expressed here. As the promise becomes more specific, it increasingly puts faith to the test and is itself more forcefully emphasized. The adverbial phrase *mibbāten*, from the womb, is by the Masoretic accentuation (Zaqeph over *gō'alekhā*), made to modify *yōtserkhā* alone, since *gō'alekhā*, who rescues you, presupposes a forsaken condition, a condition which does not apply to Israel "from the womb." *yātsar* always refers to the historical development, the cultivation, and the guidance of Israel. *'anōkhī YHWH 'ōseh kōl* expresses the essential meaning of the passage. The copula is to be supplied after *'anōkhī*— "I am the Lord." That is what is here asserted: "I am the Lord who makes (does) all things." The following attributes, most of them in participial form, develop the *'ōseh kōl* in grand detail. But whatever is said of the Lord is always related to the appositives of *YHWH* — *gō'alekhā* and *yōtserkhā*. He who does all things is Israel's Savior and Maker, as the following phrases set forth. All of these deeds of the Lord serve the redemption and guidance of Israel, and as verses 26 and 28 expressly state, the restoration of the cities of Judah, of Jerusalem, and of the temple. — *mī 'ittī*, according to the Kethibh (who was with Me), has been changed by the Qeri to *mē'ittī* ("from with Me" equals "apart from Me" equals "alone"), a change that does not affect the sense. It is a synonym of *lebhaddī*.

$$^{25}\ \text{מֵפֵר֙ אֹת֣וֹת בַּדִּ֔ים וְקֹסְמִ֖ים יְהוֹלֵ֑ל}$$

$$\text{מֵשִׁ֧יב חֲכָמִ֛ים אָח֖וֹר וְדַעְתָּ֥ם יְשַׂכֵּֽל ׃}$$

baddīm in Job 11:3 are empty words; so also in Isaiah 16:6 and Jeremiah 48:30, where the vain boastings of Moab are called *baddīm*. In those passages too the word has its original meaning. *badh, bādhadh* equals separation, isolation; *baddīm* are mere words, empty words. Cf. *lebhaddī* in verse 24. In this passage, as in

Jeremiah 50:36 (Luther: *Wahrsager*), the meaning is transferred to the persons who employ empty words, i.e., vain babblers. The LXX has ἐγγαστρἱμυθοι, ventriloquists, a word used to describe the girl with the spirit of divination in Acts 16:16. It is clear that here, where the word is a synonym of *qosemīm* (soothsayers), the reference is to necromancers, people like our modern spiritualistic mediums. Cf. 1 Samuel 28:11; Deuteronomy 18:11. The *'ōthōth*, the signs or portents that they produce, are as false as their prophesyings are vain and empty. Cf. Deuteronomy 12:2f; 1 Kings 22:11. *ḥālal* usually occurs in the Piel form in the sense of causing to shine, to glorify, to praise. Here the word is a Poel and is used in a derogatory sense: to make blind, as in Job 12:17. *hēshībh 'aḥōr* seems to be used here in a pleonastic, physical sense, meaning to thrust back, backwards, to destroy. *yesakkēl* (from an unused Qal stem, to be confused) is a Piel meaning to confuse, to make foolish. — Verse 25 refers to the heathen soothsayers and wise men; in verse 26 a contrast is drawn between them and the prophets of the Lord.

26 מֵקִים֙ דְּבַ֣ר עַבְדֹּ֔ו וַעֲצַ֥ת מַלְאָכָ֖יו יַשְׁלִ֑ים

הָאֹמֵ֨ר לִירוּשָׁלִַ֜ם תּוּשָׁ֗ב וּלְעָרֵ֤י יְהוּדָה֙ תִּבָּנֶ֔ינָה וְחָרְבֹותֶ֖יהָ

אֲקֹומֵֽם׃

In contrast to the words expressing frustration in verse 25, *mē-qīm* describes one who erects, carries out, and confirms. *'abhdō* is best understood as a collective noun parallel to *mal'ākhāyw*, His servants. Hahn, with whom Delitzsch formerly agreed, Cheyne, and others, understood the reference to be to Isaiah; but this is unnatural, because the prophet never draws attention to himself, although he certainly is a principal figure. There are much better grounds for taking *'abhdō* to refer to Israel, cf. 51:16; 59:21. The word that is said to be confirmed is the word that the Lord placed in the mouth of His servant (servants), the counsel that He revealed to His messengers. It is referred to as their word and counsel, since they proclaimed it. — *tūshābh* (with Qamets in pause) is not second person singular but third person feminine in Hophal, agreeing with the feminine Jerusalem: *she* shall be inhabited. See also the suffix in *ḥorbhōtheyhā. tibbāneynāh* likewise is third person feminine: They shall be built. Therefore the *le* prefixed to *yerūshālayim* and *'arets* is not to be translated with "to," but with "of," or "concerning." See 40:9. The last clause, "and their ruins do I restore," is not, like the preceding declarations of

the Lord, an object of *hā'omēr*, it is a separate, direct word of God.
The same is true of the second clause in verse 27.

27 הָאֹמֵר לַצּוּלָה חֲרָבִי וְנַהֲרֹתַיִךְ אוֹבִישׁ:

tsūlāh (from *tsūl*, to hiss, to swirl) is a whirlpool which breaks
forth out of the deep (cf. *thehōm* in Gen. 1:2), and *naharōthayikh*
are the waves that well forth from the whirlpool. It seems reasonable to suppose, with Delitzsch, that the reference is here to Cyrus's diversion of the Euphrates, which led to the conquest of Babylon and to the benefit of the captive Israelites. However, the setting is general. It is characteristic of the prophet to refer in such
terms to the mighty acts of the Lord in the past, to the drying up of
the Red Sea (Exod. 14:21), or of the Jordan (Josh. 3:16). Verse 27
is a continuation of verse 24b, which speaks of God's acts in the
heavens and on earth, while this verse speaks of His acts on the
sea. There He is the governing Lord of heaven and earth who
makes foolish the prophesyings of the false prophets, but fulfills
His own prophecies; here He is the Lord who rules over the deep
and makes Cyrus the fulfiller of His plans concerning Jerusalem.
That the prophet might have had in mind the Euphrates, which
served as a protection for Babylon, is certainly possible, even
though this act of Cyrus might not have been known to Isaiah.

28 הָאֹמֵר לְכוֹרֶשׁ רֹעִי וְכָל־חֶפְצִי יַשְׁלִם
וְלֵאמֹר לִירוּשָׁלַםִ תִּבָּנֶה וְהֵיכָל תִּוָּסֵד:

In Jeremiah and elsewhere a shepherd is the shepherd of people, a term that is applied to kings and rulers who are responsible
for the external welfare of their subjects, their flock. Cyrus is represented not only as the shepherd who is to control and punish the
gentile nations with the sword (cf. Ps. 49:15 [14]; Jer. 22:22; Micah
5:4f), but also, and especially, as the benign shepherd of the people
of Israel. That he shall fulfill all the Lord's pleasure does not in the
strictest sense refer to the punishment of the heathen — that is
but a means to an end — but rather to the welfare of God's people,
to their release from servitude in Babylon, to the return to their
homeland, and, as the concluding clauses declare, to the restoration of the city and the temple. It is the ideal function of the
shepherd to lead the scattered sheep of Israel back to their native
fold, cf. Jeremiah 50:6, 17-19. Cyrus represents the royal house of
David and thus becomes a type of Christ, John 10. — The *Waw*

before *lē'mōr* is epexegetical, Gr. 154, Note b, p. 485. *tibbāneh* is third person, *tiwwāsēdh* is second person masculine, since *hēykhāl* is addressed, and being without gender, is construed as a masculine.

The central thought of this discourse is contained in verse 24a and verse 28; verses 24b and 25-27 are rhetorical embellishment.

Resumé: He who formed and redeemed Israel pledges His word that the city and the temple (in verse 26 the cities of Judah are included) shall be rebuilt through the mediation of Cyrus, His shepherd of the nations.

Second Strophe: 45:1-7: *God made Cyrus an irresistible vanquisher of princes and conqueror of Babylon for the sake of His servant Jacob, in order that all the world might realize that He alone is God.*

First Half: verses 1-3:

1 *Thus says the Lord to His anointed One,*
To Cyrus, whom I grasped by his right hand,
To trample the nations before him,
That I might ungird the loins of kings
And open the portals before him,
And that the gates might not be closed.
2 *I will go before you and level the heights,*
I will shatter the doors of bronze,
And cut apart the bars of iron.
3 *The treasures of darkness will I give to you*
And the hidden hoards of secret places,
So that you may know that I am the Lord,
Who called you by name, the God of Israel.

כֹּה־ אָמַ֨ר יְהוָה֮ לִמְשִׁיחוֹ֮ לְכ֣וֹרֶשׁ אֲשֶׁר־הֶחֱזַ֣קְתִּי בִֽימִינ֗וֹ
לְרַד־ ־לְפָנָיו֙ גּוֹיִ֔ם וּמָתְנֵ֥י מְלָכִ֖ים אֲפַתֵּ֑חַ
לִפְתֹּ֤חַ לְפָנָיו֙ דְּלָתַ֔יִם וּשְׁעָרִ֖ים לֹ֥א יִסָּגֵֽרוּ׃

The anointment of Cyrus was, of course, not an anointment of the body. *meshiḥō*, on the other hand, is not just a metonymy for an instrument, a servant, a person chosen or called, 41:2,4,25. In a unique way Cyrus too received the Spirit of the Lord, cf. 42:1. Without knowing it, he was doing the Lord's work, 44:28; and he was endowed with irresistible power. His special mission, assigned to him by God, was to set Israel free, verse 4; the conquest of Babylon was the means to an end. *heḥezīq beyāmīn* or *beyadh*, to grasp by the right hand, means to support, strengthen, uphold, cf. 42:6; Psalm 73:23. It is the power of the Lord that makes Cyrus victorious; in fact, the next verses state that the Lord Himself actually does everything that Cyrus accomplishes.

Regarding the infinitive *radh* for *rōdh*, cf. Gr. 67, p, p. 180. In the series of verbs there are two infinitives (*leradh, liphtōaḥ*) and two finite verbs ('*aphattēaḥ, yissāghērū*) — cf. Gr. 114, r, p. 352. In translation this distinction need not be observed; consequently a single construction may be used in the English. The infinitives provide the idea of purpose, and the finite verbs supply the subject "I." Before "the gates" in the last line, "that" or "in order that" is to be supplied in thought. "Ungirding the loins" is an elliptical expression for loosing the girdle about the hips, the opposite of "girding the loins" (Jer. 1:17; Job 38:3; 40:7), that is, putting on armor and rendering oneself strong. Putting off the armor is then the equivalent of rendering oneself weak and defenseless. Luther expressed the thought well with *den Koenigen das Schwert abguerten. delāthayim* does not refer specifically to the gates of the palaces belonging to the kings and princes (Delitzsch), but is purely a poetic parallel of *she ῾ārīm.* Both words designate the city gates. (See the following verse.) These and the following phrases are very general. No city will be able to withstand Cyrus. In the final analysis, of course, Babylon and its mighty gates are meant.

2 אֲנִי לְפָנֶיךָ אֵלֵךְ וַהֲדוּרִים אֲוַשֵּׁר
דַּלְתוֹת נְחוּשָׁה אֲשַׁבֵּר וּבְרִיחֵי בַרְזֶל אֲגַדֵּעַ:

hadhūrīm are swelling ridges or heights; to level them ('*awashshēr*) is a figurative expression for removing all obstacles from the way. (For '*awashshēr* the Qere has '*ayashshēr,* Piel of *yāshar* in verse 13; the Kethib, '*ōshīr,* is a Hiphil in the mode of the Pe-Waw verbs, Gr. 70,2,p.192.) Although the bronze gates of the two royal palaces, one on each side of the Euphrates, and the gates of the temple of Belus, which — according to Herodotus — like the gates of the city walls, were also of brass, lie within the scope of those gates that are to be shattered, the prophet hardly is referring specifically to them. Once the conqueror had broken into the city itself, the palace and temple gates would be no bar to the plunderers. These gates might resist a mob of citizens, but not a conquering army. It was not on these palace and temple gates that

Nebuchadnezzar depended, but on the colossal threefold walls and the hundred gates of bronze that were thought to be impregnable. In fact, Herodotus relates that Cyrus stormed these gates and walls for almost two years, being derided by the Babylonians. It was only after diverting the flow of the Euphrates that Cyrus was able to enter the city, through the bed of the river. Recent discoveries by Assyriologists seem to show that there never was a siege of the city, nor even any street fighting, but that the rebellious people, wholly dissatisfied with the reign of the weakling Nabonidus-Belshazzar, delivered the city to Cyrus without the stroke of a sword. That does not invalidate the prophecy. The concrete, physical phrases are intended to say only that the Lord will render all the defenses of Babylon — walls and gates — useless and ineffective. If one insists on the literal fulfillment of all poetic phrases, he must place lightning and an ax in the hand of the Lord — and often at that! — or despair of the fulfillment. The conquest of Babylon occurred during the reign of Nabonidus-Belshazzar (some think that Belshazzar was the son of Nabonidus, and coregent) in 538. Later, after a revolt by the inhabitants of the city, Darius caused the city walls to be torn down partly and the gates to be demolished.

³ וְנָתַתִּי לְךָ אוֹצְרוֹת חֹשֶׁךְ וּמַטְמֻנֵי מִסְתָּרִים
לְמַעַן תֵּדַע כִּי־אֲנִי יְהוָה הַקּוֹרֵא בְשִׁמְךָ אֱלֹהֵי יִשְׂרָאֵל׃

The "treasures of darkness" are the treasures that were stored in underground vaults. The *maṭmuney mistārim* likewise are the gems that were hidden away in secret chambers. It is the hoards of the royal treasuries that are meant in particular, cf. Jeremiah 50:26. The Babylonian kings had unmercifully plundered the surrounding nations. The treasures that Cyrus seized in Babylon made the Persians rich and contributed greatly to the national debility, just as this same wealth had been a cause of Babylon's downfall. Cf. Isaiah 14:11; 47:1; Jeremiah 51:39; Daniel 5:1. *maṭmōn* (*ṭāman*, to bury, to hide away) is the word from which, according to some scholars, the New Testament mammon (with the assimilation of the *Teth*) was derived. Others believe that it comes from *mānāh*, to count. Still others, from *ʾaman*, to be firmly established. *qārāʾ beshēm* is identical in meaning with *qārāʾ le beshēm* in verse 4. The former phrase frequently signifies to call out a name, to proclaim, to preach; but, like the latter phrase, it may also signify to call someone by name, that is, to call him into service, as in

267

43:1. *lema'an tēdha'* refers to everything promised to Cyrus in verses 1-3. His miraculous conquests must make him realize that the Lord has called him by name and ordained him for this special work. "The God of Israel" is added as a concluding phrase in order to give Cyrus to understand that he has been called in the interest of Israel.

Second Half: verses 4-7:

4   *For the sake of My servant Jacob*
     And of Israel, My chosen one,
     I called to you by your name
     And gave you names before you knew Me.
5   *I am the Lord, and there is none other,*
     No God beside Me;
     Before you knew Me, I did gird you,
6   *So that they might know at the rising of the sun*
     And at the going down thereof, that apart from me
         there is nothing;
     I am the Lord and none other.
7   *The Maker of light and the Creator of darkness,*
     Who makes peace and creates woe.
     I am the Lord, the Doer of all these things.

lema'an 'abhdī, for the sake of My servant, says that Cyrus was called for the purpose of setting God's servant Jacob free. The *Waw* with *'eqrā'* introduces the concluding clause, the antecedent clause having been expressed by the preceding adverbs. The *Waw* need therefore not be translated. *'akhannekhā* is not to be understood as mechanically referring to titles of honor conferred on Cyrus: Shepherd, Anointed One; it is a parallel term that lends emphasis to *'eqrā' beshēm,* cf. 44:5. The two terms together refer to the call and designation of Cyrus for his mission. "Before you knew Me" does not say that Cyrus later came to know the Lord in faith, but only that the Lord had chosen him before he was born, Romans 9:11. Whether or not Cyrus ever came to a knowledge of the Lord in faith must remain undecided. An inscription, discovered in 1879 and now in the British Museum, describes him as a polytheist and indifferentist. Cf. Cheyne on 45:13 and 46:1 and *Essays* XI, p. 288 ff. From what Scripture says about him, no more can be concluded than that he did infer from his military successes that he had been divinely sent and that Israel's God was the true God. That such a belief does not constitute conversion is shown by the examples of Balaam, Pharaoh, Ahab, and others. Cf. the exposition of verse 6.

5 אֲנִי יְהוָה וְאֵין עוֹד   זוּלָתִי אֵין אֱלֹהִים
אֲאַזֶּרְךָ וְלֹא יְדַעְתָּנִי:

The repeated assertion, in the first two clauses, of the sole Godhead of the Lord emphasizes the declaration made in the third clause. *'a'azzerkhā* follows *'eqrā' lekhā bishemekhā* and *'akhannekhā* as a third member in that series of verbs. To gird someone means to make him ready for battle and victorious.

6 לְמַעַן יֵדְעוּ מִמִּזְרַח־שֶׁמֶשׁ וּמִמַּעֲרָבָה   כִּי־אֶפֶס בִּלְעָדָי
אֲנִי יְהוָה וְאֵין עוֹד:

yādha' is used here in the same sense as in the phrase *lema'an tēdha'* in verse 3. Knowledge, in verse 3, consisted in realizing that the Lord, the God of Israel, had sent Cyrus; in this verse it is the knowledge that beside the Lord, the God of Israel, there is no other God. In neither instance is this knowledge necessarily a "saving knowledge." In fact, the sentence speaks only of God's purpose, not of any result of that purpose. Luther aptly translated *yādha'* with *erfahren,* to experience. At the occurrence of such tremendous events, such as the triumphal progress of Cyrus, which transcend the grasp of ordinary reason (cf. also the exclamation of the Egyptian magicians: "This is the finger of God," Exod. 8:15(19), the unbeliever is not able to suppress the thought that the hand of God is directing the action. But he does not permit the thought to take form, does not repent, but hardening his heart rushes all the more obstinately toward his eternal doom. Exodus 8:6(10); 9:14, etc. "The *āh* of *ma'arābhāh* is not a feminine termination but a feminine suffix with Raphe over the *He* to indicate absence of Mappiq, cf. 23:17f; 34:17" (Delitzsch) Gr. 91, e, p. 256. *min* is translated with "at" or "to."

7 יוֹצֵר אוֹר וּבוֹרֵא חֹשֶׁךְ
עֹשֶׂה שָׁלוֹם וּבוֹרֵא רָע   אֲנִי יְהוָה עֹשֶׂה כָל־אֵלֶּה:

Some exegetes remark, at this point, that these words were written in intentional contrast to the dualism of the Persian religion (Ormuzd and Ahriman — Light and Darkness). Late archaeological discoveries, however, make it very doubtful that the Achaemenidae before Darius were ever adherents of Zoroaster, cf. Cheyne, *Essays*, XI, 2, 292ff. It is the consistent teaching of Scripture in both Testaments that it is God who does "all these things," that is, brings about all weal and all woe, for which here and often elsewhere in the Old Testament, especially in Isaiah, light and darkness, peace and evil are figurative expressions (*species pro genere*), the evil albeit as a consequence of sin. Since the curse was pronounced upon this visible world and all natural life, Genesis 3, God Himself works all the ruin that afflicts the world, just as it is He who stirs every leaf on the trees and produces every beat of our hearts. Deism and Naturalism have almost obliterated this knowledge of God's work from the Christian mind. Concerning the effect of the World Wars it can also be truthfully said: "Thou hast stricken them, but they have not grieved," Jeremiah 5:3. Christian preaching too seldom strikes this note. In Luther this point of Christian teaching is very much in evidence. He sees the direct working of the hand of God in the smallest affairs of his own life as well as in the momentous affairs of nations, especially in those that involve disaster. See his sermons against the Turks. Scripture abounds in passages containing this teaching. The whole book of Job is founded on it. Cf. especially Job 40 and 41; Psalm 104, 139; Romans 11:36; Amos 3:6, etc, etc.

Verse 7 is couched in general terms, but the reference is first of all to Cyrus and the destiny God has prepared for the nations through him. Cyrus is one of the great personalities of history through whom God operated to execute something special in the fulfillment of the sublime mystery of Christ and His church, even though Cyrus' role was played only on the stage of secular events. He has no place in the *same* line with Moses, Samuel, David, Isaiah, Paul, Augustine, Luther; he is not one of the spiritually great ones; but he is one of those great figures who give the events of the world a direction that must lead to the accomplishment of God's plan of salvation. Without Cyrus there would have been no deliverance of Israel out of Babylon, no continuity of the Jewish nation leading to the person of Christ, no Christ. Such men carry out their assigned work to a victorious end; they overcome their opponents even though all kingdoms of the world oppose them, Isaiah 8:9,10.

In connection with *khol ʾelleh* it is hardly necessary to refer to what our Lutheran dogmaticians expressed in these words: "*Intelligendum hoc est de malo poenae, quod juste a deo infligitur, non de malo culpae, quod a justo deo non est*" (Dietrich, Instt. p. 158).

Résumé: The Lord makes Cyrus, His chosen one, irresistible, so that he may realize that it is God who made him victorious, and that for the purpose of setting Israel free. All the world besides is to realize that there is no God other than Israel's God. The Lord alone is the doer of all things.

Third Strophe: 45:8-13: *The imminent deliverance of Israel puts to shame the people who have been murmuring against their God.*

8   *Pour out from above, O heavens,*
      And you clouds rain down salvation!
      May the earth open (her womb?) to bring forth deliverance,
      And may righteousness spring forth together!
      I am the Lord, I will create it.

9   *Woe to him who strives with his Maker —*
      A vessel of clay like other vessels of clay!
      Does the clay say to its potter: What are you making?
      And what you fashion: He has no hands?

10   *Woe to him who says to a father: What are you begetting?*
      And to a woman: To what are you giving birth?

11   *Thus says the Lord, Israel's Holy One and his Maker:*
      The future do they demand of Me!
      Concerning My children and the work of My hands,
      Do you give Me orders!

12   *(Me,) who made the earth*
      And created man upon it,
      (Me,) whose hands spread out the heavens
      And set in order all their hosts.

13   *(Me,) who in faithfulness aroused him*
      And who makes level all his paths.
      Yes, he shall build My city
      And My exiled people he shall send (homeward)
      Without ransom and without reward,
      Says the Lord of Sabaoth.

The strophe is highly dramatic. It is built up of three distinct parts, which increase in length from three to five and finally to ten clauses. The first part, verse 8, is a tableau expressed in imperatives (cf. 40:1). Streaming rain from heaven and the fruitful earth bring forth salvation in luxuriant abundance. In abrupt contrast, verses 9 and 10 describe the sinful striving of the people with God because of their unhappy lot; whereupon verses 11-13, enclosed between "Thus says the Lord" and "Says the Lord of Sabaoth," counter their striving with the majesty of the grace of Jehovah.

⁸ הַרְעִיפוּ שָׁמַיִם֙ מִמַּ֔עַל וּשְׁחָקִים יִזְּלוּ־צֶ֑דֶק
תִּפְתַּח־אֶ֣רֶץ וְיִפְרוּ־יֶ֔שַׁע
וּצְדָקָה תַצְמִ֣יחַ יַ֔חַד אֲנִ֥י יְהוָ֖ה בְּרָאתִֽיו׃

rā'aph, a rare verb, means to drip, to fall in great drops. The Hiphil is causative. Concerning *mimma'al,* above, see Gr. 119, c, p. 377. Also compare Exodus 20:4; Deuteronomy 4:39; Psalm 78:23; and Job 3:4. *shehāqīm* (sing. *shahaq,* 40:15, powder, something thin, finely spread) is a synonym of *shāmayim;* but *ether* is too poetic or too scientifically modern a translation; *clouds* is both simple and accurate. *tsedheq,* like *tsedhāqāh* in the next clause, is a synonym of *yesha',* salvation. *nāzal,* to flow, is intransitive as a rule, but here it is transitive in meaning, Gr. 117, z, p. 369. The following words are a *crux interpretum. tiphtah,* usually transitive, is perhaps an elliptical expression for "opening the womb," as in Song of Songs, 5:2,5,6 (to open a door) and Numbers 16:32; 26:10; Psalm 106:17 (to open its mouth). The heavens and the clouds are the subject of *yiphrū.* Delitzsch's remarks to the contrary are not relevant. *pārāh* never means to blossom, or to sprout forth; it means to bear fruit, to be fruitful, as in Genesis 1:28 and elsewhere, although here it is transitive as in Deuteronomy 29:17(18), with *yesha'* as its object, cf. Gr. 117, y, z, p. 369. The heavens and the clouds bring forth help. The *Waw* before *yiphrū* is consecutive: so that. So, the sentence up to this point reads as follows: You heavens above rain down, and may the clouds cause salvation to flow down; may the earth open her body so that they, the heavens and the clouds, may bring forth help. What follows is obvious. The subject of the next clause is *'erets; tatsmiah yahadh* is the predicate; *tsedhāqāh* is the object. — The construction becomes perfectly clear if one places *tiphtah 'erets* between *yesha'* and *ūtsedhāqāh:* You heavens above rain down and may the clouds pour down help and salvation! May the earth open up her body and let salvation sprout forth together!

⁹ ה֗וֹי רָ֚ב אֶת־יֹ֣צְר֔וֹ חֶ֖רֶשׂ אֶת־חַרְשֵׂ֣י אֲדָמָ֑ה
הֲיֹאמַ֙ר חֹ֤מֶר לְיֹֽצְרוֹ֙ מַֽה־תַּעֲשֶׂ֔ה וּפָעָלְךָ֖ אֵין־יָדַ֥יִם לֽוֹ׃

¹⁰ ה֛וֹי אֹמֵ֥ר לְאָ֖ב מַה־תּוֹלִ֑יד וּלְאִשָּׁ֖ה מַה־תְּחִילִֽין׃

heres designates not only a potsherd, but may also be used as the word for a vessel of clay; or even for the clay itself. There is a

272

temptation to assume that the *'eth* before *ḥarsēy* has the same
meaning as the *'eth* before *yōtserō,* and then to emend *ḥarsēy* to
read *ḥarshēy,* potters. But according to the way the words are
pointed in the text, the meaning can only be: "A vessel of clay with
(among, as one of) vessels of clay." Thus the idea of nothingness
lying in *ḥeres* is emphasized. Reference is to the single human
being who is but a tiny part of the entire human race, which before
God is but earth and ashes, Genesis 2:7; 3:19; 18:27.

   mah ta'aseh can hardly mean "*Why* are you making?" without
some addition either to *mah* or to the verb. It is true that *'asāh*
does occur in an absolute sense (44:23), but in that case its object
must be self-understood, as in 1 Samuel 26:25. *mah tōlīdh* and *mah
teḥīlīn* (Gr. 47,o,p.129, for paragogic *Nun*) could be translated
"Why beget — why give birth?" but since these phrases are parallel with *mah ta'aseh* in verse 9, they must be translated similarly.
It must be noted that all the verbs are in the imperfect, not in the
perfect. So the reference is not to something past and completed,
but to the present, to something in progress. The vessel that is in
the hands of the potter, in the process of being formed, says to the
potter: What are you making? The child that is just being born is
pictured as saying to its father and mother: What are you begetting, to what giving birth? The question is *What?* and not *Why?*
That is made clear by *upho'olkhā* and the following words, which
are explanatory of *mah ta'aseh. po'olkhā* is the Lord's word addressed to the man. *hayō'mar* must be supplied, *'eyn yādhayim lō* is
its object, and the sentence reads: Your work, does it say: He has
no hands? that is to say, he has no power, no skill, knows nothing,
can do nothing worthwhile, is a botcher. In *mah tōlīdh* the point of
comparison is the same, but the ethics of the situation receives
greater emphasis here than in the pot's rebuke addressed to the
potter. For that reason *'abh* has no suffix and *'ishshāh* is used instead of *'em* in order to show the speaker's lack of filial piety. Applied to Israel, these pictures intend to show that the people are
finding fault with the Lord, because, although He is Israel's
founder and creator in the historical sense, and the director of
Israel's destiny, He has botched His work and lacks the compe-
tence to shape Israel's fortunes according to the promise given. In
this sense Paul uses this ninth verse in Romans 9:20. Paul's τί
με ἐποίησας οὕτως "Why have You made me *thus?*" is not the
reproduction of a Hebrew "*Why* are You making?" but of the
Hebrew "*What* are You making?" The *What* refers to the person
of the speaker and asks: What are You making of me? Why do

You make me *thus* — namely, to such a vessel? Obviously, Israel utters this rebuke because of the way it conceives its present situation. In their exile the people of Israel strive with the Lord in spite of His promise to deliver them through Cyrus, because they do not believe the promise. Therefore the woe pronounced upon the people is changed in the following verses — for the sake of the believers — into a majestic assurance of the glory and power of the Lord and a reaffirmation of the promise concerning Cyrus and his mission.

11 כֹּה־אָמַר יְהוָה קְדוֹשׁ יִשְׂרָאֵל וְיֹצְרוֹ
הָאֹתִיּוֹת שְׁאָלוּנִי עַל־בָּנַי וְעַל־פֹּעַל יָדַי תְּצַוֻּנִי:

With these words begins the Lord's response to the complaints of the people. The introduction is expressed in the most solemn form. *qedhōsh yisrā'el* designates the highest perfection of the Lord in His relation to Israel as Savior. *yōtserō,* He who formed him, establishes a connection with verse 9f. The irreproachable potter of the murmuring vessel of clay, Israel, now has the word. We tentatively translate the next words: "Require the future of Me; concerning My children and the work of My hands you give Me orders." (Luther got off the track here.)

We may explain *she'ālūnī* tentatively as an imperative. *tetsawwunī,* according to its form, could be a jussive, but since it is not linked to *she'ālūnī* by a particle, it will have to be interpreted as an indicative. Commentators who take *she'ālūnī* to be an imperative, interpret *tetsawwunī* as a jussive and translate it with "entrust," that is, to commit into someone's care. Thus Delitzsch who cites 1 Chronicles 22:12 and translates: "Let My children and the work of My hands be committed to Me." But Delitzsch and the others are mistaken. *tsiwwāh* construed with the person in the accusative and the thing with the preposition *'al* nowhere means "to entrust something to someone." Here the double meaning of a German word (*befehlen,* to command and to entrust) has played a trick on the commentators. In 1 Chronicles 22:12, the passage Delitzsch refers to, *wītsawwekhā 'al yisrā'el,* does not mean "He will entrust Israel to you," as Luther translated, but rather: "He will set you, establish you over Israel," 1 Kings 2:12,24. Cf. Genesis 12:20, where one might be tempted to translate the word with "entrust." That passage too means "give a command concerning Abraham." Likewise 2 Samuel 18:5 speaks of a *command* of the king in respect to Absalom.

Such slips, common even in the better commentaries, are to be attributed in part to the fact that the rightful place of etymology has been usurped by comparison of dialects. One wonders how Kautzsch and others could have given *tsiwwāh* the meaning of "entrusting to the care of" if they had kept in mind the literal, concrete meaning of the word: "make firm, fix securely, install, establish." In this passage, too, the root meaning must be retained. For *tsiwwāh,* construed with the person in the accusative and the thing with the preposition *'al,* there are only two possible meanings: to establish someone, to install him as a regent or guardian over something, as in 1 Chronicles 22:12; or to give someone orders regarding something. Both meanings assume the subject to be a person who establishes something or has the right to command. Therefore, *tsiwwāh* in this construction is without exception used of God or of some person in a position of power. If, in our passage, the expression is used of the people or of some individual, then a sharp rebuff or condemnation is implied for the arrogance of those who, like the vessel of clay to the potter, presume to criticize the Holy One of Israel, their Maker, and to prescribe to Him how He should direct the lot of His own children and the work of His hands. For that reason *tetsawwunī* cannot be a jussive; God certainly cannot be expected to command such arrogance. It is an indicative: Concerning My own children (referring to father and woman in verse 10) and concerning the work of My hands (your own work says: "He has no hands!" verse 9) you give Me orders! This may be taken either as an assertion or as potential-voluntative reproach: "Would you be giving Me orders?" (Gr. 107, m-t, p. 317ff), or as a simple question "Do you presume to give Me orders?" (Gr. 150, l, a, p. 473). In any case it is a condemnation of the sinful wrangling of the people.

This latter statement does not apply if one looks upon *she'ālunī* as an imperative. *shā'al* expresses every shade of petitioning, from the most modest request to the strongest demand, and the Lord could here be urging the complaining exiles to seek from Him some assurance of the glorious future of His people, instead of complaining about the seemingly hopeless present and reproaching God for the way He is leading them. The fact is that the first clause yields no other meaning, so long as one accepts *she'ālunī* in the form in which it appears in the text. But the spirit of Hebrew poetry and the incongruity of the two clauses argue against that interpretation. Form and contents are so completely disparate that no kind of parallelism can be established. Gesenius and

275

Hitzig therefore take *she'ālūnī* to be an alternative form for *she'elūnī* (third plural perfect). Cheyne assumes that a *Taw* has been omitted from *tish'alūnī,* since the immediately preceding word ends in a *Taw,* and he thus achieves perfect parallelism. If any emending of the text is to be made, then Cheyne's suggestion has strong appeal. We then have two perfectly congruent clauses: Do you demand of Me to know the future? Concerning My children and the work of My hands, do you presume to give Me orders?

It is, however, not necessary to emend the text. Delitzsch's remark that the third person plural would have had to be *she'elūnī* instead of *she'ālūnī* is not necessarily decisive. *she'elūnī* occurs in Psalm 137:3, and there are several occurrences of middle-e forms of *shā'al;* but it does not therefore follow that this verb cannot have middle-a forms. See Judges 5:25; 1 Kings 3:10, etc., where *shā'al* is treated as a middle-a. The middle-e forms are, after all, really alternate forms of this verb, Gr. 64,f, p. 170. It is therefore not at all ungrammatical to treat *she'ālūnī* as a perfect and to translate: "The future do they demand of Me." That a shift occurs from the third to the second person in the next verb is nothing unusual (cf. verse 8, where there is a shift from second to third person). Delitzsch's objection that this interpretation would require *Waw* as a connecting link between the two verbs is not relevant, whether one takes both clauses as questions or as declarations. The Lord's indignant speech is blunt and requires no connecting links. In short, we have in this verse an expression of righteous anger expressed with great feeling (as a question, if one so prefers): "The future do they demand of Me? Concerning My children and the work of My hands you give Me orders!" The demand and the command are both therewith condemned as wicked. Naturally, since the complainer's demands, even regarding a good future, are made in a wicked spirit. He demands a human guarantee; he is impatient and wants the future *now.* — What follows in the next two verses will show that our interpretation has been correct. In the form of a chiasmus verse 12 connects with the second clause of verse 11; and verse 13 contains a vigorous response to the reproach expressed by the first clause of verse 11.

אָנֹכִ֤י עָשִׂ֙יתִי֙ אֶ֔רֶץ וְאָדָ֖ם עָלֶ֣יהָ בָרָ֑אתִי 12
אֲנִ֗י יָדַי֙ נָט֣וּ שָׁמַ֔יִם וְכָל־צְבָאָ֖ם צִוֵּֽיתִי׃

This verse is the Lord's answer to verse 11 and to the complaining question at the end of verse 9. *ʿasīthī* picks up the *mah ta'aseh* of verse 9, and *yādhay* here answers to *yādhay* in verse 11. The Lord is not the Maker of Israel only, but He is the Creator of all things. His works are mentioned here, as frequently elsewhere, in pairs — those above, the heavens and their hosts, the stars; those below, the earth and all mankind. Each of the four verbs expresses creation. That is also true of *tsiwwēthī,* used here in its original sense of establishing, fixing in place, calling into being, creating, and not in its other meaning of commanding, or ruling. *ʾanōkhī* and *ʾanī* occupy the position of emphasis: It is I, who, etc. Concerning *ʾanī yādhay,* (cf. Gr. 144,1,p.461). We would say: With My own hands have I, etc. The verse offers abundant proof of God's creative power and wisdom, which had been questioned by the complaining exiles. He who with His own hands so gloriously fashioned heaven and earth and all that is in them, should He not rightly and wisely lead this small people, which He not only created but adopted as His own children?

אָנֹכִי הַעִירֹתִהוּ בְצֶדֶק וְכָל־דְּרָכָיו אֲיַשֵּׁר ¹³
הוּא־יִבְנֶה עִירִי וְגָלוּתִי יְשַׁלֵּחַ
לֹא בִמְחִיר וְלֹא בְשֹׁחַד אָמַר יְהוָה צְבָאוֹת:

The initial *ʾanōkhī* says: Moreover, it is I who raised him up. The reference is to Cyrus. That he is referred to only by a suffix and not by name, constitutes a proof that it is being assumed that the complaining people had knowledge of the prophecy concerning Cyrus. They strove with God in spite of the assurance of future deliverance by Cyrus. They just did not believe that God could or would set them free. In any case, He was not acting fast enough for them. As in 42:6, *tsedheq* designates God's faithfulness to his covenant of grace with Israel. God called up Cyrus as a means, among others, that He employed to fulfill His covenant with Israel to deliver and exalt this people. He will make all ways smooth before him, will remove all hindrances to the success of this work, referring, as in verse 2, to the opposition of all enemies, specifically of Babylon. *hū'yibhneh* is like *ʾanōkhī ʿasīthī:* He it is, who, etc. Jerusalem (see 44:26,28) is called "*My* city" to bring into prominence God's personal interest in the work of deliverance. *ghālūthī, My* exiles, has the same connotation. "Not for a ransom nor for a reward" refers to anything that Cyrus might have received or expect to receive from the Lord for his services. Not for a reward, but *freely —* moved by a divine impulse. Some understand the phrase to mean that Cyrus will wrest Israel from the tyranny of Babylon without giving any recompense. The final clause assures Israel that the work of deliverance and rebuilding of the city will most certainly be accomplished.

Résumé of verses 8-13: Following an assurance of the most abundant blessings of salvation, the Lord pronounces woe upon the people, who in spite of all strive with God and do not believe. The Lord counters their complaints by reminding them of His power as revealed by the creation of all things and of the faithfulness of His grace by which He makes Cyrus victorious and impels him to rebuild His city and bring His exiles home.

Part II: 45:14-25: *The exaltation of liberated Israel is an exhortation to all the world to seek salvation in the Lord, who alone is revealed as true God.*

The second section has three distinct parts. Verses 14-17: The gentiles willingly and humbly yield themselves to the liberated Israel, and Israel's exaltation is an eternal one. Verses 18-21: The Lord, who alone is God of heaven and earth, has not deluded the seed of Jacob with dark and worthless prognostications, but has revealed to him trustworthy words of salvation, which now are being fulfilled, such as the gentiles have never possessed. Verses 22-25: Whoever in all the world turns to the Lord will share in this salvation equally with Israel; and whoever sets himself against the Lord will be put to shame. — The last two parts could also be combined into one.

First Strophe: 45:14-17: *Israel's exaltation as a result of the coming in of the gentiles and the eternal duration of its salvation.*

14　*Thus says the Lord: Egypt's labors and Nubia's gains,*
　　And the Sabeans, men of great stature,
　　They shall all fall to you and belong to you,
　　Follow you, come over in chains,
　　Bow down before you, make supplication to you;
　　Truly, God is with you alone, and there is no other,
　　　　no God besides.
15　*Truly, you are a God who hides Himself,*
　　O God of Israel, O Savior!
16　*Put to shame and confounded are they all,*
　　Driven into confusion they go, the makers of images.
17　*But Israel is saved by the Lord with an eternal salvation;*
　　Never shall you be put to shame, nor confounded for
　　　　ever and ever.

14 כֹּה ׀ אָמַר יְהוָה
יְגִיעַ מִצְרַיִם וּסְחַר ־כּוּשׁ וּסְבָאִים אַנְשֵׁי מִדָּה
עָלַיִךְ יַעֲבֹרוּ וְלָךְ יִהְיוּ אַחֲרַיִךְ יֵלֵכוּ בַּזִּקִּים יַעֲבֹרוּ
וְאֵלַיִךְ יִשְׁתַּחֲווּ אֵלַיִךְ יִתְפַּלָּלוּ
אַךְ בָּךְ אֵל וְאֵין עוֹד אֶפֶס אֱלֹהִים:

The preceding section spoke throughout of the liberation of Israel from exile in Babylon and of the rebuilding of Jerusalem. In verse 14 the aspect of the glorification of Israel is brought into the range of vision, as the prophet speaks of the conversion of the gentiles to Israel and Israel's God. Concerning the nations named here, see the remarks on 43:3. There they are referred to as ransom for Israel (cf. 18:1,2,7 and chapter 19, where beginning with verse 18 there is already mention of conversion of the gentiles). "Egypt's labors and Nubia's gains" are metonymies for rewards and gains from commerce, and in both cases the rewards and gains are meant to include those who receive them, cf. 60:6ff. Egypt, then as today, gained its wealth from the rich soil brought in by the flooding Nile; Ethiopia's profits came from its commerce in ores, precious stones, gold, spices, fabrics, and rugs (Herodotus 3:97, 114; cf. Ps. 72:10 and Ezek. 27:23,24). The Sabeans (not to be confused with Sheba on the coast of Arabia) were mentioned in 18:2 and 7, and also by Herodotus 3:20, 114, as being known for their tall and powerful bodies. *'anshēy middāh* (of *mādhadh*, to measure, cf. 40:12) are men of measure, of tall stature. The following four predicates are military expressions, borrowed from the language of war. But *ya'abhōrū* suggests voluntary subjection, and these who come over in chains present a picture of humble surrender. The obeisance before Israel and the supplication to Israel are explained in the confession, *'akh bākh 'ēl* — God is with you alone — which falls from the lips of one of these "prisoners." Israel is thus acknowledged as the genuine people of the one true God. *'akh* is at once affirmative and restrictive — the force the particle has in any one case will be determined by the context. *'ephes 'elōhīm* (end of, nothing of God) is a synonym of *'ēyn 'odh* (none besides), but more forceful. Cf. 1 Corinthians 14:25. The three names for nations really designate only two nations, since Seba is the eastern and northeastern part of Cush, or Ethiopia, lying along the Arabian gulf. Cush and Mizraim are historically two people in one, of whom now one, now the other, ruled over the

279

country. This people, more often than any other, is the subject of prophecies of doom, because from the most ancient times until the rise of Assyria it was Israel's chief enemy. Later Assyria became the foremost oppressor of Israel and drew upon itself the prophecies of judgment. That makes it all the more astonishing that especially Egypt, Ethiopia, and Assyria are mentioned as the nations that shall be converted to the Lord, 18:7; 19:18ff, especially verse 24f. The reason for this is that the glorification of Israel is to be brought out in all the more striking a way through the spiritual conquest of its most powerful enemies; on the other hand, whatever good Israel had ever received at their hands, the Lord will not leave unrewarded. These nations, however, as the foremost among the gentiles, do not stand alone; they represent the entire gentile world. The prophecy thus extends into New Testament times.

15 אָכֵן אַתָּה אֵל מִסְתַּתֵּר אֱלֹהֵי יִשְׂרָאֵל מוֹשִׁיעַ:

Most commentators look upon this sentence as an expression of marvel and astonishment on the part of the prophet or the congregation of believers. But Cheyne, no doubt, is right when he says that such a transition is too abrupt for that interpretation and that the form of address, *'elohēy yisrāēl,* is more likely to come from the lips of the converted nations. The sentence is a companion piece and conclusion of *'akh bākh 'ēl,* etc. The use of *'ēl* for God in both instances supports that interpretation. *'ēl* is the word for God insofar as He is powerful and exercises His power. As *'ēl* He proved His power against the gentiles and their worthless idols; is Israel's *mōshīa',* Savior; has exalted the despised people of Israel above all the mighty gentile world — facts that are now recognized and acknowledged by the gentiles. That is, indeed, the very confession of all gentiles who are converted to Christ — our gods are idols, salvation is of the Jews, John 4:22. We acknowledge the God of the Jews, the God of Abraham, Isaac, and Jacob to be the one true, living, eternal, almighty God, the Father of our Lord Jesus Christ, and the only true Savior. This is the supreme glory of the Jews: Only with you was God, nowhere else. We are indebted to Israel for the true God and Savior.

The predicate of the sentence lies in *mistattēr* — you are a God who keeps Himself hidden. The translation should express the characteristic of the Hithpael participle, the uninterrupted continuation of the action, Gr. 116, especially 3, f, p. 357. Not only now and then does God hide Himself; but always, without interruption, absolutely, does He keep Himself hidden from the reason and the senses of natural man, both as to His being and as to His sovereignty. Though not even we preachers are always fully aware of this characteristic of God's being, yet it is clearly set forth in Scripture: Exodus 33:18ff; John 1:18; 1 Timothy 6:16; 1 John 4:12; Isaiah 40:12ff; Romans 11:33ff; Job 38ff; 1 Corinthians 2, etc., etc. No perception by the senses or the intellect, no conclusions based on axioms of human reasoning, no scientific experiment and discovery, no natural philosophy or metaphysical reasoning will ever discover God. He has hidden Himself absolutely from the wise men of the world. Our senses only lay hold of external objects and phenomena; they cannot fully perceive God in nature or in the Word. We understand that twice three is six and that *a* equals *a*. But that kind of reasoning will never discover God. The knowledge of God that is conveyed through the senses and the understanding is essentially a matter of the emotions, of the heart. Conscience, Romans 2:14ff, the knowledge of God revealed in nature, Romans 1:19ff, or in history, Psalm 136, is not a perception of God made by the physical senses and by human reason, but rather is something that is felt, Acts 17:27. God reveals Himself, makes Himself felt in our heart in and through His works. The same is true of the saving spiritual knowledge of God. Like the former, this knowledge of God is imparted by external, physical means and acts, usually by means of the spoken or written Word; but the certain knowledge that God Himself is speaking and acting is not a matter perceived by the senses, but by the heart, an inner feeling which God Himself works directly through His Spirit. Faith — and here Schleiermacher spoke truly — is essentially a matter of inner feeling, whether it is a natural faith or the faith worked by the Spirit. And finally, God is a God, who, in spite of all revelation through conscience, nature, and Word, keeps Himself hidden from the eyes of all men and is made known to men only where He wishes to be known and where He effects such knowledge (Matt. 16:17; John 6:44,65; Matt. 11:27). Moses, David, Isaiah, and Paul did not *see* God, they beheld Him, perceived Him inwardly; they, as it were, saw Him only from the back, Exodus 33:23. Therefore, it is, if we may say so, but a trillionth part that they knew of God, 1 Corinthians 13:9ff. Human reason could not have discovered that the Savior-God was in Israel and that the ways that He chose would lead to Israel's glorification and so to the salvation of the gentiles.

16 בּוֹשׁוּ וְגַם־נִכְלְמוּ כֻּלָּם יַחְדָּו הָלְכוּ בַּכְּלִמָּה חָרָשֵׁי צִירִים:

The Lord speaks in verse 16. Repeatedly He sets the happiness of Israel and of the gentiles who have come over to God's people in sharp contrast to the utter shame of the impenitent makers and worshipers of images. *tsīr* (from *tsūr*, to make firm, to form, to fashion) is a completed image, a statue.

17 יִשְׂרָאֵל נוֹשַׁע בַּיהוָה תְּשׁוּעַת עוֹלָמִים
לֹא־תֵבֹשׁוּ וְלֹא־תִכָּלְמוּ עַד־עוֹלְמֵי עַד:

The glory of Israel is not a temporary one, like that of other nations who rise to a height and then collapse. Israel's is an eternal glory. This is said of the spiritual Israel, of the kingdom of the Messiah, toward which the temporal Israel pressed forward. — Concerning the internal or absolute accusative *teshū'ath*, see Gr. 117, 2. p, q, p. 366f.

Résumé: Israel is glorified as the gentiles acknowledge Israel's God as the hidden but true Savior-God and turn to Him; and Israel's glory endures for ever, while the unconverted are altogether put to shame.

Second Strophe: 45:18-21: *The Lord as Herald of Salvation and Truth.*

18 *Thus says the Lord, Creator of the heavens — He is God!*
Who formed the earth and made it — He established it!
He did not make it a void, He formed it for habitation:
I am the Lord, and there is none other.

19 *I have not spoken in secret, in a place of the dark land,*
I did not say to Jacob's seed: Seek Me in vain!
I am the Lord, who utters salvation and proclaims truth.

20 *Gather together and come, together draw near, you survivors*
of the gentiles;
They know nothing who drag their wooden idols after them,
Who make supplication to gods who cannot help.

21 *Tell it, bring it forth; yes, let them take counsel together!*
Who caused this to be heard beforehand, who told it from of old?
Was it not I, the Lord — and there is no other God beside Me?
A faithful God and Savior — none apart from Me.

¹⁸ כִּי כֹה אָמַר־יְהוָה בּוֹרֵא הַשָּׁמַיִם הוּא הָאֱלֹהִים
יֹצֵר הָאָרֶץ וְעֹשָׂהּ הוּא כוֹנְנָהּ
לֹא־תֹהוּ בְרָאָהּ לָשֶׁבֶת יְצָרָהּ
אֲנִי יְהוָה וְאֵין עוֹד׃

Verse 18 does not refer just to the divine power revealed in the
creation of heaven and earth, but more especially to the goodness
of God manifested in these great works. The heavens do, indeed,
first of all, proclaim God's almighty power (Ps. 19:1ff), and therefore *bōrē' hashshāmayim* is followed by the parenthesis: He is
'elōhīm — the Godhead. Concerning the earth, the fact of original
creation is not stressed. *hū' khōnenāh*, most likely, does not have
its usual meaning of "He founded it"; but, as is often the case with
kōnēn (Polel of *kūn*), it says that He prepared it, established it. Cf.
Deuteronomy 32:6; Isaiah 14:21 (Hiphil); Genesis 43:16. The
phrase embraces all the following detailed acts. He formed it with
skill, established it in perfection (*'ōsāh*). "He did not create it a
void" is paired with *khōnenāh* in that it denies the opposite. Then
there follows the positive statement, "He formed it for habitation," cf 40:22. Thus the creation, especially of the world as prepared by the hand of God, witnesses with a voice that all may hear,
that the Almighty God is truly *good*, and never anything other
than the Lord.

¹⁹ לֹא בַסֵּתֶר דִּבַּרְתִּי בִּמְקוֹם אֶרֶץ חֹשֶׁךְ
לֹא אָמַרְתִּי לְזֶרַע יַעֲקֹב תֹּהוּ בַקְּשׁוּנִי
אֲנִי יְהוָה דֹּבֵר צֶדֶק מַגִּיד מֵישָׁרִים׃

What is said of creation in verse 18, is now asserted in verse 19
of the revealed Word of the Lord. Neither the earth nor the Word
is a *thōhū*, a vain or empty thing. As the earth is a blessing for
man, providing him with a habitation and a home, so is the Word a
faithful saying, promising the grace of the Lord, Israel's salvation.
The Lord's assertion, in the first clause, that He has not spoken in
secret nor in a place of the land of darkness is a reflection on the
fortunetellers, the oracles, and necromancers of the heathen. All
pagan soothsaying was and is a shabby traffic in occult things, a
commerce with the pretended powers of an unknown world, the
underworld, the land of darkness. The expressions used in the
opening clause are borrowed from that world, cf. Job 10:21f.

283

Regarding the matter itself, see Isaiah 8:19; 29:4. The revelation
of the Lord has nothing in common with these light-shy, devilish,
contemptible, deceiving creatures. The Lord has always published
His Word freely and openly to all nations and all people, through
His prophets. Neither did He direct the chosen and beloved seed of
Jacob to seek Him in some *thōhū*, that is, in some empty, uncertain, worthless, unfulfillable promise, in the manner of the
heathen soothsayers who put off their questioners with ambiguous, worthless oracles. For *baqqeshūnī*, see Psalm 27:8.
dōbhēr, a Qal participle, is an alternate form for *medhabbēr*, a Piel
participle. It has the force of *dibbēr ṭōbh*, to utter good news, to
proclaim, to prophesy. *maggīdh*, a Hiphil participle of *nāghadh*, is a
synonym of *dōbhēr*. Whatever the Lord proclaims as a promise or
prophecy, that is, the salvation covenanted between Him and
Jacob, the blessing of Abraham, is *tsedheq*. Other interpretations
miss the point. *mēyshārīm* is in itself a formal expression like
tsedheq and means something *upright* (abstract plural) (Prov. 8:6).
It designates the same thing as *tsedheq*, viewing the salvation
from the point of view of physical uprightness, while *tsedheq*
emphasizes its certainty. Cf. the three synonyms in Proverbs 1:3
and 2:9 with the concluding words of 2:9. *tsedheq* and *mēyshārīm*
constitute a hendiadys, like *grace* and *truth* in John 1:17. This is
what the mouth of the Lord addressed as revelation to the seed of
Jacob — in contrast to the occult, deceiving, pernicious merchan-
dising of the mumbling heathen soothsayers and prophets of the
idols. See John 18:20. The Word of God is the most open thing in
the world. It is not a secret doctrine that can be interpreted only
by experts, priests, or popes. It is open to everyone. Cf.
Deuteronomy 30:11-15; Romans 10:6-8; Isaiah 48:16.

20 הִקָּבְצוּ וָבֹאוּ הִתְנַגְּשׁוּ יַחְדָּו פְּלִיטֵי הַגּוֹיִם
לֹא יָדְעוּ הַנֹּשְׂאִים אֶת־עֵץ פִּסְלָם
וּמִתְפַּלְלִים אֶל־אֵל לֹא יוֹשִׁיעַ:

In verses 20 and 21 we have once again a comparison between
God and the gentiles with their idols, in the form of a challenge to
a judicial contest to determine who it is that foretells the future
and proves Himself to be the only true God, cf. 41:1, 20ff, 26; 43:9;
44:7f. *hiqqābhetsū* and *bō'ū* are paired by the connecting *wa*. In
49:18; 60:4, the two verbs stand unconnected, side by side, as a
hendiadys, "approaching assembled." *hithnaggeshū yaḥdāw* says
the same thing. The *pelītēy*, the fugitives of the gentiles, are those

who have escaped from the judgment — looked upon as already completed — carried out by Cyrus against the nations. In this verse and the next these fugitives are addressed. Confusion results if one understands these fugitives to have been already converted, like the gentiles mentioned in verse 14, and if one assumes verse 21 to be addressed to the gentile gods. It will be noted that in verse 22 these same fugitives are exhorted to turn to the Lord, and that they are therefore here still considered as unconverted. The only question is whether these fugitives are the subject of the next verb: "they know nothing"; or whether that clause is to be taken in a general sense as a warning to the fugitives that those who drag their wooden gods along pray to a god that cannot help. We take the latter explanation to be farfetched, and prefer the former. It is the fugitives who being unconverted lack understanding; who on their flight from the judgment wearily drag along their idols. It is of such that the prophet speaks, as in 46;1, not of idols being carried in a procession, as Cheyne and others think. The shift from the third to the second person and the following participle, *hannōse'īm*, cannot be used as arguments against this explanation, because such grammatical shifts are common. That He may convert them, the Lord is showing the gentiles, who at His counsel are escaping the judgment, how foolish they are to cling to their worship of idols. They burden themselves with dead blocks of wood (*ēts*, a tree, a log — a collective) as though these idols were treasures, and they pray to gods (*ēl* is a generic) who had just deserted them in the judgment from which they were escaping. What a lack of understanding! *lō' yādhe'ū* stands isolated (cf. 1:3; 44:9): They know *nothing*, have no understanding.

21 הַגִּידוּ וְהַגִּישׁוּ אַף יִוָּעֲצוּ יַחְדָּו

מִי הִשְׁמִיעַ זֹּאת מִקֶּדֶם מֵאָז הִגִּידָהּ

הֲלוֹא אֲנִי יְהוָה וְאֵין־עוֹד אֱלֹהִים מִבַּלְעָדַי

אֵל־צַדִּיק וּמוֹשִׁיעַ אַיִן זוּלָתִי׃

The escaping gentiles, together with their idol images, are being addressed. Subject matter and phrasing are similar to 41:21,22,26. The verbs in the address do not have an object. The object is suggested by the question that follows. They are to tell, to produce, and consult about what they might be able to set alongside the age-old prophecy of the Lord that Israel should be saved and the heathen destroyed, a prophecy that is now being fulfilled. Now let them produce their proofs, their *'atstsumoth* (41:21), for the godhead of their idols. In *yiwwa'atsū* (Niphal imperfect) the third person (Jussive) takes the place of the second person of the imperative. *miqqedhem* and *me'āz* are synonyms meaning of old, or long ago, without reference to a certain time. This prophecy of Israel's ascendancy over the gentile nations has, however, been known since the time of Abraham and of the patriarchs of Israel, Genesis 12; 18; especially 22:17, etc. The prophecy was in some measure fulfilled in David and Solomon; then it appeared that with the collapse of the kingdom the promise too was doomed. The exile seemed to destroy it entirely. But it was not possible that this word of God, which had been made known to all nations, should prove to be untrue. Isaiah repeats and extends the promise. In both the first and the second parts of the book, Isaiah proclaims the victory of God's kingdom over the kingdoms of the world. In this Isaiah sees the kingdom of the Messiah who is to come. Also, the Lord had long before proclaimed this very thing through Isaiah, namely, the victory of Israel over the gentile nations that was now taking place before their eyes, cf. Isaiah 14; 21; 25; 27; 28:23ff. Has the Lord not done this? And so, this is undeniable proof that He is God and that apart from Him there is no God. At the same time, this deed shows Him to be *'el tsaddīq ūmoshīa'*, that is, the true God and Savior. *tsaddīq* is an adjective modifying *'el*, while *moshīa'* is a noun participle that identifies the *'el tsaddīq*. *'el tsaddīq*, taken literally, means only a "right God"; historically, He is the God of the covenant, "which keepeth truth for ever," Psalm 146:6. *moshīa'* explains *'el tsaddīq*. He is the Helper, Redeemer, and Savior of His people. It is this truth and the repeated assertion that there is no other God, no other true God, no Helper apart from Him, that is to turn the hearts of the heathen to Him. For one thing, they cannot produce any instance of prophecy as proof of the deity of their idols, and thus are revealed to be slaves of dead gods. And besides, in the Lord, the true God and Savior, the way to salvation is opened wide to them.

Résumé: Just as the creation, the work of the Lord's hands, is not an empty wasteland, but a blessing for mankind, so too the Lord's prophetic Word is not a no-thing, but real and true salvation. Those who are escaping from the present judgment, still idolatrous heathen, have nothing of that kind to produce as something coming from their idols. The Lord alone is a true God and Savior.

Third Strophe: 45:22-25: *Turn to me, so shall you be saved!*

22 *Turn to Me, and let yourselves be helped, all ends*
    of the earth; for I am God, and none other.
23 *By Myself have I sworn; out of the mouth of faithfulness*
    has gone forth a word, and it shall not return:
    That to me every knee shall bow, every tongue shall swear.
24 *And say of Me: Truly, in the Lord alone is salvation*
    and strength;
    But before Him shall come and be put to shame all those
    who are incensed against Him.
25 *For in the Lord shall receive salvation and in Him shall*
    glory all the seed of Israel.

This strophe brings the applications of the whole address, just as 40:26-31 did.

$$\text{22}\quad \text{פְּנוּ־אֵלַי וְהִוָּשְׁעוּ כָּל־אַפְסֵי־אָרֶץ}$$
$$\text{כִּי אֲנִי־אֵל וְאֵין עוֹד׃}$$

The fugitives who have escaped Cyrus' judgment over the nations are being admonished to turn from their impotent idols to the Lord. The *Waw* in *wehiwwāshe ū* (Niphal imperative) imparts to this second imperative (as Luther correctly concluded) the force of a final clause, as though this were *Waw* with an imperfect, Gr. 110, 2. f, p. 324f. The first imperative expresses the condition; the second, the conclusion, as in Genesis 42:18; Jeremiah 6:16; Psalm 37:27. The invitation includes the ends of the earth, all nations without exception. Cf. Mark 16; Matthew 28; 11:28. The excellent basis for the invitation, in the final clause, is often repeated because idolatrous hearts are so unwilling to receive it.

$$\text{23}\quad \text{בִּי נִשְׁבַּעְתִּי}$$
$$\text{יָצָא מִפִּי צְדָקָה דָּבָר וְלֹא יָשׁוּב}$$
$$\text{כִּי־לִי תִּכְרַע כָּל־בֶּרֶךְ תִּשָּׁבַע כָּל־לָשׁוֹן׃}$$

The solemn oath lends maximum emphasis to the invitation and its basis. The usual oath-formula in the mouth of the Lord is *ḥay ānī*, as I live, Isaiah 49:18; Numbers 14:21,28, etc. The form *bī nishba ʿtī* is less common because it is more formal, Genesis 22:16; Jeremiah 22:5; 49:13. See also Jeremiah 44:26 and Psalm 89:36(35), and Hebrews 7:20ff.

The construction of the next clause is unusual. Many commentators translate: "There goes forth from My mouth righteousness, a word that shall not turn back." It cannot properly be objected that this translation assumes a masculine predicate following a feminine subject (*tsedhāqāh*), because *yātsā'*, the predicate, is in initial position, Gr. 145, 7, o, p. 465. But the *Waw* before *lō'* prevents taking *lō' yāshūbh* as a modifying clause. Such a clause would have to read: *dābhār* (*'asher*) *lō'yāshūbh*. Those who adhere to this translation simply strike the *we*. But such violence is not necessary if one takes *pī tsedhāqāh* as a construct state, mouth of faithfulness, and *dābhār* as the subject of *yātsā'*. There goes forth out of the mouth of faithfulness a word, and it shall not return. We prefer this latter interpretation, because it adheres to the accepted text. In either case, the sense remains the same. The sentence harks back to *dōbhēr tsedheq* in verse 19. *tsedhāqāh* is here, as usual, salvation itself, like *tsedheq* in verse 19, or the will to save, the faithfulness, as we have translated it. For *lō' yāshūbh*, compare 55:11. *kī* introduces the content of the divine oath; it need not therefore be translated. *lī* applies to the second clause as well as to the first. The two clauses that follow *kī* are fully explained in verse 24.

24 אַךְ בַּיהוָה לִי אָמַר צְדָקוֹת וָעֹז

עָדָיו יָבוֹא וְיֵבשׁוּ כֹּל הַנֶּחֱרִים בּוֹ:

It is not clear why *'akh* should here be purely restrictive (Delitzsch). The affirmative meaning is the more suitable one as an introduction to a confession, for this clause expresses the substance of the oath that every tongue shall swear (verse 23). Repentant and believing, the converted gentiles confess and confirm by an oath that they have found *tsedhāqāh* and *'ōz* in the Lord, and in Him alone. Here too, *tsedhāqāh* is salvation, namely, the salvation that the Lord freely gave by His promise to Abraham, Isaac, Jacob, and their seed. It is the covenanted salvation for which all the godly believers of the Old Testament had waited, cf. Jacob, Genesis 49:18; David, Psalm 14:7; 53:7(6); 119:166. In these passages, *yeshū'āh*, the Messianic salvation, takes the place of *tsedhāqāh*. In the chapter before us, from verse 14 on, the prophesied deliverance of Israel from exile is blended into a single picture with the Messianic salvation to come. The conversion of the gentiles, foretold in verse 14, and described in verses 23 and 24, according to its inner nature becomes a reality in the work of St. Paul and continues until the Lord shall come again. *'ōz* is a word of wide signification. Here it signifies every kind of power, physical and spiritual, that the Holy Spirit imparts to the believers. But it is a power that has its source in the riches of Him

upon whom the Spirit of the Lord rests, 11:2; 61:1; yes, it is the
Lord Himself, in whom the congregation of the redeemed glory,
12:2ff; Exodus 15:2; and many Psalms. *baYHWH tsedhāqōth* (intensive plural!) *wā'ōz* is essentially the same in meaning as
YHWH tsidhqāthī wā'uzzī, or *YHWH tsidhqēnū*, Jeremiah 23:6;
33:16. The confession of the converted gentiles is their answer to
the oft repeated declarations of the Lord that He alone is God. *lī*
'āmar is a parenthesis; in the initial position it would have detract-
ed from the emotional impact of the sentence. It is impersonal,
and *lī* is less direct than "*to* Me"; it expresses a very general relation to the Lord: "concerning Me."

The *spirit* of this entire great passage is evangelical; there is no
indication of the use of force or power. It begins with the Gospel
proclamation and effects bending of the knees and believing, humble confession. And yet St. Paul in Romans 14:11 and Philippians
2:9f cites this passage as revealing the power of the Lord as Judge.
That is not false exegesis; it is rather a correct application. The
covenant of God, as the very next sentence shows, is on the one
hand Grace and Spirit, and on the other, Power and Judgment.
With His Word and Spirit, God works among men and converts
many; but those who refuse to yield to Him, He forces into submis-
sion with power and judgment. Even the damned will one day be
forced to render to Jesus Christ the honor that He is Lord. It is a
twofold truth that always remains: he who believes shall be saved,
but he who does not believe shall be damned. Both tend to the glory of God. The same truth is expressed here in the second half of
verse 24.

This clause has given commentators endless trouble and has
been translated so variously because *'ādhāw yābhō'* was wrongly
separated from the word that follows. It is a case of not seeing the
forest because of the trees. There is nothing difficult about the
sentence as it stands, if one remembers that from verse 23 on the
verb forms are jussives. *'ādhāw* (before Him), *yābhō'* (must come)
weyēbhōshū (and be put to shame), *kōl hanneherīm bō* (all who are
incensed against Him). Therefore: *Before Him*, that is, before the
Lord; they *must come*, that is, appear before His judgment seat and
be put to shame (like *yābhō' 'adh hā'elōhīm*, or *'el hā'elōhīm*, Exodus 22:7,8(8,9), which also explains Romans 14:11). Can the
singular *yābhō'* be used as an argument against this interpretation? See Gr. 145, 5, 1, p. 464. This singular is distributive in sense
and is paired with *kōl*, which is construed as a plural: Before Him
must everyone appear, and *all* must be put to shame, etc. There is

no mistake, either, in the accentuation, as Delitzsch and others maintained. The sequence of Pashta, Munach, Zaqeph occurs thousands of times at the end of a clause, cf. verses 23, b; 46:1, 3, 4, etc. The sentence division occurs after *weyēbhōshū.* In the synagog the line would be intoned thus: Before Him must appear and be put to shame — all who are incensed against Him. In 46:1b, there is an example of a Zaqeph in the middle of a sentence. The difficulty was caused by translating *'adh* either with *to* (Luther), or with *upon, against* (Gesenius). The difficulty disappears as soon as *'adh* is translated with *before.* The sentence is a companion of the New Testament "He that believeth not shall be damned," with this difference that *hanneḥerīm bō* (from *ḥārāh*; a Niphal participle) emphasizes the inner enmity of the unbelievers against God, cf. 41:11 ("they that strive against You").

25 בַּיהוָה יִצְדְּקוּ וְיִתְהַלְלוּ   כָּל־זֶרַע יִשְׂרָאֵל׃

The strophe and the entire discourse closes with a significant sentence of one line. *yitsdeqū,* does not mean to "be right," nor does it have the New Testament meaning of "to be justified." The verb indicates the possession of the *tsedheq* or *tsedhāqāh* of the Lord, that is, the salvation promised by the Lord in the covenant prepared by Him. This *tsedheq* is received *baYHWH,* through Him, in Him, with Him. It includes also the physical deliverance from all evil, 2 Timothy 4:18. The "glorying" likewise is *baYHWH* and is a result of *yitsdeqū.* "All the seed of Israel" is not Israel according to the flesh — many of those will be lost — it is the spiritual Israel, which includes the converted gentiles who have turned to Israel and to the Lord (verse 14). From *kol* in this verse, the two *kol* in verse 23 acquire their meaning. The entire strophe is summed up in this sentence; it is a summary of all the brief synopses we have appended at the end of each section.

THIRD TRIAD
Chapters 46-48

*A Preaching of Judgment
and a Call to Repentance.*

First Discourse: Chapter 46

A Preaching of Judgment and a Call to Repentance.

The significance of these last three chapters of the first third of Isaiah II will be misunderstood if one titles the chapters as Delitzsch does: 46, Fall of the gods of Babel; 47, Fall of Babel, the Capital of the Empire of the World; 48, Deliverance from Babel. — Only the first two verses of chapter 46 treat of the fall of the gods of Babel. The rest of the chapter is addressed to the *poshe'īm* (verse 8) and the *'abbīrēy lēbh* (verse 12) of the house of Jacob and is a preaching of condemnation and judgment. The fall of Bel and Nebo serves only as the occasion for this reprimand addressed to what is left of the house of Israel. Chapter 47 is even less than chapter 14 a Qinah, a lament for the dead; it is a prediction of judgment against the Babylon that still stands, expressed in Qinah rhythm. This discourse is not superfluous, nor irrelevant (Knobel); it is the logical consequence of everything that was said earlier. It brings matters to a point, and is a natural application of the preceding discourse on the Lord's counsel of salvation. It fittingly follows the preceding preaching of judgment against the house of God, which ended, however, in the glorification of Zion. To this, the fall of Babylon stands in sharpest contrast. The repetition in 48:1-11 of a preaching of judgment upon hardened Israel has its reason in the prophet's consciousness of God's designs. The gentile enemies of the kingdom of God are not of such importance that the judgment should culminate in their destruction. The climax lies in the rejection of those in Israel who harden their hearts against the covenant of grace and perish, and finally in the salvation of the elect. — All this is so clear that it cannot help forcing itself on the understanding of the reader. It would be hard to understand the failure of so many commentators to comprehend the connection of ideas, if one were not aware of their fixed idea

292

that Isaiah II was composed by a Deutero-Isaiah, different from the author of Isaiah I, who tacked together many unrelated fragments. That delusion has blinded them to the close relation between all the parts of Isaiah. What a pity that a man like Delitzsch was not able to free himself completely from the spell of an idea that rests solely on unbelief! The proper understanding of Isaiah has suffered immeasurably as a consequence.

First Discourse: Chapter 46

A Preaching of Judgment against the Rebellious People of Israel.

This short chapter has three parts: verses 1 and 2, the fall of the gods of Babylon; verses 3-7, reprimand of Israel for taking part in the Babylonian idol worship; verses 8-13, reproof of unbelief respecting the Lord's promises.

First Strophe: verses 1-2:   *The fall of the gods of Babylon.*

1   *Fallen is Bel, Nebo bows down,*
    Their images have become the lot of beasts of burden and cattle;
    Those who were carried by you are now laden
    As a burden for weary cattle.
2   *Fallen, sunk down are they altogether;*
    They are not able to carry away the burden,
    And they themselves go into captivity.

כָּרַע בֵּל קֹרֵס נְבוֹ   הָיוּ עֲצַבֵּיהֶם ¹
לַחַיָּה וְלַבְּהֵמָה   נְשֻׂאֹתֵיכֶם עֲמוּסוֹת מַשָּׂא לַעֲיֵפָה :

Bel and Nebo are the two chief gods of Babylon. Bel is the Babylonian-Assyrian form of the Phoenician-Canaanite Baal. The word designates a lord or master and was originally a title of honor or majesty, a *nomen dignitatis,* whereas the Babylonian proper name for Bel Merodach (Jeremiah 50:2), according to cuneiform inscriptions, was Marduk, or Maruduk. But Bel too became a proper name. The two names, Bel and Nebo, bear about the same relation to each other as Jehovah to Elohim in Israel. Baal is the common supreme deity of all Semitic heathen and represents the original creative power, the equivalent of Jupiter, and Nebo is represented as his son. Nebo corresponds exactly to the Greco-Roman Hermes-Mercury, the god of science, the discoverer of the art of writing, etc. The god's Babylonian name is Nabu or Nabum, the Speaker, which corresponds to the Hebrew *nābhī*, the prophet. Bel was the municipal god of Babylon, Nebo was the god of Borsippa, which lay on the other side of the Euphrates but was still within the limits of Babylon. The temple that was erected there to Nebo (the ruins are called Birs Nimrud), served, with its various levels, as a worship center for all the chief gods of the Babylonians.

The prophet sees the statues of Bel and Nebo toppled from their pedestals, viewed by him as a phase or a consequence of the fall of the city. However, it is really the Lord who describes the scene. This is the end of these "gods." Their fallen statues ('*atsabbīm,* from '*ātsabh,* to carve) fall to the lot of the draft cattle and beasts of burden. The next clause shows that asses, camels, and oxen are meant by the term "beasts of burden." *nesu'ōtheykhem,* a Niphal plural feminine participle (expressing a neuter idea) — "your lifted ones" — refers to statues of idols that were carried by the priests in solemn processions. See Baruch 6:4, the epistle ascribed to Jeremiah. The predicate of this participle is likewise a participle — they are *laden* as a burden for weary beasts. '*ayēphāh* is a feminine form expressing the neuter and is collective — *the weary,* that is, the beasts that are worn out from dragging this burden. The suffix in '*atsabbēyhem* we understand to refer to Bel and Nebo. Still, Cheyne may be right in referring it to the Babylonians, the worshipers themselves. He cites Psalm 115:4; Micah 1:7; Isaiah 10:11; 1 Samuel 31:9. The suffix in *nesu'ōtheykhem* certainly refers to the Babylonians and not, as Hahn insists, to Israel. *qāras,* to stoop down, bend over, occurs only in this and in the following verse (from *qeres,* a hook). The perfect predicates and the participles are characteristic of descriptions of present situations.

2 קָרְסוּ כָרְעוּ יַחְדָּו לֹא יָכְלוּ מַלֵּט מַשָּׂא

וְנַפְשָׁם בַּשְּׁבִי הָלָכָה׃

The verbs repeat the predicates in the first clause of verse 1, but in reverse order. The subjects of these verbs, in both sentences, are Bel and Nebo, certainly not, as Budde and other moderns thought, the beasts of burden, pictured as reeling and stumbling under the burden of the images and not being able to carry them to safety. (Would that be poetry?!) According to Herodotus, the images of Bel were made of gold. The pictures that have been discovered show them being carried by four men, and any good team of oxen would have easily borne them away without stumbling. If Herodotus can be trusted, Xerxes had no trouble carting them away. *yaḥdāw* means "all of them together"; the combined might of Bel and Nebo does not suffice to rescue their images. Bel and Nebo are also the subject of *yākhelū mallēṭ*. Here already is implied what is expressed in the following clause; "their *soul*," they themselves, their imagined divinity, is distinguished from their statues. They themselves, the deities, are not able to rescue the statues from the ravaging enemies, and they are carried into captivity by the Persians, together with their statues. As in the first verse, so here, present perfects and imperfects are used to describe the scene.

Second Strophe: verses 3-7: *Reprimand of Israel for taking part in the idol worship of Babylon.*

First Half: verses 3-5:

3 *Hearken to me, O house of Jacob,*
   And all the remnant of the house of Israel,
   Who have been borne as a burden from the mother's womb,
   Carried from the mother's lap:
4 *Even unto old age it is I,*
   And unto gray hair I will bear the burden.
   I have done it, and I will carry,
   Yes, I will bear the burden and will deliver.
5 *To whom will you liken Me and equate Me?*
   With whom compare Me, that we should be equal?

שִׁמְעוּ אֵלַי בֵּית יַעֲקֹב וְכָל־שְׁאֵרִית בֵּית יִשְׂרָאֵל ³
הָעֲמֻסִים מִנִּי־בֶטֶן הַנְּשֻׂאִים מִנִּי־רָחַם׃

shime ū 'elay is an earnest call addressed to Israel in view of the fall of the impotent Babylonian gods. The terms "house of Jacob" and "house of Israel" unite the people in one compact body, and the following testimony addressed to that body applies to every individual in it. *kol she'erīth* particularly includes in the house of Jacob whatever had up to this time remained separated from it, although a part of it. The house of Israel is Israel's progeny united under one regime. It is farfetched to identify the house of Israel with the tribes of the northern kingdom (Kimchi, Delitzsch). This would be the only passage in Isaiah II where mention is made of the ten tribes. The house of Israel is identical with the house of Jacob, as in 63:7.

minnī is a poetic form of *min*, Judges 5:14; Micah 7:12; Psalm 44:11(10), and many other passages. Luther understood it to be

295

the same as *mimmennī* and took *beten* and *reḥem* to be adverbial accusatives. In contrast to the idols of Babylon which had to be carried by men or loaded on beasts, the whole house of Jacob, from its mother's womb, since its very beginning, has been lifted up and carried by its Lord. Hahn mentions the departure of Israel from Egypt as the hour of Israel's birth. One might in like manner call the migration of the house of Jacob into Egypt, the conception of the people, Genesis 46:27. Egypt would thus be the womb from which Israel was born, cf. Hosea 11:1; Matthew 2:15. — For the charming picture of Israel being carried by the Lord, see also 63:9; Deuteronomy 1:31; 32:11; Exodus 19:4; Psalm 28:9. Moses too employs the picture, Numbers 11:12. — The passive participles express the unbroken continuance of being carried. Gr. 116, 1, a, b, e, f, p. 355ff.

⁴ וְעַד־זִקְנָה אֲנִי הוּא וְעַד־שֵׂיבָה אֲנִי אֶסְבֹּל
אֲנִי עָשִׂיתִי וַאֲנִי אֶשָּׂא וַאֲנִי אֶסְבֹּל וַאֲמַלֵּט׃

For an introductory *Waw,* following participles in the preceding sentence, see Gr. 116, v, x, p. 361f. "As for you, carried by Me, etc . . . . I am the same and will carry." For *'anī hū'* compare 41:4; 43:10, 13; 48:12. The phrase is always used in the same sense in Isaiah II: I am He, namely, God. In this verse: I am He, who carried you, and I am the same unto your old age, namely, your Bearer. The next clause repeats the thought, using indicatives instead of participles. *'anī* is repeated five times in this verse, thus emphasizing the great contrast between God and the gods of Babylon, and especially making the question in verse 5 more pointed. The use of bare verbs without expressed objects heightens the idea of action. The object is self-evident, and mention of it would introduce the idea of love, whereas the purpose is reprimand. *'anī ʿāsīthī wa'anī 'essā'* can stand very well without learned emendation. The tenses are both strictly historical: I *have* done it; I *will* carry, Gr. 106, 1, c, p. 310. *wa'amallēt* corresponds to *mallēt* in verse 2. The rescue is the true test of Godhead.

⁵ לְמִי תְדַמְיוּנִי וְתַשְׁווּ וְתַמְשִׁלוּנִי וְנִדְמֶה׃

This verse expresses the same thought as 40:18 and 25, although here there is a heaping up of the verbs of comparison. The reason for that is the great earnestness of speech, corresponding to the heaping up of the words for "I" in verse 4. The new verb is *māshal,* the original meaning of which is also "to compare." In Hebrew it is a technical term for an allegory, for figurative language, for a maxim, a proverb. The *mishlēy shelōmō* are the Proverbs of Solomon. Verse 5 is a transitional verse between this strophe and the next. The thought of this section is clear: The difference between the Babylonian gods and the Lord is so great that whereas those gods have to be carted away by cattle and cannot rescue their own images, the Lord has carried all His people from the time of their conception and will continue to carry them. How then can Israel compare its God with any idol? The subject of *nidhmeh* is the Lord and the idols — "that we should be equal," that is, to each other. The imperfect is potential in meaning.

Second Half: verses 6-7:

6 *They pour out gold from a pouch,*
   And weigh out silver with a balance;
   They hire a goldsmith that he make a god of it;
   They fall down, and even worship it;
7 *They lift him up, load him on their shoulders,*
   Set him down in his place — and there he stands,
   He does not move from his place;
   And though one cries out to him, he gives no answer,
   Nor does he help one out of his trouble.

הַזָּלִים זָהָב מִכִּיס וְכֶסֶף בַּקָּנֶה יִשְׁקֹלוּ
יִשְׂכְּרוּ צוֹרֵף וְיַעֲשֵׂהוּ אֵל יִסְגְּדוּ אַף־יִשְׁתַּחֲווּ:

This is the fourth time in Part I of Isaiah II that the manufacture of idols has been described (40:19; 41:7; 44:9ff). This verse shows why in the previous passages the makers and the worshipers of idols were merely identified. Worshipers and manufacturers are one and the same, since they order the idols from master workmen. Concerning the participial construction (*hazzālīm* is from *zūl,* to pour out, to shake) and a following finite verb (*yishqōlū*), see Gr. 116, x, p. 361. The finite verb is often preceded by a *Waw.* Since both metals are mentioned together, it is obvious that the reference is to materials used, and not to payment for the goldsmith's work. *qāneh* is the arm of the balance, a part for the whole. For *tsōrēph,* cf. 40:19, 41:7. For *waya'asēhū 'ēl,* cf. *'asāhū phesel* in 44:15; for *sāghadh,* see 44:15 and also 17. *yishtaḥawū* (Hithpael of *shāḥah*) to bow down, is stronger than *sāghadh,* hence the particle *'aph,* even.

297

ישְׂאֻהוּ עַל־כָּתֵף יִסְבְּלֻהוּ וַיַּנִּיחֻהוּ תַחְתָּיו וְיַעֲמֹד 7
מִמְּקוֹמוֹ לֹא יָמִישׁ
אַף־יִצְעַק אֵלָיו וְלֹא יַעֲנֶה מִצָּרָתוֹ לֹא יוֹשִׁיעֶנּוּ :

yissā'uhū is separated from the rest of the sentence by the pre-
positive disjunctive accent Telisha. *'al kātheph* modifies the next
verb — they lift him up, they load him on their shoulder(s). *nūah* is
the opposite of *rūah* — to be quiet — to be restless. The Hiphil
hēnīah always means to set down, to set at rest, as in Genesis 2:15:
He set him at rest in the garden Eden. *tahtāyw* (*tahath* with
suffix), literally "his under parts" is a kind of prolepsis: to the
place that will be under him, "in his place." The drastic
weya'amōdh is supplemented by the following clause: And there
he stands, he does not move from his place. *mūsh* or *mīsh* is a verb
that in its sound imitates the sound of the action, the slipping,
rushing sound of something that slips from its place. *'aph yits'aq*
and *welō' ya'aneh* are coordinated, but we have sought to express
the intended meaning by subordinating one of the clauses:
Though one cries, yet he gives no answer. *yits'aq*, like all the third
person plural verbs in verses 6 and 7, is impersonal, and the
suffixes in *mitstsārathō* and *yōshī'ennū* are to be translated accordingly.

In verses 1 and 2 the impotence of the idols is drastically pictured through the collapse of their statues; in strong contrast, in
verses 3 and 4, the glory of the Lord appears in His carrying of Israel; verses 5 and 6 then again describe the nothingness of the
idols by the manner of their creation and their inability to move
after being set on their pedestals. The purpose is to reprimand Israel for participating in the Babylonian idolatry (verses 3 and 5).
This sets the tone for the entire passage.

Third Strophe: verses 8-13: *Unbelief respecting the divine
promises is rebuked.*

8 *Remember this, and keep it in mind,*
   Take it to heart, you rebels.
9 *Remember the former things of long ago,*
   That I am God, and none other,
   God, and like Me there is no other.

10   *Who in the beginning revealed what should come afterward,*
      And beforetime what was not yet come to pass;
      Who said: My counsel shall stand,
      And all My pleasure will I perform.
11   *Who out of the East called forth an eagle,*
      Out of a distant land the hero of my counsel;
      Not only did I say it, I also bring it about —
      I set it in motion, I will also finish it.
12   *Listen to Me, you hard of heart,*
      Who are far removed from salvation:
13   *I have brought My salvation near, it is not far off,*
      And My help does not lag behind;
      Yes, I create help in Zion
      And My glory in Israel.

Commentators, with few exceptions, make two mistakes here that are a bar to a proper understanding of the passage. They refer *zōʾth* to the past, that is, to the description of the impotence of idols, the same mistake that we rejected in 44:21. The demonstrative *zeh, zōʾth,* can refer to something just mentioned, but only when circumstances clearly require that interpretation. "*zeh* almost always points out a (new) person or thing present, while *hūʾ*refers to a person or thing already mentioned or known," Gr. 136, a, p. 442. But here all circumstances require reference to what follows. Verse 9 actually repeats *zikhrū* and makes mention of the substantive to which *zōʾth* refers: *rīʾshōnōth mēʿōlām*, etc. The verse then proceeds to develop the term *rīʾshōnōth*. Furthermore, *zākhar* is not a verb suitable for referring to things just past. *zākhar* does not mean "to consider," which would be the verb to use if reference were to be made to the immediate past. *zākhar* means "to remember," "to recall to mind." And what had just been said about the impotence of the idols, and of Israel's participation in their worship, was hardly a matter that was likely to slip from the memory of the *pōsheʿīm* in Israel, for it had been so very vividly described to them. Could they so soon have forgotten that description? Was a reproof already needed? The beginning of verse 9 ought to decide the question.

The second mistake is that the participles in verses 10 and 11 are translated as referring to present time, whereas they are clearly *participia perfecti.* Since the *rīʾshōnōth mēʿōlām* (the object of *zikhrū*) are already long past, then certainly the activities of which they were the object (*maggīdh, ʾōmēr, qōreʾ*) cannot still be present activities and the object of *zākhar.*

8 זִכְרוּ־זֹאת וְהִתְאֹשָׁשׁוּ   הָשִׁיבוּ פוֹשְׁעִים עַל־לֵב :

In accordance with what has just been said, we translate *zō'th*
with "this" and refer it to what follows. No one knows the meaning of *hith'ōshāshū.* The word occurs nowhere else and is wide open
to conjecture and emendation. Cheyne translated it with "be deeply ashamed," thus following Joseph Kimchi, one reading of the
Vulgate (*confundamini*), Calvin, and Lazarde (*yithbōshāshū,*
Genesis 2:25). David Kimchi, Gesenius, Ewald, Delitzsch, and
many modern translators let the word stand as written and derive
it from *'ashash,* a word that occurs in certain old and late dialects;
some agree but change the reading to *hith'ashāshū.* Still others
suggest *hith'ashāmū* and translate: "plead guilty!" Gesenius took
'ashash to be a denominative of *'ish.* Delitzsch disagrees, but most
moderns, rather hesitatingly, follow Gesenius. It is probable that
the verb contains the concept of something firm and compact, cf.
'ashīshēy, Isaiah 16:7; and some translate: "Be firm, stand firm,"
and refer to 1 Samuel 4:9. But it is difficult to see how this translation fits into the context. Our translation is also a guess, but it at
least fits the context. Remember, call to mind, take to heart — a
climax. If anyone can suggest a better translation, he is welcome
to try. The *pōshe'īm* are the people who are really addressed. They
are the apostates who have forsaken the covenant and gone after
other gods.

9 זִכְרוּ רִאשֹׁנוֹת מֵעוֹלָם

כִּי אָנֹכִי אֵל וְאֵין עוֹד   אֱלֹהִים וְאֶפֶס כָּמוֹנִי :

The same idea, negatively expressed, occurs in 43:18, but without *mē'ōlām.* The *rī'shōnōth* in that passage are the wonderful
deeds of the Lord, such as those at the Red Sea. See our remarks
on that verse. *mē'ōlām,* an attribute to *rī'shōnōth,* describes these
deeds as having occurred in the earliest times, those referred to in
43:18. — The usual translation of *kī* as "for" or "because" is not
appropriate here. *kī* introduces a noun clause as object. *rī'shōnōth*
is the object in its external form; the object, as to its meaning, is
the sole Godhead of the Lord, as that Godhead is revealed by the
rī'shōnōth mē'ōlām. For *'ephes kāmōnī,* "nothing is like Me," cf.
45:14.

10 מַגִּיד מֵרֵאשִׁית אַחֲרִית   וּמִקֶּדֶם אֲשֶׁר לֹא־נַעֲשׂוּ

אֹמֵר עֲצָתִי תָקוּם   וְכָל־חֶפְצִי אֶעֱשֶׂה :

The participles in verses 10 and 11 tell how the Lord in the *rī'shōnōth* of ancient times showed that He alone is God, not how the Lord in general demonstrates His Godhead. They are to be translated with verbs in the past tense. *rē'shīth* and *'aharīth* are corresponding concepts: inception and outcome; beginning and end: cf. 41:22; 47:7. But *mērē'shīth* here too does not mean "since the beginning," but rather "at the beginning." I am He who at the very beginning foretold the outcome and the end. The following parallel clause expresses the same idea in somewhat different form, literally, "from before, what was not completed." I foretold beforehand what was not completed. *'ōmēr* is also a perfect participle. As in 40:8, *thāqūm* is not to be rendered "will come to pass," as it is usually translated, but "it will remain, will stand." The verb here stands alone; in 40:8, *le'ōlām* is added, "for ever." The next clause, *wekhol hephtsī 'e'eseh*, "and all my pleasure will I perform," repeats the thought. In 44:28 it is Cyrus through whom the Lord carries out His counsel. There it was already indicated, and in the next verse it is clearly expressed, what the Lord had proclaimed beforehand (*maggīdh*) as His counsel, which should stand firm, whereto He had awakened Cyrus: the fall of Babylon and all her gods named in verse 1, and the deliverance of Zion - Israel, verse 13. The discourse proceeds step by step from the general to the particular, and finally to the individual.

11 קֹרֵא מִמִּזְרָח עַיִט מֵאֶרֶץ מֶרְחָק אִישׁ עֲצָתוֹ

אַף־דִּבַּרְתִּי אַף־אֲבִיאֶנָּה יָצַרְתִּי אַף־אֶעֱשֶׂנָּה:

Cyrus is here called an *'ayit*, a bird of prey. Cf. Genesis 15:11; Isaiah 18:6. The *'ayit* is an eagle, vulture, falcon, or similar bird. Cf. Jeremiah 49:22; Ezekiel 17:3. "According to Xenophon the ensign of Cyrus and his successors was a golden eagle" (Cheyne). The point here is the fall of Babylon rather than the deliverance of Israel, which is the subject of verse 13. Babylon is the prey upon which Cyrus the eagle will swoop. Cyrus is *'īsh 'atsāthō*, the man whom His counsel has selected to carry out that counsel — a concept similar to *'abhdī* in 40:13.

'aph — *'aph* is stronger than *et* — *et*, or both-and. We have translated it with "not only — (but) also." All doubt about translating *maggīdh*, *'ōmēr*, and *qōrē'* with preterite tenses is removed by the perfect forms *dibbartī* and *yātsartī*, followed by pure futures. *dibbartī* and *yātsartī*, without expressed objects, sum up all that has gone before. The feminine suffixes of the verbs in the

future tense are of course to be understood as expressing a neuter idea. *yātsartī* and *'e'esennāh* heighten the thought in the parallel expression in the preceding clause. *yātsartī* does not mean "prepared in My counsel" (Delitzsch), but "prepared in fact, in the act." This interpretation requires the *'e'esennāh* — I will carry it to completion. *'abhī'ennāh* states that what had only been spoken is now put into action. There are in the four verbs three different concepts: to announce, to put into action; to put into action, to complete. *yātsartī* carries forward the thought of *'abhī'ennāh*.

שִׁמְעוּ אֵלַי אַבִּירֵי לֵב הָרְחוֹקִים מִצְּדָקָה: ¹²

As immediately after the beginning of the chapter (verse 3), so here immediately before its end we have an earnest call addressed to those for whom this whole discourse is meant. It is not justifiable to distinguish those called *'abbīrey lēbh,* strong of heart, from those who were called *pōshe'īm* in verse 8, as though the *pōshe'īm* were different, more vicious people, unapproachable and inclined to apostasy (Delitzsch). Even though one would entirely disregard the LXX text (*'obhedhēy* instead of *'abbīrey*), which most modern scholars have followed, the *'abbīr lēbh,* the person hard of heart, is in a worse spiritual state than the *pōshēa',* the transgressor, the disloyal, the faithless one. But why take these to be two different kinds of people? It is characteristic of our prophet that he classifies his audience, speaks to them as people of distinct spiritual peculiarities (48:1, 12; 51:1, 7; and elsewhere). But he always has only two categories: gentiles and Jews; and in Israel, the godfearing and the godless. When he apparently divides the godly into two classes, as in 51:1 (who follow after righteousness) and verse 7 (who know righteousness), those are not two different classes, but are the same persons, described from different points of view. It is a poetic, not a dogmatic, distinction. So here, the strong of heart are different from the rebels of verse 8 only in being pictured as being one degree more godless. They are the same people as those described in 48:1-11 as hypocrites, with necks of iron and foreheads of brass, who are obstinately set against every word of God, who are — as the appositive describes them — far removed from salvation, that is, completely cut off from it. That is true also of the rebellious ones to whom verses 1-11 apply. If in verses 3 and 4 the Lord reminds them of the grace and faithfulness once extended to them, something which He also declares to be unchanging in the future, it does not follow that He

looks upon them as capable of conversion. That is indicated in
48:9-11, where the same declaration is made to people with necks
of iron and brows of brass. So also, verses 8-11 are not an admonition to repent, but like verses 12 and 13, a testimony against them,
so that they are without excuse. Verse 13 is simply a summary of
verses 9-11.

13 קֵרַבְתִּי צִדְקָתִי לֹא תִרְחָק וּתְשׁוּעָתִי לֹא תְאַחֵר
וְנָתַתִּי בְצִיּוֹן תְּשׁוּעָה לְיִשְׂרָאֵל תִּפְאַרְתִּי:

The Lord has brought His salvation near. It is present. It is very
near, as *lo' thirḥaq* declares — it is *not* far away. *lo' the'aḥēr* states
that it does not tarry, as though one needed to wait for it, perhaps
in vain. *wenāthattī*, both as to content and form of the verb
(prophetic perfect of actual completion), indicates the actual completion of salvation in the immediate future. The Lord declares
this to rebels who are no longer receptive to the preaching of salvation, not as though there were still hope of their conversion, but
as a testimony against them, as a preaching of judgment.

This is the thrust of the whole chapter. In chapters 46, 47, and
48 the Lord preaches judgment and repentance. First, judgment,
in 46, 47, and 48:1-11. It is God's rule that judgment begins at the
house of God, chapter 46; Jeremiah 25:29; 49:12; Ezekiel 9:6; 1
Peter 4:17. Then follows the preaching of judgment against Babylon, 47; a repetition of the preaching of judgment against hardened Israel, 48:1 - 11; and finally, a call to repentance addressed
to those to be saved in Israel. — It is a gross misunderstanding to
interpret chapter 46 as a "pastoral sermon." It is a sermon of judgment.

Résume' of the Discourse: How can the house of Jacob, which
God lifted up from its mother's womb and carried on His shoulder
and will continue to carry to the very end, make this God equal to
fallen deities who are not able to rescue their own statues from the
enemy, statues which are manufactured to order and are unable
to move from their pedestals. These apostates ought to have
known from the wonders of ancient times that He alone is God,
and they should now know that what He has foretold, He will
surely bring about, namely, the destruction of Babylon by Cyrus,
and the establishment in the immediate future of salvation in
Zion-Jerusalem.

Second Discourse: Chapter 47

A Preaching of Judgment upon Arrogant Babylon.

This chapter has two parts: verses 1-7: the delicate and voluptuous daughter of the Chaldeans will be cast down from her high place into the dust and utterly shamed; for the Lord will avenge the mistreatment that God's people suffered at her hands; verses 8-15: voluptuous and self-assured as she is, she will with all her art and wisdom not be able to avert the coming disaster.

As for the prosody of the passage, this song of triumph marches along in most of its lines in the stirring Qinah rhythm (five stresses divided either 3 — 2 or 2 — 3 by a pause). Intermingled are also lines of a different rhythm. Modern students of meter assume that this song was originally composed only of regular Qinah verses, arranged in stanzas of uniform length, like the stanzas of one of our church hymns. Wherever this rhythm seems to be broken, they assume that the text is corrupt, and consider it to be their business to restore the "original" meter. Duhm, among others, tried that. He divides the chapter into five strophes (1-4, 5-7, 8-10a, 10b-12, 13-15), each strophe containing seven Qinah lines. Whatever does not fit into this scheme is not genuine, according to him. That is considered scientific?

First Part: verses 1-7: *Voluptuous Babylon must come down into the dust from its proud eminence, because the Lord will exercise vengeance upon her for her merciless treatment of His people.*

The first part is divided into two strophes, each containing three verses: verses 1-3 and 5-7. Verse 4 is transitional.

First Strophe: verses 1-4: *The delicate and voluptuous daughter of the Chaldeans must be reduced to slavery and be carried away as a captive, and the Lord's vengeance will be visited upon her.*

1 *Down, O virgin-daughter Babylon — sit in the dust!*
 On the ground sit down, throneless — O Chaldean daughter!
 For no longer shall one call you — delicate and voluptuous.
2 *Take up the handmill and grind flour — put away your veil,*
 Lift up the train, uncover your legs — wade through streams,
3 *So that your nakedness is bared — and your shame seen;*
 I will take vengeance — will not spare a man.
4 *Yes, our Savior is — His name is Jehovah Sabaoth — the Holy One*
 of Israel.

¹ רְדִי‌וּשְׁבִי עַל־עָפָר בְּתוּלַת בַּת־בָּבֶל
שְׁבִי־לָאָרֶץ אֵין־כִּסֵּא בַּת־כַּשְׂדִּים
כִּי לֹא תוֹסִיפִי יִקְרְאוּ־לָךְ רַכָּה וַעֲנֻגָּה:

The construct state in *bethūlath bath-bābhel* and *bath kasdīm* is not the subjective genitive, but the appositive genitive, as in 23:12; 37:22; 40:9; cf. Gr. 128, k, p. 416; not the virgin of the daughter of Babylon, daughter of the Chaldeans; but the virgin daughter Babylon, the Chaldean daughter. The city itself, the Chaldeans themselves, are being addressed. The virgin daughter is the unravished, the unconquered one. Babylon is pictured as a woman and queen. The two monosyllabic imperatives, *redhī* and *shebhī* are vigorous in the extreme. We therefore do well to adopt Luther's *herunter*, down! Duhm's *come and sit down* is too weak. The picture of Babylon as queen of the world is continued in *ʿeyn kisseʾ* and in verses 5 and 7. *ʿal ʿaphār* is in sharpest contrast to this picture. From the throne of the queen of the world down into the dust, into the dirt. *lāʾarets* and *ʿal ʿaphār* are synonymous. The accentuation connects *ʿeyn kisseʾ* with *lāʾarets*, down to the ground where there is no throne. Luther connected it with *bath kasdīm*. Our translation joins it, mainly for the sake of the rhythm, as apposition to *bath bābhel*. The sense remains the same. For the subordination of *yiqreʾū* to *tosīphī* without a conjunction, cf. Gr. 120, c, p. 385. Cf. 52:1; Hosea 1:6.

rakkāh denotes the tender, delicate person, unused to toil, gently reared; *ʿanuggāh* is stronger: pampered by comforts, luxury, and indulgence. Deuteronomy 28:54 also refers to such slaves of luxury.

305

² קְחִי רֵחַיִם וְטַחֲנִי קָמַח גַּלִּי צַמָּתֵךְ
חֶשְׂפִּי־שֹׁבֶל גַּלִּי־שׁוֹק עִבְרִי נְהָרוֹת:

The *rēḥayim* is a handmill. It consisted of two stones, a nether stone and a lighter upper stone. The upper face of the nether stone was convex in form, and in the center of the depression a stout wooden peg was fixed. In the middle of the concave face of the upper stone there was a hole which fitted over the peg in the lower stone. Near the edge of the upper stone a peg or handle was fitted with which the stone could be turned about the axis that held the stone in place. The grain was fed by hand into the hole in the upper stone that fitted over the peg that served as axis. In the lower stone a channel had been provided running from the center to the edge by which the ground meal found its way into a flat vessel or a cloth that was spread to receive it. (Riehm, *Handbook of Biblical Antiquities, II.* p. 1041; H. van Lennep, *Bible Lands,* Harper's Edition, p. 86f.) In well-to-do families, the task of grinding grain was always assigned to slaves or to prisoners, Exodus 11:5; Judges 16:21; Lamentations 5:13. Small mills were turned by one maid, larger mills by two workers, Matthew 24:41.

Babylon, the queen, is degraded to slavery and condemned to slave labor. It is not necessary to assume an ellipsis in *gallī tsammāthekh* (possibly of the word *face*). The Piel *gillāh* signifies to put off, to put away. The veil and the custom of wearing a veil varies greatly among Oriental peoples. In this instance, the reference is no doubt to the veil that covered the face, the large finely woven veil of costly materials worn by women of high station, which distinguished them from ordinary women and particularly from the slaves who wore no veils at all. — For the form *ḥespī* for *ḥispī* (Qal imperative), see Gr. 46, d, note 2, p. 124. *shōbhel* is the long trailing gown that elegant women wore on state occasions. *shōq* is the lower leg, which custom required that women of good taste should keep entirely covered by the gown. Slaves left the *shōq* uncovered. *'ibhrī nehārōth,* wade through streams, very likely pictures the deportation of prisoners of war, when streams would have to be crossed and the legs bared to the knees. The picture is carried out in detail in the next verse.

³ תִּגָּל עֶרְוָתֵךְ גַּם תֵּרָאֶה חֶרְפָּתֵךְ
נָקָם אֶקָּח וְלֹא אֶפְגַּע אָדָם:

'erwāh is nakedness, primarily nakedness of the external sexual organs, especially of the female organs, cf. Leviticus 18; Ezekiel 16:37; 23:10, 29. Public exposure of the female sexual organ was a disgrace of the most shameful kind, Lamentations 1:8. *ḥer-pāthēkh,* your shame, disgrace, is spiritual: so that your shame may be seen, namely, that it may come to light how vile you are in secret, while appearing to be so dainty. This is, of course, all figurative language to represent the spiritual and moral abomination, the idolatry, the immorality, and especially, the brutality and unfeeling hardness of Babylon (verse 6). The next clause explains why this queen, enthroned so high before all the world, acting the part of the refined lady, but inwardly vile, should be the object of such deep degradation: the Lord is taking vengeance upon her. The next strophe (verses 5-7) says why. The distinction between the two strophes is that the first (verses 1-4) describes the disgrace of Babylon in detail, and in a very short sentence states the reason; the second (verses 5-7) follows the reverse order, a brief mention of Babylon's disgrace and then in detail the reason for it.

welō' 'ephga' 'ādhām is a *crux. pāgha'* means to strike, and then to come together with someone, to encounter either as friend or as foe. In the latter sense, the verb is usually followed by *be'* or *le.* In Isaiah 64:4(5) the form is *pāgha'tā 'eth sās,* you met him who rejoiced, etc. Accordingly, Delitzsch and others translate here: I will not meet kindly (i.e., will not spare) the man. Hahn: I will not encounter a man (because everyone has either been slain or led into captivity). Some read *'ephra'* for *'ephga',* (from *pāra',* to unclothe, to dismiss) and translate: I will not release, or dismiss and set free. Still others point the consonants with the vowels of the Niphal: *'ip-pāghēa',* I will not be entreated. Later critics introduce a more drastic change. They change *'ephga'* one way or another, substitute *'amar* for *'ādhām,* connect it with *gō'alēnū* of the next clause and read: says our Redeemer. Cheyne, Duhm, Klostermann and Kittel accept this reading on the basis of Codex A of the LXX. This last emendation is attractive because it makes good sense and also restores the normal Qinah lines. Those who adhere to the text as it stands must translate: I will not encounter in friendly fashion (i.e., spare) a man. Thus, Hitzig, Knobel, Delitzsch. Since this translation is supported by 64:4(5) and fits well into the context, there is no reason to seek farther for a suitable rendering. Regarding the meter, it is a mistake to make that a factor in seeking to correct the text. The only justification for accepting a correction lies in the reading of the LXX Codex.

4 גֹּאֲלֵנוּ יְהוָה צְבָאוֹת שְׁמוֹ קְדוֹשׁ יִשְׂרָאֵל:

Verse 4 is transitional. The Lord has been speaking. Here a Hallelujah of the congregation of believers is introduced. *gō'alēnū* is either the subject of the predicate *qedhōsh yisrā'el*, or may be taken as the predicate. *YHWH tsebhā'ōth shemō* is parenthetical. Delitzsch translates: "Our Redeemer, Jehovah of hosts, Holy One of Israel is His name." If this translation were correct, it would be the only construction of that kind in Isaiah. The LXX has: He who redeemed you is Lord Sabaoth, His name is Holy One of Israel. The congregation of the believers in Israel is pictured as hearing the Lord's pronouncement of judgment. They know that the Lord judges Babylon on their account ("I will take vengeance," namely, for the injustice done to them). And the congregation rejoices that the vengeance is complete, inexorable; for their Savior, the Lord of Hosts, is mighty enough, and as Israel's Holy One zealous enough to carry it out (cf. 40:25 and 41:14).•

Second Strophe: verses 5-7: *The Chaldee daughter must be brought low, because she has grievously mistreated the Lord's people, and in her arrogance thinks herself secure against any retribution.*

5 *Sit down in silence and go into darkness — O Chaldean daughter!*
   For no longer shall one call you — mistress of kingdoms.
6 *I was angry with My people, profaned My inheritance — and gave*
      them into your hand;
   But you extended no mercy to them,
   Old men you burdened with your unbearable yoke,
7 *And thought: I shall be mistress for ever!*
   So that you did not take this to heart,
   Did not consider what must come after.

5 שְׁבִי דוּמָם וּבֹאִי בַחֹשֶׁךְ בַּת־כַּשְׂדִּים
כִּי לֹא תוֹסִיפִי יִקְרְאוּ־לָךְ גְּבֶרֶת מַמְלָכוֹת:

The beginning of this strophe is like the beginning of the first. As the Chaldean daughter was there sternly ordered to come down and sit in the dust, so she here is commanded: Sit down in silence, go into darkness. *dūmām* is an adverb which perhaps has the same meaning as the accusative of the noun *dūmāh*, complete silence (cf. Gr. 100,3.g,p.295). As a parallel to *bhaḥoshekh*, into darkness, it is then the equivalent of *baddūmāh*, into silence. Some take both phrases in an abstract sense and explain them as picturing the contrast with the former life of luxury enjoyed by this ruler over the nations, now sitting in mute misery and deepest disgrace. But it is also quite possible that the two phrases indicate the isolation and the darkness of the underground prison of these prisoners of war, as in 42:7; 49:9. Thus this exalted empress would be receiving notice of her impending defeat and imprisonment. It is furthermore possible that the two expressions refer to Sheol. In Psalm 115:17 we read *yōredhēy dhūmāh,* those who go down into silence; cf. Psalm 94:17. And *ḥōshekh* could be the same as *'erets ḥōshekh,* the land of darkness, Job 10:21; Psalm 88:13(12). This conjecture is supported by Isaiah 14:9-11, 15, where the prophet consigns the fallen king of Babylon to Sheol. Babylon is called *gebhereth mamlākhōth,* mistress of the kingdoms. The neo-Babylonian rule under Nebuchadnezzar extended from the Arabian Sea to the Black Sea and from the east coast of the Caspian Sea to the western boundaries of Egypt. That rule was brilliant but brief. It began with Nabopolassar, in 625, rose to its greatest height under his son, Nebuchadnezzar, and came to an end in 536 under Nabonidus-Belshazzar. Chaldea became a province of Persia and fell into decay. Chaldean daughter, here and in verse 1, signifies the inhabitants of Babylon.

קָצַ֤פְתִּי עַל־עַמִּי֙ חִלַּ֣לְתִּי נַחֲלָתִ֔י 6

וָאֶתְּנֵ֖ם בְּיָדֵ֑ךְ לֹא־שַׂ֤מְתְּ לָהֶם֙ רַחֲמִ֔ים

עַל־זָקֵ֕ן הִכְבַּ֥דְתְּ עֻלֵּ֖ךְ מְאֹֽד׃

Incensed by His people's sins and by its unfaithfulness regarding the Old Testament covenant of grace (Isa. 1:2ff, and often), the Lord had delivered Israel into the power of Babylon. This was in accordance with a threat that Isaiah had previously uttered in a prophecy to Hezekiah, 39:6f. Israel is called the Lord's inheritance because He had chosen this people from among all peoples to be His own special and everlasting possession. Israel is so designated as early as Deuteronomy 32:9ff, also in 1 Kings 8:51, 53, and especially in the Psalms by David and Asaph. The wording of our verse is similar to that of Psalm 78:62. God profaned His inheritance, that is, He deprived it of its consecration and of the special holiness that it had as a people set apart to be the Lord's inheritance, and He withdrew from it His special protection and treated it as a gentile people. See also the discussion of 42:24f. This statement of the reason for the subjugation of Israel under Babylon forestalls any supposition that Babylon had by its own power conquered this people, cf. 10:5, 13ff. Concerning Babylon's brutal treatment of conquered nations, of which the next verse speaks, see 14:6.

zāqēn is not a designation of the people as of ancient origin or as having become infirm through age (Gesenius, Hitzig) but refers to old persons as a class. Babylon did not spare even the feeble and venerable old men, much less others. *me'ōdh* is an adverb modifying *hikhbadht*. The abuse of power of which Babylon is here accused, the cruel treatment of the poor and weak at the hand of the rich and powerful in private and in public life, oppression, exploitation, and especially the heartless treatment of subject peoples, have throughout history been characteristic sins of great powers. This inhumanity is in itself a sign of inner decay and also an indication of approaching downfall. The blood of Abel today calls as loudly as ever to God for vengeance. The Lord is the shield of the poor. "He executeth judgment for the oppressed." The Lord shall reign forever. Psalm 146.

$$\text{וַתֹּאמְרִי לְעוֹלָם אֶהְיֶה גְּבֶרֶת עַד}^{7}$$
$$\text{לֹא־שַׂמְתְּ אֵלֶּה עַל־לִבֵּךְ לֹא זָכַרְתְּ אַחֲרִיתָהּ׃}$$

Luther regularly translated *'āmar* with *denken,* to think or imagine, when the speaker was addressing himself. That is the sense of *'āmar* in this passage. Babylon, with all its brutality, in its heart felt perfectly secure in its station as mistress of all kingdoms and nations. It had no fear of the future. In *gebhereth 'adh* everything depends on the accent. The newer critics place the Athnach in *'adh* and insist that *gebhereth* is always the construct of *gebhīrāh,* and that *'adh* is therefore a genitive: mistress of eternity, a mistress for ever. *'ehyeh* must then naturally be connected with *le'ōlām:* I shall be forever, mistress forever. The only objection that can be offered against that is the position of the Athnach and also the reading of the LXX. If one accepts the Masoretic pointing, one must assume, with Delitzsch, that the form *gebhereth,* which otherwise is always a construct, in this case is an absolute. He explains it as the feminine of *gābher,* the equivalent of *gebher.* But, be that as it may, since the Masoretes joined *gebhereth* with *'ehyeh* and placed the pausal accent in *gebhāreth,* thus marking the end of the clause, it is clear that *gebhereth* as an absolute form presented no obstacle to them. *'adh* is then a conjunction introducing the next clause, short for *'adh 'asher* (Joshua 17:14), *adeo ut,* so that, a meaning that is supported by Job 8:21; 14:6, 1 Samuel 20:41 and 2:5. (In the last passage *'adh 'aqārāh* cannot possibly

mean eternally barren; that would have to be *'aqārāh 'adh.*) We
have therefore translated "so that you," that is, so certain are you
of your everlasting supremacy, that you have not taken this to
heart, etc. *'elleh,* this is, in view of the following *'aharīthāh,* not the
threatened punishment, but Babylon's own fierce cruelty. Reference of the feminine suffix in *'aharīthāh* to *'ammī* and *naḥalāthī* is
too forced. The simplest explanation is to interpret it as a neuter
referring to the cruelty and arrogance of Babylon that were just
described: and you did not consider the end and outcome of *it.* Cf.
41:22.

Second Part: verses 8-15: *Voluptuous and secure, Babylon will
not, with all its magic and all its learning, be able to avert the
coming ruin.*

This section, like the first, is divided into two distinct parts:
verses 8-11 and 12-15. The first part emphasizes the ruin that will
suddenly and completely overcome Babylon in spite of her arrogant security and her spells and enchantments. The second part
emphasizes the inexorability of the city's doom. The two strophes
each contain two smaller strophes of two verses each.

First Strophe: verses 8-11: *The disaster will come in spite of
Babylon's arrogant security, her knowledge, and her enchantments.*

8 *But now, hear this, you voluptuous one, who sit so securely,*
  Who says in her heart: I am the one, and there is no other;
  I shall not sit as a widow, nor know the loss of children.
9 *Suddenly there will come upon you both of these,*
  In one day, loss of children and widowhood;
  *In full measure they will come upon you in spite of your many
    sorceries,*
  In spite of all the power of your enchantments.
10 *Since you have trusted in your wickedness and think: No one sees
    me;*
  Your wisdom and your knowledge, they led you astray,
  That you say in your heart: I am the one and there is no other.
11 *Therefore a disaster shall come upon you*
  Which you will not know how to ban,
  And a ruin will plunge down upon you
  That you will not be able to atone for.
  *And a sudden desolation shall come upon you of which you knew
    nothing.*

וְעַתָּ֞ה שִׁמְעִי־זֹ֤את עֲדִינָה֙ הַיּוֹשֶׁ֣בֶת לָבֶ֔טַח 8
הָאֹֽמְרָה֙ בִּלְבָבָ֔הּ אֲנִ֖י וְאַפְסִ֣י ע֑וֹד
לֹ֤א אֵשֵׁב֙ אַלְמָנָ֔ה וְלֹ֥א אֵדַ֖ע שְׁכֽוֹל׃

Depending on whether one refers *we'attāh* to the preceding verse or to the entire first half of the discourse it will be translated either "but now" or "and now," adversative or consecutive. We prefer the former. *zō'th* clearly refers to what follows. *'adhīnāh* (from *'edhen*, pleasure, Eden) is a voluptuous person. Because of the opening words of address, *hayyōshebheth* is best regarded as a second person. *lābheṭah*, a familiar form in the Psalms (4:9(8); 16:9, etc.), is, as so often, an adverb indicating a feeling of security. The next clause presents this security in concrete form, with a shift from the second to the third person as a sign of contempt — who says in her heart: I am the one, and there is no other. Delitzsch, usually so precise, uses too many words in translating *'aphsī 'odh*. *'ephes* (end) is nothingness, nothing, a stronger term than *'ayin*, 41:12; 34:12; and so *'ephes 'odh* is stronger than *'eyn 'odh*, 2 Samuel 9:3. The form *'aphsī*, occurring here, verse 10, and Zephaniah 2:15, is the same construction of *'ephes* as *minnī* is of *min* (46:3), *zūlāthī* of *zūlath* (Josh. 11:13), *'abhī* of *'abh*, *'aḥī* of *'aḥ*, etc., namely, an old construct form used either for emphasis or for poetic adornment. Giving it the old name *Chireq compaginis* does no harm to the *i*. Cf. Gr. 90, 1, a, and 3, 1, m, n, p. 248 ff. Certainly, the *i* must not be understood as the first person suffix.

Putting the same words into the mouth of this arrogant queen that the Lord uses of Himself in 45:5,6,14,18,21; 46:9 makes her guilty of the extreme of self-deification. The concrete force of *'almānāh*, widow, and *'almōn*, widowhood, is emphasized as it is contrasted with her boasting: I am the one, etc. The reference is to *gebhereth* in verse 7 and to the more specific "mistress of kingdoms" in verse 5. It is out of this exalted station that the Lord will cast her down (verse 1ff.), so that she shall no longer have a throne. Loss of her rule over the kingdoms — that is her widowhood. The kingdoms are pictured as her many husbands. Compare a similar picture in Revelation 18:7. Elsewhere the widowhood of a city means the loss of her manpower, Lamentations 1:1. Childlessness here means loss of the inhabitants of the city. In 51:20; 54:1,4,5 widowhood, maidenhood, childlessness refer to Israel's separation from the Lord as her spiritual bridegroom. A similar relation between a people and its idols was unknown to the pagan mind; much less is it possible that the Lord Himself would use this relation to picture the attachment of a gentile to his idol.

⁹ וְתָבֹאנָה לָּךְ שְׁתֵּי־אֵלֶּה רֶגַע בְּיוֹם אֶחָד
שְׁכוֹל וְאַלְמֹן כְּתֻמָּם בָּאוּ עָלָיִךְ
בְּרֹב כְּשָׁפַיִךְ בְּעָצְמַת חֲבָרַיִךְ מְאֹד׃

For the conjunctive Dagesh forte in *lākh,* see Gr. 20, f, p. 72. Luther translates *shetēy 'elleh,* both of these, with *alle beide.* The reference is to bereavement of children and widowhood, against both of which Babylon felt perfectly secure. *kethummām,* according to their completeness, that is, in full measure. *bā'u* is a prophetic perfect. *berōbh* means in, in the face of, in spite of the multitude, 5:25; 9:11(12). With *keshāphayikh* and *ḥabhārayikh* the attention turns to the Babylonian sorcery and magic. These are always the sister pursuits of the more refined mantic or divination and are common to all pagan peoples and religions, from ancient Egypt to modern astrologers, from the largest city to the remotest village. This practice of magic has its source in fear of the unknown future and in ignorance concerning God and the supernatural. It is an attempt to control the supernatural powers either for personal good fortune or for destruction of an enemy. It appears in a thousand different forms. The original homes of divination and sorcery are Egypt (Gen. 41:8; 44:5, 15; Exod. 7:9; Isa. 19:3) and Babylon (Isa. 44:25; Dan. 2:2, etc.). Excavations in Assyria and Babylon have brought to light a vast number of magic formulas.

As in Egypt, this occult art was closely linked with scientific pursuits (verse 10), and it was fostered by the government through the priestly caste. Its practitioners were known as Chaldeans. Daniel 1:20; 2:2, 27; 4:7; 5:15. The entire caste was under the direction of a chief of the magi. Luther calls him *Hofmeister,* the King James Version has "chief of the governors over all the wise men" (Jer. 39:13; Dan. 2:48). A specific form of magic art was astrology, which was allied with astronomy, verse 13. It sought to predict the fortunes of the state from the relative positions of the planets. The *ḥebher (ḥabhārayikh)* is an exorcism, by which evil may be averted, conjured away, or made harmless, Deuteronomy 18:11; Psalm 58:6(5). Why Delitzsch takes *'otsmāh* to mean number rather than power, as in 40:29, is not apparent. *me'odh* is an adverb; it modifies *bā'u,* not *'otsmāh.* It is parallel to *kethummām.*

In the entire section two verses are always paired, usually as statement and refutation. Verse 8 voices Babylon's security; verse 9 demolishes it. There is a similar relation between verses 10 and 11. Verse 13 denies the help from sorcery that is assumed in verse 12. Verses 14 and 15, however, form a pair without this contrast. The translation of the conjunction or, as the case may be, of the asyndeton is determined by this coupling of verses. Thus, the *we* in *wethabho'nah* is translated but. Babylon's security consists in her belief that she will never be stripped of her supremacy over the kingdoms nor bereft of her own inhabitants. But the Lord says to her: Both will befall you, bereavement of your children and loss of your dominion. Moreover, both, in full measure and *me'odh,* overwhelmingly. Babylon's security is *founded on* the multitude and the strength of her sorceries. The Lord says that in spite of them both, calamities shall come upon her.

וַתִּבְטְחִי בְרָעָתֵךְ   אָמַרְתְּ אֵין רֹאָנִי   10

חָכְמָתֵךְ וְדַעְתֵּךְ   הִיא שׁוֹבְבָתֶךְ

וַתֹּאמְרִי בְלִבֵּךְ   אֲנִי וְאַפְסִי עוֹד:

tibhtehi repeats the thought expressed by *labhetah* in verse 8 and therefore means "to be secure," not "to trust." *ra'ah* is not woe or disaster, as in the next verse; here it is wickedness, evil, as in Genesis 6:5; Hosea 10:15; Ecclesiastes 8:6; and *be* means in, with, in spite of, as in *berobh* in the preceding verse. Therefore: with all, in spite of all, your wickedness, you feel secure. Her wickedness is described in verse 6 as cruelty and tyranny. The *wa* at the beginning is consecutive and introduces a contrast, which again is canceled out by the *u* in verse 11. This peculiar use of *Waw* is not noted in the grammar. It is to be rendered as "yes — but," or "though — still," "since — therefore," or some such combination. For the association of the imperfect *tibhtehi* with the perfect *'amart,* see Gr. 106, g, h, i, and Note, p. 311. The thought is: you feel secure, because you said to yourself, etc. Her thought was a completed fact, on the basis of which she continued to live in security. *ro'ani* is a pause form for *ro'eni,* there is none observing me, a verbal use of the participle, Gr. 116, 3, p. 357. Babylon believes herself to be wholly unobserved, and thus denies the omniscience of God, although with uneasy conscience. Her wisdom, that is, her sorceries, and her knowledge or understanding, meaning her mathematical science, betrayed her into this hardened security in spite of conscience. The pronoun *hi',* referring to *da 'tēkh* and also to *ḥokhmāthēkh,* is inserted for emphasis. *shōbhēbh,* a Polel of *shūbh,* means to turn around, turn aside, to twist. We use the verb *turn* in a similar sense in "to turn one's head." The *wa* with *tō'merī* is consecutive. Babylon's pride in her wisdom and knowledge led her to the insane presumption: "I am the one, and there is no other." Cf. verse 8 and *'ephes kāmonī,* 46:9. She thought of herself as the supreme ruler over the earth, as the only one of her kind in wisdom and knowledge — self-deification.

וּבָ֣א עָלַ֤יִךְ רָעָה֙ לֹ֣א תֵדְעִי֙ שַׁחְרָ֔הּ 11

וְתִפֹּ֤ל עָלַ֙יִךְ֙ הֹוָ֔ה לֹ֥א תוּכְלִ֖י כַּפְּרָ֑הּ

וְתָבֹ֧א עָלַ֛יִךְ פִּתְאֹ֖ם שׁוֹאָ֥ה לֹ֥א תֵדָֽעִי׃

If the initial *Waw* in verse 10 was translated "since," then this *Waw* in *ūbhā'* must be rendered "therefore," because the two correspond to each other. *bā',* a masculine form with a feminine subject *rā'āh,* is possible when the verb precedes the subject, Gr. 145, o, p. 465. Here *rā'āh* has its original meaning of woe or disaster, but there is a play on words with *rā'athēkh* in verse 10. Supply *'asher* before *lō'. shaherāh* is an infinitive Piel, to darken, to cast a spell, to ban (from *shāhar,* to be dark) according to the Arabic. Some critics read *shahadhāh,* from *shāhadh,* to give, to bribe, to purchase a release from punishment. The former meaning is, however, supported by its parallel form *kapperāh.* The older explanation that *shaherāh* was the same as *shāhar,* the dawn, with a feminine suffix, is out of the question. The dawn of disaster, meaning the cessation of disaster, is impossible. The dawn of disaster would have to be its beginning. *hōwāh* (*hāwāh,* to fall, to tremble, Job 37:6) occurs only here and in Ezekiel 7:26, and is the same as *hawwāh,* misfortune, ruin. You shall not be able (*kapperāh*) to expiate it, that is, to avert it by paying a ransom. *pith'ōm* is the same as *bephetha',* in a wink of an eye, suddenly, unexpectedly. *shō'āh* is imitative: a rushing sound, tempest, then devastation, ruin.

As verse 10 corresponds to verse 8, so verse 11 corresponds to verse 9. As verses 10 and 8 threaten widowhood and bereavement of children, so here *rā'āh, hōwāh,* and *shō'āh* are the means by which widowhood and bereavement will be brought about, namely, by the fall of the city, which shall come like a devastating, irresistible tempest. Babylon's might and wisdom will be as nothing against it.

Second Strophe: verses 12-15: *With the fall of Babylon all her witchcraft and astrological wisdom will be put to shame.*

12 *Step forward now with your incantations and your many sorceries,*
 With which from your youth you have wearied yourself!
 Perhaps you can have success, perhaps even strike terror! —
13 *How wearied are you with all your contriving!*
 So, let those step forward and help you, who measure off the
   heavens,
 Who read in the stars, predict every new moon
 What is to befall you.
14 *Behold, they are like stubble that the fire consumes!*
 They cannot save their life from the hand of the flame;
 This is no glowing coal at which to warm oneself,
 Not a fire, by which one may sit.
15 *So are they about whom you wearied yourself,*
 With whom from your youth you have been dealing;
 Each stumbles about in his way, there is none who helps you.

עִמְדִי־נָא בַחֲבָרַ֫יִךְ֙ וּבְרֹב כְּשָׁפַ֫יִךְ 12
בַּאֲשֶׁר יָגַ֫עַתְּ מִנְּעוּרָ֑יִךְ
אוּלַי תּוּכְלִי הוֹעִיל אוּלַי תַּעֲרֽוֹצִי:

In the foregoing strophe the downfall of Babylon was pictured as about to occur. Therefore the Lord exhorts her to step forward (the original meaning of *ʿāmadh*) *now* and exercise the arts which since her youth she had acquired with such unceasing labor. The two *ʾulay* clauses are bitter mockery. *Maybe* they will be of some help. *hōʿīl* (Hiphil of *yāʿal*) means to help or serve, also intransitively (48:17) to be of some use. The next clause intensifies the mockery: Maybe you can even strike terror with them. *ʿārats*, in the transitive sense, means to cause trembling, fear, and terror. The imperfect has the same potential force as *tūkhelī hōʿīl*. Gr. 107, r, p. 318.

נִלְאֵית בְּרֹב עֲצָתָ֑יִךְ יַעַמְדוּ־נָא 13
וְיוֹשִׁיעֻךְ הֹבְרֵי שָׁמַ֫יִם֙ הַחֹזִים֙ בַּכּֽוֹכָבִ֔ים
מֽוֹדִיעִם֙ לֶחֳדָשִׁ֔ים מֵאֲשֶׁר יָבֹ֖אוּ עָלָֽיִךְ:

nilʾēyth stands in an adversative sense to *ʿimdhī-nāʾ* (verse 12), although there is no connecting conjunction. Some mocking expletive should be supplied that fits the context. In the face of impending trouble Babylon seeks counsel on every side and finds none.

She sits there exhausted and in despair. That is the sense of the first clause. Since the sorcerers and conjurors have failed her, the Lord urges her, in continued mockery, to summon her astrologers to come to her assistance with a favorable horoscope, as had otherwise always been their monthly custom. Perhaps the fortunetellers can save her!

Some translate *nil'eyth be* as: You are weary in spite of all the counseling that is at your command. But that can hardly be what is meant. Weariness would thus be pictured as resulting from impending ruin. Anticipated ruin would cause fear and terror, but hardly weariness, unless one takes *nil'ah* to mean lamed or paralyzed by terror. But the Niphal does not have that meaning. *'etsah* does not only have the meaning of objective counseling, but also occurs in the subjective sense of seeking counsel, planning, contriving, as in Isaiah 5:19; 8:10; 14:26; 19:17; 28:29; 29:15. That is the sense in this verse. *be* therefore means with, by, through. *robh*, multitude, also points to that sense. *'atsathayikh* is a singular form with plural suffix, since the word is understood as a collective. The grammar, 91, 1. p. 258 mentions similar occurrences in Ezekiel 35:11; Psalm 9:15(14); Ezra 9:15. *hobherey* (the Qere is correct because *habheru*, the perfect, does not fit at all) is a participle of *habhar*, to separate into parts. It occurs only here, and therefore offers opportunity for much needless conjecture. The reference is to persons who divide the heavens into sections (the zodiac) and who predict good or evil fortune based on the path of the sun and the planets through the signs of the zodiac and on the relative position of the planets to each other. *hozim bakkokhabhim* (participle plural) designates the same persons as professionally occupied in reading the stars, while *modhi'im* (Hiph. participle) *lehodhashim* (*l* plus article) names them as purveyors of knowledge about new moons, who each month make up a calendar of weather, fortune, misfortune, good days and bad days. The *me* before *'asher* is partitive: about that which is to come. Some combine the last clause with *yoshi'ukh* and take *me* in its meaning "away from" — seek help away from that which is coming over you. No objection can be raised to that except the position of the words, and that objection is not compelling.

14 הִנֵּה הָיוּ כְקַשׁ אֵשׁ שְׂרָפָתַם
לֹא־יַצִּילוּ אֶת־נַפְשָׁם מִיַּד לֶהָבָה
אֵין־גַּחֶלֶת לַחְמָם אוּר לָשֶׁבֶת נֶגְדּוֹ׃

317

With an opening statement in verse 14 affirming Babylon's helplessness, the discourse nears its conclusion. The affirmative *hinnēh* compares Babylon's sorcerers and diviners to stubble being consumed by fire. Whether one takes *'esh serāphātham* to be a relative clause modifying *qash,* which then must be interpreted as a collective because of the plural suffix in *serāphātham,* or simply translates "the fire consumes them, the magicians," the sense remains the same. Fire and flame are figures representing the ruin threatening Babylon, from which the magicians cannot save either themselves or their city. Before *'eyn* we insert "for," because this clause explains the one preceding it. *lahmām* is a Qal infinitive of *ḥāmam* (*laḥmām* for *lāḥōm*). Gr. 28, b, p. 93 and 67, cc, p. 182. There are many other explanations of the form, none of them satisfactory. The sense is: The fire which consumes Babylon is no fire at which one warms himself, but an all-consuming conflagration. It is not a light, or a little, fire by which one may sit in comfort. These words refer back to verse 11. "Fire" is a figure of speech for the general destruction.

$$\text{15} \quad \text{כֵּן הָיוּ־לָךְ אֲשֶׁר יָגָעַתְּ סֹחֲרַיִךְ מִנְּעוּרַיִךְ}$$
$$\text{אִישׁ לְעֶבְרוֹ תָּעוּ אֵין מוֹשִׁיעֵךְ:}$$

kēn hāyū, being a doublet of *hinnēh hāyū* in verse 14, gives verse 15 a form similar to that of the previous verse. In contents, verse 15 confirms and amplifies verse 14. As verse 14 described the fate of the magicians, just so will these wise men be to you, that is, serve to your ruin. *lākh* is *dativus incommodi.* Thus, that is, as just stated, those for whom you have gone to such trouble are or become for you the source of your destruction. Verse 14 describes them as to their own fate. Thus they will reward you (Babylon) for all your labor in their behalf. That the reference here is to the magicians and sorcerers is supported by verse 12 where Babylon is described as wearying herself over these wise men. In fact, the whole section, beginning at verse 9, treats of them. It is hardly possible that at this point, just as the gates are about to be closed, *sōharayikh* introduces an entirely new class, namely, the foreign merchants with whom Babylon carried on such an active trade. Isaiah (or Isaiah II) ought not to be charged with such an unrhetorical slip. The occurrence of the phrases *'asher yāghā'at* and of *minne 'ūrayikh,* both in this verse and in verse 12, makes it appear very likely that the *sōharīm* in verse 15 are the same people who in verse 12 dealt in incantations and sorceries. It is not necessary to picture them as peddlers who went from place to place like gypsies hawking their spells for money. Fortunetelling, like every other fraud, is always out for the money. The more it is able to surround itself with a nimbus of science and knowledge, the higher its cost. If it happens to be a monopoly, as in Babylon it was a monopoly of the Chaldees, who belonged to the priestly caste and boasted of possessing occult knowledge unattainable by anyone else, then monopolistic prices are charged. Babylon's fashionable astrologers and magicians cost the state and the well-to-do, prominent citizens dearly. It is also certain that they knew themselves to be swindlers, as was true of the augurs and soothsayers of Rome. That is why they are called *sōḥarīm*, merchants, or traffickers, who since your youth have been cheating and swindling you out of your money. And now, that disaster is about to overcome them, they stagger (*tā'ū*) about, each in his way, not to his home, as those commentators say who understand the *sōḥarīm* to be legitimate merchants. Now in the besieged city, or in the confusion of its fall, none thinks first of his home, but thinks only of saving his life. They stumble about not knowing whether they will find their way out of the doomed city or not. Let him who can, save himself! But while all are rushing pellmell seeking safety, the final word to Babylon is: There is none who can help you!

The last two words of the verse are the quintessence of the entire strophe. — This chapter, in its logic, its structure, and its poetic quality, is a perfect work of art, such as is to be found nowhere else even in Isaiah. And still, the critics, especially the fumbling metricists, cannot keep their bowdlerizing hands off it.

Third Discourse: Chapter 48

A final appeal to the house of Jacob in view of the impending deliverance: a testimony against those whose hearts are hardened and a fervent invitation to those who might still be converted.

This concluding chapter of Part I is divided into two parts of equal length. Verses 1-11 are a testimony against those of the house of Jacob who cannot be converted. This portion of the people is still hypocritical. In the hardness of its heart it did not recognize the earlier manifestations of the glory of the Lord; nor does it now, in its hardness, take to heart God's revelation of the deliverance out of Babylon. If God does not exterminate them now, but lets them suffer in the smelting furnace of affliction, it is only to prevent His name from being blasphemed. The second half, verses 12-22, is a fervent invitation extended to the Israel whom the Lord has called, to believe the Lord's word concerning the coming deliverance out of Babylon and to take part in the rescue of the people and the return to their homeland.

First Part: verses 1-11: *The testimony against the obdurate ones of the house of Jacob.*

This part is divided at the middle of verse 6. The first half deals with the hardening of Jacob against the earlier revelations, the second with the hardening of its heart against the new promises. Each half consists of two short strophes: 1 and 2; 3-6a; 6b-8; 9-11.

First Half: verses 1-6a: *The hardening against the old promises and fulfillments.*

1   *Hear this, O house of Jacob, who call themselves by the*
        name of Israel,
     Who went forth from the waters of Judah,
     Who swear by the name of the Lord and confess the God of
        Israel,
     Not in truth, and not in sincerity.
2   *Yes, they call themselves after the holy city*
     And lean on the God of Israel,
     Whose name is Lord of Sabaoth.
3   *The former things — of old I made them known,*
     It went forth from My mouth, and I let you hear it;
     Suddenly I carried it out, that it came to pass.
4   *Since I well knew that you are obdurate,*
     Your neck a band of iron
     And your brow of brass.
5   *I foretold it to you of old,*
     Before it came to pass I announced it to you,
     Lest you should say: My idol has done it,
     And my carved image and my molten image has brought it about.
6a *You have heard it; look at it all:*
     Must you yourselves not declare it?

שִׁמְעוּ־זֹאת בֵּית־יַעֲקֹב   1
הַנִּקְרָאִים֙ בְּשֵׁם יִשְׂרָאֵ֔ל   וּמִמֵּ֥י   יְהוּדָ֖ה יָצָ֑אוּ
הַנִּשְׁבָּעִ֣ים ׀ בְּשֵׁ֣ם יְהֹוָ֗ה   וּבֵאלֹהֵ֤י יִשְׂרָאֵל֙ יַזְכִּ֔ירוּ
לֹ֥א בֶאֱמֶ֖ת וְלֹ֥א בִצְדָקָֽה׃

"House of Jacob," descendants of Jacob, is an intentionally cold form of address, without any warmth of feeling. It is a lost people. It is they themselves, not the Lord, who still call themselves by the spiritual covenant name of Israel. The dispassionate "Hear this" is void of all warmth. In contrast, compare the opening words of the second half, verse 12: Listen to Me, O Jacob, etc. This perhaps is the reason for the sudden change to the third person. The "and" followed by a finite verb makes the next words the equivalent of a relative clause. *mēy yehūdhāh* is frequently explained by making reference to an assumed derivation of the name Moab, as though Moab meant *mēy ʾabh*, that is, the water, or seed, or semen of the father. But Moab is rather to be derived from *min ʾabh*, or *mē ʾabh*, "from the father." *mēy yehūdhāh*, waters of Judah, does not refer to the physical substance of procreation, but, as in Numbers 24:7

321

and Deuteronomy 33:28, it is the equivalent of the spring or source of Judah and is a figurative expression for the seed. The term "house of Israel" is hardly used here to distinguish it from the ten tribes (Cheyne), a suggestion for which there is no basis. The phrase is a parallel to "house of Jacob," and both terms are used to designate the physical origin of the people. To be a descendant of Judah was as honorable as it was to have Jacob or Abraham as father (cf. Gen. 49:8ff), but since they no longer had the faith of their fathers, this very parentage served as a judgment upon them, in the same manner as the other religious externals that were devoid of all sincerity. They swear by the name of Jehovah (cf. Deut. 6:13; 10:20), the gracious God of the covenant. When life and the soul's welfare are concerned and one ought to be most serious, they make use of this name; yes, they *yazkīru bē'lohēy yisrā'ēl*, that is, literally, "they cause Him to be remembered as holy"; on every occasion that seems to them to be important they call on Him, on the God of Israel who bound Himself in grace to Israel as a *spiritual* people; but they do not call on Him in truth and sincerity, that is, not in upright faithfulness to the covenant, but out of a lying, unfaithful, false heart, cf. 29:13,21. That is the sin that causes the ruin the prophet speaks of in 1:11ff. For *'emeth* and *tsedhāqāh,* compare 38:3; Zechariah 8:8, and 1 Kings 3:6. Both words here designate a moral condition, which, however, is based in the grace of the covenant.

2 כִּי־מֵעִיר הַקֹּדֶשׁ נִקְרָאוּ

וְעַל־אֱלֹהֵי יִשְׂרָאֵל נִסְמָכוּ יְהוָה צְבָאוֹת שְׁמוֹ:

The designation of Jerusalem as the Holy City seems to have had its origin among the Jews living in foreign lands. We find that name in Nehemiah 11:1,18; Daniel 9:24; Isaiah 52:1, and here. Nowhere but in Jerusalem was the holy place, the temple, where the Lord abode in grace, Psalm 132:13,14. Cf. Isaiah 64:9(10). *kī* in this instance is not explanatory; it continues or adds to the foregoing, like the Latin *immo,* or our English "what is more." Following a negative it has the force of "but," as in 28:27. This people has progressed so far in its blindness that they believe without faith and place a carnal reliance in matters that are purely spiritual. Cf. Matthew 3:9; John 8:39ff. Luther translates *nismākhū* with *sie trotzen auf,* they boldly rely on. This clause is in sharpest contrast to the final one, which is to be joined to it as a relative clause: They lean on the God of Israel, who, after all, is the Lord of Hosts. It was as if the hosts of the God of the spiritual people, as a matter of course, were at the service also of a carnally minded and wicked people, whereas the Lord of Hosts is at the same time also the Holy, Holy, Holy One and a consuming fire for everything unholy, 6:5 and 6:3.

הָרִאשֹׁנוֹת מֵאָז הִגַּדְתִּי וּמִפִּי יָצְאוּ וְאַשְׁמִיעֵם ³

פִּתְאֹם עָשִׂיתִי וַתָּבֹאנָה:

The first strophe, verses 1 and 2, was addressed to those who were characterized as a hypocritical and hardened people. This section, verses 3-6a, contains the opening words of the theme of the whole chapter. Under certain circumstances *hārī'shōnōth* may refer to the next things that are about to occur, as in 41:22; the word never refers to things that have been announced beforehand, as Delitzsch and others maintain (cf. our remarks at 41:22; 42:9; 43:9,18; 46:9). Here as always, *hārī'shōnōth* are *prius facta*, things that were *done* earlier. But the reference here cannot be to the beginnings of the victorious career of Cyrus, as later commentators suppose. That explanation is at once precluded by the phrase that follows immediately, *mē'āz higgadhtī,* I made them known *of old.* Where in all of Scripture is there a prophecy of the beginning of Cyrus's career of conquest, except in Isaiah II? The Scriptures, especially Isaiah I and Jeremiah, proclaim the fall of Babylon and the deliverance of Israel; but where is there any account of Cyrus's earlier career as a separate historical event of significance for Babylon's fall and Israel's deliverance? And how can the Cyrus-prophecy in Isaiah II be mechanically cut into two distinct parts, so that a campaign in the West (Lydia, etc.) would be *hārī'shōnōth,* and the departure toward Babylon, *hadhāshōth* (verse 6b)? Isaiah II, 40-48, has but a single unchanging theme from 40:1 and 2 to the end of chapter 48: Israel's deliverance out of Babylon by Cyrus; that, taken as a whole, is the *hadhāshāh,* *hadhāshōth* as distinguished from the wonderful works of deliverance in days of long ago, as the passages referred to above will show. The unfounded assumption that the author of Isaiah II was actually himself in exile has led to the stupid and un-Scriptural division of Cyrus's triumphal career into *hārī'shōnōth* and *hahadhāshōth.*

The *rī'shōnōth* that the Lord proclaimed of old, that went forth from His mouth, that He caused to be heard before they occurred, and that He then suddenly carried out, so that they came into being, are events like those named in 43:16-18, the works of deliv-

323

erance in olden times. The *ḥadhāshōth* of verse 6 refer to the deliverance of Israel from Babylon by Cyrus. Concerning the masculine suffix *ēm* for the feminine *ēn*, see Gr. 58, a, p. 155.

$$^4 \text{ מִדַּעְתִּי כִּי קָשֶׁה אָתָּה}$$

$$\text{וְגִיד בַּרְזֶל' עָרְפֶּךָ וּמִצְחֲךָ נְחוּשָׁה:}$$

midda'tī is *min* with the infinitive plus the suffix, from my knowing, that is, because I knew. *yādha'tī* in verse 8 is its companion piece. The three designations of the unspiritual character of this Jacob-Judah-Seed, *qāsheh* (hard, firm), *ghīdh barzel 'orpekhā*, and *mitshakhā neḥushāh*, describe not three, but a single attribute. The last two are amplifications of the first and explain it. In Exodus 32, 33, and 34 (cf. Deut. 9:6,13), the Lord (Moses also) calls Israel *qeshēh 'ōreph*, stiff-necked, whereas in Ezekiel 3:7 He designates the house of Israel *ḥizqēy-mētsaḥ ūqeshēy-lēbh*, of a hard forehead and a stubborn heart. Israel is untractable, goes its own unswerving way, and pays no attention to the Lord's words. In that respect it is a picture of every natural human heart (cf. Form. Conc. II, 21 — *etiam sciens volensque*). *neḥushāh* is a poetic form of *neḥōsheth*, 45:2.

$$^5 \text{ וָאַגִּיד לְךָ' מֵאָז בְּטֶרֶם תָּבוֹא הִשְׁמַעְתִּיךָ}$$

$$\text{פֶּן־תֹּאמַר' עָצְבִּי עָשָׂם וּפִסְלִי וְנִסְכִּי צִוָּם:}$$

The *wa* at the beginning continues the *midda'tī* of verse 4: because I knew — therefore. The words are an amplification of verse 3. The object of the verbs is *rī'shōnōth*. This verse states more precisely than verse 3 that the Lord announced this matter *beṭerem tābhō'*, before it came to pass; and the next clause states why these things were announced before they occurred. These people who were constantly falling into idol worship should not attribute these events to the influence of carved and molten images that they had made themselves out of wood and brass. *tō'mar* is potential. *tsiwwāh*, as in 45:12, means to call into existence, to provide. Indeed, the rational mind has no excuse for unbelief when prophecy and fulfillment are placed side by side. He who proclaims an event beforehand and then brings that event to pass, thereby reveals Himself as true God. That was the basis of the argument in Part I with the gentiles and their idols. But in spite of all these manifestations of the glory of the Lord, Israel did not recognize its God, but attributed His wonderful works to the idols, and thus became αὐτοκατάκριτος self-condemned.

שְׁמַעְתָּ חֲזֵה כֻּלָּהּ וְאַתֶּם הֲלוֹא תַגִּידוּ ⁶

kullāh (all of it) is the grammatical object of *shāma'tā* and *ḥazēh* and points to the *ri'shōnōth* as concrete accomplished facts. The first half of 6a is a condensed conditional clause; the second half expresses the consequence: If you consider (*ḥazēh*) all of this in its completed form, which you heard (*shāma'tā*) from My mouth before it came to pass, then (*we*) you yourselves (*'attem*) must confess what has always been the inevitable conclusion when prophecy and fulfillment are placed side by side: That I am God and there is no other. *thaggīdhū* is potential: Must you not of necessity confess — if you would do honor to the truth. "Confess" is a natural rendering of *higgīdh* if one thinks of that word as meaning to declare, admit, or grant. Cf. Psalm 38:19(18): "I will declare mine iniquity," that is, confess it openly. *higgīdh* does not always have the secondary meaning of proclaiming or preaching.

Second Half: verses 6b-11: *The hardening against the newer promises.*

6b *Now have I proclaimed new things to you,*
   And hidden things of which you did not know;
 7 *Only now are they being created, and not long ago,*
   And not till today, and you have not heard of them,
   Lest you should say: Lo, I knew of it.
 8 *But you do not hear, nor do you understand,*
   Nor has your ear ever been opened,
   Well do I know that you are incurably faithless,
   Known as a rebel from birth.
 9 *But for My name's sake I check My wrath,*
   For the sake of My honor, for your good, I restrain Myself,
   So as not to cut you off.
10 *Behold, I refine you, though not like silver,*
   In the furnace of affliction I try you;
11 *For My sake, for My sake I do it;*
   For how would it (My name) be blasphemed!
   And My honor do I yield to no other.

הִשְׁמַעְתִּיךָ חֲדָשׁוֹת מֵעַתָּה וּנְצֻרוֹת וְלֹא יְדַעְתָּם:

The *hadhāshōth* in this verse are in contrast to the *ri'shōnōth* of verse 3. Whether *mē'attāh* is to be translated "from now on" or "now" must in each case be determined from the context (cf. *miyyōm* 43:13, today, or from this day onward; *miqqedhem, miyyām,* to the east, to the west). That the present time is meant here is made certain by the *'attāh* in verse 7, with the following *mē'āz.* The contrasts here are: the old, the new; the days of old, now. It follows that *hishma'tīkhā* is a present perfect to be translated "Now have I proclaimed new things to you," a completed action extending into the present time; or "Now I proclaim to you a new thing," an action just brought to completion and now present as a finished thing (Gr. 106,g,p.311). It cannot be taken to be a prophetic perfect; the *'attāh nibhre'ū* forbids that, verse 7. *netsurōth,* of *nātsar,* to keep, guard, hide, is a passive participle. What the Lord is now proclaiming (or has proclaimed), namely, all that pertains to Cyrus, is that He has, up to this time, until the prophecy was brought to light by Isaiah, kept this well hidden, so that no one, not even this people, knew anything about it.

7 עַתָּ֤ה נִבְרְאוּ֙ וְלֹ֣א מֵאָ֔ז וְלִפְנֵי־יֹ֖ום וְלֹ֣א שְׁמַעְתָּ֑ם

פֶּן־תֹּאמַ֖ר הִנֵּ֥ה יְדַעְתִּֽין׃

bārā' has its usual meaning of creating, calling into existence — in contrast to mere prediction, "fulfilling," naturally by God Himself, cf. verse 16. The effect of *welō' mē'āz* is to make *'attāh* exclusive: not until now. *liphnēy yōm* is a parallel of *'attāh,* with a similar meaning. *nibhre'ū* must be added to *liphnēy yōm,* thus forming a complete sentence. Usually *liphnēy yōm* is treated as an adverb modifying *shema'tām,* but that is an impossible construction because of the *we* before *lō'.* The *we* in *welō'* cannot be construed as an introductory *Waw apodosis,* because of the other *Waw* in *weliphnēy,* if the latter phrase is explained as an adverb modifying *shema'tām.* Knobel's reference to Job 19:23 and Exodus 16:6 is unjustified. Even Delitzsch went along with that explanation. The reason for the error lies in the misinterpretation of the phrase *liphnēy yōm,* which was mechanically translated "before today." The literal meaning of *liphnēy yōm* is "to, in the face of, in respect to today" as in Psalm 72:5,17, where *liphnēy yārēaḥ* and *liphnēy shemesh* do not mean *before,* but rather *in respect to* sun and moon, as is indicated also by the use of the synonym *'im,* together with, in that passage. Luther correctly translated: *so lange die Sonne und der Mond waehrt.* So, *liphnēy yōm* means across from, in connection with, while, in the course of today, and as a parallel of *'attāh* it is affected by the contradiction in *welō' mē'āz* and receives the restrictive meaning of "not until today," in the course of this day. Accordingly, the sense is: Only now, not at some previous date, during, or in the course of today have these *hadhāshōth netsūrōth* been brought into existence; and you knew nothing of them. The *'attāh* and *liphnēy yōm* of this verse express the same thought as *pith 'ōm* in verse 3; and so, as in verse 5, the conclusion follows: So that you could not say, "I knew it."

To what particular period of time do *mē'attāh, 'attāh,* and *liphnēy yōm* refer? Those who hold that Isaiah II was written during the period of the exile say that the period referred to was somewhere between Cyrus' first great victories and the crowning achievement of his career, the conquest of Babylon. They make a point of fixing the time as close as possible to the fall of Babylon, in order to make it seem plausible that the prophet, with a little supernatural assistance, could have concluded from Cyrus' early victories that the fall of Babylon was bound to follow. Regarding that assumption there is this to say: It is impossible to contend in argument with anyone who is firm in his unbelief and denies the possibility of a real prophesying of the future, and who maintains that all prophesying of the future has its basis in present circumstances which reasonably indicate a future event. To such a person the words apply with which the Lord upbraids the house of Jacob in verses 4 and 8. Such a person must also lack all sensibility for the meaning of Scripture, particularly of Old Testament prophecy. Furthermore, the words *mē'attāh, 'attāh, liphnēy yōm* isolate the whole prophecy about Cyrus and the deliverance out of Babylon as a self-contained unit separate from all earlier bodies of events (*kullāh*), verse 6a. These three adverbs place the prophet (or the Lord), together with his audience, between these two bodies of events, without dividing either into its segments.

8 גַּם לֹא־שָׁמַעְתָּ גַּם לֹא יָדַעְתָּ גַּם מֵאָז לֹא־פִּתְּחָה אָזְנֶךָ

כִּי יָדַעְתִּי בָּגוֹד תִּבְגּוֹד וּפֹשֵׁעַ מִבֶּטֶן קֹרָא לָךְ׃

Verse 8 has been consistently misunderstood and mistranslated, because translators have intentionally or unintentionally supplied the verbs *shāmā'tā* and *yādha'tā* with *'am* as their object, whereas the verbs here are without an object. As a result this verse becomes a virtual repetition of the thought expressed in verses 6 and 7, where these verbs do appear with *'am* as their object. But the second half of verse 8 shows that this verse does not treat of the mere physical hearing and understanding of the prophecies, but rather of a moral infirmity. The translators make a second mistake when they treat the perfects as historic perfects instead of *perfecta praesentia,* Gr. 106, g, i, p. 311. The same is true of the perfect in *pitteḥā* in the next clause. The sentence is therefore not to be translated: Neither have you heard *it* (the *ḥadhāshōth*), nor have you known it. The correct translation is: Neither do you hear, nor do you understand. This is not a reference to past history, but a rebuke for a present moral condition. This verse is a pendant to verse 4. The house of Jacob is *qāsheh,* it does not yield to guidance, it neither hears nor sees. And so, the next clause must not be translated: Nor was your ear open in times past. What we have here is not a relating of past history. What would be the purpose of that? The *time* of the clause is the present: As in times past, your ear is not now open — as little today, as in the days long ago. In short, he is rebuking Israel's present hardness of heart, as in verse 4.

pitteḥā is an intensive, intransitive Piel, as in 60:11. Following a negative, *kī* is to be translated "but," not "for" or "because," Gr. 163, a, p. 500. Why cannot the exegetes see this? *yādha'tī* is "I know," not "I knew." In this connection, what could be the sense of a reference to the past? *bāghōdh* is an infinitive absolute that emphasizes the idea expressed by the finite verb. The imperfect expresses a constant repetition of the action, extending into the present time, Gr. 107, g, p. 315. The reference is here to Jacob's trickery, Genesis 27. Even then Esau complained: "He hath supplanted me these two times." The meaning of *bāghadh* is to deal underhandedly, treacherously. This faithlessness persisted in Jacob's "house" and again and again revealed itself in Jacob's relation to his God. According to the Masoretic pointing (Merkha *cum* Tiphcha), *mibbeten* modifies *pōshēa',* not *qōrā' lākh.* The house of Jacob, like its progenitor, is called *qōrā'* (a Pual), and is known as a *pōshēa',* a rebel, or a treacherous one, from the time of his youth. The participle *pōshēa'* is a noun in meaning and designates a fixed state of mind, Gr. 116, f, Note, p. 357. Since Jacob is of that kind, *bāghadh* is expressed as being constantly repeated. He is a rebel, treacherous by nature, and therefore he cannot act otherwise than treacherously. The relation of these last two clauses to each other is the same as the one that obtains between the two (or three) in the first part of the sentence: Israel's ear has never been open, and therefore it can never obey nor come to understanding. Everything in verses 8 and 7 refers primarily to the *ḥadhāshōth* that were mentioned in 6b, just as verses 4, 5, and 6a point back to the *rī'shōnōth.* Verse 8 being so general in form naturally applies also to the earlier verses.

In the following minor strophe the Lord now gives the reason why He does not exterminate this hopeless house of Israel, but afflicts it instead in the smelting furnace of affliction.

9 לְמַעַן שְׁמִי אַאֲרִיךְ אַפִּי וּתְהִלָּתִי אֶחֱטָם־לָךְ לְבִלְתִּי הַכְרִיתֶךָ:

In the absence of a connecting link we supply "but" at the beginning of verse 9 to express the unexpectedness of the statement that now follows. The Lord will extend (*he'erīkh*) His anger, will draw it out to keep it from breaking forth; He will bridle, or restrain Himself (*ḥāṭam*), for your sake (*lākh*), so as not to exterminate you, an end that Israel had deserved. Concerning *lebhiltī* with an infinitive Hiphil (*hakhrīth*) as a negative particle expressing purpose, see Gr. 165, b, p. 504. All of this the Lord does for His name's sake, for the sake of His honor and glory. *lema'an* has to be repeated before *tehillāthī*. With this thought the strophe began; with the same thought, emphasized, it ends. The one thing of importance is the honor of God. That is the reason for all things, also for His forbearance toward evildoers.

10 הִנֵּה צְרַפְתִּיךָ וְלֹא בְכָסֶף בְּחַרְתִּיךָ בְּכוּר עֹנִי:

Like the preceding imperfects, the perfect in *tsāraphtī* is future in meaning, *perfectum confidentiae,* Gr. 106, m,n, p. 312. The *Beth* before *keseph* is *Beth essentiae,* like silver (40:10; 66:15; 28:16, etc.) One will not be far off the mark if one takes it to be *Beth normae* or *modi*: "in the nature of" silver. The point of comparison is the violent heat, cf. Psalm 12:7(6); Isaiah 1:25; Zechariah 13:9. The words express the consequence of God's moderation of His anger, as described in verse 9. *bāḥar* is not used here, as Luther assumed, in its usual Hebrew sense, but in the Aramaic sense of to try, melt, refine, like the Hebrew *bāḥan**. The furnace of affliction is figurative for the sufferings of the exile. In Deuteronomy 4:20 Egypt is called an "iron furnace." The Lord will not exterminate Israel, will not cut it off entirely, but He will visit it with great affliction. The section closes with an emphatic expression of God's reason and purpose in all this.

---

*The Dead Sea Scrolls read *behanṭīkhā*.

¹¹ לְמַעֲנִי לְמַעֲנִי אֶעֱשֶׂה כִּי אֵיךְ יֵחָל
וּכְבוֹדִי לְאַחֵר לֹא־אֶתֵּן:

The forceful repetition of *lema'anī* is explained by the next two clauses. *kī 'eykh yēḥāl* is literally: how would it be blasphemed! *yēḥal* is an imperfect Niphal of *ḥāhal*. This is a strange sentence. The interjection *'eykh* (the *'eykhāh* of Lamentations: How!) is not unusual in Isaiah: 14:4, 12; 19:11; 20:6. Its meaning here is the same as in 20:6. With the imperfect in a question it expresses disapproval, something impossible, in this instance, morally impossible (cf. also 36:9). But where is the subject? We can find a subject only by turning back to verse 9, to *shemī*, a concept that is latent in *lema'anī* of this verse. But that is a forced construction. It has been suggested that this clause was originally written in the margin and was later added to the text; but this possibility is contradicted by the presence of the phrase in the text of the LXX. Some commentators read *kī 'eykh 'anōkhī 'eḥal*, how can I be profaned, cf. Ezekiel 22:26*. Duhm, followed by Cheyne and others, ascribes this phrase and twenty others of this section to a later reviser. But all of this is very uncertain. We have chosen to supply *shemī:* How dare it (My name) be profaned! That would happen if the Lord exterminated the house of Jacob. The gentiles would ascribe the extermination to the inability of the Lord to save His people. Cf. Numbers 14:16; Deuteronomy 9:28; Ezekiel 20:14ff. At the same time, the honor to be the Lord, the only true God, would be given to another, to an idol that had no right to it, 42:8; cf. 2 Samuel 7:26. The Lord's honor depends on the deliverance of His people by virtue of His election and calling of them in Abraham, Isaac, and Jacob, and by virtue of the promises given to them.

The *Résumé* will be found at the beginning of the discourse.

Second Part: verses 12-22: *The Lord invites His chosen one, Israel, to receive His word and thus participate in the salvation that is coming.*

This section is divided into two larger parts that differ sharply from each other in contents. Verses 12-16: What the God of Israel has prophesied regarding the deliverance to be effected by Cyrus, that will, at His word, be brought about just as heaven and earth

---

*The Dead Sea Scrolls read *'eyḥal*.

came into existence at His command. Verses 18-22: If Israel believes His word concerning this promised deliverance, it will experience a glorious future, after celebrating a happy return from Babylon to its homeland.

First Half: verses 12-16:   *The promised salvation is at the door.*

12   *Listen to Me, O Jacob, and Israel whom I called!*
      I am He, I am the first, and I am the last.
13   *Also has My right hand laid the foundations of the earth,*
      And My right hand spread out the heavens;
      When I called to them, they stood forth together.
14   *Come together, all of you, and hear!*
      Who among them has foretold this?
      Since the Lord loved him, he performs His pleasure on
          Babylon
      And His arm on the Chaldeans.
15   *I, even I, have spoken; and I have called him;*
      I have led him forth, and he will prosper in his way.
16   *Draw near to Me and hear this:*
      From the beginning I have not spoken in secret,
      When it came into being, I was there.
      And now: "The Lord of All, Jehovah, He sent me with
          His Spirit."

שְׁמַע אֵלַי יַעֲקֹב   וְיִשְׂרָאֵל מְקֹרָאִי 12
אֲנִי־הוּא אֲנִי רִאשׁוֹן   אַף אֲנִי אַחֲרוֹן׃

All the elements in this address have the tender, friendly quality that the Lord always employs when He speaks to His own, cf. 41:8; 43:1; 44:1,21. The Pual participle *meqorā'ī* harks back to 43:1; it is equivalent to the one "whom I have chosen" in 41:8 and 9. One must not lose sight of this, if one is to avoid going astray in what follows. The Lord is not preaching judgment in this last section of the first part; He is preaching salvation to His chosen servant, who is to be saved and who will be saved. For *'anī hū'*, see remarks on 41:4. This first half (verses 12-16) of the second part (12-22) is a brief *résumé* of the entire prophecy up to this point, and so the Lord again repeats that so often repeated chief truth: I, I alone, am God.

אַף־יָדִי יָסְדָה אֶרֶץ   וִימִינִי טִפְּחָה שָׁמָיִם 13
קֹרֵא אֲנִי אֲלֵיהֶם   יַעַמְדוּ יַחְדָּו׃

Verse 13 is also a repetition of a much proclaimed truth: 40:28; 42:5; 44:24; 45:12,18. *tippah,* like *natah,* is to spread or stretch out. The last clause (*qore',* a participle followed by *ya'amdhu,* a finite verb) really belongs among the conditional clauses, the participle being the so-called *casus pendens,* Gr. 116, w, p. 361; 159, i, p. 494, and 143, p. 457f. The clause is, however, not to be introduced by "if" in the sense of "as often as," but rather by a historical "when": When I called to them, they stood forth. It is not to be overlooked that this fact is advanced not only as proof of the Godhead of the Lord, but is at the same time cited as an example to which *qera'thiw,* verse 15, is to be joined as a pendant. Just as heaven and earth stood forth when I called them, so too shall it be with Cyrus and his work.

14 הִקָּבְצוּ כֻלְּכֶם וּשֲׁמָעוּ   מִי בָהֶם הִגִּיד אֶת־אֵלֶּה

יְהוָה אֲהֵבוֹ יַעֲשֶׂה חֶפְצוֹ בְּבָבֶל וּזְרֹעוֹ כַּשְׂדִּים:

That the gentiles are addressed here, and not Israel, although in the middle of an address to Israel, becomes immediately clear when one considers that this strophe groups into a small compass the chief points of the entire preceding prophecy. Such passages as 41:1 and 22; 43:9; 45:20 are repeated here. That accounts for the use of the third person in *bhahem.* Neither is there any good reason for applying the first clause to Israel and the second to the heathen. Since the Lord had just spoken to Israel, the summons to come together would be *post festum.* The object of *higgidh* is here the same as it was in earlier passages, namely, what the Lord intends to carry out through Cyrus. *YHWH 'ahebho,* the Lord loves him, is a condensed description of the relation existing between the Lord and Cyrus, which had elsewhere been described at greater length: 41:2 and 25; 44:28; 45:1 and 13; 46:11. "Love" is the word here instead of choose or call, as the basis for the Lord's working through Cyrus. This love does not include the kind of love that the Lord had for His Israel, His spiritual children. As is immediately explained in *ya'aseh* (Delitzsch notwithstanding), as Exodus 14:31 (*'asah yadh*) shows. *zero'o* is *concretum pro abstracto.* It is not possible to translate "and His arm (comes) upon the Chaldeans," because *kasdim* has no preposition, and besides that construction breaks up the connection of the clause with *'ahebho,* to which it clearly belongs.

15 אֲנִי אֲנִי דִּבַּרְתִּי אַף־קְרָאתִיו   הֲבִיאֹתִיו וְהִצְלִיחַ דַּרְכּוֹ:

The emphatic repetition of *'anī* connects the thought of this verse with that of 12 and 13: I, the same who called heaven and earth into being, the First and the Last, who alone am God, I proclaimed it, yea, I called him (Cyrus, of course). *'aph* connects *qerā'thīw,* as the more important act, with *dibbartī. dibbartī* is a general expression and refers to God's execution of His will against Babylon. He who alone is God, who created heaven and earth, has solemnly spoken this; and not only that, but He has already called the one whom He has chosen (*'ahebhō*), and now He has brought him forward (*habhi'ōthīw*) to carry out the mission assigned to him. The last clause states the outcome: he will carry it out to a successful conclusion. *hitslīaḥ* is a prophetic perfect.

16 קִרְבוּ אֵלַי שִׁמְעוּ־זֹאת

לֹא מֵרֹאשׁ בַּסֵּתֶר דִּבַּרְתִּי מֵעֵת הֱיוֹתָהּ שָׁם אָנִי

וְעַתָּה אֲדֹנָי יְהוִה שְׁלָחַנִי וְרוּחוֹ:

With a new summons the Lord again formally addresses Israel. He repeats what He had said in 45:19. Following the formal address we run into a number of difficulties occasioned by our differing idioms. Our idiom would require changing the order of *lō' mērō'sh* to *mērō'sh lō'* in order to arrive at the intended meaning: "from the beginning I have not spoken in secret." If we change the negative into a positive, the sentence says: "From the beginning I have spoken freely and openly, clearly and distinctly" (cf. the contrast in 45:19). The construction of the next clause is clear enough: "When it came into being, there (at this time) *was* I." The subject of both predicates is the speaker, the Lord. The question is: What had the Lord spoken? "Speaking" here is the same as pronouncing, proclaiming, foretelling, prophesying (cf. *dōbhēr tsedheq,* 45:19). In 45:19, what the Lord had said is expressly designated as *tsedheq* and *mēyshārīm* — as true salvation. But in this passage the subject matter of the Lord's speaking is precisely designated in 14b and 15 as the sending of Cyrus and the conquest of Babylon, called *teshū'ath 'ōlāmīm* in 45:17. It is of the deliverance that is to be accomplished through Cyrus that the Lord has from the beginning spoken, has prophesied, openly, clearly, and distinctly. To what does *mērō'sh,* from the beginning, refer? It could refer to the *dibbēr,* the prophesying itself, in the sense that from the beginning, as soon as the Lord began to prophesy about this matter of the deliverance through Cyrus, He prophesied

openly and unmistakably. Or could it refer to the Cyrus mission itself: From the beginning of that matter, when it first began to
develop, I prophesied openly of it. The next clause offers aid in
reaching a decision between these two interpretations. The verbal
and the adverbial parts of the second clause have their parallels in
the first clause. *mē'eth heyōthāh* corresponds to *mērō'sh; shām 'anī*
to *lō' bassēther dibbartī. mē'eth heyōthāh*, from the time of its coming into being, clearly refers directly to the promised deliverance
through Cyrus, verses 14b and 15 (called *teshū'ath 'ōlāmīm* in
45:17). It is immaterial whether one takes the suffix *āh* to refer to
some noun like *teshū'āh*, or understands it to be a neuter suffix
referring in a general way to the matter mentioned in 14b and 15.
In any event *mē'eth heyōthāh* means "when the Cyrus matter
began to be." According to the rules governing parallelism,
mērō'sh is synonymous with *me'eth heyōthāh* but not identical in
meaning. *mērō'sh* cannot be just a repetition of *mē'eth heyōthāh*,
meaning "from the beginning of this matter," or "when this matter began to be"; it must mean "from the beginning of My
prophesying," or "as soon as I began to prophesy." The Lord says
here: None of the pagan gods has foretold the career of Cyrus; I
proclaimed it beforehand, not in secret, not in dark and ambiguous
oracles, but from the very beginning of My prophecies regarding
this matter I spoke openly and unmistakably. This clause introduces nothing new; it merely summarizes what the Lord in all
previous discourses had said of Himself in contrast to the ignorant
pagan gods, as overwhelming proof of His sole Godhead (40:21,
27ff; 41:4ff, 21ff, 26ff; 42:9; 43:9,12,13,18,19; 44:6,7; 45:19-21;
46:10,11; 48:3,5). The only difference is that in this sentence
mērō'sh receives particular emphasis at the head of the clause.
The parallel clause now also becomes clear. *me'eth heyōthāh*
means "from the time of its coming into being," that is, from the
time of the beginning of the deliverance that Cyrus was to effect,
or of the *teshū'āh* that was to be his work. The passages cited
above show that "from the time of its coming into being" means to
say that before it began to be, *shām 'anī*, I was there. Since *shām*
'anī is parallel to *lō' bassēther dibbartī*, it must mean something
similar. *shām* is here an adverb of time, not of place; then, at *that*
time, at the time of its inception, I was there. *shām 'anī* is a highly
concentrated expression, much more forceful than *lō' bassēther*
dibbartī, and it includes everything that lies in that majestic *'anī*
hū', which is so common: I am; I am the First and I the Last; There
is no God beside Me; I am the Lord who does all things, and other

334

such expressions. The point to be made is that in respect to the coming of this deliverance, the Lord is He who is before all salvation and by whom all salvation is worked, whereas the pagan gods are — nothing. Other interpretations simply miss the point.

Commentators have found that the last clause of this sentence presents even greater difficulty than the first two. A wholly literal rendition of it is: "And now the All-Lord Jehovah has sent me and His Spirit." First of all, it must be established that *rūḥō* is an accusative, as well as *-anī,* the suffix of *shālaḥ.* So much is certain. The meaning then would be clear if only one knew who the speaker is. There lies the difficulty. Some say: Cyrus; others: the Messiah; still others: the prophet Isaiah. As each one tries to prove his interpretation, he comes away with the feeling that he has proved nothing. As is so often the case, the commentators range so far afield that they do not notice the truth that lies so close at hand, namely, that the prophet has come to the end of the last chapter of his first large discourse and is here summarizing, speaking very concisely. This is his very last word regarding events that are to happen. With the following *kōh 'āmar,* the application begins.

In this section the prophet has been repeating all his prophecies in condensed form; and now at the close he compresses the fulfillment of them into a single short sentence beginning with *we 'attāh,* "and now." The Hebrew scholars who supplied the text with accents, marked this word with a disjunctive *Rebia,* thus separating the word from the rest of the clause. They rightly felt that *we 'attāh* was a unit, a sentence in itself. To render the word correctly and give it its full significance, one must not hurry past the Rebia and connect the word in one breath with what follows: "And now the All-Lord has," etc. A definite pause and special intonation should follow *we 'attāh.* A question mark or exclamation point should be placed after it: And now? And now! Perhaps the clearest way of bringing out the force of this last word of the great prophecy would be to write "Now?!" The prophecy had constantly held forth the prospect of imminent fulfillment. And now, in conclusion, as an equivalent and as an answer to that prophecy, what more fitting concrete meaning could be given to that exclamatory "And now!" than the announcement: "It is finished, it is at hand, it is there!!" Cf. 48:7. And that is exactly what the sentence means to say, and it says it as dramatically as the *shām 'anī* that immediately precedes. *The promised deliverance is personified* and is introduced as speaking in its own person. It says, after the Lord has introduced it with *we 'attāh:* "The Lord of All, Jehovah, He sent me with His Spirit." To assume that Cyrus is the speaker would not affect the meaning of the passage, since it is Cyrus who is the instrument of the deliverance; but primarily it is the deliverance itself that is personified. One could render the sentence in this wise: And now it can be said: "The Lord of All, Jehovah, He sent me with His Spirit." "Me and His Spirit" is the same as "me with, or together with, His Spirit"; that is, His Spirit stands behind me and is the actual effective power. (The *Waw* in *werụ̄ho* is *Waw concomitantiae*, Gr. 154, a, Note 1, b, p. 484.) The Spirit will not let this matter halt, but will carry it through to a successful conclusion. If one thinks of Cyrus as the speaker, the result is the same. In fact, it seems that in the last clause Cyrus is indeed kept before our eyes as the speaker. That likelihood is suggested by the striking correspondence between the separate phrases in verses 16 and 15. Compare *shām 'anī* with *'anī 'anī; shelạhanī* with *qerā'thīw* and *habhī'othīw; werụ̄ho* with *hitslị̄ah darkō.* This concluding verse then says: The salvation of My people and their deliverance out of Babylon, which from the very beginning was clearly and openly proclaimed by Me, the Lord, the one true God — is now here and will be carried through to the end.

Second Half: verses 17-22: *He that believes will be saved.*

17 *Thus says the Lord, your Redeemer, the Holy One of Israel:*
    I am the Lord, your God, who teaches you what is good,
    And leads you in ways by which you should walk.

18 *Oh, if you will listen to My word,*
    Then your peace will be like a stream
    And your salvation like the waves of the sea.
19 *And your seed will be like the sand,*
    And the offspring of your body like grains of the sand,
    And his name will not be cut off nor destroyed before Me.

20 *Go forth from Babylon, flee from the Chaldeans with*
       shouts of joy,
    Announce this, and let it be heard,
    Carry it to the ends of the earth — say:
    The Lord has redeemed Jacob, His servant!

21 *They suffered no thirst when He led them through the desert,*
    From the rocks He caused water to flow for them,
    He cleft the rocks, and water gushed forth.
22 *But there is no peace, says the Lord, for the wicked.*

17 כֹּה־אָמַ֧ר יְהוָ֛ה גֹּאַלְךָ֖ קְד֣וֹשׁ יִשְׂרָאֵ֑ל
אֲנִ֨י יְהוָ֤ה אֱלֹהֶ֙יךָ֙ מְלַמֶּדְךָ֣ לְהוֹעִ֔יל
מַדְרִֽיכֲךָ֖ בְּדֶ֥רֶךְ תֵּלֵֽךְ׃

This final discourse closes with an application introduced by an
impressive *kōh 'āmar YHWH*. Everything in this sentence, from
gō'alkhā to *bedherekh tēlēkh* gives the reason and forms the basis
for a following admonition clad in the form of urgent desire. Because the Lord is Israel's *gō'ēl*, Israel's Holy One (cf. remarks on
40:25; 41:14,20), because He is Israel's God and teaches it only
what is profitable and salutary (*lehō'īl*) and constantly leads it in
the way that it should go, that is, in a salutary way (a parallel of
lehō'īl), therefore Israel should now do what follows, expressed in
the form of an ardent wish of the Lord. (Note that *melammedhkhā*
and *madhrīkhekhā* are participles expressing unbroken action.)

18 ל֥וּא הִקְשַׁ֖בְתָּ לְמִצְוֹתָ֑י
וַיְהִ֤י כַנָּהָר֙ שְׁלוֹמֶ֔ךָ וְצִדְקָתְךָ֖ כְּגַלֵּ֥י הַיָּֽם׃

Critics, especially the meter theorists, consider this entire passage from 16b through 19 to be postexilic and therefore delete it
from Isaiah's prophecy. They maintain that *lū'* with the perfect
cannot refer to the future and that this passage cannot be pre-exilic nor have been written in the hope of deliverance from exile
and of restoration to national glory. They say that a later writer,
viewing the state of postexilic Israel and despairing of the future,
was here giving voice to his grief. And so they translate: "If only
you had hearkened to My commands, then would your welfare
have been like a river, etc." But in 63:19(64:1) *lū'* precedes a verb
in the perfect (*lū' qāra'tā shāmayim*), and that surely refers to the
future. Gesenius, Gr. 151, e, p. 477, rightly lists these two passages
as examples in which *lū'* is a particle expressing a wish, with these
words: ". . . on the other hand, Isaiah 48:18 and 63:19(64:1) express a wish that something expected in the future may already
have happened." Compare the rule for conditional clauses, Gr.
159, l, m, p. 494f. This possibility being accepted, the context requires the translation: "Oh, if you will listen — then your peace
will," etc. This wish does not presuppose the impossibility or the
unlikelihood of fulfillment, but rather the exact opposite. If it were
not so, then verse 20 (and verse 21) could not follow, which in imperative form clearly anticipates the future. In order to express

the certainty of fulfillment that lies in this wish, we translate: "Oh, if you *will* listen, then your peace *will* be . . . " This clears the way for verse 20. The Lord knows that pious Israel, ensnared as it is in the ways of the gentiles and infected with unbelief, will take His word to heart and have part in the coming salvation. As to the spiritually corrupt mass, this wish remains unfulfilled and becomes a lament over a people beloved, but lost beyond recovery.

mitswoth (from *tsāwāh*, to command) is to be taken in the broadest sense of the word; it includes all the promises of the Lord and is the equivalent of the Word of God. *hiqshībh* (Hiphil of *qāshabh*) is a favorite of Isaiah, both in I and II. For *wayehī* after a hypothetical or optative clause, see Gr. 111, x, p. 330. It is also to be understood as conditional. *shālōm*, peace, as so often, is a metonym for welfare, happiness, salvation, *tsedhāqāh*, as usually, means salvation. The figures of a stream and of waves of the sea are strikingly beautiful. The point of comparison is the overwhelmingly great mass of the *shālōm*.

¹⁹ וַיְהִי כַחוֹל זַרְעֶךָ וְצֶאֱצָאֵי מֵעֶיךָ כִּמְעֹתָיו
לֹא־יִכָּרֵת וְלֹא־יִשָּׁמֵד שְׁמוֹ מִלְּפָנָי:

ḥol, in its more complete form, is *ḥol hayyām*, sand of the sea, Genesis 32:13(12); 41:49; 22:17; Isaiah 10:22. *tse'etsā'īm* (from *yātsā'*, to go out) is a favorite expression in Isaiah II: 42:5; 44:3; 61:9; 65:23; but it also occurs in Isaiah I: 22:24; and 34:1. This is the only occurrence of the word with the adjunct *me'eykhā* (*mē'īm*, plural of *mē'eh*), offspring of your bowels, that is, of your body. *me'othāyw* is derived from *mā'āh*, a word that still occurs in Rabbinic Hebrew, meaning a little stone or kernel. The comparison then is: "like its kernels," that is, of the sand. *kārath*, to cut off, to eradicate (very common in the Pentateuch) is a stronger word than *shāmadh*, to destroy. Some commentators treat the clause beginning with *lō'yikkārēth* as independent of the rest of the sentence and translate it with the indicative: "his name *will* not be cut off, etc." But that breaks up the sentence. If this clause is independent of the first clause, it will have to be connected with the end of verse 17; verses 18 and 19a must then be treated as parentheses. Ewald does so. However, the lack of an external connection between the two clauses does not necessarily separate the two from each other. Frequently an asyndeton binds the two more closely together. The *Waw* consecutive in *wayehī* still controls *lō' yikkārēth*.

²⁰ צְאוּ מִבָּבֶל בִּרְחוּ מִכַּשְׂדִּים
בְּקוֹל רִנָּה הַגִּידוּ הַשְׁמִיעוּ זֹאת
הוֹצִיאוּהָ עַד־קְצֵה הָאָרֶץ
אִמְרוּ גָּאַל יְהוָה עַבְדּוֹ יַעֲקֹב׃

Verses 20-22 comprise the closing strophe. Rhetorically, this is a
hymn of great beauty. In its form it is an admonition to pious
Israel to go forth from Babylon with shouts of joy and to sing aloud
the praise of the Lord for the deliverance that He wrought. Verse
21 describes how safe and how bountifully provided the people will
be on the way through the desert that they must cross. Verse 22,
by contrast, very briefly tells of the doom that awaits the wicked.
And thus, by means of a hymn, the end of this first great section of
Isaiah II is closely linked with its beginning, 40:1 and 2. The end
and the beginning have the same theme: Preach to her that her
warfare is at an end! Go forth out of Babylon with shouts of joy! At
the beginning, as at the end, we have the prophetic present of the
deliverance: *māle'āh tsebhā'ah —gā'al YHWH 'abhdo.* The conclusion serves as the seal of the beginning. There is but one great
theme: Deliverance of Israel out of Babylon. In connection with
nahamū, nahamū at the beginning of chapter 40, we remarked
that the imperative form was purely rhetorical. The same remark
applies to this passage. The imperatives are descriptive of the
departure from Babylon. Israel is pictured as converted, obedient,
and hopefully awaiting the hour of deliverance. They have understood what the Lord purposes to do and have believed His word.
They have been set free. They know that tomorrow or the next day
the tempest and the judgment will come upon Babylon. Their
heart pulsates with joy. They prepare for a hasty flight. They
depart with shouts of joy, and home is their goal. They praise the
Lord who saves them. They have no fear of the waterless desert,
for the Lord is their guide. He cleaves the rocks, as in the days of
old. — Is not the arrival in the homeland missing here?

Since verse 20 is already descriptive, the imperatives give way
in verse 21 to the indicative mood. Verse 21 is spoken by the departing people and is a continuation of the final clause of verse 20.
It is part of the prophet's poetic technique that he lets the Lord put
into the mouths of the people what He Himself wants to say. In
this connection the names "Babylon" and "Chaldeans" attain a
particularly bitter aftertaste: the tyrant, the idol worshiping na-

tion! *birḥu,* flee, does not contradict 52:12. In that passage there is a moral admonition, here there is description; there the point is the awakening of a trust in God's protection, here a joyful flight is being described. The verbs *haggīdhū, hashmīʿu, hōtsīʾuhā* form a sharp climax, even though *zōʾth* is interposed between the last two verbs. The climax receives emphasis by the addition of "to the ends of the earth." Compare *hōtsīʾu* with *yōtsīʾ* in 42:1. The means here, as in that passage, is the mouth, the preaching. The *zōʾth* that is to be preached is the object of *ʾimrū:* "the Lord has redeemed Jacob." *gāʾal,* as the chief thought in this sentence, occupies the position of importance, at the head. "It is finished" — that is the great theme. The Lord has saved His people Jacob. Now at the close the redeemed people once again receives the title of endearment, "Jacob," and the title of its office, "the Lord's servant." With that it is received anew into the original relationship to its God.

$$\text{21} \quad \text{וְלֹא צָמְאוּ בָּחֳרָבוֹת הוֹלִיכָם}$$
$$\text{מַיִם מִצּוּר הִזִּיל לָמוֹ}$$
$$\text{וַיִּבְקַע־צוּר וַיָּזֻבוּ מָיִם:}$$

That the verbs in this verse do not refer to the future time is indicated by *wayyibhqaʿ,* which clearly refers to past time. These verbs follow in line with *gāʾal* of verse 20. They are *perfecta frequentativa,* Gr. 112, e, h, p. 331f. They indicate an action repeated or continuing (*hōlīkhām*) in the past. The speaker (whether the Lord or the rescued people) is speaking from a position in the future and views the deliverance and the homeward journey as lying in the past. The clauses are brief, animated, and not connected by particles. *baḥorābhōth hōlīkhām* is best translated as a temporal clause: "as He led them through the waste places," Gr. 164, b, p. 501. The lively form of description accounts for the absence of *kī* or *ʾasher.* Since the situations are similar, the description of this exodus is patterned after the desert wanderings under Moses' leadership. For the divine guidance, see Exodus 13:14; Numbers 14:14; water from the rock, Exodus 17; Numbers 20; both as subject of psalmody, Nehemiah 9:12,15; Psalm 78:14f; 105:39,41. Cf. also 1 Corinthians 10:1ff. The entire description is figurative, as in 41:17-19; 43:19f; 44:3f. The purpose is to show that the deliverance out of Babylon and the return of the people to the homeland was equally as marvelous a work of the Lord as the guidance of the people through the wilderness.

22 אֵין שָׁלוֹם אָמַר יְהוָה לָרְשָׁעִים:

With an incisive word at the end, the prophet sets the doom of the wicked in contrast to the happy lot of the believers. *rāsha'* is the ἄνομος of the New Testament, the lawless one, who does not consider himself to be bound by any law, the one who is described in Luke 18:2, the one from whom every word of Law or Gospel glides off without any effect. The *rāsha'* differs from the *poshēa'* only in that he need not first have fallen away. The word designates those in Israel to whom the prophet had spoken the Lord's word in vain, who had hardened themselves against all preaching, the ἄπιστοι of Titus 1:15,16, the opposite of the *tsaddīqīm,* the believers. They did not want to be bothered by God and His preachers, because they had set their hearts on earthly things. But for them there is no peace, neither temporal happiness nor inner calm and salvation. The wicked flees when no one pursues, Proverbs 28:1; Leviticus 26:36. It is the Lord who says that. In this conclusion to chapters 40-48, we have Mark 16:16b in Old Testament form. Some modern critics take verse 22 to be an interpolation taken by a later redactor from Isaiah 57:21, since it fits in very well in that passage, but not here, according to them. They thus demonstrate that they have no understanding for the Lord's primary principle in governing the church and the world. The contents of this last strophe, of this last section, of this last trilogy, of the entire discourse from chapter 40 through chapter 48, in fact, of all of Isaiah and of all of Scripture of both Testaments is: Repent, for the kingdom of heaven is at hand. He who believes and is baptized, shall be saved; he that does not believe, shall be damned.

In connection with chapter 41 we postponed for discussion at this point the question whether the prophecies about Cyrus were written before or after his victorious campaign against the western powers. In order to avoid unnecessary repetition, we refer to the *Introduction,* where everything essential was said in the discussion of the authorship of this book.

PART II

The Redemption from the Guilt of Sin

Chapters 49-57

PART II

Chapters 49-57

The Redemption from the Guilt of Sin

The theme of the second great part (chapters 49-57) is stated in 40:2b: "Her guilt, that is, Jerusalem's, is paid in full." This theme is developed according to the point of view set forth in 40:6-8: "All flesh is grass, but the word (the promise to Abraham) of our God shall stand forever." The elaboration of the theme, as in the first part, extends through the first six chapters, 49-54, while the next three, 55-57, are given over to the application.

As in the first part, 40:1ff, the prophet with dramatic boldness introduces the Lord as the speaker with only the parenthetic remark, *yō'mar 'elōhēykhem*, so here, in the second part, without any introduction, he presents the "Servant of the Lord" as the speaker. That this Servant is the same one who, in 42:1-8, was introduced by the Lord Himself with *hēn 'abhdī* is made evident by the virtual identity of the contents of the two passages. In that passage the prophet granted us only a passing glance at this Servant of the Lord, since his primary interest was devoted to Israel's physical deliverer out of corporal captivity. It is as though the prophet with that isolated and seemingly unconnected mention of the Servant in 42:1ff wanted to say that it was not the work of Cyrus, but the work of this Servant of the Lord which was the primary and the ultimate purpose of God, and to which the work of Cyrus was but the prelude. That this is the correct interpretation of that isolated reference to the Servant of the Lord is indicated by the fact that in the second part of the book Cyrus has totally disappeared, whereas the Servant of the Lord and His work become the focus and center of the presentation. That is already indicated by the prophet's dramatic presentation of Him as speaker at the beginning of this second part and by His appearance again in the very next chapter (50:4-9) as the speaker. And then, in the sublime fifty-third chapter, the Servant is disclosed to our view in His Passion. In the last triad of this part (55-57), He is once more briefly presented as the exalted Prophet and Ruler of the nations. — The more closely the unprejudiced reader studies this figure of the Servant of the Lord, the more overpowering and irresistible becomes the conviction that this Servant cannot be the people of Israel, neither Israel *in toto* nor the spiritual core of Israel, and certainly not some collective noun or mere abstraction; He can be none other than a definite individual, a clearly defined individual.

344

It requires a Jewish, or unbelieving, or anti-Christian interpretation, besides a considerable distortion of the text, to deny this fact and to find in the Servant of the Lord a personification of the people of Israel in some form or other.

The Servant's office is equally clear. It is quite different from the mission of Cyrus. He does not appear armed with sword, spear, and shield, but endowed and anointed with the Holy Spirit (42:1; 50:4; 61:1). His weapon is not the fist, but the mouth — His Word, His Gospel, gently proclaimed to those in distress (42; 49; 50; 51:16; 55:4,5; 61:1,2). The work that He performs is not connected with war and strife, but with obedience to God, 50:4,5; preaching 42; 49; 50; 51; 55); patient suffering and weariness of soul, expiation of the sins of others (49; 50; and 53). His mission, in *résumé*, was to be the Mediator of a new covenant for Israel and a Light unto the gentiles (42; 49; 53:11,12; 55:4,5), to open the eyes of the blind and to proclaim freedom to the prisoners (42; 49:9), to bring good tidings to the poor, to bind up broken hearts (42:3; 61:1), in short, to convert Israel and the gentiles to God. His goal is to reconcile them with the Lord under His kingly rule (49:6, 10ff; 52:7,12; 56; 57:15ff), the glorification of Israel (49:14ff; 51:11; 52; 54), His own glorification (49; 53:10-12; 55:4,5), and the glorification of the Lord Himself (42:8; 49:2,7,26; 52:6). In all of this, His strength and success rest upon the faithfulness, the support, and the protection of the Lord (42:1,4,6; 49:2ff,8; 50; 51:16; 53) extended from above to Him who in weakness and the anxiety of His soul cries to His God. In short, this is not a deliverer from material ills, but a spiritual Savior; not a conqueror of nations, but a Savior of sinners; not a Cyrus, but Christ. This should make it evident that the redemption and deliverance of the prisoners of Zion out of captivity and servitude, the return to the homeland, the restoration of land and city, etc., which are in part ascribed directly to the Servant of the Lord, in part to the Lord's work in connection with that of the Servant, can no longer refer to the physical deliverance out of Babylon, to a return of exiles to their geographical home in Judah-Jerusalem, or to a physical restoration of the Old Testament Israelitic theocracy. All these are, however, at the same time a figurative representation of the spiritual redemption and glorification of the spiritual Israel, which the spiritual Servant of the Lord will bring about through His spiritual office. This accounts for the absence in this part of any mention of Babylon and its tyrannical rule over Israel, which commanded so much attention in the first part. There are still references to the captivity of

Israel, but not to the Babylonian captivity (49; 50:1; 51:11-14; all of 52, etc.). Babylon is now replaced by the gentile nations, by tyrants in general (49:7,22,23,24-26; 51:7,8,22,23; 52:5,10; 54:14-17). The prophet's view now sweeps past and beyond Babylon out into the whole wide world. Zion's captives are being freed and led homeward out of all nations, 49:12; 56:8. Yes, the gentiles themselves, enlightened by the light of the Servant of the Lord, enter as converts into Zion and the house of the Lord, 56:3,6ff.

And yet, all this is not an allegory. Not all of the individual items are types and figures of spiritual things. One cannot but acknowledge that the prophet, in his images and descriptions of the coming redemption and of the kingdom of God, is constrained by certain Old Testament limitations. Although he admits the gentiles, together with Israel, into God's kingdom of the future (49:1-6,22f; 51:4; 55:4,5; 56:3,6,7), still that kingdom is for him essentially Jewish, and the gentiles are really only guests and strangers (56:3-7), who are being added to Israel. Even in the third part of this book they still play a subordinate role (60; 61:5,6; 66:20f). The distress and misery of God's kingdom is in the view of the prophet still the destruction of city and country, the slaughter and deportation of the inhabitants. It is always the physical, albeit regenerate, seed of Jacob that is being gathered again out of all nations on earth. It is the physical Jerusalem that gathers to itself its own children in the flesh and the converted heathen. And it is this same city that is to be gloriously rebuilt, this same devastated land that is to be restored. Even the captivity in which Israel is languishing always brings to mind the Babylonian captivity described in the first part, even though it is never expressly so named. Such are the Old Testament limitations that restrict the prophet in his descriptions. Every man, also every Christian, every man of God, prophet or apostle, is a child of his times, and cannot escape the thought pattern and even the mode of expression that characterize his times, except when the Holy Spirit lifts him above and beyond those restricting bounds. Paul could not speak of railroads, steamships, telegraph and telephone, or of a hundred other items common to our time; and Isaiah must necessarily have a conception of the external forms of the future kingdom of God different from that of the Apostle Paul. Isaiah's conceptions are of those Old Testament times; Paul's, those of the New Testament. Not one prophet from Moses to Malachi, yes, to John the Baptist, ever freed himself completely from Old Testament conceptions concerning God's kingdom. That kingdom is indeed, in its essence, spiritual and within us, but at the same time God Himself has connected it to a thousand externals. God willed that salvation would be of the Jews (John 4:22), and in order to prepare for the salvation which would be effected in the New Testament and be eternal, He established an external, visible training situation amid one particular people, the seed of Abraham, the house of Jacob. Under the Sinaitic Law, which functioned as the pedagog of Israel, even the enlightened and inspired prophet was also a νήπιος, a minor child (Gal. 4:1), subject to all the limitations of a minor, except when divine inspiration lifted him above them. It is for that reason that, in depicting the kingdom of God of the future, he is not wholly free of external, concrete, historical concepts like Israel, Abraham's seed, house of Jacob, Judah, Jerusalem, temple, altar, priest and Levite, devastated lands, exile, external deliverance, return to the city and land of the Lord, and similar externals. Moreover, he could not free himself of such concepts, if he wished to be understood. It was only within the external forms of the Old Covenant that his hearers and readers were able to think about and to understand the future kingdom of God. Whenever the prophet goes beyond the limiting circle of these forms, as in chapter 53, he encounters want of understanding and unbelief. The prophet hides even the essential Godhead of the Servant, which to us of the New Testament seems *a posteriori* to be so clear, under the form of a human servant, just as the mystery of the Trinity is so often alluded to but never clearly and distinctly taught. It is impossible to establish in every case to what extent the prophet himself was conscious of the distinction between things of the spirit and material things, between figure of speech and the thing signified. The distinction, as we mentioned at the beginning of this discussion, is in many instances very clear, and in many other instances not at all so. For example, there can be no doubt that in the second chapter of Isaiah the prophet was consciously employing a figure when he wrote of the mountain of the Lord's house which in days to come should be established as the highest mountain, to which crowds of converted gentiles should stream. Neither can there be any doubt that his pious hearers understood that to be a figure. But there might be some argument over the question whether the closing paragraph of chapter 49 speaks of physical tyranny or of spiritual tyranny, if Luke 11:21f had not answered the question for us.

It is in this distinction between external material and internal spiritual things that the real difficulty in Old Testament exegesis lies, particularly that of the prophetic books. It is very simple to interpret everything external as external, as the modern skeptics do. It is just as simple to give a spiritual meaning to everything external, as the believing expositors, from Origen to the present day (including Luther), so often do. The one method is as false as the other. Both mislead us; both are untrue. The truth lies somewhere in between. There is much of the inward-spiritual, of the abstract-evangelical in Old Testament prophecy. Much that is spiritual is presented in concrete forms, and there are also many pure externals that belong entirely to the concepts of the covenant once established with minors.

It is for this reason that exegetes of the Old Testament are even less able than exegetes of the New Testament to speak with absolute certainty; often they will have to admit that "we know only in part." Besides this, every prophet is, to a greater or lesser degree, a poet, possessing poetic fancy and expressing himself in poetic fashion. He sees visions; he has glimpses of a strange world, whose language, as Paul confesses (2 Cor. 12:4), he cannot repeat in simple terms. He sees pictures which usually and for the most part lie beyond human comprehension and appear in drastic, extreme, and minutely detailed form. The prophet repeats them in the same form, and yet his purpose is to present but *one* thought, *one* fact, *one* spiritual occurrence. Note, for example, how the spiritual peace of the kingdom of the Messiah is symbolized by peace in the kingdom of beasts, Isaiah 11:6ff; the depiction of the glory of God in Ezekiel 1; and the description of the humiliation of Babylon in Isaiah 47:2: "Take the millstones, and grind meal." It is the failure to appreciate this poetic vision and manner of expression that has caused some to think that the fall of Babylon must have occurred in history exactly as Isaiah pictured it, down to the last details. It is because of this want of understanding that unbelieving theologians conclude that the prophetic pronouncements are in error, and that the believing exegetes conclude that the extra-biblical, historical accounts of the events in question must be erroneous. We unpoetic Occidentals, who live in a materialistic age, have so little feeling for the drastic, poetic symbolism of the ancient, naive, Oriental mind that our interpretation of Old Testament prophecy so often misses the point. Modesty is here most becoming for the interpreter. In the second and third parts of this book, we shall have to leave many a detail unexplained.

FIRST TRIAD
Chapters 49-51

The Faithfulness of the Lord
Accomplishes the Salvation
of Israel.

First Discourse: Chapter 49

The faithfulness of the Lord equips His Servant to be an effective Savior, and with His mighty arm He restores her children to Zion.

The discourse has two sections. The first, verses 1-13, introduces the Servant of the Lord as the Man whom the faithfulness of the Lord has *equipped to be competent* to undertake the laborious work of delivering Israel and to carry it through to success. The second part, verses 14-26, tells how the faithfulness of the Lord restores to disheartened Zion *all of her children*, after having rescued them with a mightier arm from the power of the strong one.

First Section: verses 1-13: *The faithfulness of the Lord makes His Servant competent to be the Mediator of a new covenant for Israel and to be the Light of the gentiles.*

This part is divided at the end of verse 6 into two almost equal parts, in the first of which the Servant of the Lord Himself describes the ability given Him by His faithful God to restore Israel and to be the Light of the gentiles. In the second half (verses 7-13), the Lord tells how He, because He is faithful, will honor His despised Servant before all the world, and as His faithful Helper make Him the Mediator of a covenant for the people, so that He may lead the captives of Israel unharmed, from all corners of the world, over leveled highways, back to their devastated homeland and waste inheritance.

First Strophe: verses 1-6: *The Servant of the Lord bears testimony to His mission.*

1 *Hearken to Me, O isles,*
And listen, ye distant nations!
From birth the Lord did call Me,
From My mother's womb He made My name to be known,

2 *And He prepared My mouth to be a sharp sword,*
In the shadow of His hand He hid Me,
And made Me to be a polished arrow,
And hid Me in His quiver.

3 *And He said to Me: You are My Servant,*
Israel, through whom I shall be glorified.

4 *As for Me, I thought: I labor in vain,*
Fruitlessly and to no purpose I spend My strength;
Although My cause is with the Lord
And My reward with My God.

5 *But now thus says the Lord*
Who prepared Me from My mother's womb to be His Servant,
To lead Jacob back to Him,
To gather Israel together to Him,
So that I shall be honored in the eyes of the Lord
And that the Lord shall become My Strength.

6 *He says: It is too little that You should be*
*   a Servant to Me,*
To bring back again the tribes of Jacob,
And to restore the survivors of Israel;
I will also make You the Light of the gentiles,
To be My salvation unto the ends of the earth.

שִׁמְעוּ אִיִּים֙ אֵלַ֔י וְהַקְשִׁ֥יבוּ לְאֻמִּ֖ים מֵרָח֑וֹק
יְהוָה֙ מִבֶּ֣טֶן קְרָאָ֔נִי מִמְּעֵ֥י אִמִּ֖י הִזְכִּ֥יר שְׁמִֽי׃

For *'iyyīm* and *le'ummīm mērāḥōq*, see the remarks to 41:1. It is to be noted that *mērāḥōq* is an attribute to *le'ummīm*. They are not people *from* a distance, but people *in* the distance, *distant* peoples, whereas the isles lie nearby. The two designations comprise the entire world of the gentiles. *haqshībhū* is a stronger word than *shim'ū*. The speaker summons all of heathendom to listen to Him and to pay close attention to what He has to say. His message to them is that He is divinely called and that His mission is of God. In two clauses that are almost identical in meaning, He announces to the gentiles that the Lord Jehovah, the God of Israel, who alone is true God (that is the meaning of Jehovah, according to chapters 40-48), called Him ever since the time of His birth, to an office that is yet to be named. In two details, however, the second clause is more emphatic than the first. The first has simply *mibbeṭen*, "from the womb onward"; the second clause has, purely as a poetic variation, so it would seem, *mimm ῾ey 'immī*, "from the bowels of *My* mother." It is just this *'immī* that is very important. It precludes all possibility of viewing the speaker as a personified collective noun or the people of Israel, as the Jews and the un-believing interpreters explain the phrase. *mibbeṭen*, understood figuratively, would permit that interpretation, but the next phrase, "from the womb of *My* mother," certainly does not. Only an individual speaks like that. *hizkīr shemī* means literally "He brought My name to mind"; it is a meaningful strengthening of the thought expressed by *qerā 'anī*, and it says that He named My name with a purpose, designated Me, appointed Me a name. Com-pare 19:17, to mention; 43:26, to call to mind; 62:6, to call upon; 63:7, to praise. Everywhere this Hiphil of *zākhar* goes back to the meaning of "to recall to mind, to bring to attention." These words strongly suggest Luke 2:21 (1:31), although there is no direct reference here to the name of Jesus. "Servant of the Lord," "Israel," is the name that is meant, namely a title, a name desig-nating an office, characterizing His mission, verse 3. The similarity between this passage and 41:8f and 42:1 comes to mind. His eternal election, realized within the bounds of time, and His appointment to this office, is what the Servant of the Lord here impresses upon the gentiles. Just so did the Lord Christ again and again emphasize His divine mission before friend and foe, Luke 4:18ff; Matthew 11; Luke 24; John 5; 6; 7; 8; 15-17, etc.

2 וַיָּשֶׂם פִּי כְּחֶרֶב חַדָּה   בְּצֵל יָדוֹ הֶחְבִּיאָנִי

וַיְשִׂימֵנִי לְחֵץ בָּרוּר   בְּאַשְׁפָּתוֹ הִסְתִּירָנִי׃

sīm ke, to make like or equal to, and *sīm le*, to make to some-thing, are not unlike our English phrase "to make something of." The Lord has made a sharp sword of His Servant's mouth and has made Him to be a smooth, polished arrow. Sword and arrow are weapons for killing in battle, to put an enemy to death. But physi-cal killing is, of course, not meant here. The words are figures of speech. The sharp sword and the polished, perfect arrow are the Servant's mouth. His office is first of all an office of the mouth; He is the Lord's messenger, prophet, preacher, apostle. He is to proclaim the Lord's Word to the nations. Just as the Lord at one time put His Word into the mouth of Israel, that is, revealed it to him and commanded him to proclaim it (51:16; 59:21; 43:21; Deut.

30:14; Rom. 10:8ff), so He has now placed it in the mouth of this special Servant, who is the right and proper Israel, in order that He proclaim it to the nations (verse 3). This Word is not the Law as such; it is the Word of the Lord Jehovah, the God of grace, the Gospel, the *mishpaṭ* of the Lord. Compare 42:1-8 and the following verses in this chapter. It is with this Word that the Lord will judge the nations unto salvation or unto damnation, 11:4; cf. 1:27; 59:9ff; Mark 16:16; John 3:18; 5:20-24, etc. It is a power of God unto salvation, Romans 1:16; 1 Corinthians 1:18, 24ff, but also unto damnation, John 12:48, etc. This is the Word that the Lord has put into His Servant's mouth. When He proclaims it, 11:4 is being fulfilled. Like a sharp sword or a polished arrow, it pierces through the hearts of the hearers and separates them into those for, and those against, the Lord, the God of grace, and determines their temporal and eternal lot.

The two clauses: "In the shadow of His hand He hid Me" (as a sword), and "hid Me in His quiver" (as an arrow) are poetic turns of speech which say that the Servant does not come on His own account, does not stand alone and independent, but is an instrument in the hand of His God, who chose Him and equipped Him to be an instrument which He carefully preserves for use at His chosen time, the day of salvation, verse 8. If one lays special stress on the verbs *heḥbī'anī* and *histīranī*, the hiding in the shadow of His hand and in His quiver, one might find in those words Luther's thought: *Gar heimlich fuehrt er sein' Gewalt* (in stanza 6 of his hymn, "Dear Christians, One and All, Rejoice"). Cf. Philippians 2:9: The Lord has hidden His Servant's divine glory and power in the form of the Son of man, a servant. On the basis of *'etstsorkhā* in verse 8 and 42:1,4, and 6, one might also find expressed here the powerful protection that the Lord extends to His Servant. We find the same thought expressed in Jesus' words in John 7:28; 8:16,28f; 10:36,38. The Servant declares to the nations that He, as proclaimer of the Gospel, is an especially elected and proven instrument in the hand of the Lord. This declaration is developed in the following verses.

³ וַיֹּאמֶר לִי עַבְדִּי־אָתָּה יִשְׂרָאֵל אֲשֶׁר־בְּךָ אֶתְפָּאָר׃

These words set forth the purpose of the speaker's calling; they define His mission. He is to be the Lord's Servant. For an explanation of the term, see the discussion of 42:1. *yisrā'el* is not a term of address; like *'abhdī 'attāh*, it is a predicate. The Masoretic pointing, which marked the end of the clause by an Athnach in *'attāh*, and which separated *yisrā'el* from the rest of the second clause by a Zaqeph, shows that the Masoretes favored that construction. Therefore, not: You are My Servant Israel, through whom I shall be glorified; but: You are My Servant, you are Israel, through whom, etc. This is one of the passages where negative critics violate the text in order to present the people of Israel as the Servant of the Lord.

For *'asher bekhā̆,* see the discussion of *'asher beḥartīkhā̆, qerā'thīkhā̆,* at 41:8,9. The Servant of the Lord is here called Israel; both terms are nominative predicates. As to His calling, He is Israel; that is what Jacob was, and Jacob was so named, Genesis 32:29(28); 35:10; 1 Kings 18:31; 2 Kings 17:34; Hosea 12:5,6(4,5). He is what the people, the house of Jacob, should have been, but were not: the Man who in faith wrestled with God and man and prevailed, the faithful One who in the power of the Spirit is thoroughly equipped to carry out the office of the Servant. The name *Israel* (*sārāh,* to strive, and *'el,* God) is often explained, after the analogy of similar combinations with *'el,* to mean: "God strives". (Cf. *yishmā'e'l,* Gen. 16:11; *yeḥezqe'l,* Ezek. 1:3; 3:8,9.) That could be the meaning of the name. But it would have to be understood in the sense of "God strives *for* him, on his side." But however one explains the derivation of the name, its authentic meaning, according to Genesis 32:29(28) and Hosea 12:5,6(4,5) is: "He strove with God." Genesis 35:10 hardly offers ground for a different interpretation. With these words the Lord testifies to His Servant that *He* — and not the people that indeed are still called Israel, but no longer are Israel, since they have fallen away from the Israel-character and thus become unfit for the office of Servant — is the perfect Servant, the Servant of the Lord in Spirit and in Truth, the faithful Servant, perfect in His obedience. Through Him the Lord will glorify Himself and reveal His divine glory, and His divine power, wisdom, and goodness. He will do this, as will soon be set forth briefly and then later in detail, through the salvation of Jews and gentiles.

4 וַאֲנִי אָמַרְתִּי לְרִיק יָגַעְתִּי לְתֹהוּ וְהֶבֶל כֹּחִי כִלֵּיתִי אָכֵן מִשְׁפָּטִי אֶת־יְהוָה וּפְעֻלָּתִי אֶת־אֱלֹהָי:

Since the thought in this verse stands in contrast to that of the foregoing verse, especially its last clause, the *Waw* in *wa'anī* should be translated with an adversative conjunction, *but.* The Servant's thoughts (*'āmartī*) are in a sense in opposition to the Lord's purpose to be glorified in Him. He fears that He might not be equal to this great mission, that His labor might be in vain, that He would be spending His strength fruitlessly. The same thought is suggested, in different form, in 42:4: "He will not grow weary and will not bend till He, etc." This is not an expression of unbelief; it is true modesty born of a lively awareness of His own weakness. We must not forget that He who is meant here, the Christ, is undertaking His mission to save sinners as a weak and humble human being. He "was in all points tempted like as we are, yet without sin." He was filled with fear at the thought of the baptism that He had to undergo (Luke 12:50). We are reminded of the hour of suffering in Gethsemane. He began to be very sorrowful, He trembled, and was in agony. He desired the companionship of the disciples, prayed and made supplication, His "sweat was as it were great drops of blood." "If it be possible, let this cup pass from Me." And then the bitter agony of the cross. Yes, in His days on earth as a weak human being, with no confidence in Himself, vividly conscious of His own weakness and infirmity, and yet with a trust in His God, unshakable, however violently assailed, Jesus "offered up prayers and supplications with strong crying and tears" (Heb. 5:7). — All of this is conveyed in this passage by the Holy Spirit. The words of the prophet hardly do justice to the stark reality. How these thoughts and feelings of the Servant can be fact and truth, and be set in antithesis to the appellation "Israel" in the preceding verse, which predicates perfect faith and obedience, without invalidating that name, is a problem that no one can solve. Or, to state the problem in New Testament terms, no one can explain how the temptation of the Lord, His distress, and fear, and trembling before and while drinking the cup of suffering, His prayers and supplications: "O My Father, if it be possible, let this cup pass from Me," can be harmonized psychologically with His perfect faith and obedience. Nowhere is our knowledge as inadequate as in the field of psychology. "I the Lord search the heart, I try the reins" (Jer. 17:10; Ps. 7:10 [9]). This Servant is a true man, fraught with man's weakness, but also more than a man!

The next clause presents difficulties. *mishpāṭī* does not have the same meaning as *mishpāṭ* in 42:1,3,4. It does not have the New Testament meaning of right, justice, teaching, Gospel. The suffix shows that this right is a personal prerogative of the Servant. *mishpāṭī* is parallel to *pe'ullāthī,* a word that means something like "my doing" or "my work." Cf. 40:10. *pe'ullāh* is something that has been earned or acquired, the fruit and reward of labor, cf. especially 61:8; Leviticus 19:13; Proverbs 10:16 and 11:18. And so

355

pe'ullāthī 'eth 'elōhāy means: "the outcome and success of My labor is with God." The antithesis requires this interpretation. The Servant feared that He would labor in vain and accomplish nothing, but at the same time knew that the success of His labor depended upon His God. *mishpāṭ* will then mean something similar, since it is part of the same antithesis. It cannot be allowed that *lerīq yāgha'tī* can mean something essentially different from *lethōhū wehebhel kōḥī killēythī*, and that *mishpāṭī* applies to one of the terms, and *pe'ullāthī* to the other in separate antitheses. To whichever of the preceding clauses one refers *mishpāṭī*, it always expresses an antithesis to the thought in "I labor in vain," or "I spend My strength to no purpose," and it must be translated accordingly. We prefer the parallel arrangement and connect the third clause with the first, and the fourth with the second, so that the antithesis to *mishpāṭī* lies in "I labor in vain." *mishpāṭī 'eth YHWH* can thus have no other meaning than: "My labor is not in vain." If we ask which of the many related meanings of *mishpāṭ* is best suited to the phrase "with the Lord," a consideration of the parallelism and of the antithesis leads us to some such translation as Luther's "*meine Sache*," in the sense of "My just cause," or "case," that is, the matter, or action, that has been assigned to Me, that I have been entrusted with, and that I therefore represent. In this sense we find *mishpāṭī* used, for example, in Psalm 9:5(4) and Micah 7:9. In this passage, because of the context, which deals with the Servant's calling, the word acquires the meaning of a cause directly connected with an office or calling. The Servant of the Lord is saying: I thought that I labored in vain; but that is not possible, because the cause that was assigned to Me is not Mine, but the Lord's, and the success of My labors lie in His almighty hand.

There remains the question of the relation of the two halves of the sentence to each other. *'ākhēn* is an adversative particle: but surely, however. The question is, does *'ākhēn* introduce a dependent or an independent clause? We take the clause beginning with *'ākhēn* to be dependent. Not this clause, but verse 5 contains the antithesis to 4a. That is evidenced even by the outward form: *wa'anī* in verse 4 and *we'attāh* at the beginning of verse 5; *'anī 'āmartī* is matched by *'āmar YHWH.* So the meaning must be: "I did indeed think — but now the Lord says." In respect to the contents too, the answer to 4a does not come until verse 5. That makes 4b subordinate to 4a. That's why we consider Luther's interpretation to be the correct one: *Wiewohl meine Sache des Herrn ist* ("although My cause is with the Lord"). Verse 4b is an adverbial clause introduced by the strongly adversative particle *'ākhēn* in place of the usual adversative *we*, Gr. 141, e, p. 453. And so we translate: "even though, in spite of the fact that My cause, etc. — But now the Lord says, etc." The Servant is assailed by the fear that He is laboring in vain and to no purpose, in spite of the consciousness that He is doing the Lord's work. Another possibility is that the clause beginning with *'ākhēn* is to be considered a parenthesis.

$$^5\ \text{וְעַתָּה ׀ אָמַר יְהוָה֙ יֹצְרִי מִבֶּ֙טֶן֙ לְעֶ֣בֶד ל֔וֹ}$$

$$\text{לְשׁוֹבֵ֤ב יַֽעֲקֹב֙ אֵלָ֔יו וְיִשְׂרָאֵ֖ל לֹ֣א יֵאָסֵ֑ף}$$

$$\text{וְאֶכָּבֵד֙ בְּעֵינֵ֣י יְהוָ֔ה וֵאלֹהַ֖י הָיָ֥ה עֻזִּֽי ׃}$$

The *we* in *we 'attāh*, equal in emphasis with *wa* in *wa 'anī* (verse 4), is to be translated "but." The disjunctive accent (*Munach cum Paseq*) in *we 'attāh* emphasizes the antithesis: "Now, however, this is how the matter lies." The clause beginning with *yōtserī*, followed by an infinitive, two imperfects, and a perfect, offers proof and assurance for the *'āmar YHWH*. The Lord's declaration is based on the fact that He prepared the Servant of the Lord from His mother's womb to be the Servant who is to carry out the work described in verse 6. The preparation of the Servant guarantees the fulfillment of the Lord's word. It is not in vain that the Lord has prepared His Servant from His mother's womb; His purposes and His counsels cannot be thwarted. The purpose of preparing His Servant is twofold: "to lead Jacob back to Him" and "to gather Israel together to Him." The arrangement of the members is chiastic. The Qere *lō* is to be preferred to the Kethib *lō'*.* For the construction of an infinitive with a following imperfect, see Gr. 114,r,p. 352. The repatriation of Jacob and the gathering of Israel, both to be understood in the spiritual sense, is one purpose of preparing His Servant. The second purpose follows in the next clause: "So that I shall be honored in the eyes of the Lord and the Lord become My strength." These clauses, like the one beginning with *leshōbhēbh*, are dependent on *yōtserī mibbeṭen le 'ebhedh lō*, and are parallel to it. The *Waw* links *'ekkābhēdh* with *yē 'āsēph* and both words are part of the grammatical construction described in Gr. 114,r,p. 352, whereas the perfect *hāyāh* is under the influence of the *Waw* in *wē 'lōhay*, which has the effect of a *Waw* consecutive and gives *hāyāh* the force of an imperfect.

---

*The Dead Sea Scrolls read *lō*.

Thus we have here the statement that the purpose of preparing the Servant is twofold: 1. to convert Israel, and 2. to honor the Servant. That the honor of the Servant is the Lord's purpose in saving Israel and the gentiles becomes apparent in verse 7 and then especially in chapter 53. The final clause, "and the Lord become My strength," is to be taken in the sense of verse 8; 42:6; 50:7-9, and in relation to verse 4a and 42:4, namely, as an object secondary to the main purpose. It cannot be denied that the syntax of the whole clause beginning with *we'ekkābhēdh* permits it to be understood as a parenthesis — "For I am honored in the eyes of the Lord and My God is My strength." That is the interpretation of Delitzsch and others. Delitzsch also explains "My God is My strength" as "My God is the object of My praises." That seems farfetched. Even when this clause is taken as a parenthesis, it says clearly that in the eyes of the Lord the Servant is fully prepared for His mission and that He was made fit for this work through the Lord's strength.

6 וַיֹּאמֶר נָקֵל מִהְיוֹתְךָ לִי עֶבֶד לְהָקִים אֶת־שִׁבְטֵי יַעֲקֹב
וּנְצִירֵי יִשְׂרָאֵל לְהָשִׁיב וּנְתַתִּיךָ לְאוֹר גּוֹיִם
לִהְיוֹת יְשׁוּעָתִי עַד־קְצֵה הָאָרֶץ:

wayyō'mer continues and emphasizes the *'amar* of verse 5. *nāqēl* (*qālal*) is an alternate form of *nāqal*, a Niphal perfect, Gr. 67,t,p. 181. *min* with the infinitive *heyōthekhā* is the sign of the comparative, Gr. 133,c, p. 430: "it is too little that You should be a Servant to Me, etc." The infinitives *hāqīm* and *hāshībh* are dependent on the preceding clause and express purpose. *hāshībh* is preceded by its accusative object, Gr. 115,a,p. 352. The apodosis begins with *ūnethattīkhā.* The *ū* introduces a contrast to *nāqēl*. *lihyōth* also expresses purpose. *yeshū'āthī* is an abstract designation of a person, a more emphatic equivalent of "My Savior." What was stated in 42:4,6 is repeated here and confirmed. The Servant of the Lord is ordained first of all to serve the chosen people of God. That is repeatedly emphasized in the New Testament; Jesus is the Savior of the Jews, Matthew 1:21; Luke 1:68f; 2:34; Acts 2:39; 3:26; 13:26, 46, 47; Romans 1:16, etc., etc. The Lord even speaks as though He had been sent exclusively for the Jews, Matthew 15:24. The reason for that is to be found in the special election and promise given to Abraham, Isaac, Jacob, and their seed, Romans 15:8ff, a promise of which the gentiles could not boast. They praise God solely because of His grace. The object of *lehāqīm*, to restore, is *shibhṭey ya'aqōbh*, the tribes of Jacob. The parallel to this phrase is *netsīrey yisrā'el*, according to the Kethib. The Qere substitutes *net-sūrey*, the Qal passive participle. *netsīrey* would be a construct plural of an otherwise unknown adjective *nātsīr*, which is usually explained as a derivative of *nātsar*, and translated "preserved" or "a survivor." The Qere suggestion was no doubt made on the assumption that there is no adjective like *nātsīr*, whereas *nātsūr*, in its simple form and with endings, is common, cf. 1:8.* Others explain the form as a construct plural of *nētser*, a shoot, branch, or sprout, Isaiah 11:1; 14:19; 60:21; Daniel 11:7, and read *nitsrēy*, with omission of the *Yod*. The parallelism with *shibhṭey* makes this reading seem plausible. The choice is difficult. One might prefer *nitsrēy*, if one did not have to take *lehāshībh* into account. The verb "to lead back, or return" presupposes some such object as people who had been carried off or expelled (11:12; 56:8). And so it seems reasonable, according to Isaiah 1:8 (*'īr netsūrāh*, a besieged city), to translate *netsūrey* with "imprisoned people," especially since verse 9 of this chapter also speaks of prisoners. Cf. also 48:6 and 65:4. But in Ezekiel 6:12 *nātsūr*, paired with *nish'ar*, clearly refers to one who has been preserved, who has been saved from death. This meaning fits very well with *lehāshībh*: "to return those who have been preserved from destruction who have survived." In fact, this is the meaning that is quite generally accepted. Furthermore, the idea of the remnant of those providentially preserved throughout this period of judgment and who later repent, an idea which permeates the entire first part of Isaiah (4:1,2; 6:13; 7:3; 10:20-23; 11:10-12, etc.), fairly demands such an interpretation, especially since the idea occurs in the same connection in 11:10-12. Figuratively the thought is that the Servant shall lead those back into the homeland who survived the destruction of land and city and also of the exile, cf. 35:10. In the first clause, *hāqīm* and *shibhṭey ya'aqōbh* bear the same relation to each other. The tribes of Israel are of course meant (Matth. 19:28; James 1:1). The picture is that of a staff or branch or stalk that has been broken. In the transferred sense of a stock, branch, or tribe, the picture is that of a tribe broken up and scattered, and hence degenerate. The Servant is to raise these up (*hēqīm*),

---

*The Dead Sea Scrolls read *netsīrey*.

restore them. Literally, the passage speaks of the restoration of the people of Israel that have been almost destroyed by the exile. That is the Servant's actual mission. The Holy Spirit's purpose is, however, the restoration out of the exile of the degenerate church in Israel, which in the New Testament is to be inaugurated by Christ and the Apostles, and then implemented until the consummation of the Last Day. The part played by Zerubbabel-Jeshua and Ezra-Nehemiah in the restoration of the people is hardly worth mentioning; that physical restoration served only to make possible the spiritual restoration set in motion by Christ. We have here a New Testament prophecy clothed in Old Testament forms, having the same physical and incidental characteristics found, for example, in such mighty prophecies as 53:4 (cf. Matt. 8:17) or 35:5ff (cf. Matt. 11:5), etc. One would have to close one's eyes deliberately not to see in this passage, especially when comparing it with parallel passages, the conversion of "the Remnant of Israel."

The high point of the message of verse 6 lies in the second half. The Servant is to accomplish more than just the deliverance of Israel. The Lord made Him to be a Light unto the gentiles to bring His salvation to the ends of the earth. Cf. 2:2ff; 9:1ff; 11:10; 25:6ff; 42:1ff, etc. This is that mighty prophecy, already contained in Noah's blessing, in the promise to Abraham, and which was confirmed to David and Solomon, repeated and expanded by nearly every prophet, but especially by Isaiah, that the gentiles should be received into the kingdom of God. This prophecy is the basis of the mission command of the risen Savior (Matt. 28; Mark 16) who gave His Gospel to us of the gentile world. This is the promise in which Paul found support for his mission and on which he based his majestic hymn, the Epistle to the Ephesians. Those who could not claim citizenship in Israel, who were aliens to the testaments of promise, who were without Christ, without God, and without hope, have now been brought near through the blood of Christ. Since peace has been proclaimed to them, they are no longer guests and strangers but fellow citizens with the saints and members of the household of God. To appreciate the magnitude of this grace, one must understand Romans 1:18ff.

There are two points about this mystery that must be noted. The gentiles are not an independent class of citizens in the kingdom of God, alongside the Jews, but such who have been incorporated into that citizenship which belongs to Israel by promise. In God's spiritual kingdom Israel is also God's firstborn, possessing all the rights of the firstborn. The church of the gentiles dare never forget that. The second point is that there is now no distinction between Jew and Greek, circumcision and uncircumcision, barbarian and Scythian, slave and free, for they all have the one Lord, who is generous to all who call upon Him, Christ who is our all and in us all, Colossians 3:11; Romans 10:12. We gentiles who believe are naturalized citizens in God's kingdom; the believing Jews are natives. That fact should guard us against pride, Romans 11. However, we are not for that reason treated like second-class citizens, as would be the case in earthly kingdoms. It is of great comfort to us that we are Abraham's spiritual seed, and that all the promises apply to us that were given to him. The Servant of the Lord here receives the promise that it is the will of the Lord to make Him the Light of the gentiles. Whether one takes *nethattīkhā* to be a present perfect expressing an action as completed in the past and still effective in the present, or as a prophetic perfect, the result is the same. The mission given to the Servant will be carried out in the future. This picture of the Servant of the Lord as the Light of the gentiles is developed further, with a somewhat different twist, in 60:1ff. In that passage it is the Lord Himself, respectively His "glory," which has risen over Zion and to which the nations come. But the sense is the same. The Servant of the Lord is the embodied *kebhōdh YHWH*, the glory of the Lord in person. *'ōr*, light, is in general a figurative expression for salvation, as *ḥōshekh*, darkness, signifies woe. *'ōr* is in this passage parallel to *yeshū'āthī*. But the context (verse 2) and parallel passages (42:1,2, and especially 7) clearly indicate that our passage, in particular, refers to salvation through spiritual enlightening by means of the Servant's preaching of the Word, the Gospel, which, of course, presupposes repentance (cf. Acts 26:18; Eph. 1:18, etc.). *yeshū'āthī* is an abstract term designating a person, like *'ōr gōyim*. Only unbelief would question this obvious fact. *'adh qetsēh hā'ārets* makes the entire world the scope of the preaching of salvation (Matt. 28 and Mark 16). — Christ, the Servant of the Lord, chosen from eternity and called from His mother's womb (Acts 2:22,23,36), is the Savior, not only of the Jews but also of the gentiles — that is the substance of this strophe.

Second Strophe: verses 7-13: *The Lord Himself will vindicate the honor of His despised Servant, and will make Him the Mediator of His covenant and the Savior of His people.*

361

7 Thus says the Lord, the Savior of Israel, his Holy One,
   To Him who is despised, abhorred of the people,
      the slave of tyrants:
   Kings shall see Him and rise up,
   Princes — and fall down before Him,
   Because of the Lord, who holds faith (toward You),
   Because of the Holy One of Israel, who has chosen You.

8 Thus says the Lord: In the time of favor I will answer You,
   And help You in the day of salvation,
   I will protect You and set You to be a covenant
      of the people,
   To restore the land, and to allot the ruined heritages.

9 To say to the prisoners: Go forth!
   And to those in darkness: Appear!
   They shall feed along the ways,
   And on all the heights shall their pasture be.

10 They shall not hunger, nor shall they thirst,
   Desert wind and burning sun shall not fell them,
   For He who has mercy on them will lead them
   And guide them by springs of water.

11 I will make all My mountains a road
   And My highways shall be raised up.

12 Behold, these come from afar,
   And look, those from the north and from the west,
   And those from the land of Sinim.

13 Heavens, rejoice, and exult, O earth;
   The hills break forth in rejoicing!
   For the Lord has revived His people,
   And He has mercy on His afflicted ones.

כֹּה אָמַר־יְהוָה גֹּאֵל יִשְׂרָאֵל קְדוֹשׁוֹ ⁷
לִבְזֹה־נֶפֶשׁ לִמְתָעֵב גּוֹי לְעֶבֶד מֹשְׁלִים
מְלָכִים יִרְאוּ וָקָמוּ שָׂרִים וְיִשְׁתַּחֲוֻוּ
לְמַעַן יְהוָה אֲשֶׁר נֶאֱמָן קְדֹשׁ יִשְׂרָאֵל וַיִּבְחָרֶךָ׃

Even as the Servant of the Lord came forward dramatically in verse 1, so here in verse 7 the Lord Himself appears unheralded on the scene as the speaker. *kōh 'amar* and the words that follow are the Lord's words. He is answering the discourse of the Servant. The Servant's words expressed a faith sorely tried but recovering its strength; here we have the answer, one that breaks forth in rejoicing. Verses 7 and 8 both begin with *kōh 'amar YHWH*, with assurance of the highest support, followed by two emotionally expressive appositions, "the Redeemer of Israel" and "His Holy One." These, together with *kōh 'amar YHWH,* contain the basis for the following promise and the assurance that it will be fulfilled. For its fulfillment, the Lord pledges His honor as the Redeemer of Israel, 42:8, and as Israel's zealous defender against all enemies (cf. remarks to 40:25 and 41:14). The following attributes describe the lot that has become the Servant's portion. They explain why the Servant could have been assailed by the thought that He was laboring in vain. He was received with ill-will, John 1:11; Isaiah 53:1-3. He was despised, an abomination to the people, a slave of tyrants. *bezōh nephesh* is a form that has not yet been satisfactorily explained. It is a *status constructus* with a following genitive. The verb *bāzāh* means to despise. A simple explanation would assume *bāzōh* to be a verbal adjective with volatile Qamets, meaning "contemptible." Some, however, understand the genitive as objective and arrive at the meaning "contemptible" as regards the soul or life, not worth living. Others take the genitive as subjective and arrive at the meaning "despised by (every) soul." Still others explain the form as a pure infinitive construct in the not unusual abbreviated form of *bezōh* for *bezōth.* Some make it a Qal passive participle and read *bezūy,* as in Psalm 22:7(6); while yet others suggest *nibhzeh,* a Niphal participle.* All that can be stated is that the first of these explanations is the most acceptable one. *nephesh* need not be translated. One cannot go wrong with the "despised" of Isaiah 53:3.

The second descriptive phrase is also not wholly clear. *methā'ebh* is a form of the verb *tā'abh,* which means "to be abhorred." In the Piel the meaning is "to abhor"; the Niphal meaning is "to act as an abomination" or "to be considered an abomination." The noun *tō'ebhāh,* an abomination, occurs in 1:13; 41:24; 44:19. That is all that is known about the word. If one takes *methā'ebh* to be a Piel participle with the meaning of a noun in the construct state, the result, even though one takes the genitive of *gōy* as objective, does not make sense: "the one who considers the people an abomination, or makes them that." It is erroneous to translate: "one who fills the people with abhorrence," because such a translation does not give the verb a causative meaning, since the regular Piel meaning is already causative. *tā'abh* or *tā'ebh* is an intransitive verb, which in the Piel naturally becomes transitive and causative. Only one possible explanation of this

---

*The Dead Sea Scrolls read *libezūy.*

form remains: the Piel intensifies the intransitive meaning of the Qal, and the participle *methā'ebh* is a substantive with an abstract meaning — an abomination, an abhorrence, cf. Gr. 85,e,ff, especially m, p. 236f. In passing, let it be said here, that we do not consider the grammars correct that derive the preformative *Mem* from *mī* or *māh*. The preformative *Mem* with certain participles and nouns is exactly like the German *ge*, as in *Gesetz, Gebluet, gekommen, geschlagen*, etc.; or the Latin *con, cum*, the Greek σύν and the English *con, com*. It is an intensive preformative and is therefore found only in those participles in Hebrew that are intensive in meaning: Piel, Pual, Hiphil, Hophal. *methā'ebh* as a noun means "an abomination," an "abhorred thing," so that *methā'ebh gōy* is an abhorrence of the people, that is, one whom the people abhor. *gōy* is not a people as a political body or a nation, but here designates people in general — men.

'ebhedh and *mōshelīm* are here both used in a deprecatory sense, treated by tyrants like a slave. *methā'ebh gōy* and *'ebhedh mōshelīm* are both concepts underlying *bezōh nephesh*, and like the following clauses, are further elucidated in 52:14,15 and chapter 53. Even here, this description of the Servant calls to mind the shame and the suffering of the Lord, the wild mob, the chiefs and leaders of the people, in addition to Pilate and Herod. *melākhīm yir'ū waqāmū* is an example of a common Hebrew construction — a coordination of verbs, of which the first is in reality subordinate to the second: Kings will rise when they see Him. *yir'ū* must be supplied after *sārīm*, which accounts for the *we* with *yishtahawū* (a Hithpael of *shāhāh* with reduplication of the third radical, Gr. 75,kk,p.215). — *lema'an YHWH*, for the Lord's sake, can only mean that they must acknowledge that the Lord stands behind His Servant. The phrase points backward to the concluding words of verse 4 and also of verse 5; the concrete fulfillment of the implied promise is set forth in the next verses. *'asher* for *ya'an 'asher* is causal, Gr. 158,b,p. 492; likewise also the *wa* before *yibhharekkā* suggests that *ne'emān*, a Niphal participle of *'āman*, is not to be taken in its absolute sense, "because He is faithful," but rather with reference to the Servant, "who is faithful to You." The two clauses at the end of verse 7 are the Lord's answer to the trials and temptations experienced by the Servant and expressed by Him in 4a. *lema'an* must of course be repeated before *qedhōsh yisrā'el*. This is a more expressive phrase than the name *YHWH* alone. Jehovah is the faithful God of the covenant; *qedhōsh yisrā'el* is the zealous Defender of Israel against all enemies, called

the Redeemer at the beginning of the verse. The meaning of the assurance given in verse 7 is that the Lord because of the covenant He made with His people, a covenant which above all concerns the Servant of the Lord, the true Israel, will by no means suffer Him to be so shamefully mistreated. Because of His faithfulness and His great love toward Him, He will see to it that those who profane His honor will one day fall at His feet, Philippians 2:9-11. "The zeal of the Lord of hosts will perform this," 9:6(7); 37:32.

כֹּה ׀ אָמַ֣ר יְהֹוָ֗ה 8

בְּעֵ֤ת רָצוֹן֙ עֲנִיתִ֔יךָ וּבְי֥וֹם יְשׁוּעָ֖ה עֲזַרְתִּ֑יךָ

וְאֶצָּרְךָ֗ וְאֶתֶּנְךָ֙ לִבְרִ֣ית עָ֔ם

לְהָקִ֣ים אֶ֔רֶץ לְהַנְחִ֖יל נְחָל֥וֹת שֹׁמֵמֽוֹת׃

A new and important prophecy is heralded by the *kōh 'amar YHWH*. *kōh* has been set apart from the rest of the phrase by a Legarmeh. The lector was to read: *Thus* — saith the Lord. The scholars who supplied the accents intended to mark what follows as something especially significant. It is that. *'anīthīkhā* says that it is still the Lord's concern to give an answer to the troubled words of the Servant in 4a. It is His purpose to fill His Servant's heart with comfort and rejoicing. What He stated in verse 7 does not satisfy Him; He must guide Him even more deeply into the secret of His loving counsel. The two perfects, *'anīthīkhā* and *'azartīkhā*, are prophetic perfects, and the following imperfects state the factual, concrete fulfillment of God's counsel. *'eth rātsōn*, time of favor or good pleasure (cf. *shenath rātsōn*, 61:2), is a phrase taken from the ordinance of the Jubilee Year, Leviticus 25:8ff. Paul translated it καιρὸς δεκτός, which Luther rendered with *angenehme Zeit*, an acceptable time, and with *zur gnaedigen Zeit* in this passage, a time of grace. The acceptable time is the time the Lord has fixed for manifesting His grace and help, namely, the time of Christ, also called the fullness of time, Galatians 4:4. The *yōm yeshū'ah*, the day of help, refers specifically to that time. The word "day" is, of course, not to be understood literally, but the Lord leaves nothing to chance or to so-called natural selection and evolution. Just as He ordains and regulates even the smallest things, so He has also from eternity determined time and place for all things, down to the very hour, minute, and second, especially this the greatest event of all, the deliverance of His Servant, who

365

was humiliated even unto the death on the cross. For *'anah* in the sense of deliverance see Psalm 22:22(21). That deliverance could not possibly fail; it had to occur at the predetermined moment. Second Corinthians 6 properly applies this truth also to the church. *'etstsorkha* says that the Lord always, especially in the moment of critical danger, preserves His Servant against destruction. Such critical hours were the temptation in the wilderness, Gethsemane, and the hour when the Servant commended His spirit into the hands of the Father. The heart of this promise is contained in the phrase *we'ettenkha libhrith 'am*. To avoid repetition, we refer to what was said in connection with 42:6f. In that passage "covenant of the people" and "light of the gentiles" were paired and yet distinguished from each other. "Covenant" is (like "light" and "salvation" in verse 6, and "strength" in verse 5) an abstract term used to designate a person; the mediator and executor of the covenant is meant. *'am* refers first of all to believing Israel, and then also to all believers, including those from among the gentiles. *'am* is here the equivalent of *'ammi, 'am YHWH, 'am qadhosh*.

The next two clauses tell how the executor of the covenant will fulfill His mission. That is expressed in terms that have been borrowed from the physical restitution of the land of Israel. They are quite similar to the expressions used in verse 6. *'erets* is not the earth, but the land of Israel, and the *nehaloth shomemoth* are the devastated hereditary lands of the tribes of Jacob (verse 6), which Joshua once assigned to them by lot, Joshua 13ff. It is therefore clear, as was already indicated in verse 6, that the prophet is thinking not just of the tribe of Judah and the allied tribes of Simeon and Benjamin, but also of the tribes of the Northern Kingdom and its cities. The Servant is to restore and apportion the entire land and the inherited possessions of the tribes. Actually, this prophecy, insofar as it applied to the physical restoration of the land, was fulfilled only to a limited degree after the return from exile. But the physical restoration of the land is not the essence of this promise. The restitution of land and inheritance figuratively represents the restoration to the chosen ones of Israel of their spiritual inheritance in the kingdom of God covenanted to them in the blessing of Abraham. Consequently, the believers among the gentiles, also counted as being of the seed of Abraham, belong to this people (*'am*), and the promise also applies to them, since they are "fellow citizens with the saints and of the household of God" (Eph. 2:19). And the Servant of the Lord is the Son, who will open the kingdom of heaven to whomsoever He will, Matthew 11:27ff.

9 לֵאמֹר לַאֲסוּרִים צֵ֫אוּ לַאֲשֶׁר בַּחֹשֶׁךְ הִגָּלוּ
עַל־דְּרָכִים יִרְעוּ וּבְכָל־שְׁפָיִים מַרְעִיתָם׃

lē'mōr is the equivalent of the Latin gerundive, *dicendo*, Gr. 114, o, p. 351. The language employed here and in the following verses is the language suited to the conditions of the exile and refers back to the situation described in 42:22. (Cf. 42:7; 52:2ff.; 61:1.) That there is more than just mere similarity between the deliverance from Babylon and the redemption through Christ is indicated by the closely related parallels, 42:7 and 61:1, where the opening of the eyes, which is certainly meant spiritually (35:5; 9:2; 10:20ff), is mentioned in the same breath with deliverance from the prison. The deliverance out of exile and the return to the homeland are more than just the external fulfillment of the promise given to the people; they also are a picture and symbol of the deliverance from the power of Satan. "Those in darkness" are the *'asūrīm*, the prisoners, of 42:22. The Servant breaks their bonds and frees them from the prison-house through the preaching of the Word of His Gospel: "Go forth!" Gesenius beautifully renders the Niphal of *higgālū* with "Come to the light." In the second half of this verse and in the next verse, those who have been freed by the Servant are pictured as a flock returning home under the guidance of the Lord, while the Servant remains in the background. The liberated flock finds rich pasturage along otherwise desert roads and bare hills. Or, if one is minded to make an application: On the way to heaven they find spiritual nourishment in the midst of the vanities of this world that do not satisfy the soul, 55:1-3. Cf. John 6:48ff and 1 Corinthians 10:3,4. *mar'īth*, by the way, is not pasture, but the act of feeding.

10 לֹא יִרְעָבוּ וְלֹא יִצְמָאוּ וְלֹא־יַכֵּם שָׁרָב וָשָׁמֶשׁ
כִּי־מְרַחֲמָם יְנַהֲגֵם וְעַל־מַבּוּעֵי מַיִם יְנַהֲלֵם׃

The first two phrases are a continuation of the thought with which verse 9 closes. The next phrases introduce a new picture: protection against the burning desert sun. It is very doubtful whether the explanation of *sharābh*, based on the Arabic, as *fata morgana*, or mirage, is correct. The word occurs only here and in 35:7. In that passage, mirage seems to fit: "The mirage shall become a lake of water"; but Gesenius there translates (and Luther agrees): "The sea of sand shall become a lake; the thirsty land, springs of water." This passage he translates: "Neither *heat* nor sun shall smite." The translation *mirage* would be at variance with the verb "to smite." *hikkāh*, to smite, to strike down, sometimes even to kill, in no way describes the effects of a mirage, unless one assumes the use of a zeugma, a bold figure of speech. It seems beyond doubt that *shārābh* is derived from the same stem as *sāraph* (spelled with *Sin*), which means "to burn," a verb from which such nouns are formed as *serēphāh*, brand; *sāraph*, a fiery serpent; and *serāphīm*, the seraphim. Gesenius, in all likelihood, is correct in translating the word with "glowing heat." The use of *hikkāh* to describe the smiting of the sun or of the moon is familiar, Psalm 121:6. The two words, "heat" and "sun," are apparently to be understood as a hendiadys: "the sun's heat." If *shārābh* is to be taken in the sense of *mirage,* then the word would seem to have been chosen because of the torrid atmosphere that causes the reflection. It is interesting that the Koran (Sura 24:39) describes *shārābh* as a haze in the desert that the thirsty traveler takes to be water until he arrives at the spot and finds nothing. — The next two clauses give the reason for the five preceding clauses. "He who has mercy on them will lead them" applies to all five statements, whereas "guiding them by streams of water" refers only to protection against thirst and heat. The nominal participle *merahamām* is very loving and full of comfort. It depicts the mercy and pity of the Lord as continuing uninterruptedly, as a fixed and settled attitude on His part. For examples that illustrate this compassion of the Lord (σπλαγχνίζεσθαι in the New Testament), see Matthew 9:36; 14:14; 15:32. Compare also 54:10, Psalm 23, Psalm 121.

11 וְשַׂמְתִּי כָל־הָרַי לַדָּרֶךְ וּמְסִלֹּתַי יְרֻמְוּן׃

He will make the hills into highways by tearing them down and leveling them, 40:4. A *mesillāh* is a road that has been constructed to serve as a highway. *yerumūn* is the masculine form of the verb following a feminine subject, Gr. 145, u, p. 466. The final *Nun*, as in *yerumūn*, usually expresses marked emphasis. The Lord makes the road passable for His people who are returning home, in fact, fills the whole world with smooth highways, because His people who have been freed shall return home from all corners of the world.

12 הִנֵּה־אֵלֶּה מֵרָחוֹק יָבֹאוּ וְהִנֵּה־אֵלֶּה מִצָּפוֹן וּמִיָּם וְאֵלֶּה מֵאֶרֶץ סִינִים׃

hinnēh directs the beholder to a startling scene. The regions named here, from which the redeemed are returning, are clearly the four corners of the earth. Knobel remarks that "the sea, when it is mentioned as opposite to the north, is the south sea, as in Psalm 107:3." The regions are mentioned in chiastic form: north and south occupying the middle position, the far region and the land of the Sinim, the beginning and the end. The land of the *sīnīm* is perhaps China; nothing positive can be said about the name, cf. Genesis 10:17; Ezekiel 30:15. *raḥōq* must then be the west, as in 60:9. But *raḥōq* in many other cases refers to the east, and if that is the case here, then the *'erets sīnīm* must be a western, Mediterranean land. In any case, the redeemed of the Lord are returning from all corners of the world, back to Zion, cf. 43:5,6.

13 רָנּוּ שָׁמַ֫יִם֙ וְגִ֣ילִי אָ֔רֶץ יִפְצְח֥וּ הָרִ֖ים רִנָּ֑ה
כִּֽי־נִחַ֤ם יְהוָה֙ עַמּ֔וֹ וַעֲנִיָּ֖ו יְרַחֵֽם׃

Heaven and earth and all the hills are exhorted to break forth in rejoicing. As in the parallel passage, 44:23, *shāmayim* is a vocative without the article, Gr. 126,a,p. 404. The verbs are arranged in climactic order. In *yiphtseḥū* we have followed the reading of the Kethib, since the shift from second person to third person is nothing unusual in Isaiah. The Qere reads *ūphitseḥū rinnāh*, imperative, which is the usual form of this phrase. Literally, "open rejoicing wide," that is, "open the mouth wide in rejoicing." The second half of the sentence contains, in abstract form, the reason for the exhortation to all of nature to rejoice. It is an explanation and a summing up of verses 1-12. In the translation of *niham*, the Piel of *nāham*, to breathe heavily, we have not followed the usual translation: "The Lord has comforted." We feel that this translation does not do full justice to the sense. The lexicons have not yet listed all the nuances of this much-used word. The commonest meaning of the word is, without doubt, "to comfort," as for example, in 51:19; 61:2; 66:13; and at the very beginning, 40:1. But in 51:3 that meaning of the word is hardly suited to its object, or to the comparison. In 52:9, and even in 51:12, a somewhat different meaning seems to be required. *nāham*, in the physical sense, means "to breathe heavily." The Piel has a causative meaning: to cause heavy breathing, to restore the breath, to revive, to renew, and, in a transferred sense, to comfort, that is, to quiet or gladden someone with words of encouragement. In a similar way the Niphal arrives at its meaning: to let oneself be moved to compassion, to feel sorry for, to regret, to take revenge. So, it seems to us that here the meaning "to revive, to renew, to heal, to raise up again, to restore" (physically, in the sense of *heqīm*, verse 6), comes nearest to the intended meaning. Compare the remarks on 51:3. It is the synonym closest to *gā'al,* redeem, or ransom, 52:9. We believe that the translation here must be: "The Lord has healed, or restored again, His people." That translation is in accord with *yeraḥēm.* That word expresses not merely the feeling of compassion; it includes the practice of it, the concrete exercise of compassion. Whereas the perfect *niḥam* expresses an accomplished fact that has now become a fixed situation, the imperfect in *yeraḥēm* designates an act beginning in the present, continuing in the future, endlessly repeated.

It is the Lord's purpose to exalt this Servant whom He has chosen from eternity above all the kings of the earth by giving Him power to be the Savior of His people and of the gentiles. Those whom He has saved the Lord leads back to Zion and has unending compassion on them. That is the gist of this section.

The first part of the discourse dealt with the exaltation of the Servant of the Lord; in the second part the prophet portrays the corresponding exaltation of Zion, pictured as a mother.

Second Section: verses 14-26: *The faithfulness of God glorifies and exalts Zion when He leads to her the troops of children that were born to her in strange lands, when princes bow down before her, and when the "Giant" from whom the children have been rescued has received his punishment.*

This section is divided into two parts, one longer (verses 14-23) and one shorter (verses 24-26). The first part is divided into four subparts: 14-17; 18,19; 20,21; 22,23. This section is emotionally one of the most moving passages in Isaiah. The last clause in the preceding section *wa'aniyaw yeraḥēm,* He will have mercy on His poor people, is, in the manner of our prophet, here developed at length. How the Lord, in His sincere love and compassion, deals with His people in their distress, is set forth in this section. Every word is fraught with fervent compassion, which in the concluding verses gives way to an equally hot anger directed against Zion's oppressors.

First Half: verses 14-23: *The faithfulness of the Lord leads back to Zion all her lost children, and compels kings to bow down in homage before her.*

14 *But Zion says: The Lord has forsaken me,*
    And my Lord has forgotten me!
15 *Can a woman forget her little child,*
    To have no pity on the child of her womb?
    And even though she should forget,
    Yet will I not forget you.
16 *Behold, I have carved you in the palms of My hands,*
    Your walls are always before Me.
17 *Your children are coming (to you) in haste;*
    Those who destroyed and laid you waste, go forth from you.
18 *Lift up your eyes round about and see:*
    All these are coming to you in throngs.
    As I live, says the Lord,
    You shall put on all of them like an adornment,
    And gird yourself with them, like a bride.
19 *For your ruins, your waste places, and devastated land —*
    Now shall you be too narrow for your inhabitants,
    And those who swallowed you up shall be far away.
20 *They shall yet say in your ears,*
    The children of your barrenness: The place
       is too narrow for us,
    Make room for me, where I may dwell.
21 *Then shall you say in your heart:*
    Who has borne me these?
    For I was childless and barren,
    Rejected and deserted on the way;
    But these — who has reared them?
    Behold, I was left alone,
    Whence can these have come?
22 *Thus says the Lord God:*
    Behold, to the gentiles will I lift up My hand,
    And to the nations will I lift up My banner;
    So that they bring your sons to you in their bosom,
    And your daughters — they will be carried
       at their shoulders.
23 *Kings shall be your foster fathers,*
    And queens your nursing mothers.
    With faces to the ground they shall bow down before you
    And shall lick the dust of your feet.
    Then shall you know that I am the Lord,
    In whom none that trust in Me shall be put to shame.

14 וַתֹּאמֶר צִיּוֹן עֲזָבַנִי יְהוָה וַאדֹנָי שְׁכֵחָנִי׃

It is inconceivable how commentators can seriously identify
tsīyon in this verse and in verses 16-23 with the people lying cap-

tive in Babylon. The ruined city, Zion-Jerusalem, in the devastated land of Israel, together with its inhabitants, is being addressed here and in almost all other cases where these names are employed. Zion is described as the mother of an exiled people and as the spiritual bride of the Lord, as in chapters 54, 60, and 62, although that relation is not so clearly indicated here as in the other chapters. Evidence for that is the similarity in contents between this chapter (especially in the wording of verses 20, 21, and 22) and chapter 54, verses 5 and 6; and also the ardent tone of various expressions in the course of the address.

It is the ruined city with its few remaining inhabitants, the city that in Lamentations is described as afflicted and almost in despair, that utters the complaint in verse 14. The city is here the counterpart to the sorrowing Servant in verse 4, except that this is a much more dismal picture, the grief is more profound, the complaint more extreme, almost completely despairing. Zion speaks of the Lord as Jehovah, thus giving Him the name of her Covenant-God. She calls Him *'adhōnāy*, that is, my Lord, in the sense of Psalm 45:12(11), and Judges 19:26, and as Sarah addresses her spouse as *'adhonī*. *'adhōnāy* with the long Qamez is the conventional name for God, but in the final analysis, it still means "*my* Lord." The wife complains that she has been put out of the house by her lord and master, that her husband has forsaken and forgotten her. *'azābhanī* denotes physical separation; *shekhehanī*, banishment from thoughts and feelings. The Lord has not only separated Himself from her, but His love for her is dead. This is not godless talk, but the expression of the most severe trial of faith; it is the experience of hell in one's soul. — An external heightening of the effect is achieved by the chiastic arrangement of the members.

הֲתִשְׁכַּח אִשָּׁה עוּלָהּ מֵרַחֵם בֶּן־בִּטְנָהּ 15
גַּם־אֵלֶּה תִשְׁכַּחְנָה וְאָנֹכִי לֹא אֶשְׁכָּחֵךְ ׃

Without transition the prophet responds to the anguished cry of the despairing woman with the Lord's answer, which pours forth like a stream from the overflowing well of His compassion. The answer is given with unparalleled psychological insight and in strikingly poetic phrases. It begins with a rhetorical question and continues with the most fitting comparison that could possibly be found to describe such a situation — a mother's love. The answer then goes beyond this comparison to a climax that cannot be surpassed. The fifteenth verse is like a suddenly swelling stream that bursts through all dams and overflows its banks. The strophe grows longer. The wellspring of pity cannot be exhausted; it rises and rises, until it finally subsides in another tremendous burst of anger against those who brought this agony upon the beloved spouse. In all of secular literature, even in the Scriptures, there is not to be found another description of the fervent love of God for His children to match this one. Oh, if we could only taste even a drop from this measureless sea of God's burning love!

We cannot bring ourselves to make any change in Luther's seemingly inspired translation of this passage. Should Luther's *Kann auch ein Weib ihres Kindleins vergessen?* ("Is it possible that a woman should forget her little child?") be set aside for the prosaic *Vergisst etwa ein Weib ihres Saeuglings?* ("does a woman ever forget her sucking child?")? Or should Luther's *und ob sie desselben vergaesze* ("and even though she should forget it") yield to the prosaic, literal translation *und ob diese* (plural!) *vergaeszen* ("and even if these should forget")? The plural in this clause indicates no more than that *'ishshāh* is used in the generic sense. We challenge anyone to translate this verse more precisely, in better German, or more poetically, than Luther has done. The question "Is it possible?" is fully expressed in *hathishkaḥ.* The poet uses "woman" instead of "mother," because the mother concept is already contained in *ūlāh* "her sucking child." Thus an unpoetic repetition is avoided. Moreover, the expression *'em benāh* "a mother her son" instead of the *'ishshāh ūlāh* of the text would not have brought out the element of ardent love and tenderness that is here the prophet's intention. Mother love is most tender, warm, and heartfelt toward the baby, the sucking child. For that reason the prophet does not employ the picture of a father's love, which is used in many other places, 63:16; Psalm 103:13, etc. Cool, calculating reason may enter into a father's love. A pure, warm, and tender love, uninhibited by calculation, must usually be sought in the woman and mother. This mother love has its physical basis in *ben biṭnāh,* just as all love rests upon some unity that brings together a separated subject and object. A child is a thousand times more the flesh and blood and soul of the mother than of the father. She *cannot* tear her child out of her heart; and if compassion is required, then she *must* show compassion. The prophet simply accepts a moral necessity. Nor does he in the following words surrender this inevitability. It would be grammatically incorrect to translate: "even these will forget." *gam* is here as much

as *gam kī*, even if, even though, Gr. 160,b,p. 498. The verb is
strictly potential: and even if she should, assuming that she could,
forget. See Gr. 107, r, p. 318, especially in conditional clauses, p.
319,x,5. This holds true notwithstanding cases such as Lamentations 4:10. Those were unnatural exceptions occasioned by inhuman need; the prophet here speaks of the inherent nature of a
mother's heart. The clause is simply the expression of an assumed
possibility. Theoretically there is such a possibility, and the force
of the following clause rests on that possibility. The *we* before
'anōkhī is adversative, and as a conjunction it also belongs to the
verb. *'anōkhī*, a stronger form of *'anī*, emphasizes the person —
Yet, will *I* still not forget you, even though there were a possibility
of a mother forgetting. As the auxiliary "can" was latent in
tishkaḥ and *tishkaḥnāh*, so here also in *'eshkaḥ*: I cannot forget
you. This is morally a total impossibility.

16 הֵן עַל־כַּפַּיִם חַקֹּתִיךְ   חוֹמֹתַיִךְ נֶגְדִּי תָּמִיד׃

The expression, "to carve in the palms of the hands," has its origin in a custom still widely observed in the Orient of tattooing
various parts of the body to indicate dedication to a god, or to a
person, or even to a dead person. Cf. Exodus 13:9,16; Leviticus
19:27f; Deuteronomy 6:8; 11:18; 14:1. Thus, in a certain respect,
such marking was forbidden. See also Galatians 6:17; Revelation
13:16ff; 14:9,11; 15:2; 16:2; 19:20; 20:4. Tattooing, especially of the
wrist, is said to have been customary among worshipers of the
Syrian Astarte. Prohibition of the practice is not a bar to the use of
pictures. The custom was prohibited insofar as it lent support to
superstition and idol worship and turned the heart away from
God. In the present instance the picture seems clearly to be that of
a man inscribing the name or symbol of a loved one in his hand.
Zion is pictured as a city, and it is Zion's image that the Lord has
inscribed in the palm of His hand. When the Lord looks into His
hands, the walls of Jerusalem lie before His eyes, which means
that the Lord's thoughts are directed always toward Zion and that
His heart is concerned wholly with her welfare. The one object of a
young lover's thoughts, feelings, and desires is the loved one! This
is not sentimental talk, it is truest truth and most real reality. God
is love. God *so* loved the world. God has one supreme thought: the
consummation of the mystery, which is Christ and His bride, and
the exaltation of both, chapters 54, 61, 62, Ephesians 5, all of
Ephesians and Colossians, Revelation 21 and 22, the new

Jerusalem, the Bride. All of God's purposes and plans, His rule and control of the history of the world, serve to bring about the realization and consummation of this mystery. There is no need to debate whether the walls of Jerusalem in ruins or the walls in their ideal form are meant, because the two conditions are inseparably bound together. At the moment the walls lie in ruins before Him. But from eternity God has had compassion with us in our wretchedness, and from eternity His pity is directed toward our salvation. Chapter 54:11ff must be fulfilled. If one could but fully grasp the Lord's thoughts of love toward us! For that love with which the heart of the Lord burns toward His Church is love for me, for you!

$$^{17} \text{מִהֲרוּ בָּנָיִךְ מְהָרְסַיִךְ וּמַחֲרִבַיִךְ מִמֵּךְ יֵצֵאוּ:}$$

How the Lord restores the *'anīyah,* the *sō'arah,* the *lōʾ nuḥamah* of 54:11 and makes them to be a *tehillah,* an object of praise in earth (62:7) is stated here as a theme and described fully in the following verses. *miharū* is a prophetic perfect, and poetically the word pictures the children running as though they could not come quickly enough to save their mother from her pitiable state and to exalt her. Luther, following the Vulgate and the LXX, read *bōnāyikh* instead of *bānāyikh,* "your builders" instead of "your children."* But it is the *children* who are pictured as builders, and that needs to be expressed. And as her own children rush to her side as builders, the former *meḥāresīm* and *maḥaribhīm* (Hiphil participle of *ḥārēbh*) take to their heels.

$$^{18} \text{שְׂאִי־סָבִיב עֵינַיִךְ וּרְאִי כֻּלָּם נִקְבְּצוּ בָאוּ־לָךְ}$$
$$\text{חַי־אָנִי נְאֻם־יְהוָה כִּי כֻלָּם כָּעֲדִי תִלְבָּשִׁי וּתְקַשְּׁרִים}$$
$$\text{כַּכַּלָּה:}$$

To the mother, who in her misery and grief sits staring hopelessly before her, comes the Lord's comforting call to lift up her eyes and look round about her. The connection of the adverb *sābhibh* with *seʾī* instead of with *reʾī* is perhaps to be explained by the Oriental's more vivid perception, which is more true to nature than ours is. We would be more likely to omit *seʾī* altogether. The Lord directs her attention to something that still lies in the future, but is so certain that it is pictured as happening at this very mo-

---

*The Dead Sea Scrolls read *bōnayikh.*

ment before her eyes — they are all gathering together, they are coming to you. "They all" refers, of course, to her children, verse 17. Luther combined the two verbs into a single concept, "they come gathered to you." We have rendered the Niphal *niqbetsū* with an adverbial phrase "in throngs." That is the intended meaning. Not scattered, not singly, but in troops, as though by agreement, under God's direction, led by the same impulse of love toward their mother, at the same moment, from all directions they come to her as their common focus and goal. In the certainty that this vision of the returning children is already beginning to banish the shades of dull despair from the heart of the so dearly loved one, the heart of the Lord too beats with stronger feeling. He binds Himself with an oath, to make her all the more sure and to hasten her happiness, and shows her what great glory is contained for her in this spectacle of returning children. "As I live, says the Lord, you shall put on all of them like an adornment, and gird yourself with them, like a bride." Cf. 61:10. *ḥay 'anī* is the usual oath formula, literally "living I." See the remarks on 45:23. In this formula, *'anī* always has the long *a*, not only in pausal forms, but also with lesser disjunctive accents, and even with conjunctives Merkha and Munach, Gr. 32, c, p. 105f. *kī* is used after the oath formula in place of the usual *'im lo'*. Phrases suggesting the finery of a bride's wardrobe are employed, because a woman's children are her chief honor, pride, and joy. The unnatural, deliberate childlessness of our day is a shame to the female sex.

$$\text{19} \quad \text{כִּי חָרְבֹתַ֙יִךְ֙ וְשֹׁמְמֹתַ֔יִךְ וְאֶ֖רֶץ הֲרִסֻתֵ֑יךְ}$$
$$\text{כִּ֤י עַתָּה֙ תֵּצְרִ֣י מִיּוֹשֵׁ֔ב וְרָחֲק֖וּ מְבַלְּעָֽיִךְ׃}$$

In verse 19 the Lord turns His attention to the land that had been devastated by the enemies and since then had lain waste, and to the ruins of Jerusalem and the other cities. *'erets harisuthēkh*, the land of your ravishment, your ravished land, is like *har qodhshī, 'ir qodhshī, shēm qodhshī*, Gr. 135,n,p. 440. *kī* at the beginning of this sentence is hardly substantiation of the preceding sentence, rather the three *kī* following the oath all belong to the same construction and introduce three objective clauses. *'attāh* introduces a sharp contrast. While the land lay waste and devastated, the inhabitants were few (cf. 7:21-25); but now there shall be so many inhabitants that they are pressed for room. For a discussion of the construction of this sentence — three impersonal nouns and a personal subject of the verb — see Gr. 144,1, p. 461. It is, however, also possible to construe the impersonal nouns as accusatives of reference: "as regards your ruins, etc." For *tsar min* see Gr. 133,c,p. 430. The form *tētserī* is an imperfect of *tsar* or *tsārar*, Gr. 67,p,p. 180. The sense is: "you shall be too confined for all your inhabitants" (a collective noun!). *mebhalle'ayikh* is a Piel participle of *bala'*, to swallow up. The destroyers of the land shall be forced out by the troops of children that shall flock to Jerusalem.

עוֹד יֹאמְרוּ בְאָזְנַיִךְ בְּנֵי שִׁכֻּלָיִךְ 20
צַר־לִי הַמָּקוֹם גְּשָׁה־לִּי וְאֵשֵׁבָה:

Verse 20 projects the same thought into the future. *'odh* (literally, repetition, continuation) is therefore to be translated: "it will yet come to pass that, etc." *be'oznayikh* does not here refer to quiet, secret whispering in one's ear, but means "before your ears," so that she must hear it, not just occasionally, but as an often repeated unpleasing discussion of the difficult problem of the lack of *Lebensraum*. "The children of your barrenness" are those who were produced by Jerusalem during the time of her barrenness, that is, during the time when she had been put out of the house and exposed by her husband to the destructive power of her enemies, the time of the exile. All other explanations are artificial and farfetched. The phrasing of the passage rests on the assumption that the spiritual marriage between the Lord and Zion has continued to exist. The Lord had not, as Zion had supposed, dissolved that marriage when He delivered Zion into the hands of the gentiles (verse 14); He had merely suspended the relation for a time. Since the office of king, and of priest, and to some extent also the office of prophet were no longer functioning, the Lord was in that respect no longer spiritually her spouse; she was *de facto* put out of the house, was shut out by her husband, was widowed, and therefore barren (cf. verse 21 and chapter 54). That is the meaning of *shikkulīm*.

tsar is a Qal perfect of *tsārar* in the intransitive sense of that verb. *geshāh* is the imperative (*gash*) of *nāghash*, with a paragogic *āh*. Gr. 66,c,p. 173. *lī* is best construed as a *dativus commodi*, Gr. 119,s,p. 381, and so she is to be understood as saying: "Make room for me." The prefix *we* with *'eshēbhāh* is final or consecutive, Gr. 165, and 166,p. 503f. The form is an imperfect Qal of *yāshabh* with paragogic *āh*.

21 וְאָמַ֣רְתְּ בִּלְבָבֵ֔ךְ מִ֣י יָֽלַד־לִ֣י אֶת־אֵ֗לֶּה
וַאֲנִ֤י שְׁכוּלָה֙ וְגַלְמוּדָ֔ה גֹּלָ֣ה ׀ וְסוּרָ֔ה וְאֵ֖לֶּה מִ֣י גִדֵּ֑ל
הֵ֤ן אֲנִי֙ נִשְׁאַ֣רְתִּי לְבַדִּ֔י אֵ֖לֶּה אֵיפֹ֥ה הֵֽם׃

Zion, the mother, who had been speechless with joy and wonder at sight of the thronging crowds of her children (the departing enemies are no longer in evidence), now regains her tongue. She asks herself: Who can have borne these for me? *yāladh* is used in Genesis, in the poetic books, and in Isaiah 65:23 of the father as well as of the mother; and if one translates it here with "beget," one should keep in mind that Zion does not at all think of herself as having borne these children. In the following she stresses the fact that she did not bear them and could not have borne them. The Lord is, of course, assumed to be the bearer of them. She is really asking who can have been the mother of these children of hers. Situations like those in the case of Abraham (Hagar) and of Jacob (the handmaids) are presupposed. The prefix *we* with *'ani* introduces a circumstantial noun-clause, in the sense of "I having been left alone," Gr. 156, p. 489. Four successive expressions from the mouth of the mother, a pair of adjectives followed without connecting link by a pair of participles, strongly emphasize her barrenness. *shekhūlāh*, childless, and *galmūdhāh* (perhaps borrowed from the Arabic), barren, are the adjectives. *gōlāh*, rejected, is an active participle; *sūrāh*, deserted, left by the wayside (from *sūr*, to turn aside) is passive in meaning. The two adjectives describe her condition of being childless and barren, while the two participles supply the reason for that condition — she had been put aside by her husband. Because her children come to her fully grown, she asks: "Who reared these for me?" And because she still has not recovered from her joyous amazement, she repeats the thought: "Behold, I was left alone, by myself (*lebhaddī*; these, where were they? Whence can these have come?" For the sake of variety and vividness, the question is added without a conjunction.

22 כֹּֽה־אָמַ֞ר אֲדֹנָ֣י יְהוִ֗ה
הִנֵּ֨ה אֶשָּׂ֤א אֶל־גּוֹיִם֙ יָדִ֔י וְאֶל־עַמִּ֖ים אָרִ֣ים נִסִּ֑י
וְהֵבִ֤יאוּ בָנַ֙יִךְ֙ בְּחֹ֔צֶן וּבְנֹתַ֖יִךְ עַל־כָּתֵ֥ף תִּנָּשֶֽׂאנָה׃

With climactic effect, as though stirred by Zion's happiness, the Lord answers her with the usual assuring *kōh 'amar*, except that *'adhōnāy*, the Ruler of all things, has been added to the *YHWH*, as still further assurance that the promise to Zion will be fulfilled. At the sign and signal of the Ruler over all the world, the gentile people shall in joyful obedience bring back Zion's sons and daughters. The question may be raised whether this promise is an explanation of the previously described gathering of the children about the mother, or whether an influx of further children is being held in prospect. It is hard to say which is meant, since the promise is being constantly augmented. In any case the verse adds the new thought that the heathen shall accompany the children back to their mother in the friendliest and most loving manner. A Jewish diaspora in all quarters of the world is presupposed here (cf. verse 12), a deportation violently carried out and forcefully maintained against unwilling people, such as the Assyrian and the Babylonian Golah (captivity). Not only will they be freed from the power of the gentiles, as in the case of Babylon, and of their own free will return home (as in verse 17), but the Lord raises His commanding hand as a signal to the nations that hold the people in captivity and moves them to a cheerful obedience. The raising of a banner for the nations says the same thing, the only difference being that a direction is thereby indicated. Cf. especially 11:10 and 12; 62:10. If one now notes what is said in the next verse, it becomes clear that the raising of the hand and of the banner at the same time effects the conversion of the gentiles. It is the *converted* nations who bring back the converted Jewish *gōlāh* (captivity) to Zion, cf. chapter 60. The whole promise is thus shown to be indicative of the day of salvation (verse 8), the time of the New Testament. See Romans 11, especially verses 14 and 25ff. The Christian mission among the Jews has been assigned to the church among the nations as a task that continues till the Day of Judgment. "In the bosom" and "at the shoulder" (not *on* the shoulder) shall the children be carried to Zion, a picture of gentle and loving devotion. — The interpretation misses the mark entirely that takes these returning children to be only the spiritual children of Zion, that is, gentiles who have come to the faith. Gentiles and Jews are too clearly distinguished here to permit of that explanation. One might debate that question in connection with 60:4, but not here where gentiles appear as the subject and Jerusalem's children as the object.

וְהָיוּ מְלָכִים אֹמְנַיִךְ וְשָׂרוֹתֵיהֶם מֵינִיקֹתַיִךְ 23

אַפַּיִם אֶרֶץ יִשְׁתַּחֲווּ לָךְ וַעֲפַר רַגְלַיִךְ יְלַחֵכוּ

וְיָדַעַתְּ כִּי־אֲנִי יְהוָה אֲשֶׁר לֹא־יֵבֹשׁוּ קוָֹי:

The discourse continues to build up to a climax. Kings and queens of the nations are meant. Even the greatest and most powerful, the rulers over the gentile nations, will humble themselves before the church and place their power and their treasures at her disposal. The *sārōthēyhem* are, of course, not women of lower rank (concubines), but wives of the princes. Queens are meant. The participles *'ōmenīm*, nurses, and *mēynīqōth*, wet-nurses, are intended like *hēbhī'ū* and *tinnāse'nāh* (Hiphil) of the preceding verse, to bring out the tenderness of their loving care. The next clause reaches the climax. The kings and queens (queens are included in the third person masculine plural) shall with face bowed down to the ground (adverbial accusative) do obeisance before Zion. That they lick the dust of her feet is a picture of deepest abasement. They will accord to her what their own subjects must accord to them, honor that is due to majesty. Kings and queens will accord that honor to *their* queen, that is, the kind of honor due to God, for she is *sārāthō*, the spouse of the King of kings. History tells us how this promise has in various instances been literally fulfilled. Every prayer of a Saxon Elector, or of a Gustavus Adolphus, every hymn by Aemilie Juliane or by Ludaemilia Elizabeth is a literal fulfillment of this promise. It is well known how this prophecy was abused by the papacy to lord it over kings and princes. But even though one should not be able to cite a single instance of the literal fulfillment of this prophecy, the promise nevertheless remains true. In the vivid fashion of the Oriental poet, the prophet is portraying, ideally, the homage paid to the church by kings and nations.

With mention of the mental and moral condition that the Lord desires to create in Zion, the final clause brings the promise to its conclusion. The *we* before *yādha'at* is the *Waw* consecutive perfect (following imperfect verbs), with strong emphasis. The perfect is frequentative, Gr. 112, e,p. 331: "then you will continue always to remember, etc." Luther rightly felt that *yādha'* should be rendered with *erfahren*, to learn to know. This experience of the mind and the senses that Zion shall have, is that those who trust in Him shall never be put to shame, for He is Jehovah, the eternally faithful and eternally gracious God. Concerning the grammatical reference of *'asher*, see Gr. 138, d,p. 445: "I who — shall not be put to shame in Me, etc." Cf. *'asher beḥartīkhā* (accusative) 41:8.

The development of the thought is arranged with consummate skill in the following sequence: 1. I can never forget you, verses 14-17; 2. Your children come in unthought-of numbers to build and beautify you, verses 18 and 19; 3. So great is their number that for very joy you shall not know what to say, verses 20,21; 4. The gentiles and their princes shall do homage before you, verses 22,23.

The promise then retraces its step to answer a possible objection. Zion's children are still lying helpless in the unbreakable chains of their powerful enemy; how is it possible that this promise shall ever be fulfilled? The next strophe provides the answer.

Second Half: verses 24-26: *The zeal of the Lord rescues Zion's children from the "Giant" and wreaks vengeance upon him.*

24   *Can the prey be taken away from the strong one*
    And the prisoners be rescued from the conqueror?
25   *Thus says the Lord:*
    The prisoners shall indeed be taken away from
      the strong one,
    And the tyrant's prey shall be taken from him.
    For I will oppose those who oppose you,
    And your children — I will rescue them.
26   *And your oppressors will I feed with their own flesh,*
    And like new wine shall they drink unto drunkenness their
      own blood,
    And then shall all flesh know
    That I, the Lord, am your Savior,
    And that your Redeemer is the Mighty One of Jacob.

²⁴ הֲיֻקַּח מִגִּבּוֹר מַלְקוֹחַ וְאִם־שְׁבִי צַדִּיק יִמָּלֵט׃

The Hophal *yuqqaḥ* with the interrogative *ha* is potential, like *hathishkaḥ* in verse 15: "*Can* prey be taken away?" Gr. 107,r,t,p. 318. A *gibbōr* is a strong warrior who has overcome an opponent and plundered him. *malqōaḥ*, booty, and *yuqqaḥ* (both from *lāqaḥ*, to take) are a play on words. In the parallel question that follows, the word *tsaddīq* offers some difficulty. Delitzsch's solution does not, in our opinion, seem to be correct: "a host of captives consisting of righteous men" (epexegetical genitive, and *tsaddīq* a collective noun). That translation completely upsets the strict chiastic arrangement of the members of the parallelism. Delitzsch correctly says that "the question is logically one, and only divided rhetorically into two"; but for that reason alone the perfect correspondence between the members of the two clauses must not be disturbed. It is clear that *tsaddīq* refers to the same person or persons as *gibbōr*. The original meaning of *tsaddīq* also points in that direction. For the meaning of *tsādhaq* is "to be at all times what one ought to be, capable, fit, perfect in one's way." Here the reference is to one who is capable in war and battle, a synonym of *gibbōr*, but stronger than *gibbōr*. And so, if one translates *gibbōr* as hero or warrior, one must render *tsaddīq* with a stronger expression, such as, giant, unconquerable one. That is the point of the comparison. The one who is holding the *shebhī* captive is pictured as unconquerable. For that reason the question is: "Is it possible that, etc.?" The *gibbōr-tsaddīq* refers primarily to the seemingly unconquerable Babylon, but one must not forget that in this section the prophet purposely and consistently takes no note of Babylon, but directs his gaze into the whole wide world, as is clearly indicated in verses 12 and 22. In the combination, *gibbōr-tsaddīq*, he visualizes the power of all the gentile peoples and their kings. What is impossible for men, that is possible for God, the *'adhōnāy YHWH,* Luke 11:21f.

25 כִּי־כֹה ׀ אָמַ֣ר יְהֹוָ֗ה

גַּם־שְׁבִ֤י גִבּוֹר֙ יֻקָּ֔ח וּמַלְק֥וֹחַ עָרִ֖יץ יִמָּלֵ֑ט

וְאֶת־יְרִיבֵךְ֙ אָנֹכִ֣י אָרִ֔יב וְאֶת־בָּנַ֖יִךְ אָנֹכִ֥י אוֹשִֽׁיעַ׃

kī is used here in its primary and most general meaning as an affirmative particle, as in verse 18 after the oath-formula: "Yes, indeed" (cf. the lexicon). And now, with only a slight change in the wording, the question asked in verse 24 is repeated in the form of an affirmation. The verbs remain the same; but *shebhī* is now joined with *gibbōr*, and instead of *tsaddīq, malqōah* now is joined with *'ārīts*, the mighty one, the tyrant, the terrible one, the one who fills others with terror.* This is proof enough that Delitzsch's interpretation of *tsaddīq* in verse 24 is not correct. Just as wrong are the text critics who, being at a loss how to explain *tsaddīq* in verse 24, substituted *'ārīts* from this verse. How long must the master of language, the poet Isaiah, suffer at the hands of these stumbling critics? The next clause, with a *we* preceding *'eth,* gives

---

*But in the Dead Sea Scrolls the words *shebhī* and *malqōah* are reversed in verse 25 to read: *gam malqōah gibbōr yulqah ūshebhī 'ārīts yimmālēt.*

the reason why the seemingly impossible will become possible and become a reality: "for with your strivers will *I* strive; those who oppose you will *I* oppose." *'anōkhī* is very emphatic: "and your children will *I* rescue." That is how this promise will become truth and reality.

וְהַאֲכַלְתִּי אֶת־מוֹנַיִךְ אֶת־בְּשָׂרָם וְכֶעָסִיס דָּמָם יִשְׁכָּרוּן 26

וְיָדְעוּ כָל־בָּשָׂר כִּי אֲנִי יְהוָה מוֹשִׁיעֵךְ וְגֹאֲלֵךְ אֲבִיר יַעֲקֹב:

As a conclusion to this line of thought, Isaiah adds, as he so often does, a short presentation of the reverse thought, in this case, the Lord's vengeance upon the enemies who have oppressed Zion. *mōnayikh* is a Hiphil participle of *yānāh*, which is related to *'anāh* (spelled with *Ayin*), but is always transitive: "to oppress." *he'ekhīl*, a Hiphil, has two objects: "I will make your oppressors to eat their flesh." The suffix in *besārām* and *dāmām* is emphatic: "their own flesh and own blood," Gr. 135, k,p. 439. *dāmām* is an accusative. *yishkārūn* is a transitive Qal: "they shall drink (unto drunkenness) their own blood, like new wine." *weyādhe'ū* is a counterpart to *weyādha'at* in verse 23. Through this act of vengeance on the part of the Lord, all flesh shall come to the knowledge that the Lord is Zion's Helper and that the Mighty One of Jacob is Zion's Savior. Note the chiastic arrangement of members! The two subjects are the extremes, and the predicates are the means. In the first clause the predicate has the emphasis, in the second clause the emphasis is on the subject. In His fixed purpose, the Lord is Zion's Helper; in His unconquerable power, He is her Savior. The Lord has brought Zion to understand this through the experience of His salvation; through the experience of His judgment He has brought His and Zion's enemies to a knowledge of the love and faithfulness that He bears toward His own. With that, the thought comes to a close.

Second Discourse: Chapter 50

Through the perfect obedience of His Servant, the Lord, in His faithfulness, makes amends for the misery that His people have brought upon themselves through their sin and guilt.

In dramatic array the chapter presents the discourse in three parts. In verses 1-3 the Lord speaks. Not unfaithfulness or lack of power on the part of the Lord, but Israel's guilt, was the cause of its misery. In verses 4-9 the Servant of the Lord becomes the speaker and proclaims His perfect obedience and the Lord's help in His suffering. In the concluding section, verses 10 and 11, the Lord again speaks and makes the application: He who believes shall be saved; he who does not believe shall perish.

Vitringa, followed by Ewald, mistakenly attaches verses 1-3 to the foregoing chapter. The tone of this chapter is quite different from that of chapter 49. There the tone is one of merciful comfort; here it is reproach. The two chapters do, however, have in common the thought of spiritual marriage between the Lord and Israel (49:14ff).

First Strophe: verses 1-3: *Not unfaithfulness or lack of power on the part of the Lord, but Israel's transgressions were the cause of its chastisement.*

1 *Thus says the Lord:*
 Where is your mother's letter of divorce, with which I put her away?
 Or where is a creditor of Mine, to whom I sold you?
 Truly, because of your iniquities have you been sold,
 And because of your transgressions was your mother put away.

2 *Why was no one there when I came?*
And when I called, why did no one answer?
Is then My hand too short to redeem?
Or am I lacking in power to save?
Truly, at My rebuke do I dry up the sea,
I change the streams into a dry waste,
That their fish stink because there is no water
And die of thirst.
3 *I clothe the heavens in darkness,*
And sackcloth I make their covering.

1 כֹּה ׀ אָמַר יְהֹוָה

אֵי זֶה סֵפֶר כְּרִיתוּת אִמְּכֶם אֲשֶׁר שִׁלַּחְתִּיהָ

אוֹ מִי מִנּוֹשַׁי אֲשֶׁר־מָכַרְתִּי אֶתְכֶם לוֹ

הֵן בַּעֲוֹנֹתֵיכֶם נִמְכַּרְתֶּם וּבְפִשְׁעֵיכֶם שֻׁלְּחָה אִמְּכֶם:

ʾey changes the demonstrative *zeh* into an interrogative pronoun — "which?" Gr. 137, a, p. 443. Our idiom, however, requires
"Where is the letter of divorce?" rather than "Which is the letter?" In this case, *zeh* might also be interpreted as an enclitic emphasizing the *ʾey,* Gr. 136, c, p. 442. Regarding the letter of divorce,
see Deuteronomy 24:1ff; Jeremiah 3:1; Matthew 5:31f. In *ʾim-
mekhem* the people themselves are meant, in distinction from the
mother Zion-Jerusalem, a purely poetic personification of the
mass of the people. In 49:14ff the mother is Zion-Jerusalem.
shillaḥ, a Piel, means to divorce, to put away, to reject. The picture
in the next clause is of the compulsory surrender of children to
satisfy a debt to a hardhearted creditor, cf. 2 Kings 4:1; Matthew
18:25. The regulation covering such situations is set forth in Exodus 21:7ff; Leviticus 25:39ff.

mī minnōshay, "which of (*min partitivum*) My creditors is it,"
does not, of course, assume that there are such creditors, but as in
the case of *ʾey zeh* and the letter of divorce: "Where is there a creditor of Mine to whom I might have sold you?" The verbs in the
relative clauses have potential force, since the form of the questions actually denies the existence of either a letter of divorce or of
a creditor. The particle *hēn* throughout the chapter (verses 1,2,9,-
11) does not direct the attention to something, but is used in an assertive sense: "Truly." *ʿawōn* is sin viewed as guilt; *peshaʿ* is
breach of faith, rebellion, transgression, sin against the conscience. These strong expressions were chosen because it is the

prophet's purpose to throw a strong light on Israel's guilt as the cause of her exile. The Lord had not been unfaithful, had broken no promise; but the people had persistently transgressed, had repeatedly rebelled against their gracious and faithful God. That is why Israel was rejected and delivered into the hands of gentile tyrants.

² מַדּוּעַ בָּאתִי וְאֵין אִישׁ   קָרָאתִי וְאֵין עוֹנֶה
הֲקָצוֹר קָצְרָה יָדִי מִפְּדוּת   וְאִם־אֵין־בִּי כֹחַ לְהַצִּיל
הֵן בְּגַעֲרָתִי אַחֲרִיב יָם   אָשִׂים נְהָרוֹת מִדְבָּר
תִּבְאַשׁ דְּגָתָם מֵאֵין מַיִם   וְתָמֹת בַּצָּמָא׃

maddūa' (*mah* and *yādhūa'*, a Qal pass. part. of *yādha'*, literally, "how known," that is, why, for what reason) *bā'thī we'eyn 'īsh* is a case, common in Isaiah, of co-ordination instead of subordination; the interrogative really belongs to *'eyn 'īsh*, and *bā'thī* is an adverbial clause: "Why was no one there *when* I called?" Cf. Gr. 150, m, p. 476. Also Isaiah 5:4 and 58:3. A similar case is that of *qārā'thī* and *'eyn 'ōneh*. The reference is to the time of the exile. The Lord had approached His people again and again through His Word preached to them by Moses and the prophets, particularly from the time of Isaiah to the period of the exile, and had always encountered deaf ears and hardened hearts, cf. chapters 1-5; and finally the people responded only with scorn and contempt for the Word that was preached to them, and with blows, imprisonment, and death for those who preached it, cf. Jeremiah 26, 34, and 35; Matthew 23:34ff. *qātsōr qātserāh* is an infinitive absolute with a finite verb, a construction that strengthens the meaning of the finite verb. The *min* in *mippedhūth* is *min comparativum* — too short to save, Gr. 133, c, p. 430. See Isaiah 59:1 and Numbers 11:23 for the same thought.

The parallel clause that follows differs only in that *lehatstsīl* (Hiphil of *nātsal*) is stronger and more vivid in meaning than the prosaic *mippedhūth*. For proof of His "long" hand and for the "fullness of His strength" (40:26) the Lord points to the miracle of the Red Sea, Exodus 14:22; cf. Isaiah 51:10. Joshua 3:16 is another case in point. *ga'arāh* (from *gā'ar*, to shout at) is onomatopoetic. It signifies shouting, rebuking, and in a more spiritual sense, threatening, withstanding. It is one of Isaiah's favorites: 17:13; 30:17; 51:20; 54:9; 66:15. The word suggests first of all a storm. *midhbār* is an accusative of the product, Gr. 117, ii, p. 371. *tibh'ash deghāthām*, etc. is a consecutive clause without a conjunction. *tibh'ash* is jussive, Gr. 166, a, p. 504. The singular *deghāthām* from *dāghāh* is a collective, Gr. 122, s, p. 394. The LXX reading is here based on the Hebrew verb *yābhēsh*, to dry up, to wither; not on *tibh'ash*, from *bā'ash*, to rot, to stink. The *min* in *mē'eyn* is the causative *min*, Gr. 152, y, p. 483. *thāmōth* is another jussive, like *tibh'ash*, Gr. 109. k, p. 323.

אַלְבִּישׁ שָׁמַיִם קַדְרוּת וְשַׂק אָשִׂים כְּסוּתָם: ³

This sentence is a further development of *ga'arāthī* in verse 2. In the second half it might be debated whether *saq* or *kesūthām* belongs in the predicate. The meaning is about the same as in the first half, but with intensification: the entire heavens like a single dark blanket; whereas the first part might be understood to refer only to a partial darkening. God being so completely a Lord of the elements, it was for Him a slight matter to protect His people against the might of their enemies, or to rescue them again out of the hands of tyrants. And so, it was not because the Lord was lacking in power or in love and faithfulness that He delivered His people to the enemy, but it was the people themselves that brought this misery upon themselves as a chastisement for their unfaithfulness. But the Lord is faithful, and He will not permit this condition to continue; He will provide help through His Servant.

Second Strophe: verses 4-9: *The Servant of the Lord is the true Comforter of the weary, because He was completely obedient even in His suffering, in which the faithfulness of the Lord upholds Him.*

4 *The Lord God has given Me the tongue of the learned,*
   That I may know to give rest to the weary with the word;
   He awakens every morning — He awakens My ear,
   That I may hear like those well skilled.
5 *The Lord God opens My ear for Me,*
   And I — I do not resist,
   Nor do I turn away backward.
6 *I offer My back to those who smite Me*
   And My cheeks to those who pluck out the hair;
   My face I do not hide against shame and spitting.
7 *Because the Lord God helps Me,*
   Therefore I do not perish because of shame,
   Therefore do I make My countenance like flint,
   And I know that I shall not be confounded.

8 *He is near who vindicates Me.*
   Who is he that will strive against Me? — Let us stand up together!
   Whoever challenges Me, let him step forth to Me!
9 *Truly, the Lord, the Lord God helps Me —*
   Who is it that can condemn Me?
   Truly, they will wear out like a garment,
   Moths will consume them.

This section is divided into two equal parts — verses 4-6 and 7-9. The first part treats of the *obedience* of the Servant; the second part tells of the *help* that the Lord provides. The passage reads like a prelude to chapter 53. Here it is the obedient and suffering Servant of the Lord who is saying of Himself essentially the same things that the prophet proclaims of Him in chapter 53, with the difference that the major points are arranged in opposite order. The fruit of the Servant's suffering, namely, the winning of souls through His preaching, is mentioned at the very beginning (verse 4a) of this strophe, whereas chapter 53 closes with the account of the fruits (verses 10-12). The middle portion of this section as well as of chapter 53 describes the Servant's obedience and patience in suffering (50:4b-6; 53:1-9). In this section the vindication of the Servant closes the section, whereas that appears at the beginning of chapter 53 (52:13-15). The subject matter of verses 10 and 11 in this chapter is divided in chapter 53 among verses 1 and 2 at the beginning and verses 10 and 12 at the end. This difference in the arrangement of the material, which has not been noted by the commentators, is deliberate. It must be noted that the subject discussed in both passages is one and the same. In many features of the person described, they complement each other. Only when the two are taken together do we get a complete picture. And then it becomes so much the more clear that the person portrayed in both passages is not the people of Israel, as the Jews and the modern unbelieving commentators assume, but the perfect Servant of the Lord Himself, our Lord Jesus Christ. — We have rendered the perfect tenses of the first three verses and the imperfects of the last three with the present tense, since the entire monologue is not narration but description of absolute, timeless facts.

4 אֲדֹנָי יְהֹוִה נָתַן לִי֙ לְשׁוֹן לִמּוּדִים
לָדַעַת לָעוּת אֶת־יָעֵף דָּבָר יָעִיר ׀
בַּבֹּקֶר בַּבֹּקֶר יָעִיר לִי אֹזֶן לִשְׁמֹעַ כַּלִּמּוּדִים׃

As in chapters 49 and 61, the Servant of the Lord appears as the speaker, without any introduction. As in those chapters, His appeal here is to the Lord who sent Him. His speech is grave and solemn. Four times He speaks of His God as *'adhōnāy YHWH,* the Lord of all, Jehovah, and four times He uses the assertive "behold," "truly." What He is saying will become fact and truth through His Covenant-God, who rules over all created things. His God endows Him with a *leshōn limmūdhīm,* with a tongue of the learned. A *limmūdh* (from *lāmadh,* to practice, become accustomed, to learn) is in general a skillful, a learned person, *qui artem adeptus est;* a *leshōn limmūdhīm* is, therefore, a tongue skilled in speaking, teaching, preaching, the tongue of a speaker. But in 8:16 and 54:13, the *limmūdh* is *limmūdh YHWH,* who has been taught by the Lord Himself (John 6:45), who has been initiated into and made conversant with His mysteries, a διδακτὸς θεοῦ. Concretely then, the tongue taught of God is the tongue of the prophet, preacher, teacher, a tongue that has been enlightened by the Holy Spirit. The Servant is speaking of His endowment for His prophetic office, as in 49:2ff; 42:1ff. His mouth is a sharp sword, a polished arrow, shaped by the Holy Spirit. He proclaims the mysteries of God with the tongue of a master, and therefore with the power of God to convert. His words are spirit and life; "never man spake like this man," John 7:46; Matthew 7:29. The purpose of His endowment with such a tongue is that He should know how to refresh the weary with His word. A *yāʿēph* (40:29ff) is one who is spiritually weary, one with a broken and contrite spirit (57:15; 66:2), a bruised reed, a smoking flax (42:3), the weary and heavy laden of Matthew 11:28, as Zion is pictured in 49:14.

ūth (lāʿūth) occurs only here, and its meaning can only be guessed at, since even the dialects offer no assistance. The LXX translation was evidently based on a text that had *leʿittō,* "in its time." This accounts for Luther's *zu rechter Zeit.* But that reading makes the Hebrew construction very awkward. One cannot go far wrong in the interpretation if one translates *ūth* in the light of the "I will give you rest" of Matthew 11:28. For the unusual use of *'eth* before *yāʿēph* without the article, cf. Gr. 117, c, p. 363. *dābhār* is an adverbial accusative, "with the word." *yāʿīr lī 'ozen* in this clause recalls the *nāthan lī leshōn limmūdhīm* of the first clause. The first phrase speaks of the endowment for the prophetic office, this one of the preparation for His perfect obedience. Delitzsch is mistaken when he explains this as referring to the manner in which the Servant receives revelation, namely, that the Servant receives His revelation by the full light of day, as Moses did, and not by night in dreams or visions, as was the case with other prophets. But *babbōqer babbōqer* does not refer to the early hours of the day when He is awakened, in contrast to being awakened in the night time. The phrase refers to the daily repetition of the awakening. Cf. *yōm yōm*. Since awakening normally occurs in the morning, *bōqer* was chosen rather than *yōm*. But the reference is not at all to a physical awakening. "Opening the ear" is a figurative expression for the inner, moral preparation for *hearing, lishmōa'*, which immediately follows. This hearing is not primarily a spiritual understanding, a spiritual perception in contrast to deafness or spiritual dullness of hearing. The reference is not to a purely intellectual hearing, but rather to a *willing*, spiritual hearing, a listening, a glad obedience as opposed to not wanting to hear and resisting, as is at once made clear in verse 5, where the same phrase occurs. "He awakens My ear every morning (or morning for morning)" means that He arouses Me anew each day, through the Holy Spirit, 42:1; 61:1, unto cheerful spiritual obedience. *limmūdh* in *kallimmūdhīm* is here, as earlier with *lāshōn*, the virtuoso or master; in this instance the virtuoso in *obedience,* namely, the one who yields perfect and complete obedience to God. In short we have here the Man who is described in Psalm 40:7ff(6ff) and Hebrews 10:5ff according to His twofold office: the perfect Prophet, such as the world had never seen, and the perfect High Priest, who by His willing, gladly given obedience, whether doing or suffering, expiated our guilt and atoned for all our sin (40:2). His willing obedience atones for the disobedience, the rebelliousness, the obstinacy ("we have turned every one to his own way," 53:6) of Israel and the gentiles. It is not in the performance of the outward work or in the endurance of great agony, but in the absolute willingness of His doing and suffering that our redemption lies — "I delight to do Thy will, O My God," Psalm 40:9(8). Our Lord Christ, the Servant of the Lord, is not only a Master of speech, skilled to give powerful and thorough comfort with the Word of God to despondent souls; He is also a Master in obedience toward God, a Master of the art, otherwise unknown in the world, of wiping out the sin of the entire lost world, as the sun dispels fog and clouds, 44:22; 43:25, and Romans 5:19.

5 אֲדֹנָ֤י יְהוִה֙ פָּֽתַֽח־לִ֣י אֹ֔זֶן

וְאָנֹכִ֖י לֹ֣א מָרִ֑יתִי ׀ אָח֖וֹר לֹ֥א נְסוּגֹֽתִי׃

The Servant repeats the thought of verse 4 in somewhat different words. That the sense is as we have just explained, is made clear by the second clause of this sentence: "And I — I do not resist, nor do I turn away backward." *nesūghōthī* is a perfect Niphal of *sūgh,* to turn back, and *'aḥōr* is an adverb modifying and emphasizing the idea expressed by the verb, the whole being an expression in more concrete form of the concept of nonresistance, *lō' mārīthī.* In the whole life of the Servant there was never a moment when there arose in His soul an impulse to resist. His fear of the baptism with which He was baptized, His trembling, His agony, etc., were externally caused emotions, which His human (and divine) spirit suffered. They were not expressions of a reluctant and resisting will, Psalm 22:12ff(11ff); 1 Peter 2:22f; Isaiah 53:7ff.

6 גֵּוִי֙ נָתַ֣תִּי לְמַכִּ֔ים וּלְחָיַ֖י לְמֹֽרְטִ֑ים

פָּנַי֙ לֹ֣א הִסְתַּ֔רְתִּי מִכְּלִמּ֖וֹת וָרֹֽק׃

In verse 6 the speaker describes in concrete terms His unresisting, uncomplaining obedience. It is not the first duty of the exegete to show how these words of the Servant were literally fulfilled in His own body, Matthew 26:67f; 27:26ff; John 19:1ff; his first concern is with the text. What the Servant says of Himself here shows by examples how He willingly yielded perfect obedience. Beatings with staves and scourges, blows in the face, malicious blasphemies (*kelimmōth*) and spitting (whether one understands these expressions literally or as figures to represent inhuman degradation, 52:14) are indignities that everyone can endure; but no natural human being, no Christian, so long as he is still clothed with flesh and blood, can endure such things willingly and gladly without any inner rebellion. Cf. Jeremiah 20:9, 14ff; Job 3. Only the Holy One of God, He who was without sin, was capable of that. If the people of Israel were meant here, even Israel according to the spirit, Isaiah would be painting an untrue picture. No, this portrayal is of an individual, of *the* Servant, who is Christ, the one true Seed of Abraham, Galatians 3:16. The prophet is describing the Man of complete and perfect obedience. That is the purpose of his description.

makkīm is a Hiphil participle of *nākhāh. leḥāyayim* is the dual form of *leḥī,* a cheekbone, which Luther discerningly translated with *Wangen* (cheeks), a word that is well suited to go with the verbs to scratch, pluck, tear out the hair. Cf. Nehemiah 13:25. *kelimmōth* may be a variant of *kelimmūth,* "shame." It may also be taken to be an intensive plural of *kelimmāh. rōq*, "spit," a noun, is from the stem *rāqaq* and is onomatopoetic.

 וַאדֹנָי יְהוִה יַעֲזָר־לִי עַל־כֵּן לֹא נִכְלָמְתִּי 7
עַל־כֵּן שַׂמְתִּי פָנַי כַּחַלָּמִישׁ וָאֵדַע כִּי־לֹא אֵבוֹשׁ׃

Verse 7 treats of the strong and effective help that the Servant receives in His suffering. It is the power of His God, the Lord God, that upholds Him under treatment that for men would be unbearable. But it is not so much outward, physical support, as spiritual support for His soul; it is preservation in obedience, in patience, in the holy will. Cf. Luke 22:43; Psalm 22:12(11), 25(24). The *Waw* with *'adhōnāy* could be taken as adversative, expressing contrast with the foregoing; but we prefer to connect it with *'al kēn* and take it in the causal sense — "because — therefore." The Niphal *nikhlāmtī* is stronger than *'ebhōsh* at the end of the verse. What is meant by the same is expressed in Psalm 69:21(20): "Reproach has broken my heart." Cf. verse 15(14) He would succumb under the shame if the Lord did not give Him the inner support to withstand the disgrace. And now, strong in the Lord's support and in the consciousness that He shall not be finally put to shame, but be raised up through shame to glory, He makes His countenance like flint, that is, He opposes the shame with the unbreakable determination to let it pour over Him, defies it, and gains the victory.

קָרוֹב מַצְדִּיקִי מִי־יָרִיב אִתִּי נַעַמְדָה יָּחַד 8
מִי־בַעַל מִשְׁפָּטִי יִגַּשׁ אֵלָי׃

To the inner, spiritual victory there is now added the vindication of the Servant in the face of the enemies, who had thought Him to be alone, deserted of God, Psalm 22:9(8); Matthew 27:43. *qārōbh* is figurative. Here we have the answer to the prayer in Psalm 22:12(11), 20(19), and the fulfillment of Isaiah 65:24. *qārōbh matsdīqī* is an explanation in concrete terms of *ya'azor lī* in verse 7. The question is one of the guilt or innocence of the Servant. Because His enemies considered Him guilty of the most heinous sins, the greatest crimes, they mistreated Him most shamefully. Cf. Matthew 26:65-67. Then the Lord God Jehovah, who pronounces the last and eternally valid judgment upon all men, including the enemies of His Servant, steps forth and justifies Him, pronounces Him innocent. That is the Servant's strong comfort. It is this comfort that makes Him happy and determined to set His countenance like flint, and calmly and without fear to defy His enemies.

The next clause, *mī yarībh 'ittī,* must not be joined with *qārōbh matsdīqī.* The scholars who provided the accents, correctly separated *qārōbh matsdīqī* from the rest of the sentence by means of a Zaqeph, so that it stands apart as the great fact from which the following statements flow as practical consequences. *mī yarībh 'ittī* and *na'amdhāh yāḥadh* belong together as protasis and apodosis. *mī* may be understood to be the interrogative: "Who will strive with Me?" But we prefer to treat it as the indefinite pronoun, as in verse 10 (Gr. 137,c,p.443): "Whoever will strive with Me, let us come together." In the certainty that the Lord, who is near, justifies Him, the Servant defies His accusers. The next clause repeats the same thought in intensified form. The expression *ba'al mishpāṭ* (cf. *ba'al pīphīyōth,* 41:15; *ba'al haḥalōmōth,* Gen. 37:19; *ba'aley bhrīth 'abhrām,* Gen. 14:13) designates a person who in some way is connected with *mishpāṭ,* with the cause, that is, with the Servant's cause in this instance, namely, the person who is His accuser and opponent before a judicial tribunal. This phrase goes beyond *mī yarībh* in that the adversary is not just an occasional accuser, but has now become a formal accuser before a court of justice, a recognized adversary pressing for a decision. Likewise, *yiggash 'ēlāy* is more forceful and defiant than *na'amadhāh yāḥadh.* The Servant knows that He shall never be put to shame, verse 7.

⁹ הֵן אֲדֹנָי יְהוִה יַעֲזָר־לִי מִי־הוּא יַרְשִׁיעֵנִי
הֵן כֻּלָּם כַּבֶּגֶד יִבְלוּ עָשׁ יֹאכְלֵם׃

The ninth verse contains a summing up and the outcome of the case at court. Again we have the assertive *hēn* and the Lord God Jehovah, followed by the general statement, "He helps Me." *mī hū'* is more emphatic than *mī* (Gr. 136,c,p.442) and is the equivalent of the Latin *quisnam:* "Who is it then that could condemn Me — *yarshī'ēnī?*" *hirshīa',* a Hiphil of *rāsha',* is the exact opposite of *hitsdīq* in verse 8 and means "to condemn, declare guilty." Cf. Matthew 26:66. Paul's application of this passage to the Christian is well known, Romans 8:31ff.

The second half of the sentence tells of the outcome of the court action: Truly, every one of them, all of His accusers and persecutors fall to pieces like a garment that the moth (collective) devours. The same picture appears in 51:8. Job 13:28; Hosea 5:12; Psalm 39:12(11); Job 4:19 indicate that moths are thought of as the *cause* of the disintegration of a garment. Here the picture is not to be understood as referring to physical disintegration (although that too would not be out of place); but the meaning is that the accusations of the enemies will collapse before the righteous judgment of the Lord and be put to shame like the moldering of a moth-eaten garment. The point of comparison lies in the ease with which the rabid accusers will be exposed as vicious persecutors and slanderers.

Through the steadfast support of the Lord God Jehovah, the Servant of the Lord, the Preacher of salvation, perfect in His obedience while mistreated and condemned by His enemies, will stand before the judgment of His God vindicated and justified, while His accusers are put to shame. Of a truth, He is "My salvation unto the end of the earth."

Third Strophe: verses 10-11: *He that believes shall be saved; but he that believes not shall be damned.*

10   *He among you who fears the Lord,*
     Who gives ear to the voice of His Servant,
     He who walks in deep darkness,
     Where no light shines for him,
     Let him trust in the name of the Lord
     And rely upon his God.
11   *But all of you who kindle a fire, who tie firebrands,*
     Go into the flames of your own fire
     And into the arrows that you set afire!
     By My hand shall all this befall you,
     In torment shall you lie.

10 מִי בָכֶם יְרֵא יְהוָה שֹׁמֵעַ בְּקוֹל עַבְדּוֹ
אֲשֶׁר ׀ הָלַךְ חֲשֵׁכִים וְאֵין נֹגַהּ לוֹ
יִבְטַח בְּשֵׁם יְהוָה וְיִשָּׁעֵן בֵּאלֹהָיו׃

mī, as in verse 8, is an indefinite pronoun introducing several noun clauses; the verb of the independent clause is *yibhṭaḥ*. Three different qualities are listed under *mī*. The first is "fearing the Lord"; the second, "obedient to the voice of His Servant"; the third, "walking in darkness without a ray of light." The first is designated by an adjective, the second by a participle, the third by a finite verb, which shows that the speaker's intention is to describe characteristics, not just something transient. The correction of *shōmēa'* offered by the Grammar, 137, c, p. 443, is unjustified. The use of the participle is intentional. The purpose is to describe a characteristic. The *yerē' YHWH* is usually referred to as *yerē' 'elōhīm*. The fear of God is basically always fear in the presence of God, awe before the majesty of God. This is seen from passages like Psalm 33:8. It is the result of a consciousness of one's guilt and powerlessness over against God's holiness and omnipotence. But in the person who is characterized in the Scriptures as God-fearing there has been a change in the conditions that caused the feeling of awe before God. In Genesis 22:12 Abraham is called God-fearing, because he believed God's promise and therefore was ready to sacrifice that which was dearest in life to him; God and God's Word were for him high above everything else. Whereas the wicked man, because of his wicked nature, trembles before God, Psalm 14:4f, the God-fearing man does the right and shuns the evil (Job 1:1,8), because he possesses true reverence for the Almighty, who has shown him, a lost and condemned creature, grace, and received him as His child and heir. How can he dishonor the gracious God who has become to him his One and All! So Joseph felt, Genesis 39:9. These are the people to whom the Lord, who here again is the speaker, is addressing His words. "Who among you" — these are not the enemies of the Servant, who have just been put to shame, but the children of the Zion-Mother who were addressed in verses 1-3 of this chapter. In whomsoever of those children there is still found real reverence for the Lord, the all-powerful and gracious God of Israel, "let him trust ... !" *shōmēa' beqōl 'abhdō* does not denote a further characteristic but is included in *yir'ath YHWH*. He who honors and fears the Lord, honors His Messenger also, John 5:23. The proof of the fear of the Lord lies in giving ear to the word and voice of the Servant and yielding obedience to Him, for the Servant's word is God's Word, which He has placed like a sharp sword in the Servant's mouth, 49:2, by which He brings comfort to the weary, verse 4; 42:3; 61:2,3; by which He sets the prisoners free and opens the eyes of the blind, 42:7, etc. It is faith, obedience to the Gospel, that is meant. The third phrase is connected with the other two by *'asher* with a verb in the perfect and describes a different kind of person: one who walks in deep darkness, etc. *hashēkhīm* (intensive plural) is an accusative of place or reference, Gr. 117, bb, p. 370 and 118, d, r, p. 373ff. *we'ēyn nōghah lō* emphasizes the darkness. It is a darkness that is not even relieved by a gleam of light. This portrays extreme misfortune and misery, such as Zion experiences, 49:14, and the Servant endures. The *'asher* makes the clause conditional or temporal. It is similar to *gam kī* in Psalm 23:4, except that in that passage the *gam kī* is potential, while here the verb in the perfect tense represents the situation as already having come to pass. The translation is then: "When he wanders in darkness where there is no gleam of light . . . ." He who fears God and believes the word of the Servant must endure much tribulation with Him and pass by way of a cross to the crown, Matthew 10:22-39; Acts 14:22, etc. Often there will be no gleam of light on the way. Outward circumstances all seem to portend disaster, the heart finds no comfort, sees no hope. To him the Lord says: Let him trust in the name of the Lord. Luther quite consistently translated *bāṭaḥ* with "to hope." That fits the sense in this case too. *bāṭaḥ* means to be calmly certain in the hopelessness of the present, of glory in the future. The name of the Lord is, in its outward form, that by which the Lord is made known to us, what the Lord has revealed to us of His being, His will, His nature, and His works. That is His eternal and sole Godhead, His grace and truth, His power and His lordship over all the world, which He has put in our service. All this is concentrated in the names *YHWH* or *YHWH 'elōhēykhem*. See Exodus 34:6; Isaiah 42:8. In this name that has been revealed to us, there is complete security for all who hope in Him, even for those who walk in the valley of the shadow of death, Psalm 23:4. *yishshāʿen* (Niphal of *shāʿan*) is a stronger word than *yibhṭaḥ:* "Let him rely on his God." As God is the God of His Servant, so also is He the God of those who listen to the Servant's voice.

11 הֵן כֻּלְּכֶם קֹדְחֵי אֵשׁ מְאַזְּרֵי זִיקוֹת
לְכוּ ׀ בְּאוּר אֶשְׁכֶם וּבְזִיקוֹת בִּעַרְתֶּם
מִיָּדִי הָיְתָה־זֹּאת לָכֶם לְמַעֲצֵבָה תִּשְׁכָּבוּן :

This final word of the chapter is addressed to the unregenerate enemies of the Servant, who persist in unbelief. *hēn* is once more assertive: "Surely." The persistent unbelievers are portrayed as enemies who kindle flames and tie flaming arrows or firebrands (*zīqōth*). The Piel of *ʿazar* is not like the Hithpael a reflexive, but is strictly transitive; it is not to be rendered: "They surround themselves with firebrands," but: "They bind arrows and firebrands" with tow soaked in pitch, which they set afire in the flames they have just kindled. The picture is taken from the siege of a city, into which burning arrows are shot, or which is set afire after being taken. In their bitter rage the enemies of the Lord and His Servant employ the most extreme means of destruction, cf. Psalm 2. But they must needs hear the Lord's judgment: "Go into the flames of your own fire, and into the arrows that you set afire." They are destroyed by their own weapons. This judgment is like that in Matthew 25:41. Their lot is measured out to them by "My" hand, that is, by the hand of God, who had sent His Servant to be their salvation; but they, instead of receiving Him in faith, fought against Him and unceasingly persecuted Him. Cf. Matthew 21:33-46; 23:34-39.

zō'th includes what immediately precedes and what follows. *ma'atsēbhāh* occurs only here. It is a noun formed from the stem *ātsabh* with the intensive prefix *Mem*. It means pain, torment. For the meaning of *Lamed*, see Gesenius, item 9, under *le;* it has the meaning of *in*, as in *lebhādhādh* and *lābheṭaḥ* in Psalm 4:9(8). *tishkābhūn* is equally expressive with its emphatic Nun-ending. That is their lot — to lie bedded in torment, unable to help themselves. — He that believes shall be saved, he that does not believe shall be damned.

In His faithfulness the Lord delivers Israel from the misery it had brought upon itself by its sin; with His mighty power He supports the Servant whom He had sent to be the people's Savior; to the believers He promises security, to the unbelievers perdition.

Third Discourse: Chapter 51

All flesh is as grass; but God's promise of salvation to His people stands firm for ever (40:6-8) .

In the preceding chapter the people as such were addressed; now the Lord turns to address the believers among them and exhorts them not to be afraid of the power of the oppressors, for they are like grass; but His promised salvation is at the door, and the promise will be fulfilled in Israel's deliverance and glorification, and in retaliation against their oppressors.

The discourse consists of two parts of equal length, verses 1-11 and verses 12-23. The two parts treat the same theme, but present it in different form. There is warmth of feeling in both parts; but in the second part it becomes impassioned, so that even tender comfort takes on the form of reproach (verses 12 and 13). The chapter displays a high degree of technical skill. Everywhere there are corresponding parallels and contrasts, even in the shortest passages, and dramatic passages are not lacking. In content and form the chapter is one of the most perfect in Isaiah II.

Each larger part is divided into two smaller parts — I: 1-6, 7-11; II: 12-16, 17-23. Since the two main parts treat the same theme, we will supply headings only for the four subparts.

First Part: verses 1-6: *The Word that promises new salvation for Zion and conversion of the gentiles will outlast both heaven and earth.*

1   *Listen to Me, you who pursue salvation,*
   You who seek the Lord,
   Look to the rock out of which you were hewn,
   And to the hollow of the well out of which you were dug.

2   *Look to your father Abraham,*
    And to Sarah, who bore you in pain;
    For, as I called him when he was alone,
    And blessed him and multiplied him —

3   *So also will the Lord build Zion again,*
    All her ruins shall He restore,
    Her desolation shall He make to be an Eden,
    And her wastes like a garden of God;
    In her shall joy and rejoicing be found,
    Praise and the voice of singing.

4   *Listen to Me, O My people,*
    And My nation, hearken to Me!
    For instruction shall go forth from Me,
    And My right will I order as a light for the peoples.

5   *My deliverance draws near, My salvation goes forth,*
    My arms shall judge the nations;
    The isles wait for Me
    And they trust in My arm.

6   *Lift up your eyes to heaven,*
    And look down to the earth beneath;
    The heavens shall vanish like smoke,
    And the earth fall to pieces like a garment,
    And those who dwell on it shall die just like that.
    Yet My deliverance shall remain forever
    And My salvation shall never be broken.

שִׁמְעוּ אֵלַי רֹדְפֵי צֶדֶק מְבַקְשֵׁי יְהוָה 1

הַבִּיטוּ אֶל־צוּר חֻצַּבְתֶּם וְאֶל־מַקֶּבֶת בּוֹר נֻקַּרְתֶּם:

The Lord is speaking. He exhorts those who press for salvation and who seek the Lord, to listen to Him. The *rōdhephēy tsedheq* are those who penitently recognize that their deportation out of their city and land, called their "warfare" or time of service (40:2) under tyrants of this earth, was really a banishment from the gracious rule of the Lord, which they had brought upon themselves by their sin and guilt (50:1,2). They now pursue *tsedheq*, that is the covenanted salvation, grace, and the God of grace, with troubled hearts, not yet daring to grasp with joyful faith the new promise of salvation. The Lord comforts them by reminding them how miraculous and contrary to all reason were the origin and increase of the people out of that ancestral pair, Abraham and Sarah, when both were incapable of begetting or bearing children. The reminder is first expressed figuratively: "Look to the rock out of which you were hewn." Regarding the suppression of the sign of the relative with the preposition before *ḥutstsabhtem* and *nuq-*

qartem cf. Gr. 155, k, p. 488. *tsūr*, a hard rock, is a picture of barrenness. Abraham is meant, verse 2. Not in himself, but because of his barren wife, he was a barren rock, incapable of producing progeny. Out of such a one the people of Israel were hewn. They should consider also the hollowed-out well (*maqqebheth*, from *nāqabh*, to bore out) from which they were dug. As the next verse explains, this refers to Sarah. A *bōr* is a cistern excavated out of the solid rock; it is itself dry, being used for storage of water that has its source elsewhere. So Sarah was in herself barren, incapable of conceiving and giving birth to a child.

הַבִּ֙יטוּ֙ אֶל־אַבְרָהָ֣ם אֲבִיכֶ֔ם וְאֶל־שָׂרָ֖ה תְּחוֹלֶלְכֶ֑ם ²
כִּי־אֶחָ֣ד קְרָאתִ֔יו וַאֲבָרְכֵ֖הוּ וְאַרְבֵּֽהוּ ׃

And yet Abraham became the father of this people, and Sarah gave birth to this people in a wholly natural way, laboring and suffering all the pains of childbearing (that is the meaning of *ḥōlēl*, a Polel of *ḥīl*). The imperfect is used to represent the act of childbearing more vividly, Gr. 107, b, p. 314. Why are the people to turn their attention to this miraculous birth? The Lord's explanation follows in the next clauses. The *kī* in *kī 'eḥādh* and *kī niḥam* belong together and form a correlative: "just as — so." "As I called him when he was alone and then blessed and increased him, so will the Lord, etc." The calling of Abraham was a single completed act and is expressed in the perfect tense; the blessing and increasing, being repeated and continued, is expressed in the imperfect. From this naturally barren pair the Lord produced a multitude of descendants. He called one lone man into His service and solely by His blessing caused a great nation to grow up. From that example they should learn to believe what now follows.

כִּי־נִחַ֣ם יְהוָ֣ה צִיּ֗וֹן נִחַם֙ כָּל־חָרְבֹתֶ֔יהָ ³
וַיָּ֤שֶׂם מִדְבָּרָהּ֙ כְּעֵ֔דֶן וְעַרְבָתָ֖הּ כְּגַן־יְהוָ֑ה
שָׂשׂ֤וֹן וְשִׂמְחָה֙ יִמָּ֣צֵא בָ֔הּ תּוֹדָ֖ה וְק֥וֹל זִמְרָֽה ׃

Just so, that is, as He dealt with Abraham and Sarah, will the Lord cause Zion (city, land, people) to rise out of its present barren state to new prosperity and glory. It is hard to understand why translators insist on rendering *niḥam* with a stiff and mechanical "to comfort," a word that does not at all fit the picture. The original meaning of *nāḥam* is "to breathe deeply." In the other conjugations the word can represent any of the actions connected with hard breathing: to have compassion, to repent, to take revenge, to take comfort, to comfort others, etc. In the Piel the word denotes breathing, sighing with relief, alleviating fear, reanimating. When applied to Zion lying in ruins the word means "to cause to rise again, to rebuild," a meaning which the specific object of the word requires. What could be the meaning of "to comfort ruins"? The following concrete explanations show how *niham* is to be understood: the waste places shall be like an Eden, and the desolation like a garden of God. Just as the Lord, solely by His word of blessing, in a manner contrary to all nature, created Israel out of this barren pair, out of one lone man, so also shall He by His word of blessing bring forth out of these desolate ruins new life and new glory. That is the subject of verse 4. The pictures are extreme: ruins, waste, desolation on the one hand, paradise and the garden of God on the other. Just as the first group pictures a condition that is to come, so also does the second group picture a future reality of joy, rejoicing, and the sound of music. The prophet foresees the renewal of Zion in its perfection. The bodily, spiritual, New Testament, heavenly Zion is conceived as a single unit. To the physical Zion the other concepts of Zion are joined, not as different, separate Zions, but as the lone body of Zion in spiritual, New Testament, heavenly glorification, Revelation 7; 14; 21.

4 הַקְשִׁיבוּ אֵלַי עַמִּי   וּלְאוּמִּי אֵלַי הַאֲזִינוּ
כִּי תוֹרָה מֵאִתִּי תֵצֵא   וּמִשְׁפָּטִי לְאוֹר עַמִּים
אַרְגִּיעַ:

The first three sentences of this part (verses 1-6), contain 14 clauses, the next three have 15 clauses. Verse 4 begins with the same kind of address as verse 1, but in somewhat stronger terms of exhortation. Where verse 1 had *rōdhephēy tsedheq*, we now have *'ammī*, and *le'ummī* in place of *mebhaqqeshēy YHWH*. *'ammī* and *le'ummī* already express divine fulfillment of the act of pursuing salvation and seeking after salvation expressed in the verbs used in verse 1. And so God speaks of these seekers and pursuers as a people (united under one government) and a nation (united by descent), the congregation of His people. Those who seek salvation and the God of salvation in a penitent spirit are to know that they are His *'am*, living under His government of grace; and His *le'ōm*, begotten by Him and reared by Him as His family and beloved children.

The noun-clauses introduced by *kī* are the object of the verbs in

401

the first two clauses. This is what they are to hearken to and take
to heart as God's word: A *thōrāh* shall go forth, etc. For the meaning of *thōrāh* and *mishpāṭ,* see the explanation under 42:3,4.
thōrāh does not mean Law as distinct from Gospel; it means
doctrine, instruction, God's word. *mishpāṭ* in its formal sense is the
justice which prevails as the rule of right in God's kingdom,
namely, grace; *thōrāh* in its essence is the Gospel. The old order of
the economy of laws is now a thing of the past. Now a different instruction goes forth from the Lord, a new justice is being established, which is grace and truth, John 1:17; Jeremiah 31:31ff. This
administration of grace, this doctrine of salvation, the Lord will establish not only in His people Israel, but He will also make it a
light, that is, a converting power unto salvation for the gentiles, cf.
Luke 2:32; Acts 26:18. Note how the New Testament era is joined
immediately to the rebuilding of the ruins of Jerusalem. The inter-
vening postexilic period of 500 years is, in the prophet's view,
wiped out. The external glory of the people of Israel was destroyed
by the exile, and it was never restored. The promised renewal is
that of the New Testament, a heavenly renewal, which the
prophet clothes in Old Testament garb, as John also did in the
Book of Revelation.

5 קָר֤וֹב צִדְקִי֙ יָצָ֣א יִשְׁעִ֔י וּזְרֹעַ֖י עַמִּ֣ים יִשְׁפֹּ֑טוּ

אֵלַ֤י אִיִּים֙ יְקַוּ֔וּ וְאֶל־זְרֹעִ֖י יְיַחֵל֥וּן׃

tsedheq and *yesha'* in verse 5, and *yeshū'āh* and *tsedhāqāh* in
verse 6 are all one and the same thing, the promised salvation,
which consists in deliverance, pardon, renewal, glorification. Each
word views the same thing from a different angle. The predicates,
qārōbh, an adjective, *yātsā',* a verb in the perfect, and *yishpōṭu,* an
imperfect, all refer to the future, as did also the verbs *thētsē'* and
'argīa' in verse 4. The first line of verse 5 — *qārōbh* to *yishpōṭu* —
explains the phrase in verse 4 beginning with *thōrāh.* The second
line of verse 5 explains the final clause of verse 4. *qārōbh* says that
the *thōrāh* and *mishpāṭ* of verse 4, and *tsedheq* and *yesha'* of verse
5, that is, the salvation prepared by the Lord and its fulfillment,
are now near at hand, fully completed in the mind of God. The second and third clauses of verse 5 explain that the Lord will mightily
"judge" the nations with that justice which He has set to be a light
unto the gentiles, and says that they are already longing for the
revelation of its power. And so these two clauses also express the
nearness of salvation. *zerō'ay* (plural, a poetic variation of *zerō'ʕ*)
does not represent the judging, punishing power of God, but rather

His power unto salvation, as is indicated by the longing with which the gentiles await it. This is the arm of the Lord which secures justice for them, namely, the justice of grace, salvation, deliverance (*yesha*ʾ) from the misery of sin. The waiting and yearning (both are intensive Piel forms of *qāwāh* and *yāḥal,* or *ḥūl*) of the isles is poetic description and must not be dogmatically misapplied. In content, verses 3-5 are the equivalent of 42:6f and 49:6, with the addition of one new thought: it is near.

⁶ שְׂאוּ לַשָּׁמַיִם עֵינֵיכֶם וְהַבִּיטוּ אֶל־הָאָרֶץ מִתַּחַת

כִּי־שָׁמַיִם כֶּעָשָׁן נִמְלָחוּ וְהָאָרֶץ כַּבֶּגֶד תִּבְלֶה וְיֹשְׁבֶיהָ כְּמוֹ־

כֵן יְמוּתוּן

וִישׁוּעָתִי לְעוֹלָם תִּהְיֶה וְצִדְקָתִי לֹא תֵחָת׃

The theme of the sixth verse is the certainty of the promised salvation. This verse is Luke 21:33 in vivid poetic form, a part of the development of 40:6-8. Those who wait with yearning for the promised salvation are bidden to look at the heavens and the earth. They impress us as being imperishable, and so too there seems to be an unbroken sequence in the generations of the earth's inhabitants. Their continuation is, however, not absolute. They will melt away like the snap of a finger; but the promised salvation of the Lord is absolutely eternal; it is everlasting. *kī* with *shāmayim* again introduces an object-clause. The point of comparison in *ʿāshān* and *beghedh* is their nothingness. The verbs fit into the picture. *nimlāḥū* (Niphal of *mālaḥ*) means to be worn away, to be scattered like dust, to dissolve; *bālāh* means to fall to pieces for rottenness.

kemō khēn is the subject of much dispute. *kemō* is a poetic form of *ke*. Gr. 103, k, p. 303. Many later commentators translate *kēn* as mosquitoes or midges. But *kēn* in the singular never occurs in that sense elsewhere in Scripture. In Exodus 8:12-15 (16-19) (Luther: *Laeuse*) *kinnīm* and *kinnām* occur, but not *kēn*. Modern Hebrew defines *kinnāh* as a louse, with a plural *kinnīm*, where one would expect *kinnōth*. The only sure thing seems to be to take *kēn* in its simple meaning of "so." They will dissolve and melt away like "so," like "that." "Just like that," with a snap of the fingers. They will dissolve into nothingness. The point of comparison is again their nothingness. *ḥāthath* denotes a physical breaking; the Niphal *niḥath* (imperfect *yēḥath*) is passive. Combined with the negative *lōʾ* it is the perfect opposite of *nimlaḥ, bālāh,* and *mūth.*

This verse is the focal point of the whole passage. The promise of the renewal of Zion and of the conversion of the gentiles will soon be fulfilled, and this salvation will be everlasting.

Second Part: verses 7-11: *The enemies can put nothing in the way of the fulfillment of this salvation; the strong arm of the Lord initiates it and carries it through to completion.*

7   *Hearken to Me, you who choose salvation,*
    O people, in whose heart My doctrine dwells!
    Do not fear the reproach of mortal men,
    And do not tremble at their revilings.

8   *For like a garment the moth will devour them,*
    And like wool the worm will devour them;
    But My salvation will stand forever,
    And My redemption to all generations.

9   *Awake, awake, clothe Yourself in power, O arm of the Lord,*
    Awake as in the days of old, in generations of long ago!
    Is it not You who cut down Rahab, pierced through the crocodile?

10 *Is it not You who dried up the sea,*
    The great deep of waters —
    Who made the depths of the sea a way,
    Over which the redeemed could pass?

11 *So shall the ransomed of the Lord return*
    And rejoicing come home to Zion,
    Eternal happiness shall be on their head,
    Joy and gladness shall take hold of them,
    Woe and sorrow shall flee away.

שִׁמְעוּ אֵלַי יֹדְעֵי צֶדֶק עַם תּוֹרָתִי בְלִבָּם 7

אַל־תִּירְאוּ חֶרְפַּת אֱנוֹשׁ וּמִגִּדֻּפֹתָם אַל־תֵּחָתּוּ:

The address of this second part is similar to that of the first part. Those who were in the first part designated as pursuers after salvation and seekers after the Lord, here are called *yōdheʿey tsedheq* and *ʿam tōrāthī belibbām* (weaving verse 4 into the pattern). These are the same people, somewhat differently described, as those addressed in the first part. *ʿam tōrāthī belibbām* is an explanatory parallel to *yōdheʿey tsedheq. yādhaʿ* is therefore clearly something more than "to know." It designates an act of will, *nosse cum affectu,* to delight in, to love, to choose, a sense that this verb often conveys. Cf. Psalm 40:9 (8), where *thōrāthekhā bethōkh mēʿay* corresponds to our *tōrāthī belibbām* in the sense of love for the Word of the Lord. As in verse 1, the believers are here described as lovers of salvation, lovers of the Lord and of His Word, by which salvation is conveyed. The believers are not to fear the mockery and revilings (the words are synonyms, *gidduphōth* being the stronger of the two) of human beings (*'enōsh,* a collective singular, that emphasizes the nothingness of man). In the exile, the believers in the word of promise were mocked by the unbelievers of their own people because of their belief in deliverance and in the renewal of Zion (66:5) and by their enemies who heaped mockery and abuse upon them (Ps. 137). It is against that mockery and abuse that this comfort is directed.

⁸ כִּי כַבֶּגֶד יֹאכְלֵם עָשׁ וְכַצֶּמֶר יֹאכְלֵם סָס
וְצִדְקָתִי לְעוֹלָם תִּהְיֶה וִישׁוּעָתִי לְדוֹר דּוֹרִים:

These mockers and scoffers are so worthless that vile worms destroy them as they devour garments and shreds of wool. Their mockery is of no account and no more able than moths and worms to hinder the realization of the promised salvation. The promise of salvation, however, and the assurance of deliverance, which always accompanies that promise, stand firm for ever. This verse is an amplification of 40:6-8: All flesh is grass, etc.

⁹ עוּרִי עוּרִי לִבְשִׁי־עֹז זְרוֹעַ יְהוָה
עוּרִי כִּימֵי קֶדֶם דֹּרוֹת עוֹלָמִים
הֲלוֹא אַתְּ־הִיא הַמַּחְצֶבֶת רַהַב מְחוֹלֶלֶת תַּנִּין:

Instead of continuing this comforting exhortation in words spoken by the Lord, as in 50:2b, 3; 48:12,13; 44:7,24; 43:15-18; 42:5; 40:21ff, the prophet now dramatically introduces the Lord's hearers as speakers and lets *them* supply the historical foundation for the Lord's words. They have heard the Lord's repeated assurances, have received them in faith, and now break forth with the enthusiastic plea that the Lord come to their rescue with His powerful arm, as He once did at the Red Sea. The three following verses are of great poetic beauty. The arm of the Lord, not the Lord Himself is invoked, and for that reason the verbs and the pronouns have the feminine form. The urgent repetition of *ūrī,* awake! pictures the Lord's arm as inactive, at rest, cf. Psalms 44:24(23); 57:9(8); 108:3(2). Indeed the arm is viewed as a purely physical member, for it is called upon to exert *'ōz,* strength, as for the execution of a difficult piece of work. The work is the rescue from exile and the return of the people to their homeland, verse 11. The next words hark back to the olden days and to that mighty work of the Lord which outshone all His other works for Israel and which is equaled only by the impending promised rescue (43:16-19). The reference is, of course, to the deliverance out of Egypt. He who directed that deliverance of the people, will also carry out this rescue. That rescue of ancient times is sketched in a few broad terms.

For the *ke* in *kīmēy* with a following genitive, see Gr. 118, s, u, p. 375f — in the manner of the days of old time. *dōrōth 'ōlāmīm* (double plural, Gr. 124,q,p.400f) generations of the old days of Israel, an accusative of time, Gr. 118, i, p. 374, merely emphasizes *yemēy qedhem*. The negative rhetorical questions that follow are an emphatic way of expressing the positive: Is it not You, etc.? *rahabh,* the raging one, and *tannīn,* a long, snake-like creature, perhaps a crocodile, are symbols of Egypt, as in Psalm 87:4; Isaiah 30:7; 27:1; Ezekiel 29:3; 32:2. The verbs and their forms (Hiphil participle of *ḥātsabh* and Polel participle of *ḥālal*) are vigorous expressions: hew down, pierce through. The destruction of the power of Pharaoh is pictured. The implication is: Thus will the Lord destroy the power of Babylon and every other power that holds us captive.

הֲלוֹא אַתְּ־הִיא֙ הַמַּחֲרֶבֶת יָם֙ מֵי תְּהוֹם רַבָּה 10
הַשָּׂמָה֙ מַעֲמַקֵּי־יָם֙ דֶּרֶךְ לַעֲבֹר גְּאוּלִים׃

The "sea" and the "great deep of waters" refer to the Red Sea, which Israel crossed on the way out of Egypt. Whereas the verbs following *halō' 'att hī'* are all participles with an attached article, the word *hassāmāh,* which one would naturally assume to be another participle with the accent on the ultimate, has the accent on the penultimate and is therefore a third singular feminine form of the perfect. (The postpositive Pashta is used with Azla when the accent is not on the final syllable.) Whether the Masoretes were right in thus accenting this word can be questioned. If this is a finite verb, then the article functions as a relative, the equivalent of *'asher.* There are a number of instances of this use of the article, cf. Gr. 138, g, i, k, p. 446f. Some critics move the Zaqeph away from *yām* and place it on *derekh,* but even with the accent where it now rests, *derekh* must be taken as part of the predicate. Grammatically *la'abhōr* belongs to *derekh,* but logically it belongs to *ma'amaqqēy yām.* — In those days the Lord made a highway for the people through the deeps where otherwise there lurked only destruction. And so also He is now able to make paths and highways for the children of Zion to return home from captivity all over the world, impossible as that might seem to them.

וּפְדוּיֵי יְהוָה יְשׁוּבוּן וּבָאוּ צִיּוֹן בְּרִנָּה 11

וְשִׂמְחַת עוֹלָם עַל־רֹאשָׁם שָׂשׂוֹן וְשִׂמְחָה יַשִּׂיגוּן נָסוּ יָגוֹן

וַאֲנָחָה׃

With one very slight difference, this verse is a repetition of 35:10. *pedhūyēy* (from *pādhāh*) is a Qal passive participle plural in the construct state. The literal meaning of *pādhāh* is to pay a ransom. It is commonly used in the extended sense of redeem, or set free. One might understand these words as having been spoken by the believers in Israel, but since the redeemed are referred to in the third person, it is more likely that the Lord Himself is being quoted. This is the Amen to the rapturous shouts of joy of the pious throngs of captives. The *ū* before *pedhūyēy* is to be taken as assertive: "yes," they shall return; although it may also be understood as a consecutive *Waw*. As in the days of old, *so* shall the redeemed return. *pedhūyēy* is a concise expression; in this instance there is not the usual assurance that the captives shall first be freed. They are portrayed as already free and on their homeward journey. They *are returning,* returning to Zion, and that with great rejoicing, the two phrases of the second clause adding details descriptive of the return. Now a new element is added: *Eternal.* "Everlasting joy," like the crown of a bride, shall rest on Zion's head. This theme is continued in two clauses, one positive, one negative. "Bliss and happiness" are a hendiadys: blissful joy and happiness. *sāsōn* and *simḥāh* (not *pedhūyēy*) are the subject of *yassīghūn* (Hiphal of *nāsagh*), as is evidenced by the parallel structure of the second half of the sentence. *yāghōn* (grief, pain, heartache) and *'anāḥāh* (sighing, sobbing) will flee from there (literally: "fled from there are," perfect tense). The parallel arrangement of the last two clauses is chiastic — the predicates form the means, the subjects the extremes. With this, the subject is exhausted; what follows must be a new thing.

Third Part: verses 12-16: *Israel should not be afraid, for the Lord, who governs the elements of all creation, is instituting a new regime of grace with those who are soon to be freed, in spite of all enemies.*

12 *It is I, I, who am creating a new thing for you.*
  Why should you be afaid of men, who must die,
  Of children of men, who become like grass?

13 *Why do you forget the Lord, who made you,*
  Who spread out the heavens and established the earth,
  Why tremble all the day, unceasingly, at the tyrant's fury,
  When he threatens to kill; where is now the tyrant's fury?

14 *Those who are imprisoned will soon be set free,*
  They shall not sink toward the grave,
  And food shall not be lacking for them.

15 *For I — I am the Lord, your God,*
  Who stirs up the sea, that its waves roar;
  The Lord Sabaoth is His name.

16 *And I will put My words in your mouth,*
  And will hide you in the shadow of My hand,
  To stretch out a heaven and lay the foundations of an earth,
  And proclaim to Zion: My people are You.

12 אָנֹכִ֧י אָנֹכִ֛י ה֖וּא מְנַחֶמְכֶ֑ם

מִי־אַ֤תְּ וַתִּֽירְאִי֙ מֵאֱנ֣וֹשׁ יָמ֔וּת וּמִבֶּן־אָדָ֖ם חָצִ֥יר יִנָּתֵֽן׃

The general theme is the same: the deliverance and glorification of Zion in spite of the opposition of enemies who shall come to naught. Only the manner of developing the theme is new. Regarding the emphatic addition of *hū'* to *'anōkhī,* see Gr. 141, h, p. 453. The participle of *niham,* as in verse 3, does not mean "to comfort," but rather "to renew"; hence our translation: "who is creating a new thing." The Lord repeats the theme of the first part with new and firm assurances. *mī 'att,* "who are you, that, etc." is rhetorically connected with *halō' 'att hī'* in verses 9 and 10. The usual rendering of this phrase, "are you then so helpless, that," hardly does justice to this idiomatic phrase. The entire history of the relation between Israel and its gracious God, and especially the *menahemkhen* of this verse lies in this phrase. We would say in our idiom: "God is your *menahēm;* why then are you afraid?" Cf. Gr. 111, m, p. 328. *yāmūth,* with a preceding *'asher* understood, is a relative clause with adjectival meaning: "Why then are you afraid of men who are mortal, destined to die," Gr. 155, f, p. 487. In the next clause, *ben 'adhām* and the reference to perishable grass emphasize the feebleness of the enemies. Before *hātsīr* we must supply *'asher ke,* "who is like." In view of the fact that the Lord (I, I, the one true, eternal, almighty, and gracious Covenant-God) is the Restorer of His people, there is no reason why they should fear the feeble attempts of their enemies to hinder the restoration.

408

13 וַתִּשְׁכַּח יְהוָה עֹשֶׂךָ נוֹטֶה שָׁמַיִם
וְיֹסֵד אָרֶץ וַתְּפַחֵד תָּמִיד כָּל־הַיּוֹם
מִפְּנֵי חֲמַת הַמֵּצִיק כַּאֲשֶׁר כּוֹנֵן לְהַשְׁחִית וְאַיֵּה חֲמַת הַמֵּצִיק׃

The Lord's consolation here takes on a tone of reluctant reproach — purely out of cordial concern. In their despondency
God's people are forgetting that their very existence (verses 1 and
2) and the continued existence of heaven and earth are due alone
to the power of the Lord their God. Because of their heedlessness,
the people live in constant fear of their oppressors, *ka'asher kōnēn
lehashhīth,* that is, in the same manner that they make preparations to destroy. *mētsīq,* oppressors, a collective noun, is a Hiphil
participle of *tsūq,* which means to choke, to strangle. Every new
measure that these stranglers devise fills the people with new
fear. But, says the Lord, where is the fury of these tyrants? To understand this question it is necessary to think of verse 14 as taking place. The doors of the prison are already open; the purpose of
the *mētsīq* to starve the prisoners is frustrated. And now in view of
this release of the prisoners, the Lord asks: Where is now the tyrant's fury? As much as to say: Don't you see that the fury of the
oppressors is powerless to offer any hindrance to your release?

14 מִהַר צֹעֶה לְהִפָּתֵחַ וְלֹא־יָמוּת לַשַּׁחַת וְלֹא יֶחְסַר לַחְמוֹ׃

For an explanation of the construction, *mihar lehippāthēah,* "it
hastens to be opened," see Gr. 114, m, p. 350, also Note 1 on that
page. The chief thought lies in the infinitive. *mihar* is to be rendered as an adverb: "Soon, quickly, will the *tsō'eh* (Qal participle)
be freed." *tsō'eh* is a Qal participle of *tsā'āh,* a word derived from
the Arabic, meaning to bend, crouch, to be bowed down. In the Old
Testament the word occurs also in 63:1, where it is usually translated "proud," a meaning suggested by the backward bending of
the neck. It occurs in Jeremiah 2:20, where it signifies a harlot
reclining by the way; and there are two occurrences in Jeremiah
48:12, which the LXX translates with κλίνοντας and κλινοῦσι
(the first a Qal participle and the second a Piel perfect). Those examples do not throw much light on the meaning of the word in this
passage. Luther's *Schroeter* in the Jeremiah passage, one who
handles winecasks, is pure conjecture. Nothing more is certain
than that *tsā'āh* does mean "to be bowed down, to crouch, to be
bent over." Our guess is that the word describes the prisoners as

sitting or lying in a crouching or bent position, and we translate the collective singular as "those who are imprisoned." *hippātheaḥ* supports that translation. What else may be suggested by the word is uncertain. The next clause, "They shall not sink toward the grave," quite clearly says that the *tsō'eh,* by being freed from prison, shall escape death by starvation in prison. Freed from prison he shall have bread in abundance.

$$\text{15 וְאָנֹכִי יְהוָה אֱלֹהֶיךָ רֹגַע הַיָּם וַיֶּהֱמוּ גַּלָּיו}$$
$$\text{יְהוָה צְבָאוֹת שְׁמוֹ:}$$

Verse 15 sets forth the reason for offering this consolation to Israel. He who makes this promise is *YHWH* (Israel's God of grace) and *'elōheykhā* (the Ruler over all things). *rōgha'* is a shorter alternate form of *rōghēa'* its accented final syllable connects it closely with *hayyām.* Nevertheless, *rōgha'* is in the absolute state and *hayyām* is an accusative, Gr. 65, d, p. 172. It is Israel's God who whips up the sea in the storm so that its waves roar. He is the Lord, the God of the hosts (in this phrase *'elōhēy* must always be supplied, Gr. 125, h, p. 403), who governs the world with all its forces and elements, according to His good pleasure.

$$\text{16 וָאָשִׂים דְּבָרַי בְּפִיךָ וּבְצֵל יָדִי כִּסִּיתִיךָ}$$
$$\text{לִנְטֹעַ שָׁמַיִם וְלִיסֹד אָרֶץ וְלֵאמֹר לְצִיּוֹן עַמִּי־אָתָּה:}$$

The *wā* before *'āsīm,* since it is not preceded by a perfect, is not *Waw* consecutive imperfect. *'āsīm* refers to the future, and the Qamets under the *Waw* is an echo of the Qamets under *Aleph.* In respect to the time of the action *kissīthīkhā* accommodates itself to *'āsīm,* although the action itself is completed (perfect). This *wā* forms a correlative with *we* in verse 15: "for — and therefore" or "as — so." Just as the Redeemer of Israel holds the sea in His hand (verse 15) and is the Creator of Israel, of heaven and of earth, so will He create a new heaven and a new earth, and to that purpose put His words into Israel's mouth and keep Israel in the shadow of His hand. This is no different from what was said in 49:2 and 42:1-4 (cf. 59:21) and what appears in Luke 21:15. In the first two of these passages the Savior Himself is addressed; here the word is spoken to Israel after the Spirit, whose mission is the same as that of the Savior, even though it comes to complete fruition only through Him as its perfect representative. The powers that will bring about Israel's release and glorification are the covenant with spiritual Israel, of which the Servant is the Mediator (according to 42:6 and 49:8), and His Spirit, and His Word (59:21), which shall endure forever. Also Israel's preservation in faith and in grace is effected through these powers ("I will hide you in the shadow of My hand"). Thus the Lord will create a new heaven and a new earth and restore the covenant-relation with Israel to its fullest power. "Heaven and earth" do not, of course, refer to those now existing. They have already been "stretched out" and "planted." A new creation is meant in 65:17; 66:22; Revelation 21:1ff, and we have here primarily a symbol of the perfection of the new order that will be established through Christ. Instead of *nāta' shāmayim*, the usual verb used in this phrase is *nātāh*. The meaning of *nātāh* is to stretch out; *nāta'* means to plant, to set in the ground, to drive into the ground like a tent-stake.

There is no reason why God's people should fear the fury of their enemies. Their fury is as nothing before the Almighty Lord, who through His word will accomplish Israel's redemption and perfect glorification.

Fourth Part: verses 17-23: *Yes, the people are like grass; but the Word of our God endures into eternity (40:7,8).*

This part is made up of two distinct paragraphs joined by the parenthetical verse 21.

17 *Rouse you, rouse you, rise up, O Jerusalem,*
Who has drunk out of the hand of the Lord the cup of His wrath,
Has drunk out of the bowl of intoxication, drained it.

18 *Of all the children that she has borne,*
There was none who guided her;
And none who took her by the hand,
Of all the children that she had reared.

19 *These two have befallen you — who sorrowed with you? —*
Devastation and ruin, sword and hunger —
Who was your comforter?

20 *Languishing your children lay*
At all the street corners —
Like antelopes caught in a net,
Filled with the wrath of the Lord and the rebuke of your God.

21 *Therefore, hear this, you afflicted one,*
And drunk, but not with wine:

22 *Thus says your Lord, the Lord,*
He who contends for His people, your God:
Surely, I will take out of your hand the cup of intoxication,
The bowl of the cup of wrath —
And you shall drink it no more.

23   *Instead, I will give it into the hand of your tormentors,*
     Who said to you: Bow down, that we may walk over you! —
     And you had to make your back like the earth
     And like a street for those that walked across.

The first paragraph, verses 17-20, describes Jerusalem at the moment when she drained the intoxicating cup of the wrath of the Lord to the dregs, and the spectacle she presented immediately after the conquest by Nebuchadnezzar. The verses emphasize that she received no help or comfort from her own children. In verses 21-23, the city, afflicted and drunk with the cup of the wrath of God, is comforted with the promise that she shall no longer have to drink of this cup and that the Lord will instead give it to her enemies to drain.

17 הִתְעוֹרְרִי הִתְעוֹרְרִי קוּמִי יְרוּשָׁלַ֜ם

אֲשֶׁר שָׁתִית מִיַּד יְהוָה אֶת־כּוֹס חֲמָתוֹ

אֶת־קֻבַּעַת כּוֹס הַתַּרְעֵלָה שָׁתִית מָצִית:

Jerusalem is pictured as staggering drunkenly and lying stretched out from having drunk of the cup of the Lord's anger. Three times the Lord calls to awaken her out of her stupor. In structure the verse is similar to verse 9. The entire passage is dramatic in the extreme. To appreciate this verse fully, one should read the first two chapters of Lamentations.

hith'orerī, a Hithpael imperative has the same meaning as *ʿūrī* in verse 9, but intensified. As in that passage the arm of the Lord is pictured as at rest, so here Jerusalem is portrayed as a woman physically feeble and bereft of feeling and sensation. *hith'orerī* is repeated with emphasis in order to rouse her to consciousness. With *qūmī* the Lord appeals to her to use what physical strength may be left to her. But both imperatives are creative words which give to Jerusalem what is required of her; they are quickening words of comfort and renewal, the *niham* of verse 3 and *menahemkhem* of verse 12. It was He who had afflicted Jerusalem, who had given her the cup of *hēmāh* to drink. *hēmāh* is wrath, fury, hot anger, a stronger word than *'aph*, anger. *qubba'ath kōs* is a poetic broadening of the simpler *kōs*. The entire cup is thus designated, with handle and foot, the *qubba'ath* being the bowl of the cup. This is the same word as *qōbha'* in 1 Samuel 17:38 and is the construct form of *qubbā'ah*. The syllable *qub* is no doubt a hardening of the syllable *gab*, which appears in *gābhīa'*, a cup, Genesis

44:2,12, and which regularly designates something bowl-shaped. *qubba'ath kōs* is to be understood literally: the bowl of the cup. *tar'ēlāh*, from *rā'al*, to stagger, to reel, denotes drunken staggering. That is the contents of the cup. This cup, filled with reeling, that is, with the hot anger and wrath of the Lord, which the Lord Himself has poured and pressed to her lips, she must drink, must drain to the last drop. The asyndetic arrangement of the verbs makes the statement drastically impressive. "You have drunk out of the bowl of intoxication, drained it."

אֵין־מְנַהֵל לָהּ מִכָּל־בָּנִים יָלָדָה 18

וְאֵין מַחֲזִיק בְּיָדָהּ מִכָּל־בָּנִים גִּדֵּלָה׃

And in the midst of all this woe and misery, there was among all the children that she had borne and reared, no *menaḥēl* (cf. 40:11; 49:10; Ps. 23:2), no one to guide and lead her, no one who would take her by the hand, none to support, strengthen, or comfort her. The repetition of the same thought in the same grammatical structure is melancholy in the extreme. Cf. Lamentations 1:2,9, 17,21. The emphasis lies on the *mikkol bānīm. 'akhēn ḥatsīr hā'ām*, 40:7! The people of God too are as grass where the rescue of Zion from the wrath of the Lord is concerned. Oh, those miserable, shallow, humanistic babblers who by some kind of philosophy, or by moralizing preaching, or social institutions, or by cultivation of natural human character seek to rescue from the woes of this life a humanity that is destroying itself by its own sin and languishes under the wrath of God! Man's woe is man's sin. Where there is sin, there is God's wrath, and only the grace of this same angry God can rescue, redeem, and restore to new life and happiness.

שְׁתַּיִם הֵנָּה קֹרְאֹתַיִךְ מִי יָנוּד לָךְ 19

הַשֹּׁד וְהַשֶּׁבֶר וְהָרָעָב וְהַחֶרֶב מִי אֲנַחֲמֵךְ׃

These words describe the physical destruction and the helplessness of the city. In *shtayim hēnnah,* these two things, the *hēnnah* is abstract, Gr. 122, q, p. 393. *shtayim* here means "of two kinds." See the lexicon under *shnayim. qōre'othayikh,* a Qal participle in the feminine plural, is from *qāra'* spelled with *Aleph,* but here it has the meaning of *qārāh* spelled with *He* (to meet), as is frequently the case in Isaiah. The word is the predicate: It was these two things that befell you. *mī yānūdh lākh* is a rhetorical question. No one showed her any sympathy. The literal meaning of *nūdh* is to sway back and forth, and in a transferred sense denotes the wagging of the head at sight of great trouble to show sympathy. The two kinds of woe that befell her are expressed by two pairs of words. On the one hand the woe is *shōdh,* devastation (from *shādhadh,* to be violent, to destroy) and *shebher,* ruin (from *shābhar,* to break in pieces); and on the other hand it is hunger and sword, that is death, by starvation and by the sword of the enemy. Destruction and ruin refer to the city; death by hunger and the sword refer to the inhabitants. For *mī 'anaḥamēkh* the commentators commonly offer *mī menaḥamēkh* as a correction, "Who was your comforter?" But one can manage with the former. It can be taken in the sense of *mī 'anī wa'anaḥamēkh:* "Who am I that I should be able to comfort you?"* Since these words are attributed not to the prophet, but to the Lord Himself and are obviously parallel to *mī yānūdh lākh,* it does seem unnatural to put this question into the mouth of the Lord. But we must not forget that we here have to do with Oriental poetry.

20 בָּנַיִךְ עֻלְּפוּ שָׁכְבוּ   בְּרֹאשׁ כָּל־חוּצוֹת   כְּתוֹא מִכְמָר
הַמְלֵאִים חֲמַת־יְהוָה   גַּעֲרַת אֱלֹהָיִךְ :

"Your children" are not children as distinguished from adults, but are the inhabitants of the city that Zion has reared. *'ālaph* (the form is here a perfect Pual) cannot mean to cover with a veil. In Amos 8:13 the meaning of the Hithpael is clearly "to faint with thirst." That the Pual is used here in the same general sense seems very probable because of the connection with hunger and the sword. The inhabitants are being described as perishing or already lying lifeless. They lie at the head, that is, at the corners of all the streets, like an "antelope of the net," that is, caught and hopelessly enmeshed, exhausted and in the throes of death. With *hamelē'īm* the thought returns to verse 17 and gives the reason for all these external woes: the anger and rebuke of the Lord. *ge'ārāh* denotes the verbal expression of anger. The voicing of God's anger wreaks ruin, destruction, and death.

21 לָכֵן שִׁמְעִי־נָא זֹאת עֲנִיָּה   וּשְׁכֻרַת וְלֹא מִיָּיִן :

Since Jerusalem has had to drain the cup of God's anger to the last drop, therefore, and for that very reason, the Lord in His love now turns to her in boundless compassion. She is called upon to listen to what the Lord has to say to her. *nā'* adds emphasis to the

---

*The Dead Sea Scrolls read: *yenaḥamēkh* (3rd person).

414

imperative. Jerusalem's misery is once more summed up in the one word *'anīyāh*. This word, which sounds forth so often in Isaiah and all of Scripture, is very general and yet so meaningful. The German *elend* comes close to expressing its meaning; the English "misery" and "miserable" have overtones not contained in *'anīyāh*. The word is descriptive of the lot of the children of God in this world. *shekhurath* is in the construct state, Gr. 130, a, b, c, p. 421. What is there remarked in b is pure conjecture.

22 כֹּה־אָמַ֞ר אֲדֹנַ֣יִךְ יְהוָ֗ה וֵאלֹהַ֙יִךְ֙ יָרִ֣יב עַמּ֔וֹ

הִנֵּ֥ה לָקַ֛חְתִּי מִיָּדֵ֖ךְ אֶת־כּ֣וֹס הַתַּרְעֵלָ֑ה

אֶת־קֻבַּ֙עַת֙ כּ֣וֹס חֲמָתִ֔י לֹא־תוֹסִ֥יפִי לִשְׁתּוֹתָ֖הּ עֽוֹד׃

The plural *'adhōnīm* usually refers to human lords and only occasionally to God, Psalm 147:5; Malachi 1:6. Delitzsch suggests that it is used here because Jerusalem is pictured as a woman; he might have said *wife* of the Lord. In any case, *'adhōnayikh* says that the Lord, as *'adhōnīm*, is her Lord and Master, and therefore the spiritual Husband and Lord of Jerusalem, the wife. As Spouse and God (*'elōhayikh*), the Lord contends *for* His people. *'asher* is to be supplied before *yārībh*. With the accusative *rībh* is also used in this sense, Isaiah 1:17; Deuteronomy 33:8. The striving and contending for Jerusalem consists in taking the cup of intoxication out of her hand and pressing it to the lips of the enemies in retribution for the torment inflicted on Jerusalem. *hinnēh* is assertive; *lāqahtī* is a prophetic perfect; *thosīphī lishtōthāh* is to be construed like *mihar lehippātheah* in verse 14 (Gr. 114,m,p.350). *ʿōdh* with preceding *lōʾ* means as much as "never again."

23 וְשַׂמְתִּ֙יהָ֙ בְּיַד־מוֹגַ֔יִךְ

אֲשֶׁר־אָמְר֥וּ לְנַפְשֵׁ֖ךְ שְׁחִ֣י וְנַעֲבֹ֑רָה

וַתָּשִׂ֤ימִי כָאָ֙רֶץ֙ גֵּוֵ֔ךְ וְכַח֖וּץ לַעֹבְרִֽים׃

The *Waw* after a preceding negative is exclusive, emphasizing the antithesis: "but, rather," Gr. 154, a, p. 484f. *samtīhā* is a prophetic perfect. *mōghayikh* is a Hiphil participle of *yāghāh*, although some commentators read *mōnayikh* from *yānāh*, to oppress. The following clauses develop this thought. The *mōghīm* have humiliated Jerusalem in inhuman fashion. The figurative expressions in the concluding clauses symbolize this humiliation: "to bow the soul," that is, one's self; "to make one's back a highway upon which one may walk."

Jerusalem lay prostrate, stunned, and insensible under the wrath of God; her own children were impotent to offer any help; but the Lord Himself will raise her up, take away the cup of wrath from her lips and give it to the enemies to drain.

The entire chapter, as is indicated by our heading, carries out the theme expressed in 40:6-8.

The three chapters, 49, 50, and 51, are woven into a unit, a Triad, by the thought that the faithfulness of the Lord makes Israel's deliverance and renewal a reality in spite of all the raging of the enemy and Israel's total impotence.

SECOND TRIAD
Chapters 52-54

*The Lord's zealous love leads His Servant
safely through His vicarious suffering,
and together with Him,
His afflicted congregation,
to sublime glory.*

First Discourse: Chapter 52:1-12

Because of the triumphant howling of the tyrannical enemies, and because of their blasphemies against His holy name, the Lord will glorify the newly sanctified Jerusalem and reveal His holy arm by redeeming His people and leading them safely home.

The discourse consists of two parts of equal length. Verses 1-6: The Lord will reveal His name to His people by resanctifying Zion-Jerusalem and delivering her captive people, because the enemies howl in derision at His people and daily blaspheme His name. Verses 7-12: On the hills surrounding Jerusalem messengers of joy appear and proclaim to Zion the return of her liberated people under the guidance of the Lord, their King. The Lord confirms the joyful message and exhorts Jerusalem to rejoice. The returning people are admonished to cleanse themselves of all pagan practices, and they receive assurances that the Lord will conduct them to safety.

First Strophe: verses 1-6: *Jerusalem shall be sanctified anew and her captive people shall be liberated, because their oppressors mock them and daily blaspheme the name of the Lord.*

1 *Awake, Zion, show your strength,*
   Put on your beautiful garments, O holy city Jerusalem;
   For no longer shall the uncircumcised and unclean set foot in you.
2 *Shake yourself free of dust, arise, O captive host of Jerusalem,*
   Free yourself of the chains about your neck, O captive daughter Zion!

418

3   *For thus says the Lord: You were sold for nought,*
    You shall also be redeemed without money.
4   *Yes, thus says the Lord, the Lord of all:*
    At the first My people went down to Egypt to sojourn there,
    And Assyria oppressed them without cause;
5   *And now, what is here before Me? says the Lord.*
    For nought was My people led away,
    Their oppressors howl, says the Lord,
    And always, all day long, they mock My name.
6   *Therefore My people shall know My name,*
    Therefore, on that day — that I am He, who says: Here am I.

עוּרִי עוּרִי לִבְשִׁי עֻזֵּךְ צִיּוֹן ¹

לִבְשִׁי ׀ בִּגְדֵי תִפְאַרְתֵּךְ יְרוּשָׁלַם עִיר הַקֹּדֶשׁ

כִּי לֹא יוֹסִיף יָבֹא־בָךְ עוֹד עָרֵל וְטָמֵא:

✕The twofold exhortation, "awake, awake," is addressed to the city Zion-Jerusalem. The city is not viewed as being asleep (Delitzsch), but as sunk into a stupor of grief and despondency because of her total destruction. This is an echo of 51:17-23. *ūrī, ūrī,* here echoes the *hith'ōrerī, hith'ōrerī* of that passage. Zion is admonished to put on her strength. She still possesses such strength, but she cannot rouse herself out of her stupor and put it to use. *libhshū 'uzzēkh* is therefore like our "pull yourself together." Regarding coordination without a copula, see Gr. 120, h, p. 387.

The *bighdhēy thiph'artēkh,* your beautiful garments, contrast with the sackcloth (not mentioned here) in which she had been sitting in the ashes (cf. 58:5, *saq wā'epher*). She is to change from her garb of sorrow to her beautiful garments (*bighdhēy thiph'artēkh* is construed like *har qodhshī,* Gr. 135,n,p.440), because she is again called the *'ir haqqōdhesh* (cf. 48:2), the city of holiness, the holy city (Gr. 128,p,p.417). Jerusalem had been the holy city, since it was the dwelling place of the Lord, the habitation of the glory of His grace, Psalm 46 and 84 (cf. Isaiah 63:15). But the Lord had Himself profaned it, when He departed from it and gave it over to the gentiles to desecrate and destroy it, 47:6; 43:28. But now the Lord again calls it the holy city, because in His heart it was still that and would soon be that again in the eyes of men. So, this designation of the city is prophetic prolepsis, which is intended to shake the city out of its dull grief, enliven it with new spirit, and fill it with new hope, joy, and strength. The picture of adorning itself with beautiful garments means to say that Jerusalem is to appear outwardly in a manner befitting the glory for which it is destined. Zion will soon again be a kingdom of priests and a holy nation, Exodus 19:6; therefore she is to be clothed in priestly garments and in the finery of a bride, cf. 61:10. Grounds for this exhortation are to be found in "for no longer shall the uncircumcised and unclean set foot in you." Concerning *yōsīph yābhō'*, see Gr. 114, m, p. 350; 120, c, p. 385; cf. also 47:1, at the end of the verse. "Not shall continue, not shall go," that is, "not shall continue to go," "no longer shall go." *'ōdh* adds emphasis. *'ārēl*, uncircumcised, is a Levitical designation for non-Israelites. The uncircumcised is outside the fellowship of Israel's God of grace and outside the sanctified congregation of the people, Genesis 17; Exodus 12:48. *ṭāmē'*, unclean, is likewise Levitical uncleanness; it is the abstract term corresponding to the concrete *'ārēl*. The *'ārēl* is in himself an unclean person, whose presence and contact renders all about him unclean, so that he is an abomination before God. That is what happened to Jerusalem, the holy city, and to the holy people (cf. Ps. 79 and 80), particularly in the last catastrophe. The Lord promises that that shall never happen again; she shall for all time be the unprofaned, pure, and holy city. The Lord will dwell in and with her and govern her without interruption as her King of grace.

It is the future, uninterrupted, spiritual government of the grace of the Lord in His church that is here expressed in negative terms, the same thought that appears at the beginning of the next section in verse 7: your God has taken over the government, *mālakh 'elōhāyikh*. The prophet presents in a single picture the entire future of the church into all eternity — the restitution of Jerusalem after the exile being the feeble beginning, followed by the Lord's government of grace in the New Testament Church and its fulfillment in eternity. The prophet views this rule of the Lord and presents it in terms of what the Lord is doing for the holy city of Jerusalem. But what the prophet says here is really nothing new. These are the old, familiar "sure mercies of David," so well known to the faithful in Israel, which are fulfilled in the coming of the Servant of the Lord, 55:3; 2 Samuel 7:12ff; 1 Kings 8:25; which are echoed again and again in the Psalms, Psalm 2, 89, 93, 97, 98, 99, 110; of which all the prophets testify, beginning with the first of them, Obadiah (verse 21); and which are the theme of the entire book of the prophet Isaiah, chapters 7-12; 25-27; 34 and 35; and throughout Isaiah II. This is the *melūkhāh* of Obadiah, the βασιλεία τῶν οὐρανῶν of Matthew, and the new Jerusalem that descends from heaven in the Revelation of St. John. Isaiah

sees it realized in the restitution of the ruined city and in the
return to the city of her *gōlāh,* or *shebhī.*

²הִתְנַעֲרִי מֵעָפָר קוּמִי שְׁבִי יְרוּשָׁלָם

הִתְפַּתְּחִ֗י מוֹסְרֵי צַוָּארֵךְ שְׁבִיָּה בַּת־צִיּוֹן׃

Most commentators understand this verse as being still addressed to Jerusalem and construe *shebhī* as a verb: "sit down,"
that is, be seated on the throne — in contrast to the virgin daughter of Babylon, who is commanded in 47:1 to be seated on the
ground, *shebhī lā'arets.* The Masoretes seem to have construed
shebhī as an imperative of *yāshabh,* since they combine *qūmī* and
shebhī by means of the Merkha and Tiphcha accents. That interpretation seems to be supported also by *hithna'arī mē'aphār,*
shake yourself free of dust, shake the dust out of your clothes; for
she had been sitting on the ground in ashes, a condition that
clearly forms the basis for the exhortation to put on her beautiful
garments. The exhortation in verse 1, to put on beautiful garments and to rise, is in verse 2 addressed to the same person.
Furthermore, *bath tsīyōn* (epexegetical genitive, daughter,
namely, Zion) in the next clause is a parallel to *yerūshālāyim* and
refers primarily to the city itself. It cannot be denied that
shebhīyāh (fem. of *shābhī*), meaning deported, taken captive, led
into captivity, is an attribute of *bath tsīyōn* and would have to be
understood in a greatly weakened sense if *bath tsīyōn* is taken to
refer to the city. Certainly, the city was not led away captive; but
that is what *shebhīyāh* says. So the word must refer to the inhabitants, and the term *bath tsīyōn* is a designation of the inhabitants
of the city who languish in the Babylonian exile. In the following
section, verses 3-6, it is clearly they who are being addressed, not
the city as such. But the phrase could hardly have been so understood if the inhabitants had not been mentioned before. And since
the last clause of verse 2 refers to the *gōlāh* of Jerusalem in
Babylon, the first clause must likewise refer to the *gōlāh,* for the
parallel structure of the sentence requires that. It then follows
that *shebhī* in the first part of the sentence must have *shebhīyāh*
as its synonymous parallel, and *shebhī* is therefore a substantive
denoting captivity, a body of captives. It is then immaterial
whether one construes *yerūshālāyim* as epexegetical genitive or as
possessive. — Our interpretation is therefore that verse 1 refers to
the city, and verse 2 to the people lying captive in Babylon. The
people are pictured as *shebhī,* a captive people, lying on the
ground, in the dust, in prisons, caves, and dungeons; and now they

are being exhorted to take heart, to rise up and shake the dust out
of their clothes, that is, to free themselves entirely of the shattered bonds and chains. The second half of the sentence serves
only to make the first half more concrete. — *hithpatteḥū*, a
Hithpael, third plural perfect, is pointed in the Qere as an imperative, second feminine, *hithpatteḥī.*

³ כִּי־כֹה֩ אָמַ֨ר יְהוָ֜ה חִנָּ֣ם נִמְכַּרְתֶּ֗ם וְלֹ֥א בְכֶ֖סֶף תִּגָּאֵֽלוּ׃

As the exhortation to Jerusalem in verse 1 is based on the fact
that no uncircumcised and unclean persons shall ever again profane her, so this exhortation addressed to the captive people in
Babylon is based on the Lord's assurance that He has determined
to free the people and will now carry out His promise. The solemn
kōh 'amar YHWH makes that certain. *ḥinnām* means "for
nought," without remuneration. The Lord has sold the people;
Babylon and the other powers are pictured as buyers. The Lord received nothing from them for delivering His people into their
power. The last clause avows that Israel shall be delivered out of
the hands of the enemy without money, that is, that the Lord will
offer no ransom or any compensation for their deliverance. They
will have to free the people whether they want to or not. The Lord
will use force. He will do that through Cyrus, even as in Egypt He
forced Pharaoh by the ten plagues to do His will. The forceful, concise form *ḥinnām* — *we* can be rendered almost exactly, if we
translate *we* with "just so": "As you were sold for nought, just so
shall you be freed without money."

⁴ כִּ֣י כֹ֤ה אָמַר֙ אֲדֹנָ֣י יְהוִ֔ה מִצְרַ֛יִם יָרַֽד־עַמִּ֥י בָרִֽאשֹׁנָ֖ה לָג֣וּר
שָׁ֑ם וְאַשּׁ֖וּר בְּאֶ֥פֶס עֲשָׁקֽוֹ׃

Verses 4-6 contain the grounds for the promise of deliverance
and glory made in verses 1-3. *'adhōnāy YHWH* lends special emphasis to the *kōh 'amar*. *'adōnāy* has the power, *YHWH* has the
will to carry out what *'amar* says. The unjust oppression that Israel, since the beginning (*barī'shōnāh*) of its history, suffered in
succession under the three great world powers, Egypt, Assyria,
and Babylon, is given as the reason for the deliverance and restoration to glory. This oppression of the people was at the same time
sin against the Lord Himself. For that reason Israel is consistently
called "My people." Each succeeding world power outdid the preceding one in brutality. At the beginning of their history the
Lord's people journeyed to Egypt (*mitsrayim* is accusative of direc-

tion) to sojourn there, as Egypt's invited guests. The people went there on Pharoah's invitation, Genesis 45:18ff; 47:5f; and so they should have been treated as guests. But Egypt exploited the people, brutally oppressed them, kept them in bonds in defiance of the Lord, Exodus 1; 5. The prophet makes no mention of this, because the story was so well known. The Assyrian oppression, which followed the Egyptian, is treated with equal brevity. *be'ephes,* "for nought," here has the meaning of "without ground or reason." Egypt and Assyria are so briefly mentioned, because the emphasis lies on the Babylonian oppression, to which the next verse is devoted.

וְעַתָּ֥ה מַה־לִּ֛י־פֹה֙ נְאֻם־יְהוָ֔ה 5

כִּֽי־לֻקַּ֥ח עַמִּ֖י חִנָּ֑ם מֹֽשְׁלָ֤יו יְהֵילִ֙ילוּ֙ נְאֻם־יְהוָ֔ה וְתָמִ֥יד כָּל־

הַיּ֖וֹם שְׁמִ֥י מִנֹּאָֽץ :

phōh here designates Babylon as distinct from Egypt and Assyria. It is altogether arbitrary to insist that *may-lī-phōh,* on the basis of 22:16, must mean "What have I to do here?" In that passage too it has only the general meaning of "What have you here and whom have you here, that you, etc." What special meaning is implied in the question must be determined by the context. Cf. 22:1; Judges 18:23; Psalm 114:5. If *ki* follows the interrogation *may-lī-phōh,* as in the passages cited and in this verse (*ne'um YHWH* is a parenthesis), then the *kī* is consecutive, Gr. 166, 2, p. 505, and 107, u, p. 318. Examples are Psalm 114:5: "What ailed you, O sea, that you fled?" Isaiah 29:16: "What *right* have you that you, etc."; Judges 11:12: "What controversy lies between me and you?"; 2 Samuel 16:10; 19:23(22), *mah-lī welākhem,* "What right have you over against me, that," etc. Cf. τί ἐμοὶ καὶ σοί John 2:4. Similarly, *may-lī-phōh* in this verse can mean: "Under what legal obligation was I *here* (in the case of Babylon) that My people were led away for nought?" But with this construction, the following clauses are but loosely connected and follow rather lamely. It seems to us that a different construction is to be preferred, since it is simpler. *may-lī-phōh* means "What have I?" or "What return have I here for having let My people be led away for nought?" We are reminded of the question in Matthew 19:27: τί ἄρα ἔσται ἡμῖν What shall we have therefore? The answer to the question follows in the next two clauses. This is the return I have for having let My people be led away without cost: Their taskmasters howl at them, and continually, all the day long, My name is blasphemed.

For *luqqah* in the sense of taken captive, led away, see Jeremiah 48:46. *ḥinnām*, here, as in verse 3, means without cost, for nought. The *mōshelāyw* (Qere) are of course not the Jews, but the Babylonian tyrants. *yeḥēylīlū* is the uncontracted form in the Hiphil of *yālal*, cf. Gr. 70, c, p. 193. The word otherwise is used always of mournful wailing. Here it is used of the *mocking* howling of the taskmasters which is similar to wailing cries of woe. *minnōˀats* is Hithpolal participle for *mithnōˀats,* Gr. 55, b, p. 152.

$$
\text{לָכֵן יֵדַע עַמִּי שְׁמִי לָכֵן בַּיּוֹם הַהוּא}^{6}
$$

$$
\text{כִּי־אֲנִי־הוּא הַמְדַבֵּר הִנֵּנִי:}
$$

lākhēn, therefore, joins the two halves of this first section together. The Lord had restrained His arm because of His plans for salvation and judgment, but now Babylon's mistreatment of the people and mockery of the Lord have removed all restraints, and He will quickly redeem His people. Because the Babylonians mocked the name of the Lord, He will show His people how holy that name is and how powerful it is to redeem His people and to destroy the enemy. In the second clause *lākhēn* is repeated for emphasis: yes, therefore. *bayyōm hahūˀ,* on that day, says that the redemption will take place at the time foretold in the promise. *yēdaˁ* is to be supplied from the first clause. The third clause says more specifically what the people shall experience: "That it is I who gave the assurance (*medhabbēr* is intensive): Here am I," that is, that I am He who fulfills His promises of salvation — which is what the enemy denied and those of little faith in Israel doubted. The contention of the modern critics that verses 3-6 must be an interpolation because the poetic form varies from that of verses 1 and 2 and the content is mainly reflection is wholly devoid of weight. (Cf. Cheyne, *Introduction,* p.303 and Duhm, *Das Buch Jesaia,* p.351,2d Ed.)

Second Strophe: verses 7-12: *The joyful message of the homecoming of the captives and the admonition that they cleanse themselves and be of good cheer.*

7 *How beautiful on the mountains are the feet of the heralds of joy,*
   Who proclaim peace, preach good tidings, announce the redemption,
   Who say to Zion: Your God has become King!
8 *Hark, your watchmen raise their voices, rejoice altogether,*
   For eye to eye they see,
   That home to Zion the Lord is returning.

9 *Break forth, rejoice all together, O ruins of Jerusalem,*
For the Lord has given His people a new birth,
He has redeemed Jerusalem again.

10 *The Lord has revealed His holy arm*
Before the eyes of all the gentiles,
And all the ends of the earth see the redemption of our God.

11 *Away, away, go forth from there,*
Touch no unclean thing!
Go forth from the midst of them, cleanse yourselves,
You who bear the Lord's vessels!

12 *For you need not depart in haste,*
And not as in flight do you need to go forth;
For the Lord shall go before you,
And it is the God of Israel who gathers you.

7 מַה־נָּאווּ עַל־הֶהָרִים רַגְלֵי מְבַשֵּׂר
מַשְׁמִיעַ שָׁלוֹם מְבַשֵּׂר טוֹב מַשְׁמִיעַ יְשׁוּעָה
אֹמֵר לְצִיּוֹן מָלַךְ אֱלֹהָיִךְ׃

In form, this section is entirely independent of the preceding
section, but in contents it is closely connected with that section.
What is there promised is here described as fulfilled. The Lord's
hinnēnī (verse 6) has come true. Zion's captives have been freed
and are described as being on their way home. Zion receives the
glad tidings from messengers who sped on ahead. These words can
be understood as having been spoken by the prophet, or else as
coming directly from the mouth of the Lord. The description
begins by directing the attention to the heralds who appear on the
mountains surrounding Jerusalem with their glad tidings of
deliverance.

nā'wū used to be construed as a Pilel of *nā'ah*, or *nā'aw*, but today it is explained as a Niphal of *'āwāh*, to desire, Gr. 75, x, p. 212f,
and 23, d, p. 80. "How desirable, how beautiful!" The feet are
called beautiful because they are looked upon as the bearers of the
glad news. The picture is a synecdoche, *pars pro toto*. They are presented as hastening over Jerusalem's hills toward the city.
mebhassēr is a collective. For the meaning see the remarks on
40:9. It is a general term for the εὐαγγελισταί of the New Testament. They preach *shālōm, ṭōbh,* and *yeshū'āh,* not three separate
messages, but a single item described by three different terms. It
is the salvation promised in the days of old, which now begins with
the *yeshū'āh,* the deliverance of the people out of Babylon, which

has as its consequence nothing but good, namely, peace with God, the perfect condition of salvation. The conclusion of the message announces the reason for all this good: Zion's God has become King, has taken over the rule. That is the translation required by *mālakh*. The assumption is that the Lord, angry with His people, had, during the exile, given the rule over Israel and over the kingdoms of the world into the hands of the gentiles. With the deliverance of His people out of the power of the gentiles, He again took into His own hands the rule of grace over Israel and the reins of world government, never again to let them out of His hand. Thus full salvation is guaranteed the people of God for all future time. Psalms 93 and 96-99 strike the same note. It is the consummate rule of God, which John depicts in Revelation 11:15,17 and 19:6 as already accomplished, of which all the prophets, beginning with Obadiah, speak. See 41:27. Delitzsch refers to Nahum 2:1 (1:15) as the original of our passage, thus denying authorship of our passage to Isaiah and ascribing it to a Deutero-Isaiah. Nahum prophesied during the reigns of Manasseh and Josiah, after the destruction of No-Ammon (660). Why must it always be assumed that the lesser spirits, like Nahum, are the originals, and that the great ones, like Isaiah (or an assumed Deutero-Isaiah), are the copyists?

קוֹל צֹפַיִךְ נָשְׂאוּ קוֹל יַחְדָּו יְרַנֵּנוּ 8

כִּי עַיִן בְּעַיִן יִרְאוּ בְּשׁוּב יְהוָה צִיּוֹן׃

Concerning *qōl* as an exclamation, cf. 40:3,6, Gr. 146, b, p. 467. The plural form *nāse'ū* agrees with the plural in *tsōphayikh*. The *tsōphīm* can hardly be prophets, as Delitzsch thought; in any case, it is a mistaken view to take them to be companions of the returning captives. Zion is being addressed, verse 6; the *tsōphīm* are her watchmen. They are sentinels, whose station is on the watchtowers, on the walls of the city, or out in the field, and it is their duty to scan the surrounding country and to report any signs of danger, as in 21:5-9; 2 Samuel 13:34; 18:24ff. It is they who at sight of the heralds approaching over the hills of Jerusalem, as one man (*yaḥdāw*) raise up their voices and shout for joy, for eye to eye they behold (*rā'āh* with *be* means to look upon something) the return of the Lord to Zion. The "eye to eye" does not refer to sentinels standing close together, eye to eye, as Duhm explains, but means that their eye looks into the eye of the one who is approaching. First they see the heralds of joy who are hastening on ahead of the others, and then they behold eye to eye, face to face, the Lord Himself returning to Zion at the head of the redeemed. Older translators and commentators, following the LXX, construed *shūbh* as causative or transitive. It is undeniable that *shūbh* is so used, as the lexicon will indicate, but it is not necessary to take it in that sense in this passage. From verse 7 onward, the subject of the discourse is, besides the heralds of good tidings, God who has become the King of Zion. It does seem more natural to look eye to eye upon the One returning (the Lord) than upon someone leading (*shūbh* in the causative sense) others home. In our translation *tsīyōn* is an accusative of direction, cf. Gr. 117, a, Note 2, p. 362. If one takes *tsīyōn* to be the object of *shūbh*, the result is that the Lord is pictured as returning Zion to Zion, that is the people of Zion to the city of Zion, which seems quite unpoetic.

⁹ פִּצְח֤וּ רַנְּנוּ֙ יַחְדָּ֔ו חָרְב֖וֹת יְרוּשָׁלִָ֑ם

כִּֽי־נִחַ֤ם יְהוָה֙ עַמּ֔וֹ גָּאַ֖ל יְרוּשָׁלִָֽם ׃

Now the ruins of Jerusalem, pictured as lying deep in sorrow, are exhorted to break forth in rejoicing. The two imperatives, co-ordinated without a copula, are emphatic (*pitsehū, rannenū* instead of the more usual *pitsehū rinnāh*, 14:7; 44:23; 49:13; 54:1; 55:12). In the second half of the verse and in verse 10 the reason for the exhortation is given. *niham,* as in 51:3, is more fittingly understood in the physical than in the moral sense, especially since it is parallel with *gā'al* which here refers to physical deliverance. In *gā'al* there lies the idea of repurchasing, regaining possession, a connotation that we are prone to overlook. Babylon is pictured as conquered and broken. The Lord has wrested Jerusalem out of its hands and regained possession of the city, and so the Lord has revived the people which He has brought with Him out of Babylon to a new life of bliss. It is with this understanding that we have translated *niham* with "reborn." The Lord has regained possession of the people for Himself. That is, in fact, the reason why the sorrowing ruins of Jerusalem should rejoice, for now they are to be gloriously rebuilt.

¹⁰ חָשַׂ֤ף יְהוָה֙ אֶת־זְר֣וֹעַ קָדְשׁ֔וֹ לְעֵינֵ֖י כָּל־הַגּוֹיִ֑ם

וְרָאוּ֙ כָּל־אַפְסֵי־אָ֔רֶץ אֵ֖ת יְשׁוּעַ֥ת אֱלֹהֵֽינוּ ׃

Verse 10 is an extension of the thought expressed in 9b. The Lord has shown His omnipotent power to the unbelieving, scoffing enemies, to all heathen. Babylon, the unconquerable, lies broken, and the people are free. The entire gentile world must recognize and acknowledge the salvation that the Lord has prepared for His people. The picture in *ḥāsaph zerōaʿ qodhshō,* He has bared His holy arm, is extremely vigorous and forceful. It is the arm of God that from out of the tempest destroys the enemies with the sword of vengeance.

11 סוּרוּ סוּרוּ צְאוּ מִשָּׁם טָמֵא אַל־תִּגָּעוּ
צְאוּ מִתּוֹכָהּ הִבָּרוּ נֹשְׂאֵי כְּלֵי יְהוָה:

Verses 11 and 12 refer back to the hour when the exodus of the delivered people from Babylon began. The people are urgently exhorted to go out and depart from "there," the name of Babylon being carefully avoided here, as always in the last two parts of the book. The exhortation to touch no unclean thing is in contrast with the command given to the Israelites when they departed from Egypt, to borrow from their neighbors vessels of gold and silver (Exod. 11:2). In that instance it was the Lord's wish to give to His people, which was yet to be sanctified, a part of the wages they had earned but that had been withheld. Here the redeemed are made from the very beginning to be *nōseʿey keley YHWH,* bearers of the temple vessels that had been carried off by Nebuchadnezzar, that is, appointed to serve as priests and Levites (Num. 1:50ff). It makes no sense to translate *keley YHWH* with "weapons of the Lord." Since they are appointed to this service, they must now be Levitically clean, must separate themselves outwardly from the abominations of the people of Babylon ("go forth from the midst of them"), and not lay hands on even a shred of Babylonian belongings. *hibbārū* is the Niphal imperative of *bārar* with lengthening of the vowel to compensate for the doubled consonant Gr. 67, v, p. 181. For the fulfillment of this prophecy through Cyrus, see Ezra 1. What the departing people took with them in the form of freely offered gifts was not really Babylonian goods, but gifts bestowed on them by Cyrus, the servant of God. Paul's use of this verse in 2 Corinthians 6:17 is well-known. Compare also Abraham and the king of Sodom, Genesis 14:22ff.

12 כִּי לֹא בְחִפָּזוֹן תֵּצֵאוּ וּבִמְנוּסָה לֹא תֵלֵכוּן
כִּי־הֹלֵךְ לִפְנֵיכֶם יְהוָה וּמְאַסִּפְכֶם אֱלֹהֵי יִשְׂרָאֵל:

This verse gives the reason for the admonition to cleanse themselves thoroughly of all Babylonian filth. There is no hurry (*hippāzōn*), as there once was at the exodus from Egypt (Exod. 12:11); here they are not in flight as their fathers were before the sword

428

of Pharaoh, for Babylon's power is broken and the Lord has assumed the rule (*mālakh*). The Lord goes on before the redeemed, preparing a way for them, and He also follows after them, gathering up those who might faint on the way. The expressions in the second half of the verse are descriptive of an army taking to the field. The Lord is both vanguard and rear guard of His departing people. They leave completely secure against any threat of the enemy.

Résumé: The chapter is a fervent exhortation to Zion, whether at home or among strangers, to shake off all sorrow and to give herself over to joy and rejoicing, because the hour of her deliverance, and with it, the hour of her rebirth and eternal glorification has arrived, verses 1-6. The second half describes the arrival of the Lord at the head of the delivered hosts in Jerusalem after resuming His kingly rule and destroying the gentile power. Going back in point of time, the second part of the chapter concludes with the exhortation to the redeemed in Babylon to purge themselves of all uncleanness in complete reliance on the protection of the Lord, and to sanctify themselves for the Lord's service, into which they are now to enter anew. — Verses 11 and 12 can also properly be considered as a separate strophe.

Second Discourse: Chapters 52:13-53:12

The Lord exalts to divine glory the Servant who had been
sent to humble Himself and take upon Himself the guilt of
all as their substitute.

The traditional chapter division, which dates back to the early
part of the thirteenth century, went astray at this point. The
chapter begins at 52:13, where the Servant of the Lord is introduced, who from that point on to chapter 53:12 is the subject of the
discourse. The discourse is divided into five parts: 1) 52:13-15: The
exaltation of the humbled Servant; 2) 53:1-3: The inhuman
degradation of the Servant; 3) 4-6: He bore our chastisement; 4)
7-9: He suffered patiently, although He was innocent; and 5)
10-12: The superhuman exaltation of the Servant.

First Strophe: 52:13-15: *The Servant of the Lord, who was humbled beneath what is human, is exalted far above what is human.*

13 *Behold, My Servant will prosper,
    He will rise, He will be lifted up, He will be
       highly exalted.*
14 *As many were amazed at You —
    So disfigured was His appearance beyond that of a man,
    And His form beyond that of the sons of men —*
15 *So will He strike the nations with amazement,
    Kings will shut their mouths before Him;
    Then will they see what had never been told them,
    And discover what they had never heard.*

13 הִנֵּה יַשְׂכִּיל עַבְדִּי יָרוּם וְנִשָּׂא וְגָבַהּ מְאֹד:

This strophe is a brief summing up of the contents of the following chapter (53:1-12), with deep stress on the chief thought of the
chapter. The theme of the 53rd chapter is not the suffering of the

430

Servant as such, but rather His triumph over suffering and His exaltation out of this humiliation. — *hinnēh,* as so often, does more than call attention to something; it is affirmative. The primary meaning of *yaskīl* is "to be prudent," "to act wisely," namely so, that the proposed goal is attained. Often it refers to the attainment itself: to have success, to prosper, to carry a thing through to completion. In 41:20 and 44:18 the word is used in the first of these two meanings. It also occurs often in the latter sense, as for example in 1 Samuel 18:14 and Jeremiah 23:5. We prefer the latter meaning for this verse, since it expresses the chief thought of verses 13-15 and of the entire section to the end of chapter 53. In 42:1-9; 49:1-9, and 50:1-9 this same thought also comes clearly into the foreground. In the face of all difficulties the Servant of the Lord will carry through to a successful end the task that has been assigned to Him. The next three verbs unfold the thought expressed in *yaskīl.* They presuppose the inhuman degradation of the Servant referred to in verse 14, and they form a climax. *yārūm* says only that He will not remain in the state of humiliation and perish, but will rise out of it, prevail, and triumph. *nissā˒* designates the process of this rising as being lifted up or lifting Himself up. *gābhah* expresses the state or condition of His exaltation, cf. 5:16 and Job 36:7. *me˓ōdh* emphasizes this high state, which in verse 15 is defined more concretely. The Servant is being exalted to a state of lordship over all the nations and their kings. How wonderful that the Spirit of inspiration has in these three verbs so precisely foretold the resurrection *(yārūm),* the ascension into heaven *(nissā˒),* and the sitting at the right hand of the Father *(gābhah me˓ōdh)!* — According to the rule governing the sequence of tenses the imperfect *yārūm* is followed by two perfects.

כַּאֲשֶׁר שָׁמְמוּ עָלֶיךָ רַבִּים 14

כֵּן־מִשְׁחַת מֵאִישׁ מַרְאֵהוּ וְתֹאֲרוֹ מִבְּנֵי אָדָם :

The construction of verses 14 and 15 has long been misunderstood, even down to our own time. The King James Version construes the passage correctly, but Luther misunderstood the construction. The sentence beginning with *ka'asher - rabbīm* is not continued until the *kēn yazzeh* of verse 15. The two clauses from *kēn mishḥath* to *˒ādhām* are a parenthesis. In the opening clause, the Lord intimately addresses the Servant in the second person *(˓aleykhā),* whereas in the following clauses and in the next sentence the more impersonal third person is again employed. *shāmēm* denotes a state of barrenness, sterility, lifelessness; here it describes the overwhelming amazement over the disfigured form of the Servant. The poetically extreme expression tends to emphasize the contrasts. The parenthesis *kēn mishhath* to *'ādhām* gives the reason for this amazement, literally: "so disfigurement more than man was His appearance, and His form (supply 'was disfigurement') more than sons of men." Awkward as the connection with *kēn* may appear to us, *mishhath* is nevertheless a substantive in the construct state, before a comparative introduced by *min*, Gr. 130,a,p.421. There is also a possibility that *mishhath* should be read *moshhath* (a Hophal participle). The Babylonian punctuation is said to have *mushhath*. There is, however, no doubt about the meaning: His appearance, as well as His form, have been inhumanly disfigured. *mishhath* is to be supplied before *mibbenēy*. *'īsh* was chosen rather than *'ādhām* or *'enōsh*, and *tō'ar* rather than *pānīm*, as more expressive of the nobility of His natural appearance. "Men mock and taunt and jeer Thee, Thou noble countenance." For *tō'arō* instead of *to'orō* (Hateph Pathah instead of Hateph Qamets), see Gr. 93,q,p.267, also 1 Samuel 28:14; Isaiah 1:31. The disfigurement of the Servant, it may be added, is to be understood of the body as well as of the spirit and the emotions, as verses 3,4,5, and 7 of chapter 53 and its fulfillment in the Passion history show.

15 כֵּן יַזֶּה֙ גּוֹיִ֣ם רַבִּ֔ים עָלָ֛יו יִקְפְּצ֥וּ מְלָכִ֖ים פִּיהֶ֑ם
כִּ֠י אֲשֶׁ֨ר לֹֽא־סֻפַּ֤ר לָהֶם֙ רָא֔וּ וַאֲשֶׁ֥ר לֹֽא־שָׁמְע֖וּ הִתְבּוֹנָֽנוּ׃

kēn yazzeh now continues the sentence that began with *ka'asher* in verse 14 and that was interrupted by the parenthesis. Intense as was the amazement over the disfigurement of the Servant, the amazement over His exaltation will be equally intense. The *rabbīm* of verse 14 is now enlarged to *gōyim rabbīm*. Concerning the meaning of *yazzeh*, a Hiphil of *nāzāh*, there is today virtually only one opinion. *hizzāh* in the sense of "sprinkle" with a person as its accusative object does not occur; and the context, both that which precedes (the contrast to *shāmemū rabbīm*) and that which follows (the kings in mute astonishment), precludes any thought of a priestly act of cleansing the nations by sprinkling. The context requires an act that would have as its consequence something akin to the mute astonishment of the kings. *nāzāh*, as a Qal intransitive, means to spatter, to spurt forth in scattered drops (cf. 63:3 and 2 Kings 9:33). The Hiphil would then mean to cause to spring forth, so that the nations, like spattered drops of water,

scatter in consternation over the sudden spectacle of the glory of
the Servant. As those "many" (*rabbīm*) were stunned at the sight
of the inhuman disfigurement of the form of the Servant, just so,
at the sight of His divine glory, will they spring up and scatter in
terrified amazement. The parallel clause describes the kings of
the nations as shutting their mouths before Him, struck with fear
and amazement as they view the glory of the Servant. This refers,
in its final analysis, to the speechless terror of the unbelievers at
the sudden appearance of the Servant on the Day of Judgment, cf.
Matthew 24:30; 25:31f; Luke 23:30; Revelation 6:15,16; Isaiah 2;
and Hosea 10. Other revelations of the glory of Jesus, including
the spiritual manifestation that is regeneration, are, however, not
ruled out (see 49:7). The following clauses, headed by *kī*, explain
why the glory of the Lord struck the nations and their kings with
such overpowering amazement. They are seeing something wholly
unexpected, unheard-of, unbelievable. *'asher* introduces a relative
clause which is the accusative object of a verb that follows: "That
which was not told to them, they see, etc.," cf. Gr. 138,e,p.445. *rā'ū*
refers to physical perception; *hithbōnānū* to inner perception. *lō'*
suppar lāhem and *lō' shāme'ū* are poetic expressions and must not
be pressed. In our everyday speech such expressions as "unheard-
of" and "impossible" have also outgrown their etymology.

Second Strophe: 53: 1-3: *The inhuman degradation of the Servant.*

1   *But who believes our preaching?*
    And to whom is the arm of the Lord revealed?
2   *For like the shoot of a plant He grew before Him,*
    Yes, like a root-sprout out of dry ground,
    He had neither form nor beauty,
    When we saw Him, there was no semblance that could
      please us.
3   *Despised was He and shunned by everyone,*
    A man of sorrows and acquainted with grief,
    Like one before whom one covers his face,
    So despised that we esteemed Him not.

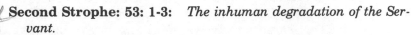

¹ מִי הֶאֱמִין לִשְׁמֻעָתֵנוּ וּזְרוֹעַ יְהוָה עַל־מִי נִגְלָתָה:

Even though there is nothing literally contained in 52:15 that
points to a *conversion* of the gentiles and their kings, and though it
is only their stunned amazement at the sudden sight of the majesty of the Servant that is expressed, still 53:1 stands out in clear

contrast to that verse. Verse 15 treats of the impression that the
exalted Servant made upon the *gentiles;* in contrast, in chapter 53
the Servant is confronted by people of His own nation, among
whom He walks, and who can observe Him in everyday life. The
pronouns *we* and *our* in verses 1-6 refer to Israel; the pronouns in
lephānāyw (2), in *'ammī* (8), and in *'aḥalleq* (12) refer to the Lord
who is mentioned in verses 1, 6, and 10. To interpret the *we* in 53:1
as referring to the gentiles mentioned in 52:15 is a sheer case of
violence exerted by those who refuse to see the person of the
Messiah in the Servant, but insist that the Servant is Israel personified. We repeat: There is nothing whatever in 52:15 to indicate
that the gentiles come to the obedience of faith through the spectacle of the exalted Servant. Conversion of the gentiles is not
referred to until 53:11 and 12, and the *we* in chapter 53 are always
persons who have come to acceptance of the Servant in penitent
faith. The opening words of chapter 53: "Who believes our preaching?" are in contrast to the last verse of 52 and therefore are to be
connected to it by the adversative conjunction *but.* The unexpressed connection between 52:15 and 53:1 is this: This despised
Servant will in due time be so highly exalted that the whole remaining unbelieving world will stand stunned and silent before
Him in amazement. To us, the people of the Lord, this exaltation
has always been preached. But who — even among us — believed
it! For, etc... To insist that preaching (*shemu'āh*) is not preaching
in the subjective sense, but always preaching in the objective
sense, namely, the content of what is heard by us, is a mechanical
use of language. In John 12:38 and Romans 10:16 ἀκοή is the
preaching, as Luther correctly understood. There has been a transition in sense from the objective to the subjective. In this connection, see Obadiah 1 and Jeremiah 49:14, where *tsīr*, a messenger,
is used alongside *shemu'āh*. Who, then, are the *we* referred to in
the suffix of *shemu'āh?* As we have said, they are not the unconverted gentiles of 52:15. From verse 2 onward it is the people of
Israel who are meant in the pronoun *we,* and so it seems natural to
assume that it is they who are meant by the suffix in
shemu'athēnū, and that the prophet identifies himself with them.
Delitzsch favors that interpretation. But this makes sense only if
one translates *lishemu'athēnū* as "to what we have heard," as
Delitzsch in fact does, and if one then takes *shemu'āh* in the sense
of sermon or message, the result will be a monstrosity: "Who of us
believed his own message?" *shemu'athēnū* can certainly be taken
in the objective sense. The prophet, speaking in the name of the

people, would then be saying: In contrast to the gentiles, who had never heard of the majesty of the Servant and will one day tremble before it, we, of Israel, have heard very much about it; but who of us believed it? One might accept that explanation, especially since it is homogeneous to, and parallel with, the revelation of the arm of the Lord in the next clause. But those who take *shemu ̔athenu* in its subjective sense, as in John 12:38, do not need such an explanation, but may understand the *we* lying in the suffix of *shemu ̔ah* as referring to the prophet in conjunction with all his fellow prophets. If someone objects to this, he should remember that in this sublime section Isaiah speaks like a dramatic poet who often brings his speakers forward without first introducing them. Thus, in 52:13-15 it is the Lord that speaks (*My* Servant, etc.); in 53:1 it is the prophet speaking in the plural for the school of the prophets; in verses 2-7 it is the people; in verse 8 it is again the Lord (*My* people); in verses 9-10 it is again the people or the prophet; and in verse 11 it is once more the Lord. It is in this situation that the critics, when it suits them, find their excuse to alter the text, as in the case of *'ammi* in verse 8.

The question "Who believes our preaching?" is rhetorical, more an exclamation than a question. The point is that hardly anyone, even in Israel, had put any faith in the glorious exaltation of the Servant. Cf. Gr. 150, d, p. 474 and 151, a, p. 476. The perfect *he'emin* represents the past continuing into the present, or the perfect of common experience, both of which are well expressed by our present tense, Gr. 106, g, k, p. 311f. Isaiah, more than anyone else, had preached of the exaltation of the Servant of God, chapters 4,7,9,11, 32-35, 40,42,49,50; but up to the present he had preached in vain. Only now, when in spirit he is among the apostles at Pentecost, are the eyes of the elect opened, Acts 2:36ff. The second clause: "To whom is the arm of the Lord revealed?" repeats the contents of the first clause in somewhat different poetic form, cf. 52:10. This refers to the true spiritual recognition that God was in Christ, 2 Corinthians 5:19.

2 וַיַּעַל כַּיּוֹנֵק לְפָנָיו וְכַשֹּׁרֶשׁ מֵאֶרֶץ צִיָּה

לֹא־תֹאַר לוֹ וְלֹא הָדָר וְנִרְאֵהוּ וְלֹא־מַרְאֶה וְנֶחְמְדֵהוּ:

Verses 2 and 3 are explanatory of verse 1. The *Waw* consecutive imperfect is sometimes explanatory, without a change of time, Gr. 111, d, p. 326; Genesis 2:25; 36:14 and 32; 1 Kings 1:44. The modern conjecture that *ki 'alah* ought to take the place of *wayya'al* is altogether unnecessary. Israel failed to recognize the divine glory of the Servant, because He appeared in such humble form. The two comparisons: "like the shoot of a plant He grew up before Him" and "like a root-sprout out of dry ground" clearly are a reference to His earthly parentage. *yōneq,* from *yānaq,* to suck, is literally a sucker, a small shoot that unexpectedly and unnoticed springs up somewhere on the branch of a tree. In 11:1 it is called *ḥoṭer,* the Greek μόσχος. *shoresh,* a root, or root-sprout, is used here, as in 11:10 in the sense of *nēṭser mishshorāshāyw* of 11:1. He grew out of a land of dryness (*tsīyyāh* is a noun). This clearly represents a fulfillment of 11:1. The branch from which this shoot (*yōneq* or *ḥoṭer*) springs forth is the stem (*geza'*) of Jesse, and the root-sprout that grows out of dry land is the *nēṭser mishshorāshāyw,* a sprout from his (Jesse's) roots. The house of Jesse or of David, which brought forth the Servant of the Lord, is pictured as dried-up land out of which a root would by nature not send up a new shoot, or as a branch from which an offshoot could no longer grow. To ignore this explanation, which is practically forced upon the passage by 11:1, and to explain the dry ground as referring to political situations (the exile) or to spiritual conditions in Israel, is ranging far afield, while the true explanation lies so near at hand. On the other hand, one is not justified in explaining this dry ground by what Mary says in Luke 1:34. The aridity of the royal house of David alone is meant. "Is not this the carpenter's son?" Matthew 13:55ff; Mark 6:3. "Can there any good thing come out of Nazareth?" John 1:46; 7:41,52.

In the next clause, the reference to form and beauty is, of course, not to be understood as a description of His physical form and appearance, although that is not to be ruled out entirely. The paintings of the head of Christ represent the ideal of ancient and modern artists. The Scriptures tell us nothing about Christ's outward appearance. There is nothing here of rank or position, wealth, power, or outward pomp or grandeur, nothing of what appeals to the eye of natural man as brilliant and imposing. Cf. Matthew 8:20; 9:9ff, and the humble form of the Servant, Philippians 2:7. The final clause of this verse has three members, each of which is introduced by *we: wenir'ēhū, welō' mar'eh, wenehmedhēhū.* The first *we* is temporal or conditional: "when we saw Him." The second is the *we* of the apodosis: "then there was no semblance." The third *we* is consecutive: "so that He pleased us" or "that could please us." For temporal clauses, see Gr. 164, b, p. 501; for conditional clauses, Gr. 159, g, p. 494; for consecutive clauses, Gr. 166, a, p. 504. His appearance did not attract the eyes, but rather made one look away.

נִבְזֶה֙ וַחֲדַ֣ל אִישִׁ֔ים אִ֥ישׁ מַכְאֹב֖וֹת וִיד֣וּעַ חֹ֑לִי ³
וּכְמַסְתֵּ֤ר פָּנִים֙ מִמֶּ֔נּוּ נִבְזֶ֖ה וְלֹ֥א חֲשַׁבְנֻֽהוּ׃

The third verse intensifies the thought of verse 2b. *nibhzeh,* a participle Niphal of *bazah,* is a stronger expression than *welo' neḥmedhehū,* which is only negative, whereas this in a positive way asserts the abject appearance of the Servant. The abstract *nibhzeh* is paired with the more concrete *waḥadhal 'ishīm,* shunned of men. The real meaning of *ḥadhal* (construct of *ḥadhel)* is "lacking"; *'ishīm,* a plural of *'ish* that occurs only here and in Psalm 141:4 and Proverbs 8:4, is quite properly rendered by some as "persons of note," a meaning that it frequently has, especially in connection with *gebher* or in contrast to the common people (2:9). There is no intercourse between Him and the prominent people because they avoid Him, John 7:48f. He associates with ordinary people, on occasion with publicans and sinners. As the description continues, it rises in intensity: "a man of sorrows." *makh'obhoth* (from *ka'ebh)* are pains or sorrows of all kinds, physical and mental. He is marked by pain and sorrow; they characterize Him; suffering is His chief distinction, in life. *widhūa' ḥolī* means "acquainted with grief or suffering." *ḥolī* does not always mean sickness; it can mean grief, trouble, woe, misfortune, evil, Ecclesiastes 6:2; Isaiah 1:5; Hosea 5:13. *widhūa'* is *we* plus *yedhūa',* a construct form of *yādhūa',* the Qal passive participle. Literally the phrase means "known of grief," but not in the sense that grief is the subject and "the known or acquainted one" the object, namely, that grief knew Him. *yedhūa'* is the subject and *ḥolī* the object; He knew grief. The passive, in this case, is active in meaning, like the perfect participles of the Latin deponent verbs. Delitzsch and others construe it thus. It is grammatically possible, however, to interpret *ḥolī* as a genitive of cause and *yedhūa'* as the object: the one acknowledged or known by grief, whom grief elected. Cf. *bezūy 'am,* "despised of the people," Psalm 22:7; *yeludh 'ishshāh,* "born of a woman," Job 14:1, Gr. 116 k, l, p. 358f. The phrase acquires more force through the latter interpretation. Before all others, the Servant was the object of suffering, sought out, so to speak, by suffering as the one object on earth to whom suffering pertained. All the suffering that pertained to this cursed world, He attracted to Himself, verse 6b. This suffering and these sorrows are not physical infirmity; they are the guilt of sin, wrath, curse, and punishment, taken from us and laid upon Him, as verses 5 and 6 explain. The next clause, "like one before whom one covers his face" brings the concept of degradation to its climax, cf. 52:14. *master* is not the Hiphil participle (*mastir*), nor can it be a Hophal participle (*mostar*), since the verb *sathar* has no Hophal. It must be taken as a substantive formed from the Hiphil with causative force: "like the causing to hide the face away from Him," that is, His form aroused such dread in the beholders that they hid their faces from Him. No one could bear to look upon Him. *nibhzeh* repeats the word with which the sentence began and sums up the contents. *welo' hashabhnuhu* is a consecutive clause with frequentative perfect following a participle, Gr. 166, a, p. 504 and 112, k, p. 332, cf. *wenehmedhehu*, verse 2. *lo'* is more than a simple negative; we esteemed Him *nothing,* we despised Him.

Third Strophe: 53:4-6:   *He bore our chastisement.*

4 *Truly, He took upon Himself our pains,*
   And our sorrows — He bore them;
   But we accounted Him as one stricken,
   As smitten of God and afflicted.

5 *But He — pierced is He for our transgressions,*
   Crushed for our iniquities;
   The chastisement lies upon Him that we might have peace,
   And by His wounds have we been healed.

6 *We all were wandering astray like sheep,*
   We turned each one to his own way;
   While the Lord cast upon Him the iniquity of us all.

אָכֵן חֳלָיֵנוּ הוּא נָשָׂא   וּמַכְאֹבֵינוּ סְבָלָם
וַאֲנַחְנוּ חֲשַׁבְנֻהוּ נָגוּעַ   מֻכֵּה אֱלֹהִים וּמְעֻנֶּה:

This strophe explains the mystery of the inhuman humiliation of the Servant, which was described in the preceding section. It is not His own guilt, but the guilt of another, of us, the people of God, that the Lord laid upon Him. This guilt takes the form of punishment which smites Him and makes Him the most deeply stricken with suffering and the most despised of all. Here is revealed the very essence of God's plan of redemption, more plainly than anywhere else in the Old Testament. This section sets all of the Messianic prophecies from Genesis 3:15 to Malachi 4:2ff into their proper light, particularly Isaiah's own prophecies of the Son of the Virgin, of the Prince of Peace, the Rod out of the stem of Jesse, the

Victor over death (Isaiah 25:8), the Cornerstone in Zion (28:16), the Way of Holiness (35:8), and everything that he proclaimed concerning the Servant of the Lord. The entire New Testament Gospel of the righteousness of faith, as St. Paul in particular expounded it, rests upon these three verses. "The chastisement of our peace was upon Him; and with His stripes we are healed." These words are all of the New Testament Gospel in a nutshell; not a word need be added. This is the truth which manifests itself as the power of God unto salvation through faith (Romans 1:16f), creates faith, regenerates, and sanctifies unto eternal life. Isaiah 53 is in fact what Strauss says of the 22nd Psalm, "the program that the disciples of Christ followed when they presented the life and sufferings of the Lord" — through inspiration of the Holy Spirit, we may add. The words, "Truly, He took upon Himself our pains, and our sorrows — He bore them," have been interpreted to mean that the people of Israel bore our sorrows. Every believer, in whom there dwells the power of the Holy Spirit, must find this interpretation to be wholly repugnant, an ungodly distortion, and blasphemy of the Holy One of Israel.

The three verses of this section are made up throughout of contrasting phrases. *'ākhēn,* too, which is usually affirmative, here takes on an adversative meaning because of its connection with the preceding verse. It may be translated "but surely," and even though the "but" is not expressed, the effect of *'ākhēn* is adversative (Delitzsch notwithstanding). *holāyēnū,* our sicknesses, our sorrows, is a plural with a defective *Tsere* in the suffix. *hū'* emphasizes the subject of the verb, and some manuscripts add another *hū'* after *ūmakh'obhēynū* but it is not like Isaiah to emphasize the same thought twice with the same word. In the first clause the emphasis is on the person; in the second clause it is on the thing which here is the suffix in *sebhālām: "He* bore *our* sorrows; our *pains,* He bore *them."* As for Luther's translation, *Er trug unsere Krankheit, und lud auf sich unsere Schmerzen,* which from our youth seems sacred to many of us, we are loath to change a syllable of it. Still, it is the duty of the exegete to note that Luther in his translation reversed the order of *nāsā'* and *sābhal.* The meaning of *nāsā'* is "to lift up, to take up a burden"; *sābhal* means "to carry away." Isaiah always uses these verbs in that sense when they are used as synonyms, as in 46:4, at the end of the verse, and in 46:7. Matthew, too, correcting the φέρει . . . ὀδυνᾶται of the LXX, has ἔλαβεν καὶ . . . ἐβάστασαν (8:17). Luther really should have said: *"Fuerwahr er lud auf sich unsere Krankheit und trug un-*

sere Schmerzen."The action in *sābhal* advances a step beyond that in *nāsā'*, cf. 46:1, *nesu'othēykhem 'amūsōth.* What the Servant lifted up on Himself and carried were *holāyēnu* and *makh'obhēynu*. Those are not, first of all, our sins (the next verse speaks of them), but rather the consequences of our sin, the sorrows and pain, all the woe and suffering of time and eternity that sin has brought upon us, death, the wages of sin, Romans 6:23. This clause speaks only of the consequences and the punishment of sin, not specifically of the guilt of sin, although that is, of course, implied. The accent lies here entirely on *He — our*, on the substitutionary suffering; and the following clause puts even greater stress on that thought. The *we* with *'anahnū* is adversative, since *'anahnū* stands here in contrast to *hū'* of the first clause. Since He was suffering not His own, but an alien punishment — *our* punishment, which *we* had incurred — we looked upon Him as a *nāghūa'*. This form, a Qal passive participle, is in the absolute state, like *me'unneh* at the end, while *mukkēh* is a construct form. *mukkēh 'elōhīm* defines the act inherent in *nāghūa'; me'unneh* expresses the meaning or purpose of the act. Job's words, 19:21, express what is meant here: "The hand of God has touched me," *nāgha' bī.* Cf. 1 Samuel 6:9, where "chance" is the opposite. The noun *negha'*, accordingly, is used to designate such plagues as famine, pestilence, drought, fire, locusts, caterpillars (1 Kings 8:37), which God visited as punishment for sin upon a nation or a person (cf. the plagues visited on Pharaoh and his people, Exod. 11:1), and especially leprosy and every incurable disease, Leviticus 13:2ff. And so, Israel, as the prophet testifies, looked upon the Man of Sorrows as one overtaken by God's judgment because of His transgressions; or as one stricken, not by the Lord, the God of grace, but by *'elōhīm*, the Ruler and Judge of the world. This judgment, as Israel imagined, consisted in His being a *me'unneh,* one bowed down, humiliated, crushed into the dust, who had to be inhumanly humbled, as though He had violated the majesty of the Almighty. Cf. the accusation actually made against Him, John 10:33.

5 וְהוּא֙ מְחֹלָ֣ל מִפְּשָׁעֵ֔נוּ מְדֻכָּ֖א מֵעֲוֹנֹתֵ֑ינוּ
מוּסַ֤ר שְׁלוֹמֵ֙נוּ֙ עָלָ֔יו וּבַחֲבֻרָת֖וֹ נִרְפָּא־לָֽנוּ׃

The *we* with *hū'* may be understood either as adversative or as adverbial (whereas). In either case, the contrast with what precedes is expressed: but, although, however, yet. Gr. 141, e, p. 453. We prefer to follow the tenor of the whole section and accept Luther's translation: *"aber"* (but). *meḥolāl,* a Poal participle of *ḥalal,* literally, "pierced," designates the act of putting to death, or at least the mortal wounding, like the Poel in 51:9. The parallel, *medhukkā',* crushed, confirms this meaning. Verse 5 is not merely a repetition of verse 3; it carries the idea of suffering and being laden with sorrows forward to the idea of being killed and destroyed. With that, the description of the suffering and the chastisement comes to a conclusion. *medhukkā',* a stronger form than *meḥolāl,* carries the picture to its extreme limit. It portrays complete personal destruction. *min,* the prefix of *peshāʿenū,* is not tᵣ be understood in its physical sense: "pierced by our sins," but in its ethical or causal sense, "because of." That is borne out by 4a, 5b, and 6, and also by the parallel *ʿawonōtheynū,* which accentuates the element of guilt in *peshāʿîm.* The *causa efficiens* of His suffering was God (verse 4), the Lord (verse 6); our transgressions and our guilt were the ethical cause. The LXX correctly rendered *min* with διά and the accusative. Luther's translation of the next clause, *mūsar shelōmēnū ʿālāyw: "Die Strafe liegt auf ihm, auf dass wir Friede haetten,"* is as exact and beautiful a rendering as it is possible to achieve. The element of *"Strafe,"* punishment, is simply inseparable from chastisement; *mūsar* (consult the verb *yāsar*) and the preceding clauses force that meaning upon the word. Concerning the genitive *shelōmēnū,* see Gr. 128, q, p. 417: "the punishment inflicted for the purpose of our peace (salvation)." The meaning of the genitive here is close to that of the dative of advantage. Cf. *berîth ʿabhdekhā:* the covenant made for your servant, Psalm 89:40(39); *tsōʾn ṭibhḥah:* sheep meant for slaughter, Psalm 44:23(22). *shālōm* is here and elsewhere one of the many special terms for the full salvation that the Lord has prepared for His people, through His Servant. The thought that is latent in *mūsar shelōmēnū* receives full and clear expression in the final clause. Not only was our salvation the intended purpose of the punishment that lay upon Him, it was actually the consequence of that punishment. The article *(ba)* with *ḥabhurāh* indicates that the word is to be taken in a generic sense: By that which on Him was wound and swollen welt (1:6) has healing come to us. The Niphal *nirpā'* with *le* is impersonal (Gr. 121,a,p.387). The New Testament and the Christian preaching, and especially the Christian hymns, have repeated this oxymoron in many different forms, cf. 1 Peter 2:24; 2 Corinthians 5:21; 8:9; Romans 8:3,4; Galatians 3:13; 4:4,5. This is the Christian mystery: He took our place, became our substitute.

6 כֻּלָּ֙נוּ֙ כַּצֹּ֣אן תָּעִ֔ינוּ אִ֥ישׁ לְדַרְכּ֖וֹ פָּנִ֑ינוּ
וַֽיהוָה֙ הִפְגִּ֣יעַ בּ֔וֹ אֵ֖ת עֲוֹ֥ן כֻּלָּֽנוּ׃

kullānū, all of us, has the emphatic position at the head of the
sentence, an emphasis that is increased by *'īsh*, everyone, in the
next clause. The entire people was one great *massa perdita*, without exception. The article in *katstsō'n* does not specify any one
flock; it is the article of comparison, Gr. 126, o, p. 407, the point of
comparison being the unawareness and helplessness. Like a flock
of foolish sheep, unaware that they had gone astray and drifting
blindly toward their destruction, so we were going astray, cf. Matthew 9:36; Mark 6:34. "Everyone wandered his own way," that is,
all of us blindly followed our impulses and desires, giving no
thought to the dangers of death that surrounded us. Delitzsch
thought that the conditions of the exile were being described here,
but the prophet, in the Spirit, is already standing with those of his
people who had come to faith at the first Pentecost, and what the
Lord says of the people in Matthew 9:36 is meant in this verse. The
prophet is speaking of spiritual aberration. From time immemorial that had been Israel's sin, from the Red Sea (Exod. 14:11)
to the time of Christ, and even unto the present day. What all the
prophets condemn, what Isaiah deplores in the first chapter, what
continued unabated in the exile: Israel's alienation from the faith,
its constantly recurring defections from the God of the covenant,
its thousand *peshā'īm*, its breaches of faith, from which it refused
to be healed and which brought about the exile and the final rejection, that is what these two clauses refer to. Israel had become like
the gentiles, whom God since Abraham's time had permitted to go
their own wrong way, Acts 14:16, Psalm 81:13(12). And so, like
the gentiles yes, more than the gentiles, they were deserving of rejection. But God did not reject His people. While they were blindly
stumbling along on their own false path, "the Lord cast upon Him
the iniquity of us all." Sin is guilt before God, and because God is
holy and just, sin's punishment lies within itself. Sin slays its own
perpetrator. The soul that sinneth, it shall die, Ezekiel 18:20. But
now it is God's holy purpose that the punishment for sin should
not strike *us*, the guilty doers, but *Him*, the Servant, who willingly
took upon Himself (*nāsā*) the sorrows that were ours. For the
meaning of the Hiphil *hiphgīa'*, consult the lexicon under *pāgha'*.
So, the Servant was one who was condemned, smitten of God, and
humiliated; not for His own transgressions, but for ours. The *Lord*
cast upon Him the sin of *all of us*.

Fourth Strophe: 53:7-9: *Patiently He suffered every wrong, although He was innocent.*

7 *Mistreated was He; but He — He humbled Himself
And He opened not His mouth,
Like a lamb that is being led to the slaughter;
And like a sheep that is dumb before its shearers,
So He opened not His mouth.*
8 *Through violence and judgment was He carried away,
And His generation — who gave thought to it
That He was snatched out of the land of the living?
Because of the wickedness of my people the judgment fell
upon Him.*
9 *They would give Him a grave with the wicked;
But He was with the rich in His death,
Since He had done no wrong,
And no deceit was found in His mouth.*

For a proper understanding of this section it should be noted that it reveals three aspects of the sufferings of the Servant: His mistreatment, His patience, and His innocence. Outwardly, the chief of these is the first. It is contained in *niggas,* which Isaiah characteristically places at the head of the entire passage; it forms the contents of verse 8, and then fades out in the first part of verse 9. The emphasis on mistreatment, however, serves only to accentuate the Servant's patience, which is to be brought more clearly to light. His patience contrasts with the terse and powerful *niggas* when it appears in the tender and appealing picture of the Lamb and the sheep. At the end of verse 8 it appears once more, by implication, it is true, and yet with powerful effect (*mippesha' 'ammī*). The third aspect, His innocence, magnifies the great patience with which He bore mistreatment. An appreciation of this relation will be of aid in understanding the details.

נִגַּשׂ וְהוּא נַעֲנֶה וְלֹא יִפְתַּח־פִּיו 7
כַּשֶּׂה לַטֶּבַח יוּבָל וּכְרָחֵל לִפְנֵי גֹזְזֶיהָ נֶאֱלָמָה
וְלֹא יִפְתַּח פִּיו :

Concerning the compound sentence *niggas wehū' na'aneh* cf. Gr. 141, e, g, p. 453. By subordinating the participial clause *wehū' na'aneh* to the finite verb *niggas,* a preciseness of expression is achieved that is difficult to approximate in our language. The main clause is *niggas,* a Niphal perfect: "He was mistreated." *nāghas* refers to the forced labor imposed by one in power; a *nōghēs* is the Egyptian oppressor, Exodus 3:7,etc. The perfect tense denotes an action completed in the past and continuing in its consequences into the present. He had been mistreated, then, and for all time. Under the continuation of this mistreatment He was a *na'aneh,* one who bowed Himself without interruption (cf. Gr. 116,f,p.357). If we follow the construction and translate: "He was mistreated, while He was bowing Himself down," the emphasis falls on the wrong part of the sentence, namely, on the main clause, whereas this characteristic Hebrew construction emphasizes the subordinate clause: *na'aneh.* This is achieved by insertion of the pronoun *hū',* which picks up the subject of *niggas,* emphasizes it, and makes what is grammatically a subordinate clause into an actual main clause, which then is aligned with the following clause by a simple connecting *we.* If we reverse the grammatical order: "While He was mistreated, He was one who bowed Himself down," we do not do justice either to *niggas* or to *hū',* for both words ought to retain their emphasis. We can come near to approximating the original, if we do not disturb the grammatical position of *niggas,* place the verbal concept at the head, render the *we* as adversative, translate *hū'* separately, and subordinate everything that follows to *niggas.* That is what we have done in our translation of verse 7. "He humbled Himself" does not do justice to the Hebrew participle, and we should have preferred to render it: "He willingly yielded to it," but we were fearful of deviating too far from the basic meaning of *na'aneh.*

wehū' na'aneh is more precisely and concretely explained by *welo' yiphtaḥ pīw* and the two comparisons. "He opened not His mouth," that is, in protest or contention, or even in complaint. "Who, when He was reviled, reviled not again; when He suffered, He threatened not, but committed Himself to Him that judges righteously," 1 Peter 2:23. It is self-evident that the Lord's responses to the high priest or to the secular court, or what He said to Judas and to the soldiers in the garden, do not detract from the truth of this statement. No prophet or poet should be subjected to such literal interpretation. The rest of this sentence is not an addition to *na'aneh,* but an explanation of the word. The Servant's attitude is meant here, which at the proper time is expressed either by silence or by words. No word of the Lord that He addressed to those who mistreated Him bears a mark of impatient or sinful protest. The two comparisons that follow are exceedingly tender and appealing. It is debatable whether the reference in *seh,* lamb, is to the sacrificial lamb. The point of comparison in the word is the outward silence and the inner nonresistance, and for that reason, in addition to the lamb, there is mentioned in second place the *rāḥēl,* the mother-sheep. It is difficult to bring out the tenderness intended in these expressions, which in German might be expressed by *Laemmlein* and *Schaeflein,* which have no exact equivalent in English. After *kasseh* and *kerāḥēl* a relative pronoun must be supplied, and relative clauses follow as attributives, Gr. 155, g, p. 487. Regarding the parenthetical note in the grammar that it would be better to read *keseh* instead of *kasseh,* see Gr. 126, o, p. 407. *yūbhāl* is a Hophal imperfect in pause, of *yābhal;* *ne'elāmāh* is a Niphal perfect. There is a clear division after *yūbhāl,* and the two clauses, separated by a Zaqeph, are in chiastic parallelism. The *w'* before the final *lō'yiphtaḥ* continues the comparison begun by *ke* in *kerāḥēl:* "and *like* a sheep, etc., *so* He, etc."

מֵעֹצֶר וּמִמִּשְׁפָּט לֻקָּח וְאֶת־דּוֹרוֹ מִי יְשׂוֹחֵחַ 8
כִּי נִגְזַר מֵאֶרֶץ חַיִּים מִפֶּשַׁע עַמִּי נֶגַע לָמוֹ :

This verse deals throughout with the violent treatment suffered by the Servant. It is a development of the curt *niggas* at the beginning of verse 7. The prophet could not dismiss the matter of the violent treatment of the Servant with that one short word. In the same manner in which he enlarged on *hū' na'aneh,* so he turns his attention in vivid detail to *niggas.* In *'otser* there is contained the same concept of force that is denoted by *niggas. luqqaḥ* too suggests violence; He was taken by force and carried off. And so the opening statement is that He was carried off by force and judicial action. It is altogether unlikely that *min* can here have been used in the local sense — "He was carried away from violence and judgment" — as Luther and Delitzsch thought. That interpretation requires that it would have to be God Himself who carried Him away from violence and judgment. One cannot imagine what the connection would be between this interpretation and the following clauses. That thought is premature. The death of the Servant has, up to this point, not yet been described; and so, the rescue from violence and judgment would have been described before the death itself! Or else those words would imply that God snatched Him away from violence and judgment and thus actually prevented His death. There is only one meaning of *min* that fits into the context, and that is the causative sense, as in Genesis 49:12; Job 14:9; Ezekiel 19:10. Here the means is denoted, as in Genesis 9:11; Job 4:9; 7:14; 39:26: "through, by means of, violence and judgment was He snatched away." *'ōtser* and *mishpāṭ* are clearly a hendiadys, and *mishpāṭ* is understood to be a court action or a judicial decision. And so, without much strain, we come to the simple statement: "through violent judicial action, or through judicial violence He was snatched away." And so, *niggas* of verse 7 has received concrete expression; we now know what the prophet meant to say with that one short word. What now follows fits nicely into this interpretation.

There is only one acceptable translation of *dōr*, and that is the γενεά of the LXX, meaning generation, contemporaries. The *'eth* with *dōrō* is the sign of the accusative, not a preposition. It is an accusative of respect: "and respecting His generation, that is, His contemporaries," Gr. 117, m, p. 365f. The accusative τὴν γενε - ὰν αὐτοῦ in the LXX is literally correct, and, given the right punctuation, the entire sentence in the LXX, which Acts 8:32f copied, can be correctly interpreted, although the first clause shows that the LXX obviously is based on a different text. *mī yesōḥeah* (Pilel of *sīah*) follows directly upon *'eth dōrō* — . "And as for His generation, who (of His generation) gave thought that He, etc." In Psalm 143:5 *'asōḥeah* occupies the top of a three stage climax: *zākhar*, to consider; *hāghāh*, to speak quietly; *sōḥeah*, to speak with vehemence. In view of such passages as Job 7:11; Psalm 55:18(17); 77:4(3) (Qal), one cannot resist the feeling that the Pilel here denotes lamenting, bewailing. This interpretation is appealing, because it carries on the line of thought contained in the opening clause; on the one hand, the Servant is brought to His death by a cruel court action, and on the other hand, there is no one among the people who bewails His death. The following *kī* introduces an objective clause: No one laments *that* He was *nighzar* (cut off, snatched away) out of the land of the living. He was treated either with cruel brutality, or passed over with complete indifference. The last clause, *mippesha'*, etc., may be treated as an independent statement, unconnected with the foregoing clause. But since *mippeshā'ēnū* preceded it in verse 5 in an ethical-causal sense, it is altogether unlikely that *min* would be used here in physical-causal sense: "*by* the crime of My people the deathstroke was dealt Him." We repeat: The source of the *negha'* (verses 4,5) is God; the ethical cause of His being struck down is the *pesha' 'ammī* or the *peshā'ēnū*. For a discussion of *negha'*, see *nāghūa'*, verse 4. For *lāmō* as a singular, see Gr. 103, f, Note 3, p. 302, and chapter 44:15. The various emendations proposed here by the learned critics are, without exception, unsatisfactory.

There is no reason whatever for deviating from the Masoretic text. Taking the last clause to be independent, we have this sequence of thought: Through the violent treatment of those in possession of earthly power He was snatched away; among His contemporaries none bewailed His cruel death; He was judged by God for His people's sin. These three thoughts concretely express the content of *niggas* in verse 7. It seems very doubtful that the last clause should still be dependent on *kī*. Joining this clause to the foregoing clause without a connecting particle seems awkward, and as for the sense, one would then have to give *yesōḥēaḥ* the meaning of "recognizing," "understanding," together with that of "giving thought to," "bewailing." And finally it seems unpoetic to repeat in emphatic interrogation what had already been said in verse 4 and was therefore self-evident. How could anyone reason in his mind that the Servant had been put to death because of the sin of His people, when no one could have had any knowledge of that fact!

9 וַיִּתֵּן אֶת־רְשָׁעִים קִבְרֹו וְאֶת־עָשִׁיר בְּמֹתָיו
עַל לֹא־חָמָס עָשָׂה וְלֹא מִרְמָה בְּפִיו׃

Verse 8 dealt with the death of the Servant. Verse 9 deals with His burial. The subject of *wayyittēn* is impersonal, since the circumstances forbid making God the subject. It is possible, but it would be farfetched, to make *'ammī* the subject. (See Gr. 144,d,p.460.) The imperfect is the modal imperfect, which represents the action as willed, or as in some way conditional: "They would, or wished to, give Him." Gr. 107, m, n, p. 316f. *'eth* is a preposition: with, or together with, in the company of, the wicked. Since they considered Him wicked, they wished also to bury Him with the wicked.

The next clause has, to this day, been a crux. The words, as they appear in the text say either: "and with the rich in His state of death" or "with the rich He was in the state of death." Modern interpreters have given up *'ashīr* and *bemōthāyw* as corruptions. Most of them substitute *'oseh ra'* (evildoer) for *'ashīr;* and for *bemōthāyw* they propose *bēyth mōthō* (house of death, tomb). Cheyne remarks: "The well-known rendering of AV, 'and with the rich in His death,' is more than probably based on a corruption of the text." He then proposes: "And His grave was appointed with the rebellious, and with the wicked His tomb, although, etc." The text of the LXX is also obscure and offers no assistance, although the text on which it is based did have the form *bemōthāyw. be* is

447

the preposition, *mōth* is the construct form of *māweth*, death, and *ayw* is a plural suffix. The plural form of the word occurs also in Jeremiah 16:4 and Ezekiel 28:8,10. To take the word in the sense of *bāmāh*, a height, or burial mound, is mere speculation since the passage in Ezekiel (43:7) upon which this conjecture is usually based has itself had doubt cast upon it, and the sense in which the word occurs here would not be at all suitable in the Ezekiel passage. If we adhere to the text as we have it before us, then *bemōthāyw* means "in the state of His death," and nothing else. If we accept *ʿashīr* as the correct reading, then we are compelled to translate the *we* before *ʾeth* with "but," thus placing this clause in contrast to the preceding clause: "but with the rich (or with a rich person) was He in the state of His death." His enemies had meant that His body should be laid in the grave of a criminal, but God ordained that it should lie in a splendid tomb. And so, while the first clause still describes the state of humiliation, the second clause touches on the state of exaltation. To take *ʿashīr* as the equivalent of a wicked person or an evildoer is out of the question, for the simple reason that *ʿashīr* never occurs in that sense. Neither is there any reason why the second clause should not be interpreted as antithetical to the first. It is not unusual that a noun-clause should follow upon an adverbial clause, as the second half of our verse demonstrates. The chief argument against the interpretation that the first two clauses are in antithetical parallelism is that this explanation does not fit in with the next clause introduced by *ʿal lō*, since *ʿal lō* is a concessive conjunction and would have to be translated "although," "notwithstanding that not." But that objection is answered by Psalm 119:136, where *ʿal lō* means "*because* not." See also Gr. 160, c, p. 499 and 104, b, p. 306 on Job 16:17. For a discussion of *ʿal* (*ʿal ʾasher*, in its complete form) as a conjunction meaning "because" see Gesenius, Lexicon, at the end of the article. The translation would therefore be: They meant to give Him a grave with the wicked; but He was with the rich (or: with a rich man) in His death, *because* He had done no wrong and no deceit was found in His mouth. The last half of the verse contains the reason for the statement made in the second clause of the sentence. If this second half of the verse is not the theme (as is often the case in Isaiah), yet it is the transition to the next verse and the next section, which deals with the exaltation of the Servant. — Again it is demonstrated by this difficult passage that adherence to the text is the simplest and the only safe way toward the goal.

Fifth Strophe: 53:10-12:   *The more than human exaltation of the
Servant.*

10   *Yet it pleased the Lord to smite Him with pain.*
     When His soul shall have brought a guilt offering,
     Then should He see His seed, should live long years,
     And by His hand should the Lord's plan prosper.

11   *For the travail of His soul shall He see refreshing,*
     Through knowledge of Him shall My Servant, the Savior,
         pronounce salvation to many,
     For He Himself bears their guilt.

12   *Therefore will I give Him many as His portion,*
     And the powerful will He divide as His spoil —
     Because He gave His life into death
     And was numbered with the transgressors,
     And had taken upon Himself the sin of the many,
     Yes, became the Intercessor for the transgressors.

¹⁰ וַיהֹוָ֞ה חָפֵ֤ץ דַּכְּאוֹ֙ הֶֽחֱלִ֔י אִם־תָּשִׂ֤ים אָשָׁם֙ נַפְשׁ֔וֹ

יִרְאֶ֥ה זֶ֖רַע יַאֲרִ֣יךְ יָמִ֑ים וְחֵ֥פֶץ יְהוָ֖ה בְּיָד֥וֹ יִצְלָֽח׃

The fourth strophe (verses 7-9) described the Servant suffering
under the mistreatment of His people; the present strophe, continuing the thought of the third (verses 4-6), reveals to us the counsel
of the Lord which ruled throughout His Servant's suffering. The
ninth verse served as a transition to this thought. Verse 10 may be
connected directly with verse 9, and the *we* prefixed to *YHWH*
translated with "for" or "because", but we understand the entire
section as being in contrast to the foregoing one and translate the
we as "yet" or "however." (Concerning the pointing of the *we*
before *YHWH,* see Gr. 102, m, p. 300.) The opening clause dominates the thought of the rest of the section. The literal translation
is: "Yet it pleased the Lord to crush Him; He caused (Him) to
suffer." *YHWH* is emphatically placed at the head in order to
stress the contrast to what the people (verses 7-9) had in mind to
do. At the same time *YHWH* is in contrast to *'elohīm* in verse 4.
Not only had the Servant been delivered by the God of all the
world, but also by Jehovah, the God of Israel. The perfect form
hāphēts has here the force of a noun-clause: "It was the pleasure of
the Lord." *dakkʿō* is an infinitive Piel with accusative suffix: "to
smite Him." The implication is that the Servant was put to death,
cf. verses 5 and 8. It was the people who put Him to death, but in
all of this, even in His death, it was the pleasure, the counsel, of
the Lord that was being fulfilled. Jesus, the Christ, is the Lamb
that was slain from the beginning of the world, "delivered by the

449

determinate counsel and foreknowledge of God," Revelation 13:8; Acts 2:23; 4:28; Luke 22:22; 24:26f. *heḥelī* cannot be another form of *heḥolī,* sickness, suffering, in the accusative of instrument or material. Such a change of vowel from *o* to *e* is unheard of, and besides, this would be an incorrect pointing of the article. This form is a Hiphil perfect of *ḥālā'* (with final *Aleph),* *heḥelī',* the *Aleph* being omitted. The *Aleph* may have been dropped because the next word *'im* begins with an *Aleph.* In Jeremiah 32:35 *(haḥatī)* and 2 Kings 13:6 *(heḥetī)* the *Aleph* is dropped in similar circumstances. But, compare also Gr. 74, k, p. 206; 75, ii, p. 215; and 75, rr, p. 216. *heḥelī,* then, means "He made sick, made to suffer." The lack of grammatical connection with the other clause makes this word emphatic. In our translation we have rendered it as an adverbial modifier.

The following clauses explain at length what God's plan and counsel were in permitting His Servant to be so smitten. If we accept the text as it is written: *'im tāsīm 'ashām naphshō,* then *naphshō* is the subject, *tāsīm* (third, singular, feminine) the predicate, and *'ashām* the object. The imperfect after *'im* has the force of a future perfect: "When His soul shall have brought a guilt offering." It would be forcing the construction to render *tāsīm* as a second person masculine with God as the subject and *naphshō* as part of the predicate. Only insofar as the Servant Himself brings the guilt offering does what follows accrue to Him as a reward. Much has been written about the meaning of *'ashām.* Special attention should be given to Leviticus 5,6,7,14,19,22; Numbers 5:5-10; 6:1-12; also 2 Kings 12:17(16); Ezra 10:19. *'ashām* is that sin by which harm is done to what belongs to God or to one's neighbor, for which recompense must be made. *'ashām,* as an offering, is then that material thing of value that is offered as a recompense. It does not expiate a sin through punishment (as a sin offering); it makes good some damage done, by rendering abundant compensation. It is particularly to be noticed that this trespass offering is brought because of one's own consciousness of trespass and free admission of wrongdoing. The Lord's Servant, as a substitute sufferer, took our sin as a trespass against God upon His own conscience, assumed it as His own guilt, and with His own life willingly rendered satisfaction for it to God.

The apodosis begins with *yir'eh.* Since the prophet is speaking of God's purpose, the verbs should be thought of as subjunctives. "When His soul, etc. . . . then should or would He see His seed." Out of His willingly offered sacrificial death new life, a new spiritual progeny, should spring forth. This is the "corn of wheat" (John 12:24) which falls into the ground and dies and brings forth much fruit. This is the truth of Ephesians 1:19ff; 2:1-7; Colossians 2:12,13; Romans 6:3ff, concerning the death and resurrection of Christ, out of which proceeds the Holy Spirit, giving new life to spiritually dead souls; the Gospel as the power of God unto salvation; our faith as the new man in our rebirth; the church as the spiritual body of Christ the Head. The death of Christ as a trespass offering is the source of all salvation and of all spiritual and eternal life. Cf. Psalm 22:31 (30). But we read not merely *yihyeh zera' lō,* "He shall *have* seed"; but *yir'eh zera',* "He shall *see* seed" — with His own eyes. That phrase indicates His survival of death and His resurrection. For it is only as one who had risen again from death that He could see His seed. The following clause, *ya'arīkh yāmīm,* says that in so many words: "He shall live long years." Out of this voluntary death, offered once as a sacrifice, there flows for the Servant Himself eternal life, Romans 6:9f; Revelation 1:18. That is His reward from God for offering Himself as a sacrifice. On this passage rest the Lord's repeated declarations that He would rise again.

The last clause, *wehēphets,* etc., expresses the statements that He shall "see seed," and shall "live long years" in terms of the Lord's plan and counsel. For just that is the very acme of God's plan: To give His Servant eternal life and spiritual seed. Through the Servant's own hand (*beyādhō*), that is, through His act of mediation, His guilt offering, this plan shall *yitslāḥ,* prosper, succeed, in spite of all opposition. The total scope of this plan is outlined in such passages as 9:2-7; 42:6,7; 49:6 (covenant of the people, Light of the gentiles, creation of the eternal kingdom of peace), also in 2:1-5, and chapters 12, 35, 60-63, 65, and 66:14.

11 מֵעֲמַל נַפְשׁוֹ יִרְאֶה יִשְׂבָּע בְּדַעְתּוֹ

יַצְדִּיק צַדִּיק עַבְדִּי לָרַבִּים וַעֲוֹנֹתָם הוּא יִסְבֹּל׃

Verses 11 and 12 develop and extend the main prophecy of verse 10 that He shall see seed and live long years, actually only the first of these two statements. *yir'eh zera'* corresponds to *yir'eh yisbā',* "He shall see seed — He shall be refreshed, satisfied." The content of this latter statement and its basis are contained in the phrase *bedha'tō yatsdīq,* etc. The *lārabbīm* of this sentence is picked up by the *bārabbīm* of verse 12 and developed into a new thought. Whatever else is contained in these two sentences is not an unfolding of a new line of thought, but rather an addition of details explaining the foregoing prophecy. This is typical of Isaiah's style. If commentators had taken notice of this fact, they would not so often have taken the wrong turn and would have saved themselves much labor in the interpretation of verse 12.

min, the prefix of *'amal,* is ethical-causal, as in *mippeshā'ēnū,* verse 5, and *mippesha',* verse 8: "*because* of the travail of His soul." Luther correctly paraphrased it with: *"Darum, dass seine Seele gearbeitet hat."* Because of the travail of His soul — for His soul as well as His body suffered and patiently bore what has so far been described — there shall come to Him what now follows: *yir'eh, yisbā',* He shall see, He shall be satisfied, refreshed. Concerning the coordination of the verbs without the copula, see Gr. 120, g, h, p. 387. The satisfaction follows immediately after the seeing. We have therefore translated: "He shall see refreshing." The refreshing, or satisfaction, that He sees, is the *zera',* the seed, the fruit of His trespassoffering. He had thought that He labored in vain, 49:4, and now these! In the next clause the seed are called *hārabbīm,* the many, that is, the great multitude that God apportioned to Him for His faithful labor in His office as Servant, a multitude gathered from among His own people and from the gentiles. To these the exalted Servant shall through His knowledge pronounce (*yatsdīq*) salvation, justification. The emendation of the text that the critics have proposed here may well be ignored. The Hiphil *hitsdīq,* which usually is construed with the accusative, here is followed by *Lamed,* the sign of the dative (*lārabbīm*), a construction that is not uncommon with other verbs, Gr. 117, n, p. 366. It is quite arbitrary to explain this construction as characteristic of a later period and to draw the conclusion that Isaiah II was composed at a late date. If that conclusion were correct, one would logically have to assign other passages and books in which *Lamed* with the dative is used instead of the regular accusative, to the period of the exile or later, such as: Genesis 45:7, Leviticus 19:18, 34; Numbers 10:25; Job 5:2; 9:11; 12:23; 19:28; Psalm 69:6(5); 73:18; 86:9; 116:16; Isaiah 11:9; 61:1. Actually, this looser construction is borrowed from the language of the people, which *precedes* all literary language, always exists alongside it, and is often employed in poetry when a clear and forceful expression is desired. *hitsdīq lārabbīm* is simpler and clearer than *hitsdīq hārabbīm.* The meaning of the clause is that the Servant pronounces to the many that justification, or salvation, which through His perfect obedience (50:4-9; 53:4-9) He acquired by the suffering of body and soul, as their portion assigned to them by the

Lord. *tsaddīq* is not an adjective attribute of *'abhdī* ("My just Servant"), but is a substantive and is the subject of *yatsdīq*. The point is to be made that the salvation is pronounced (*yatsdīq*) by someone who is himself *tsaddīq*, and *'abhdī* follows as an apposition identifying the *tsaddīq* as "My Servant." *hitsdīq* pertains originally only to the Lord, as to one who alone is *tsaddīq*. But now has He given all *hitsdīq* into the hands of another (cf. John 5:22). But only one who Himself is *tsaddīq* can carry out the act of *hitsiq*. And such a one, yes, the only *tsaddīq*, is *'abhdī*, My Servant, in the perfect exercise of His office of Servant. Concerning the grammatical relation of *tsaddīq* and *'abhdī*, see Gr. 132, b, p. 428. We have frequently pointed out that *hitsdīq, tsaddīq, tsedheq, tsedhāqāh* are not to be understood in the rigid sense of "just," "justice," etc., but are always used to denote deliverance, salvation, the salvation promised in the covenant. Nevertheless, *hitsdīq* is still a forensic concept — not in the strict sense of the pronouncement of righteousness to someone because he has been found to be righteous, but as a pronouncement of salvation to him, without regard to his personal state of righteousness. There is presupposed a state of perdition and ungodliness, cf. Romans 4:5. *tsaddīq* in this passage is not simply a righteous one, or the righteous one, but rather, the One who in His office as Savior is perfect and triumphant. Always keep in mind chapters 42 and 49! Only the German, and no other modern language, has a fully adequate expression for the concept that is in *tsaddīq — Heiland* (Savior).

A literal translation of the clause is: "Through His knowledge will the Savior, My Servant, pronounce salvation to the many." There still remains the question whether the suffix of *bedha'to* is objective or subjective. It must, first of all, be noted that *bedha'to* is an adverbial modifier of *yatsdīq*. The question is not at all whether *da'ath* can be construed objectively, cf. 11:2 (11:9, *dē'ah 'eth YHWH)*; Habakkuk 2:14; Jeremiah 22:16; Hosea 4:1,6; 6:6; Malachi 2:7. It is equally clear that knowledge of salvation, Luke 1:77; knowledge of God, Romans 11:33; knowledge of Christ, Philippians 3:8, are a fixed New Testament concept taken from the Old Testament. The knowledge of the Lord, the acceptance of Christ, faith in Him are the means that God has wrought, by which we receive and accept the salvation that is His gift to us. The righteousness of God is revealed "from faith to faith." But it cannot be maintained that this, the objective sense, is in this instance the most likely one. To be noted is that *da'ath* with a suffix occurs almost only in the subjective sense, Proverbs 22:17. But it is decisive that Isaiah regularly ascribes the Servant's exercise of His office, the successful completion of His work, and especially the blessed deliverance of Jews and gentiles, to His knowledge and understanding. Upon Him rests the spirit of wisdom, of understanding (*da'ath*), and of the fear of the Lord, in which He judges the *dallīm* with righteousness (11:4a). That is essentially also the meaning of our passage — He will pronounce "righteousness" to the needy. In 42:1 the same Spirit is bestowed on Him, in the power of which He brings judgment, or salvation, to the gentiles. In chapter 49 the same line of thought appears, as also in 61:1. If one compares 50:4, where the Servant is endowed with the tongue of the learned, so that He should know — *lādha'ath* — to speak relief to the weary, then the thought forces itself upon us that here it is the same *da'ath*, the wisdom of the Servant, *da'to*, that is the means of carrying out the Servant's last work — the blessing of the many with salvation. It is His own *da'ath*, the knowledge given Him of God, to know and understand God's eternal counsel, its means and its ways, by which the Servant brings salvation to the many. With *bedha'to* the prophet points back to *yaskīl* in 52:13 ("act wisely") as the means of the triumphant completion of His whole work. The last clause, "for He Himself bears their guilt," sets forth the basis on which the foregoing statements rest. *yisbōl* is an imperfect of the same kind as those that preceded, denoting an act that continues uninterruptedly in the future. The Servant of the Lord is a priest forever, from eternity to eternity, after the order of Melchizedek, Psalm 110:4.

לָכֵ֞ן אֲחַלֶּק־ל֣וֹ בָרַבִּ֗ים וְאֶת־עֲצוּמִים֮ יְחַלֵּ֣ק שָׁלָל֒ 12
תַּ֗חַת אֲשֶׁ֨ר הֶעֱרָ֤ה לַמָּ֙וֶת֙ נַפְשׁ֔וֹ וְאֶת־פֹּשְׁעִ֖ים נִמְנָ֑ה
וְהוּא֙ חֵטְא־רַבִּ֣ים נָשָׂ֔א וְלַפֹּשְׁעִ֖ים יַפְגִּֽיעַ׃

lākhēn, therefore, refers to the labor of the Servant as the substitute for the sinner and the worker of salvation, as described in the preceding two verses and expressed in verse 11 as "travail of His soul" and as bearing "their guilt." Cf. διό in Philippians 2:9. *Because* the Servant willingly took upon Himself such deep humiliation, *therefore* the Lord will now — do what? Most modern commentators, including Delitzsch, seem to feel that they must translate the next two clauses in such a way that they say: "Therefore I will give Him an inheritance among the many" (Budde). Or: "Therefore will I give Him a portion among the many" (Kautzsch). Or: "Therefore do I give Him a portion among the great"

(Delitzsch). Or: "With the great, will He divide the spoil." Or: "With a great multitude will He divide the spoil." Or: "With the great will He distribute booty." And Duhm suggests: "Therefore will He inherit among the great and with the strong divide the spoils." The commentators agree only in missing the point, but each in his own way. We let the Hebrew text stand as it is written; the LXX, although it reaches a correct conclusion, need not be considered. We maintain that the *rabbīm* in this verse are the same *rabbīm* as in verse 11. Good exegesis is made impossible if the same word in the same general connection is given one meaning in one sentence and another meaning in the next. It was Delitzsch's mistake that he gave this word two different meanings. The *rabbīm* referred to in *'aḥalleq lō bārabbīm* are identical with those to whom the Savior, the Servant of God, pronounced salvation in verse 11. The second mistake of the commentators is that they take *'aḥalleq lō* to mean "I will let Him take part in," in the sense of the Latin *participare* with accusative of the person and ablative of the thing, "I will make Him a participant in." The Hebrew *ḥālaq* does not have that meaning in any conjugation, least of all in the Piel. The word always means to divide, to distribute, to measure out someone's portion to him, to give him the portion that has been designated as his. *ḥeleq*, accordingly, is not *a* part of something, but as Luther correctly understood, it is *the* appointed portion, the lot, the inheritance. It is carelessness that has permitted the concept of an appointed portion or inheritance to be weakened into merely granting participation. *'aḥalleq lō* is therefore not to be rendered: "I will grant Him participation," but: "I will give Him His part, His portion, His lot, His inheritance." If the object now follows as accusative or with the particle *be* or *le*, that is immaterial; it is still the object. In this instance the object is preceded by *be*, and the translation is: "I will give Him His portion in many," that is, consisting in, or in the form of, many. Not: among, together with many. Concretely the meaning is that the many whom the Servant redeemed, and to whom He gave salvation as their eternal lot, shall be His eternal portion and inheritance — His seed. Following the LXX and the Vulgate, Luther caught the meaning of the passage in his translation: *"darum will ich ihm grosse Menge zur Beute geben."* An exact translation of the passage is: "Therefore will I give Him the many as inheritance."

If that translation is accepted, then the following parallel clause should present no difficulty. It says: "And the strong, or powerful, will He apportion as booty"; or, "He will acquire them as booty, appropriate them as His own portion." Construing *'eth* before *'at-sūmīm* as a preposition produces this thought: "In company with the great will He distribute booty, or acquire booty." But who are these great persons? To imagine them to be the angels would be introducing an entirely un-Biblical thought. The angels are not redeemers and inheritors together with Christ, with the right to expect a share of the booty, or lot, or inheritance that He had won. Or are the angels to figure as mere assistants or members of His court? And other powers, together with whom the exalted Servant might distribute spoils, do not exist. If we take *'eth* to be the sign of the accusative and translate: "He will divide the mighty as spoils," the question is asked: "To whom will He apportion these spoils?" The question is Delitzsch's. The question is, however, unjustified, because it could be asked everywhere, when recipients of spoil are not expressly mentioned, as in Genesis 49:27; Exodus 15:9; Psalm 68:13(12), etc. In poetry the phrase is not to be subjected to rigidly literal interpretation, but in the poetic passages cited nothing more is indicated than the *possession* of rich spoil. Luther's interpretation: *"und er soll die Starken zum Raub haben,"** is again correct. The thought is by no means a new one. It appears in Psalm 2:7f; 22:27ff(26ff); Isaiah 45:23f; 49:7,23,25; 52:15. This thought in 52:15, at the beginning of the chapter, is thus closely linked with the same thought in this verse at the end of the chapter, and notice is thereby given that its development has come to a conclusion. Cf. Philippians 2:10f. Whether the acquisition or distribution of the mighty as booty refers to the conversion or merely to the subjection of those who constitute the booty is not said. The wicked too are booty and spoil belonging to the exalted Servant as His possession over which He has sway according to His good pleasure. We are of the opinion that the spiritual gifts are meant here, of which Paul speaks in Ephesians 4:7ff, on the basis of Psalm 68:19(18). The Church is the recipient of these gifts. We repeat: verses 10,11,12 are very closely related to one another. They treat of the fruit, respectively of the reward, of the vicarious suffering of the Servant. Verse 10: He shall see seed and live long years; verse 11: This seed shall be His refreshing and rejoicing, and to the many will He pronounce salvation; verse 12: This multitude is His eternal inheritance, and He shall also gain the mighty as His spoil. *That* is both fruit and reward for His suffering.

The next four clauses repeat and bring to a conclusion the expo-

---

*"and He shall have the strong as His spoil."

sition of the reasons for His exaltation and for His rewards. The last two clauses are made subordinate to the first two by the adverbial *we* with *hū'*. The first clause: "He gave His life into death" repeats "When His soul shall have brought a guilt offering" (verse 10). "He was numbered with the transgressors" recalls the opening words of verse 11, "the travail of His soul." "He took upon Himself the sin of many" repeats the closing words of verse 11, "He Himself bears their guilt." The final clause, "He became the Mediator (or Intercessor) for many," stands alone.

The conjunction *taḥath 'asher* originally meant "instead of," but here it has the more usual meaning of "because," that is, "as a reward for." *he'erāh* is a Hiphil of *'ārāh,* to strip, to empty. *he'erāh nephesh,* literally: "to empty or pour out the soul" *lammāweth,* unto death, is a poetic expression for "to give up His life." According to Old Testament conception, the soul or life resided in the blood, Leviticus 17:11. He poured out His blood to the last drop and thus gave up His life for us, as an offering, a trespass offering to compensate for our guilt (verses 4,5,6,10). To *nimnāh* of the next clause Delitzsch makes the discerning remark: *Niphal tolerativum!* Cf. Gr. 51, c, p. 137. He lets Himself be counted *'eth pōshe'īm,* with the evildoers, that is, He lets Himself be treated as an evildoer. This repeats the thought of 9a. The Lord Himself foretold the literal, physical, fulfillment of this prophecy, and Mark quotes it in 15:28. To this, to *this extreme,* He gave *Himself* up, while it was the sin of the many that He had taken (perfect!) upon Himself; yes, He prayed for the evildoers. The final clause, *lappōshe'īm yaphgīa',* is connected with the one before it by a simple *Waw* copula. This *Waw* does not merely connect *yaphgīa'* with *nāsā'* as another completed action, as Delitzsch remarks, but in this case — something no exegete seems to have noticed — the *Waw* adds something new, something that has up to this moment not been mentioned. It is an emphasizing, strengthening *Waw,* the equivalent of *gam* or *wegam,* to which one can do full justice only by translating it with "yes," or with "even." The grammar does not give a full discussion of this *Waw.* There is a passing reference to it in a footnote to Gr. 154, a, footnote(b), p. 484, where 2 Samuel 1:23 is at least cited. If this *Waw* were no more than the usual copula "and," then this most majestic chapter in Isaiah II would end in a dragging close, which appears in Luther's translation too. A climactic "Yes" gives the close of the chapter a fresh, ringing note. His reward, His portion, His eternal inheritance are made proportionate to the unheard-of shame and suffering of soul which, according to God's plan, He took upon Himself willingly, for others, for His people, for His enemies.

We cannot leave this greatest of all chapters of Isaiah, indeed of the entire Old Testament, without reviewing in their essential parts the tremendous contents of the chapter. The theme is set forth in 52:13: The great exaltation of the Servant of the Lord. The next two verses develop this theme from the inhuman degradation of the Servant to His exaltation and His rule over all the gentiles and their kings. Chapter 53 then describes, first, His humiliation in four paragraphs, verses 2 and 3; 4 and 5; 6 and 7; 8 and 9a. From 9b to the close of the chapter, the exaltation is described in similar short divisions. The chief aspects of the humiliation are 1) the *depth* of His humiliation — He was the most despised of all men, verses 2 and 3; 2) the *vicarious nature* of His suffering — He suffered the punishment for *our* sins for our salvation, verses 4 and 5; 3) His *attitude* in His suffering — He suffered without complaint, willingly, although innocent, verses 6 and 7; 4) the *cause* of His suffering — the brutality of men, the faithlessness of His people, God's judgment *(negha')*, verses 8 and 9a. The four steps in the description of His exaltation are: 1) the *honorable entombment,* verse 9b; 2) His *eternal life and progeny* (seed), verse 10; 3) *the refreshing of His soul* in the blessedness of the multitude of seed, verse 11; 4) His *rule* over the multitude of the redeemed and over the mighty. The bond that unites all these descriptions into one is the fact that this was God's plan and counsel. That this was God's plan is mentioned in the very first verse of 53. In 4b there is mention of a contrary view. The plan appears again in verse 6. There is a shimmering of it in the *negha' lāmō* of verse 8. It is more clearly stated in verse 9b, and in verse 10 it is brought into the foreground to dominate the conclusion of the chapter.

The more one studies this chapter, the more one is filled with wonder and admiration for the artistic skill displayed in its composition. The idea of a *suffering* Servant of the Lord, who through *suffering* rises to superhuman glory, is indicated at the very beginning of the Old Testament (Gen. 3:15), and now and then in later passages (Num. 21); it was symbolized by the sacrificial offerings, and typified in David (Ps. 8,16,22,etc.). But it was not until Isaiah began to prophesy that this idea was directly and thoroughly developed, first, by a prelude in 50:4-9, and then in this great chapter, where it is presented in such fullness, depth, and vivid clarity, as though Isaiah had lived 700 years later and had seen the suffering Savior with his own eyes, enlightened by the Holy Spirit. The prophet has ordered his thoughts with such clarity, completeness, and firm coherence that his portrayal of the Christ is not surpassed even by that of the evangelists and apostles. Before the smooth outpouring of thought in one unbroken stream the cramped attempts of such critics as Duhm and Cheyne to improve the text with their emendations, corrections, and conjectures, melt away like butter in the hot sun, indeed, they seem childish. Modern unbelieving commentators and modern Jews profess to see in the figure of the suffering Servant of the Lord the people of Israel, who will rise through suffering and shame to dominion over all the nations of the world. Their attempts founder in the face of the undeniable clarity and faithfulness with which Isaiah has portrayed, not an idea, not a collective something, not a personification, but rather an individual person. Even Duhm admits that. The very idea that any one nation could bear the sins of all other nations and thereby save them in order to rule over them is foolish and altogether lacking in support. It is an idea that turns the hope of Israel into something carnal, though this hope wherever it is mentioned is something spiritual and never appears in *this* precise form of glory obtained by vicarious suffering. And furthermore, even though every other feature of the picture here portrayed could be applied to a nation, still verse 9 would be an absolute bar to such an interpretation. Assignment of a grave with evildoers, respectively, letting him lie in death with a rich man, can be said only of an individual, not of a nation. And finally, the words themselves, or rather the Holy Spirit in the words, provide the correct understanding of the prophecy. Since the Lord Himself, Luke 22:37, applied this chapter to Himself, and the entire New Testament testifies that it refers to Him, and since step by step and line for line the chapter finds its fulfillment in the "Son of man," no cleverness and no art will ever succeed in applying this greatest of all prophecies to anyone but Christ the Savior. Faith stands before this portrayal of the Lord and with Paul Gerhardt prays:

> *Be Thou my consolation,*
> *My shield when I must die;*
> *Remind me of Thy passion*
> *When my last hour draws nigh.*
> *Mine eyes shall then behold Thee,*
> *Upon Thy cross shall dwell,*
> *My heart by faith enfold Thee.*
> *Who dieth thus dies well.*

Third Discourse: Chapter 54

The Glorification of the Afflicted Congregation

Chapter 52, the first discourse in this Triad, promised deliverance to the holy city that lay in ruins, and the return of her children out of captivity; chapter 53, the second discourse, set before her eyes the form of her Deliverer in His exaltation out of unheard-of humiliation and suffering into ineffable bliss and glory. The concluding chapter 54 promises to the redeemed congregation, already described in 53 as repentant and believing ("we," "seed" of the Servant, the "many" upon whom salvation was bestowed), that it likewise shall be glorified, since it has been apportioned to Him as His *ḥeleq*. The Redeemer, the Servant of the Lord in chapter 53, is no longer just the deliverer out of the Babylonian exile, but is the Deliverer from the punishment of sin. The work that He has performed is that He bears His people's sins; and the redemption that He has won for them is "justification," the redemption He bestows upon His own through the covenant of grace. And so, the subject to whom the Lord in chapter 54 promises this glorification is certainly Zion-Jerusalem, which in chapter 52 is still repeatedly called by that name, but now is no longer just the earthly, physical Jerusalem.

This is a conclusion that follows as self-evident from the nature of the Redeemer and His salvation as described in chapter 53. This understanding is further supported by the fact that from chapter 53 on to the end of the center section, chapters 49-57 Jerusalem-Zion is no longer referred to by name. In chapter 52 the Lord's people are still referred to as Zion (four times) and as Jerusalem (four times). But after that, these names disappear, just as the name of Babylon no longer appears throughout the second and third sections of the book. With the portrayal of the purely spiritual Redeemer in chapter 53 the prophecy discards entirely, until the end

460

of chapter 57, the narrow and restraining garb of nationality and becomes wholly spiritual and all-inclusive. The outward form of the physical and national is indeed still employed, but that is now purely a picture of spiritual things. Chapter 54 speaks of the future glory of the church, of the congregation of the saints, in pictures that have been derived from the modes of life in the Old Testament.

This chapter is divided into three sections of almost equal length. Strophe 1, verses 1-5, addresses the church as the reinstated spouse of the Lord and promises her the blessing of many children. In strophe 2, verses 6-10, the Lord swears to her eternal love and unfailing faithfulness. Strophe 3, verses 11-17, portrays her as a city (Jerusalem) and promises her a glorious restoration, inner happiness, and complete security from her enemies.

First Strophe: verses 1-5: *The Church, as the reinstated Bride of the Lord, shall be richer in children than before, and shall rejoice in new honors, because her Husband is the zealous and almighty God.*

The strophe is divided at the end of verse 3. The first part speaks of the church's wealth of children; the second, of her new state of honor, setting forth the reason for both promises.

1   *Sing, O barren one, you who never gave birth;*
    Break forth in rejoicing and sing, you who never travailed!
    For more are the children of her that was desolate
    Than the children of her that is married, says the Lord.
2   *Enlarge the place of your tent*
    And let them spread wide the curtains of your habitation,
    Do not hold back! Lengthen your cords,
    And fasten well your tent-stakes!
3   *For you shall spread out to the right and to the left,*
    And your offspring shall inherit the gentiles,
    And shall repopulate cities that lay in ruins.
4   *Do not be afraid, for you shall not be put to shame;*
    And fear no disgrace, for you shall not be shamed.
    Yes, the shame of your youth you shall forget
    And no longer remember the reproach of your widowhood.
5   *For your husband is He who made you,*
    His name is the Lord Sabaoth;
    And your Redeemer is the Holy One of Israel,
    God of the whole earth is He called.

461

¹ רָנִּי עֲקָרָה לֹא יָלָדָה פִּצְחִי רִנָּה וְצַהֲלִי לֹא־חָלָה
כִּי־רַבִּים בְּנֵי־שׁוֹמֵמָה מִבְּנֵי בְעוּלָה אָמַר יְהוָה:

That the church of the Lord is here thought of as His bride is clearly set forth in the very first sentence. She is addressed as the "barren one." The following relative clause in the third person without the sign of the relative (thus, especially after a vocative, Gr. 155,f,p.487) says why she is so called: she has not given birth. The perfect *yālādah* here is adjectival in meaning, and describes a finished situation which continues to exist, cf. Gr. 106, g, p. 311. Thus also Judges 13:2. *lō' thēlēdh*, an imperfect, instead of *yālādah*, perfect, would have described her as one who could not give birth, Gr. 107, w, p. 319, as in Job 24:21. Concerning the abrupt transition from one person to another, see Gr. 144, p, p. 462. The church of that day is characterized as barren, as one who had never given birth, whom the Lord, through the exile, had put out of the house and with whom He had suspended the spiritual relationship of husband to bride. He had turned away from her in anger and left her forsaken and alone, 49:14ff, especially verse 21. Israel according to the flesh did indeed produce offspring during the exile; but spiritual Israel did not produce spiritual children, because the Lord had withdrawn His grace from it. In this connection compare what is said in 49:14ff. *lō' halāh* is a relative clause modifying *'aqārāh* and is a rhetorical repetition of its parallel, *lō' yālādah*. This barren one is now most urgently exhorted to break forth in rejoicing. The three imperatives, *ronnī, pitshī rinnāh*, and *tsahalī* form a climax. The rare verb *tsahal* is also used to designate the neighing of a horse, and so means to shout aloud in joy. The reason for this exhortation is that she who had been barren shall now have a multitude of children, yes, more children than the children of the married one. With *be'ūlāh* she herself is designated in her condition before the exile. At that time a right marital relation still existed between her and her God. So long as the Davidic royalty, especially the priesthood and with it the prophetic office, were functioning, the Lord communed spiritually with Israel and spiritual children were daily born to the congregation. That ended with the exile. The house of David was rejected, divine worship ceased, and prophecy subsided into a murmur. The spiritual congregation had become widowed, Lamentations 1:1. But now it shall be blessed with a multitude of children greater than ever before.

462

² הַרְחִ֣יבִי ׀ מְק֣וֹם אָהֳלֵ֗ךְ וִירִיע֧וֹת מִשְׁכְּנוֹתַ֛יִךְ יַטּ֖וּ אַל־תַּחְשֹׂ֑כִי

הַאֲרִ֙יכִי֙ מֵֽיתָרַ֔יִךְ וִיתֵדֹתַ֖יִךְ חַזֵּֽקִי׃

As the possessor of her own tent (wives of the more prominent persons each had their own tent, Genesis 24:67; 31:34) she is now exhorted to extend her tent widely and to fasten it firmly, to make room for the multitude of children that have been promised to her. The parts of a tent mentioned here are those mentioned in connection with the tabernacle: *yerī'ōth,* the tent-cloths; *mēythārīm* (from *yāthar,* to stretch), the tent-cords; and *yethēdhōth (yāthedh),* the tent-stakes. The plural *mishkenōth* does not denote a plurality of tents, but rather the magnificence and grandeur of the one, as in Psalm 46:5(4); 84:2(1); etc. *yaṭṭū,* a third person plural Hiphil of *nāṭāh,* means to spread out, to stretch out, and here has jussive force: "Let them, or may they spread out." The servants who are to carry out the instructions of the mistress of the dwelling are the subject of *yaṭṭū. 'al taḥsōkhī,* "do not hold back," without an object, and grammatically independent of the rest of the sentence, is a vivid interjection. The mistress is not to fear that the enlargement of the tent might be overdone. No matter how widely she stretches out her tent, it will never be too large for the multitude of the children that are to dwell in it. The admonition to fasten the tent-stakes firmly *(ḥazzēqī)* is hardly intended to suggest that the tent is secured against collapse forever, but rather that the new spaciousness of the tent requires stouter stakes than the former small ones.

³ כִּֽי־יָמִ֥ין וּשְׂמֹ֖אול תִּפְרֹ֑צִי

וְזַרְעֵךְ֙ גּוֹיִ֣ם יִירָ֔שׁ וְעָרִ֥ים נְשַׁמּ֖וֹת יוֹשִֽׁיבוּ׃

Verse 3 gives reasons for the admonition in verse 2, but the description of the extension of the church now goes far beyond the picture of a tent. The church will "break forth." *pārats* always contains the idea of breaking, breaking up, breaking through; here it conveys the idea of bursting because of overabundance, spreading abroad like a flood, multiplying greatly, as in Genesis 28:14; Exodus 1:12; Hosea 4:10. To the right and to the left, in all directions, shall the church spread out, and her offspring shall possess, shall inherit the gentiles *(yīrāsh).* As in Deuteronomy 2:12; 9:1, 11:23, and elsewhere, the term represents victory over the gentiles, conquest of their cities, and taking their place, as is made clear in the next sentence. *neshammōth* is a Niphal feminine plural participle of *shāmēm*. The cities lie in ruins because of the conquest and because their gentile inhabitants have been exterminated. All of that, however, is but a picture of the spiritual conquest of the gentile world by the New Testament Church through the preaching of the Gospel. That is what is meant, above all, by the ancient promise given to Abraham, Genesis 22:17; 24:60, etc. The Hiphil *yōshībhū* is not causative, "cause to inhabit"; it is an intensive Qal: fill with inhabitants, populate.

⁴ אַל־תִּירְאִי כִּי־לֹא תֵבוֹשִׁי וְאַל־תִּכָּלְמִי כִּי לֹא תַחְפִּירִי
כִּי בֹשֶׁת עֲלוּמַיִךְ תִּשְׁכָּחִי וְחֶרְפַּת אַלְמְנוּתַיִךְ ᵃ לֹא תִזְכְּרִי־עוֹד:

The second half of the strophe describes the mother's pride in the many children with which she has been blessed. She is thought of as being fearful and slow to believe the promise that had been made to her. She has had two unhappy experiences: her *'alūmīm*, her youth, i.e., the time of her spinsterhood as a slave in Egypt, before the Lord had taken her to wife (that was done at Sinai), when she as *'almāh*, unmarried, could not give birth. That was her first great reproach. And now the exile, when the Lord, her Husband, put her aside and made her a widow. This last reproach was greater than the first. She had never believed that the Lord would let such shame come upon her; and yet it happened. She was and remained a weak woman, easily seduced. Is it not true that she would again be unfaithful and sin against her Husband, provoke Him to reject her finally, and thus bring upon herself irrevocable shame? Verse 4 is directed against such thoughts. She shall never again experience such shame. *bōsh*, to be put to shame, and the stronger Hiphil *hehpīr* are intransitive, the latter being an intensive Qal, which we can render only with the passive. *'al tikkālemī*, an imperfect Niphal, is a peculiar form. As a negative imperative, it cannot mean: "do not be put to shame," but rather is a parallel to "do not be afraid." There is an inner sensation of shame, and therefore this phrase is perhaps best rendered with "fear no shame." *kī*, in the next clause, is not causal, but adversative, since the clauses that it governs express a plus quantity; and so, it will be translated "but rather," "yes," *immo vero*. The church will be so secure in her new honor as bride that she will not even remember her former shame.

⁵ כִּי בֹעֲלַיִךְ עֹשַׂיִךְ יְהוָה צְבָאוֹת שְׁמוֹ
וְגֹאֲלֵךְ קְדוֹשׁ יִשְׂרָאֵל אֱלֹהֵי כָל־הָאָרֶץ יִקָּרֵא:

464

The fifth verse concludes the first strophe with a statement of the basis on which the admonitions and promises of the preceding four verses rest. One might be tempted to follow Luther and make *'osayikh* the subject of the opening clause and *bō'alayikh* the predicate, but the word order and the parallel *gō'alēkh* point to the opposite relation of the two words. *bō'alayikh* is the subject, as *gō'alēkh* is the subject of the next clause. The emphasis in the first clause lies on *'osayikh*, and in the second clause on *qedhōsh yisrā'ēl*. It is assumed to be well known that the Lord is Israel's wedded Husband and Redeemer, who acquired her by payment of the ransom. What Israel is to remember and inscribe upon her heart, in order to comprehend the promise just made to her, is that her Husband is the Almighty and her Redeemer, who is able to make all His promises come true. The adjuncts to *'osayikh* and *qedhōsh yisrā'ēl* also guarantee that fulfillment. Her Husband is He who with an almighty hand made her what she is, who is the sole Source of all her fortunes, of joy and sorrow, of honor and of shame. And His name is Jehovah of the hosts, Israel's Covenant-God, whom all the hosts of heaven serve for the fulfillment of His counsels, to overcome every hostile power. Her Redeemer, her Ransomer, is the Holy One of Israel, who in the zeal of His love for His people destroys all her enemies and is the God and Ruler of all the world. In short, His absolute omnipotence and rule over all things are the church's guarantee for her future greatness and honor. The same thought is conveyed by the plurals of excellence in *bō'alayikh* and *'osayikh*, Gr. 124, k, p. 399.

Second Strophe: verses 6-10: *The new love and unswerving faithfulness of the Lord toward His bride as warrant for the fulfillment of the preceding promises.*

This section also has two parts. The first half, verses 6-8, assures the church of the Lord's love and faithfulness in abstract terms; the second part, verses 9 and 10, employs comparisons, the first of which is taken from history, the second from nature. In both parts the discourse rises to a climax. The entire section manifests an intensity of deep love, is extremely vivid, and through the repetition of "says the Lord," supremely powerful. It is one of the most powerful passages in our book.

6   *For like a wife forsaken, and like one embittered of*
    heart the Lord calls you,
    And like a wife of one's youth who once was rejected,
    says your God.

7 *In a brief burst of anger I forsook you;*
   But with much compassion will I again take you to Me.

8 *In an outburst of wrath I hid My face from you for a moment;*
   But with everlasting grace will I have compassion on you,
   *   says the Lord, your Redeemer.*

9 *This shall be to Me like the waters of Noah;*
   Just as I swore that the waters of Noah should not
   *   again overflow the earth,*
   So do I swear that I shall not be wroth with you nor rebuke you.

10 *Even though the mountains are removed and the hills fall,*
   Yet My grace will not be removed from you,
   And My covenant of peace shall not waver;
   The Lord, your Redeemer, has said it.

כִּי־כְאִשָּׁה עֲזוּבָה וַעֲצוּבַת רוּחַ קְרָאָךְ יְהוָה 6
וְאֵשֶׁת נְעוּרִים כִּי תִמָּאֵס אָמַר אֱלֹהָיִךְ׃

The preceding strophe closed with mention of the Holy One of
Israel. That name expresses the Lord's zeal *for* Israel against her
enemies. In the section now before us the Lord's zeal toward His
church, His inner compulsion of love toward her, His deep
heartfelt pity are developed. In 49:15 mother love is the comparison; here that emotion of pity is made vivid by the picture of
the beloved wife of one's youth. — *'atsūbhath rūaḥ* is a substantive
adjective and is an independent concept alongside of *'ishshāh
'azūbhāh*. but it is usually translated as an adjective attribute to
'ishshāh: "like a forsaken and embittered wife." But that is incorrect. Cf. 1 Samuel 1:10; Proverbs 31:6; Job 3:20. The phrase should
be translated: "like a forsaken wife, and one embittered in heart."
One need not be disturbed by the absence of *ke* before *'atsūbhath*;
it is not even used before *'esheth* in the next clause. *qerā'akh* (a
euphonic form for *qerā'ekh)* is a perfect designating something
that in fact lies in the immediate present. *Now* He is calling her
after her affliction is past. This verb and *ke* are both to be supplied
before the following clause. "Wife of one's youth" is employed
because at that time a man's love toward his wife is most heartfelt,
so that in later life a man's love constantly remembers his wife as
the love of his youth. — The many-faceted *kī* before *thimmā'ēs* is
difficult to reproduce accurately in English. The thorough treatment of *kī* in the Gesenius lexicon (15th edition) under point 5,
and in Koehler-Baumgarten under point 18, offers an explanation
that at least approximates the meaning of this particle. It is there
explained as a temporal particle in the sense of "as," "when."
Therefore: "and like the wife of one's youth when it was spurned."

But that is not idiomatic English. We have to take the clause in a relative sense: "and like the wife of one's youth who had been spurned." The *kī thimmāʾes* clause is a relative attribute, the equivalent of the adjective *ʿazūbhāh* in the first clause, with this difference that the verb form in the imperfect expresses the action as momentary, transient, happening only once, whereas the adjective expresses an enduring state. In a moment of anger a man might sometime spurn the love of his youth, but he does not intend to reject her permanently; when he comes to his senses, the old love gains the upper hand and he retracts his hasty action. It is just this point that is developed in what follows. The assurance "says your God" is, in its content, an antithesis to *kī thimmāʾes*. This is being spoken by Him, who, although He once rejected you, still was and is, and will always be, your God.

בְּרֶגַע קָטֹן עֲזַבְתִּיךְ וּבְרַחֲמִים גְּדֹלִים אֲקַבְּצֵךְ: ⁷

The opening clauses of verses 7 and 8 take up the theme of *kī thimmāʾes*. It is remarkable that almost all translate *beregaʿ qātōn* with "a little moment." Everyone seems to have followed the LXX which has χρόνον μικρὸν κατέλιπόν σε. It is of course true that *regaʿ* means a moment, a brief period of time, that it often appears in the plural, that it occurs as an adverbial accusative even in the plural, that it may have a modifier such as *ʾehādh,* and that even with the preposition *ke* it may still refer to a brief moment of time. It is also admitted that *beregaʿ qātōn* can mean "in a small moment." But it does not follow that it has that meaning here. First of all, it must be noted that *beregaʿ qātōn* and *beregaʿ* occur only in these two verses. It is therefore necessary to examine whether the analogy of *regaʿ, keregaʿ, kimeʿaṭ regaʿ, regaʿ ʾehādh* justify the translation "a small moment" in this passage. The immediate context always determines the special meaning of an expression. *regaʿ* has the meaning of "a moment" only in its derived and applied sense; originally the word had the meaning of movement, unrest, the unexpected rousing out of rest to unrest and the return to rest; therefore *rāgaʿ* means not only to become restless, but can also mean to return to rest. Cf. the lexicon under *rāgaʿ* I and *rāgaʿ* II. That *regaʿ* must here be understood in its original sense of movement, unrest, excitement, burst of anger, as we have translated, is made apparent by the context. Its antithesis is *rahamīm gedhōlīm,* great or much compassion; and so, *regaʿ qātōn* is a small, a brief anger. But it is not the *duration* of the emotion on the one hand and of the action on the other hand that are contrasted with one another, but rather the comparative greatness of the two emotions, anger and compassion. Moreoever, the *be* with *rega'* is no doubt used in the same sense as the *be* with *rahamīm*. And *gādhōl* can hardly refer to a period of time, least of all with a concept like *rahamīm*.

We would have preferred to translate the perfect of *'azabhtīkh* with a pluperfect. The rejection is now, after pity and compassion have returned, part of the distant past, but the thought is also conveyed by the simple past tense. *'aqabbetsēkh* stands in contrast to *'azabhtīkh*. One must therefore not rigidly translate "I will gather," since that verb presupposes a plurality of objects. To take or draw to oneself expresses the intended thought. As for the contents: If that was a small burst of anger when the Lord rejected the wife of His youth, how great must then the compassion be with which He again received her, for He Himself calls it great in comparison with His anger. Or is that merely poetic exaggeration, as Delitzsch supposes in another connection? Rather, the case is, that human language simply cannot express the greatness and the depth of divine mercy adequately, not even in part. Cf. Romans 11:33.

8 בְּשֶׁצֶף קֶצֶף הִסְתַּרְתִּי פָנַי רֶגַע מִמֵּךְ
וּבְחֶסֶד עוֹלָם רִחַמְתִּיךְ אָמַר גֹּאֲלֵךְ יְהוָה׃

This emotionally rich passage has several plays upon words that are similar in sound but different in sense. Thus in verse 6 *'azūbhāh* (with *Zayin*) and *'atsūbhath* (with *Tsade*); in verse 10, *mūsh* and *mūt*, each used twice in the verse. In verse 8 *shetseph* and *qetseph*. *shetseph* is derived from *shātsaph* and is the same as *sheteph*, Proverbs 27:4, from *shātaph*, to overflow, to overwhelm, the shift from a T-sound to an S-sound being not at all unusual. The word signifies an overflowing. *qetseph* is a sudden rush of anger, which as suddenly subsides. And so, *shetseph qetseph* signifies an overflowing of anger, an outburst of hot temper. The picture is of a sudden outburst of anger that momentarily overflows and overpowers the heart. For the moment, overcome by violently rising anger (this is, of course, an example of anthropopathy) the Lord has hidden His countenance from her, turned away from her in displeasure — for a moment, *rega'*, an adverbial accusative. Not until *this* verse are anger and mercy (which is called *'ōlām*, eternal) compared as to their duration, whereas in verse 7 they were contrasted as to their greatness. *qetseph* contains in itself the quality of a momentary *shetseph*, which quickly breaks down and subsides. Although Luther's translation of the first part of the verse* has become very dear to us, the correct translation is: "In an outburst of anger I have for a moment hidden My face from you." Luther's translation of the latter part of the verse is above reproach: "but with eternal mercy will I have compassion upon you, says the Lord, your Redeemer."** The perfect *riḥamtīkhā* can properly be translated with the future, since it denotes a completed present condition that endures into the future. In verse 6, the subject of *'āmar* was *'elōhāyikh*; here it is *YHWH*, with no difference of meaning. The addition of *gō'alēkh*, your Redeemer, presupposes the Lord's great compassion.

9 ‏כִּי־מֵי נֹחַ זֹאת לִי

אֲשֶׁר נִשְׁבַּעְתִּי מֵעֲבֹר מֵי־נֹחַ עוֹד עַל־הָאָרֶץ

כֵּן נִשְׁבַּעְתִּי מִקְּצֹף עָלַיִךְ וּמִגְּעָר־בָּךְ:

The *kī* at the beginning of this sentence is not causal, "for" or "because," as translated by most commentators. As in Job 6:21 and Isaiah 5:7, it introduces a fact at the beginning of an independent clause. It need not be translated at all. The "like" in our translation is not a translation of this *kī*, but is introduced to explain the whole passage, which employs the waters of Noah as a comparison. Luther mistakenly translated *kī* as *"denn"* (for), but then correctly continues with *"wie"* (as). *kī* might also be rendered with "truly" or "yes": Truly, like the waters of Noah this shall be to Me. Or — since this is highly condensed discourse — Truly, as at the waters of Noah shall this be to Me! *zō'th*, of course, refers to the present flood of anger that has come upon Israel. *'asher*, before *nishba'tī* could be taken in a temporal sense, but it is safer to understand it as a correlative of the following *kēn*, "as — so," expressing a comparison, Gr. 161, b, p. 499. See also the lexicon under *'asher* B, 6. The verb is a historical perfect; in the next clause the same form is a perfect with present force, Gr. 106, i, p. 311. The comparison with the waters of Noah is so comforting to the spiritual Israel, because together with all the world it knew from that experience that God faithfully had performed what He had sworn. *gā'ar be* here refers not to a rebuke with words, but with actual chastising blows that give vent to His anger.

---

* *"Ich habe mein Angesicht im Augenblick des Zorns ein wenig von dir verborgen."*
** *"aber mit ewiger Gnade will ich mich dein erbarmen, spricht der Herr, dein Erloeser."*

כִּי הֶהָרִים֙ יָמ֔וּשׁוּ וְהַגְּבָע֖וֹת תְּמוּטֶ֑נָה 10
וְחַסְדִּ֞י מֵאִתֵּ֣ךְ לֹֽא־יָמ֗וּשׁ וּבְרִ֤ית שְׁלוֹמִי֙ לֹ֣א תָמ֔וּט
אָמַ֥ר מְרַחֲמֵ֖ךְ יְהוָֽה׃

kī is here not causative but concessive: "even though." The independent clause is introduced by *we* before *ḥasdī*: "*yet* My grace,
etc." The two imperfects in this first clause are potential, Gr. 107,
r, p. 318. The article with *hārīm* and *gebhā'ōth* is generic. Mountains and hills are conceived as firm and immovable because of
their mass and height; cf. Genesis 49:26; Deuteronomy 33:15; Habakkuk 3:6; Psalm 90:2. But even though these firmest of all features of the earth should waver and move, yet shall My grace not
waver. *mē'ittēkh* is to be understood first in a physical sense, but it
also denotes an inner relation and fellowship. *mūṭ* means to
waver, to weave back and forth; *mūsh* means to slip, to slide; as a
transitive *mūsh* has the meaning of to touch, to feel. *berīth shelōmī*
is not "the covenant of My peace," but "My covenant of peace,"
like *har qodhshī*, etc. Gr. 135, n. p. 440. It is the covenant that the
Lord concluded with Israel in Abraham, Genesis 17:7, and which
He confirmed again and again, which was also the basis upon
which the covenant of Sinai rested ("I am the Lord, thy God, thou
shalt not, etc."). Its content was peace, and grace, and salvation
for Israel, since it proclaimed: I am your God; you are My people.
The foundation upon which the promise rests is the Word (*'āmar*)
of Him who has compassion, *meraḥamēkh*, just as compassion was
the basis of the promise of the Redeemer in verse 8.

In connection with verse 9, Delitzsch makes this remark: "The
prophecy refers to the converted Israel of the last days, whose Jerusalem shall never be destroyed again." Delitzsch believed in a
general conversion of the Jews before the Day of Judgment. But
there is even less basis in the New Testament than in the Old Testament for such a belief. This and all similar promises apply to the
church of the New Testament as a whole. It is written for our
sakes, for us to believe, for our rejoicing and our comfort.

This section sets forth the depth and inviolability of the love of
the Lord for His church as the guarantee for its future glorification. In the following section this glorification again becomes the
subject of the prophecy. However, in that section the church is not
pictured as the bride of the Lord but as the city of Jerusalem.

470

Third Strophe: verses 11-17: *As the City of the Lord, the Church shall rise again in great splendor, shall be filled with spiritual understanding, and shall dwell safely with salvation as its bulwark, while the Lord holds all her foes at a distance.*

The first half, verses 11-14, describes the future splendor, the inner happiness, and the security of the church; the second half, verses 15-17, tells how all the designs of the enemies will be defeated by the Lord.

11 *O you afflicted one, tempest-tossed, and without comfort!*
Truly, I will lay your stones in stibium
And build your foundations with sapphires.
12 *Your pinnacles will I make to be rubies,*
And your gates into carbuncle stones,
And your walls all of jewels.
13 *And all your children shall be taught by the Lord,*
And great shall be the peace of your children.
14 *With salvation shall you be fortified,*
You shall be far removed from violence; for you need have no fear;
And far from destruction, for it shall not come near you.
15 *If anyone does strive against you, it will be without Me;*
Whoever strives against you, to you must he fall.
16 *If I created the smith, who blows the fire of coals,*
And produces a weapon, according to his skill,
So have I also created the destroyer to bring it to naught.
17 *Any weapon forged against you shall not succeed,*
And every tongue that rises in strife against you shall you condemn.
This is the inheritance of servants of the Lord, says the Lord,
And this is their salvation, by My hand.

11 עֲנִיָּה סֹעֲרָה לֹא נֻחָמָה

הִנֵּה אָנֹכִי מַרְבִּיץ בַּפּוּךְ אֲבָנַיִךְ וִיסַדְתִּיךְ בַּסַּפִּירִים:

The three attributes in the opening address show how deeply the loving heart of the Lord was moved at sight of the ruined city. *'anīyāh* is a substantive designating in a general way an afflicted one. *sō'arāh* is most likely not, as Delitzsch explains the form, a Qal feminine participle, which would have to be translated, as in Jonah 1:11 and 13 and Habakkuk 3:14, as "stormy" or "tempestuous." That is not what the prophet wishes to say. The form is a Pual perfect, third person feminine plural of *sā'ar*. The relative *'asher* is to be supplied: "who has been battered by the tempest." With striking effect an identical Pual form follows in *lō'nuḥāmāh* (in pause): "who has not been comforted." The translation "without comfort" can be justified only if one for a moment leaves the personified city out of consideration and imagines in its place an actual person. Storm-tossed, lashed by the tempest, is again said of the city itself, and it is natural to assume that *lō'nuḥāmāh* also applies to the city. To describe the city as without comfort leads to the concept of unrestored, not rebuilt, that is, still lying in ruins, which exactly describes the condition of the city. We should have preferred to translate *lō'nuḥāmāh* with "not rebuilt." The translation "without comfort" is purely a concession to tradition and to poetic euphony. For *lō'* in the sense of un-, see Gr. 152, a, Note, p. 478. *hinnēh* is here asseverative, not merely an interjection. The Hiphil participle *marbīts* is used here in place of the finite verb *'arbīts* as a so-called *futurum instans*, which denotes the immediate future. Gr. 116, p, p. 359. *rābhats* occurs for the first time in Genesis 4:7: "sin *lieth* at the door." The root is the same as that of *rābha'* from which *'arbā'ah*, four, and *rōbha'* and *rebha'*, a fourth part, are derived. The meaning of lying down, crouching on all fours, is suggested by *rābhats*. The Hiphil is causative: to cause to lie down, to lay. The Lord represents Himself as a stonemason or master builder, who is rebuilding Jerusalem. He will lay all her stones in *pūkh*. *pūkh* is a cosmetic made from antimony or from other charred ingredients, and it was used by Oriental women as eye-shadow to bring out the white of the eye. Cf. 2 Kings 9:30 and Jeremiah 4:30. The Lord uses *pūkh* to bind the building blocks together and achieves the effect of making each block appear like a woman's eye set off by cosmetics. This applies not only to the city walls, as is usually assumed. The concluding clause of the sentence refers to the city walls, while the first two clauses refer to all the stones out of which the city itself with all its houses is to be built. So also *yesadhtīkh* (it is possible that the word should be pointed *yesōdhōthayikh*, your foundation walls) refers not only to the foundations of the walls, but to all foundations of the city, with all its buildings. The Lord will construct the foundation of the entire city out of what seems to be pictured as a single great block of sapphire. As the use of the word *pūkh* indicates, it is the beauty of the precious stones that here comes into consideration. There may be a question whether the stones are intended to have a symbolic meaning. The blue of the sapphire, sky blue, in the Old Testament, is the color of the condescending gracious majesty of God. In that case the foundation of sapphire suggests the majestic, sovereign grace of God as the foundation of the church.

12 וְשַׂמְתִּי כַּדְכֹד שִׁמְשֹׁתַיִךְ וּשְׁעָרַיִךְ לְאַבְנֵי אֶקְדָּח
וְכָל־גְּבוּלֵךְ לְאַבְנֵי־חֵפֶץ :

shimshōthayikh, plural of *shemesh*, the sun, are the pinnacles, that is the uppermost rims of the serrated walls of the city, the buildings, and the towers. Again, there is no reason to think only of the pinnacles of the city walls, although these are chiefly meant. The meaning of *kadhkhōdh* is not known. Like all the other materials mentioned here, it must be some sort of precious stone, perhaps one of flaming, bright red color, suggesting — like everything fire-red — anger and terror for the enemies of the city. *kadhkhōdh* is an accusative and is part of the predicate. The accusative here has the same force as that of the *le* connected with *'abhney* in the next two clauses. *'eqdāḥ* is usually translated with carbuncle, since the word is derived from *qādhaḥ*, to burn, to blaze. This stone is not only beautiful, but is also for the enemy symbolic of terror. *kol gebhūlekh* now brings us to a description of the city walls, of which there had been no direct mention up to this point. The primary meaning of *gebhūl* is not territory, but boundary, rim, hedge, or fence, in accordance with the meaning of the verb, to fence in, to encircle. Cf. Ezekiel 43:13,17,20; 40:12. That must be the meaning of the word in this instance, since a "territory" of precious stones would hardly make sense. Here the word is used in its most attractive sense as an enclosing hedge, meaning the city walls. *gebhūlekh* is the most poetic equivalent of *hōmōthayikh*. *'abhney ḥephets*, stones of delight (said of their effect rather than of their quality), are stones of beauty, jewels. Compare this description with that of the New Jerusalem in the Revelation of St. John 21:18ff. It need hardly be said that this physical splendor is purely a picture of the spiritual glory of the future church in its perfection. The same is true of the Revelation of St. John. It would be a mistake to attempt to interpret each separate item.

13 וְכָל־בָּנַיִךְ לִמּוּדֵי יְהוָה וְרַב שְׁלוֹם בָּנָיִךְ :

The prophecy now proceeds from the external splendor to a description of the inner glory of the City of God. *kol bānayikh* are all her inhabitants. The *limmūdhey YHWH* are the disciples, the pupils and adherents of the Lord, that is, those who have been taught by the Lord Himself, who know Him by faith and have yielded their hearts to Him, cf. John 6:45; Jeremiah 31:33. The church of the New Testament is made up solely of true believers; it

473

is the communion of saints. The second inner ornament of the inhabitants is "great peace." Inner peace, peace of conscience, peace of heart, the peace of God which passes all understanding (Phil. 4:7; Col. 3:15) is meant, which is founded on the knowledge that Almighty God is reconciled and gracious, and therefore no longer needs fear any evil, Psalm 23:4. This "proud peace" is the lot of all believers, the *naḥalath 'abhdhēy YHWH,* verse 17.

בְּצְדָקָה תִּכּוֹנֵנִי 14

רַחֲקִי מֵעֹשֶׁק כִּי־לֹא תִירָאִי וּמִמְּחִתָּה כִּי לֹא־תִקְרַב אֵלָיִךְ׃

tikkōnāni is Hithpolel with assimilated *Taw;* Qamets has replaced Tsere in Pause. As is often the case, the Hithpael here has a passive meaning. The new church shall be strengthened and fortified with salvation (*be* of the material). This is the basis for what is said in verse 13. The Lord clothes His church wholly in righteousness and salvation, (61:10). That is her strength; and since she is founded on this covenant of salvation, on grace, and the righteousness of grace, all her inhabitants are the "taught of the Lord," who are made so secure against all enemies that the peace of God rules in their hearts and they need fear no evil.

raḥaqī is an imperative of assurance or promise. By His promise God provides what it would otherwise be impossible for man to obtain, Gr. 110, c, p. 324. *'osheq* does not mean fear, as the word is often translated, but refers to outrage, violence, or oppression that comes from without, cf. 30:12; 59:13; Psalm 73:8, or it refers objectively to that which has been seized by violence. The concept of fear is, however, contained in *raḥaqī mē,* be far from. An inner removal far from oppression is meant: be not afraid of it, do not think of it! The reason for this assurance lies in *kī lō' thīrā'ī.* This potential imperfect (Gr. 107,r,p.318) is to be translated: you will have no need to be afraid. The last clause again supplies a reason. Before *mimmeḥittāh, raḥaqī* must be supplied. *meḥittāh* never refers to subjective fear, but always to that which causes fear, the fearful thing, Proverbs 21:15. The original meaning of the word is physical ruin, from *ḥāthath,* to break to pieces, to wreck, to shatter. This word, too, indicates that *'osheq,* its parallel, is objective, and that *raḥaqī* refers to an inner attitude. All fear and anxiety are unnecessary, because *'osheq* and *meḥittāh* shall not come near the church. With this thought the prophet leads over to the following verses, which speak of the protection of the church against external foes.

¹⁵ הֵן גּוֹר יָגוּר אֶפֶס מֵאוֹתִי מִי־גָר אִתָּךְ עָלַיִךְ יִפּוֹל:

hēn does not here have the meaning *behold!*. It is in this case a conditional particle, Gr. 159, w, p. 497. The infinitive absolute *gōr* emphasizes the actuality of *yāgūr*: if actually, if in spite of all, someone does set himself to strive against you. The verb is impersonal. *'ephes* begins the apodosis: "then without Me," that is, he does so without Me, without or against My counsel, and therefore his undertaking cannot succeed. *mē'ōthī* is the same as *mē'ittī*, Gr. 103, b, p. 300, literally: "not of Me" is it. *mī*, in the following clause, is an indefinite pronoun, not the interrogative, Gr. 137, c, p. 443. *ʿalayikh yippōl* cannot mean "on you will he come to grief." The meaning here is: He will fall to you, that is, be converted and go over to you, cf. 1 Samuel 29:3; 2 Kings 7:4; Jeremiah 21:9; 37:13,-14. We have here a plus in addition to what was prophesied in 41:11ff. Cf. 45:14.

¹⁶ הֵן אָנֹכִי בָּרָאתִי חָרָשׁ נֹפֵחַ בְּאֵשׁ פֶּחָם

וּמוֹצִיא כְלִי לְמַעֲשֵׂהוּ וְאָנֹכִי בָּרָאתִי מַשְׁחִית לְחַבֵּל:

hēn (Qere has *hinnēh*) may be understood as declarative, but we have taken it in its conditional sense, as in the previous verse. Our translation of the Hiphil participle *mōtsī*, "who withdraws or produces," namely, out of the fire of the forge, is not literal, but it is factual. *lema'asēhū* is "according to his handicraft, or his skill." *ma'aseh* is used in that sense in Isaiah 3:24; Numbers 31:51; 2 Chronicles 16:14. It is the Lord who has control of the formation of a weapon from its very beginning, who endows the smith with the strength and skill needed for his work, but at the same time is ready with the *mashḥith* to destroy these very weapons (*leḥabbēl*, inf. Piel) before they can be used to do harm. This abstract statement is applied to the present situation in the next verse.

¹⁷ כָּל־כְּלִי יוּצַר עָלַיִךְ לֹא יִצְלָח

וְכָל־לָשׁוֹן תָּקוּם־אִתָּךְ לַמִּשְׁפָּט תַּרְשִׁיעִי

זֹאת נַחֲלַת עַבְדֵי יְהוָה וְצִדְקָתָם מֵאִתִּי נְאֻם־יְהוָה:

yūtsar is a Hophal of *yātsar*. *yātsar* is the term used to denote skillful workmanship; but here no human skill is of any consequence. The reference, in the next clause, to verbal strife before a court shows that the subject of the prophecy is now intellectual strife, and no longer physical strife, as in the preceding verse.

Against all intellectual and scientific aggression the church will prevail and hold the field forever. *mishpāṭ* here refers to the judicial action, the strife or contest itself. The Hiphil *hirshīa'* means to refute, to prove something to be wrong and to expose it publicly as something to be condemned.

The next clause serves as a separate, comprehensive, emphatic conclusion to the section. *zō'th* points backward. *naḥalāh*, the equivalent of *ḥēleq* is the assigned and apportioned lot. *'abhdhēy YHWH* resolves the concept of the personified city into its component parts, the true servants of the Lord. Cf. "all your children" in verse 13. *tsedhāqāh* again refers to salvation, that salvation guaranteed by the covenant. The *we* is explicative. Before *mē'ittī* it is necessary to supply "given," "created," or some similar word. *ne'um YHWH* is the powerful Amen to the whole prophecy.

THIRD TRIAD
Chapters 55-57

*An Appealing Invitation
to Accept the Lord's Salvation;
Renunciation of Those
Who Despise the Call.*

First Discourse: Chapter 55

An Appealing Invitation to Accept the Lord's Salvation; Renunciation of Those Who Despise the Call.

The chapter division between 56 and 57 misses the mark. Chapter 56 should close with verse 8, because 56:9-12 forms a unit of thought with 57:1 and 2. As in Part I (40-48), so here too the last three chapters of Part II (49-57) are an application of the foregoing prophecy. Chapters 55 and 56 are an evangelical call to the spiritually despondent and to the erring who may yet be converted to repent and accept the Lord's proffered grace. Chapter 57, by far the longest section of this Part (56:9-57:13a), begins with a declaration of God's wrath directed first to the wicked shepherds of the people (56:9-57:2), and then (57:3-13a) to the people themselves. Beginning with 57:13b, there is a repetition of the promise of salvation to the believers, and in verses 20 and 21, Part II concludes with an enlarged form of the refrain which marked the end of Part I (48:22).

First Discourse: Chapter 55

Invitation and Call to Repentance

The chapter is to be divided between verses 5 and 6. The first, the shorter part, is a general call addressed to all among the *gentiles* who are in need of salvation, to share in the "sure mercies of David," which the Lord is now making a reality. The larger second part calls the sinners in *Israel* to repent, because the Lord's bountifully offered grace, powerfully assured by His word, makes the joyful deliverance of Israel a fact.

First Strophe: verses 1-5: *The invitation to all among the gentiles who are in need of salvation to partake of the sure mercies of David.*

478

The first portion, verses 1-3, in fervent and appealing words, contains the invitation itself; the second portion, verses 4 and 5, sets forth the mercies of David.

1 *Ho, every one who thirsts, come to the waters!*
  And you, who have no money, come, buy, and eat!
  Yes, come, buy without money, and without cost, both wine and
    milk!
2 *Why do you spend money for that which does not nourish,*
  And your labor for that which does not satisfy?
  Do but hearken to Me and eat what is good,
  That your soul may delight in fatness.
3 *Incline your ears and come to Me!*
  Listen, so that your soul may live;
  For I will establish an eternal covenant for you:
  The mercies of David, that have been made sure.
4 *Truly, I have set Him to be a witness to the people,*
  A Prince and a Commander of nations.
5 *Truly, a people that You did not know, You will call,*
  And a people will run to You that knew You not —
  Because of the Lord, Your God,
  And for the sake of the Holy One of Israel, because He glorifies
    You.

Why is it that the commentators cannot see that the gentiles, not the people of Israel, are addressed in this passage? Not one word in the entire section points to Israel; everywhere the gentiles are indicated. — Up to this point, Israel has been in the foreground of the prophecy; what is more natural than that the Lord should now finally turn His attention to the gentiles? Chapter 53, for example, began and ended with the prophecy to the Servant that He should have as His spoil many nations, kings, great multitudes, and the mighty of the world. Part II likewise began with a call to the gentiles (49:1-7) and with the express promise that through their conversion the Lord would glorify His Servant. From that point on, to the close of chapter 54, the Lord, so to speak, poured out His heart to Israel. Is it likely that now, in the application, He should overlook the gentiles altogether? But the strophe itself, by its contents, clearly shows that it is specifically the gentiles who are here being addressed. It is true that the invitation itself, the terms of address, the admonitions, and the abstract promises are couched in general terms. But the promise of the "mercies of David," because of the very form of that promise, must apply to the gentiles. If that promise were in this instance meant for Israel, it would hardly have been expressed by *kārath berīth*, "to make a covenant," but by *heqīm berīth*, "to confirm, or fulfill, the covenant," or by the still more general phrase *nāthan berīth*, because the Davidic covenant of grace had been established since 2 Samuel 7 and it needed only to be fulfilled. And self-evidently, the promise to David's seed applies at the same time to the people. If no more were meant here than the covenant as it applied to Israel, then we might have expected the prophet to write *'ekhrethāh 'ittekhem*, "I will make a covenant *with* you," which is the usual form of the expression. But instead of that usual form, we have here *'ekhrethāh lākhem* — *for* you. Although the gentiles are thus indicated as beneficiaries of the covenant, which had indeed always included them, yet it had not been concluded *with* them, but *for* them. Cf. Romans 15:8ff. Absolute proof that this passage is directed to the gentiles lies in the fact that in verses 4 and 5 the mercies of David are referred to only insofar as they apply to the gentiles. Thus the use of *kārath* and *lākhem* in verse 3 is clarified. The Lord here promotes the *promises* given to David that he should rule over the gentiles to the higher level of a *covenant* meant for the gentiles, by virtue of which He decks a banquet table with His grace and earnestly invites them to partake most freely, verses 1-3.

¹ הֹוֹי כָּל־צָמֵא לְכוּ לַמַּיִם וַאֲשֶׁר אֵין־לֹו כֶּסֶף לְכוּ
שִׁבְרוּ וֶאֱכֹלוּ וּלְכוּ שִׁבְרוּ בְּלוֹא־כֶסֶף וּבְלוֹא מְחִיר יַיִן
וְחָלָב:

hōy is an interjection expressing encouragement; *tsāme'* is an adjective used as a generic noun; *'ekholū* is the pausal form of the imperative *'ekhelū*. The threefold *lekhū* brings out the urgency of the invitation. The *Beth* in *belo'* is *Beth pretii*, for no money, at no cost. The negative is thus made into a positive. It needs hardly to be mentioned that these are all physical expressions for spiritual things, and yet the modern naturalists and the older rationalists, who were unable to discern anything but physical features in Jerusalem, Israel, walls, and ramparts in all the prophecies, now see only material things and acts in water, wine, milk, thirst, money, run, eat, and buy. That passes for scientific scholarship! — Matthew 11:28ff is a New Testament form of these Old Testament words. Thirst expresses the lack of every form of salvation. It is the natural emptiness in the breast of every sinner, which cannot be satisfied by any goods, joys, or glories of this world. Oh, the wealth of the American, the culture of the Germans, Faust's thirst for knowledge and his yearning to savor of every boon the world had to offer — all is *habhēl habhālīm*! It is all vanity, said the Preacher — every glory, including that of Solomon, all of it is vanity. The thirst remains, only more fevered than before. The same plaint pervades the literature of every age. So too, the youthful Goethe, that brilliant genius, the darling of his age, cries out in bitter disappointment:

> *Ach, ich bin des Treibens muede!*
> *Was soll all der Schmerz und Lust!*
> *Sueszer Friede, sueszer Friede,*
> *Komm, ach, komm in meine Brust!*

Disillusioned, weary of the mad chase, seeing no good in all the pain and passion, he cries out: "Sweetest peace, come, oh, come into my breast." But peace cannot come into the natural heart of man, and therefore, He, our Lord, has Himself come down from heaven and brought it to us. *He* is our peace. Now He calls to everyone and everything on earth that is without peace to come to Him, and offers to them without cost, as a free gift, that which no person and no earthly power can convey. But long before He appeared in the flesh, the God of all grace, who had never desired the death of the sinner, had called Jews and gentiles to Him who was to come. Our text is one of those great invitations directed to the gentiles to come to the great Prince of Peace, His Servant. *kol tsāmē'*, "all, everything that suffers thirst"; none is excluded, not a single soul. *lekhū, lekhū, lekhū*! Here are water, wine, and milk. That quenches the thirst, that rejoices the human heart, Psalm 104:15; that is pure, nourishing food and sweet refreshing, 1 Peter 2:2; Exodus 3:8, and frequently. The text has *shibhrū*, buy; but that is a picture which in view of the two modifying adverbs, "for no money, at no cost" means but to get, to take, to receive, to accept. The chief emphasis, indeed, lies on this idea of an offer free of all cost. Everything in the world costs something; only this one thing, the mercies of David, the salvation in Christ, costs nothing, absolutely nothing. In connection with the mention of wine, see Isaiah 25:6 and Proverbs 31:6.

לָ֤מָּה תִשְׁקְלוּ־כֶ֙סֶף֙ בְּֽלוֹא־לֶ֔חֶם וִיגִיעֲכֶ֖ם בְּל֣וֹא לְשָׂבְעָ֑ה
שִׁמְע֨וּ שָׁמ֤וֹעַ אֵלַי֙ וְאִכְלוּ־ט֔וֹב וְתִתְעַנַּ֥ג בַּדֶּ֖שֶׁן נַפְשְׁכֶֽם:

The first half of this verse describes the foolishness of those who with much labor and at great cost seek in other things their salvation and the nourishing and refreshing of their souls. This is not

481

empty rhetoric; it is purest fact. The entire life of natural man, his family life, his social life in land and city, his clubs and societies, all of the intercourse of men, even on the national and international levels, all of their anxious striving is given over to the one purpose of satisfying the thirst for happiness, one laborious, uninterrupted, self-tormenting striving for that which is not bread and can never satisfy. And no one understands, no one believes, till the last hour strikes. That is the curse of this life of sin, Genesis 3:17ff; 5:29; Psalm 90; Job 7:14. The task of Sisyphus!

In *shime 'u 'elay*, an imperative strengthened by an infinitive absolute, the Lord, speaking in the spirit of the sure mercies of David, calls all who are so hopelessly plaguing themselves to come to *His* Gospel. Luther rightly translates: *"Hoeret mir doch zu!"* "If only you would listen to Me!" The accent lies on *Me*, as opposed to all those things outside of Him, to which the world lends its ears and its heart. *'ikhlu tobh*, "eat what is good," is joined by the copula directly to *shime 'u*. The eating and the satisfaction of hunger, which follow immediately upon the hearing, occur through, or by, the hearing of faith, for God has placed all salvation in the Word, in preaching, *His* preaching, the Gospel. This is what is called *tobh*, the true and eternal good, which truly imparts peace and satisfying to the soul. The final clause, introduced by *Waw*, carries the thought onward: "That your soul may delight in fatness." Fatness, *deshen*, is the oil of the olive tree, which was in general use for food. Here fatness is used figuratively to designate abundance, gratification, spiritual satisfaction, joy and gladness, as in Psalm 63:6(5); Job 36:16; Jeremiah 31:13(14). *'anagh*, here in the Hithpael, is the exact opposite of *'anah*, to be plagued. Truly, *with* Him and *in* Him is true rest, peace, comfort (66:13), spiritual satisfaction, joy, and happiness. Matthew 11:28! "Jesus, priceless treasure, Fount of purest pleasure!" — Joh. Franck.

הַטּ֤וּ אָזְנְכֶם֙ וּלְכ֣וּ אֵלַ֔י שִׁמְע֖וּ וּתְחִ֣י נַפְשְׁכֶ֑ם 3
וְאֶכְרְתָ֤ה לָכֶם֙ בְּרִ֣ית עוֹלָ֔ם חַסְדֵ֥י דָוִ֖ד הַנֶּאֱמָנִֽים׃

The first half of the third verse is a repetition in somewhat different words of the thought in the second half of verse 2. The purpose is to make the admonition all the more urgent. *hattu* is a Hiphil imperative, second person plural. *'oznekhem* is a collective; *utehi* is an apodosis; the *Waw* before *'ekhrethah* is causal. Luther correctly construed the verse. *'ekhrethah berith lakhem* was discussed above. The covenant of David, as it applies also to the gen-

tiles, is called an *eternal* covenant as distinguished from the temporary covenant made with Israel on Sinai, a covenant that has its
end in Christ, Romans 10:4; 2 Corinthians 3:11; Galatians 3:11,19,
24f. This is the first and the last, there will be no third. The covenant is referred to here as the *ḥasdhēy dhāwidh*, the mercies of
David, a *terminus technicus*, cf. 2 Chronicles 6:42. Isaiah could
assume that every pious Jew was familiar with the term. The mercies of David, rather than the promises to Abraham, became the
prime object of the hopes of Israel, although those hopes were to a
large extent carnal. The name refers to the promises given first to
David in 2 Samuel 7:12ff, repeated in Psalms 2, 18, 72, 89, 110, and
in the prophets, especially in Isaiah 9:2, and treasured as the gracious promise of the eternal kingdom embracing all nations of the
Prince of Peace, the Seed of David, the Christ. They are described
as *hanne'emānīm*, "the sure and unbreakable" promises. Cf.
Psalm 89:35-38(34-37). How these promises will be brought to
those who are invited is told in the next two verses.

4 הֵן עֵד לְאוּמִּים נְתַתִּיו נָגִיד וּמְצַוֵּה לְאֻמִּים:

It should hardly be necessary for commentators who do not *seek*
difficulties, to discuss the question whether the *ʿedh* introduced in
this verse is the historical David, or that *Seed* of David, the Christ,
in and through whom the promised mercies should be realized.
How does a *historical* perfect, as *nethattīw* has been construed, fit
into this context; or what place has this sentence, taken as a mere
historical note, in this connection where, so many years *after*
David's time, the subject is the invitation to the future kingdom of
his *Seed*? In the next verse it is clearly the David who is yet to
come who calls unknown gentiles into His kingdom. It is equally
clear that in both sentences the subject is the same. Or is it possible that verse 4 is only a comparison in this sense: As I once called
David to be a witness (verse 5) so shall You, David's Seed, call a
people? That sense would have to be expressed more clearly than
by means of *hēn* with a perfect and a following *hēn* to introduce an
apodosis. In 54:15 a conditional *hēn* is followed by an apodosis
without introductory particle; in 54:16 a conditional *hēn* is
followed by *Waw apodosis*, the usual construction, cf. Gr. 159, w, p.
497. But *hēn — hēn*, as — so, is not grammatical. In verse 4, He
through whom the mercies of David are to be realized is the subject. That is not David the king, although he too is a type of his
great Son and even in his day cast his shoe over Edom and made
Moab his washpot, Psalm 60:10(8); 108:10(9). Nor is it David's

483

next descendant, Solomon, who constructed a very imperfect type of the promised kingdom, whose oppressed and impoverished subjects groaned under his yoke, 1 Kings 12:4. The subject here is the Seed of David, of whom David speaks in Psalm 110, whom Jeremiah (30:9), Ezekiel (34:23f; 37:24), and Hosea (3:5) expressly call by the name of David, and whose kingdom they describe, as Psalms 72 and 89 and Isaiah 9 do. Into this kingdom of grace and peace the Lord is now inviting the gentiles. This David the Lord has set as a witness (*ʿedh*) to the nations, as their Prince (*nāghīdh*) and Commander (*metsawwēh*). It is not necessary to advance a proof that this does not refer to a witness before court or to one who testifies as to the facts of a case; this is a witness in the capacity of Preacher, Proclaimer, and Prophet, as in Revelation 1:5; 3:14; John 1:4,8; 3:11; 18:37; Acts 1:8, etc. He is to be a witness *to* the gentiles, since the mercies were not known to them as they were known to Israel. It is necessary that out of His own mouth they hear the sure, and powerful, and convincing testimony that they too have part in the mercies of David and that they together with Israel have been made fellow citizens with the saints in the household of God, Ephesians 2 and 3. And Paul was the spokesman through whom the Heir of the mercies of David became a witness to the gentiles of their salvation and called them into His kingdom. As *ʿedh* is the "Prophet," so *nāghīdh* is the "Head, the Chief, the Prince" of His people. *nāghīdh* is used to designate the priestly and the high-priestly office, as well as the office of king, Jeremiah 20:1; Daniel 11:22; 1 Chronicles 9:11, etc. In Daniel 9:25 the Messiah too is called *nāghīdh*, and so one might be tempted in this passage to take *nāghīdh* to mean a high priest, thus completing the threefold office of the Messiah — Prophet, Priest, and King — but that would be reading something into the text. There is nothing in the context that suggests the office of priest. The word is here a synonym of *metsawwēh*, a commander, and the context speaks only of the prophetic and the kingly activity, as in most of Isaiah's prophecies. *nāghīdh* and *metsawwēh* are one concept; the first word designates the king according to His greatness, the second according to the exercise of His office. We have here the Child and the Son, whose government is upon His own shoulder, so that of the increase of His government and peace there shall be no end upon the throne of David, 9:5f(6f). Of Him all the prophets testify. It is to the peace of His kingdom that the gentiles are being invited, as they were earlier invited to partake freely of water, wine, milk, and all good.

484

5 הֵן גּוֹי לֹא־תֵדַע תִּקְרָא וְגוֹי לֹא־יְדָעוּךָ אֵלֶיךָ יָרוּצוּ
לְמַעַן יְהוָה אֱלֹהֶיךָ וְלִקְדוֹשׁ יִשְׂרָאֵל כִּי פֵאֲרָךְ׃

The prophecy now turns to address the King, the Son of David Himself, who in verse 4 was called Witness, Prince, and Commander. It is not the people that are here being addressed; the masculine form of the verbs and of the suffixes indicates that. Verse 5 is a counterpart to verse 4. As in that verse, *hēn* is again assertive rather than merely directive, for the matter at issue here is the awakening of faith in the sure mercies of David. *gōy* is in both instances used in its most indefinite sense: not, *a* people, or peoples, but people as a mass, people in general. "People whom You do not know You will call" into Your kingdom and under the rule of Your peace. *Call* is used here in the sense in which the apostles used the word, namely, to extend an effective call, to convert, to bring people *de facto* into Your kingdom. Herein lies the glorious wonder of the mercies of David that this Son of David will rule not just over those who were known as God's people, but over unknown strangers living in distant lands, over wild and strange people, over the remotest gentiles — that is really the point of the promises given in chapters 42, 49, and 53. The second half of the sentence is a poetic variation of the first half, but it does contain the result of the call that had been issued. That result was already mentioned in 2:2ff, and in many other passages. Cf. 65:1; Hosea 2:23; Romans 9:25; 10:20.

The adoption of the gentiles into the kingdom of the Messiah occurs "because of the Lord, your God, and for the sake of the Holy One of Israel." The two prepositions *lema'an* and *le* are identical in meaning and they indicate that the purpose of this is to fulfill the counsel of God and thus to glorify Him who, as your God, joined Himself to you, and who for the welfare of His people Israel zealously contends against all its enemies. The phrases in these last clauses take the place of the customary *lehithpā'ēr*, "that I may be glorified," 60:21; 61:3. The final phrase, *kī pe'arākh*, pointedly makes God's purpose the glorification of His *Servant*, David's Seed, the King of this great and eternally blessed kingdom. Cf. Ephesians 1:10,22; Colossians 1:18. The perfect is the same as that in *nethattīw* in verse 4 and expresses future action, Gr. 106, m, p. 312. The form *pe'arākh* is not, as might appear at first glance, a third person masculine with a second person feminine suffix in pause (instead of *pe'arekh*, as in 60:9); it is the equivalent of

485

pe͞'arekhā͞, with a second person masculine suffix in pause, Gr.
58, g, p. 156. The prophet is not speaking of Israel's glory, but
of the glorification of the Son of David, the Servant of the Lord
κατ' ἐξοχήν.

This strophe has called all the gentiles, all who are in need of
salvation, to come and receive the sure mercies of David. By virtue
of these mercies the Lord has ordained the Son of David to be a
Preacher of grace and a Lord of grace to the gentiles, and through
these mercies the Lord has given Him the gentiles as His inheritance, in order to glorify both Him and Himself.

Second Strophe: verses 6-13:   *A call to Repentance addressed*
   to the sinners in Israel.

This strophe consists of four stanzas, each made up of two
verses. The first two stanzas contain six lines each; the last two
have eight lines each.

6,7   *Oh, seek the Lord while He may be found,*
      Call upon Him while He is near!
      Let the wicked forsake his way
      And the evildoer his designs,
      And turn to the Lord; He will have compassion on him,
      And to our God, for He forgives abundantly!

8,9   *For My thoughts are not your thoughts*
      And My ways are not your ways,
      Says the Lord.
      As far as the heavens are higher than the earth,
      So are My ways higher than your ways
      And My thoughts than your thoughts.

10,11 *For as the rain and the snow fall down from heaven*
      And do not return thither
      Without moistening the earth and making it fruitful and
         productive,
      Giving seed to the sower and bread to the eater —
      So shall My word be that goes forth from My mouth;
      It shall not return to Me fruitless,
      Without having done what pleases Me,
      And having accomplished what I directed it to do:

12,13 *That you shall depart with rejoicing*
      And be returned home in peace.
      Mountains and hills shall break forth in rejoicing before you,
      And all the trees in the field will clap their hands.
      Cypress shall sprout forth in place of the thorn,
      Instead of briers, the myrtle shall flourish.
      And this shall be to the honor of the Lord,
      An everlasting memorial that shall never fall.

Since the picture in verses 12 and 13 is still of the return to the homeland, it is clear that this section is addressed to the Israelites. Cf. 41:17-20; 42:16; 43:2; 43:19f; 49:9-11; 51:11; 52:11f.

⁶ דִּרְשׁ֤וּ יְהוָה֙ בְּהִמָּ֣צְא֔וֹ קְרָאֻ֖הוּ בִּהְיוֹת֥וֹ קָרֽוֹב׃

The meaning of *dārash* is "to step, to tread, to enter"; with the accusative of the person: "to approach"; here, to approach the Lord with the plea for help and salvation. "Seek Him alone, Who did atone, Who did your souls deliver." The suffix in *behimmātse'o* (Niphal infinitive) is not nominal (genitive), "in His being found," but verbal (accusative), "in His letting Himself be found," Gr. 51, c, p. 137 and 115, d, p. 354. The suffix of the infinitive Qal *bihyōthō* is, however, nominal. Sinners are exhorted to make use of this one opportunity for repentance. That opportunity is given and remains only so long as the Lord lets Himself be found, so long as He is near. That opportunity is there whenever and so long as the Lord *calls*, 50:2; 65:12; 66:4. Cf. John 12:35; 2 Corinthians 6:2. His voice, His call, His inviting word alone has the power to convert. Where that voice no longer is heard, there is no more opportunity to come to grace.

⁷ יַעֲזֹ֤ב רָשָׁע֙ דַּרְכּ֔וֹ וְאִ֥ישׁ אָ֖וֶן מַחְשְׁבֹתָ֑יו
וְיָשֹׁ֤ב אֶל־יְהוָה֙ וִֽירַחֲמֵ֔הוּ וְאֶל־אֱלֹהֵ֖ינוּ כִּֽי־יַרְבֶּ֥ה לִסְלֽוֹחַ׃

A *rāshā'* is a "wicked, ungodly person," one who has inwardly forsaken God and follows his own lusts. The *'ish 'āwen* is the man of evil deeds, the hardened sinner, who no longer is troubled by sin. It is significant that the prophet speaks of the *way* of the *rāshā'*, which leads away from God into destruction; and of the *maḥashābhōth* of the *'ish 'āwen*, namely, his *thoughts* and *designs*. The Lord's call is intended to reach the *sinners*, the publicans and the adulterers in Israel, Matthew 9:13. He calls them *away* from the service of sin, back to Himself where they belong, to YHWH and *'elohēynu*, to Him who has bound Himself to Israel in grace and made Himself Israel's "dear" God. *'elohēynu* in the mouth of God is not an error in the text, nor is it a slip that the prophet commits; it is a term that God takes out of the mouth of the people, where it has become a familiar expression, or *terminus technicus*, very commonly paired with YHWH. The two promises at the end of the verse, contained in *wīraḥamēhu* and *yarbeh lislōaḥ* ("He increases to forgive"), are especially inviting and comforting. The

487

first assures to every sinner God's personal compassion, the second tells of the eternal constancy of God's grace. Cf. Romans 5:20; Isaiah 1:18; 1 Timothy 1:13-17. "Though great our sins and sore our woes, His grace much more aboundeth." In these qualities lies the divinely persuasive power of the Gospel.

8 כִּי לֹא מַחְשְׁבוֹתַי מַחְשְׁבוֹתֵיכֶם וְלֹא דַרְכֵיכֶם דְּרָכָי נְאֻם־יְהוָה׃

9 כִּי־גָבְהוּ שָׁמַיִם מֵאָרֶץ כֵּן גָּבְהוּ דְרָכַי מִדַּרְכֵיכֶם וּמַחְשְׁבֹתַי מִמַּחְשְׁבֹתֵיכֶם׃

For the most part these two verses are clear. There is only one question: What is the point of contrast between the thoughts and ways of God and those of the persons addressed? Since our catechism days we have assumed that here the ways and thoughts of God are set in contrast to the ways and thoughts of men in general, to impress upon us the incomprehensibility of God's rule over the world, as in 40:13f; Romans 11:34, etc. But that is a mistaken interpretation. God's ways are here set in contrast to the ways of the *rāshā'*, and the thoughts of God to the thoughts of the *'īsh 'āwen*. Their thoughts are evil and lead to destruction; God's ways and thoughts are good, just, and holy, and lead to salvation. For these are ways, not only of God, but of *our* God, the Lord, as is emphasized by *ne'um YHWH* at the end of verse 8. Verses 12 and 13 state to what deliverance the ways and thoughts of God lead. The Lord's *mahashābhōth*, His "counsels and plans," His *derākhīm*, His "practical measures" regarding us sinners, all pertain finally to the eternal salvation of His elect people. Romans 8:28. *kī* in verse 9, even if it were not followed by *kēn*, is the *kī* of comparison, as in 62:5 and elsewhere. The *kēn* just emphasizes that fact. *gābhehū* is a perfect, expressing state or condition, Gr. 106, g, p. 311.

10 כִּי כַּאֲשֶׁר יֵרֵד הַגֶּשֶׁם וְהַשֶּׁלֶג מִן־הַשָּׁמַיִם
וְשָׁמָּה לֹא יָשׁוּב כִּי אִם־הִרְוָה אֶת־הָאָרֶץ
וְהוֹלִידָהּ וְהִצְמִיחָהּ וְנָתַן זֶרַע לַזֹּרֵעַ וְלֶחֶם לָאֹכֵל׃

Regarding *kī 'im*, see Gr. 163, c, p. 500. It means "unless previously." The imperfects *yēredh* and *yāshūbh* are present as to time, expressing what is customary, Gr. 107, f, g, p. 315f. It is their nature to fall, etc. The perfects following *kī 'im* are regular perfects, Gr. 106, b, p. 309f. The subject of *nāthan* lies in *geshem* and *sheleg*.

11 כֵּן יִהְיֶה דְבָרִי֙ אֲשֶׁ֣ר יֵצֵ֣א מִפִּ֗י לֹא־יָשׁ֤וּב אֵלַי֙ רֵיקָ֔ם
כִּ֤י אִם־עָשָׂה֙ אֶת־אֲשֶׁ֣ר חָפַ֔צְתִּי וְהִצְלִ֖יחַ אֲשֶׁ֥ר שְׁלַחְתִּֽיו׃

This is a beautiful comparison, the point of which lies in the assurance that "it shall not return to Me fruitless," without having
accomplished its purpose. "To Me," that is, into the sky, above
which God dwells. The sky is conceived as the point of departure.
Rain and snow fall from the sky, moisten the earth and make it
fruitful, then vaporize or flow to the sea, where they become vapor
and return again to their place of origin. For a description of the
course of the waters, see Ecclesiastes 1:7. It is impossible that rain
and snow should *not* have that wholesome effect, which assures
bread for the present year and seed for the year to come, thus sus-
taining the life of mankind from year to year. "So shall My word
be." Rain and snow, too, are God's, and it is He who sends them
forth from His abode. They are His messengers, do His will and
carry out His commands, and only because of His will do they have
their wholesome effect. Just so does His *Word* go forth from His
mouth as His herald, fulfilling the mission assigned to it by God.
That mission is defined in verse 12. It is impossible that the Word
should not fulfill its mission, for it is His creative, commanding
Word, alive with His power. It is the Almighty God Himself in action, even as He performs His will in the rain and the snow.
Romans 1:16; Hebrews 4:12f; Jeremiah 23:29ff.

12 כִּֽי־בְשִׂמְחָ֣ה תֵצֵ֔אוּ וּבְשָׁל֖וֹם תּֽוּבָל֑וּן
הֶהָרִ֣ים וְהַגְּבָע֗וֹת יִפְצְח֤וּ לִפְנֵיכֶם֙ רִנָּ֔ה וְכָל־עֲצֵ֥י הַשָּׂדֶ֖ה
יִמְחֲאוּ־כָֽף׃

The initial *kī* is not causal. It introduces an object clause and indicates the contents of the Word that goes forth from the mouth of
the Lord. Compare Genesis 4:23, where after *'imrāthī* it introduces
direct discourse; after *wayyō'mer*, Genesis 21:30; 22:16; and commonly after the oath formula. And so, in this instance, *kī* introduces in direct discourse the contents of the assurance given in
verses 10 and 12. That assurance is the equivalent of an oath. *kī*
here has the force of a colon and does not need to be translated, except perhaps by "namely" followed by a colon. The meaning of the
passage is that you shall depart in joy and be led in peace. For
tūbhālūn, a Hophal of *yābhal*, see 53:7. The background of the pic-

489

ture is still Israel's imprisonment in Babylon and other lands. But that is here only a figure for the captivity of the elect in this world of sin and pain in which they live as strangers so long as they are in the flesh. It is a world in which the elect too, while yet unregenerate, are bound as slaves to the lust of sin, living in constant fear because of the guilt of their sin. Even after they have been reborn, they are still in "captivity to the law of sin" which is in their members. Laden with the tribulation of this earthly time, they cry with St. Paul, Romans 7, for release from the "body of this death." But they have the promise that they shall depart in joy homeward to Zion. Verily, in peace shall we be led to the Jerusalem that is *above*, where our citizenship is and whence we now await the coming of our Savior, Jesus Christ, the Lord, Philippians 3:20f. Cf. Psalm 126; Isaiah 57:1f; 2 Timothy 4:18. "Turn again our captivity, O Lord, as the streams in the south." With rejoicing! What is here said of the rejoicing of the mountains, the hills, and the trees over the final deliverance of Zion is, of course, not to be understood literally — and yet it is true! It is as true as what is said of the groaning of the whole creation under the vanity and in the service of the "bondage of corruption" in this world of sin, of the curse, and of the captivity of the children of God, Romans 8 — of which this passage is a counterpart.

13 תַּחַת הַנַּעֲצוּץ֙ יַעֲלֶ֣ה בְר֔וֹשׁ תַּ֥חַת הַסִּרְפַּ֖ד יַעֲלֶ֣ה הֲדַ֑ס
וְהָיָ֤ה לַֽיהוָה֙ לְשֵׁ֔ם לְא֥וֹת עוֹלָ֖ם לֹ֥א יִכָּרֵֽת׃

na'atsuts, which occurs only here and in 7:19, and *sirpadh*, which occurs only here, are unidentified weeds of the desert, "thorns and thistles," Genesis 3:18. In their place, cypress and myrtle, precious trees and shrubs shall sprout forth. This again is poetic fancy, as in 12b, but will nevertheless be fulfilled a thousandfold in the palingenesis of Matthew 19:28 upon the new earth of 2 Peter 3:13 and Revelation 21:1, where the creature too will be made free of the bondage of corruption and share in the glorious freedom of the children of God, Romans 8:21. The prophet certainly does not believe that the hills will sing and the trees clap their hands, nor that the physical wilderness will be transformed into a paradise in this world, but he does believe in the final deliverance and glorification of the children of God and the heavenly transfiguration of their future abode. As in all prophecies of the future, the prophet does not view this transfiguration in the perspective of its fulfillment, but as directly connected with the coming of the Christ that he had prophesied, in the same manner as he had connected the coming of Christ directly with the deliverance from the Babylonian exile. He does not distinguish between temporal deliverance and spiritual, eternal deliverance, but unites both in a single picture. In a strict sense, the subject of *hāyāh* lies in *thētsē'ū* and *tūbhālūn*, but the circumstances connected with the departure and the arrival in the homeland are not excluded. The salvation and glorification of His people is God's greatest honor and a memorial to His honor that will endure into all eternity.

The sinners in Israel are called upon to turn in repentance to the Lord who has come to them with abundant forgiveness. In contrast to their evil and pernicious thoughts, the Lord has for them only thoughts of salvation. Through the power of His almighty and unchangeable Word of promise His thoughts toward them will be fulfilled in their salvation and eternal glorification.

Second Discourse: Chapter 56:1-8

Whosoever repents with his whole heart shall receive grace abounding and shall be glorified, even though he is physically cut off from association with the people of God.

Preliminary Remarks. After the modern critics had for a time contented themselves with their discovery of a Deutero-Isaiah, hailed by them as the author of chapters 40-66, Bernhard Duhm, in the early 1890's, announced his discovery of a third author, whom he labeled Trito-Isaiah and to whom he ascribed the authorship of chapters 56-66. Duhm based his theory on the assumption that in these chapters we are suddenly confronted with a situation entirely different from the one that prevailed before chapter 56. Babylon, the tyrant over the people of Jehovah, has disappeared from view; there is no longer any reference to a return out of exile; the people are again settled in their own land; internal disorders, godlessness of the people and their shepherds, dissension, apostasy, idol worship, self-righteousness, and dull despair characterize a situation which obtained only in the time of Ezra, before the coming of Nehemiah. The author of this section, he said, was a far less talented man than Deutero-Isaiah. Here we encounter a somewhat different vocabulary, an inferior poetic gift, a gloomy and legalistic spirit, even though the author here and there does rise to rosy expectations for the future. That is, in brief, Duhm's conception of his Trito-Isaiah. This theory, vigorously supported by Marti, had hardly been generally accepted as scientifically based theology, when Cheyne, who in the course of the years had made a complete turnabout from a positive to a negative position, proved that Duhm's theory of a single author of chapters 56-66, a Trito-Isaiah, was untenable. Cheyne then ascribed the chapters from 56 to 66 to ten different authors who all lived during Nehemiah's time, who were much inferior to Deutero-Isaiah, and who in mechanical fashion adopted that author's phraseology and rhythm. Chapters 63:7 to 64:11, he said, were of much later origin, belonging to the time of Artaxerxes Ochus, 363-345 B.C. Cheyne's hypothesis received general acceptance, and since then his followers have busied themselves with outstripping the master and have ascribed not only this group of chapters but also some of the earlier ones to various editors who made revisions and compilations of hundreds of leaflets to put together these chapters. Since Cheyne has already disposed of Duhm, we can be spared a repetition of that task. In order to set into their proper light the scientific methods of the Cheyne propositions, we point only to the manner in which Cheyne treated Isaiah 64:9-11 (Jerusalem and the temple burned and restored). Of Isaiah 63:18 Duhm had said that the author, Trito-Isaiah, simply ignored the second temple as being too unimportant in relation to the first temple. When it was discovered that with a little manipulating the text could be made to read: *lammāh tsi'arū reshā'īm qodhshekhā,* "why do the godless despise Thy holy place and desecrate (*bōsesū*) Thy holy place," 64:10,11 still were found to stand in the way. How could one get over or around this barrier? That was simple. Some *assumed* that the second temple had probably been destroyed by the hostile Samaritans, and that Scriptures had forgotten to record the fact. Cheyne himself explained that *most probably* a destruction of the temple had occurred under Artaxerxes Ochus. (Introduction to the Book of Isaiah, p. 356ff.) That is a sample of the "scientific" method of modern theology. And yet the critics consider us hopelessly backward if we do not fall for the "scientifically established results" of modern criticism. The fact is that there is not one scientifically established fact to support the entire modern Isaiah criticism (Deutero-Isaiah, Trito-Isaiah, Fragmented Isaiah). Everything has been hatched and edited by the light of the study lamp. Their slogans are: a different vocabulary, different phraseology, an inferior spirit, strange environment, etc. If the gaps in the argument are altogether too great, it is always possible to assume corruption of the text and to "restore" the reading. Even historical facts, of which there is otherwise no evidence whatever, can be assumed as "most highly probable," and all difficulties standing in the way of their hypotheses are conveniently swept aside.

At this point we cannot resist mentioning a parallel. After 1914 England filled the entire world with the assertion that the German emperor was the proven and only originator of World War I,

493

that it was Germany's purpose to conquer the whole world with the sword, and that its method of waging war was so inhumanly barbaric and bestial, that it was the duty of the whole world to join the allies in fighting against Germany to render that nation forever impotent. Year in, year out, day after day, that story was repeated in all newspapers, magazines, and thousands of books, repeated and allegedly proved, until the whole world and England itself believed it. They believed their own manufactured propaganda. So-called scientific theology operates in the same fashion when it goes beyond a presentation of observed facts and launches into explanatory theories.

Modern scientific theology, and particularly scientific Bible criticism, has been guilty of fraud. If Bible criticism presented the facts and stopped there, who would not accept them with thanks! But it resorts to hypotheses and theories in order to come up with a *natural* explanation, since it will not and cannot admit a supernatural intervention in nature, without sacrificing its nimbus of scientific method. In spite of an occasional bad conscience that now and then speaks up, they repeat their theory so long and so often, and search after proofs — which, naturally, they manage to uncover — until the theological world under the spell of the critical school takes its theories to be everlasting gospel. *Mundus vult decipi, ergo decipiatur!*

We decline to go along with them. Up to the present moment no one has come forward with a single proof that all of Isaiah II was not written by the son of Amoz, who lived in the time of Uzziah, Jotham, Ahaz, and Hezekiah, kings of Judah. It is difficult to understand why just our so-called scientific theological world cannot give up its efforts to roll the Sisyphean stone and cannot cease to persuade itself that it has at last reached the summit. A much more wholesome and profitable work would be to repent and to accept the salvation that is in Christ. That is what the prophet recommends in this section.

This short discourse may be divided into three parts. Verses 1 and 2 characterize the repentant man in terms of his outward behavior; verses 3-7 contain a promise of salvation to God-fearing proselytes and eunuchs; verse 8 holds forth the prospect of the addition of yet others to Israel.

1 *Thus says the Lord:*
   Preserve the right and do righteousness!
   For My salvation is near to appear,
   And My help, that it be revealed.

2 *Blessed is the man who does this,*
   And every child of man who holds fast to it,
   That he keep the Sabbath, not profaning it,
   And hold back his hand, that it do no evil.
3 *Let not the son of a strange land, who turns to the Lord, say:*
   The Lord will surely separate me from His people;
   And let the eunuch not say:
   Behold, I am a dry tree.
4 *For thus does the Lord say to the eunuchs,*
   Who keep My sabbaths,
   Who choose what I delight in,
   And who hold fast to My covenant:
5 *In My house and within My walls*
   I will make for them a memorial and a name
   Better than that of sons and daughters.
   I will give them everlasting honor that shall not be cut off.
6 *And the aliens who cleave to the Lord and serve Him,*
   Who love His name, to be His servants —
   Whosoever keeps the sabbath, not profaning it,
   And holds fast to My covenant,
7 *Them will I lead to My holy mountain,*
   And will delight them in My house of prayer;
   Their offerings and sacrifices shall be welcome on My altar;
   For My house is called a house of prayer for all peoples.
8 *The Oracle of the Lord, the Almighty,*
   Who gathers to Himself the scattered ones of Israel:
   To those already gathered will I gather to him still more.

The poetic quality of this passage does not bear comparison with many other preceding and following passages. But to draw the conclusion that these verses must therefore have been written by a different author is unscientific procedure. No poet ever writes at the unchanging height of his creative genius. Luther, Paul Gerhardt, Goethe, occasionally wrote just verses. The spirit of Biblical poets and prophets also sometimes seems muted and repressed. The reason for that is to be found in the unpoetic quality of the material that is being dealt with. How can the poetic spirit be moved to heights by materials such as those in 40:19,20; 41:5-7; 44:12-20; 46:6,7, etc? If anyone needs to be convinced that the poetic verve can be severely dampened by the material being treated, he needs but to turn to those hymns that preach Law and repentance, the Christian life, and especially Christian "duties." The prophet is here charged with extending an invitation to take part in the Lord's grace to two different classes of persons: to proselytes and to eunuchs, who because of certain statutes had

495

reason to fear that they were excluded from the community of the Lord. That is not highly poetic material. The poet cannot call these people to repentance as he had called to the wicked and the unfaithful. Here there is no lightning and thunder, here it is not wickedness and impenitence, but lukewarmness and neglect of the ordinances of the Lord and fear of the statutes regarding aliens and eunuchs that stood in the way of ready contrition. The admonition to repent is here of necessity an admonition to observe those things that under Old Testament conditions were the genuine proofs of a God-fearing heart: observance of the right (*mishpāṭ*) laid down in the Law, and observance of that institution that brought the sinner into immediate contact with his God, the Sabbath and the Sabbaths. For the Sabbath had been instituted for man's sake, that is, above all, for the sake of his soul's salvation. It shows a lack of spiritual understanding to charge the prophet with legalistic bias because he speaks in these terms.

$$\text{כֹּה אָמַר יְהֹוָה שִׁמְרוּ מִשְׁפָּט וַעֲשׂוּ צְדָקָה}$$
$$\text{כִּי־קְרוֹבָה יְשׁוּעָתִי לָבוֹא וְצִדְקָתִי לְהִגָּלוֹת:}$$

mishpāṭ and *tsedhāqāh* in the first half of this verse cannot be identical in meaning with *yeshū'āthī* and *tsidhqāthī* in the second half, because the coming of the latter two depends on the doing of the first two. They describe righteousness of life in the forms of the Old Testament as sincere devotion to the revealed God of grace and a conduct of life in accordance with the ordinances of His covenant. The admonition is nevertheless a call to repent. *shimrū* and *'asū* presuppose nonobservance and nonconformance to the ordinances of the Lord. *yeshū'āthī* and *tsidhqāthī* are the Messianic salvation. This is the preaching of John the Baptist and of Christ Himself: "Repent, for the kingdom of heaven is near at hand," Matthew 4:17, especially in the spirit of Matthew 3:8.

$$\text{אַשְׁרֵי אֱנוֹשׁ יַעֲשֶׂה־זֹּאת וּבֶן־אָדָם יַחֲזִיק בָּהּ}$$
$$\text{שֹׁמֵר שַׁבָּת מֵחַלְּלוֹ וְשֹׁמֵר יָדוֹ מֵעֲשׂוֹת כָּל־רָע:}$$

The Book of Psalms begins with the word *'ashrēy*, in Isaiah it appears only here and in 30:18 and 32:20. The word occurs only in the form of the construct plural. It is a form of the noun *'esher* or *āshār* (of the verb *āshar*, to be happy). It is used as an interjection: Happiness of! Blessed is, or are! *'enōsh* designates man as frail and mortal, although in poetry the word is often used for *īsh.*

Before *ya'aseh*, *'asher* is to be supplied, Gr. 155, f, 1, p. 487. *zo'th* points both backwards and forwards; *bāh* refers to *zo'th*. *hallelō* is a Piel infinitive with suffix, of *hālal*, to loosen, in the Piel, to profane. The words *mishpāt* and *tsedhāqāh* in verse 1 are here defined as observance of the Sabbath and refraining from committing evil deeds. In verse 4 this is described as keeping the Sabbath of the Lord and holding fast to His covenant, likewise in verse 6. The covenant of Sinai is meant, of which the Sabbath was the chief outward symbol. The covenant of Sinai was grounded wholly in the covenant with Abraham and was in reality nothing other than a preliminary fulfillment of that covenant in certain fixed outward legal forms. Israel was therein formally adopted as God's people, and was hedged about with the Law for the purpose of its preservation until Christ should come. And just as the covenant of Sinai was, first of all, a covenant of blessing by which the Lord gave Himself to Israel as its God of grace, so was the Sabbath a day of blessing for Israel, a means of grace — "a Sabbath made for man," Mark 2:27. It was a day of blessed communion of God with Israel, a thoroughly evangelical institution, which was for that reason to be held as sacred as the covenant itself. Along with circumcision it was the genuine *sign of the covenant*, Exodus 31:13ff; Ezekiel 20:12ff. The keeping of the Sabbath was therefore, together with circumcision, the accepted outward proof of faithfulness to the Lord's covenant. It was a sign of membership by grace among the people of the covenant, as desecration of the Sabbath was a sign of the opposite. If then our passage is an exhortation to keep the Sabbath and the ordinances of the Lord, that is not to be interpreted as proceeding from an external, legalistic conception of "righteousness," but rather as an exhortation to return to faithfulness to the Old Testament covenant.

3 וְאַל־יֹאמַר בֶּן־הַנֵּכָר הַנִּלְוָה אֶל־יְהוָה לֵאמֹר
הַבְדֵּל יַבְדִּילַנִי יְהוָה מֵעַל עַמּוֹ
וְאַל־יֹאמַר הַסָּרִיס הֵן אֲנִי עֵץ יָבֵשׁ:

The *ben hannēkhār*, son of a foreign land, is the non-Israelite, the foreigner, the alien. From this point onward he plays a role in Isaiah; cf. 60:10; 61:5; 62:8. *hannilwāh* describes him as a proselyte. The form, a perfect Niphal with the article, from *lāwāh*, is a malformation. Possibly the participle *hannilweh* (cf. verse 6, *hannilwīm*) was intended, or the article is used for the relative *'asher*, Gr. 138, k, p. 447. The participle too would have the meaning of a

497

perfect, expressing state or condition, Gr. 116, v, p. 361. The ordinances regulating the relative and the absolute separation of the gentiles from the Israelitic community are set forth in Deuteronomy 23:1-8. Verse 1 of that passage excludes eunuchs absolutely. Cf. Leviticus 22:24 and Acts 8:27ff. The eunuch's words have reference to his impotence, because of which his name, even if he could have been accepted into the community, would still have been blotted out in Israel.

4 כִּי־כֹה ׀ אָמַ֣ר יְהוָ֗ה

לַסָּֽרִיסִים֙ אֲשֶׁ֣ר יִשְׁמְרוּ֙ אֶת־שַׁבְּתוֹתַ֔י

וּבָחֲר֖וּ בַּאֲשֶׁ֣ר חָפָ֑צְתִּי וּמַחֲזִיקִ֖ים בִּבְרִיתִֽי׃

5 וְנָתַתִּ֙י לָהֶ֜ם בְּבֵיתִ֤י וּבְחֽוֹמֹתַי֙ יָ֣ד וָשֵׁ֔ם ט֖וֹב מִבָּנִ֣ים וּמִבָּנ֑וֹת

שֵׁ֤ם עוֹלָם֙ אֶתֶּן־ל֔וֹ אֲשֶׁ֖ר לֹ֥א יִכָּרֵֽת׃

To the description of the God-fearing eunuch as one who keeps the Sabbath and is faithful to the covenant, verse 4 now adds that he chooses those things that are well-pleasing to the Lord, in order to stress that it is not outward things that matter, but the sincere attitude of the heart toward the Lord. For their faithfulness toward the covenant and toward the laws governing outward things, verse 5 promises them *yādh* and *shēm* in the house and within the walls of the Lord (both terms denote the temple and its courts). *yādh*, being coupled with *shēm*, must have a similar meaning. Some therefore translate *yādh*, in this case, with memorial, as in 1 Samuel 15:12; 2 Samuel 18:18; or with place, a meaning that it has in Numbers 2:17; Deuteronomy 23:13(12); Jeremiah 6:3 (cf. Isa. 57:8). Since either meaning fits well here, it would be difficult to defend one choice over the other. The meaning of *shēm* together with the immediately following attribute is clear. The Lord will accord to those who by the Law are excluded from the community of Israel, a better recognition and a more lasting memory than physical sons and daughters could provide. The Lord will provide for them an everlasting and ineradicable memory. This, of course, paraphrases the complete acceptance into grace and the future kingdom of grace.

6 וּבְנֵ֣י הַנֵּכָ֗ר הַנִּלְוִ֤ים עַל־יְהוָה֙

לְשָׁ֣רְת֔וֹ וּֽלְאַהֲבָה֙ אֶת־שֵׁ֣ם יְהוָ֔ה לִהְי֥וֹת ל֖וֹ לַעֲבָדִ֑ים

כָּל־שֹׁמֵ֤ר שַׁבָּת֙ מֵֽחַלְּל֔וֹ וּמַחֲזִיקִ֖ים בִּבְרִיתִֽי׃

7 וַהֲבִיאוֹתִים אֶל־הַר קָדְשִׁי וְשִׂמַּחְתִּים בְּבֵית תְּפִלָּתִי
עוֹלֹתֵיהֶם וְזִבְחֵיהֶם לְרָצוֹן עַל־מִזְבְּחִי
כִּי בֵיתִי בֵּית־תְּפִלָּה יִקָּרֵא לְכָל־הָעַמִּים:

Verses 6 and 7 speak of the lot of the alien sons. Verse 6 describes them in respect to their relation to the Lord; verse 7 tells of the promises that are given to them. For *hannilwīm*, see verse 3. *shēreth* (only in Piel) is used to denote voluntary, honorable service, whereas *'abhadh* is used for service of any kind, but usually for menial, burdensome labor, as of a slave. The form is a Piel infinitive with a prefix and an accusative suffix. *'ahabhāh* is a Qal infinitive with paragogic *He*. The participles *hannilwīm, shōmēr*, and *maḥazīqīm* are emphatic, in the so-called *casus pendens*; their concluding clause in verse 7 is introduced by the *Waw apodosis*, Gr. 143, d, p. 458. The final infinitives: "to serve Him," "to love the Lord's name," "to be His servants"(the intensification of the thought should not be overlooked) characterize the cleaving to the Lord (*hannilwīm 'al YHWH*) as being sincere and from the heart. Those who so cleave to Him God will take to His Holy Mountain (Zion, the mount of the temple is meant, Isa. 2:2; Ps. 2:6), that is, into the temple itself and receive them into His house of prayer. (For *bēyth tephillāthī* and *har qodhshī* compare *berīth shelōmī*, 54:10). Within the walls of the temple they shall be refreshed by the spiritual refreshment that goes forth from the Lord. For it is there that the Lord dwells among Israel, where He "will come unto thee and bless thee," Exodus 20:24, 29:42ff. It is there that He hears prayers and accepts sacrifices, Deuteronomy 12. Cf. Psalm 84, 87, etc. *'ōlōth*, burnt offerings, and *zebhāḥīm*, sacrifices, are two kinds that represent the whole genus of offerings. With spiritual quickening the Lord serves them and is pleased to accept their offerings, thus betokening the granting of all His grace, even to guests and strangers, cf. Ephesians 2:19. The basis for these promises is found in Solomon's dedicatory prayer, 1 Kings 8:41-43. Even in the Old Testament, exclusion of the gentiles from the kingdom of God was not absolute, Deuteronomy 4:7,8; Psalm 147:19f, etc. Solomon's temple was built for them also; the temple, and with it, the access to God's grace was open. Indeed, it was Israel's calling to be God's servant and preacher to the gentiles of God's salvation, 43:21, until the time when the wall between Israel and the gentiles should be torn down, Ephesians 2:14, and the difference between them cease to exist, Romans 3:9; Ephesians 2.

499

נְאֻם ֫ אֲדֹנָי ֤ יְהוִֹה מְקַבֵּץ נִדְחֵי יִשְׂרָאֵל 8
עֹוד אֲקַבֵּץ עָלָיו לְנִקְבָּצָיו:

Since *ne'um* does not ordinarily appear at the beginning of a sentence, the critics remove it to the end of the foregoing sentence. But it is too emphatic for that position. *ne'um*, to which *'adhōnāy* and *YHWH* are added, is used instead of *'āmar* in order to bring out the grandeur of the promise that follows. He who gathers the scattered ones of Israel (in the form *nidhḥey* from *niddāḥ*, Niphal participle plural *niddāḥīm*, both the vowel and the Dagesh have dropped out) will also gather *'ālāyw*, in addition to him (Israel), *leniqbātsāyw*, namely, in addition to his (Israel's) gathered ones — others also. For permutation, a variety of apposition which is not complementary, but rather defines the preceding pronoun (here with a change in prepositions which is an explanation of *'ālāyw*) see Gr. 131, k, 1, p. 425. He who gathers the scattered ones of Israel, He will gather together yet others in addition to Israel's gathered children, others who are "not of this fold," John 10:16.

Third Discourse: Chapters 56:9-57:21

Renunciation of hardened apostates and the promise of healing extended to those who repent.

As to contents, this discourse divides into three distinct parts. The first part, 56:9 to 57:2, describes the neglect of the flock of Israel by its shepherds and the removal of the godly from the impending disaster; the second part, 57:3-13, denounces in the first half, verses 3-8, the spiritual adultery of the shameless idol worship, and in the second half, verses 9-13, the selfish worldliness of the apostates, and, in contrast to the blessings of the godly, denies to them the mercy of God; the third part, 57:14-21, promises peace to those who repent and the healing of all wounds.

First Strophe: 56:9-57:2: *The shameful neglect of the flock of Israel by its godless shepherds.*

9 *Come, all you beasts of the field!*
   Come to devour, all you beasts of the forest!
10 *Altogether blind are their watchmen, they know nothing,*
   All are like dumb dogs who cannot bark,
   Lazy dreamers, who love to slumber.
11 *Strong in greed are these dogs, never satisfied,*
   And they are shepherds! They are unable to understand,
   They turn to their own way, all of them,
   Every one, without exception, to his own profit.
12 *Come, I will fetch wine, let us drink strong drink,*
   And tomorrow shall be as today — very great, overflowing!
57:1 *The faithful man perishes, and no one takes it to heart,*
   Godly people are carried away, but no one takes note
   That the righteous are being removed from disaster.
2 *He enters into peace; they rest on their beds,*
   Who have walked in an upright way.

9 כָּל־חַיְתוֹ בַיָּעַר   כָּל־חַיְתוֹ שָׂדַי אֵתָיוּ לֶאֱכֹל׃

A comparison with Jeremiah 12:9 and Ezekiel 34:5,8 will contribute to an understanding of these verses. The prophet views his
people as betrayed and deserted by their shepherds, and abandoned to their enemies like a helpless flock of sheep to wild beasts.
Dramatically, he addresses the enemies as wild beasts of the fields
and the forest. They are being summoned to fall upon the sheep of
Israel, to kill and devour them, for they are lying there defenseless, while their shepherds neglect their duty and follow their
lustful desires. This is a dramatic form of speech, which is intended to bring out in a drastic manner the hopelessly depraved
physical and spiritual condition of Israel. *ḥayethō sādhāy* is "all
the beasts of the field." *ḥayethō* is an old form of the construct
state, for *ḥayath*. It occurs also in Genesis 1:24, Gr. 90, o, p. 254.
sādhāy is an original form of *sādheh*, the Patach being lengthened
to Qamets in pause. In *'ethāyū*, the imperative of *'athāh*, to come,
the original *Yod* has likewise reappeared, together with its preceding vowel. The regular form would be *'ethū*, Gr. 29, t, p. 98. In the
usual sequence of accents, *sādhāy* has an Athnach, followed by
'ethāyū with Zaqeph Gadol. These words are thus set off from the
rest of the sentence. In the second half of the sentence, *le'ekhōl*
and *kol ḥayethō* are linked together by Merkha cum Tiphḥa, thus
making *kol ḥayethō* the object of *le'ekhōl* and producing this
thought: All beasts of the field, come to eat all beasts in the forest.
That would identify the sheep of Israel with the beasts in the
forest, which could hardly have been intended. But Delitzsch has
called attention to another scheme of accentuation that places a
disjunctive Tiphḥa in *le'ekhōl* and a conjunctive Merkha in *kol
ḥayethō*, thus producing what is quite clearly the correct relation
of the words to one another. The first clause ends with *'ethāyū*, the
second begins with *le'ekhōl*. *'ethāyū* is not repeated but must be
supplied, so that we have two synonymous clauses in chiastic arrangement: "All beasts of the field, come; (come) to eat, all beasts
of the forest!" The construct form of a noun preceding a noun with
prepositional prefix is not unusual, Gr. 130, a, p. 421. The beasts of
the field and in the forest are naturally the enemies, who will
swallow up the people of God completely. The next verse tells how
favorable the opportunity is for the enemies to carry out their purpose, for the flock of Israel lies altogether unguarded and unde-
fended, an easy prey. Israel's watchmen do not watch.

צֹפָו עִוְרִים כֻּלָּם לֹא יָדָעוּ 10
כֻּלָּם כְּלָבִים אִלְּמִים לֹא יוּכְלוּ לִנְבֹּחַ
הֹזִים שֹׁכְבִים אֹהֲבֵי לָנוּם:

tsōphāw, as the Qere notes, should be written *tsōphāyw*. A *tsōpheh*, participle of *tsāphāh*, is a lookout on a wall or a watch-tower, who is to warn of the approach of an enemy to the city or of a wild beast to a flock. In this case the watchmen are the prophets of Israel, cf. Ezekiel 3:17; 33:7. It is clear that the prophet is referring to the spiritual depravity of Israel, not to its physical troubles. The reference is perhaps primarily to the spiritual conditions in the exile. Israel was more wretched spiritually than physically. There were no prophets sent from God, and the people were betrayed by pseudo-prophets who sought only their own gain. If the prophets in Jerusalem after the first deportation were "lying prophets," Ezekiel 13:3ff, 17ff., those that professed to minister to the wretched people in the exile were equally unreliable (Ezek. 34:1-8). They abandoned the people to spiritual depravity, while they greedily "fed themselves and not My flock." Israel in Babylon, for the most part, sank into paganism and became a prey to unbelief, self-righteousness and every form of pagan idol worship, as is set forth in the next section (57:3-13a) and in chapters 58, 59, 64, and 66. But these conditions are not confined to the time of the exile; they characterize the entire period till the coming of Christ, which Isaiah always includes in his description of the exile. Only during a short period after the first return to Jerusalem and at the time of the building of the temple under Haggai was there a brief resurgence of the spirit. At the time of Malachi everything had again sunk into the mire and spiritual life had become a hardened self-righteousness. The exile marked not only the permanent collapse of Israel's external glory, but also its spiritual ruin. Christ Himself and His apostles were able to rescue only the "elect" in Israel, the rest were hardened, Romans 11:7, and the flock of Israel became the prey of deceivers out of their own midst and of foreign despots. This is the prophet's theme. The guilt for this ruin lay first of all with the unfaithful watchmen and shepherds of Israel, with the prophets, teachers, and priests of the people. The watchmen are depicted as blind, who *lō'yādhā'ū*, have no understanding, namely, of the truth of God, of the salvation of His covenant, of the Gospel of the Old Testament. That applied *kullām*, to all of them.

The decay of the church begins with its servants, its teachers and preachers, and it starts with the failure among them of an understanding of the Gospel. The head may still comprehend it, but the heart gradually becomes indifferent and cold, while the world with its goods and its lust slowly takes possession. Form and outward show of godliness may still be present, but the power has failed, 2 Timothy 3:5. And so they become dumb dogs who cannot bark. The shepherds are compared to sheep dogs whose duty it is to bark at the wolves and scare them away from the flock. Instead of performing a similar function faithfully, the shepherds no longer have the moral strength to oppose the deceivers of Christianity, for fear that they might suffer loss of popularity, income, and comfort. The next clause continues the comparison. *hōzīm* (participle plural of *hāzāh*) are dreamers, and not only that, they are *shōkhebhīm*, reclining, reposing, lazy dreamers, who instead of feeding the flock with the Word of God that had been given to them, busy themselves with their own revelations and love to slumber. *lānūm*, an infinitive with prefix following a construct state, is the same construction as *hayethō bayyā'ar*, verse 9. Physical laziness is the inseparable companion of spiritual lethargy. If zeal for the kingdom of God governs the pastor's life, he will conquer his comfortable flesh and bring his own body into subjection, 1 Corinthians 9:25,27. When comfortable living and love of luxury take control of the heart, the spirit dies.

11 וְהַכְּלָבִים עַזֵּי־נֶפֶשׁ לֹא יָדְעוּ שָׂבְעָה
וְהֵמָּה רֹעִים לֹא יָדְעוּ הָבִין
כֻּלָּם לְדַרְכָּם פָּנוּ אִישׁ לְבִצְעוֹ מִקָּצֵהוּ :

nephesh can have no other meaning here than desire, lust, greed. The verb *nāphash* is imitative of the sound of breathing, puffing, panting. *nephesh* consequently also represents the seat of the feelings. The next clause indicates what particular desire of the dogs is meant here. They do not know satiety, are gluttonous. The gluttony of the dogs represents the greed of the shepherds. Greed on the part of pastors is common enough to have become proverbial among the people. There is a saying in Mecklenburg: "*Papengiez is nich to stillen, Papenbuk is nich to fuellen.*" That is: Parsons' greed cannot be stilled, parsons' belly cannot be filled. *rō'īm*, shepherds, in the next clause, is not in apposition to *hemmāh*, as Luther translates, but is a predicate: And they are shepherds! That is an ironic commentary on the contradiction between the nature of the shepherds and the office they should fill. The greed is the greed of dogs that would devour the sheep; the office is that of shepherds who should be devoted to the welfare of the sheep. The next clause emphasizes that point. They do not know understanding, that is, they neither feel nor understand that they should not be hungry dogs, but shepherds who watch over their flocks. But everybody goes his own way, following the lusts of his evil heart (cf. 53:6), thinking only of his own gain. *miqqatsehu*, literally: from his end, like *miqqedem*, to the east, means *to* his end, that is, to his own highest profit. Each one squeezes the high-possible gain for himself out of the flock.

אֵתָיוּ אֶקְחָה־יַיִן וְנִסְבְּאָה שֵׁכָר 12

וְהָיָה כָזֶה' יוֹם מָחָר גָּדוֹל יֶתֶר מְאֹד:

The preceding description has been arranged in the form of a climax, which in verse 12 reaches its height. One of the shepherds is represented as summoning the others to a carousal. The verb *sabha'* is the specific word for drinking to excess, for drinking for the sake of drink. *kazeh* is an adverb: "like this that follows" (Gr. 100,f,p.295). *mahar* is in this instance an adjective modifying *yom*. Some prefer to read *mohar* (Hateph Qamets), cf. Gr. 100, c, p. 294 and the lexicon. *gadhol* is also an adjective modifying the predicate, tomorrow's day. *yether*, however, like *me'odh*, is an adverb. "Like this, so shall tomorrow's day be, great, abundantly overflowing."

הַצַּדִּיק אָבָד וְאֵין' אִישׁ שָׂם עַל־לֵב 1

וְאַנְשֵׁי־חֶסֶד נֶאֱסָפִים' בְּאֵין מֵבִין

כִּי־מִפְּנֵי הָרָעָה נֶאֱסַף הַצַּדִּיק:

This sentence follows verse 12 directly, without a connecting link, thus indicating that the actions of the two verses are simultaneous. While the shepherds carouse, forgetful of their office, the righteous perish. The *tsaddiq* is the faithful Israelite who holds fast in faith to the promises of the covenant and therefore also walks according to the ordinances of the covenant, the counterpart of the Christian believer. *'anshey hesedh*, men of the love of God, is a synonym of *tsaddiq* and is a designation of those who have received the grace of God, who are faithful to the Lord, humble, God-fearing. *'abhadh* is used in its physical sense, denoting a violent death, not the death that comes as a natural end of life. The faithful will be swept away by a sudden, early death, possibly

505

through an accident that has the appearance of a judgment, while no one mourns or ever realizes that the hand of God is in this and that He in His grace is removing the righteous man out of the way of the impending judgment. The two participles, *ne'esāphīm* and *mēbhīn* form the predicate. They express unbroken duration of the two actions which occur simultaneously. The clause introduced by *kī* is the object of *mēbhīn*.

$$\text{2 יָבוֹא שָׁלוֹם יָנוּחוּ עַל־מִשְׁכְּבוֹתָם הֹלֵךְ נְכֹחוֹ׃}$$

shālōm is not an adverbial accusative, but the accusative object of *yābhō'*. The verb *bō'* is used not only with following particles, *b*, *l*, *'el*, and the locative *āh*, but may also be construed with the accusative. Its meaning is then "to enter," Gr. 116, h, p. 358. The subject of both predicates, *yābhō'* and *yānūhū*, is the phrase at the end of the sentence, *hōlēkh nekhōhō*, "who walks his upright way." *nākhōah* is a substantive in the adverbial accusative, Gr. 118, q, p. 375. Although the word is singular in form, it is a collective; hence, one of the verbs can appear in the singular while the other is plural. The emphasis lies entirely on the predicates: he enters into peace, they rest on their beds — who walk their upright way. The reference is to the *tsaddīq* of the preceding verse. *mishkābh*, a bed, here denotes a deathbed, the grave, as in Ezekiel 32:25; 2 Chronicles 16:14. See also Job 17:13. Luther beautifully expresses it with "*sie ruhen in ihren Kammern.*" Cf. also 2 Kings 22:20. The lot of those who will be snatched away from the coming judgment is described as something more than the mere negative fact that they will not experience that judgment, for they shall enter into positive peace and a state of well-being. *shālōm* always denotes a positive state of peace and happiness, never a mere absence of misfortune.

The interpretation is far-fetched that identifies the *tsaddīq* with faithful shepherds as distinguished from the unfaithful watchmen. According to 56:9, it is the flock which the wild beasts threaten with disaster, and so it is most natural to think of the faithful members of the *flock* when the prophet speaks of deliverance from a future judgment. It must not be overlooked that the enemy nations are the wild beasts through which the *rā'āh*, the disaster of the judgment, is to be carried out. Otherwise, *tsaddīq* and *'anshēy hesedh* are quite general terms.

This section says that the people of God, in its external aspect, is ripe for judgment because it has been so neglected by its shepherds. But the Lord will in good season remove His faithful elect out of the way of the impending catastrophe and will bring them home into eternal peace, a deliverance that will not be recognized by the hardened part of the people.

Second Strophe: 57:3-13: *The Lord's renunciation of the hardened apostates, and a brief blessing upon the faithful.*

First Half: verses 3-8: *Idolatry, the shameful spiritual adultery of the apostate people.*

3   *But you, come forward, you children of the sorceress,*
    Brood of the adulterer and the harlot!
4   *You are laughing — at whom?*
    You open wide your mouth, stick out your tongue — at whom?
    Are not you yourselves the brood of sin, the false seed?
5   *You, who under the terebinths,*
    Yea, under every green tree, burn with lust,
    And slaughter your children in the valleys,
    And in the clefts of the rocks.
6   *The smooth stones of the brook are your portion,*
    They, they, are your lot.
    Therefore you pour out drink-offerings to them,
    You bring offerings of grain —
    And shall I remain silent to that?
7   *When you prepare your bed on a high and lofty mountain,*
    You ascend it, to offer sacrifice.
8   *Behind the door and on the doorpost you hang your symbols.*
    Turned away from Me, you uncover and go up (to your bed),
    And you bargain for your pay from them,
    Made a fool by intercourse, you look about for a sign.

This first half of the second strophe is so constructed that each succeeding stanza has one more line than the one before. The first, verse 3, has two lines, verse 4 has three lines, and the last stanza, verses 7 and 8, has six lines. The theme is contained in the two lines of verse 2, and the following stanzas develop it. Two statements are made: the apostates are the offspring of the sorceress, and they are the brood of a harlot. There are two forms of expression, but factually only *one* thing is meant: idol worship. Adultery and harlotry are but the image; what they portray is the idol worship of the people. That representation of idol worship is common in the Old Testament especially in Hosea, Ezekiel, chapters 16 and 23, and in Isaiah.

³ וְאַתֶּ֥ם קִרְבוּ־הֵ֖נָּה בְּנֵ֣י עֹנְנָ֑ה
זֶ֥רַע מְנָאֵ֖ף וַתִּזְנֶֽה ׃

The emphatic *we'attem* brings out the contrast between the apostates and the faithful who have entered into their rest. The Lord speaks and summons them to step forward before His face to hear judgment pronounced against them. If *hēnnāh* is translated with now, referring to time instead of place, that translation could be justified, because *qirbhū* already is a command to step forward before the face of the Lord (cf. Gen. 15:16b; 2 Sam. 4:6). *'onenāh*, from *'anan*, to practice witchcraft, is a Polel feminine participle, from which the preformative *Mem* has been dropped. Israel, as the mother of an idol-worshiping people, is called a sorceress, because sorcery or witchcraft was always a conspicuous feature of all idolatry, 44:25; 45:19; 47:9-13; Nahum 3:4. As the apostates are children of the idolatress, they also have the nature of their mother and are themselves idolaters. *zera' menā'eph wattizneh* designates them as apostates from the Lord and charges them with infidelity and with breach of the spiritual wedlock of the Lord and His chosen people. *wattizneh* is a short way of expressing the relative clause *wa'asher tizneh*. The finite verb is more emphatic than the feminine participle *zōnāh* would have been. Israel is thus designated as a harlot who practices lewdness as part of the cult of idol worship. It is not necessary to try to identify the *menā'eph*, the adulterer, with some certain person, such as the idol Israel was serving. Both parties to the adultery, the male and the female, are mentioned merely for the sake of emphasis. Those who are being addressed are as adulterous as it is possible for one to be whose father and mother are both adulterers and for whom adultery is inborn.

⁴ עַל־מִי֙ תִּתְעַנָּ֔גוּ

עַל־מִ֛י תַּרְחִ֥יבוּ פֶ֖ה תַּאֲרִ֣יכוּ לָשׁ֑וֹן
הֲלֽוֹא־אַתֶּ֥ם יִלְדֵי־פֶ֖שַׁע זֶ֥רַע שָֽׁקֶר ׃

This verse censures the malicious glee of the brood of spiritual adultery. *tith'annāgū* (a pausal form) refers to the self-satisfied inner enjoyment of those who open wide their mouths and thrust forth their tongues to display their malicious glee. Their derision is not directed only to the faithful in general, but is meant particularly for those who were mentioned in verses 1 and 2 as having perished. The scoffers never understood the salutary meaning of the death of those faithful ones but assumed that they had been deluded by the worship of Jehovah and had been abandoned by Him. In contrast, the Lord charges that, not those who died, but precisely they themselves, who are the offspring of infidelity, the adulterous, false seed (*zera' shāqer*), are those who should have been carried off by the judgment and should have been the proper objects of derision. The vivid description of malicious joy suggests the observation that Semites, especially the Jews, have a talent for mimicry. The shortening of *yaldhēy* to *yildhēy*, which occurs only here, may be a way of expressing contempt. *pesha'* and *sheqer*, like *'onenāh* in verse 3, are here represented as the mother of the apostates. *pesha'* is personified infidelity toward the Lord. *sheqer* is not untruthfulness, but sham, falseness. Israel is portrayed as the faithless bride of the Lord, who has "played the harlot with many lovers," Jeremiah 3:1, and by them conceived and given birth to children who call themselves by the name of God but are the brood of idols. They have been brought forth by infidelity and falseness and are themselves a faithless and false brood, who are therefore deserving of scorn and derision. The following verses describe how this false and counterfeit brood expresses itself in loathsome and fanatical lewdness in the worship of idols.

⁵ הַנֵּחָמִים֙ בָּאֵלִ֔ים תַּ֖חַת כָּל־עֵ֥ץ רַעֲנָ֑ן

שֹׁחֲטֵ֤י הַיְלָדִים֙ בַּנְּחָלִ֔ים תַּ֖חַת סְעִפֵ֥י הַסְּלָעִֽים׃

To begin with, we have in verse 5 a pair of participial phrases in apposition, which are later followed by independent clauses with a verb in the perfect, and then, in verse 9, with an imperfect, and again with a perfect. As the participles denote a condition or a characteristic without any fixed time, so too the following perfects should not be construed as historic perfects followed by imperfects with *Waw* consecutive indicating the same time as the perfects. These are perfects of present time, which describe customary and habitual actions on the part of the people, Gr. 106, k, p. 312. They correspond to the Greek gnomic aorist. Consequently, all the verbs that carry the thread of thought forward are to be translated with the present tense to indicate customary action, as Luther construed them. These words are not being addressed to the impenitent people languishing in exile. The details of the description do not fit them. It is true that the people in exile did give themselves up to Babylonian idol worship, but the plains of Babylon did not have overhanging cliffs, rocky streams, and high hills for the kind of idol worship that is described here. The situation described here fits only the homeland of the exiles. For that reason, most commentators understand this indictment to refer to idol worship committed before the exile and take the perfects to be historical. But that interpretation makes the threat of punishment meaningless, because Israel was suffering even at this moment, as exiles in Babylon, the punishment for idolatry committed before the exile. Furthermore, the sentence: "And shall I remain silent to that?" can hardly apply to abominations practiced long ago, but must apply to the present time; and verses 12 and 13a certainly do not speak of a past or even of a present judgment, but of a judgment of God that lies in the future. The impression cannot be avoided that the entire passage, 57:3-13a, deals with present sins and future judgment. As unnatural as the interpretation mentioned above, that the passage refers to sins that lay in Israel's past history, is another interpretation which assumes that Isaiah, who in all other prophecies speaks in the spirit as from a position in the future, now suddenly gives up that position and speaks as from a natural historical point of view, of things that were taking place during his own time. Such a sudden change in point of view would have had to be more clearly indicated.

The context clearly points to events quite different from those that were contemporary with Isaiah. In 56:1-8 the prophet had already spoken of the temple as a house of prayer for all people. Since the first temple, as Isaiah saw it from the ideal point of view that he has taken in the exile, lies in ruins and ashes, he can in 56:7,8 be referring only to a time in which the new temple has been built, that is, to the time when the people have returned home out of the exile and have rebuilt the temple and established the worship of God in it. The section from 56:9 to 57:2 refers to this postexilic congregation. The congregation of the people newly established in the homeland and in Jerusalem has again been deserted by its shepherds and given over as prey to wild beasts. A new judgment confronts the people, and the few faithful are taken away before it arrives and enter into their peace. The wicked portion of the people, however, who have again made themselves guilty of idolatry, as their fathers had practiced it before the time of the exile, and who thus have proved that they are of the same incorrigible nature as their fathers, are being rebuked in this section and receive notice of their final rejection from the Lord. From chapter 56 onward this is now the situation which the prophet has before his eyes, if not exclusively, yet primarily. This is his usual point of view from here to the end.

From chapter 56 to chapter 66 the prophecy is for the most part directed to the people who have returned from the exile and again live in Jerusalem. But, at the same time, it must not be forgotten that prophecy does not observe sharp divisions in periods of time. Thus, in chapters 40 to 48, the prophet, speaking from the point of view of the exile, in general prophesies the deliverance of the people through Cyrus and their return to the homeland; but chapter 42 and the beginning of 44, without any transition whatever, take us into New Testament times. So also, Part II, chapters 49-57, for the most part deals with the deliverance through Christ, but repeatedly speaks of that deliverance in terms of the external conditions of the exile. At the end of Part II, in the chapter now under discussion, the description reaches beyond the exile into postexilic times, and in general maintains this point of view throughout Part III, chapters 58-66, in order to portray from that point of view a new future glory, to which God's people had not yet attained in the deliverance out of Babylon. But postexilic conditions are constantly interwoven with conditions of the exile because they are of the same character as those of the exile. Both periods are characterized by humiliation and degradation. From the prophet's point of view the period between the exile and the coming of Christ is blotted out, and he associates Christ directly with the exile. In fact, when Israel was deported to Babylon, that marked for all time the end of the glory of the Old Testament people of the covenant. The period from the exile to the New Testament deliverance and glorification of Israel is one long, unbroken interval of judgment, misery, and disgrace of the people of God. In the several divisions of Part III, the prophet is in his thoughts sometimes in the middle of the exile, and then suddenly with the people newly established in their homeland. But never do the people rise from their condition of moral and outward misery; they must continue to languish under the rule of heathen conquerors until Christ appears. Since modern commentators have no understanding of this prophetic point of view, they fall back on the familiar literary trick of explaining the structure of Isaiah II as being a composite of many isolated pieces dating from many different periods.

Regarding the concrete description of the special kind of idolatry that the people are said to have practiced, the objection has little weight that we have no knowledge that the people after the exile were guilty of that particular kind of abomination. Ezra, chapters 9 and 10, describes how the people, and even their priests, became intermingled with surrounding nations whose idol worship was characterized by that kind of abomination. Such intermarriage shows plainly enough that the people had lost their abhorrence of that form of idol worship or at least gave it sanction by their silence. Family relationships must also have influenced them to take part in the idolatrous rites. The attitude of the postexilic people toward the heathen and their idols was no different from that of the people before the exile. Intermingling with the gentiles, which had been forbidden in order to isolate Israel from pagan idol worship, lay in the very blood of the people and repeatedly proved to be the means that led them to fall away from the Lord and to defile themselves with the horrible worship of heathen idols (Ezek. 23:43). In spite of all reforms, this worship repeatedly cropped forth, and Old Testament history closes with an account of the last attempt, certainly also ineffectual, to eradicate that evil, Nehemiah 13. However, it is a mistake on the part of the commentators on prophetic books, of which we have frequently made mention, to interpret such concrete descriptions in a rigidly literal fashion. Prophecy speaks out in drastically concrete and extreme terms; often enough it employs external acts and occurrences to describe what actually existed only as an attitude of mind or heart; paints a picture that only in its outlines had historical reality. That is especially the case when moral decay is being described. See, for example, the very first chapter of Isaiah. And so, in this section the scene is laid in the land of Judah; the form of the concrete occurrences is taken from the history of Israel before the exile; and the burden of these sins, in their essence, is laid upon the postexilic people.

hannēḥāmīm, "those who burn," is said of those who burn with wanton, idolatrous sexual lust. The word is a Niphal participle of *ḥāmam*, in which the Dagesh is missing from the *Mem* of the stem, Gr. 67, dd, p. 183. They burn with lust *bā'ēlīm*. That can be translated: "toward the idols." But since the principle of parallelism of members is no doubt observed in this verse, it is more likely that the *'ēlīm* are terebinths, which are a single species of green trees corresponding to the entire genus mentioned in the next clause. *nēḥāmīm* must accordingly be supplied in the second clause. When the people find a terebinth or for that matter any other green tree, they begin to burn in lust toward the idol and worship it there. Green trees, like the high hills, mountaintops, dry stream beds, and clefts in rocky cliffs were the sites where the heathen and the apostate Israelites customarily worshiped the idols. Cf. Jeremiah 2:20; 3:13; Ezekiel 6:13; Isaiah 1:29,30; Hosea 4:12,13; 2 Kings 16:4; 17:10-12. Like the worship of idols on all high places, so also the worship under green trees, most likely in honor of Astarte, was accompanied by sexual excesses. According to Jeremiah 19:5; Hosea 13:1f, and other passages, the slaughter of children in the river valleys was also a part of the worship of Baal, in particular of the Moloch (Molech) of the Ammonites and Moabites. Baal, Molech, Moloch, Milkom, and Malkam (1 Kings 11:5,33; Jer. 49:1,3, etc.) were not different gods, but merely different names for the same chief god of the Canaanite tribes (cf. Jer. 32:35). The children were first slaughtered and then burned. Under Ahaz, Manasseh, and Amon this abomination was practiced without restraint in the valley of Ben Hinnom. Cf. 2 Kings 3:27; 16:3; 17:17,31; 23:10,13; Jeremiah 7:31; 19:5; 32:35; Ezekiel 16:20f, 36; 23:37,39, etc. The *neḥalîm* are not the streams themselves, but the stream beds, which carried water after rain storms, but were otherwise dry. Today they are called wadies. The *se'iphēy hasselaʿîm* are clefts in the rocks, and, in contrast to the broad wadies, are narrow ravines or gulches (2:21; Judges 15:8), perhaps even caverns in the rocks where the sacrifice of children took place.

ḥalleqēy, the smooth ones, is a plural construct of the adjective *ḥalaq*, smooth. (The Dagesh forte makes the Shewa more audible.) "The smooth ones of the stream" are the rocks that have been worn by flood waters into grotesque shapes which the people regarded as images of the gods and to which they brought offerings of food and drink. Some modern interpreters take the word to mean small, smooth flat stones or gravel, but that meaning does not fit the context. The combination of *ḥalleqēy* and *ḥelqēkh* is a play on words that can hardly be imitated in English. The literal meaning is: "Of the smooth ones of the stream bed is your portion." Budde's translation is amusing: "In the gravel of the dry stream beds in the clefts of the cliffs, they (the idolaters) receive their portion of land, which is their punishment for their idolatrous worship of the rocks." Just as the Lord is the believer's chosen "portion forever," his comfort (Psalm 73:26; 16:5; Lamentations 3:24), and the object of all his faith and hope, so too, the rock-gods in the stream beds are the idolaters' portion, their property and their goods, their one and all, their trust and confidence. *hēm, hēm, gōrālēkh* — "they, yes, they, are your portion" — expresses the same thought, but with greater emphasis. They have renounced the Lord as their portion and as the comfort of their hearts, and have made senseless dead stones their portion and trust. To these stones they bring offerings of meat and drink to win their favor. *gam*, in spite of the Maqqeph, does not serve *lāhem* in particular, but is connected with the verbs *shāphakht* and *he'elīth*. *gam* has consecutive or conclusive force and may be rendered with "accordingly." Cf. 1 Samuel 12:16; Malachi 2:9; Psalm 52:7(5). The last clause is translated by some moderns: "And shall I feel remorse because of that?" They deny that the Niphal *niḥam* can mean "to comfort oneself," "to quiet oneself about something." But one needs only to accept the meaning "to have compassion, to pity, to feel sorry for," to arrive at the right meaning of the phrase. Cf. Jeremiah 15:6; Genesis 24:67; 38:12; 2 Samuel 13:39; Psalm 90:13. The interrogative form of the phrase says with emphasis that God in the face of these idolatrous abominations has put away all feelings of compassion and must now smite with His judgment. In content this phrase is parallel to verses 12 and 13a.

7 עַל הַר־גָּבֹהַּ וְנִשָּׂא שַׂמְתְּ מִשְׁכָּבֵךְ
גַּם־שָׁם עָלִית לִזְבֹּחַ זָבַח:

Verses 7 and 8 treat of the cult of Astarte and Baal which was practiced in the high places. The offering of sacrifices on the hilltops no doubt was suggested by the thought that those places were closer to the gods. This cult was common to all the Canaanite nations. Even in Israel, before the temple was built and long afterwards, the hilltops were permitted and favored places for the worship of the Lord. Cf. 1 Kings 18:19ff; 19:10,14. In Judah such worship was forbidden after the building of the temple (Deut. 12 and 16:5; 1 Kings 15:14, etc.), although the practice here and there nevertheless persisted until the time of Josiah, 2 Kings 23. But in both kingdoms this practice regularly degenerated into the heathen cult of Baal and Astarte. Altars, carved posts, asherahs, and "houses of the high places" were erected on high hills (1 Kings 12:31; 13:32, etc.). These houses of the high places were in all

514

likelihood temples combined with buildings and rooms provided for the exercise of idol worship coupled with abominable lewdness. It was only natural that the unbelieving people who returned from the exile and intermarried with the neighboring gentile peoples, especially with Moabites and Ammonites, should again take up the worship of Baal, Moloch, and Astarte as their fathers had done before the exile. This cult of idols, this spiritual whoredom, is portrayed in terms of physical whoredom, with which it was accompanied.

mishkabhekh, your bed, refers to the bed that Israel had prepared for the practice of her adulteries with the pagan gods. *gam*, in the next clause, has the same force as *gam* in verse 6. Its connection is not solely with *sham*, but with the whole clause. In our translation we tried to express the logical connection between the two clauses by making the first clause the protasis and the second its apodosis. Israel begins by preparing a bed on the hilltop, she then ascends the hill bearing gifts (offerings) for her paramours (the idol gods), with which she hopes to seduce them into sexual orgies, Ezekiel 16:33f.

$$^8 \text{וְאַחַר הַדֶּלֶת וְהַמְּזוּזָה שַׂמְתְּ זִכְרוֹנֵךְ}$$
$$\text{כִּי מֵאִתִּי גִּלִּית וַתַּעֲלִי הִרְחַבְתְּ מִשְׁכָּבֵךְ}$$
$$\text{וַתִּכְרָת לָךְ מֵהֶם אָהַבְתְּ מִשְׁכָּבָם יָד חָזִית:}$$

deleth and *mezuzah* are the door and the doorposts of the brothel where she had prepared her bed. There are two different opinions regarding the meaning of *samt zikhronekh*, "you set up your memorial." One opinion is that the *zikkaron* is the memorial tablet that the head of the house in Israel used to attach to the door of his house. This memorial, in accordance with Deuteronomy 6:9; 11:20; Exodus 13:9, was inscribed with the Ten Commandments; but Israel, in order not to be reminded whenever she entered her house of her relation to the Lord, hangs the memorial *behind* the door inside the house. But, say those who hold the other opinion, that would be making worse out of bad, because now she would have that reminder always before her eyes within the house. The memorial therefore would have to be some kind of heathenish symbol that would call to mind her paramours, the idol gods. This latter opinion is very likely the correct one. This bed that she has prepared is not found in an ordinary dwelling, but in some structure connected with idol worship, located on a hilltop. What could suggest to her that she prepare a memorial reminding her of the

515

Lord's Commandments, which she then hangs *behind* the door in order to make such a reminder ineffective? There is still a third possibility: that the *zikkārōn* is neither a reminder of the Lord nor of her new lovers, but of her for the benefit of the latter. The *zikkārōn* is a sign of some kind that identifies her profession and gives notice to her paramours of her presence in this house.

The difficulty in *kī mē'ittī gillīth watta'alī* is that *gillīth* has no expressed object. It would seem most natural to supply *'erwāthekh*, your shame (cf. Ezekiel 16:26; 23:18), rather than to reach beyond the next verb *hirḥabht* to *mishkābhekh* for the object of *gillīth*. The meaning of *mē'ittī* can only be, "away from Me," and toward the idols. The object of *ta'alī* is *mishkābhekh*, your bed, as in verse 7, and again at the end of this verse. *hirḥabht mishkābhekh* refers to the uncovering of her bed in expectation of her bedfellow. In the next clause the masculine form *tikhroth* is used for the feminine *tikhrethī*. This is not something unusual, cf. Jeremiah 3:5; Ezekiel 22:4; 23:32; Gr. 145, t, p. 466, and for a general discussion of *enallage generis*, Gr. 144, p. 459f. *berīth* must be supplied to *tikhroth lākh*: "You make for yourself a covenant from them," that is, you bargain with them for your compensation. In the next clause, *'ahabht mishkābhām* refers not to the bed as such, but to the lewd act committed on it. As for the last phrase, *yādh ḥāzīth*, we cannot agree with Delitzsch, Cheyne, and others who follow Doederlein, that *yādh* refers to the *membrum virile*, in spite of Ezekiel 16:26f; 23:20 (note the Hebrew text!). This translation would go beyond what is said in the two Ezekiel passages. *yādh* could be used here in the sense of 56:5; 1 Samuel 15:12; 2 Samuel 18:18, designating either the *zikkārōn* of the first clause or an Astarte pillar that stood in the place, Deuteronomy 16:21; Judges 6:28, etc., some sign that stirred her to lustfulness. Our translation admittedly attempts to draw a veil before the details.

Second Half: verses 9-13: *The ceaseless wooing of the people for the favor of those in power, and the renunciation of the people in contrast to the blessing of the faithful.*

9 *You journey to the king with oil,*
You have gathered great store of ointments;
You send your envoys far into the distance,
And you stoop down to Sheol.

10 *You weary yourself with many journeys,*
You do not think: It is in vain!
You find support for your life,
Therefore you do not grow weary.

11 *Of whom are you afraid, and whom do you fear,*
    That you have become faithless and do not remember Me,
    And do not take it to heart?
    Have I not been silent, yes, for a long time,
    So that you did not fear Me?
12 *But I will expose this justification of yours,*
    And your doings — they shall be of no use to you.
13 *When you cry out, then let your assembly help you;*
    But a wind will carry them away, a breath will take them hence —
    But he who trusts in Me shall inherit the land
    And possess My holy mountain.

וַתָּשֻׁרִי לַמֶּלֶךְ בַּשֶּׁמֶן וַתַּרְבִּי רִקֻּחָיִךְ 9
וַתְּשַׁלְּחִי צִירַיִךְ עַד־מֵרָחֹק וַתַּשְׁפִּילִי עַד־שְׁאוֹל:

In this second half of the strophe, Israel is still being pictured as the unfaithful bride of the Lord, but not as the paramour of the pagan idols. Now she is the faithless coquette, a spiritual adulteress, courting the favor of the great king of a world power, because she no longer trusts in the protection of the Lord and fears the might of the great powers — Egypt at one time, then Assyria and Babylon, and now Persia. Ahaz, and his embassy to Tiglath Pileser, comes to mind, 2 Kings 16:7,8,17,18; Isaiah 7; and Hezekiah, 2 Kings 18:14ff; 20:12ff. In the first clause, the question is whether the oil, the salves, and the ointments with which the coquette Israel journeys to the king are intended as a tribute or gift to the king, or whether they are meant to be used as cosmetics to beautify her own person. If they are to be a gift to the king, then *bashshemen* would have to be translated "with oil"; if they are meant for her own person, then perhaps "anointed with oil" would be the proper rendering. There is no way of deciding which is meant. Oil and spices and ointments were favorite gifts for a king, 1 Kings 10:10; Hosea 12:2(1). Delitzsch thought she took these things with her as "sensual stimulants with a view to amorous pleasures," and he refers to Ezekiel 23:41. But if she provided herself with these things in order to make herself more ravishing, then they can no longer be considered a gift for the king, as Delitzsch also supposes.

The second clause speaks of delegations that minor nations sent to the great powers, as Ahaz sent to Tiglath Pileser, or that they sent to other small nations in order to form a coalition against the dominating power. *'adh merāḥōq*, a double preposition, "to a faraway place," indicates that in this case it is the king of a great power to whom Israel makes this journey and for whom the delegation is meant. The first clause is figurative, the second is factual. She plays the coquette toward the king by sending gift-bearing delegations to him. To win his favor she stoops and debases herself to Sheol — a hyperbole that describes her total lack of character. Duhm understands *melekh* to refer to Milkom of the Ammonites, and Sheol to the oracles at which the gods of the underworld were consulted. He takes the oil to be material used in worship of the idols.

$$^{10} \quad \text{בְּרֹב דַּרְכֵּךְ יָגַעַתְּ לֹא אָמַרְתְּ נוֹאָשׁ}$$
$$\text{חַיַּת יָדֵךְ מָצָאת עַל־כֵּן לֹא חָלִית:}$$

The singular *darkēkh* is a collective, and in the term *rōbh darkēkh* are grouped Israel's journeys to the king and the embassies bearing gifts. There is so much of everything that she is wearied by it, and yet she does not say: *nō'āsh*, "it is useless." *nō'āsh* is a Niphal participle of *yā'ash*. Here, as in Jeremiah 2:25 and 18:12, it is neuter, although the form is masculine. She does not admit that all her trouble is in vain, since she still finds in it the "life of her hand." The usual explanation of this phrase (Delitzsch, Cheyne, Hitzig) is that *hayyāh* (life) is a concrete expression for restoration, and that *yādh* ("hand") represents strength, hence: "restoration of your strength." But that sounds too contrived to be satisfactory. The attempted corrections of the text are vain. A much simpler explanation is: "You find life by your hand," that is, your hand is a means of gain and of supporting your life. The genitive is a genitive of cause, as in Psalm 128:2, *yegīa' kappeykhā*, "of the toil of your hands you shall eat." There is no good reason either why one should not take *yādhēkh* to be a paraphrase of the whole person, "your life," your self. She is still supporting her life with the activities of her hand, and for that reason (*'al kēn*) she does not slacken her efforts to win the king's favor.

$$^{11} \quad \text{וְאֶת־מִי דָּאַגְתְּ וַתִּירְאִי כִּי תְכַזֵּבִי}$$
$$\text{וְאוֹתִי לֹא זָכַרְתְּ לֹא־שַׂמְתְּ עַל־לִבֵּךְ}$$
$$\text{הֲלֹא אֲנִי מַחְשֶׁה וּמֵעֹלָם וְאוֹתִי לֹא תִירָאִי:}$$

This sentence asks the reason for this unfaithful activity in the service of men. The *Waw* in *we'eth* is explicative: "*After all*, whom do you fear and of whom are you afraid?" For the force of *'eth mī* at the head of the sentence, cf. Gr. 117, e, p. 364. *dā'agh* expresses a lesser degree of fear than *yāre*. The *kī* of the next clause is consecutive, "so that." Just as Israel's fear is the reason for her efforts to win the favor of the great power, so is it the consequence of that fear that she becomes unfaithful to the Lord, *thekhazzēbhī*, and forgets Him. And what is more, *lō' samt 'al libbēkh*, "she did not take her unfaithfulness to heart," made nothing of it. It is not easy to determine the logical connection between the clause beginning with *halō'* and the clause preceding it, and still less easy to determine the connection between the clause beginning with *we'othī* and the one just preceding it. Because of this difficulty, critics since early times have been suggesting alterations in the text. But such alterations are always uncertain and usually, as in this case, unnecessary. A literal translation of the first clause is: "Am not *I*" (the pronoun in a participial clause always is emphatic) "the silent one" (Hiphil participle of *ḥāshāh*) "and that since long ago?" That is a partial answer to the question: Of whom then are you afraid? Certainly you are not afraid of Me, for I have long been silent, that is, according to 42:14: I have not come with wrath and punishment, as one who had to be feared. You were afraid of others, but not of Me. And now the *w* in *we'othī*, which introduces the next clause, is also clear. If it had been connected directly with its verb *tīrā'ī*, it would have been written as the *Waw* consecutive, *wa*, but since it is separated from its verb by *'othī lō'*, it is written *Waw* with a Shewa; but it retains its consecutive force and the clause is: "so that you do not fear Me." The Lord's silence, referring back and looking forward, is given as the reason why Israel, unfaithful (*thekhazzēbhī*) and indifferent (*lō' samt 'al libbēkh*) to the Lord Himself (*we'othī* in the position of emphasis!), forgot Him (*'othī* again emphatic!) and did not fear Him. That it was the Lord Himself whom she forgot and did not fear, is emphasized. This simple construction becomes confused if one construes the *we* as temporal and translates it with "while," as Delitzsch does. It must be construed as consecutive, because a participle (*maḥsheh*) preceding a clause with *we* usually has causal meaning, as in the *casus pendens*.

אֲנִי אַגִּיד צִדְקָתֵךְ וְאֶת־מַעֲשַׂיִךְ 12
וְלֹא־יוֹעִילוּךְ׃

'anī 'aggīdh stands in contrast to *'anī maḥsheh* in verse 11. *tsidhqāthēkh* is used ironically. The true *tsedhāqāh*, righteousness, is faithfulness to the covenant. But Israel's *tsedhāqāh*, as was shown in verse 11, is her unfaithfulness in regard to the covenant.

ma'asayikh refers to Israel's faithless activity as described in verses 9 and 10. *we'eth ma'asayikh* is not a second object of *'aggīdh*. As the Athnach indicates, the first clause ends at *tsid-qāthēkh*. *'eth* is here the *'eth* of respect: "and as for," or in respect to, your activities, your doings, etc. *ma'asayikh* is not used in the objective sense of deeds or works, but in the subjective sense of doings or activities. The subject of *yō'īlūkh* is *ma'asayikh*. The Lord will no longer remain silent, but will expose Israel's abominable adulterous practices as vain and unavailing.

בְּזַעֲקֵךְ֙ יַצִּילֻ֣ךְ קִבּוּצַ֔יִךְ 13

וְאֶת־כֻּלָּ֤ם יִשָּׂא־ר֙וּחַ֙ יִקַּח־הָ֔בֶל

וְהַחוֹסֶ֥ה בִ֙י יִנְחַל־אֶ֔רֶץ וְיִירַ֖שׁ הַר־קָדְשִֽׁי׃

za'aqēkh is an infinitive Qal of *zā'aq* with suffix: "in your crying, when you cry." Wailing will certainly come, because her *ma'asīm* are altogether unavailing (verse 12), and the Lord will expose them and judge them in His anger. *hitstsīl*, a Hiphil of *nātsal*, means to pull forth, to rescue. *qibbūts*, from the root *qābhats*, to gather, is an intensive noun formed off the Piel, and signifies a gathering or assembly. The word occurs only in this passage and is usually explained as referring to a gathering of gods, a pantheon. The word clearly expresses contempt, and quite likely includes also the human powers whose help Israel has been seeking. When you cry out, let them come to the rescue! But they are so impotent that a single blast of wind, yes, a breath will carry them all away together. And so, on the day when the Lord lays bare her practices, she will stand there helpless and defenseless because she has rejected her only true Helper.

In contrast to the detailed description of the fate of the unfaithful, the second half of the verse concludes this section with a brief mention of the happy lot of those who remained faithful. "But he who trusts in Me shall inherit the land and possess My holy mountain." The phrases are taken from the conditions of the exile, but the promises also refer in full measure to those who had returned to the homeland, who were formally in possession of the land and the mountain, but not as wholly free and true owners, since they were still servants of the Persian world-power and could not fully enjoy their inheritance. But the promise extends to the full, free, and true possession under the immediate rule of the Lord.

Third Strophe: 57:14-21: *The supreme God from heaven will dwell with those who repent, and He will bestow healing and peace upon them, whereas the wicked are incapable of peace.*

14 *There is One who says: Make level, make level, clear the way,*
   Remove every obstacle from the way of My people!

15 *For thus saith the high and exalted One,*
   Who is enthroned forever, and whose name is Holy:
   I dwell on high and in holiness,
   With the contrite and with him who is bowed in spirit,
   To quicken the spirit of the humble
   And to give new life to the heart of the contrite.

16 *For I will not contend forever*
   And will not be angry forever,
   When the spirit shrouds itself before Me,
   And souls that I Myself created.

17 *Because of the iniquity of his cruelty I was wroth and smote him;*
   I hid Myself and was angry,
   So that to the ways of his own heart he turned aside.

18 *Now have I seen his ways and will heal him,*
   And I will lead him and recompense him with consolations,
       namely, for his mourning ones,

19 *Fruit of the lips will I create: Peace, Peace*
   For those far off and those who are near! says the Lord,
       and I will heal him.

20 *Yet, like the angry sea, which cannot be still,*
   And whose waves cast up slime and filth, are the wicked.

21 *There is no peace, says my God, for the wicked.*

14 וְאָמַר   סֹֽלּוּ־סֹלּוּ פַּנּוּ־דָרֶךְ   הָרִימוּ מִכְשׁוֹל מִדֶּרֶךְ עַמִּי׃

Chapter 40:3f. spoke of the preparation of the way for the Lord; here it is the way of the people returning to the homeland that is to be made smooth. A similar, even more forceful exhortation appears in 62:10. Again, the situation is that of the exile. *we 'amar* should not be connected with the subject of the verbs in verse 13b. The summons with which this new strophe begins is based on the concrete results that will flow from the promises contained in the following verses. *'amar* is impersonal, like *qōl qōrē'* and *qōl 'ōmēr* in 40:3 and 6. The subject is purposely left unexpressed. It is a mysterious voice that speaks, but it is at the same time a voice that is sufficiently familiar without special mention. The *we* is not easy to reproduce in English. This is the second time that this call, although in somewhat different form, has sounded. The Word of grace still proclaims a deliverance that is yet to come. The homeland awaits the arrival of the released captives, verse 13, and the call still sounds forth: "Smooth out the way for My people." So, the *we* must in some way be causal in meaning.

$$15\ \text{כִּי כֹה אָמַר רָם וְנִשָּׂא שֹׁכֵן עַד וְקָדוֹשׁ שְׁמוֹ}$$
$$\text{מָרוֹם וְקָדוֹשׁ אֶשְׁכּוֹן וְאֶת־דַּכָּא וּשְׁפַל־רוּחַ}$$
$$\text{לְהַחֲיוֹת רוּחַ שְׁפָלִים וּלְהַחֲיוֹת לֵב נִדְכָּאִים׃}$$

After opening with a positive statement of the fact of the return to the homeland, the prophet introduces the grounds for that statement with the familiar and impressive: *For thus says*, etc. He who issues this command to prepare the homeward way for the people is *rām*, the Highest, the absolute Majesty. He is *nissā'*, "exalted" above all things and above all powers. He is *shōkhēn 'adh*, "enthroned forever," whom no one shall ever remove from power, whose name is the Holy One, or Holy (a proper noun). Cf. 40:25 and the preceding thoughts, very similar to these. As in chapter 40, *qādhōsh* is here the One who alone is Holy, the Unapproachable One, who dwells in light "which no man can approach unto" (1 Tim. 6:16), but who reveals Himself in grace and is therefore to be worshiped. But He is also a consuming fire for all who despise His grace. This absolute supremacy, holiness, and eternal being, together with abounding grace, are the guaranty for the fulfillment of the promise in verse 14.

Beginning with *mārōm*, there is now a clear declaration of what had before been indicated only in the form of attributes: "Yes, I dwell," etc. *mārōm* and *qādhōsh* may be construed as predicate adjectives: "I dwell as the Supreme and Holy One"; or they may be construed as neuter objects of *'eshkōn*: "I dwell in, or am enthroned in, exaltation and holiness." Our preference is for the first of these constructions, even though the following parallel phrase, *'eth dakkā'*, makes the construction of the two words as objects seem the more likely. He who is enthroned as the absolutely supreme and holy One dwells *with*, that is, in His grace He dwells *in* the *dakkā'*, in him who is crushed and contrite of spirit. *dakkā'*, as a passive concept (cf. 53:5,10; Ps. 34:19[18]), expresses the cause; *shāphāl*, the effect: brought low, that is, humbled in spirit as a result of being bruised and crushed. In 66:2 the order is reversed, *'ānī ūnekhēh rūaḥ*. Cf. Psalm 34:19(18); 51:19(17); John 14:23. God's purpose in taking up His dwelling with the humbled in spirit is *lehaḥayōth rūaḥ* and *lēbh*, in order to resuscitate spirit and heart. *rūaḥ* is the spirit of life, the life principle; *lēbh* is the seat of all feeling of joy and sorrow. However, one must never be too painfully exact in dissecting the psychological references of poets and prophets. The Lord will revive the despondent hearts, make them joyful again, and fill them with new hope and comfort.

16 כִּי לֹא לְעוֹלָם אָרִיב וְלֹא לָנֶצַח אֶקְצוֹף
כִּי־רוּחַ מִלְּפָנַי יַעֲטוֹף וּנְשָׁמוֹת אֲנִי עָשִׂיתִי :

rībh denotes the anger that expresses itself in reproach and punishment; *qātsaph* refers to the feeling of anger. The meaning of the clause introduced by the second *kī* is not immediately clear. Usually the *kī* is understood to be causal: "*For* the spirit *would* waste away before Me," namely, if I should be angry and punish continually. But there is no good reason why *kī* should not be construed as temporal or conditional: I will not be angry forever, or, positively expressed, I will restrain My anger, *if,* or *when,* etc. The verb *'ataph* means to bend, fold, wrap up, and has a variety of transferred meanings based on this concrete meaning. Here the meaning would be: "to cover oneself for fear or shame, or to be shrouded as to the spirit, to become weak, unconscious, to perish." Cf. Psalm 73:6; 65:14(13); 61:3(2) (*ba'atoph libbī*); 102:1 (superscription) (*kī ya'atoph*). The Lord forgoes His anger, which otherwise would rage without end, as soon as the sinner's spirit is broken before it and shrouds itself before it or is engulfed in fear and begins to perish, for the Lord does not desire the death of the sinner. Before *neshāmoth, kī ya'atoph* or, more properly, *ta'atophnāh* must be supplied, likewise *'asher* before the emphatic *'anī.* The Lord has mercy on the souls which He Himself created, and *because* He brought them into existence. God's work of creation is frequently given as the grounds for His compassion with His creatures, especially in Isaiah, cf. 43:1ff.

17 בַּעֲוֹן בִּצְעוֹ קָצַפְתִּי וְאַכֵּהוּ הַסְתֵּר וְאֶקְצֹף
וַיֵּלֶךְ שׁוֹבָב בְּדֶרֶךְ לִבּוֹ :

The second half of this strophe is a more detailed explanation of the first half. If the Lord does not remain angry forever, why do His people languish so long under His chastising hand? Verse 17 gives the answer. *'awōn* is sin in its aspect of *guilt;* the *sin* of Israel, referred to here as a male person, is *betsa'.* The verb *bātsa'* means to break or cut off, and the noun denotes a breaking or cutting off, and concretely, what is broken off, plunder, profit, unjust gain, and the injury inflicted upon others by insatiable greed which grasps at their goods and property, at wife and child, house and home, body and life, and thus becomes the murderer of the greedy man's hapless neighbors. Avarice was of old the national sin of Israel. Along with apostasy from the Lord, there is in Israel no sin that is so often and so severely punished as the hard-hearted oppression of the poor, the weak, the helpless, and the widows and orphans. Cf. Exodus 20:17; Leviticus 19:13; Jeremiah 2:34; 6:13; 8:10; 22:13; Ezekiel 33:31; Psalm 119:36; Isaiah 1:15-17,23, and 58:1-8. Under Nehemiah (chapter 5), the rich and powerful had already completely pauperized the poor and weak, and Nehemiah notes it as something unusual that he had, in contrast, behaved himself selflessly. Jacob, the father of the nation, took advantage of his own brother Esau; he outwitted Laban at every point in acquiring the property of others; and he was even unable to keep his bargaining instinct from mingling with his piety, Genesis 28:20ff. *betsa'* was Israel's national sin. That is why the New Testament so often speaks of πλεονεξία. But avarice, Israel's most conspicuous sin, is not restricted to that nation; it is the sin of the whole world, ever since God forsook the human heart and laid His curse upon the earth, and especially is it the sin of recent times and of those people who rule the world today and live in times of unlimited opportunities. Opportunity makes thieves. Since money-making is the real object in life of our own people, the land reeks of the blood of the downtrodden. The World War offered as a sacrifice to the worldly avarice of particularly the so-called Christian Protestant nations millions upon millions of their young men. Greed is a root of all evil.

It is therefore not surprising that our text should name avarice as the real guilt of Israel, because of which the Lord rejected His people. It was at the same time a falling away from God and fratricide, the source and representative of all the sins that were prevalent in Israel. Not as one sin among many, but as the predominant sin, is avarice presented here. As is manifested in 58:2, 3ff (cf. 1:10-17), it is this sin that makes all forms of worship a reeking hypocritical show.

The second clause, introduced by *we* not by *wa*, *we'akkēhū*, etc., is explanatory of *qātsaphtī.* "Namely, I smote him," etc. *we'akkēhū*, a Hiphil of *nākhāh*, represents the visible effects of God's anger. The Hiphil infinitive absolute *hastēr* (*sāthar*) is an adverbial adjunct to *'akkēhū* (Gr. 113,h,p.341), likewise also *we'eqtsōph*, which follows immediately (Gr. ibid., Note 1). Therefore: "I smote him, hiding My face and venting My anger." The last clause is consecutive: "And so he went," etc. The chastisement brought about no betterment, but resulted only in his becoming *shōbhabh*, rebellious, walking in the ways of his evil heart. Cf. Isaiah 1:5; 9:13; Jeremiah 5:3. Such will also be the experience of the nations after the present World War. Those who are defeated will not repent, and, still less, the victors. The poor German people! They overthrew the Gospel with their "learning." And if victors in the war, they will be doubly poor and pitiable.*

דְּרָכָיו רָאִיתִי 18

וָאֶרְפָּאֵהוּ וְאַנְחֵהוּ וַאֲשַׁלֵּם נִחֻמִים לוֹ
וְלַאֲבֵלָיו:

The *derākhāyw* are the erring and disastrous ways that Israel walked, as dictated by the *derekh libbō*. The Lord observed Israel's plight and His heart was moved to pity, as once before in the history of the people, Ezekiel 16:6. And now He will heal him of all his wounds, and *lead* (*hinḥāh, nāḥāh*) him *bema'geley tsedheq*, in the paths of righteousness, Psalm 23:3, and will recompense him with consolations for all his suffering. *wela'abhēlim* is explanatory, namely, "his mourning ones." Of course, God's pity does not mean that the misery is removed while the sin remains. As the healing of Israel and the leading in paths of righteousness are purely the action of God's grace, so can they be bestowed only upon those who repent.

בּוֹרֵא נִוב שְׂפָתָיִם 19

שָׁלוֹם ׀ שָׁלוֹם לָרָחוֹק וְלַקָּרוֹב אָמַר יְהוָה וּרְפָאתִיו:

Delitzsch and some other commentators connect the participial phrase *bōrē' nībh* with *'amar YHWH*. However, *'amar YHWH* is parenthetical, as usual, and the phrase beginning with *bōrē'* is adverbial and should be connected with *ūrephā'thīw* as its apodosis. The *ū* is the *Waw apodosis*, Gr. 116, x, p. 361. "Creating fruit of the lips, I heal him." Or, the *bōrē'* phrase may be treated as a *casus pendens*: "As, or, when I create fruit of the lips," Gr. ibid. w, p. 361. The sentence is an explanation of *'erpā'ehu* in verse 18. The Lord effects the healing of Israel by creating fruit of the lips. (The Qere *nībh* replaces *nōbh* or *nūbh* of the verb *nūbh*, to grow or sprout, which is the Kethib reading.) On the basis of Hosea 14:3(2) and Hebrews 13:15, Gesenius, Ewald, Delitzsch, and others in-

---

*Note: These last few sentences were written while the first World War was still raging.

terpret fruit of the lips as prayers of praise and thanksgiving. The Rabbis, followed by Calvin, Hitzig and a number of moderns explain the fruit as referring to the Lord's words: "Peace, Peace," etc. This is the more likely interpretation, since otherwise the words "Peace," etc., would have no grammatical connection with the rest of the sentence. However, one must not think of fruit as being fruit of the lips of God because that explanation would not harmonize with *bārā*: The Lord is *bōrē*, He *creates* fruit of the lips, that is, He puts the message, "Peace, Peace, to those afar and those who are near," into the mouths of His heralds. The Lord saves His people and sends the joyful message out into the wide world. This refers first of all to the conditions of the exile, but applies also to the people living in postexilic subjugation, is completely fulfilled in the mission command of Christ, Mark 16 and Matthew 28, and absolutely and finally fulfilled when the Lord delivers us from *all* evil and will preserve us "unto His heavenly kingdom," 2 Timothy 4:18. "There remaineth therefore a rest to the people of God," Hebrews 4:9. See also Ephesians 2:17 where Paul applies *lārāḥōq* to the gentiles and *laqqārōbh* to the Jews. God brings salvation and healing to the world through the Gospel, which according to chapters 42 and 49, 50:4; 51:4ff; 61:1ff, He has placed into the mouth of His Servant.

20 וְהָרְשָׁעִים כַּיָּם נִגְרָשׁ כִּי הַשְׁקֵט לֹא יוּכָל
וַיִּגְרְשׁוּ מֵימָיו רֶפֶשׁ וָטִיט:

21 אֵין שָׁלוֹם אָמַר אֱלֹהַי לָרְשָׁעִים:

The three subsections of this discourse (56:9-57:21) share the peculiarity that each section closes with a statement that in contents is in direct contrast to the rest of the section. The first two sections describe first the ways of the ungodly and threaten them with God's wrath, and then close with a blessing upon the godly: 57:1f and 57:13b. The third section sets forth the happiness of those who repent, and closes with a judgment upon the *reshāʿim*, the ungodly, 57:21. *reshāʿim* is the designation for those who wholly reject God's salvation. In a striking figure they are compared to the tempest-tossed sea (*nighrāsh*, a Niphal participle), which cannot come to rest, *kī hashqēṭ lō' yukhāl*. *kī* is indeed not a relative particle but is nevertheless to be interpreted as a relative: "*as, insofar as*, it cannot come to rest." It is similar to the Latin *ut* with the indicative. *hashqēṭ* is a Hiphil infinitive absolute treated as a substantive and object of *yūkhāl,* although it precedes the verb, Gr. 113, d, p. 340. The sentence closes with the forceful and effective picture: "Whose waves cast up slime and filth." Such are the people who have conclusively shut themselves off from God's grace. Driven by insatiable desire and secret fear, they pursue fortune in this or that illusory form, never attain peace or come to rest, and only serve to bring to light more sin, uncleanness, and wickedness.

Like Part I, this second part closes with the Amen of the prophet, differing only from 48:22 in having *'elōhay* instead of *YHWH*: "There is no peace, says my God, for the wicked."

PART III

*The Spiritual, Eternal
Deliverance*

Chapters 58-66

PART III

Chapters 58-66

The Spiritual, Eternal Deliverance

The theme announced in 40:2c that Israel "has received of the Lord's hand double for all her sins" is carried out to its completion in Part III. The restoration and glorification of Zion, according to 40:9-11, is carried out by the coming of the Lord *beḥāzāq,* with a strong hand, to quell the enemies with His power, while as the Shepherd of His flock He receives His people into grace. The arrangement of the thoughts in Part III is different from that in Parts I and II in that the call to repentance here appears at the beginning, chapters 58 and 59, followed without transition by a majestic description of the glory of the church, in chapters 60-62, and of the destruction of the enemies, in chapter 63. In chapter 64, there follows the repentant confession of the church, which we would have expected to appear after chapter 59. The book closes, in 65 and 66, with the final separation of the faithful from the ungodly.

FIRST TRIAD
Chapters 58-60

*Only if the house of Jacob
repents fully and sincerely,
can the glory of God's grace
rise upon it for its outward
and inward, its temporal
and its eternal glorification.*

First Discourse: Chapter 58

If Israel will turn from its shamelessly hypocritical show of repentance to true godliness, it can again enter into its inheritance, in renewed strength.

The discourse proceeds from bitter rebuke to a heartfelt promise. The division into two parts occurs between verses 7 and 8. Verses 1-7 contain a preaching of judgment, in three sections: 1-3a; 3b-5; 6 and 7. The first section exposes the unabashed insolence of the hypocrites; the second lays bare the hypocrisy of their sham piety; and the third describes true fasting.

The second part of the discourse, verses 8-14, is in the form of a promise, and it likewise may be divided into three subsections. The first two sections, verses 8 and 9 and verses 10-12, join the promise of healing and renewal to the love for the neighbor, which had been preached in the first part (verses 1-7). In verses 8 and 9 the promise comes first and the condition that they cease to oppress the poor comes afterward. In verses 10-12 the condition, active love for the neighbor, is briefly stated at the beginning, and then follows the promise in detail. The third section, verses 13 and 14, leads the call to repentance, in the form of a promise, into a different theme: True observance of the Sabbath. It then assures to the penitent the possession of the inheritance of Jacob.

First Section: verses 1-7: *The call to repent of their hypocritical fastings.*

First Strophe: verses 1-3a: *The shameless insolence of the hypocrites.*

1 *Cry aloud, do not hold back,*
  Like a trumpet lift up your voice
  And show My people their sinfulness,
  And to the house of Jacob their sin.
2 *For every day do they seek Me*
  And desire knowledge of My ways,
  Like a people who had done righteousness,
  And had not forsaken the right of their God;
  Righteous judgments do they ask for,
  They desire the drawing near of God.
3 *"Why do we fast and You do not see it,*
  And are not aware that we afflict ourselves?"

קְרָא בְגָרוֹן אַל־תַּחְשֹׁךְ כַּשּׁוֹפָר הָרֵם קוֹלֶךָ 1
וְהַגֵּד לְעַמִּי פִּשְׁעָם וּלְבֵית יַעֲקֹב חַטֹּאתָם:

The Lord is speaking. The mandate seems to be directed to the prophet, but, like 40:1, this is merely a rhetorical form expressing what God wants to have proclaimed to His people. Whereas the form here is like that of 40:1 and 2, the content is the exact opposite; there it was comfort, here it is rebuke. But in both cases *'ammī* is addressed, here as the house of Jacob, there as Jerusalem. *hārēm qōlekhā kashshōphār* is an echo of *hārīmī bhakkōaḥ qōlekh* in 40:9, and it indicates that the prophet is taking up the matter for the last time and that now 40:9-11 is to proceed to fulfillment.

qerā' bheghārōn, cry out with the throat, that is, at the top of your voice. *'al taḥsōkh* (cf. 54:2), do not hold back, adds emphasis to the summons, which is raised to a still higher pitch by the comparison to a *shōphār*. The *shōphār* was the trumpet that called to battle, Judges 7:8; Job 39:25, or that gave the signal that a new year had begun, Leviticus 25:9, or that gave notice of the beginning of other festivals. The purpose is to drive home to the hearts of the people the seriousness of their sin. The singular *pish'am* gathers together all their *ḥaṭṭō'thām* into a single fundamental collective sin. It is the sin of *'ammī*, My people, their breach of faith, falling away from the Lord, their God. The house of Jacob is the designation of the people as a nation, who were descended from him and were his family. The term is commonly one of reproach. It is so used in this passage. Cf. also 2:5,6; 8:17; 10:20; 14:1; 29:22; 46:3; 48:1. But the term is at the same time also a re-

533

minder of the Lord's loving kindness toward Jacob and his seed. The seed of Jacob, so richly blessed, the Lord's chosen people, precious in His sight, this people — fallen away from the Lord! Cf. 1:2-4. Therefore: "Cry out from your throat, with all your might!"

$$2 \quad \text{וְאוֹתִי יוֹם ׀ יוֹם יִדְרֹשׁוּן וְדַעַת דְּרָכַי יֶחְפָּצוּן}$$

$$\text{כְּגוֹי אֲשֶׁר־צְדָקָה עָשָׂה וּמִשְׁפַּט אֱלֹהָיו לֹא עָזָב}$$

$$\text{יִשְׁאָלוּנִי מִשְׁפְּטֵי־צֶדֶק קִרְבַת אֱלֹהִים יֶחְפָּצוּן:}$$

we does not connect *'othī* with *pish 'ām* and *ḥaṭṭō'thām*, but connects the imperatives in verse 1 with what follows in verse 2 and sets forth the special reason why the preaching of Israel's sin should sound forth with such strength. Their apostasy from the Lord had made them unbelievably blind, self-righteous, and shameless. *we 'othī* occupies the position of emphasis. Me, Me, from whom they have fallen away, Me do they seek day after day and crave knowledge of My ways. Concerning *dārash*, see 55:6. *dha'ath* is most naturally construed as a substantive, but there is nothing to hinder taking it as an infinitive. *ḥāphēts* (literally: to bend forward) occurs here in the strongest sense of the word: to desire, crave, demand. They demand knowledge of God's ways and of the purpose of His rule. But the following shows clearly that it is more than just God's ways in general that they want knowledge of; they want to know the reason for the way that He is leading them now, why He still does not free them from their misery, even though they, etc. For an account of how this prophecy was fulfilled, see Ezekiel 14:1-8 and Ezekiel 20:1-8. They act like people (*ghōy* is used in its most general sense) who had fully performed and never forsaken the covenant Law of Israel, the righteousness that God had established for them. They demand judgments of righteousness, righteous judgments, that is, the intervention of the Lord on their behalf, against their oppressors, on the ground that He had sworn to remain faithful to His covenant. They were of the opinion that they had faithfully done their part in keeping the covenant, but that the Lord had not done His. They demand the drawing near of God, namely, to deliver them and to destroy their enemies.

$$3 \quad \text{לָמָּה צַּמְנוּ וְלֹא רָאִיתָ עִנִּינוּ נַפְשֵׁנוּ וְלֹא תֵדָע}$$

The self-righteous people are quoted. Sometimes one interrogative governs two coordinate clauses (*tsamnū*, from *tsūm*, and *rā'ithā),* while the sense requires that the first should be subordinated to the second: "Why do You not notice that we fast?" Gr. 150, m, p. 476. The King James Version translates *'innāh nephesh* with "afflict our soul," which is a paraphrase of "fasting." *nephesh* here denotes the natural feelings of the body, the discomfort that accompanies the deprivations of fasting. The divine ordinances ordained only one day of fasting, the Day of Atonement, Leviticus 16:29ff; 23:27ff; Numbers 29:7. Fasting as a penitential exercise was also practiced on other occasions, however, as is reported in 1 Samuel 7:6; 1 Kings 21:9; 2 Chronicles 20:3f; Jeremiah 36:6,9; Joel 2:12; Jonah 3:5ff. The people of the exile, after that great disaster, observed four special fast days: the anniversary of the beginning of the siege of Jerusalem on the tenth day of the tenth month; the occupation of Jerusalem on the ninth day of the fourth month; the destruction of the temple on the tenth day of the fifth month; the assassination of Gedaliah and the flight of the remaining Jews to Egypt on the third day of the seventh month (cf. 2 Kings 25 and Jer. 41 and 52). In Zechariah 7:1ff and 8:19 the Jews consult the prophet whether they should continue to observe these fast days, and they receive the same answer that the Lord gives here in His own person. We note that the people after the exile continued to fast on these special days.

The two coordinated perfects in the first clause are followed in the second clause by the imperfect *thēdhā',* which is the equivalent of our "and You do not *want* to take note of it." So, that is their grievance and their complaint against the Lord, that He does not appreciate and acknowledge their bitter penitential works. The Lord's answer to this unseeing self-righteousness follows in the next verses. He calls their fasting hypocrisy.

Second Strophe: verses 3b-5:   *The hypocrisy of their fasting.*

3b   *Yes, when you fast you seek profit,*
And you oppress all your laborers.
4   *Behold, you fast with strife and quarreling*
And smiting with wicked fist,
You do not now fast in order to make your voice heard on high.
5   *Is that a kind of fast that I should choose,*
A day when a man afflicts himself:
To bow down his head like a bulrush,
And make sackcloth and ashes his bed?
Will you call that a fast
And a day acceptable to the Lord?

הֵן בְּיוֹם צֹמְכֶם תִּמְצְאוּ־חֵפֶץ וְכָל־עַצְּבֵיכֶם תִּנְגֹּשׂוּ׃
4 הֵן לְרִיב וּמַצָּה תָּצוּמוּ וּלְהַכּוֹת בְּאֶגְרֹף רֶשַׁע
לֹא־תָצוּמוּ כַיּוֹם לְהַשְׁמִיעַ בַּמָּרוֹם קוֹלְכֶם׃

beyōm tsōmekhem, on the day, or in the time of your fasting, that is, whenever you fast, your fasting is linked with *matsāh hephets*. In *timtse'ū* there lies the idea of wishing, or wanting, that is, you wish or desire to find *hephets*. "Business" as a translation of *hephets* is mere conjecture. While they fast, they seek something that gives them satisfaction, and according to the context, that would be their own profit and welfare, which they extort from their laborers. *'atstsebhēykhem* does not mean "your efforts," a plural of *'etsebh*, since *nāghas* means much more than just "to carry on." In *nāghas* there lies the idea of oppression, and the verb requires an object that fits with the concept of oppression (cf. remarks on *nāghas* at 53:7, and *nōghēs*, the word for taskmaster). *'atstsebhēykhem* must come from *'atsēbh* or *'atstsābh*, meaning either forced labor and indebtedness, or in a personal sense, a laborer, a peon, one forced to do hard labor. Since *nāghas* is the word regularly used for the methods of the taskmasters in driving the laborers, it would seem most likely that *'atstsebhēykhem* has the personal meaning of peon, or oppressed laborer, cf. Exodus 5:6,10,13,14 and 3:7. They drive their laborers as the taskmasters drove the slave-laborers in Egypt. The situation is described in Nehemiah 5:1-5. The fighting, quarreling, and smiting with the fist, of which the next sentence speaks, was said of the treatment accorded to the laborers, not of fellow men in general, as verses 6ff indicate. The *'atstsebhēykhem* are people who are under their power. The prefix *le* before *rībh* indicates the connection between the fasting and the striving and quarreling. It is a fasting connected with strife, quarreling and smiting, and it is therefore a hypocritical fasting and repentance. *'eghrōph* is usually translated with "fist," on the authority of the LXX, and *'eghrōph resha'* is the "fist of godlessness," violence without regard to rights and without mercy. *kayyōm* is the equivalent of *kehayyōm* and, like *hayyōm*, means this day, today, now (cf. 1 Sam. 9:13; 1 Kings 1:51). It is linked by Masoretic accent with *lō' thātsūmū*: "you do not fast now in order to let your voice be heard on high." Again their fasting is thus marked as hypocritical. A proper fasting is a repentant pleading for forgiveness directed to the ears of God on high. The essence and virtue of fasting is repentance. It turns away from sin and from injustice toward one's neighbor, and turns to God with a plea for grace and forgiveness. But their fasting does neither; it is nothing but an external *opus operatum* and therefore worthy of condemnation.

הֲכָזֶה יִהְיֶה צוֹם אֶבְחָרֵהוּ יוֹם עַנּוֹת אָדָם נַפְשׁוֹ ⁵
הֲלָכֹף כְּאַגְמֹן רֹאשׁוֹ וְשַׂק וָאֵפֶר יַצִּיעַ
הֲלָזֶה תִּקְרָא־צוֹם וְיוֹם רָצוֹן לַיהוָה׃

khāzeh literally is: like this, such, of such kind. With the interrogative *ha* the meaning is: Should such a thing be a fasting, etc.? The next clause, since it is a parallel of the first, is still part of the question and *hakhāzeh yihyeh* must be repeated: Should such a day be a day of affliction of the soul of a man? *'innāh nephesh* is again the equivalent of *tsōm*, fasting. *yōm 'annōth*, etc., is to be construed as an abbreviated form of *yōm 'asher ye'anneh bō 'ādhām naphshō*. The dependent clause begins with *halākhōph*: "(Is it this) to bow one's head like a bulrush and to make sackcloth and ashes his bed?" (Concerning the Dagesh forte in *yatstsīa'*, a Hiphil imperfect of *yātsā'*, see Gr. 71, p. 193. The *lā* in *halāzeh* is the sign of the dative which usually follows *qārā'*. The *la* in *laYHWH* is adverbial, pleasing *to* the Lord. A bowed head, sackcloth and ashes, the usual signs of mourning, do not constitute a fasting that is pleasing to the Lord. The eyes of the Lord observe the heart and its motives, not the outward works.

Third Strophe: verses 6-7:   *The true fast.*

6   *Is not this the fast that I choose:*
  To loose unjust bonds,
  To untie the knots of the yoke,
  To set at liberty the bond-laborers,
  And that you burst asunder every yoke?
7   *Is it not, to share your bread with the hungry,*
  And that you take into your home the homeless poor,
  That when you see one naked, you clothe him,
  And do not hide yourself from your own flesh?

הֲלוֹא זֶה צוֹם אֶבְחָרֵהוּ ⁶
פַּתֵּחַ חַרְצֻבּוֹת רֶשַׁע הַתֵּר אֲגֻדּוֹת מוֹטָה
וְשַׁלַּח רְצוּצִים חָפְשִׁים וְכָל־מוֹטָה תְּנַתֵּקוּ׃

tsōm is made definite by the abbreviated relative clause *'ebhḥārēhū*, therefore: not, *a* fast, but *the* fast that I choose. Regarding the absolute infinitives with object in this sentence, see Gr. 113, b and f, p. 340. *hartsubbōth*, from *ḥātsabh*, to hew out, to dig out, has a pleonastic *Resh. resha'*, in the phrase *hartsubbōth resha'*, is a qualitative genitive: unjust bonds. *'aghuddōth mōtāh* (*'āghadh*, to bind together) are not the rope-knots with which the shaft of the wagon or plow is fastened to the yoke, but the cords that came together at the throat of the ox and made the yoke secure. Not until these knots were untied, could the ox be freed of the burden of the yoke. These expressions are, of course, all figurative. The plural *retsūtsīm* is from *rātsats*, to bruise, to break, and describes the bond-laborers as exploited, weak, and defenseless. The word *rātsūts* occurs also in 42:3, in the phrase "a bruised reed." *hophshīm* is an adjective derived from the verb *hāphash*, to be free, which occurs only once, in the Pual, in Leviticus 19:20. *hophshīm* is a part of the predicate, and combined with *shillaḥ*, the phrase means "to set free, to set at liberty," Deuteronomy 15:12,- 13,18; Jeremiah 34:9ff. All forms of oppression, whatever they may be, are summed up in the closing clause. The Piel form of the onomatopoetic word *nāthaq* occurs also in Psalm 2:3: "Let us break their bands asunder." This verse treats the true kind of fast from a negative aspect: to cease and desist from all manner of injustice that had been practiced against the weak. The seventh verse turns to the positive practice of works of mercy.

7 הֲלוֹא פָרֹס לָרָעֵב לַחְמֶךָ וַעֲנִיִּים מְרוּדִים תָּבִיא בָיִת
כִּי־תִרְאֶה עָרֹם וְכִסִּיתוֹ וּמִבְּשָׂרְךָ לֹא תִתְעַלָּם:

The construction of the opening words is still dependent on *zeh tsōm 'ebhḥārēhū* of the sixth verse. As in that verse, the first verb to follow the opening clause is an absolute infinitive. But the next verb reverts to the finite form. "Breaking one's bread with the hungry" is the Hebrew equivalent of our "sharing one's bread with the hungry." *merūdhīm* is the plural of *mārūdh*, a Qal passive participle of *māradh*, which here has the same meaning as *rūdh*, to wander about. It is an attribute of the substantive *'anīyyīm*, the wandering, homeless poor. *bāyith* is not the Israelite homeland (thus Cheyne), as opposed to foreign Babylon, but the private home of the person addressed, the onetime oppressor of the poor and homeless. The same may be said of clothing the naked. Note *kī* with the imperfect in the protasis and the perfect with *we* in the apodosis, Gr. 112, hh, p. 336. "When and wherever you see him naked, then and there clothe him." The last clause is a general admonition, which includes within itself the reason for it. The oppressed neighbor is of your own flesh, of the same nature, with the same feelings, therefore, etc. Whether the reference is here to the whole human family, or particularly to the family of the people of Israel, it is difficult to decide. Cf. Genesis 37:27; 2 Samuel 5:1; 19:13. The oppression of which the prophet has been speaking was practiced in the midst of his own people.

This section reproves the self-righteousness, the hypocrisy, and the insolence of the people of God according to the flesh. Because they observed the outward forms of fasting, they presumed to have a right to deliverance at the hands of the Lord, while at the same time refusing to give up the oppression of their neighbor and their apostasy from the Lord. The prophet informs them that the proof of repentance consists in leaving off from oppressing their brethren and in being merciful to them.

Second Section: verses 8-14:   *The blessing of true repentance.*

First Strophe: verses 8-9:   *Putting an end to oppression will be followed by the healing of Israel and an answer to her prayers.*

8   *Then will your light shine forth like the dawn*
    And your healing will quickly sprout forth;
    Your salvation will go before you,
    And the glory of the Lord will be your rearguard.
9   *Then will the Lord answer when you call,*
    And when you cry for help, He will say: Here am I!
    If you remove oppression from your midst,
    The shaking of the finger and the speaking of evil.

אָז יִבָּקַע כַּשַּׁחַר אוֹרֶךָ וַאֲרֻכָתְךָ מְהֵרָה תִצְמָח 8

וְהָלַךְ לְפָנֶיךָ צִדְקֶךָ כְּבוֹד יְהוָה יַאַסְפֶךָ ׃

'ōr, light is here, as usual, a figure of happiness, a condition of happiness and blessedness, cf. 60:1 and 3. For *'arukhāh,* from *'arakh,* to draw out in length, see the lexicon. *mehērāh,* a substantive, is here used adverbially. Quickness is the point of comparison in both of the opening clauses. In southern climes, dawn and full daylight follow dark night much more quickly than in the north. At the equator, the change from night to full daylight takes place in a few minutes. The pictures in the next two clauses,

"to go before you" and "to gather you up," are military terms, vanguard and rearguard, cf. 52:12. *tsedheq* again has the meaning "salvation," and *kebhōdh YHWH* is the protective glory of the grace of God, the pillar of cloud and the pillar of fire, while Israel wandered in the wilderness, Exodus 13:21; Numbers 14:14; Psalm 68:8(7); 78:14, etc. It is "the glory of God in the face of Jesus Christ," 2 Corinthians 4:6; it is Jesus Christ Himself, 1 Corinthians 10:4.

אָז תִּקְרָא וַיהוָה יַעֲנֶה תְּשַׁוַּע וְיֹאמַר הִנֵּנִי ״

אִם־תָּסִיר מִתּוֹכְךָ מוֹטָה שְׁלַח אֶצְבַּע וְדַבֶּר־אָוֶן :

These words refer to the complaint directed against the Lord in verses 2 and 3: *lō'rā'ithā welō'thēdhā'*. *shiwwa'*, to cry for help, occurs only in the Piel. When the Lord says *hinnēnī*, Here am I!, that is a set expression indicating that the Lord has heard the plea for help and has come to grant it. The clause beginning with *'im tāsīr* (Hiphil of *sūr*) states first in summary form, then in a pair of particulars, the conditions upon which the coming of help depends. The summary statement echoes verse 6, and the two particulars recall verse 4a. *shelaḥ* is an infinitive for *shelōaḥ*, Gr. 115, b, p. 353. Pointing the finger is a threatening gesture. It is doubtful that it can be interpreted as a gesture of contempt (Prov. 6:13), since there is nothing in the context (verses 4,6, and 7) to support that meaning. *dabber 'āwen* repeats the thought of *rībh* and *matstsāh* in verse 4.

Second Strophe: verses 10-12: *Complete renewal is the blessing of mercifulness.*

10   *If you open your heart to the hungry,*
     And satisfy the soul that is bowed down,
     Then will your light shine forth in darkness,
     And your gloom of night become like noonday.

11   *Yes, the Lord will continually lead you,*
     And will satisfy your soul in desert places,
     And renew the strength of your bones,
     And you shall be like a well-watered garden,
     And like a spring of water whose waters never fail.

12   *Your children will rebuild the old ruins,*
     The ancient foundations will you build up anew,
     And you shall be called mender of broken walls,
     Renewer of streets — so that men may dwell there.

וְתָפֵק לָרָעֵב נַפְשֶׁךָ וְנֶפֶשׁ נַעֲנָה תַּשְׂבִּיעַ ¹⁰
וְזָרַח בַּחֹשֶׁךְ אוֹרֶךָ וַאֲפֵלָתְךָ כַּצָּהֳרָיִם :

The strophe begins with a statement of the conditions set for
the promised renewal. The *we* continues the construction begun
with *kī* in verse 7, and another *we* apodosis follows at the beginning of the second half of the verse. *thāpheq* is the jussive form of
the Hiphil imperfect of *pūq*. *pūq* occurs only in the Hiphil, with the
single exception of the Qal in Isaiah 28:7. *pūq* means "to strike, to
happen on something, to strike against something, to thrust forward," and then in an extended sense of these three meanings: "to
receive or acquire; to stagger or reel"; and finally, "to proffer or
present." Cf. Psalm 140:9(8); 144:13; Proverbs 3:13; 8:35; 12:2;
18:22; Jeremiah 10:4 (to totter). *hephīq nephesh* must mean "to
offer or proffer one's soul." Delitzsch's explanation on the basis of
Deuteronomy 24:6 seems to us to be too contrived and daring:
"The name of the soul, which is regarded here as greedily longing,
is used for that which nourishes it . . . the longing itself (*appe-
titus*) for the object of the longing." He then translates: "and
offerest up thy gluttony to the hungry," that is, what you yourself
would rather eat. It is possible to arrive at the meaning of the sentence without recourse to such artfulness. *hephīq nephesh* means
to offer one's soul or heart, to open up one's heart and evince pity
and compassion for one's neighbor. The word *nephesh* would not
have been used twice in quick succession if in one case it were
used in one sense, and in the other case in a much different sense.
The first clause is abstract and general; the second, concrete and
specific: If you open your heart and satisfy with food the heart
that is bowed down. The LXX translates *naphshekhā* with τòν
ἄρτον ἐκ ψυχῆς σου. The four substantives in the second half
of the sentence are all used figuratively: *ḥoshekh* and *'aphelāh* for
trouble and affliction, *'or* and *tsohorayim* for happiness and
blessedness.

וְנָחֲךָ יְהוָה תָּמִיד וְהִשְׂבִּיעַ בְּצַחְצָחוֹת נַפְשֶׁךָ ¹¹
וְעַצְמֹתֶיךָ יַחֲלִיץ וְהָיִיתָ כְּגַן רָוֶה
וּכְמוֹצָא מַיִם אֲשֶׁר לֹא־יְכַזְּבוּ מֵימָיו :

The first clause promises those who are compassionate —
meaning the people — secure guidance for all future time. The
second promises that they shall be satisfied and restored in

541

drought-ridden places (*tsaḥtsaḥoth*, from *tsāḥāh*, to shine, to glow, be hot). The third promises strengthening of the bones, that is, rejuvenation of their strength. The second half of the verse combines the two preceding promises into the comparison with a garden well-watered by springs that never fail. Cf. Jeremiah 31:12. Springs that do not deceive are springs that never disappoint the thirsty traveler when he comes to them.

12 וּבָנ֤וּ מִמְּךָ֙ חָרְב֣וֹת עוֹלָ֔ם מוֹסְדֵ֥י דוֹר־וָד֖וֹר תְּקוֹמֵ֑ם
וְקֹרָ֤א לְךָ֙ גֹּדֵ֣ר פֶּ֔רֶץ מְשֹׁבֵ֥ב נְתִיב֖וֹת לָשָֽׁבֶת׃

'asher must here be supplied before *mimmekhā*, as in Psalm 118:26 before *mibbeyth*: "those who are *of you*, that is, your descendants, will build." The *ḥorbhoth 'olām*, the old ruins, and the *mosedhēy dhor wādhor*, the ancient foundations, do not refer to the conquered and dilapidated cities of the gentiles, but to the ruined walls and cities of their own homeland, particularly to Jerusalem. They are not the *'arim neshammoth* of 54:3, according to Genesis 22:17; the reference is rather to what Ezekiel says in chapter 36:10 and 33.

godhēr has the verbal character of the participle governing the accusative *perets*, whereas one would have expected the noun construction after *qorā' lekhā*, Gr. 116, f. p. 357. The same is true of *meshobhēbh* (Polel participle of *shūbh*) *nethibhoth. perets* is collective. The people who will be returned to their homeland will not build new cities in other locations, but will rebuild the ruins of the cities that they loved and will restore the familiar streets, and they shall be called menders of broken walls and restorers of streets. *lāshābheth* does not refer to the rebuilt streets alone, it includes also the restored foundations of the dwellings. Living in their own homes will again be a possibility and a reality.

Verse 12 adds a promise to the exiled people that the homeland will be restored and rebuilt and that they shall again dwell in the homes that they so ardently longed for.

Third Strophe: verses 13-14: *The enjoyment of the inheritance of Jacob as a blessing of the right observance of the Sabbath.*

13 *If you turn back your foot from the Sabbath,*
   That you do not gratify your pleasures on My holy day,
   And if you call the Sabbath a delight,
   And call the holy day of the Lord Honorable
   And honor Him by not carrying on your affairs,
   And by not seeking your pleasure and by idle talk,

14 *Then you will have your delight in the Lord*
    And I will cause you to travel over the high places of the land
    And give you the inheritance of Jacob your father to enjoy,
    For the mouth of the Lord has spoken it.

אִם־תָּשִׁיב מִשַּׁבָּת רַגְלֶךָ עֲשׂוֹת חֲפָצֶיךָ בְּיוֹם קָדְשִׁי ¹³
וְקָרָאתָ לַשַּׁבָּת עֹנֶג לִקְדוֹשׁ יְהוָה מְכֻבָּד
וְכִבַּדְתּוֹ מֵעֲשׂוֹת דְּרָכֶיךָ מִמְּצוֹא חֶפְצְךָ וְדַבֵּר דָּבָר׃

From true piety as it is evidenced in one's behavior toward his
neighbor, the final strophe now moves forward to the real theme:
Full faithfulness toward the Lord. This thought was just incidentally touched on at the end of verse 4: "to cause your voice to be
heard on high." Regarding the meaning of Sabbath observance,
compare the discussion of 56:1,2. The development of the thought
in verse 13 shows that the Lord looks above all at the attitude of
the heart.

The first clause, "If you turn back your foot from the Sabbath,"
is figurative. The Sabbath is pictured as holy ground upon which a
profane foot must not tread. Cf. Exodus 3:5: "Draw not nigh hither
. . . for the place whereon thou standest is holy ground." Ecclesiastes 4:17(5:1). The clause beginning with 'asōth is an explanation in concrete terms of the first clause. It is unnecessary artifi-
cially to seek in 'asōth, as Delitzsch, Hahn, and others do, "an explanatory permutative of the object raghlekhā." The governing
power of the preposition min in mishshabbāth is extended
to 'asōth, Gr. 119, hh, p. 384. 'asōth is to be translated as though it
were written mē'asōth.* It is difficult to understand why one commentator after the other, here and in verse 3, translates ḥēphets
with "business," since the usual meaning of the word is quite
satisfactory here. If one understands "business" to mean ordinary
affairs or concerns, then too much ground is covered; if the word is
taken to mean "business transactions," then too little ground is
covered. ḥaphātsīm are those things that give pleasure and satisfaction. The Sabbath is called yōm qodhshī, My holy day, because
the Lord blessed and sanctified it as a day of His own rest after the
work of creation (Exod. 20:11; 31:15; 35:2), and because He had
made it a special memorial of the deliverance out of Egypt, a day
for the sanctification of His people, Deuteronomy 5:15; Ezekiel
20:12f.

---

*The Dead Sea Scrolls read: mē'asōth ḥaphātseykhā.

Israel is admonished to call this day *'onegh,* that is, a refreshing or restoration, because that is what observance of the day should mean both for body and spirit. *liqdhōsh* is a dative object of *qārā'thā.* The phrase would have been written *qādhōsh l'adhōnāy,* if the prefix *le* had not already been used with *qedhōsh.* Since the Sabbath is the Holy (scil., day) of the Lord, therefore Israel is to call it Honored, or Honorable, a proper noun. The Pual participle *mekhubbādh* is followed immediately by a finite form of the same verb in the indicative as an indication that honor is to be shown by deed as well as by word. The deed is expressed in three negative clauses. As in the case of *'asōth* earlier in this verse, the *min* in *mimmetsō'* applies also to *dabbēr.* The *derākheykhā* are your *own* concerns and affairs. *ḥephtsekhā* here means nothing more than your own pleasure and profit. *dabbēr dābhār* is idle, empty talk.

14 אָ֣ז תִּתְעַנַּג֮ עַל־יְהוָה֒ וְהִרְכַּבְתִּ֖יךָ עַל־בָּ֣מֳותֵי אָ֑רֶץ

וְהַאֲכַלְתִּ֗יךָ נַחֲלַת֙ יַעֲקֹ֣ב אָבִ֔יךָ כִּ֛י פִּ֥י יְהוָ֖ה דִּבֵּֽר׃

The promise contained in this verse is connected by the verb *tith'annagh* with *'onegh* in verse 13. But now the expression is not just *tith'annagh 'al shabbāth,* but *tith'annagh 'al YHWH:* "You shall have restoring in the Lord," for that is the purpose of the Sabbath. It is neither certain nor necessary that *hirkabhtīkhā* should be rendered with a different translation from the obvious one: to take into possession. The statement about the inheritance of Jacob shows that this promise has to do with the return to the homeland in Canaan. The Lord will let His repentant people range over the highlands (*bomothēy 'ārets*) of their own land, that is, He will give them secure possession of it. The original promise in Deuteronomy 32:13 and 33:29 is of identical import. It is just these "high places" of Canaan that were the inheritance of "your father Jacob," Genesis 28:4,13, etc. Israel shall again be lord in its own land and enjoy the products thereof, cf. 65:9, 10, 13, 21f; Ezekiel 34:14; 36:1-8.

The solemn declaration at the close is like that in 40:5; 1:20. It should be noted that the wording of the prophecy indicates that the promise is not completely fulfilled in the mere return out of exile back to Canaan. After the return from the exile Israel never became mistress of the land, much less of the whole world. The prophecy has spiritual intent and reaches into the New Testament, Matthew 5:5; cf. Romans 4:13.

544

To those who in truth fear God, this strophe promises inner rejoicing in the Lord and also a physical resettlement in the inheritance of the fathers. But Israel will come into possession of the promised inheritance only if it turns away from its self-righteous, insolent, and hypocritical repentance, and turns again in sincere repentance to love of the neighbor and the fear of God. That is the basic thought of this discourse.

Second Discourse: Chapter 59

"The Lord's people, the house of Jacob" (58:1) , is so completely ensnared in apostasy and sin, that no one, by himself, can come to the rescue of the people. Therefore, the Lord Himself, with His own arm must intervene to wreak vengeance on His irredeemable enemies and to save those who repent.

The chapter may be divided into three main sections. The first section, verses 1-8: The guilt of the people stands like a wall of separation between them and their God, and their sins continually lead them farther away from peace. The second section, verses 9-15a: Because the people are so completely entangled in sin, they grope about blind and helpless, and deliverance cannot come to them. The third section, verses 15b-21: In view of this hopeless situation, the Lord decides that He Himself must arise to judgment, to destroy His irredeemable enemies and to deliver those who repent.

Each main section is again divided into two almost equal halves, which in contents correspond to each other in different ways. In the first section the halves are parallel; in the second there is a palindromic relation; in the third, a progression.

Throughout the chapter, the verses are of four lines each. Exceptions are the first verse of the chapter, the conclusion of the second section, and the opening verse of the third section. The Masoretic division of verses in 20 and 21 is incorrect, and we have adjusted the division as well as we were able.

First Strophe: verses 1-8: *The people's guilt stands as a wall of separation between them and their God, and their sins continually lead them farther away from peace (salvation).*

546

First Half: verses 1-4: *The vicious attitude toward their own brethren and their faithlessness toward the Lord constitute the wall of separation between the people and their God.*

1   *Truly, the Lord's hand is not so short that He cannot save,*
    Nor His ear so dull that He cannot hear;
2   *No, it is the guilt of your sins that between you*
    And your God has become a wall of separation,
    And your evil deeds
    Have hidden His face before you, so that He does not hear.
3   *For your hands are stained with blood,*
    And your fingers with guilt;
    Your lips speak deceit,
    And your tongue utters maliciousness.
4   *There is not one who calls on Me in righteousness,*
    Not one who strives (with Me) in good faith;
    Each one trusts in vanity and utters folly,
    They conceive injury and give birth to ruin.

1 הֵן לֹא־קָצְרָה יַד־יְהוָה מֵהוֹשִׁיעַ וְלֹא־כָבְדָה אָזְנוֹ מִשְּׁמוֹעַ:

Chapter 59 continues the reprimand that was begun in 58. This second discourse of Part III is a companion piece to the first and sharply rejects the complaint there made by the hypocritically repentant people. It is sterner and more threatening than the first discourse. While the first was mainly concerned with the *hypocrisy* of the people's repentance and with an exposition of the nature of true and honest fasting and with a promise of deliverance as a reward of such fasting, this second discourse characterizes the sinful state of the people as *hopeless,* as a wall that separates them from their God. It portrays their sinful state in darkest colors and ends with the portrayal of an unavoidable judgment. A clear understanding of this state of affairs is crucial for a correct interpretation of verses 4, 8, and several other verses that follow.

The chapter begins with *hēn,* which here does not merely point forward, but asserts with emphasis. "Truly" stamps what follows as a more emphatic restatement of something that was said before, in 58:1-5. This entire chapter is based on the direct assumption that up to the present time Israel had been without help. The very first clauses and the whole section from 1 to 15a intend to explain the situation. The reason why Israel still languishes in its misery is not that the Lord perhaps is not able to rescue the people — that is the meaning of the figure of speech in: "The hand of the Lord is not so short that He cannot save." Nor is

it that He is unwilling to help — that is the sense of the second
figure: "Nor is His ear so dull that He cannot hear." But:

כִּי אִם־עֲוֹנֹתֵיכֶם הָיוּ מַבְדִּלִים בֵּינֵכֶם לְבֵין אֱלֹהֵיכֶם 2
וְחַטֹּאותֵיכֶם הִסְתִּירוּ פָנִים מִכֶּם מִשְּׁמוֹעַ:

"It is the guilt of your sins that between you and your God has
become a wall of separation, and your evil deeds have hidden His
face before you, so that He does not hear." Every word is important here. *ʿawōn* is sin viewed as guilt, and the plural indicates the
multitude of repeated deeds that increase the guilt. Instead of a
simple indicative *yabhdīlū,* the predicate is a participle with *hāyū:*
"they have become separators," thus emphatically portraying the
finality and unbroken continuation of guiltiness. That is why we
translate: "has become a wall of separation." It is the guilt of sin
that erects a wall of separation between the sinner and his God.
Sin is a violation of the law of God, a *crimen laesae majestatis,* that
turns God's good will into displeasure and anger, until the violated
honor of God has been restored by an act of atonement, that is, by
the suffering of God's punishment. Sin, as a wrong against God, as
an attack on His honor, lays upon him who commits sin the obligation to make amends, or it condemns him to eternal separation
from God, that is, to damnation.

ḥaṭṭā'th is sin viewed as error, a transgression of the bounds set
by God, a deviation from the path of righteousness, a going astray.
And so, it leads away from God, either to one side or backwards;
and as the *ḥaṭṭā'ōth* multiply, they more and more "hide the face
of God before you so that He does not hear," that is, they make
Him unwilling to listen to your prayers and answer them. Israel's
persistence in its guilty ways and its impenitent continuance in
the error of its ways raised that wall that separated it from God,
that cast His grace aside, and thus absolutely barred the way to
help. What now follows, to the end of 15a, is nothing more than an
expansion of these two thoughts. Verse 3 develops the first of
these thoughts, Israel's guilt; verse 4 develops the second, Israel's
persistence in error. Because they fail to recognize this, the commentators all go astray in interpreting verse 4.

כִּי כַפֵּיכֶם נְגֹאֲלוּ בַדָּם וְאֶצְבְּעוֹתֵיכֶם בֶּעָוֹן 3
שִׂפְתוֹתֵיכֶם דִּבְּרוּ־שֶׁקֶר לְשׁוֹנְכֶם עַוְלָה תֶהְגֶּה:

The form *negho͞'alū* is abnormal, compounded of a Niphal perfect and a Pual perfect, cf. Gr. 51, h, p. 138, where it is called a *forma mixta*. Of this peculiar vocalization Vitringa says: "*Emphasin addit dicto.*" "Your hands are stained with blood and your fingers with guilt" clearly refers to the offenses mentioned in the second verse — *'awōnōthēykhem* (plural there) and *'awōn* (collective here). Their guilt, referred to here, in 58:4, and elsewhere, consists in their merciless treatment of their own brethren. The judgment pronounced here on this sin is harsher than that in the earlier passage. Here it is called fratricide; their hands are stained with the blood of their brothers; they are guilty of the sin of Cain, even though they are not charged with actual murder. Physical acts against one's neighbor of a lesser degree of violence than outright killing are designated as murder in 58:4 and 6, and also in 59:5,6,7 (cf. Matt. 5:21f; 1 John 3:15).

The next two clauses, "your lips," etc., refer to sins of the tongue, whose source, however, is the falseness and deceit of the heart. *sheqer*, especially when combined with *dibbēr*, is that untruthfulness with which one seeks to delude, deceive, defraud or harm one's neighbor; hence: trickery, deceit. *'awlāh* is a stronger expression: fraud, knavery, wickedness. *hāgāh*, to contemplate, to think over, to murmur, when combined with *'awlāh*, means contemplating with evil intent, to plan fraud and harmful deceit. Cf. Psalm 2:1.

אֵין־קֹרֵא בְצֶדֶק וְאֵין נִשְׁפָּט בֶּאֱמוּנָה
בָּטוֹחַ עַל־תֹּהוּ וְדַבֶּר־שָׁוְא הָרוֹ עָמָל וְהוֹלֵיד אָוֶן:

Nearly all commentators translate this verse incorrectly, because they understand the verse to refer to sins against one's neighbor, instead of the sin of unfaithfulness toward the Lord. The LXX, the Vulgate, Vitringa, Maurer, Knobel, Delitzsch, Cheyne, Kautzsch, Budde, Duhm, Marti, Driver, Luther, Schlachter, all have sins against the neighbor in mind. A remark by Vitringa seems to indicate that the Chaldaic paraphrase understood the passage correctly: *Chaldaeus . . . Non est qui oret in veritate.* Since the commentators take the verse to refer to sins against neighbors — perhaps because of its position between verses 3 and 5ff — they have difficulty in explaining what *qōrē' bhetsedheq* must mean. Following Coccejus, who according to Vitringa has *Litem intendit cum justitia* ("pleads his case truthfully"), they translate: "*In jus vocare*"! Delitzsch says that *qārā'* here has the meaning of the

Greek κηρύσσειν, and he translates: "No one gives public evidence with justice," this coming somewhat nearer to Luther, who usually translates *qārā' bheshēm* with "preaching the Name," and in this instance renders *qārā' bhetsedheq* with "preaching of righteousness." Those who take *qārā' bhetsedheq* to be the equivalent of *in jus vocare*, understand *nishpāt* to mean "going to law with" one's neighbor and translate the following clauses accordingly. All of this results from a failure to observe that the strophe, verses 1-8, divides into two halves between verses 4 and 5, so that verse 4 is not an intermediate member between verse 3 and verse 5, but concludes the section verses 1-4, while verse 5 begins a new thought. It has also escaped observation that chapter 59 is a companion-piece to chapter 58, and that our verse 4 refers back to 58:2 and 3. Everything is clear when one realizes that the subject of discourse is the unabashed hypocrisy with which the people display their "fasting" before God. *bhetsedheq* must not be combined with *qōrē'* into an idiomatic expression like *qārā' bheshēm*, but it simply modifies *qōrē'* just as *be'emūnāh* modifies *nishpāt*. The first clause then reads: "There is no one who calls in righteousness," namely, upon the Lord. In 58:9 *tiqrā'* is actually used in that very same sense. The next clause, *we'ēyn*, etc., is equally simple: "There is none who contends in sincerity," namely, with the Lord, a charge that is also raised in 58:2 and 3. Just as *be'emūnāh* is translated with "in sincerity" or "in truthfulness," so also *bhetsedheq* is translated with "in faithfulness," that is, in faith, in "Christian" *bona fides*. So also the last two phrases *bātōah 'al tōhū* and *hārō 'amāl*, etc., speak of the attitude of these people toward the Lord, not toward their neighbors, an idea to which *bātōah* is not at all suited. (For the infinitive absolute *bātōah*, see Gr. 113, ff, p. 346. *hārō* is infinitive absolute of *hārāh*, for *hārōh*.) In their arrogant appeals to the Lord and in their insincere contention with Him, they rely on *tōhū*, nothingness, that is, they labor under the delusion that they had fulfilled all righteousness, 58:2; and their lips speak vanity in that they boastfully display their fasting before the Lord, 58:2 and 3.

The last clause, *hārō 'amāl*, etc., is taken from Job 15:35. It is a proverbial expression of broad application. It occurs also in Psalm 7:15(14), except that there *sheqer* replaces *'awen* in the second part of the phrase. *'amāl* is trouble or anguish that one causes for himself or for others. *'awen* is a stronger expression and means misfortune, disaster, or even wickedness. The first part of the phrase, according to Job 15 and Psalm 7 (cf. Prov. 22:8 and Job

4:8) means "to conceive evil plans against someone." The meaning of the second phrase is that while conceiving evil they plunge themselves into disaster. The only question is whether the evil designs of the first phrase are directed against the Lord or against the neighbor. In Job 15, as the 25th verse shows, they are directed against the Lord; in Psalm 7 (cf. the beginning of the Psalm and verse 16f [15f]) against the neighbor. The clauses immediately preceding indicate that the evil designs were directed against the Lord. But since these last two clauses at the same time form a conclusion to the preceding lines and a transition to the second half of this strophe, which treats of hard-heartedness toward their neighbors, the first clause ought to be understood as referring in general to evil plans directed against both God and the neighbor. The clause is not intended to be specific. The same may be said of the second clause. The mischief that they design does not necessarily, as in Psalm 7, fall on their own heads; but the product of their thoughts in general is mischief and ruin. In the next section it is the neighbor who falls victim to the mischief that these scoundrels conceive and propagate.

Second Half: verses 5-8:   *Their thoughts and designs are nothing but misfortune for their neighbor and for themselves.*

5   *They hatch out vipers' eggs,*
    They weave spiders' webs;
    He who eats of their eggs must die,
    And an egg that is broken splits into an adder.
6   *What they weave is useless for a garment*
    And no one can cover himself with their product;
    Their works are works of mischief,
    And working of violence is in their hands.
7   *Their feet run to evil*
    And they hasten to shed innocent blood;
    Their thoughts are thoughts of destruction,
    Ruin and devastation are in their paths.
8   *They know not the way of peace,*
    There is no salvation in their tracks,
    They have made their paths crooked for themselves;
    Who walks on them will have no salvation.

5 בֵּיצֵי צִפְעוֹנִי בִּקֵּעוּ וְקוּרֵי עַכָּבִישׁ יֶאֱרֹגוּ
הָאֹכֵל מִבֵּיצֵיהֶם יָמוּת וְהַזּוּרֶה^b תִּבָּקַע אֶפְעֶה:

Verses 5 and 6 are couched in figurative terms; verses 6 and 7 repeat the thought in abstract terms. It is not at all certain what kind of serpent the *tsiph ʿonī* is (11:8; 14:29; Jer. 8:17; Prov. 23:32). Since the word designates an especially wily and venomous serpent, we have translated it with *viper*. Under the picture of a viper their plans are marked as malicious and deadly. The weaving of spiders' webs describes their machinations as being designed to ensnare their neighbors in their nets as a spider entangles insects in its web. He who let himself be deluded by their schemes is like the man who eats vipers' eggs, which are assumed to be poisonous. *zūreh*, a Qal passive participle of *zūr*, to crush, is explained, Gr. 80, i, p. 224, as an "obtuse form" of the feminine *zūrāh*. The article is generic: *the, a* crushed, scil., egg. The construction of the concluding phrase is: As for the egg that is crushed — an adder, *'eph ʿeh*, splits itself (*tibbāqaʿ* is Niphal), that is, slips forth to snap at the eater.

קוּרֵיהֶם֙ לֹא־יִהְי֣וּ לְבֶ֔גֶד וְלֹ֥א יִתְכַּסּ֖וּ בְּמַעֲשֵׂיהֶ֑ם 6
מַעֲשֵׂיהֶם֙ מַעֲשֵׂי־אָ֔וֶן וּפֹ֥עַל חָמָ֖ס בְּכַפֵּיהֶֽם׃

"What they weave is useless for a garment" suggests by contrast the threads of the silkworm, cf. Ezekiel 16:10 and 13. Of the threads of silk one may make a garment with which to clothe himself, but their *maʿaseyhem*, the products of their malice, are useless for that; they are *ʿawen* which work only misfortune and destruction; they are *pōʿal ḥāmās*, the practice of violence with which their hands are occupied.

רַגְלֵיהֶם֙ לָרַ֣ע יָרֻ֔צוּ וִֽימַהֲר֔וּ לִשְׁפֹּ֖ךְ דָּ֣ם נָקִ֑י 7
מַחְשְׁבֽוֹתֵיהֶם֙ מַחְשְׁב֣וֹת אָ֔וֶן שֹׁ֥ד וָשֶׁ֖בֶר בִּמְסִלּוֹתָֽם׃

"Feet" here are personified. *raʿ* is not evil in general, but the malicious act that causes injury. The parallel clause, "they hasten to shed innocent blood," repeats the thought in concrete, more potent form. The subject of the Piel *yemaharū* is not "their feet," but they themselves. The *maḥshebhōth* of the next clause could be translated with machinations, which has a somewhat similar sound. We have translated with "thoughts," since evil intent is the chief element in the concept. The consequence of their plans and thoughts is expressed in the last clause: *shōdh* and *sheber*, wreck and ruin, are the result of their devastation and destruction.

8 דֶּרֶךְ שָׁלוֹם לֹא יָדָעוּ וְאֵין מִשְׁפָּט בְּמַעְגְּלוֹתָם
נְתִיבוֹתֵיהֶם עִקְּשׁוּ לָהֶם כֹּל דֹּרֵךְ בָּהּ לֹא יָדַע שָׁלוֹם:

derekh shālōm is the way *to* peace, and *yādhā'ū* is a present perfect: "they have not understood, do not know," Gr. 106, g, p. 311.
But *shālōm*, it must be noted, is something more than just a state
when there is no war. This is a case of *species pro genere*, and *peace*
includes all well-being, deliverance and salvation, and the meaning of *lō'yādhā'ū* is: "they do not experience" or "come to know it."
The clause does not say merely that they are not peaceably inclined, as Delitzsch and others would have it, but it declares that
they do not experience *shālōm*, deliverance and salvation, and
thus the closing statement in this section returns to the opening
words in verses 1 and 2 (palindrome). It is also a mistake to translate *mishpāt* with *justice*. It would be putting a feeble expression
into the prophet's mouth to have him say, after so drastically
describing the deadly malice of the godless, that there is "no
justice in their tracks." He had already said much stronger things
than that. *mishpāt* is here a synonym of *shālōm*, as well as of
tsedhāqāh in verse 9, and, like *tsedheq* and *tsedhāqāh*, it denotes
that *right* which God pronounces in His judgment and which conveys freedom, life, deliverance, salvation and happiness. It has the
same meaning as *mishpetēy tsedheq* in 58:2. And so, these first two
clauses are perfect parallels. As one clause says that they do not
know or experience help and salvation, so the other says that
there is no help or salvation in their tracks. That is, the tracks or
paths that they follow do not lead to help, salvation, and happiness. Expressed in positive terms: All their paths lead to misfortune and destruction.

The second half of the verse applies this thought specifically to
the persons involved, both with reference to the persons themselves and to their victims. "They make their paths crooked," that
is, they twist them into hopeless, destructive paths for themselves
(*lāhem*), so that they themselves perish by following them, and *kōl
dōrēkh bāh*, everyone else who follows them, likewise finds no help
(*shālōm*) and also perishes. And so, the closing thought returns in
emphasized form to that of the beginning of the strophe and also
serves as a transition to the next strophe.

Second Strophe: verses 9-15a: *Deliverance remains far distant
from the people, because their wickedness is far too great.*

553

First Half: verses 9-11: *The desperate condition of the people.*

9   *Therefore is a judgment of freedom far from us,*
     And deliverance cannot come to us;
     We long for light, and lo! — darkness —
     For the breaking of dawn — and we walk in gloom.

10 *We grope like blind men along the wall,*
     We grope like those that have no eyes,
     By broad daylight we stumble as in twilight,
     We are like dead men among those in the strength of manhood.

11 *We growl like bears, all of us,*
     We coo like doves,
     We wait for rescue and it is not there,
     For deliverance, and it is far from us.

עַל־כֵּן רָחַק מִשְׁפָּט מִמֶּנּוּ וְלֹא תַשִּׂיגֵנוּ צְדָקָה ⁹
נְקַוֶּה לָאוֹר וְהִנֵּה־חֹשֶׁךְ לִנְגֹהוֹת בָּאֲפֵלוֹת נְהַלֵּךְ :

A comparison of verse 9 with verse 11 reveals that this section is constructed as a palindrome. If *'al kēn*, "therefore," is understood to refer to the contents of verses 2-8, then the meaning of this section is briefly: Because of our hopelessly sinful state, deliverance remains far from us, and we grope about, helpless and hopeless.

This entire chapter, beginning at the end of the first main strophe (verse 8), cannot be understood, indeed, the sense must remain hopelessly confused, if one does not grasp the fact that *shā-lōm* and *mishpāt* in verse 8; *mishpāt, tsedhāqāh, 'or*, and *neghōhōth* in verse 9; *mishpāt* and *yeshū'āh* in verse 11; *mishpāt* and *tsedhā-qāh* in verse 14; *mishpāt* in verse 15; *tsedhāqāh* and *yeshū'āh* in verses 16 and 17, are all concepts having to do with God's plan of salvation. All of these terms, from different points of view, express different aspects of *deliverance*. The fundamental concept is *tsedhāqāh*, or, more fully, *tsidhqath YHWH* or *tsidhqāthō*, "the righteousness of the Lord," which denotes the faithful attitude of the Lord regarding His covenant and His plan of salvation toward His people (verses 16 and 17), or conversely the faithful attitude of the people toward the Lord of the covenant, like *tsedheq* in verse 4; or the exercise of that attitude in the act of deliverance, verses 9 and 14; or the objective deliverance itself. *tsedhāqāh* in the second clause of verse 9 (here personified, like *mishpāt* in the first clause) is clearly the *exercise* of the Lord's counsel of salvation toward His people, His help, His deliverance, or, if one will, the objective help

and deliverance. "That remains far from us." And so, *mishpāṭ* in
the first clause, as a parallel term to *tsedhāqāh*, is the act of
deliverance or the deliverance itself, insofar as this proceeds from
the Lord's judicial act, by which He adjudges the rights and the
salvation of the covenant to the people, or it may be the fruit itself
of the adjudged right. For that reason we have translated *mishpāṭ*
with "judgment of freedom" and *tsedhāqāh* with "deliverance."
But each one of these concepts might have been rendered with
rescue, help, salvation and similar terms; however, *mishpāṭ* should
not be translated with justice and *tsedhāqāh* with righteousness,
unless it has been first made clear that these terms are used in the
sense of rescue, help, salvation, etc. The perfect *rāḥaq* is a present
perfect: help has remained, is far, from us. The imperfect
thassīghēnū indicates that the effort to draw near has continually
been repeated in the present time, but always unsuccessfully. The
imperfects *neqawweh* and *nehallēkh*, "we long for, we walk,"
likewise indicate continuance in the present time. *'or*, light, and
ḥoshekh, darkness, and the stronger plurals *neghōhōth*
and *'aphēlōth*, are figurative expressions for fortune and misfortune, happiness and suffering.

נְגַֽשְׁשָׁה כַֽעִוְרִים֙ קִיר וּכְאֵ֥ין עֵינַ֖יִם נְגַשֵּׁ֑שָׁה 10
כָּשַׁ֤לְנוּ בַֽצָּהֳרַ֙יִם֙ כַּנֶּ֔שֶׁף בָּאַשְׁמַנִּ֖ים כַּמֵּתִֽים׃

The cohortative *neghasheshāh* is a Piel of *gāshash*, to grope; it occurs only in this verse, and its second occurrence in this verse in a
pausal form is intended perhaps only for euphony or for emphasis,
Gr. 108, g, p. 320. The first two parallel clauses denote figuratively
the futile attempts of a people shackled by sin and apostasy to find
the door that would open the way out of the prison of their misery.
The next two clauses emphasize that thought. The preposition *ba*
which appears with *tsohorayim* must be supplied between *ka* and
nesheph, cf. 1:26; Jeremiah 33:7,11. "We stumble by broad
daylight as *in* twilight." *nesheph*, from the verb *nāshaph*, is
literally the moving or blowing of the evening breeze, and in a
transferred sense, the evening or the evening light. The prophet
continues his picture of the people groping futilely for the door
that might lead to freedom from the prison of their misery, by
adding that they stumble about in a half-light. That we stumble,
trip, and fall while groping blindly about means that we but increase our misery while seeking to free ourselves. It is Luther's
"Yea, deep and deeper still I fell . . . So firmly sin possessed me."

Cf. Romans 7:14. The meaning of "broad daylight" becomes clear if one understands gloom and darkness to represent the misery resulting from the horror of their sinful state. The term "broad daylight" describes the immutability of the ancient covenant of grace, the availability of the righteousness of salvation, and the constancy of God's grace. Although the grace of God shines as bright as midday, God's people lie in the misery brought on by their apostasy and sinfulness, and they fall always deeper into misery while groping about blindly for an escape from it. The reason for their blind groping is given in Romans 9:32f and Isaiah 58:2f.

Commentators and lexicographers are uncertain about the meaning of *'ashmannīm*, since the word occurs nowhere else. This has led to comments and conjectures, and has also opened the way for emendators to try to "correct" the text. The obvious course to follow, however, is to take the word as it stands and to try to extract a meaning from it that fits the context. Derivation from *'āsham*, fault, or *shāman*, waste, is out of the question. A simple and possible explanation is that the word is a substantive with prosthetic *Aleph* derived from the root *shāman*, to be fat, Gr. 85, b, p. 235. The meaning fat or strong is then a perfect antithetic parallel to *mēthīm*, the dead. "We are the dead (generic article) among the healthy and living." Whereas all about us flourishes in the joy of life, we have become the prey of helplessness, despair, and perdition. "Surely the people is grass!" 40:7.

נֶהֱמֶה כַדֻּבִּים֙ כֻּלָּ֔נוּ וְכַיּוֹנִ֖ים הָגֹ֣ה נֶהְגֶּ֑ה 11
נְקַוֶּ֤ה לַמִּשְׁפָּט֙ וָאַ֔יִן לִֽישׁוּעָ֖ה רָחֲקָ֥ה מִמֶּֽנּוּ׃

Growling like bears and cooing or moaning like doves (the intensifying absolute infinitive *hāghōh* should not be overlooked) are figurative expressions for the dull and hopeless sorrow voiced in the last two clauses of this verse and that also appeared in the words at the beginning of this section, verse 9. We wait in vain for deliverance.

Second Half: verses 12-15a: *It is our insincerity toward the Lord that prevents our deliverance.*

12 *For too great before You is our transgression,*
And our trespasses — that testifies against us;
For our transgressions (lie open) before us,
And our iniquities — we cannot deny them.

13   *Being unfaithful to the Lord and lying to Him,*
      And turning backwards away from God!
      Preaching violence and rebellion,
      Conceiving lying words and uttering them from the heart!
14   *And so, salvation has been driven back,*
      And deliverance remained far off;
      For faithfulness has fallen in the street,
      And uprightness could find no entrance.
15a   *And so, faithfulness was not to be found,*
      And he who shuns evil is everyone's prey.

12 כִּי־רַבּוּ פְשָׁעֵינוּ נֶגְדֶּךָ וְחַטֹּאותֵינוּ עָנְתָה בָּנוּ
כִּי־פְשָׁעֵינוּ אִתָּנוּ וַעֲוֺנֹתֵינוּ יְדַעֲנוּם:

Commentators usually introduce confusion into this passage by interpreting the sins of which it speaks as sins against the neighbor. But everything in the passage is immediately clear when it is recognized that the passage treats only of rebellion and unfaithfulness toward the Lord, and that *mishpāṭ* and *tsedhāqāh* in verse 14, and *hā'emeth* in 15a, denote God's faithfulness regarding His counsel of salvation.

The *peshā'īm* referred to here are not gross sins in general, but are transgressions against the covenant of grace; they are the *pesha' rābh*, the "great transgression" of Psalm 19:14(13), repeated over and over, the sins of rebellion and unfaithfulness toward the Lord so often mentioned by Isaiah (Isa. 1:2-4; 57:4, and elsewhere). That is made clear by verse 13, which develops the contents of verse 12. *pāshōa' wekhaḥēsh ba YHWH* of verse 13 is a description of the twofold *peshā'eynū* of verse 12. Cf. also *shābhēy pesha'*, "those who turn back from rebellion," in verse 20. The *peshā'eynū* are therefore our sins of rebellion, our sins of unfaithfulness. *ḥaṭṭō'theynū* and *'awōnōtheynū* are poetic generalizations of the same concept. Regarding the singular form *'anethāh* in place of a plural *'anū,* cf. Gr. 145, k, p. 464. "Answers against us" is the equivalent of "testifies against us, accuses us." The idiomatic Hebrew phrase "our faithlessnesses are *'ittānū,* with us," usually translated "are known to us," says that our breaches of faith lie at hand, open to view. The phrase depicts the sins of the faithless rebel as lying by his side just as stolen articles lie at the side of a thief caught in the act. *yedha'anūm,* "we know them," says that we must acknowledge them, cannot deny them. Three things are said of the breaches of faith committed by the people: they are many, they accuse the people, they are open to view.

פָּשֹׁעַ וְכַחֵשׁ בַּיהוָה וְנָסוֹג מֵאַחַר אֱלֹהֵינוּ 13

דַּבֶּר־עֹשֶׁק וְסָרָה הֹרוֹ וְהֹגוֹ מִלֵּב דִּבְרֵי־שָׁקֶר׃

The six verb forms in this sentence are without exception absolute infinitives, which in a lively manner list the people's sins of disloyalty. Cf. Gr. 113, ff, p. 346. The preposition *ba* belongs to both verbs in the opening clause (cf. *pashe'u bhi,* Isa. 1:2). The meaning of *pasha'* is to fall away from, to be disloyal, defect; *kahesh* means to lie, play the hypocrite, to deceive. Although they have actually in their hearts already fallen away from the Lord, they still feign loyalty, cf. 58:2f. *nasogh* is an absolute infinitive of *sugh,* to turn aside, to turn away from. In the *nasogh* clause the *pashoa'* and *kahesh* of the first clause are combined into a single figurative expression.

Delitzsch and many others interpret *dabber 'osheq wesarah* as referring to sins against one's neighbor and translate *'osheq* with oppression and *sarah* with infraction against the law, untruth, or similar terms. But the context points to sins against the Lord. *sarah* is a noun derived from *sur,* to turn aside, to turn away from. In one instance, Isaiah 14:6, it has the meaning of "stop" or cessation; but it never refers to a deviation from the Law in the sense of an infraction. It always refers to a turning aside or away from *God,* even in Deuteronomy 19:16, where the reference is not to some slight infraction, but rather to *pesha',* the one great sin, falling away from the *Lord.* In all other passages (Deut. 13:6[5]; Isa. 1:5; 31:6; Jer. 28:16; 29:32), *sarah* is defection from the Lord, a synonym of *pesha'.* And now, in this clause (*dabber 'osheq wesarah*), although it is certainly possible, it would be very strange if in this listing of sins against the Lord one of the terms (*sarah*) should refer to disloyalty toward the Lord, while the other (*'osheq*), which comes first, in the position of emphasis, would refer to oppression of one's neighbor, not to a sin against the Lord. It is undoubtedly true that *'osheq* always means oppression of one's neighbor and is never used in the sense of a sin against the Lord Himself. But in Isaiah 30:12 *'osheq,* according to the clear context and the parallel *naloz* (from *luz*), stands for *'oqesh,* in the sense of falseness, crookedness, disloyalty, unbelief, from *'iqqesh,* to bend, twist, confuse, cf. 59:8. And that is almost certainly the meaning here, since the transposition of consonants common to two different words is not at all an unusual occurrence. And so, the sentence reads: "Speaking falseness and disloyalty," namely, against the Lord.

The forms *hōrō* and *hōghō* from *hārāh*, to conceive, be pregnant, and from *hāghāh*, to meditate, to mumble — instead of the Qal forms *hārō* (*hārōh*) and *hāghō* (*hāghōh*) — are usually explained as absolute infinitives in Polel. These particular forms do not occur elsewhere. They are intended to give added emphasis to the concept: "they bear within themselves" and "they give utterance from out of their hearts." *millēbh* is not to be understood as being the same as our "from the heart." The difference between *hārō* and *hāghō* is like the difference between being pregnant and giving birth, cf. verse 4. *dibhrēy sheqer* are words that are untrue and at the same time injurious. They are constantly planning and on every occasion they give vent to untruthful and vicious speeches designed to induce apostasy from the Lord and to promote disloyalty.

14 וְהֻסַּג אָחוֹר מִשְׁפָּט וּצְדָקָה מֵרָחוֹק תַּעֲמֹד
כִּי־כָשְׁלָה בָרְחוֹב אֱמֶת וּנְכֹחָה לֹא־תוּכַל לָבוֹא:

The 14th verse proceeds to the conclusion of this part of the prophecy. The *we* before *hussagh* is the *Waw* consecutive perfect after the absolute infinitives in verse 13, which represented the imperfect, Gr. 112, 2 and 3, p. 331ff. Luther correctly rendered it as "therefore," "and so." *hussagh* is a Hophal perfect of *sūgh*, to take leave, remain behind, to depart. *mishpāṭ* and *tsedhāqāh* clearly convey the idea of help and deliverance, or salvation. The judgment, or "right," which the Lord in His grace had pronounced upon His people and had supported by His promise, has been, so to speak, violently driven backwards and held at a distance by Israel's unceasing and constantly increasing apostasy. And so, the *tsedhāqāh*, which is the manifestation of His grace in delivering His people, remains (imperfect!) in the distance, does not draw near, as verse 9 has set forth. That fact is once more briefly accounted for in the two clauses introduced by *kī*: "for faithfulness has fallen in the street and uprightness can find no entrance." *reḥōbh* is the open square found in every city in the East, open to common traffic, available for public speeches, a place where court could be convened, the Greek ἀγορά, the Roman forum, our marketplace, the plaza of the Romance nations. The meaning of the picture is that *'emeth* no longer comes to public attention, no longer can make itself heard. There is still a question regarding the meaning of *'emeth*. One can hardly go wrong so long as one keeps in view its relation to the Lord. Whether one interprets it subjectively as firmness, reliability, constancy, or objectively as

559

truth, the result is that either faithfulness toward the Lord, or the Lord's truth, His Word, can no longer get a hearing among the people. In any case, it means that he who is still faithful to the Lord is no longer allowed to speak openly of the truth of the covenant between the Lord and His people. That is the meaning of these words. The next clause, *ūnekhōhāh lō*, etc., has a similar meaning. Uprightness, or objectively, what is upright, "is not able to come," that is, he who is upright in heart toward the Lord can no longer gain a hearing with anything that is upright before the Lord.

15 וַתְּהִי הָאֱמֶת נֶעְדֶּרֶת וְסָר מֵרָע מִשְׁתּוֹלֵל

As in verse 14, *'emeth* is faithfulness toward the Lord. That interpretation is confirmed by *sār mērā*, which in negative form says the same thing. *ne'dereth* is a Niphal participle of *'ādhar*, to fail, to remain behind, cf. 34:16 and 40:26, and joined with *wattehī* the meaning is: "And faithfulness became an abandoned one." This rather formal construction is emphatic and expresses the development of a constant and permanent condition. *'emeth* has become like an orphan or an abandoned child. The expression reminds one of *nibhzeh waḥadhal 'īshīm*, 53:3, and *bezūy 'am* in Psalm 22:7(6). Permanently deserted and forsaken, faithfulness stands there, and — to complete the thought — whoever now turns away from evil, or repents of his disloyalty toward the Lord, he becomes an object of mistreatment, or as Luther so strikingly translated, "*musz jedermannes Raub sein*," becomes the victim of every form of violence.

This description of the cruelty practiced in Israel is by no means just poetic exaggeration. There was a striking parallel to it in our own country during World War I, when persons suspected of pro-German sympathies were flagrantly abused, and that with the sanction of the government. When the soul of a nation has been thoroughly poisoned with hate by the shameless, systematic defamation of another nation, then faithfulness toward God and His Word, toward truth and justice, simply has no abiding place. Whoever revolts against the wickedness becomes everybody's prey. In the name of patriotism every scoundrel is granted the right to mistreat the best of men, and no one raises a hand against the injustice. We Christians, who thought that our guaranteed freedom of religion protected us against any possible persecution because of our faith in Christ, have now learned by experience that no form of government, no law, no constitution, and no authority can protect us against persecution, Matthew 10; John 16. The only escape lies in denial. Will we persevere, like Jeremiah?

Third Strophe: verses 15b-21: *Because no help is to be found among men, the Lord clothes Himself in His saving righteousness, to judge the enemies and to deliver His own.*

First Half: verses 15b-18: *Because there is no Helper among God's people, the Lord invests Himself in His saving righteousness and avenges Himself on His enemies.*

15b *When the Lord saw that, He was filled with displeasure*
  That there was no longer any help.

16 *When He saw that there was no man,*
  He was amazed that there was no mediator.
  Then His own arm had to become the Helper,
  And His faithfulness — that imparted strength to Him.

17 *And He drew on faithfulness as a coat of mail,*
  And on His head He set the helmet of salvation,
  And drew on the garment of vengeance as clothing,
  And wrapped Himself in zeal as in a war-garment.

18 *According to their deeds, so will He repay:*
  Wrath to His adversaries,
  Recompense to His enemies;
  To the isles will He pay retribution.

Because of technical irregularities in the poetic structure of verses 15 and 18, the division between the second and the third main strophe splits verse 15 in the middle, and verse 18 seems to be too short to form the normal four-line stanza. The text critics therefore assume either that a line has been omitted or that redactors did some patchwork — an assumption that does not infuse one with respect. As for the splitting of verse 15, why should not the prophet, who writes entire discourses in logical periods without indicating paragraphs *externally,* as we are accustomed to do for our exegetical purposes, use a four-line verse to join two large sections together? And verse 18 does actually contain four lines, if one is willing to acknowledge that for purposes of forceful expression a three-stress line in the middle of the verse is reduced to two stresses. The learned critics have been too mechanically pedantic!

וַיַּרְא יְהוָה וַיֵּרַע בְּעֵינָיו כִּי־אֵין מִשְׁפָּט׃

The two *Waws* consecutive in this verse, and also in the first half of verse 16 are coordinate pairs: when — then, cf. Gr. 111, d,

p. 326. The prophet pictures the Lord as viewing the hopeless condition of His forlorn people, and in anthropomorphic terms he describes the Lord's intervention in the situation. What the Lord sees causes His great displeasure (*yēra' be 'ēynāyw*, "it was evil in His eyes"), for there was no *mishpāt* to be seen and there was none who would step forward as judge and helper. Here too, *mishpāt* is a term that denotes the salutary promises of the covenant.

וַיַּרְא כִּי־אֵין אִישׁ וַיִּשְׁתּוֹמֵם כִּי אֵין מַפְגִּיעַ 16
וַתּוֹשַׁע לוֹ זְרֹעוֹ וְצִדְקָתוֹ הִיא סְמָכָתְהוּ׃

'ish here means more than just "someone"; it has the weightier meaning of a manly person, a hero, a man who steps forward bravely to render help, as in 1 Samuel 4,9; 26:15; 1 Kings 2:2. The parallel term *maphgīa'* in the next clause goes farther than this but does not differ in meaning. The meaning of *pāgha'* is "to happen on something, to meet"; and from that point the meaning broadens out to cover a variety of feelings and emotions. As a Hiphil in the causative sense in 53:6 and 53:12 the word is used in widely differing senses. Jeremiah 15:11 and Job 36:32 are almost opposites. It seems to us that mediator is the only possible meaning here, mediator in the sense of Ezekiel 22:30, or as Phinehas became a mediator in Numbers 25:11. The hopeless state of the church in a period of greatest decay is made altogether complete when even the believing remnant has lost courage and no one can be found among all those who tremble and complain who is able to pull himself together sufficiently to arouse God by earnest and powerful prayer and himself to grapple with the situation with self-sacrificing firmness. That explains the employment of such a forceful expression as *yishtōmēm*, to be amazed (Hithpoel of *shāmēm*, to be arid, waste, rigid), used anthropomorphically of God. Even among the believers there is not one real man to be found.

With *wattōsha'* the main concluding clause begins, following the two clauses introduced by *wayyar'* which together form the introductory clause. When the Lord saw, with amazement, the absolutely hopeless condition of His people, then, etc. By means of consecutive imperfects, the description places all of the acts in the past, because the prophet views the intervention of the Lord into the historical conditions that have just been described as a single picture and presents the scene in epic form. (The one perfect verb, *semākhāthhū*, is joined in a special way to the first imperfect.) The

change to the future in verse 18 shows that for the prophet himself all of this lies in a future time. For a correct understanding of
the prophet's presentation of events, in respect to the time of their
occurrence, one would have to translate the two *wayyar'* in 15b
and 16a and also *wayyishtomēm* in verse 16 with the present tense,
and the following verbs with the future tense, in this wise: And the
Lord sees it and is filled with displeasure, that, etc. (verse 15b)
. . . and He sees it and is amazed (verse 16) . . . therefore His
own arm will help him, etc. The *lō* that follows *tōsha'* is a regular
dative, not the ethical dative. Not only is there no *'ish* or
maphgīa' to be found, but helpers too are lacking to assist the
Lord in His work. The Lord Himself must supply that assistance
because of His covenant with Israel. Since no one will assist Him,
He must rely on His own arm, that is, His almighty power, to be
His help, and on His *tsedhāqāh*, that is, His faithfulness to His
covenant-promise and His zealous will to save His own people, as
He had promised. The same thought occurs in 63:5, with this difference that in that passage *ḥēmāh* takes the place of *tsedhāqāh*,
because the issue is exclusively the destruction of the enemies,
while here it is chiefly the salvation of the Lord's own. This is, of
course, poetic language and highly anthropomorphic. It is quite
similar to what we sing in Luther's hymn: "But God beheld my
wretched state Before the world's foundation, And, mindful of His
mercies great, He planned my soul's salvation." To help His people, the Lord draws on His omnipotence and His grace, here called
tsedhāqāh, that is, His gracious purpose, which was guaranteed by
His promise — His faithfulness to His covenant. *hī'* serves to
repeat *tsedhāqāh* and to make it most emphatic: His *tsedhāqāh*,
that is what imparted strength and supported Him.

וַיִּלְבַּ֤שׁ צְדָקָה֙ כַּשִּׁרְיָ֔ן וְכ֥וֹבַע יְשׁוּעָ֖ה בְּרֹאשׁ֑וֹ 17
וַיִּלְבַּ֤שׁ בִּגְדֵ֤י נָקָם֙ תִּלְבֹּ֔שֶׁת וַיַּ֥עַט כַּמְעִ֖יל קִנְאָֽה׃

The description now becomes very vivid. We see how the Lord as
a man of war eager for the fray clothes Himself in His armor. He
clothes Himself in *tsedhāqāh*, the grace promised to His people, as
in a coat of mail (for *shiryān* cf. Gr. 29,u,p.98), that is, He protects
His heart as with an impenetrable breastplate, so that nothing
can possibly weaken His zeal to save; He sets the helmet of salvation upon His head, that is, He kindles within Himself the spirit of
battle, with the certainty of victory, cf. 1 Thessalonians 5:8. As
these two clauses treat of the deliverance of His own, so the next

two treat of the destruction of the enemies. "He draws on garments of vengeance as clothing, and wraps Himself in zeal as in a
war-garment" says in a general way that His heart is filled with
anger against His enemies and with the determination to carry
out His judgment against them. The Lord has armed Himself, and
the next verse describes how He proceeds to action.

¹⁸ כְּעַל גְּמֻלוֹת כְּעַל יְשַׁלֵּם חֵמָה לְצָרָיו גְּמוּל לְאֹיְבָיו
לָאִיִּים גְּמוּל יְשַׁלֵּם :

Regarding *ke'al . . . ke'al,* "according as . . . so," cf. Gr. 118, 6,
especially Note 2, p. 375f. *gemūlāh,* like *gemūl,* has a double meaning and may designate the act that deserves retribution, whether
in a good or a bad sense, as well as the act of retribution itself.
Here the word is used in the first of these two senses. "According
to their deeds, so will He recompense." This general declaration is
made more specific in the next three clauses: "The heat of His
anger against His adversaries, retribution for His enemies." The
division into two statements is rhetorical; actually, the direct object (recompense) is the same, and likewise the indirect object (the
enemies). The single concept of God's angry retribution is resolved
into the two components, anger and retribution, which are then
applied separately to the synonymous terms, adversaries and
enemies. The *'iyyīm,* the isles, in the last clause, are the gentile
nations inhabiting the islands and the coasts of the Mediterranean Sea. As representatives of all gentile nations they are made
the object of retribution, not as Delitzsch supposes, "to hide the
special judgment upon Israel in the general judgment upon the nations," but because the judgment upon the gentile nations is
linked together with the judgment upon God's people, according to
the rule "that judgment must begin at the house of God" (Jer.
25:29; 49:12; Ezek. 9:6; 1 Peter 4:17). The chief object of the judgment, in the Old Testament and in the New Testament, is always
the people of the Lord, who even more than the heathen world
ground the grace of God under foot. See chapters 65 and 66 of
Isaiah and also Jeremiah and Ezekiel. Cf. Matthew chapters 11,
23, 24, and 25.

Second Half: verses 19-21: *After the judgment upon His enemies, the Lord glorifies His name, and with His promised salvation brings deliverance to gentiles and to Jews.*

19 *And in the west shall the name of the Lord be revered,*
    And His glory at the rising of the sun;
    For He shall come like a pent-up stream
    Which the breath of the Lord drives on.
20 *And He shall come to Zion as a Savior,*
    And to those in Jacob who turn back from rebellion, says the Lord,
21 *For I — this is My covenant with them, says the Lord:*
    My Spirit, which is upon you.
    And My words that I have put in your mouth,
    They shall not depart from your mouth, nor from the mouth of your
        seed,
    Nor from the mouth of your seed's seed, says the Lord,
    From now on, even forever.

¹⁹ וְיִֽירְא֤וּ מִֽמַּעֲרָב֙ אֶת־שֵׁ֣ם יְהוָ֔ה וּמִמִּזְרַח־שֶׁ֖מֶשׁ אֶת־כְּבוֹד֑וֹ
כִּֽי־יָב֥וֹא כַנָּהָ֖ר צָ֑ר ר֥וּחַ יְהוָ֖ה נֹ֥סְסָה בֽוֹ:

yīre'ū is from *yārē'*, to fear. Some old Hebrew Bibles have *yir'ū* from *rā'āh*, to see, a meaning which would be out of place here. But the Ḥireq in those Bibles was written defectively. Cf. Psalm 86:11; 102:16(15); Deuteronomy 28:58, etc. *mimma'arābh* and *mimmizrāḥ* could indeed mean from the west and from the east if the verb required that meaning. But that is not the case here. To fear from the west and from the east does not make good sense. Nor is there any reason why "they," or "people," should be inserted as a subject, when the mere designation of directions, east and west, fits the context perfectly (cf. *miqqedhem* and *miyyām*, "in or toward the east," "in or toward the west"). These two most commonly mentioned directions stand for all points of the compass and for all places on the earth. When the Lord shall come to judge the impenitent rebels among the gentiles and among the Jews, then it shall come to pass that in the west and in the east the name of the Lord shall be revered (*yīre'ū* is impersonal!). A *universal* judgment is meant, for the Holy Spirit has in mind the inauguration of the New Testament, a renewal of the former covenant with Abraham. This reverence or fear of the name of the Lord can, according to the passages referred to above, only be the true, believing childlike fear of God, not just a wholesome terror among the gentiles. Many gentiles will come to the healing, believing knowledge of the saving name of the Savior and of the glory of the grace of the Lord, for that is the primary meaning of *kebhōdh YHWH*, as was proclaimed in Exodus 33 and 34.

Verses 19ff. contain the theme that is developed in the following chapter, the last in this triad. Cf. 60:3: "the gentiles shall come to Your light." The final outcome of the judgment upon incurably hardened Israel and the gentile world is the acceptance and conversion of the πλήρωμα from among the gentiles which takes the place of the ἥττημα, the "diminishing" of Israel, and in the conversion and salvation of the "remnant" of Israel, as St. Paul sets forth in Romans 11, with reference to this passage in Isaiah (verse 20).

The next clause tells why the judgment has this outcome. "For He shall come like a pent-up stream which the breath of the Lord drives on." Most commentaries miss the mark here, as is so often the case when too much art is employed where the facts are quite clear and simple. First of all, the above translation and construction must be accepted as the simplest, most natural, and as alone being appropriate to the context. The Lord is the subject; *tsār* is a modifier of *nāhār*, nothing more; *rūah YHWH*, etc., is a relative clause; *bō* refers to *nāhār tsār*. The next question is: What is it that is substantiated by the coming of the Lord in the power of a pent-up stream? Naturally it is the *conversion* of people from the east and the west, as foretold in the first half of the verse. And what actually is this power of the Lord, as represented by an impetuous stream? Can it be the execution of judgment on gentiles and Jews as described in verse 18? If so, that would mean that the prophet is simply repeating himself, although not in the same words. And yet, verse 19b is reminiscent of verse 18. Violence in that passage, violence here.

This is the picture of the stream: The storm waters, driven by a hurricane wind, drive down a narrow bed between high cliff walls, rushing and roaring and irresistibly carrying everything before them. But, and this is the key to an understanding of the passage, it is the *rūah YHWH* that drives the stream with such force. *rūah YHWH* sometimes denotes a mighty wind, but in other passages it is the spirit of the Lord. Here the phrase has a double meaning. In the picture it is a mighty wind; in the interpretation of the picture it is the spirit of the Lord. That is the spirit of retribution for the enemies and of *tsedhāqāh* and *yeshū ʿāh* for those who are His own, the spirit of the name and the glory of the Lord, which appears in the bow of grace, but at the same time dwells in the blazing and consuming fire, Ezekiel 1. The coming of the Lord is the rushing, roaring stream driven by the spirit of vengeance and of salvation, "the spirit of wisdom and understanding, the spirit of counsel and might, the spirit of knowledge and of the *fear of the Lord*," 11:2.

That is the spirit that creates and brings to pass all things. And thus will verses 18 and 19b be fulfilled, and the name and the glory of the Lord of grace be known in faith and be revered from the rising of the sun to the going down thereof. That fulfillment began with Paul (cf. Romans, Ephesians, Colossians), is being fulfilled today, and will continue to be fulfilled till the Day of Judgment. *nōsesāh* is the Polel perfect of *nūs*, "to flee."

20 וּבָא לְצִיּוֹן גּוֹאֵל וּלְשָׁבֵי פֶשַׁע בְּיַעֲקֹב נְאֻם יְהוָה:

This verse turns to the other side of the picture. Verse 19 treated of the conversion of the gentiles; this verse treats of the forgiveness of those in Israel who repent. The subject of the sentence lies unexpressed in *bā*; it is the Lord, not *gōʾel*. *gōʾel* is a part of the predicate: He comes to Zion as a Redeemer. *gōʾel* is to be understood in its literal sense of redeemer, ransomer. Zion and Zion's children were unjustly in Babylon's power, 52:3ff. The spiritual Zion, God's beloved children, elect and glorious, His peculiar people, were unjustly held captive under sin and under the power of the Law and of the devil. That is why the Lord comes to them as their Ransomer, and in particular — *ū* before *leshābhēy* has this explanatory and particularizing meaning — "for those in Jacob who turn back from rebellion." *shābhēy* is a Qal participle plural of *shūbh*, to turn back, and *peshaʿ* is an objective genitive, Gr. 116, h, p. 358. Rebellious, but not hardened and rejected Jews are meant. They are *in* Jacob. They lie in *peshaʿ*, in rebellion, but they turn back from it. This passage is essential for the correct understanding of Romans 11, particularly of verse 25. As proof of his statement, Paul refers in verse 26 to this passage. These temporary rebels against their God are the ἥττημα of Israel, which is being filled out, supplemented, by the πλήρωμα from among the gentiles. When this rebellious, but still not hardened, part of Israel repents, then "all Israel" has been saved. In the course of the New Testament this is always and again and again being fulfilled by the conversion of many in Israel. Only a part of Israel, the part beyond recovery, of whom this chapter has treated up to this point, is doomed to permanent hardening; as for the rest, Romans 11:31f describes their happier lot. *neʾum YHWH* is not just an idle phrase. Such total depravity of a whole people as has been described in this chapter, especially in view of verse 16, makes the promised conversion and salvation of some in Jacob seem altogether unbelievable. That promise calls for some special assurance. That is given in *neʾum YHWH*, and in detail in the next verse.

²¹ וַאֲנִ֞י זֹ֣את בְּרִיתִ֤י אוֹתָם֙ אָמַ֣ר יְהֹוָ֔ה רוּחִי֙ אֲשֶׁ֣ר עָלֶ֔יךָ וּדְבָרַ֖י אֲשֶׁר־
שַׂ֣מְתִּי בְּפִ֗יךָ לֹֽא־יָמ֡וּשׁוּ מִפִּ֩יךָ֩ וּמִפִּ֨י זַרְעֲךָ֜ וּמִפִּ֨י זֶ֤רַע זַרְעֲךָ֙ אָמַ֣ר יְהֹוָ֔ה
מֵעַתָּ֖ה וְעַד־עוֹלָֽם׃

The *wa* with *'anī* is subordinating and might be translated *for* or *because.* *'anī,* in the position of emphasis at the head, forms a complete sentence with the next three words: "For I — this is My covenant with them," says the Lord (Gr. 143, a, p. 457). The language of the entire verse is very emphatic. The twofold *'amar YHWH* strengthens the emphasis still more. The critics, who discount the intended emphasis, are ready with their theory of text corruption. The words explain why the Lord has not rejected the entire rebellious and reprobate people (cf. verses 14-16), but will, as was just set forth in verse 20, save a remnant: "For, as for Me — this is My covenant with them (*'ōthām = 'ittām,* as in Jeremiah), says the Lord." This is not being said of an entirely new covenant, which the Lord at some future time will conclude with those who shall be saved out of Israel, but the reference is to the ancient covenant made *aforetime* with them, *in Abraham.* In Genesis 17:4 that covenant was inaugurated with almost identical words (*'anī hinnēh bherīthī 'ittākh*) and was expressly termed "an everlasting covenant," verse 7, firmly established for all of Abraham's descendants, from generation to generation. *Because* the Lord had long before concluded this covenant with Abraham, therefore He must and will come to Zion as a Redeemer, verse 20. The substance of that covenant is expressed in the words *rūḥī 'asher,* etc. "My spirit, which is upon you, and My words that I have put in your mouth." The first words refer first of all to 42:1, but the spirit that is there bestowed upon the Servant of the Lord, 61:1, also became the portion bestowed upon spiritual Israel, 63:10f, and that will again be poured out upon them, 44:3. This spirit rested upon the prophets, the kings, and the priests, on David, Samuel, Gideon, Joshua, Moses, Jacob, and Abraham. This is the spirit of 11:2. The words that are "put into Israel's mouth" are the words of promise that were given to Israel ever since the covenant with Abraham, which Israel had heard, which were "very nigh unto thee, in thy mouth and in thy heart," Deuteronomy 30:14; Romans 10:8; words in which it can put its trust, which it should proclaim and preach, Isaiah 43:21. This spirit of the Lord, the gracious God of the covenant, the spirit of grace and salvation, the promise of God's pardoning grace, the word of salvation — all of which were given to

Israel by virtue of the covenant with Abraham — shall never depart from the seed of Abraham. "The word shall not depart from your mouth" is just a more graphic way of saying that it shall not depart from you. The word is received through the ear, it lies in the heart, it is given voice through the mouth, Romans 10:9f. It is a way of saying that the word, an inner, spiritual possession, lies close to the lips for ready utterance.

In verse 21 we have actually nothing different from what was said in 54:10 and elsewhere: God's covenant of grace with Israel will never lapse. May Israel sink ever so deep, God's gifts and His calling of Israel will never be repented of, Romans 11:29. God will keep faith with this people forever, as He had sworn to them, and to the end of time there will always be some in Israel (the *shābhēy pesha' beya'aqōbh*, the ἐκλογή, the spiritual Israel) whom He shall save. This verse is a confirmation of the covenant with Abraham.

All of chapter 59 is marked by a clear progression of thought, and in its entirety and in its parts it moves on to an expression in the last verse of the thought with which the chapter began. It is not the Lord, but Israel itself in its sins and its unfaithfulness, who is responsible for its unavoidable ruin. There has been all too much of sin and rebelliousness (verses 12ff). There is not a single man to be found in Israel who would become a redeemer for the people, 15b, 16. Therefore, the Lord Himself is forced to come to judgment with His almighty power against this depraved people and the gentile world. But because of God's faithfulness to IIis covenant, this same judgment will serve as a blessing for many gentiles from the east and from the west, and by virtue of the covenant once made with Abraham, God will also in His faithfulness save all in Israel who have not been hardened beyond recovery.

Chapter 60 enlarges on the salvation that the Lord has prepared for the saved remnant in Israel and for those who will be saved among the gentiles, and clothes it in glowing words that display its full beauty and glory.

Third Discourse: Chapter 60

The glorification of Israel is realized, as the "glory of the Lord" descends upon it.

The two parts of the chapter have essentially the same content. The first part, verses 1-12, begins with the inner glorification and proceeds to the external; the second part, verses 13-22, follows the reverse order — the familiar chiastic arrangement. Everything that up to this point has been said about the future glorification of Zion (40:2,5,11; 41:19,20; 42:10ff; 43:4ff; 44:26; 45:14,23,24; 49:6,12,18ff; 51:3,11; 52:1-10; 54; 56:6,7; 57:14-19; 58:10ff; 59:17-21) is now summed up in a single great picture, depicted in great detail. A parallel picture is found in Isaiah 2:1-4 and Micah 4:1-7; Isaiah 47 is its antitype, picturing the downfall and abasement of Babylon.

The Spirit of God, speaking through the prophet, is not describing the physical glorification of an earthly Jerusalem, although He employs physical terms in the description. The picture is of a spiritual, eternal, New Testament glorification of Israel according to the spirit. This is self-evident to the New Testament Christian, and the church has always so interpreted the chapter. Even the most unbelieving of the exegetes feel that they are here dealing with symbols, and in almost every verse they feel compelled to distinguish between the symbols and what they stand for. These exegetes, however, prefer to look upon this chapter, and indeed on all of Isaiah II, and even on John's picture of the new Jerusalem (Rev. 21:10ff) as a dream, a fantasy in which the authors envision a future, earthly glorification of the Jewish nation and its great city. They refuse to be persuaded that a prophet could possibly be so moved by the Holy Spirit that he could make use of Old Testament terms and pictures to portray the spiritual glory of Christ and His church in the New Testament. There is no use arguing with men who hold a position that is *a priori* so prejudiced. Their position is acceptable only to such as are equally prejudiced. For us Christians it is as clear as the sun that this is a prophecy of what John says of Christ in his Gospel (e.g., 1:1-17), in his first Epistle, and in the Book of Revelation (ch. 21); of what Paul wrote of the church in Ephesians, and what the entire New Testament says of both. It is understandable that an entire mass of people like those that made up the Jewish nation, whether of high or low degree, educated or uneducated, can turn its spiritual hope into something carnal, for the mass always tends to become unbelieving and to embrace what is earthly and carnal; but it is psychologically not to be explained how a prophet, moved by the Holy Ghost, who otherwise has such a clear conception of the spiritual nature of Christ and His kingdom, could possibly picture the future kingdom of the Messiah as an earthly utopia.

First Part: verses 1-12: *Drawn by the Glory of the Lord which has risen over Zion, the gentiles come from all parts of the world, bringing Zion's children and placing themselves and all their wealth in Zion's service.*

This part of the chapter may be divided into five smaller sections: verses 1-3; 4 and 5; 6 and 7; 8 and 9; 10-12.

1 *Arise, shine, for your light has come,*
   And the glory of the Lord has risen upon you.
2 *For, behold, darkness covers the earth,*
   And gross darkness the nations;
   But over you the Lord has arisen,
   And His glory shines over you.
3 *And the gentiles will come to your light,*
   And kings to the brightness of your rising.
4 *Lift up your eyes and see round about you:*
   All of them gather together and come to you!
   From far distances your sons are coming,
   And your daughters are being borne on the arms.
5 *When you see it, you will be radiant,*
   And your heart shall throb and swell,
   When the multitudes of the sea turn to you,
   And the wealth of the gentiles comes to you.
6 *The multitude of camels shall cover you,*
   The young camels of Midian and Ephah;
   All those of Sheba shall come;
   They carry gold and frankincense,
   And they proclaim the praises of the Lord.

7   *All the flocks of Kedar gather together to you,*
    The rams of Nebaioth dedicate themselves to you,
    They mount, as a sacrifice pleasing to Me, My altar,
    So that I may glorify the dwelling place of My glory.
8   *Who are these that fly like a cloud,*
    Like doves to their windows?
9   *The isles, yes, they wait for Me,*
    And the ships of Tarshish, as the foremost,
    To bring your children from afar;
    Their silver and their gold with them,
    For the name of your God, the Lord,
    And for the Holy One of Israel, because He has so glorified you.
10 *And strangers will build your walls,*
    And their kings will minister to you.
    Because in My anger I smote you,
    So have I in My mercy had pity on you.
11 *Your gates shall always be open by day and by night,*
    They shall never again be closed,
    So that the wealth of the gentiles may be brought to you,
    And their kings coming with them in state.
12 *Every people and kingdom that does not serve you shall perish,*
    And the nations shall be utterly destroyed.

1 קוּמִי אוֹרִי כִּי בָא אוֹרֵךְ   וּכְבוֹד יְהוָה עָלַיִךְ זָרָח:

For remarks on *qūmī 'orī*, see 51:17 and 52:1f. Zion personified is being addressed, pictured as sitting in ashes, troubled and despondent. *qūmī* is addressed to the body, *'orī* to the spirit. Let Zion be bright, radiant, and shining, that is, cast aside her sadness, and with all her heart be glad. There is a play on words between *'orī* and *'orēkh*. The present perfect *bā'*, has come, expresses an action accomplished in the past and now present and enduring in its effects, Gr. 106,2, g, p. 311. *zārah* at the end of the verse is the same kind of perfect. *Your* light is the light that is Zion's peculiar possession by virtue of the ancient and constantly repeated promise, according to 40:8, that "the word of our God" shall stand forever. That word is now being fulfilled. The next line tells us what the light of Zion is: It is the *kebhōdh YHWH*, "the glory of the Lord." The *ū* before *kebhōdh* is explicative: that is, "namely." Regarding the physical appearance of the "Glory of the Lord" and its meaning, we have spoken at length in connection with 40:5. Here too it is represented as an external phenomenon, shining brilliantly over the ruined city, Ezekiel 11:23; 43:4f; 44:4. The meaning of *zārah* is that the light has broken forth and now shines brightly *'alayikh*, over you.

2 כִּי־הִנֵּה הַחֹשֶׁךְ יְכַסֶּה־אֶרֶץ וַעֲרָפֶל לְאֻמִּים
וְעָלַיִךְ יִזְרַח יְהֹוָה וּכְבוֹדוֹ עָלַיִךְ יֵרָאֶה:

Verse 2 expands the picture. *'erets* is the earth, not just the land
of Israel, because *le'ummīm,* the nations, in the following clause, is
a parallel to it. Darkness lies over the whole earth and gross darkness (*'arāphel* is literally "black clouds") covers all the nations.
The article with *hōshekh* is most likely a dittograph, the final *h* of
hinnēh having by mistake been carried over to the next word, Gr.
126, n(c), p. 407. In contrast to all the rest of the world, which lies
in darkness, there has gone up over Zion (*yizrah*) and now is shining (*yērā'eh*) this great light of the glory of the Lord. The imperfects here express a beaming of light that exists in the present and
continues to shine, Gr. 107,f, p. 315. *yizrah* and *yēra'eh* must not be
translated with past tenses or with terms that suggest a dawning
of light just coming into view. "Your light has come" for *yizrah* no
more suggests that light is just becoming perceptible than does
Luther's "*erscheinen*" for *yērā'eh* suggest only the beginning of
dawn. A present beaming and streaming of light is meant. Zion is
not being exhorted to observe how light is beginning to dawn over
it, but to observe that her light is already brightly beaming. This is
not a picture of something that is just developing, but of something that is already there. The next clause gives life to the picture.

What the prophet here represents as a bright light shining over
Jerusalem is what in 40:2 he called *kiphlayim,* double, and in 61:7,
"a double measure," that Jerusalem is to receive out of the Lord's
hand: an undreamed of glorification, the consummation of the in-
dwelling of the grace of God in His church, including salvation and
every gift of God's grace in time and eternity. It is the union of
Christ with His church, which in chapter 62 and elsewhere in both
Testaments is represented as the union of bridegroom and bride
and as the marriage of the Lamb. It is the perfect fulfillment of all
prophecy, the final realization of the hope of Israel, of the believing congregation — that is what the prophet presents to our eyes
in this picture. He does not separate time from eternity, nor does
he intermix the two; but the description of the details of conditions
and events extends beyond time into eternity. He sees first of all
the time of the New Testament, which, at the birth of Christ, God
inaugurated by the appearance of the glory of the Lord to the
shepherds in the field — a shining light, like the light in this verse.

The light of Jesus Christ shone not only when He wished it to appear in visible brightness, Matthew 17; 2 Peter 1:16f, but He was Himself the Glory of the Lord, as John testifies, John 1:14,16; 1 John 1:2ff; which Isaiah also saw (chapter 6 and in this chapter), as John testifies of him, John 12:41. The manifestation of the eternal Word in the flesh, His dwelling among us with all His grace in the Word, with the abrogation of the Law, with all spiritual blessings in heavenly places in Christ (Eph. 1:3), with the outpouring of His Holy Spirit in the power of God for the gathering, renewing, and perfecting of His church unto eternal life — that is what Isaiah here sets forth before us in his portrayal of the manifestation of the *kebhŏdh YHWH* over Jerusalem, not indeed defining it from all sides, but only setting forth certain aspects of it. Toward the end of the chapter his description culminates in the glory of eternal life. He sets this glorious light that shines over Zion in sharp contrast with the darkness that broods over the rest of the world. Light is a symbol of truth, goodness, life, happiness, salvation; darkness is a symbol of ignorance, sin, grief, woe, damnation. God Himself is Light, the Father of light, and He clothes Himself in light as a garment; He dwells in light, and fills everything with truth, life, and blessedness. Apart from God there is only darkness, lies, death, wailing and gnashing of teeth. The world lies altogether in darkness. What the world knows is either not true or it is a false show; what it aspires to is evil or vain; its emotions are deception or heartache.

It was the wisdom, the virtue, the highest culture of the world that united to devote all the world's knowledge, power, and wealth to the titanic struggle of the nations in this World War, bent on destroying themselves and each other — to what end? For nothing, absolutely nothing, except only to deceive and cheat each other with hollow phrases. When the wars come to an end, men remain what they always were: sinful and evil, altogether evil. The world remains the same vale of tears that it always was, not an iota the better for all the wars. So was it, and so it will continue to be in every part of the world where the Lord has not arisen to shine in the glory of His grace through the Gospel, or where men have turned their backs on this sun of life, of temporal happiness and eternal blessedness, and instead worship at the altar of human reason and human virtue, wantonly turning back to their own darkness. However, not all those who still sit in darkness and the shadow of death are doomed past all help to eternal darkness.

The prophet beholds the salvation of multitudes upon multitudes from the lands that still lie in darkness.

³ וְהָלְכוּ גוֹיִם לְאוֹרֵךְ וּמְלָכִים לְנֹגַהּ זַרְחֵךְ:

The word is *gōyim*, gentiles, not *haggōyim*, the gentiles, or *kol haggōyim*, all gentiles. In stating his theme, the prophet is here using exact terms. It is clear from verse 12 that he does not have all gentiles in mind. He sees not only the children of Israel but great multitudes of gentiles from all over the world coming in haste to the glory of Israel. The promise given to Abraham, Genesis 12:3; 26:4; 28:14, is very well known to him. Fulfillment of that promise was mentioned as early as 40:5. Israel, the seed of Abraham, the friend of God, 41:8, is the bearer of that promise; and the Servant of the Lord, who is to spring forth out of the midst of Israel, the one seed of Abraham, will bring righteousness to the gentiles and establish it upon the earth to be a light unto the gentiles and God's Savior to the ends of the earth (9:1[2]; 42:1,4,6; 49:6,7). The gentiles and their kings will be amazed at Him (52:10,15); He will extend His call to gentiles whom He does not know, and gentiles who do not know Him will come running to Him (55:5). Thus will He glorify His people. He will set free Zion's children who are captives in Babylon (42:7; 43:14, etc.); her children who are scattered throughout the world will be brought home (43:5-7; 56:8, etc.); He will convert many gentiles to Zion and bestow their wealth upon her (45:14; 49:12-23; 56:6,7), so that there will no longer be room for the multitude of her children (49:18ff; 54:1ff); and Zion shall rise out of her ruin and ashes to a new and undreamed of glory (44:28; 49:23; 54:11,12); her people shall all be taught of the Lord (54:13), shall all be holy (52:1), shall all live in peace (54:13) under the Lord's protection (54:14ff), happy under the guidance of their Shepherd's staff (40:9-11) through all eternity (45:17; 51:11; 52:9), while all her enemies must perish and be confounded (41:11ff; 42:13ff; 43:14ff; 46:1,2; 47:1ff; 49:26; 51:22f; 54:17). All of this the prophet sees coming into fulfillment, now that the Glory of the Lord has come down upon Zion. The hour that Zion has awaited with such fervent longing has now arrived. Gleaming in the radiance of her heavenly Lord, she radiates light into the dark world, with the result that the ancient promise of Abraham is fulfilled: the gentiles stream to her light. The prophet here views on a grand scale what the Magi from the East experienced as the forerunners of the elect from among the gentiles: "We have seen His star in the east and have come to worship

Him." Kings too, the lords of power, intellect, and wealth, come to the light that streams forth from Zion.

שְׂאִי־סָבִיב עֵינַ֫יִךְ וּרְאִי כֻּלָּם נִקְבְּצוּ בָאוּ־לָךְ ⁴
בָּנַ֫יִךְ מֵרָחוֹק יָבֹאוּ וּבְנֹתַ֫יִךְ עַל־צַד תֵּאָמַֽנָה :

Verse 3 contains the theme that will be developed throughout the first part of this chapter. Zion is exhorted to lift up her eyes and look about to see what is happening to her. In our translation we have connected *sābhībh* with *re ī* instead of *se ī,* since that arrangement is more in accord with our Western idiom. The next clause states in clearer words what had been said in verse 3. *kullām,* all of them, refers to all of those that are on their way to Zion. These are no longer just the gentiles and kings that had been named before, but are also "the sons and daughters" whom the gentiles and lords bring along with them. The masculine forms of *kullām* and of the verbs *niqbetsū* and *bā'ū* represent both genders, as is usually the case when there is a prolepsis of pronominal subjects. See Gr. 122, v, p. 394. Compare also 49:18, where these very same words appear, and for the subject matter see 43:6; 49:12, 22; Deuteronomy 28:64. The verb *niqbetsū* can be expressed by an adverbial modifier of *bā'ū:* "they come in crowds," instead of "they are gathered and come." The two verbs separate the action into gathering and coming, although the idea is a single action, a hendiadys. The daughters too come from afar, *mērāhoq,* but of them it is said that they are carried *'al tsadh,* upon the side, or on the hip. Little children were carried resting on the hip and supported by an arm, or else on the arm and supported by the hip. The expression is applied here to grown-up daughters as well as to children to indicate the tender consideration that is accorded to Zion's children by the converted gentiles, who are here pictured as the bearers. This tenderness shown by gentiles to weaker ones on the long journey indicates that the gentiles are thought of as being converted to faith in the glory of the Lord that shines from Zion. The Masora already looked upon the form *tē'amānāh* as being irregular. It is a pausal form, eliminating the doubling of the *Nun* and changing the Tsere to Pathah, Gr. 51, m, p. 139. The occurrence of perfects and imperfects almost side by side in this verse shows how closely these two modes may approach each other in meaning in poetic descriptions. Cf. Gr. 106, 1, p. 312.

5 אָז תִּרְאִי֙ וְנָהַ֔רְתְּ וּפָחַ֥ד וְרָחַ֖ב לְבָבֵ֑ךְ
כִּֽי־יֵהָפֵ֤ךְ עָלַ֙יִךְ֙ הֲמ֣וֹן יָ֔ם חֵ֥יל גּוֹיִ֖ם יָבֹ֥אוּ לָֽךְ׃

This verse pictures the almost indescribable joy that fills the heart of Zion at sight of the multitudes that come to her. The coordination of *tirʾi* and *wenāhart*, usual in Hebrew, is best expressed in English by subordinating the first of the two verbs. *nāhart*, from *nāhar*, can hardly be the verb *nāhar*, which means "to flow." It is more likely to be the verb *nāhar*, to burn, to blaze, a verb which also occurs in Psalm 34:6(5). *nāhar* in this sense is related to an Arabic and Syriac root *nūr*, which occurs frequently in the Aramaic portions of Daniel in the sense of "fire." There is in Hebrew a noun *tannūr*, a furnace, a derivative from the root *nūr*, Genesis 15:17; Exodus 7:28(8:3), et al. The meaning of the clause is: When you see, then your heart will burn. Or: When you see, then your face will glow. It is hard to say which of the two thoughts was in the prophet's mind. One might even take *nāhar* in the sense of flowing or streaming: Your heart shall overflow. In any case, the great joy is meant with which Zion sees the approaching multitude. *pāḥadh*, to tremble, and *rāḥabh*, to be wide, to swell, tell how Zion's heart trembles and swells with joy. One has the feeling that the prophet is searching for pictures that describe what is in reality indescribable — the blessed joy that fills the heart.

The next clauses continue the description. In verse 4 it was chiefly Zion's children to which her gaze was directed; in verse 5 it is the gentiles with their wealth which come streaming toward her, over which she is to rejoice. The unexpressed object of *ʾaz tirʾi wenāhart* is the sons and daughters mentioned in verse 4; *uphāḥadh werāḥabh lebhābhekh* has as its object the gentiles streaming toward Zion, bringing treasures and leading Zion's children, verse 5b. *kī* here introduces an object clause, Gr. 157, b, p. 491. It makes little difference whether one translates *kī* with "that" or with "if" or "when," so long as it remains clear that the stream of gentiles with their treasures is the object of Zion's great joy. To give clear expression to the thought it is necessary to supply *tirʾi* from the first clause and again to subordinate it, thus: And your heart shall tremble and swell, *when you see* how they come to you, etc. Whether *hamōn yām* refers to the treasures of the inhabitants of the isles, as Delitzsch, Cheyne, the LXX, and most modern interpreters believe, or to the people who inhabit the isles, as Vitringa, Luther, Jerome, and Symmachus believe, cannot be decided. *hamōn* can well mean either the one or the other. The Niphal *yēhāphekh*, to turn, is used of things as well as of persons, cf. Lamentations 5:2 and Ezekiel 4:8. The parallelism is not decisive either, for although *hēyl* certainly means wealth, proper-ty, treasures (Zech. 14:14), there is still room in the parallelism to place persons and things alongside each other, as verse 11b shows, where goods and kings are parallel to each other. The context fails to shed any light on the matter. It is true that the next verses, taken literally, speak of the treasures of the gentiles, but it is generally agreed that this is figurative language and that the na-tions are included who are the bearers of the treasures, also that "isles" in verse 9 is a personification. In fact, in verses 10, 11, and 12 the persons of the gentiles and their kings are expressly named. The only passage in the New Testament that contains a reference to our verse is Revelation 21:24: "The kings of the earth (persons) do bring their glory and honor into it," and verse 26: "And they shall bring the glory and honor (things) of the nations into it." In the hope of expressing the sense of the whole passage we have translated *hamōn yām* with "multitudes of the sea," to agree with Luther's "*Menge am Meer*," that is, the nations inhabit-ing the islands and the coasts of the Mediterranean Sea, and *hēyl gōyim* with "treasures of the gentiles." The last clause becomes the theme of the next sentences. When Luther writes of the "*Menge am Meer*" as being *converted*, he is not factually in error, since the nations that are streaming toward Zion are not being driven by any external force but are drawn by the bright light that shines over Zion.

6 שִׁפְעַת גְּמַלִּים תְּכַסֵּךְ בִּכְרֵי מִדְיָן וְעֵיפָה

כֻּלָּם מִשְּׁבָא יָבֹאוּ

זָהָב וּלְבוֹנָה יִשָּׂאוּ וּתְהִלֹּת יְהוָה יְבַשֵּׂרוּ:

shiph'āh, a word of rare occurrence, denotes "great abundance, a multitude." The expression "will *cover* you" is suggested by the fact that a heavily laden camel occupies considerable ground, and the multitude of them is pictured as being so great that they cover all open spaces, streets, and lanes of the city. *bekher* is not, as Je-rome and Luther supposed, the dromedary as distinguished from the two-humped Bactrian camel, because the camel of the Ara-bians and Syrians was always the dromedary and not the Bactrian camel. *bekher*, from *bākhar*, to be the firstborn, refers to the young dromedary in his youthful strength and tractability. Cf. *bekhōr*, the first-born, Genesis 49:3: "my first-born, my might, and the beginning of my strength." The first clause emphasizes the multitude, the second adds the concept of strength and excellence.

Midian (Gen. 25) was the son of Keturah, Ephah was the first-born of Midian, whereas the brothers Kedar and Nebaioth, mentioned in the next verse, were Ishmaelites. The Midianites inhabited the territory about the Elanitic Gulf (the Gulf of Aqabah) and also the lands east of the Dead Sea as far north as Hauran, cf. Judges 6 and 7. Ephah was a subordinate tribe, an appendage of Midian. The descendants of Nebaioth are thought to have been the Nabateans, who inhabited Edom at the time of Alexander the Great. The Kedarites, mentioned so often in the Old Testament (Ps. 120:5; Song of Sol. 1:5; Isa. 21:16f; 42:11, 60:7, et al.), are thought to have been the forebears of the nomadic Arabians, the Bedouins. They dwelt in the part of Arabia between Babylon and the Elanitic Gulf (Gulf of Aqabah). They were very rich in flocks of sheep. Sheba, the land so named after the grandson of Keturah, is *Arabia felix*, the southwest coast of the Arabian peninsula, the home of the queen of Sheba, 1 Kings 10; Matthew 12:42. This was the land of spices, of gold and precious stones, whose trade extended to Tyre and the Euphrates, to Egypt and Somaliland, and perhaps also to the East Indies. Although the Sabaeans transported most of their stock in trade in their own numerous caravans, the Midianites and even the Ishmaelites also took over a considerable portion of it in their caravans between Sheba and other countries. Whether *kullām*, the first word in the third clause, refers to Sheba's own caravans, or to those of Midian and Ephah coming from Sheba, cannot be determined. The sentence structure would suggest that the latter is the most likely; the second half of the verse treats of the treasures coming from Sheba, while the first half speaks of the bearers. Still, to make the picture complete, one would expect that the caravans of the Sabeans would also be mentioned as journeying to Zion. Gold and frankincense, the most costly of the treasures, are representative of all the goods with which the camels are burdened. These are gifts for Zion; it is not said whether or not the incense is intended for use in the temple. Frankincense in Matthew 2:11 is intended only as a costly personal gift. Those who have already arrived and those who are still on the way all proclaim, *yebhassērū*, the praises of the Lord. They have seen and acknowledged His glory, and out of the fulness of their hearts their mouths speak. *tehillōth* is an intensive plural, and therefore not to be translated "deeds of honor." It is not likely that these onetime heathen should have known much of

the glorious deeds of the Lord, but they are now seeing the glory of
His grace, and that is the subject of their praise.

7 כָּל־צֹאן קֵדָר יִקָּבְצוּ לָךְ אֵילֵי נְבָיוֹת יְשָׁרְתוּנֶךָ
יַעֲלוּ עַל־רָצוֹן מִזְבְּחִי וּבֵית תִּפְאַרְתִּי אֲפָאֵר׃

"All the flocks," as the chief possession of the Kedarites, represents their total possessions, and so also the rams of Nebaioth
stand for the best that their land has to offer, like *shiph'ath
gemallīm* and *bikhrēy* above. Flocks of sheep as well as rams are
gifts from each of the tribes; it is only the poetic mode of expression that separates the terms. *shērēth* occurs only in the Piel. The
verb denotes an honorable, usually voluntary, service, whereas
'ābhadh is used to denote forced service. Service in the sanctuary
is here indicated. The next clause shows that this service, in its literal sense, is meant. The rams of Nebaioth, the pick of the flock,
and therefore suitable as sacrificial animals, ascend the Lord's
altar (freely, not under compulsion) to serve as an offering to the
Lord. *'al rātsōn* is the same as *lerātsōn*, for "well-pleasing," pleasing to Me, as an offering acceptable to the Lord. *ū*, before *bēyth*, introduces a final clause, Gr. 165, a, p. 503. "The house of My glory"
is usually translated according to the formula of *har qodhshī, bēyth
tephillāthī*, "My glorious house," Gr. 135, n, p. 440, but we prefer to
take it in the sense of Psalm 26:8: *mishkan kebhōdhekhā*, "the
dwelling place of My glory," the "place where Mine honor
dwelleth."

Without taking *hamōn yām*, verse 5, into consideration, it is
clear from verse 3 that *ḥeyl gōyim* and the various gifts especially
mentioned in verses 6 and 7 are metonymies and include gifts of
all kinds together with the givers. The prophet draws a picture of
streams of gentiles coming in haste from all directions to the light
that shines so brightly over Zion, in order to bring to the city of the
Lord and to the Lord Himself all their goods and possessions to
thank and glorify Him for His grace. This is a prophecy concerning the New Testament, but it is a picture of an ideal. The prophecy has been fulfilled and in its fundamental meaning is being
fulfilled every day in every believer, even though performance
lags behind the will. And yet there are many who excel in performance. Men like Paul and other apostles, like Luther and many
theologians, princes and principalities, men of great talent, widows with their mites, missionaries, school teachers, pastors in
lonely outposts, and itinerant preachers still freely give to the

Lord and His church everything that they possess and thank Him for the privilege of serving Him. No one achieves complete self-sacrifice. We carry with us into the grave something of Peter's "What shall we have therefore? " (Matt. 19:27) and of Elijah's "It is enough; now, O Lord, take away my life" (1 Kings 19:4); and yet, what the prophet says here is perfect truth and reality, since it has become a fact and glorious truth in the radiance of the glory of the Lord that shines over the church of the New Testament — in Christ and His Gospel.

8 מִי־אֵלֶּה כָּעָב תְּעוּפֶינָה וְכַיּוֹנִים אֶל־אֲרֻבֹּתֵיהֶם׃

In this verse the prophet once more directs the attention of the church toward the west. For there, not in the east or the south, lies her future. According to the Lord's plan, Zion's recruits are to come from the nations of the west. In reality it was the church that went out to gather the gentiles, but the prophet pictures the gentiles as streaming toward the church, toward Zion-Jerusalem. That is a poetic presentation that is founded on the fact that the church is God's one great community of nations in comparison with which all other combinations of peoples and nations are unimportant and of no account — and who would represent the greater going to the lesser, and not the lesser to the greater! And besides, it had once pleased God to make Israel His chosen people and first-born son, and Jerusalem His dwelling place on earth and the source from which the blessing of Abraham should flow out to all nations, as the Lord said: Salvation is of the Jews, John 4:22. And so it is that whenever prophecy is presented in pictures, it naturally makes Zion-Jerusalem and the Jewish people the center also of the future kingdom of God on earth, about which all nations that participate in the Lord's salvation gather together. But that prophecy is well aware of the actual domain of the church on earth is clear from such passages as Hosea 2:1(1:10); 2:25(23); Romans 9:25f; 1 Peter 2:10.

Before *kā'ābh* the relative *'asher* must be supplied, which also serves to introduce the next clause. The picture of a mighty fleet appearing over the horizon and bearing the nations to Zion is highly poetic. It is compared to a mass of clouds and a flock of doves. The interrogative form heightens the effect. The point of comparison in both cases is the mass; *te'ūpheynāh* suggests haste, and the *'arubbōth* of the doves ("cotes, windows") brings out the idea of "home." Cf. Ephesians 2:12,13,19.

כִּי־לִי ׀ אִיִּים יְקַוּוּ וָאֳנִיּוֹת תַּרְשִׁישׁ בָּרִאשֹׁנָה ⁹
לְהָבִיא בָנַיִךְ מֵרָחוֹק כַּסְפָּם וּזְהָבָם אִתָּם
לְשֵׁם יְהוָה אֱלֹהַיִךְ וְלִקְדוֹשׁ יִשְׂרָאֵל כִּי פֵאֲרָךְ׃

The first phrase *kī lī 'iyyīm yeqawwū* (Piel) has been changed by
text critics to *kī lī tsīyyīm yiqqāwū* (Niphal), or to *keley 'iyyīm yiqqāwū*, "the vessels of the isles gather together." They argue that
the combination of "the isles wait for Me" and "the ships of Tarshish foremost" does not make sense, if one takes into consideration that the next clause is a final clause. Isles, they contend, cannot be conceived of as waiting to bring people to Zion in the same
sense as the ships of Tarshish bring them. The parallelism, so they
say, requires that the first clause contain a synonym like *tsīyyīm*
(ships) or *keley* (vessels) to balance the ships of Tarshish in the
second clause, and in any case, "they gather together" would be
better suited to the picture than "they wait for Me." We take up
the matter here in order to expose the vanity and heedlessness of
the critics, which so readily impresses the inexperienced. One mistake that these critics make is that they do not pay proper attention to the rules of parallelism. There are perfect parallelisms in
which all elements are present, as for example, verse 7:

All the flocks of Kedar gather together to you,

The rams of Nebaioth dedicate themselves to you.

Here the elements of one sentence perfectly balance those of the
other: flocks and rams, Kedar and Nebaioth, gather together and
dedicate themselves, to you and to you. But much more common is
the incomplete parallelism, in which one or more of the elements
are unexpressed in one clause and have to be supplied out of the
other. An example is verse 8:

Who are these that fly like a cloud —

and — like doves to their windows?

In the first clause the adverbial phrase of destination is missing
and must be supplied by some fitting phrase to match "to their
windows." In the second clause the verb is missing and must be
supplied out of the first. "Who are these that" is expressed in the
second clause by a simple "and." The situation is similar in the
first two clauses of verse 9:

The isles, yes, they wait for Me, —

And the ships of Tarshish —, as the foremost.

Here the first clause must borrow a phrase to match "as the foremost"; and the second clause must borrow "they wait for Me" out of the first. The meaning conveyed by this pair of clauses is: The isles and the ships of Tarshish as the foremost (at the head) wait for Me to . . . The adverb *bārī'shōnāh*, "as the foremost," or "at the head," modifies "they wait for Me" and applies to the ships as well as to the isles. It is here that the critics make their first mistake. They take "ships of Tarshish" to be an adverbial adjunct of "the isles wait for Me" as though the sentence read: The isles wait for Me with the ships of Tarshish at the head, leading the way. They ignore the "and" between the two clauses. They set up a comparison between the ships and the isles, showing the ships of Tarshish as occupying the first position and the isles following in second place. But that is not at all what is meant. The prophet treats the isles and the ships of Tarshish as a pair, places them side by side over against all other lands and nations. But the objection still is raised that the prophet would hardly treat the isles as a means of transportation together with the ships of Tarshish. It must, however, not be forgotten that the Hebrews, like all Orientals, make much more use of figures of speech, particularly in poetry, than we do. In the immediately preceding verses the metonymy prevails: camels, sheep, and rams represent their owners. Here the ships of Tarshish, the characteristic vessels of the island inhabitants, represent the inhabitants themselves. Fortunately, in Isaiah 23:1 we have this very same figure of speech: "Howl, ye ships of Tarshish, for it (Tyre) is laid waste, so that there is no house." There the ships represent the inhabitants of Tyre, and so here too the ships of Tarshish represent their owners, the isles. The sense of the passage is quite simple: The isles with their ships of Tarshish are waiting for Me in the forefront, namely, of all the other nations. During the great World War, we in America could say: The Germans *with* their submarines wait in the forefront to destroy our ships and our sons; after them, sickness and the battlefield will do the rest.

The objections of the critics have no merit. The learned critics make elementary mistakes in understanding the grammatical, poetical construction of the text and then emend what they call the corrupt text as though they were endowed with wisdom from on high. Whoever does not accept their work is considered ignorant and behind the times. Even such an eminent scholar as Cheyne goes along with this clumsy criticism when he translates in the Rainbow Bible, the crowning achievement of textual and literary criticism of his time, "Yea, to Me the ships gather, in the van the vessels of Tarshish." But the Masoretic text scoffs at the critics. The sentence, "The isles wait for Me," is genuinely Isaianic. It appears in 51:5, and 42:4 is almost identical. Why should the phrase not be used here where we have a summary of the essence of Isaiah's prophecy? One need only note that before *'onīyōth* there is a *wo*. Because of this *wo*, the words that follow cannot be construed as an adverbial modifier of the preceding clause, but must be understood as another clause of equal standing with the first, so that *wo'onīyōth tarshīsh bārī'shōnāh* is a complete clause parallel to the first clause, *kī lī 'īyyīm yeqawwū.* The ships of Tarshish figuratively represent the personified isles, as in 23:1, and the perfectly sound and highly poetic sense of the passage is: The isles and ships of Tarshish, as the foremost, wait for Me, etc. As the foremost, or in the forefront, is just by chance a correct translation here. Most exegetes take "in the forefront" strictly in the local sense, as ships in a fleet are stationed. Cf. Cheyne's "in the van." We are not prepared to say positively that *bārī'shōnāh* never has a purely local sense, because we have not given every occurrence of the word a thorough study, but we are certain that the word was originally an adverb of time and not of place, as in 52:4; Genesis 13:4; 2 Samuel 7:10; 1 Kings 20:9; 1 Chronicles 15:13; Jeremiah 7:12. From this original meaning, no doubt, the other meaning of "forefront" or "in first rank" was derived; but even when the word has that meaning, the concept of time is still prominent, as in Deuteronomy 13:10(9); 17:7; 1 Kings 17:13; Zechariah 12:7. We know of no passage where it has a purely local meaning. The prophet wishes to say that the isles with their ships of Tarshish have long been waiting for the time to bring her children to Zion. They are those who are farthest away among the gentiles (verses 4 and 9), and they must make haste if they are to arrive in good time. They come flying like clouds, like doves they speed homeward. The mention of ships of Tarshish also suggests fleetness, for these ships were known as swift, seagoing vessels, chosen for that reason by the merchants of Tyre for their commerce with the distant ports of Tartessus (a city or province on the Guadalquivir River in Spain, or Spain itself) and the western Mediterranean lands. The gentiles of the west, always referred to by Isaiah as the isles, are, among all the heathen, those whom God had chosen to be the first in point of time to receive the Gospel (42:1,4; 49:1; 51:4; 59:19 compared with 66:19 and this passage), and in the history of the church they were the first. As we remarked in connection with 42:4 and 51:5, "they wait for Me" must not be misused by pressing the phrase dogmatically. This is a poetic description of what the prophet sees. The same remark applies to *barī'shōnāh.*

The gentiles of the distant western seas have waited long for the Lord's signal "to bring your children from afar." Who are these children? Are they Jews of the Diaspora, or are they spiritual children of Zion, gentiles who have been born to her through faith? There is no doubt whatever that the prophet pictures the gentiles who come to Zion as having been converted, 42:6; 45:14; 49:6; 52:10,15; 55:4f; 59:19; 60:3ff; 65:1; 66:19ff. It is also clear that in our passage he has made a distinction between converted gentiles and the children of Zion as those who are bearers and those being borne. And so we are forced to conclude that "your children" are the physical children of Israel who had been scattered among gentile nations, the *nidhhēy yisrā'el* of 56:8. But a closer examination of chapter 60 reveals that much more is said in the chapter of converted gentiles than of returning children of Zion. Only verses 4b and 9 of this chapter treat of the latter; otherwise, all of verses 3 to 12 refer to converted gentiles coming to Zion with their treasures. By far the greater mass of the multitude pictured as journeying to Zion consists of converted gentiles, whereas the smaller number of the children of Zion are portrayed as children who are being led back to their home, and for whose sake the entire movement among the gentiles was instituted. That is the point of view of the entire Old Testament from the story of Abraham onward to the last of the prophets. Nor is this point of view entirely abandoned in the New Testament; it is still present, but forced into the background by the emphasis that is given to the entrance of the gentiles into God's kingdom as equals with the believers of Israel, cf. Ephesians 2 and 3. The fact is, and it will continue to be so, that Japheth does not occupy a tabernacle of worship of his own, but dwells in the tents of Shem, Genesis 9:27. Israel, except for that part that is hardened, is and remains the Lord's first-born son, Exodus 4:22, and God's calling of Israel and His gifts will never be withdrawn; God will not repent of His promise, Romans 11. Respecting our physical parentage, our relation to physical Israel is that of fellow heirs, sharers of the same body and sharers of the same promise in Christ, Ephesians 3:6; spiritually, there is no distinction between them and us, Romans 11:32. Believers in Israel do have a right to the title of children of Israel and children of Zion superior to that of all gentiles, but that does not justify any expectations that there will ever be a universal conversion of the Jews. The current Zionist movement is but of the flesh. Enthusiasts among Jews and Christians during World War I gave themselves over to the delusion that when the Allies gained the victory, Isaiah 60 would come into fulfillment in the physical sense and that the Jews from all over the world would stream back to Palestine and Jerusalem, where, according to the expectations of the Jews, the Messiah would appear and establish a kingdom of this world. That hope has not been fulfilled, nor will it ever be fulfilled. But what our text does say, has ever since the days of St. Paul been richly fulfilled and will continue to be fulfilled until the Day of Judgment. Through the stumbling and fall of the Jews, we gentiles who have fallen heir to the promise of salvation, Romans 11:11,12,15, "to provoke them to jealousy," bring Zion's physical children from all corners of the earth to their spiritual mother Zion, the church of Christ. According to the Lord's promise, our preaching of the Gospel to them shall not be in vain.

The suffixes in *kaspām* and *zehābhām* refer to the isles and the ships of Tarshish, as is evident from the context. The suffix in *'ittām* might be made to refer to *bhānayikh*, but to what purpose? Zion's children and the gentiles' treasures are being brought along "for the name of your God, the Lord, and for the Holy One of Israel, because He has so glorified you." The gentiles come, leading Zion's children and bringing their own treasures with them, in order to glorify Jehovah, Zion's God, as the one true God and the Holy One of Israel, who so jealously defends Israel against her enemies that she appears crowned with divine glory, but for her enemies He is a terrible judge. Humbly they come forward to devote themselves and all their goods to His service.

10 וּבָנוּ בְנֵי־נֵכָר חֹמֹתַ֫יִךְ וּמַלְכֵיהֶם יְשָׁרְתֽוּנֶךְ
כִּי בְקִצְפִּי הִכִּיתִיךְ וּבִרְצוֹנִי רִחַמְתִּֽיךְ:

In verse 1 Zion was portrayed as languishing in deep sorrow; here she appears as lying in the midst of ruins. Her walls are broken down, but she shall be gloriously restored. Those who have torn down her walls shall rebuild them: the children of foreign lands, the gentiles, those same gentiles of whom the entire passage speaks, who being converted, come in streams from the east and the west, bearing their gifts and leading the children of Zion with them. This they do as freely and as willingly as they brought along their possessions to honor God and to glorify Zion. That this service is voluntary and freely yielded is also indicated by the verb *yeshārethūnekh*, as we explained earlier in verse 7. For this service of the kings, cf. 49:23. For the fulfillment of this prophecy one might refer to Cyrus (Ezra 1) or to Artaxerxes Longimanus (Ezra 7 and Nehemiah 2), but the prophecy is quite general, and as the context shows, it is converted kings who are meant, verses 3 and 11. The true fulfillment came with the New Testament. For the second half of the verse, *kī bheqitspī*, etc., compare 54:7 and 8. In that passage the Lord's pity is spoken of as lying in the future; here it is an accomplished fact, and the glorification of Zion is pictured as already consummated.

11 וּפִתְּחוּ שְׁעָרַיִךְ תָּמִיד יוֹמָם וָלַיְלָה לֹא יִסָּגֵרוּ
לְהָבִיא אֵלַיִךְ חֵיל גּוֹיִם וּמַלְכֵיהֶם נְהוּגִים :

pittehū, although a Piel, is intransitive as in 48:8. The critics prefer *niphtehū*, a Niphal, although an intransitive Piel occurs in Arabic. The two adverbs (*tāmīdh*, always, continually, and *yōmām wālayelāh*, by day and by night) show that the prophet intended that the verb should express an intensive, not just a passive or reflexive, idea. The Masoretic accentuation joins *yōmām wālayelāh* with *tāmīdh* by placing a subordinate accent (Tebir) in *tāmīdh* and the more important disjunctive accent (Tiphcha) in *yōmām wālayelāh*. The same sequence of accents is to be found in the second clause of verse 13. The intentionally abbreviated clause, *lō'yissāghērū*, at the end of the half-verse, thus becomes especially emphatic. We have attempted to express this emphasis in our translation by rendering the negative *lō'* with "never again." The obviously free quotation of this verse in Revelation 21:25 does not argue against the correctness of this accentuation. The wide-open doors of Zion that shall never be closed vividly signify that the grace and spirit to seek the conversion of the gentiles shall never fail on earth until Christ comes for the last judgment. Or, to employ a picture from the New Testament, Matthew 11:28, the arms of the Lord Christ will always be extended in gracious invitation toward all sinful men until the time when these same arms shall wield the avenging sword over a hardened and impenitent world. Isolated, individual judgments in the meantime are of course not excluded. The doors are held constantly open in order to admit the treasures of the gentiles and their kings — that My house may be filled, Luke 14:23.

For *nehūghīm*, a Qal passive participle of *nāhagh*, to lead, to escort, the critics propose the active participle *nōhaghīm*, as being more readily intelligible. But the words that immediately follow show that the form must be *nehūghīm* and cannot be *nōhaghīm*. Those nations and kingdoms that refuse to become *nehūghīm*, that is, led as captives to Zion, are threatened with destruction. The kings of the gentiles are actually pictured as being led to Zion by their own people, naturally not as unconverted, resisting prisoners, but as believers willingly following their escort, as verses 3 and 10 have already set forth. Little imagination is required to picture the converted nations as joyfully leading their own converted kings in triumph to Zion with costly treasures and rich gifts.

12 כִּי־הַגּוֹי וְהַמַּמְלָכָה אֲשֶׁר לֹא־יַעַבְדוּךְ יֹאבֵדוּ וְהַגּוֹיִם חָרֹב יֶחֱרָבוּ׃

This verse is identical with Genesis 12:3, as particularized in Zechariah 14:16ff. And note how seriously this is meant: *hārōbh yeherābhū*, the emphatic infinitive absolute construction, threatens complete devastation.

Résumé of verses 1-12: The Lord in all the glory of His grace comes down to His church, which still lies in distress, and by the radiance of His grace converts many gentiles, who now lead Zion's own children back to her and offer themselves and their riches to the service of the Lord and His church.

Second Part: verses 13-22: *The glory of the Lord which has appeared over Zion will make Zion itself altogether glorious. To the honor and the gifts bestowed upon Zion by the great ones of the world, the Lord Himself will add improvement of all external conditions, security from all enemies, perfect happiness under perfect grace, complete spiritual renewal, and unlimited fruitfulness and growth.*

This part, like the first, is divided into five smaller strophes: verses 13 and 14; 15 and 16; 17 and 18; 19 and 20; 21 and 22.

13 *The glory of Lebanon shall come to you,*
    The cypress, the pine, and the cedar, all of them,
    To beautify the place of My sanctuary,
    That I may make My footstool glorious.
14 *Bending low shall the children of your oppressors come to you,*
    And all who reviled you shall fall down at the soles of your feet,
    And they shall call you the city of the Lord,
    The Zion of the Holy One of Israel.

15 *Instead of your being the forsaken and hated one,*
   To whom no one came,
   I will make you to be a glory forever,
   A joy from generation to generation.

16 *And you shall suck the milk of the nations,*
   And shall suck at the breast of kings,
   And shall know that I, the Lord, am your Savior,
   That your Redeemer is the Mighty One of Jacob.

17 *I will bring you gold in place of bronze,*
   And bring silver in place of iron,
   Bronze in place of wood,
   Iron in place of stone,
   And will make Peace to be your government
   And Righteousness to be your rulers.

18 *No more shall report of violence be heard in your land,*
   Nor of ruin and devastation in your borders,
   For you shall call Salvation your walls,
   And your gates Praise.

19 *No more shall the sun be your light by day,*
   No more shall the moon give you her light,
   Instead, the Lord shall be your light forever
   And your God your glory.

20 *No more will your sun set*
   Nor the moon go down,
   For the Lord will be for you an eternal light,
   And the days of your sorrow shall be at an end.

21 *And your people shall all of them be holy,*
   And forever shall they possess the land —
   A shoot of My plantation, the work of My hands,
   For My glorification.

22 *The smallest shall become a thousand*
   And the least a strong nation.
   I, the Lord, will in its proper time hasten it.

כְּבוֹד הַלְּבָנוֹן אֵלַיִךְ יָבוֹא   בְּרוֹשׁ תִּדְהָר וּתְאַשּׁוּר יַחְדָּו 13
לְפָאֵר מְקוֹם מִקְדָּשִׁי וּמְקוֹם רַגְלַי אֲכַבֵּד׃

Verses 13,14 and 15,16 form two pairs of similar content. Verses 13 and 15 each recite the glories of Zion; 14 and 16 tell of the reverence that her children accord her. These four verses form a larger stanza, which is balanced by another stanza of four verses (17-20), in which the opening verse 17 is similar to verse 13, and the closing verse 20 similar to verse 16.

Verse 13 should be compared with 35:2. The glory and pride of Lebanon lay in the unmatched beauty and vigor of her forests. For the three varieties of trees named here, cf. the remarks at 41:19. Naturally, the finest and most beautiful varieties would be chosen for mention. Commentators are at odds whether these trees are chosen for their usefulness in building or for their ornamental value. Those who contend for the first of these views refer to 44:26ff; 45:13; 52:9; 54:12ff; 61:4, where the promise is given that city and temple shall be rebuilt. The others refer to 35:1 and 2, where it is the desert (the large one, or the land of Judah?) that shall be beautified. No definite answer can be found in the text or the context. The words are indefinite enough to accommodate either interpretation. The purpose the trees are to serve is mentioned in the next clause: the beautification of "the place of My sanctuary" and the glorification of "My footstool." In a strict sense the temple is meant, 1 Chronicles 29:2; Psalm 132:8: "Arise, O Lord, into Your rest," and verse 14: "This is My rest for ever, here will I dwell." In a broader sense the city itself is meant, and it is the city of Zion that is the subject of prophecy in the entire chapter. Zion, the city, in all its parts, and especially the temple, is to be so splendidly rebuilt and beautified (cf. verse 17) that the gentiles who are streaming toward it will recognize and praise it at once as the city, not of an earthly king, but as the city of the Lord, who is revered in Zion as the Holy One.

וְהָלְכוּ אֵלַיִךְ שְׁחוֹחַ בְּנֵי מְעַנַּיִךְ וְהִשְׁתַּחֲווּ עַל־כַּפּוֹת רַגְלַיִךְ 14
כָּל־ מְנַאֲצָיִךְ
וְקָרְאוּ לָךְ עִיר יְהוָה צִיּוֹן קְדוֹשׁ יִשְׂרָאֵל׃

This verse describes the reverence shown to Zion by the children of her erstwhile gentile oppressors. *me'annayikh*, a Piel participle of *'anāh*, is correctly rendered by some commentators as "persecutors," which gives the Piel *'innāh* its proper intensive meaning. The reference here is to one-time tormentors of the children of Zion. This is the form of vengeance that the grace of God takes: It converts the most rabid enemies of the church into her ardent lovers and champions, to the glorification of God Himself and of His church. *shehōah*, a Qal infinitive construct, is used as a *casus adverbialis*, Gr. 113, h, p. 341, and 118, q, p. 375. Like *me'annayikh*, the Piel *mena'atsāyikh* is intensive — those who revile and scoff at you. Corresponding to these expressions that denote enmity are those that express the veneration of the former enemies. The "bending low" of *shehōah* is continued in the more

lengthy phrase *hishtaḥawū 'al kappōth raghlayikh.* The confession
of their mouths yields all honor to Zion; they hail the city of the
Lord as the Zion of the Holy One of Israel, that is, the dwelling
place of the one eternal God, the beloved of the Exalted One who
says: "My glory will I not give to another, neither My praise to
graven images," 42:8; 48:11. The proper noun Zion, followed by a
genitive, is like *'ūr kasdīm,* Ur of the Chaldees, and *YHWH
tsebhā'ōth,* Jehovah of the hosts. The appellative *'īr* is omitted
after *tsīyōn,* Gr. 125, h, p. 403.

תַּ֣חַת הֱיוֹתֵ֤ךְ עֲזוּבָה֙ וּשְׂנוּאָ֔ה וְאֵ֖ין עוֹבֵ֑ר ¹⁵
וְשַׂמְתִּיךְ֙ לִגְא֣וֹן עוֹלָ֔ם מְשׂ֖וֹשׂ דּ֥וֹר וָדֽוֹר׃

The Qal passive participles *'azūbhāh* and *senū'ah* are substantive predicates expressing a continuing state. Therefore, not: "Instead of your being forsaken," but: "Because you were a forsaken
one." The conjunction *taḥath,* instead of, easily takes on the meaning of compensation: "in compensation for," or as Luther has it,
dafuer, dasz. In the entire Third Part of Isaiah II the thought that
lies in *kiphlayim* (40:2c) is being carried out. The Lord will abundantly compensate His people for all the injustice that, according
to His counsel, it has suffered at the hands of its enemies. It should
be observed that *'eyn 'obhēr* is a noun clause describing a continuing state, Gr. 152, 1, p. 480. It emphasizes the forlorn state of the
people and the animosity of its enemies. The *we* in *wesamtīkh* is
the *Waw apodosis. gā'ōn* is majesty, or exalted state. The figure is
the opposite of personification, the person being designated by the
abstract term "majesty" or "exaltation." This is a climax of poetic
feeling. Compare the similarity of content in verses 15 and 13.
Zion, at one time misery itself and a thing despised, shall now be
splendor itself.

וְיָנַ֙קְתְּ֙ חֲלֵ֣ב גּוֹיִ֔ם וְשֹׁ֥ד מְלָכִ֖ים תִּינָ֑קִי ¹⁶
וְיָדַ֗עַתְּ כִּ֣י אֲנִ֤י יְהוָה֙ מֽוֹשִׁיעֵ֔ךְ וְגֹאֲלֵ֖ךְ אֲבִ֥יר יַעֲקֹֽב׃

ḥalēbh is a construct of *ḥālābh.* "To suck the milk of the gentiles" (or perhaps "drink" would be the better word, as the effect
of sucking) is a figurative expression for the enjoyment of the
treasures that the gentiles are bringing to Zion; so, too, the next
clause expresses Zion's utilization of earth's noblest and most glorious gifts. *melākhīm* is an indefinite genitive with the force of an
adjective: "royal breasts." Some commentators consistently trans-

late *shōdh* with "abundance" (in this verse, in Isaiah 66:11, and Job 24:9) and distinguish it from *shadh*, mother's breast. But in Job 24:9 *shōdh* certainly does mean "breast," and in both Isaiah passages the word is used in connection with the verb "to suck." It seems certain that the passage says that Zion shall lie at royal breasts. For the shift from the prophetic perfect *yānaqt* to the imperfect *tīnāqī* (pausal for *tīneqī*), see Gr. 106, n, p. 312. The imperfect denotes continuation of the action. The thought is the same as in 49:23a. The *Waw* in *weyādha'at* is *Waw* consecutive perfect, and Luther correctly translated: *auf dasz du erfahrest*, "and so you shall know." This is said of the spirit, rather than of the intellect. Through this actual, external glorification, Zion gains the inner spiritual understanding and certainty that He whose promises had not been able to comfort her heart, because she could not rightly believe His truth and power, is really her true Helper and Almighty God. The Lord's faithfulness is expressed by *YHWH* and *gō'alekh*; His almighty power by *mōshi'ekh* and *'abhīr ya'aqōbh*. The point of these four verses is that the Lord's glorification of Zion will bring about the veneration and love of those who before had hated and reviled her.

17 תַּחַת הַנְּחֹשֶׁת אָבִיא זָהָב   וְתַחַת הַבַּרְזֶל אָבִיא כֶסֶף

וְתַחַת הָעֵצִים נְחֹשֶׁת   וְתַחַת הָאֲבָנִים בַּרְזֶל

וְשַׂמְתִּי פְקֻדָּתֵךְ שָׁלוֹם   וְנֹגְשַׂיִךְ צְדָקָה׃

The new stanza, verses 17-20, begins as did the preceding one, verses 13-16. As the Lord promises in verse 13 to bring the glory of Lebanon to Zion, so here He promises to supply her with the finest of materials to rebuild and adorn the temple and the city. The description moves, without transition, from an enumeration of articles of adornment to a list of those that will make Zion secure against conquest: gold, silver, bronze, iron; and it ends with a statement that Zion shall dwell in peace. No mention is made of the purpose for which each material is to be used. What formerly had been made of bronze will now be made of gold; what had been iron shall now be of silver; what had been of wood shall now be of bronze; and what had been of stone shall in the renewal be of iron. This is no doubt said of the structure of the temple and its utensils, of the utensils and materials of private dwellings, and of the materials of which streets, walls, and towers are to be constructed. The city and all its vessels and utensils are to be made of precious or of durable materials. The precious metals will serve for adornment, the durable ones for defense of the city. All of this is, of course, figurative. Zion is to be both splendid and secure from assault. In Revelation 21 the glory of the new Jerusalem is portrayed in altogether different terms.

The element of security is set forth in the last two clauses. The only correct interpretation of these clauses is to construe *shālōm* and *tsedhāqāh* as direct objects of *samtī,* and *pequddāthēkh* and *nōghesayikh* as secondary objects: "He will make Peace to be your government," etc. Peace and Righteousness will henceforth be Zion's ruling body, that is, her inner control and her external security, so that personal rulers and defenders will no more be needed. The figure is personification. The opposite construction: "I will make your government to be Peace," etc., does not make good sense. This is confirmed by the next sentence.

לֹא־יִשָּׁמַע עוֹד חָמָס בְּאַרְצֵךְ שֹׁד וָשֶׁבֶר בִּגְבוּלָיִךְ 18
וְקָרָאת יְשׁוּעָה חוֹמֹתַיִךְ וּשְׁעָרַיִךְ תְּהִלָּה:

These words do not refer to Zion's own citizens. Their nature is not discussed until verse 21. Verse 18 is a continuation of the words at the end of verse 17 and refers to violence and ruin caused by enemies from without. The state of peace described here is in contrast to the destruction of city and land by neighboring enemies, in particular to the destruction wrought by the Babylonians. *weqārā'th* once more takes up the thought of the closing words of verse 17. The *Waw* is causal. The construction is like that of verse 17: *yeshū'ah* and *tehillāh* are direct objects; *ḥomōthayikh* and *she'ārayikh* are secondary objects. "You shall call Salvation your walls, and your gates Praise" (note the chiasmus). Walls and gates are no longer needed. Their function has been taken over by Salvation and the good name that by God's grace Zion now enjoys. The *tehillāh* of Zion consists in the esteem in which she is held in all the world as the City of the Lord, the Zion of the Holy One of Israel, verse 14.

This part of the prophecy has also been richly fulfilled in the church of the New Testament. The inescapable natural enmity of the world, of humanistic science and culture, of industrial, commercial, and national-political life against the church and its Gospel, have not only never been able to suppress the church, but from century to century, from one period of development to another, they have been constrained to grant her more and more outward freedom and space in the world. At various times and in various places, it is true that the church still exists under the sign of oppression and persecution. The church will to the very end be an *ecclesia pressa*, and toward the end of all things it will have to suffer extreme persecution. But in spite of all, the church has historically emerged from the state of persecution of the first few centuries into a state of public tolerance, and in most modern times into one of outward freedom. In the course of time God has granted the church as a body more and more outward respect in the world. Freedom of religion has more and more become an accepted principle of government among civilized nations, whereas in Old Israel the church was under constant siege and under attack from all sides. The complete fulfillment of all these prophecies will take place only in the world to come. The following verses show that the prophet does not draw a line between the time of the New Testament and eternity.

19 לֹא־יִהְיֶה־לָּךְ עוֹד הַשֶּׁמֶשׁ לְאוֹר יוֹמָם
וּלְנֹגַהּ הַיָּרֵחַ לֹא־יָאִיר לָךְ
וְהָיָה־לָךְ יְהוָה לְאוֹר עוֹלָם וֵאלֹהַיִךְ לְתִפְאַרְתֵּךְ׃

yihyeh with its predicate nominative differs only in form from the intransitive verb *yāïr* with its adverbial modifier *lenōghah*. *nōghah* can, as in verse 3 and 62:1, be "a bright gleaming light," or, as in 13:10 and in this passage, "a gentle gleam" — akin to our *light* or *gleam*. "For light the moon will no longer shed its beams upon you." *ʿodh* is to be supplied from the preceding clause. The *we* that introduces the second half of the sentence is rendered in Revelation 21:23 with γàρ; St. John's interpretation is therefore: The City no longer has need of sun and moon. Sun and moon are pictured as having been abolished. The prophet envisions the new creation of 65:17, which is final and eternal. Therefore: The Lord shall be for you an *eternal* light. One would have expected *nōghekh* instead of *tiph'artekh*, but perhaps the word could not be used in that way (besides *nōghah* the only other form of the word that occurs is *noghhām*). The writer chose a word with the same general root-meaning (*pe'ēr*) and thus gave the description a slightly different turn, which fits into the tone of the whole chapter. The emendation which substitutes *layelāh* for *ūlenōghah* is a shallow notion.

20 לֹא־יָבוֹא עוֹד שִׁמְשֵׁךְ וִירֵחֵךְ לֹא יֵאָסֵף
כִּי יְהוָה יִהְיֶה־לָּךְ לְאוֹר עוֹלָם וְשָׁלְמוּ יְמֵי אֶבְלֵךְ׃

shimshekh and *yerehekh* are not to be understood of sun and moon in a physical sense, but as designations of the Lord, who has taken their place. "Your sun," that is, your Lord, etc. *yeʾaseph*, a Niphal of *ʾasaph*, does not mean "shall wane," a meaning that readily suggests itself, but it is a synonym of *yabho*, "shall set," and refers to the setting of the moon and may be translated with "disappear" or some similar term. The statement is, in part, made on the same basis as that in the preceding verse, the difference being that *ʿolam* introduces a new element — not a future endless duration, but unbroken permanence. Cf. James 1:17: "With whom is no variableness, neither shadow of turning." So, the verse is not at all identical with the one that precedes it. As verse 19 concludes with an unexpected *tiph'artekh*, so this one also ends with an unexpected shift of expression: "And the days of your sorrow shall be at an end." The prophet's thoughts keep returning to the central concept of the glorification of Zion. The days of misery are at an end. Never, not even for a short time, shall they return. Uninterrupted happiness, never-ending joy will be the portion of the church under the total rule of the grace of the Lord. "Old things are passed away; behold, all things are become new." Cf. 25:8; 35:10; 65:19; Revelation 7:17; 21:4.

²¹ וְעַמֵּךְ֙ כֻּלָּ֣ם צַדִּיקִ֔ים לְעוֹלָ֖ם יִ֣ירְשׁוּ אָ֑רֶץ נֵ֧צֶר מַטָּעַ֛י מַעֲשֵׂ֥ה יָדַ֖י לְהִתְפָּאֵֽר׃

From the portrayal of the happy state of the church, the prophet now moves on to a description of the moral and spiritual character of the inhabitants of Zion, and of its importance. The prophet had attributed all of Israel's suffering and misery to her sin and impenitence. Cf. the section from 40:18 and 21 to chapter 59. Israel's repeated rebelliousness was the cause of all her misery. But now the Lord takes away from His people not only the guilt of their sin but wipes out its very existence. The citizens of Zion are without exception *tsaddiqim*. What that means was expounded at length at 41:10. They are now the new creatures that the covenant of grace requires and which the perfect fulfillment of that covenant has made them: perfect in their trust in this grace (faith); perfect in the love of God their Savior; perfect in childlike fear of His name. The essence of the requirements of the Law (Rom. 8:4ff; Exod. 20:2,3; etc.) has, by their perfect apprehension of the glory of God's grace, become their personal characteristic; they are altogether spiritual and holy — holy in the same sense in which St.

Paul calls all believers saints, namely, washed clean by grace, born again by the Spirit of Christ, not just in part, but wholly. Sinful lust is destroyed within them, they are sanctified in heart and mind. As *tsaddīqīm* and saints they shall inherit the land eternally. *'erets* is not to be rendered with "earth," but with "land." The reference is to the original promise given to Abraham, Genesis 12:1 and 7; 13:15; 15:18, etc., etc. In the final analysis that promise does include possession, inheritance, and government over all the world, Romans 4:13; cf. also the first part of this chapter, especially verse 12. Still, Canaan is always thought of as Israel's own land and the seat of Israel's government, since the promise did include physical ownership and was in that respect fulfilled; dominion over all the world would, and should remain, purely spiritual, Matthew 5:5; 19:28ff; 25:21; Luke 22:30. The last verse of this chapter shows, however, that the prophet has not yet advanced beyond a description joining the temporal with the eternal character of the kingdom of the Messiah, and it is a part of the limitations that the Old Testament point of view necessarily imposes, that the description of the future kingdom of God, even that of eternity, is tied to the land and to the city of *this time*, "the Jerusalem which now is," Galatians 4:25. And still, this promise is not to be understood in a physical sense, but just as the covenant with Abraham in reality applied only to his spiritual seed among Jews and gentiles, so also is the possession of land and earth, promised here, a spiritual possession, as is evident from the New Testament passages just cited. This possession includes not only "the land" and the earth, but also the Jerusalem, the land, and the world above, the entire future creation with all its wealth and treasure.

nētser mattā'ay (the Qere pointing) is in apposition to the words immediately preceding. There seems to be no reason why the Qere prefers the plural *mattā'ay* to the singular *mattā'i*, since in either case the change in the text is from *Waw* to *Yod*, and the singular yields a more satisfactory sense. In all passages where *mattā'* occurs (here; 61:3; Ezek. 17:7; 31:4; 34:29; Micah 1:6) it has the objective meaning of plantation, garden, vineyard, cf. 5:2ff; Matthew 21:33ff; Mark 12:1ff; Luke 20:9ff. The word nowhere occurs in the subjective sense. Therefore: Zion's citizens, the holy people, are a shoot from My plantation, from My garden; not "of My planting." Furthermore, what could be the purpose of the plural plantations or gardens? Delitzsch seems to have taken the plural in a subjective sense, for he explains *mattā'ay* as meaning acts of grace. But that is arbitrary. The word does not have the meaning of "im-

planting"; a *matṭā'* is a plantation or garden. The second apposition, "the work of My hands," does introduce the necessary subjective element and with it the real basis for *yīreshū 'ārets*. Because
this people is a sprout out of *His* garden, because it is the work of
His hands and of the favors of *His* grace, therefore it shall never
again be deprived of the possession of its land.

The object of *lehithpā'ēr* is the Lord. One might be tempted to
connect this verb with the first part of the sentence, but the conclusion of 60:3 shows that its connection is with the preceding appositives. Israel, in its state of holiness is a work of the hands of
the God of grace, which through the gifts of His grace He created
for the glorification of Himself.

הַקָּטֹן יִהְיֶה לָאֶלֶף וְהַצָּעִיר לְגוֹי עָצוּם ²²
אֲנִי יְהוָה בְּעִתָּהּ אֲחִישֶׁנָּה׃

This verse takes us again entirely into the temporal realm. It is
not in harmony with the context to interpret *haqqāṭōn* and
hatstsā'īr as referring to Israel as a people, whether as the least
among the nations, or in the sense of Amos 7:2 and 5, as weakened, feeble, decimated. The reference is to individuals in Israel,
and the positives have the force of superlatives, Gr. 133, g, p. 431.
The promise, in its literal sense, pertains to natural reproduction
and expansion, in contrast with Israel's inability to expand while
in exile, cf. 54:1ff. This is, of course, to be understood figuratively
as a picture of the spiritual fruitfulness of the church of the New
Testament, as Paul himself interprets 54:1 in Galatians 4:27.

The final clause treats of the fulfillment of this promise. *be'ittāh*
(with neuter suffix), "in its time," is "the fullness of time" of Galatians 4:4 and "the time of Christ" of Ephesians 1:10. *'ahīshennāh*
(Hiphil of *ḥūsh* or *ḥīsh*), again with neuter suffix, says that the
Lord will quickly and suddenly, at the time that He Himself has
fixed, bring into being all the glorification that He has promised in
this chapter. That is the way God acts in all of His momentous
visitations on earth. His preparations for the great events are slow
and unhurried. But when all conditions are ripe, then the new
bursts forth unexpectedly and in a short time becomes established. It is thus that the World War so unexpectedly engulfed the
world. No one foresaw at the beginning what new things would
result from it, but in not too long a time the revolution was
complete and the world was changed. The same was true of the
great Deluge, of Israel's deliverance from Egypt, of the Babylonian

exile, of the fall of the old Roman Empire, of the Reformation, and finally that will also be true, on the grandest scale of all, of the Day of Judgment. After long and silent preparation, the Lord will come suddenly like a thief in the night. Oh, that the church in our day might not misread the signs of the times!

After two penitential sermons, this triad, consisting of chapters 58, 59, and 60, continues with a prophecy of the future perfect glorification of Zion. The first discourse, in chapter 58, denounces the hypocritical penitence of the people and preaches a right repentance. The next chapter exposes the irremediable spiritual decay and proclaims the coming of the Lord in judgment to reject the incurably impenitent and to save those who repent. The last discourse describes the perfect salvation which shall be the lot of those who repented and were saved by the revelation of the glory of the Lord.

SECOND TRIAD
Chapters 61-63:6

*The Glorification of Zion in
its Highest Perfection and
the Destruction of all Her Enemies.*

First Discourse: Chapter 61

The Glorification of Zion in its Highest Perfection and the Destruction of all Her Enemies.

Modern critics leave chapters 61 and 62 in their present location, as related pieces, but they detach 63:1-6 from this section and attach it to 59:15b-20 because of the similarity of phrases and expressions. The reasons they give are not convincing. The Day of Vengeance announced at length in 63:1-6 is also mentioned in this section (61:2), as a counterpart to the "Year of the Lord's Grace." This would indicate that the first verses of chapter 63 are quite properly connected with chapters 61 and 62.

First Discourse: Chapter 61

The Year of Grace proclaimed by the Servant of the Lord brings freedom and happiness to the Church and leads her back to a rightful priesthood with a twofold inheritance in the newly rebuilt city.

This discourse may be divided into four short strophes: verses 1-3; 4-6; 7-9; 10 and 11. In the first of these the Servant speaks; in the second and the third and at the very end of the fourth, the Lord Himself is the speaker; verse 10 is a brief interlude, a hymn of the church rejoicing in her salvation.

First Strophe: verses 1-3: *The Servant of the Lord as Herald of Freedom and Messenger of Joy.*

1   *The Spirit of the Lord is upon Me,*
    Because the Lord anointed Me to proclaim good news to the
      heavy-laden,
    Sent Me to bind up the broken-hearted,
    To proclaim freedom to the captives,
    The opening of the eyes to the prisoners,

600

2   *To announce the Year of Grace of the Lord,*
    And a Day of Vengeance of our God,
    To comfort all those that mourn,
3   *To place upon the mourners of Zion —*
    To give them — a crown instead of ashes,
    The oil of joy instead of mourning,
    A garment of praise in place of a drooping spirit,
    So that they will be called Terebinths of Righteousness,
    The Lord's planting, which shall render Him praise.

רֽוּחַ אֲדֹנָי יְהוִה עָלָי   יַעַן מָשַׁח יְהוָה אֹתִי   1

לְבַשֵּׂר עֲנָוִים שְׁלָחַנִי   לַחֲבֹשׁ לְנִשְׁבְּרֵי־לֵב

לִקְרֹא לִשְׁבוּיִם דְּרוֹר   וְלַאֲסוּרִים פְּקַח־קֽוֹחַ׃

The first sentence of this chapter is a summing-up of 11:2; 42:1;
49:8; 50:4 and 5. What was promised there, is now being fulfilled.
The events here foretold are those that follow immediately after
Matthew 3:16, and the point of time is that of Luke 4:18. Armed
with the Spirit of God, the Servant of the Lord, the Messiah, now
steps out before the world as the Lord's Herald and Preacher. It is
of course true that His preaching is couched in terms suited to the
conditions of the exile, and the images that the prophet employs
are such as are suggested by the exile. It follows therefore that the
fulfillment of the prophecy must in its form be adapted to exilic
conditions, even though they might appear to be only of minor importance. But to assume that the momentous prophecies in chapters 2, 7, 9, 11, 12, 25, 26, 35, 40, 42, 49, 50, 53, and 60 find their
fulfillment in this one minor event of the exile would be like having a tremendous mountain travail and bring forth a tiny mouse.
Such an assumption denies the reality of all prophecy and divine
revelation; it stamps Christ Himself as a deceiver and rejects the
authority of the entire New Testament. But why waste time arguing, when Christ Himself has said, Luke 4:21: "This day is this
scripture fulfilled in your ears." This verse tries the spirits whether they are of God or not. The position that men in general, and exegetes in particular, take regarding the word of Christ in Luke
8:10 ("Unto you it is given to know the mysteries of the kingdom
of God, but to others in parables, that seeing they might not see,
and hearing they might not understand") reveals whether the
spirit that is in them is of God or not. Those who permit themselves to remain forever bound by the external details of this picture without ever being able to penetrate to the truths portrayed

in it, have been hopelessly blinded by the prince of this world. This prophecy, presented in pictures suggested by the Babylonian exile, describes conditions as they exist in the New Testament and in eternity.

'adhōnāy coupled with *YHWH* is not without special significance. The Spirit of Him who governs all things and who effectively performs all His counsel, rests upon the Servant, the Lord. At the same time He is also the Spirit of the God of salvation, who is the Giver of life and salvation to His people. *ya'an* (short for *ya'an 'asher*), when followed by a verb in the perfect, always means "because." The term οὗ ἕνεκεν, with which the LXX translates *ya'an*, and which the Lord employed in Luke 4, was understood in no other sense by Greek-speaking Jews, who made little distinction between cause, purpose, and effect. Cf. also Gr. 158, b, p. 492. *māshaḥ 'othī* and *shelāḥanī*, "He anointed Me," "He sent Me," are synonymous, the first being the sign and the second the thing signified, since anointing signified calling or sending. Both verbs are followed by infinitives with *le*, signifying purpose. The pronominal object *'othī* is emphatic and is in harmony with the strong emphasis on the divine mission of the Servant in 49:1.

His mission is *lebhassēr 'anāwīm*. *bissēr* is the Greek εὐαγγελίζεσθαι (cf. 40:9). The *'anāwīm* are the poor and miserable, not the pious and godly. Modern exegetes, who welcome support for their unbelief, have wherever possible forced upon *'anāw* the meaning of "humble," "obedient," "godly." A shameful amount of capital had been squeezed out of *'anāw me'odh*, Numbers 12:3, in order to bolster the theory that Moses was not the author of the Torah. The Numbers passage is made to say that Moses was an exceedingly obedient or godly man above all men on earth instead of an exceedingly troubled or much plagued man. *'anāw* is derived from the same stem as *'anī*, and both words have the primary meaning of poor, miserable, afflicted, unfortunate. Since in Scripture the poor in this world are commonly also the faithful (cf. especially 1 Cor. 1:26ff, Matth. 11:5), *'anāw* can indeed take on the meaning of pious, humble, meek, etc. But in most cases the word still means poor, troubled, afflicted, plagued. It never wholly loses this meaning, and in our passage that is obviously the meaning of the word.

The contrast between *lebhassēr* and the synonyms of *'anāw*: *nishberēy lēbh* (heartbroken), *shebhūyim* (captives), *'asūrīm* (prisoners), makes it clear that *ʿanāw* must here refer to the poor and afflicted people. The corresponding πτωχοί of the LXX and the New Testament is added testimony for the correctness of this translation. And yet, the 17th edition of the Gesenius-Buhl lexicon cites Isaiah 61:1 in support of the meaning "subordinate to Jahve." The passage in Matthew 11:5 would accordingly then have to be read: "Those who subordinate themselves to Jahve are having the Gospel preached to them." In Isaiah 66:2 *ʿanī* is used instead of *ʿanāw* (cf. 57:15). It follows that here *ʿanāw* must designate the poor and afflicted, etc. Naturally, moral and spiritual affliction is meant, and the *ʿanāwīm* are the πτωχοὶ τῷ πνεύματι of Matthew 5:3, that is, those who have felt the rod of the Law and whose consciences have been smitten because of their sin. They are those who see in all affliction the heavy hand of God, Psalm 32:4. To these the Servant of the Lord shall preach the glad tidings of forgiveness, life, freedom, and salvation.

Whereas *lebhassēr* is followed by an object in the accusative, *laḥabhōsh* has an indirect object. Cf. Gr. 117, n, p. 366. *nishberēy lēbh* characterizes the *ʿanāwīm* as spiritually afflicted; *shebhūyim* and *ʾasūrīm* refer to such as are in physical captivity and imprisonment. As in 42:7; 49:9; 52:2, this is a reference to conditions of the exile, but that this is not exclusively exilic terminology is shown by the more general use of the terms in Isaiah 49:24 (Matt. 12:29) and Psalm 14:7; 147:3. The reference is first of all to the children of Zion who are captives and prisoners in Babylon or among other gentile people; but just as *bissēr*, the preaching of the Gospel, applies to all the afflicted on the earth, so also does the binding-up apply to all the broken-hearted; and the proclamation of freedom and the opening of eyes likewise applies to all who by sin are made spiritual captives of "the strong man armed." As in chapters 42 and 49, so here the mission of the Messiah, the Servant of the Lord, the Savior Jesus Christ, is being described. This is Matthew 11:28.

qārāʾ derōr is a phrase taken from the terminology of the Year of Jubilee (Lev. 25:10; Jer. 34:8f). Ezekiel (46:17) calls it the *shenath hadderōr*. Cf. Leviticus 25:9ff. *peqaḥ qōaḥ* is usually explained as an error of the copyist, a dittograph, and the text critics substitute *peqōaḥ* for it, from 42:7. Cf. Gr. 84b, n, p. 234f. But the dittograph theory in most cases rests on very shaky ground. Could this perhaps be a formation like *qetaltōl* from *qātal* (Gr. p. 234)? Nothing certain can be said about the form.

² לִקְרֹא שְׁנַת־רָצוֹן לַיהוָה וְיוֹם נָקָם לֵאלֹהֵינוּ לְנַחֵם כָּל־אֲבֵלִים׃

The *le* before *YHWH* and *'elōhēynū* is an alternate form expressing the genitive relation. *shenath rātsōn* and *yōm nāqām* are unit concepts. Not "the year of the grace of the Lord" and "the day of the vengeance of our God," but "the Lord's year of grace" and "our God's day of vengeance," like the more familiar "judgment day," Gr. 129, d, p. 420. *qārā'* here too means to proclaim, to preach. The year of grace and the day of vengeance are of course not two separate times. This is one time, a time of grace for the poor and needy, and a time of retribution for all the enemies of God's people. The verse harks back to 49:8f. Cf. 2 Corinthians 6:2. The purpose and the effect of the preaching of the Servant and of the heralded time of grace is the comforting of all that mourn. They are the *'anāwīm* of verse 1, the broken-hearted who, because of their sins, mourn under the weight of God's wrath. They are the mourners of Zion mentioned in the next verse. *lenahēm* means something more than to give comfort. The short clause of purpose, *lenahēm kol 'abhelīm*, is the theme of the following verse, which develops the term *lenahēm*. Its meaning is the equivalent of quickening or restoring to life.

³ לָשׂוּם! לַאֲבֵלֵי צִיּוֹן לָתֵת לָהֶם פְּאֵר

תַּחַת אֵפֶר

שֶׁמֶן שָׂשׂוֹן תַּחַת אֵבֶל מַעֲטֵה תְהִלָּה תַּחַת רוּחַ כֵּהָה

וְקֹרָא לָהֶם אֵילֵי הַצֶּדֶק מַטַּע יְהוָה לְהִתְפָּאֵר׃

The phrase *latheth lahem*, which seems to interrupt the flow of the sentence, is a rhetorical emphasis of the opening phrase, *lāsūm la'abhēley tsīyōn*. *sūm*, coupled with such a specific object as *pe'ēr*, a crown, an ornament for the head, a wreath (cf. verse 10; 3:20; Ezek. 24:23; 44:18), here has the more specific meaning of "to set or place upon." The comfort mentioned in verse 2 is pictured as an ornamental wreath placed on the heads of the mourners in place of the ashes which they had sprinkled on their heads as a sign of mourning, cf. 2 Samuel 13:19; Job 2:12. There is a play on words in *pe'ēr* and *'epher*. As ashes were a sign of grief, so *pe'ēr* was a sign of rejoicing, signified in English by a crown or wreath. According to the Masoretic text, the sign of rejoicing is followed in the next clauses each time by a corresponding emotion of sorrow: *shemen sāsōn* by *'ēbhel*; *ma'atēh thehillāh* by *rūah kēhāh shemen* *sāsōn*, oil of rejoicing, occurs elsewhere only in the bridal psalm, 45:8(7). The expression has its origin in the custom of anointing oneself with aromatic oils on joyous occasions, Ecclesiastes 9:8; 2 Samuel 12:20; Song of Songs 4:10. *ma'aṭēh thehillāh*, if our text is correct, is a garment of praise, or less specifically, festive garments (cf. *bighdhēy thiph'artēkh*, 52:1). *rūaḥ kēhāh* (cf. 42:3 and the verb in verse 4), a drooping, flagging, glimmering spirit, is parallel to *'ebhel* and is a sign of extreme grief or despair. And so, in place of sorrow, the redeemed shall have the oil of gladness, and in place of a fainting spirit, festive garments. It strikes one as strange that in the first member of the clauses the *sign* of the emotion is made parallel to the emotion itself in the second member, whereas one would have expected to find sign corresponding to sign, and emotion to emotion. That arrangement can be achieved by placing *ma'aṭēh* before *'ebhel*, thus: *shemen sāsōn taḥath ma'aṭēh 'ebhel, tehillāh taḥath rūaḥ kēhāh*, "oil of gladness for garments of mourning," "praise for a despairing spirit." This change in the arrangement of the words is the more inviting since the LXX also has an arrangement that differs from that of the Masoretic text. But who can be sure?* That the decorative head-covering, the oil of gladness, and *ma'aṭēh thehillāh* are external signs of a happy joyful emotion of the heart, not just pictures of gladness, is suggested by the predicates *lāsūm* and *lāthēth* and evidenced by the following clause. Because of the signs of inner joy that will be observed in the redeemed, they shall be called (*weqōrā' lāhem*, Perf. Pual) *'ēylēy hatstsedheq*, terebinths of salvation. Because the terebinth is evergreen and long-lived, it is a symbol of fresh and enduring strength. *tsedheq* is here, as elsewhere, the salvation that the Lord has covenanted to provide for His people through His Servant. They are therefore called terebinths, or oaks, of salvation, that is, men who have been made fresh and strong and happy in the salvation that by the grace of God is theirs. *maṭṭa' YHWH*, a planting of the Lord, has essentially the same meaning, cf. 60:21. *lehithpā'ēr* has the same meaning that the phrase has in 60:21.

By His preaching, the Servant of the Lord, anointed with the Spirit of the Lord, will bring to the captive mourners of Zion freedom and happiness, and He will make strong trees of salvation of those who had despaired.

---

*The Dead Sea Scroll reads exactly like the Masoretic text.

Second Strophe: verses 4-6: *The Redeemed as Priests of the Lord.*

4 *And they shall rebuild the old ruins,*
And restore the ancient desolations;
And they shall rebuild the ruined cities
And the desolations of generation after generation.
5 *And strangers shall stand and feed your flocks,*
And sons of aliens shall be your plowmen and vinedressers.
6 *And you shall be called priests of the Lord,*
Ministers of our God shall you be named;
On the wealth of the nations shall you feast,
And in their glory shall you revel.

‎4 וּבָנוּ חָרְבוֹת עוֹלָם שֹׁמְמוֹת רִאשֹׁנִים יְקוֹמֵמוּ
‎וְחִדְּשׁוּ עָרֵי חֹרֶב שֹׁמְמוֹת דּוֹר וָדוֹר :

The subject of verses 1-3 was the spiritual renewal of the redeemed. This section of ten lines, verses 4-6, treats of the restoration of the external conditions in which the church of the new
order will exist. In verse 4 the prophet envisions the restoration of
the cities and villages of the homeland, of Jerusalem in particular
(44:26), which had been lying in ruins since the exile. In the rebuilding of Jerusalem he includes also the restoration of the ruins
of ancient times. Lines 1 and 3 of verse 4 speak in general terms of
old ruins (*horbhoth ʿolam, hiddeshu ʿarey horebh*), lines 2 and 4
hark back in the terms *rīʾshonim* and *dor wadhor* to most ancient
times. Thus the completeness of the restoration has been prophesied. Cf. the account of the renewal of the building materials in
60:17. At first glance one would take the strangers mentioned in
verse 5 to be the subject of *bhanu* since they are expressly mentioned as builders in 60:10. But the structure of the passage requires that *ʾabheley tsīyon* be taken as the subject of *bhanu*, since
60:10 is too far removed and there are no examples to support an
assumption that *bhanu* anticipates as subject the *zarim* of verse 5.
The children of Israel, now rejoicing in their redemption, are to be
considered the renovators of the ruins, while the *zarim* and *beney*
nekhar are workmen who carry out the plans. Cf. 58:12.

‎5 וְעָמְדוּ זָרִים וְרָעוּ צֹאנְכֶם וּבְנֵי נֵכָר אִכָּרֵיכֶם וְכֹרְמֵיכֶם :

These are not unconverted, hostile strangers, but as chapter 60
clearly shows, they are gentile converts. Tending the flocks, plow-

ing the fields, and dressing the vineyards are activities representative of all the forms of labor necessary for the physical support of the Lord's congregation on earth. As the gentile converts in 60:5-17 devote their treasures to Zion and rebuild the city, so here they are represented as voluntary providers of the needs of the church, each according to his calling or skill, so that the church, as will appear in the next verse, is nourished by the wealth of the gentiles and glories in the free use of it.

וְאַתֶּם כֹּהֲנֵי יְהוָה תִּקָּרֵאוּ מְשָׁרְתֵי אֱלֹהֵינוּ יֵאָמֵר לָכֶם ⁶

חֵיל גּוֹיִם תֹּאכֵלוּ וּבִכְבוֹדָם תִּתְיַמָּרוּ :

The promise given in Exodus 19:6 is described in the first half of this verse as being ideally fulfilled. In the church of the New Testament there is no longer a specially designated class of priests, but the church consists entirely of functioning priests, who without any special human mediation stand before God as true priests and offer up true, spiritual, God-pleasing sacrifices, 1 Peter 2:9; Romans 12:1. *meshārethēy 'elohēynū*, ministers of our God, has a more general meaning than *kōhanīm. shērēth*, a verb that occurs only in the Piel, always denotes an honored or preferred service, in contrast to *ʿābhadh*.

Some modern commentators, following the lead of Saadya Gaon and Solomon Rashi, derive *tithyammārū* from *yāmar* (*mūr*), of which a Hiphil form *hēymīr* occurs in Jeremiah 2:11. They then translate: "they give themselves in exchange," with *bikhebhōdhām* as object, thus making the priestly services an article of exchange or barter — a most unusual thought! But, since *Yod* quite frequently is substituted for *Aleph*, and since Psalm 94:4 has *yith'ammerū* in the sense of "to boast, to glory in," it seems quite likely that such an exchange of consonants took place in this instance and that the verb expresses the idea of boasting or glorying in — a thought that suits well to the context.* This is the interpretation of the LXX, the Syriac, and the Vulgate, which Luther followed. Delitzsch and many others agree, while the modern negative critics resort to attempts to correct the text.

It leads to un-Scriptural conclusions to suggest that the services of the *kōhanīm* (priests) and of the *meshārethīm* (servants or min-

---

*The Dead Sea Scrolls read *tithya'mmārū*. The Masoretic reading appears only in this place, while a form similar to that of the Dead Sea Scrolls may be found in Psalm 94:4.

isters) in the New Testament church — for it is of the New Testament that the prophet speaks, Luke 4:17ff — are assigned exclusively to Jewish Christians who are to render the spiritual service of priests, while the gentile Christians serve mainly as Gibeonites, as hewers of wood and drawers of water. Since the New Testament church is made up chiefly of converts from paganism and is constantly being recruited by the conversion of gentiles who are in possession of the world's riches, it can be said that the church lives on the wealth of the gentiles and glories in the use of the best of their treasures. According to chapter 60, the converted gentiles lay all their treasures, even the wealth and services of kings, at the feet of the church, not only at the time of their conversion, but as a continuing gift and service. Whatever the source of their income may be, whether from service as shepherds and plowmen, or from business or otherwise, they serve the church with it. Moreover, not only the goods and services of converts, but also those of unconverted gentiles belong by divine right to God's dear children, and insofar as such wealth is withheld from the church, it is a "robbery of iniquity," verse 8. It is, however, altogether natural and unavoidable that the exilic and postexilic Jewish congregation should be represented as having the priesthood in trust, since the postexilic and the New Testament church merge into one in the mind of the prophet. And furthermore, it is the Jewish congregation, not a congregation of gentile converts, that advances out of the Old into the New Testament, perpetuates the kingdom of God and, before all gentile nations, takes precedence in the New Testament. This was the promise that Israel had received from the Lord. Of all nations it should be the firstborn of the Lord, a pre-eminence that is everywhere attested in the New Testament, Matthew 10:5, 6; 15:24; John 4:22; Acts 3:25f; 13:46; Romans 1:16; 9:4ff; 11:16,18,24,28,29; 15:8f; Matthew 8:12; Ephesians 3:6, etc. Therefore, neither are the gentile Christians excluded from the priesthood of the New Testament, nor are the Jewish Christians exempted from the obligation of supporting the church.

Some commentators — mostly unbelieving — on the basis of this and similar passages, make the prophet out to be a bigot, narrow-minded and hedged in by a false nationalism in respect to the position to be occupied by Israel and the gentiles in the kingdom of the New Testament. They assume also that the prophet is speaking only of external conditions. Mistaken are also the believing commentators who give loose rein to all manner of allegories in their interpretation of the passage and divest it of its prophetic quality.

This strophe tells us that the church of the New Testament is made up of Jewish and gentile believers, here represented by the believers of Israel, the Lord's firstborn, and consists entirely of priests of God, who shall receive such generous material and moral support from non-Jewish and gentile nations that their material requirements of life will be abundantly satisfied. The fulfillment began with the centurion of Capernaum (Luke 7) and since then has proceeded without interruption.

Third Strophe: verses 7-9: *Previous suffering shall be doubly requited.*

7 *Instead of your shame you shall have double,*
   And instead of their disgrace they shall rejoice in their
      inheritance;
   Therefore in their own land they shall possess double,
   And shall have everlasting joy.
8 *Because I am the Lord who loves justice,*
   Who hates the iniquity of robbery,
   I will assure them of the fruit of their labor
   And will make an eternal covenant with them.
9 *And their seed shall be known among the gentiles*
   And their offspring among the nations;
   Whoever shall see them, will recognize them,
   That they are a seed that the Lord has blessed.

תַּחַת בָּשְׁתְּכֶם מִשְׁנֶה וּכְלִמָּה יָרֹנּוּ חֶלְקָם 7
לָכֵן בְּאַרְצָם מִשְׁנֶה יִירָשׁוּ שִׂמְחַת עוֹלָם תִּהְיֶה לָהֶם:

These lines have been variously construed. Because of the *lākhēn*, some translators have understood the entire first line as causal, followed by a clause introduced by "therefore." They take both *mishneh* and *kelimmāh* to be attributes of *boshtekhem.* This construction requires some manipulation of the text: "Because of your double shame and contempt, therefore," etc. But such skillful maneuvering is not called for. The construction is really quite simple. The completed parallelism would be:

   taḥath boshtekhem mishneh (tārōnnū)
   (taḥath) kelimmāthām ḥelqām yārōnnū.
   Instead of your shame you shall rejoice in double,
   Instead of their disgrace they shall rejoice in
         their inheritance.

609

In the first clause *tārōnnū* is missing, *taḥath* and the suffix of *kelimmāh* in the second. But *taḥath* and *tārōnnū* are readily supplied from *taḥath* and *yārōnnū* in the second line of the parallelism.

rānan is here construed with an object in the accusative instead of the usual *le*. The change in person, from second to third, is not at all unusual for Isaiah. Regarding the omission of *taḥath* before *kelimmāh* cf. Gr. 119, hh, p. 384. *yārōnnū ḥelqām*, they shall rejoice in their inheritance, is presented as the antithesis of *bōsheth* and *kelimmāh*, because the expulsion of Israel out of their homeland constituted their greatest degradation and shame. Loss of the homeland would seem to indicate to them that Israel had lost all claim to be the chosen people of the one true God. Had not God sealed this land to them as their inheritance for ever? Genesis 12:7; 13:15, etc. Now the land had been forcibly taken from them, and that seemed to prove that the promise and the Giver of the promise had been a delusion and Israel's claim a mere figment of their imagination. *ḥelqām*, their inheritance, refers to Israel's homeland. *lākhēn* refers back to *boshtekhem* and *kelimmāh* without consideration for the predicate of the first clause; but this predicate receives emphasis and more exact definition in the second sentence. *lākhēn* has a meaning similar to our "in such a way that." In the first line *mishneh* and *ḥelqām* were separated, in the second they appear together, since *'artsām* is an exact equivalent of *ḥelqām*. They shall possess double in their own homeland and inheritance. The LXX seems to be based on a different text and renders the first *mishneh* as an adverb: "again," "a second time."* It may be noted that our text picks up the *kiphlayim* of 40:2 and suggests the idea of "double glory." The last clause expresses the emotion of the heart that follows as a result of the restitution of the inheritance: "everlasting joy" shall be theirs.

⁸ כִּי אֲנִי יְהוָה אֹהֵב מִשְׁפָּט שֹׂנֵא גָזֵל בְּעוֹלָה
וְנָתַתִּי פְעֻלָּתָם בֶּאֱמֶת וּבְרִית עוֹלָם אֶכְרוֹת לָהֶם:

Most commentators, Delitzsch included, explain verse 8 as a statement of the reason for the promise given in verse 7 and translate *kī* with "for." That interpretation leads to a misunder-

---

*In the LXX the first half of this verse is missing. In the second half *be'artsām* and *mishneh* are reversed and the latter taken adverbially ἐκ δευτέρας . These words are also reversed in the Dead Sea Scrolls.

standing of the entire verse, especially of the phrase *ghāzēl be'ōlāh*, and of *pe'ullāthēm* and *be'emeth*. The construction is really quite simple. *kī* does not refer to the preceding verse and is not to be translated "for." *kī* introduces an opening clause that contains the reason for the action expressed by *wenāthattī*, and is to be translated "because." Because I am the Lord, who . . . , I will give, etc. *'ōlāh* is a contraction of *'awlāh* (cf. Job 5:16, the marginal note to Psalm 92:16(15), and the plural *'ōlōth* in the lexicon). *'ōlāh* here is not a burnt offering, but denotes injustice, evil, crime, iniquity, like *'awel*. *ghāzēl* denotes something that has been got by robbery. *ghāzēl be'ōlāh* is that which has been unjustly taken, the plunder of iniquity. Because the Lord is a God who loves righteousness and hates robbery and iniquity, therefore will He . . . etc. The text does not read *wenāthattī lāhem*, etc. Hence *nāthan* must not be translated with "give": "and I will give them." The text says: *nāthattī pe'ullāthām be'emeth*, that is, I will set or put their *pe'ullāh* in security, and *pe'ullāh* is not wages, but the fruit or product of one's labor. Continuing the statement in the preceding verse, the Lord promises: "After I shall have compensated My people for the shame they have suffered, and placed them in their inheritance, and given them double to enjoy in their homeland, they shall forever continue in the enjoyment of their inheritance. They shall never again be the plunder of iniquity, as now, but I will make them secure in possession of the product of their labor against all unjust robbery." The same thought is carried out in 62:8,9. Technically the verse is an elaboration of the last clause of verse 7, and for that reason it closes with a similar phrase: "and an eternal covenant will I make with them" — one that ensures to them possession and enjoyment of all the products of their labor. The *ū* before *berīth* indicates that what follows is in the nature of a reason.

וְנוֹדַע בַּגּוֹיִם֙ זַרְעָם וְצֶאֱצָאֵיהֶם בְּתוֹךְ הָעַמִּים 9
כָּל־רֹאֵיהֶם֙ יַכִּירוּם כִּי הֵם זֶרַע בֵּרַךְ יְהוָה׃

Verse 9 adds to the double inheritance which Israel shall receive the element of honor which was contained in the first *mishneh* of verse 7. The Niphal *nōdha'* here has the pregnant meaning of "acknowledged," "esteemed," cf. Psalm 76:2(1); Proverbs 31:23. The Hiphil *yakkīrūm* is intensive in meaning: They will stare at, examine closely as something strange, and so: They will recognize them with certainty. The following *kī* introduces an objective clause. What they recognize in them is that they are a seed, a generation that the Lord has blessed. What here is promised in the form of physical descriptions to the postexilic church, consisting of Jewish believers, has been richly fulfilled in the true spiritual meaning of the promise in the New Testament church of gentile and Jewish Christians. All such things will be added in abundance to those who seek first the kingdom of God and its righteousness. The meek — and they are the afflicted and pious children of God — possess nothing and yet have all things and possess the kingdom of the world, not only as a right, but also as to the use and enjoyment of it. Only they who in their hearts have renounced this world's goods, can rightly use and enjoy them; whereas no one whose heart is bound to earthly things can truly enjoy them. The true honor and respect of men is also the lot of the Christian. That respect consists in this that the children of the world, at the same time that they revile, persecute, and crucify us, cf. 2 Corinthians 4:2; 5:11, are convicted by their conscience that we Christians are indeed the truly good and blessed children of God. Our double portion both of wealth and of honor will be fully revealed when our Lord appears, according to promise, in all His glory.

Fourth Strophe: verses 10-11: *The Church in its garments of salvation.*

10 *I greatly rejoice in the Lord,*
My soul glories in my God
That He has clothed me with garments of salvation,
Covered me with the mantle of righteousness,
Like a bridegroom who, priestlike, adorns his head,
Or a bride who puts on her jewels.
11 *For, like the earth that sends forth its shoots,*
And like a garden that makes its seed that is sown spring up,
So will the Lord God cause righteousness to spring forth,
And praise before all nations.

שׂוֹשׂ אָשִׂישׂ בַּיהוָה תָּגֵל נַפְשִׁי בֵּאלֹהַי 10
כִּי הִלְבִּישַׁנִי בִּגְדֵי־יֶשַׁע מְעִיל צְדָקָה יְעָטָנִי
כֶּחָתָן יְכַהֵן פְּאֵר וְכַכַּלָּה תַּעְדֶּה כֵלֶיהָ:

It would be out of harmony with the rest of Scripture to put these words into the mouth of the Servant of the Lord, who spoke the words in verses 1-3. Nowhere in Isaiah or elsewhere in Scripture does the Messiah say that the Lord has clothed Him with salvation and righteousness. Everywhere He is the Bringer of salvation (chapters 42, 49, 50, 53, 55, 61:1-3), never the recipient of salvation. Chapter 49:8 speaks cf help and preservation, not of salvation and righteousness. On the other hand, rejoicing over salvation is always placed in the mouth of the soul that has been blessed with this grace — for example, Moses and Miriam, Exodus 15; Hannah, 1 Samuel 2; Mary, Luke 1 — or in the mouth of the grateful church as a whole, as in many of the Psalms. In our passage the singer rejoices, not over salvation that he imparts to others, but over salvation that he receives. It is Israel, the congregation of believers, the church, that is here represented as rejoicing over the Lord's gift of salvation.

The absolute infinitive followed by a finite verb (*sōs 'asīs*) emphasizes the sincerity of the rejoicing. *YHWH* and *'elōhay* denote the God of salvation, and the prefix *be* indicates that He is the object and the source of the rejoicing. *tāghēl* (a jussive!) *naphshī* continues and heightens the thought expressed by *sōs 'asīs*. *kī* introduces the reason for the rejoicing. The congregation of believers sums up everything that the Lord has done for its deliverance and salvation in this picture: He has clothed me with garments of salvation and with the mantle (*me 'īl* is the flowing outer garment that completes the attire of the rich, the noble, the princes, prophets, and priests) of righteousness. *ye 'ātānī,* He has completely arrayed me. The genitives are genitives of apposition. *tsedhāqāh* is not to be understood as righteousness in the moral sense, but as a synonym of *yesha'.* As a *terminus technicus*, the word denotes the salvation that has been wrought in accord with the eternal election of God and God's covenant of grace made with Abraham in Christ, the Servant of the Lord. It includes all temporal and eternal, physical and spiritual, gifts that lie in God's power to bestow, — the δικαιοσύνη θεοῦ that is imputed to faith without any human merit or contribution whatsoever. *tsidhqath YHWH* embraces everything that Israel of old, the church, every believer, has ever received or still receives of help and salvation. In this poor life of ours we possess it in faith, and therefore in imperfect form, a form in which our flesh does not delight. Therefore we savor its blessedness only in smallest measure and delight in it only faintheartedly. But where it is apprehended and understood even in smallest measure, the Christian heart will join in with the song of joy in our text.

The next two comparisons vividly set forth the joy of the church and her glorious attire. The joy of a bridegroom and of a bride is chosen as representing the deepest and sincerest happiness. Lying hidden in the heart, it does not express itself in noisy behavior, but rather in its adornment. The bridegroom gives evidence of his joy by his priestlike headdress — for that is the meaning of *kihēn* — while the bride proudly adorns herself with her jewels. The priestly turban, the *mighbā'ah* (from *gābha'*, to be loftily domed) was considered to be the ultimate in elegant male headdress, because of its fine white material and its attractive form. So too, the bride's jewels were her proudest adornment.

Finally, the *ke* prefixed to *ḥāthān* and to *kallāh* is a preposition, not a conjunction. The two phrases are relative attributes: Like the bridegroom who, etc.; and like the bride who, etc., Gr. 155, g. p. 487.

11 כִּי כָאָרֶץ תּוֹצִיא צִמְחָהּ וּכְגַנָּה זֵרוּעֶיהָ תַצְמִיחַ
כֵּן ׀ אֲדֹנָי יְהוִה יַצְמִיחַ צְדָקָה וּתְהִלָּה נֶגֶד כָּל־הַגּוֹיִם:

In the last verse of the chapter the Lord again speaks, as in verses 4-6 and 7-9. In these words the basis is set forth on which the whole discourse, not merely verse 10, rests. Here the promise of salvation is made still more certain. The comparison is based on the law of nature (a clear reference to Gen. 1:11,12; 2:9; 8:22) that the earth and every garden will without fail cause the seed to sprout that is sown in it. As certainly as this will come to pass, so certainly will the Almighty Lord, Israel's God of grace, who creates and rules over all things, cause salvation and honor to spring up before all nations, so that they cannot fail to observe and acknowledge it. The *ke* before *'arets* and *ghannāh* is a particle of comparison. *'asher* must be supplied before *tōtsī'* and *zērū'eyhā*. The suffixes in *tsimḥāh* and *zērū'eyhā* must not be overlooked. Its plants and His seeding, that is, that which was entrusted to it for growth. God, who annually fulfills the pledge which He attached to nature, will just as surely keep His promise of salvation which He gave to His people.

Second Discourse: Chapter 62

Jerusalem in glorious array as the bride of the Lord.

We have divided this chapter into three parts: verses 1-5, 6-9, 10-12, because, on the one hand, the thought in 1-3 is repeated in another form in 6-9. The Lord will not rest until Zion has been restored to her full glory; and the watchers on the walls of Jerusalem shall not cease to call out until the Lord shall have raised her to highest honor in the world. Verses 4 and 5, on the other hand, in common with verses 10-12, express the thought that all the world shall seek out Zion-Jerusalem and frequent her borders. A different division is preferred by other commentators.

Rhetorically, the climax of chapters 58-66 is reached in this central triad of 61-63, of which in turn chapter 62 is the climax. The prophet's heart bursts forth in an expression of joyous enthusiasm over the realization of the supreme promise of revelation, which he now views in the spirit: the redeemed congregation as the Lord's masterpiece, as the bride and wedded wife of the Lord. Because of the overflowing fullness of his heart his mouth overflows in speech of matchless power. The speech attains still greater sublimity by being put into the mouth of the Lord Himself. Thus the speech gains authority, emphasis, and vividness, since the Lord Himself as speaker addresses Zion directly. The speech begins on an elevated note, advances rapidly to an even higher pitch, until at the end of the first half it comes quietly to rest. At the beginning of the second half it rises again to a climax, rests seemingly in exhaustion in a solemn oath in verses 8 and 9, and then once more rises to enthusiastic heights in the resounding trumpet call of a herald, before descending to the calm of a short description of the glory of Zion. In verse 4 the speech changes from the usual rhythm of three or four stresses in a verse, to the powerful Qinah rhythm; and hardly anywhere are the iambic-anapestic cadence of solemn Hebrew speech and the melodious effect of the vowel sounds of the language so strikingly manifest as in this passage.

First Strophe: verses 1-5:   *The Lord will not rest until He has placed Jerusalem as His gloriously appareled bride at His side and has made her known as such to all the world.*

1   *For Zion's sake I will not keep silent,*
    And in behalf of Jerusalem I will not rest,
    Until her salvation goes forth like a bright light,
    And her deliverance like a torch that flares up,
2   *And until the nations see your salvation,*
    And all the kings see your glory;
    And you shall be called by a new name,
    Which the mouth of the Lord shall determine,
3   *And until you are a beautiful crown in the Lord's hand*
    And a royal diadem in the right hand of your God.
4   *No more shall you be called "Forsaken,"*
    No more shall your land be called "Desolate";
    But you shall be called "My Delight"
    And your land "Married,"
    For the Lord's pleasure is in you
    And your land shall be espoused.
5   *For as a young man takes a maid to wife,*
    So shall your children espouse themselves to you,
    And with the joy of a bridegroom in his bride,
    So will your God rejoice in you.

לְמַ֤עַן צִיּוֹן֙ לֹ֣א אֶחֱשֶׁ֔ה   וּלְמַ֥עַן יְרוּשָׁלַ֖͏ִם לֹ֣א אֶשְׁק֑וֹט 1
עַד־יֵצֵ֤א כַנֹּ֙גַהּ֙ צִדְקָ֔הּ   וִישׁוּעָתָ֖הּ כְּלַפִּ֥יד יִבְעָֽר׃

Verse 6 clearly indicates that the speaker is the Lord. The situation is that preceding that of chapter 60. What that chapter describes as being present, is here in a state of preparation. The Lord will not rest until what is there described has become fact and reality. As in that chapter, so here too, a light rises over Zion, and the nations and their kings behold its glory. The bestowal of a new name is also foretold in 60:14b. In verse 3 the prophecy takes a new turn and pictures the preparation of Zion as the bride of the Lord. *lema'an* is essentially a particle expressing purpose, and for that reason we have, in its second occurrence, given it a meaning that suggests God's intention in respect to Zion-Jerusalem. God's purpose is the glorification of His church. God will not rest or be silent until the glory of His church has become fact and truth indeed, cf. 42:14; 57:11; 64:1; 65:6. It is the zeal of the love of the Lord that accomplishes this work, cf. 9:7; 37:32, and *'ahīshennāh* in 60:22. *shāqat* is a stronger verb than *hāshah*, as resting is stronger than pausing. Whereas in 60:1-3 light and radiance are direct designations of salvation, here the words are used by way of comparison. *tsedheq* and *yeshu'ah* are the terms that denote salvation. *nōghah*, radiance, a bright light, does not as a rule signify a glaring light, but rather a soft, mild light, 50:10; 60:19. Here the word is paired with a burning torch, since it is the dawning light of salvation that is being depicted. The antithesis is here, as in 60:2, the darkness. *yibh'ar*, as is indicated by its masculine form, is not the predicate of *wishu'āthāh*, but is a relative clause (with suppressed *'asher*) modifying *lappīdh*, Gr. 155, g, p. 487 (cf. 61:10), like a torch that flares up.

וְרָאוּ גוֹיִם צִדְקֵךְ וְכָל־מְלָכִים כְּבוֹדֵךְ ²

וְקֹרָא לָךְ שֵׁם חָדָשׁ אֲשֶׁר פִּי יְהוָה יִקֳּבֶנּוּ:

We have construed the perfects *rā'u* in verse 2 and *hāyīth* in verse 3 as being linked to *yētsē'* in verse 1 by the connective *Waw* and as being governed by the conjunction *'adh* in verse 1. This is not only the most natural explanation of the construction, but the particulars mentioned in verses 2 and 3 belong essentially to the glorification that the zeal of the Lord will, without pause or rest, bring to pass. In addition, the entire section is divided between verses 3 and 4 into two strophes, each of ten clauses; and in verse 4 a new subject, without *Waw*, is introduced.

Zion's salvation and glory shall be revealed not to her alone, but to all the world, in limited measure during the time of this world, but in all its fullness at the coming of the Lord, 2 Corinthians 4:10f; Romans 8:18; Colossians 3:4; 1 John 3:2; cf. 61:9. The new name by which Zion shall be known appears at the end of the chapter in verse 12. Cf. 65:15c. But the Lord, as if unwilling to withhold mention of the name any longer, makes known in verse 4 a few names that, like the name in verse 12, are an indication of Zion's relation to her Lord. The mouth of the Lord Himself, who makes Zion glorious, who alone knows her real character, and who determines all things, will confer that name — *yiqqobhennū*, an imperfect Qal of *nāqabh*, to cut, chisel, engrave.

וְהָיִ֛יתְ עֲטֶ֥רֶת תִּפְאֶ֖רֶת בְּיַד־יְהֹוָ֑ה וּצְנ֥וֹף מְלוּכָ֖ה בְּכַף־
אֱלֹהָֽיִךְ׃

The church will be a glorious diadem, a regal turban, a royal crown in the hand of the Lord. The kingly crown here represents the most glorious and most beautiful ornament available. It is an ornament made of the most costly materials and is a sign of the most exalted human dignity, Ezekiel 21:31f(26f). Here the reference is not to the crowns with which brides and bridegrooms in the Orient (Song of Songs 3:11) were accustomed to deck themselves on the day of their espousal (Cornill, Intro. p. 272). In this picture it is the church that is being depicted as the most precious and glorious work of the Lord, as His masterpiece, in comparison with which even heaven and earth, which are doomed to pass away (51:6; 65:17) are as nothing. It is the church, which is held in the hand of the Lord, to the wonder and amazement of the whole world. Up to this point the meaning of the text is clear. Whether "in the hand of the Lord" is to indicate that He intends to place this crown on His head as a crown of honor, we shall not attempt to decide. It would, however, be a genuinely Biblical thought, since God's greatest glory is His grace, His gracious working in His church. That is His masterwork.

Cf. Proverbs 12:4 for the picture of the wife as the husband's crown, and Philippians 4:1 and 1 Thessalonians 2.19 for the picture of the congregation as Paul's crown of rejoicing. Since the church is the bride of the Lord, she might also be represented as the crown which He has set upon His head.

לֹא־יֵאָמֵר֩ לָ֨ךְ ע֜וֹד עֲזוּבָ֗ה וּלְאַרְצֵךְ֙ לֹא־יֵאָמֵ֥ר עוֹד֙ שְׁמָמָ֔ה
כִּ֣י לָ֗ךְ יִקָּרֵא֙ חֶפְצִי־בָ֔הּ וּלְאַרְצֵ֖ךְ בְּעוּלָ֑ה
כִּי־חָפֵ֤ץ יְהֹוָה֙ בָּ֔ךְ וְאַרְצֵ֖ךְ תִּבָּעֵֽל׃

The repetition of the *le* in *lākh* and *le'artsēkh* makes a distinction between the city and the territory in which it is situated. The city was *'azūbhāh*, a wife forsaken by the Lord, her Husband, a mother forsaken by her children; the homeland was *shemāmāh*, a desolation, made such by its enemies. Both friends and enemies so named the city and the homeland. That, however, shall be changed. The city, in her relation to the Lord shall be *hephtsī bhāh*, "My joy in her" (according to 2 Kings 21:1 this was the name of Hezekiah's wife, the mother of Manasseh), and her land shall, in relation to her children, be *be'ūlāh*, the wedded one. The *kī* before *lākh,* following an earlier *lō'* is not causal but antithetical, equivalent to *kī 'im,* Gr. 163, a, p. 500. The *kī* in the final clause introduces the reason for what precedes. The Lord rejoices in the city, and therefore she is *hephtsībhāh;* and the land is *be'ūlāh,* because she shall be wedded. In connection with the latter name it should be noted that it is derived from *bā'al,* which means "to take possession of as a husband." As the next verse shows, it is the children of Zion who carry out the function of a *ba'al* and take possession.

כִּי־יִבְעַל בָּחוּר בְּתוּלָה יִבְעָלוּךְ בָּנָיִךְ 5
וּמְשׂוֹשׂ חָתָן עַל־כַּלָּה יָשִׂישׂ עָלַיִךְ אֱלֹהָיִךְ:

kī, meaning "for," does not in this case include the sense of "like" or "as." The "as" of the comparison (*ke*) is implied, Gr. 161, a, p. 499. The thought that children espouse their mother has by some been considered so monstrous that they felt compelled to assume a corruption of the text. But the LXX too has essentially this text, and according to the context, in spite of the feminine suffix in *yibh'ālūkh,* it is the homeland, not the city, that the children of Zion will take to wife. Moreover, the point of comparison is not the sexual relation, but the idea of possession that lies in the word *bā'al.* The homeland will again come into the possession and under the control of the children of Zion, its legitimate lords. The true bridegroom and husband of Zion is, however, the Lord Himself, as the following clause makes clear: "And with the joy of a bridegroom in his bride, so will your God rejoice in you." *mesōs hāthān — yāsīs* is the so-called internal accusative — with joy He rejoices, etc., Gr. 117, p, p. 366. Cf. 45:17. The sincere and supreme joy of a bridegroom in his bride is chosen to picture God's joy in His bride the church. God's highest joy is the glorification of His church and His union with her. "This is a great mystery," Ephesians 5:32. Therefore He "gave Himself for it," Ephesians 5:25. See also Isaiah 54:5-10.

Second Strophe: verses 6-9: *Those who watch and pray over Jerusalem should give the Lord no rest, till He makes her the object of praise in all the earth.*

6 *On your walls, O Jerusalem, have I set watchmen,*
Who all the day and all the night shall never be silent.
You who appeal to the Lord, grant yourselves no rest,
7 *And give Him no rest,*
Till He establish and make Jerusalem a praise in the earth.

8   *The Lord has sworn by His right hand and His strong arm:*
     I will not again give your grain as food for your enemies,
     Nor shall strangers drink your wine for which you labored;
9   *But those who gathered the harvest shall eat it and praise the Lord,*
     And those who gathered the vintage shall drink it in My holy
         courts.

6 עַל־חוֹמֹתַ֨יִךְ֙ יְר֣וּשָׁלִַ֔ם הִפְקַ֖דְתִּי שֹׁמְרִ֑ים

כָּל־הַיּ֧וֹם וְכָל־הַלַּ֛יְלָה תָּמִ֖יד לֹ֣א יֶחֱשׁ֑וּ

הַמַּזְכִּרִים֙ אֶת־יְהֹוָ֔ה אַל־דֳּמִ֖י לָכֶֽם׃

In the first strophe it is the Lord who gives Himself no rest until
the glorification of Zion is complete; here He admonishes the
watchmen whom He has Himself placed on the walls of Zion, to
grant neither themselves nor the Lord any rest, until He shall
have established Jerusalem as a *tehillāh* on the earth. It is not
clear whether the walls are to be considered as complete or still
uncompleted; at any rate, in whatsoever state they may be, they
are in existence, and what is promised in 54:11f lies in the future,
as does also the glorification of the city itself. The *shōmerīm* are
watchmen stationed on the walls, whose duty it is to be on the
lookout for the approach of possible enemies and to give the alarm
in case of need. They are *tsōphīm* (52:8), as distinguished from the
night watchmen within the city itself (Song of Songs 3:3; 5:7) and
from the guards at the gates (Nehemiah 3:29). These watchmen
are the prophets and preachers, spiritual watchmen, who guard
and watch over the church lest it suffer injury. That they are
never silent and never cease to call out by day or by night cannot
mean that they are summoning defenders to battle against approaching enemies, since enemies are no longer present. Their unceasing calling is intended either to summon the citizens to put
their hands to the building of Zion — for by means of their own
labor God intends to accomplish the glorification of Zion, 61:4;
58:12 — or to exhort the heathen converts, who are streaming to
the city, to join in the work of glorification. Cf. 60:10ff. Possibly
the unceasing call is intended for the ears of both. Zion's inhabitants and the children of strangers from afar off are admonished
by the prophets not to rest from their work of building the Lord's
city, until its glory is fully established.

The *mazkirīm 'eth YHWH* (verbal function of the participle, Gr.
116, f, p. 357), those who remind the Lord, who appeal to Him, are
hardly to be identified with the Lord's watchmen or other official

remembrancers such as the priests. That thought would have been expressed by *mazkirēy YHWH*. These *mazkirīm* are all those who pray to the Lord and confess Him, all who call upon Him — prophets, priests and laymen, teachers and hearers. Whosoever prays to the Lord and in his prayer believingly reminds Him of His promises, must allow himself no rest, namely in prayer, until, etc. *hammazkirīm* is vocative. Between *'al* and *domī* one needs to supply *yehī,* Gr. 152, g, p. 480.

וְאַל־תִּתְּנוּ דָמִי לוֹ   עַד־יְכוֹנֵן ⁷

וְעַד־יָשִׂים אֶת־יְרוּשָׁלַ͏ִם   תְּהִלָּה בָּאָרֶץ:

Verse 7 continues the thought of verse 6: As you give yourselves no rest, so give Him, the Lord, no rest until He, etc. The Piel *yekhōnēn* does not here mean "to lay the foundation," since it is the completion of the building of Zion that is being described, and the word here has the more general meaning of preparing or constructing, as in Isaiah 45:18. *tehillāh bā'arets* is a part of the predicate of *yasīm*: He will make Jerusalem a praise in the earth. The prophet has chosen this personification as a sublime representation of the glorification of Zion. By the hand of the Lord, Zion shall become a praise in the earth.

נִשְׁבַּע יְהוָה בִּימִינוֹ   וּבִזְרוֹעַ עֻזּוֹ ⁸

אִם־אֶתֵּן אֶת־דְּגָנֵךְ עוֹד   מַאֲכָל לְאֹיְבַיִךְ

וְאִם־יִשְׁתּוּ בְנֵי־נֵכָר תִּירוֹשֵׁךְ   אֲשֶׁר יָגַעַתְּ בּוֹ:

In the last clause of verse 7 the discourse reached a climax. Verses 8 and 9 now add the Lord's oath as a solemn Amen. Regarding the use of the perfect in the oath formula, see Gr. 106, g and i, p. 311f. The Lord swears that with His right hand and the almighty power of His arm He will perform the words of His oath. *'im* after *nishba'* — that not. Whenever the land of Israel was invaded by its enemies, and especially when the land was conquered by Babylon, the produce of the land and the fruits of the labor of the people became the spoil of the enemies, but that shall not happen again. On the contrary:

כִּי מְאַסְפָיו יֹאכְלֻהוּ וְהִלְלוּ אֶת־יְהוָה ⁹

וּמְקַבְּצָיו יִשְׁתֻּהוּ   בְּחַצְרוֹת קָדְשִׁי:

Those who reap the grain shall eat it, and those who harvest the new wine shall drink it. They shall themselves enjoy the fruits of their labors and have the use of what their hands produced upon their own land. The phrases "and praise the Lord" and "in My holy courts" have reference to the offerings of the firstfruits of the land (Deut. 26:1ff; 14:22f) which the people brought to the holy place and of which they and the priests and Levites, the fatherless, the widows, the poor, and the strangers joyfully partook. Jerusalem shall be a praise upon the earth, adorned with all spiritual gifts; and with thanks and praise to God it shall enjoy in peace perfect spiritual and temporal happiness.

Third Strophe: verses 10-12: *The children of Zion in all the world are invited to join her in the enjoyment of her glory. Zion receives a new name.*

10   *Go forth, go forth through the gates,*
    Level the way for the people;
    Raise up, raise up the highway, clear it of stones;
    Lift up a banner for the people.
11   *Behold, the Lord will let the ends of the earth hear it:*
    Say to the daughter of Zion: Behold your salvation!
    Behold, His reward is with Him
    And His recompense goes forth before Him.
12   *And they shall be called the holy people, the Redeemed of the Lord,*
    And you shall be called Frequented, the city not forsaken.

עִבְרוּ עִבְרוּ בַּשְּׁעָרִים פַּנּוּ דֶּרֶךְ הָעָם ‏10

סֹלּוּ סֹלּוּ הַמְסִלָּה סַקְּלוּ מֵאֶבֶן

הָרִימוּ נֵס עַל־הָעַמִּים :

    The summons that begins with verse 10 has in its essentials already been published twice (40:3; 57:14), and portions thereof more frequently (40:9,10; 49:22; 52:7,8; 59:20). In connection with verse 11, see also Zechariah 9:9. It is not mere accident that the summons each time is a little different. Identification of the addressees of the summons with certain persons gives a false picture of the situation. The imperatives are rhetorical. In this connection see the remarks on 40:1. The subject is quite impersonal: One is to go out through the gates and the highway is to be prepared. *'ibhrū, 'ibhrū bashshe'arīm* does not, of course, mean to go in or to go out from the gates of Jerusalem. The gates are those of the cities of the gentiles and they are to go forth through these toward the gates of Zion, for the purpose is to summon the Diaspora of Zion in all the world to return to the mother-city, whose glorification is now complete. The gates through which the heralds pass with their invitation are not those of Babylon alone, but those of all the cities of the gentiles in which the *nidhḥey yisrā'el* now live as sojourners. That sense is supported by the admonition to lift up a banner for the people. We cannot agree with Gesenius that *hā'ammīm* has the specific meaning of "tribes." Those who level the ways may be the heralds themselves or other persons, but the point is that they are *for* the people who are returning home and who shall not be hindered by obstacles on their way. Some call the children of Israel together, others prepare the way. The raising of a banner for (*'al*) the nations is not meant for the nations themselves, but for the children of Zion living among them, as a sign for them to gather together for the return home, and it is assumed that the nations stand ready to help them in their journey.

הִנֵּה יְהוָה הִשְׁמִיעַ אֶל־קְצֵה הָאָרֶץ ¹¹
אִמְרוּ לְבַת־צִיּוֹן הִנֵּה יִשְׁעֵךְ בָּא
הִנֵּה שְׂכָרוֹ אִתּוֹ וּפְעֻלָּתוֹ לְפָנָיו:

The summons to go forth through the gates is now followed by the Lord's statement that He will let the ends of the earth hear it, namely, hear His command to say to the daughter of Zion: Behold your salvation! The heralds through whom the Lord announces this message to all the earth are those who were addressed in verse 10 with: Go forth! The daughter Zion (cf. Gr. 128, k, p. 416, for the epexegetical genitive) is not the city, but the scattered children of Israel in all the world. As in 60:1, *bā'* means that He has come and is here. *yish'ekh,* your salvation, like *yeshū'athī* in 49:6, represents the person of the Savior in abstract terms. *His* reward and *His* recompense, in 40:10, indicate that this is the meaning of the abstract terms. 60:1 is to be understood in the same way. The Son, the Servant of the Lord, is the personal glory of the Lord; and His reward and recompense are the prize that He, or respectively the Servant, has wrested in battle from the enemy and bestowed on His people Zion for its glorification. Chapter 63 speaks of the battle in which He has won reward and recompense.

וְקָרְאוּ לָהֶם עַם־הַקֹּדֶשׁ גְּאוּלֵי יְהוָה ¹²
וְלָךְ יִקָּרֵא דְרוּשָׁה עִיר לֹא נֶעֱזָבָה:

lāhem refers to the children of Zion who were called together and who are now represented as having reached their home. They are called *'am haqqōdhesh*, the people of the sanctuary, the holy people. This holiness is founded in the righteousness, the salvation and the glory of verses 1 and 2a, as is shown by 2b; and it is identical with the *tsedhāqāh* of 60:21, which gives their name to the *tsaddīqīm*, the righteous. *ge'ūlēy YHWH* is a synonym of *'am haqqōdhesh* and explains the term. They are now fully clothed with the *tsidhqath YHWH*, the salvation of grace, which the Lord Himself has prepared for them.

The city is now called *dherūshāh* and *'īr* (*'asher*) *lō' ne'ezābhāh*. Since the fundamental meaning of *dārash* is to tread upon, it is not necessary to translate *dherūshāh* with sought, or desired. The parallel phrase, *lo' ne'ezābhāh*, suggests the intended meaning. *dherūshāh* is the opposite of its parallel *ne'ezābhāh* and therefore means the much visited, whose streets are crowded with a constant stream of visitors. According to verses 4 and 5, it is the Lord Himself who goes in and out at her gates. For the emphasis in *lō' ne'ezābhāh* see Gr. 152, a, Note and d, p. 478f. The note on page 478 advises that *ne'ezābhāh* is not to be taken as a participle (adjective), but as the third singular perfect. *'asher* is to be supplied before *lō'*. Perfect salvation and abundant richness of life are now Zion's lot. This is the basis for her new name; she is the metropolis of the world.

A *résumé* of this discourse may be found in the headings of the three main strophes: 1. The Lord will neither pause nor rest until Jerusalem shall have been presented to all the world as a royal crown in His hand, as the espoused of her children, and as the bride of the Lord. 2. The watchmen on her walls and all those who pray within her walls shall give the Lord no rest until He has made her a praise in the earth and assured her of possession and enjoyment of the fruits of her land. 3. To all the scattered children of Zion in all the world the message shall be brought that the glorification of the mother-city has been completed and that her new name is the Frequented, the city Not-Forsaken.

Third Discourse: Chapter 63:1-6

The Lord's judgment of annihilation against the enemies, and the complete deliverance of those who are His own.

This brief prophecy (63:1-6) completes the second trilogy (chapters 61-63:6) of the third great part of Isaiah II. Verse 1 hails the conquering Hero on His return from victorious battle; verses 2 and 3 account for His startling appearance; verses 4-6 state the reason for the conflict and give a description of it. It should be noted that the description includes not only the destruction of the enemy, but also the deliverance of those who are the Lord's. — Of the three discourses (chapters 61, 62, and 63:1-6) the first is quiet, objective description; the second adopts a tone of loud rejoicing; the third is a dramatic, poetic climax.

1 *Who is this who comes from Edom,*
   From Bozrah, His garments glowing?
   He, who in His attire so splendidly appareled,
   Marches in the fullness of His strength? —
   It is I, the Proclaimer of Salvation, the great Deliverer.

2 *Why is Your clothing red?*
   And Your garments like those of one who treads in a winepress?

3 *The winepress, yes, I trod it all alone,*
   And of the nations there was no one at My side,
   So did I tread them in My anger,
   And trampled them in My wrath;
   With their lifeblood I sprinkled My garments,
   And I have stained all My clothing.

4 *For I had in mind a day of revenge,*
   The year to deliver My own had come.

5 *I looked about, but there was no helper,*
   Amazement overcame Me, but no one stood by Me.
   So My own arm helped Me, and My wrath sustained Me.

6 *I trod down the peoples in My anger*
  And made them drunken in My wrath,
  And I let their lifeblood run into the ground.

The prophet concludes his portrayal of the glorification of Zion with a dramatically vivid account of the destruction of all her enemies. As in a vision, he sees a conquering Hero, clad in shining garments of deep red coloring, with head uplifted, returning in the fullness of His strength, from Bozrah, the capital city of Edom. Filled with wonder at this amazing sight, he asks himself who this may be. The Hero Himself answers his question. But the prophet wishes to know more than just the identity of the Hero. His second question regarding the red-stained garments leads the Hero, who has already identified Himself in His first answer as the Savior of Israel, to report that He has at last carried out the long-planned judgment upon the heathen, His own and Zion's enemies. Without any help from without, sustained by His consuming wrath, He had slain His enemies, and their blood had drenched and stained His garments a deep red.

1 מִי־זֶ֣ה ׀ בָּ֣א מֵאֱד֗וֹם   חֲמ֤וּץ בְּגָדִים֙ מִבָּצְרָ֔ה
    זֶ֚ה הָד֣וּר בִּלְבוּשׁ֔וֹ   צֹעֶ֖ה בְּרֹ֣ב כֹּח֑וֹ
    אֲנִ֛י מְדַבֵּ֥ר בִּצְדָקָ֖ה   רַ֥ב לְהוֹשִֽׁיעַ׃

zeh, here joined to *mī* by Maqqeph and together with *mī* separated from the rest of the sentence by Munach legarmeh, is practically enclitic and serves only to emphasize the interrogative *mī.* Here it expresses amazement: Who then is this? Who can this be? Cf. Gr. 136, c, p. 442. *bā'* is a finite verb, present perfect, Gr. 106, g, p. 311. If it were a participle it would have been supplied with the article, *habbā',* because of the following adjectival and participial appositives. *'asher* is to be supplied before *bā'.* The questioner sees the Hero advancing on the highway that leads from Edom through Bozrah toward Jerusalem. Bozrah was situated about 25 miles southeast of the southern point of the Dead Sea. It was at least for a time the capital of Edom and was a city of considerable size (Gen. 36:33; 1 Chron. 1:44; Isa. 34:6; Jer. 48:24; 49:13,22; Amos 1:12). Its significance here is that it was a royal city and, in all likelihood, a strong fortress, as the name Bozrah, the unassailable, seems to indicate. Bozrah was to Edom what Jerusalem was to Judah, 34:6. The prophet makes Edom the scene of the great judgment upon the nations, since Edom was from of old the bitterest and most implacable enemy of God's people, an enmity that

dated back to Genesis 27. Cf. Obadiah 10-16; Amos 1:6,11; Ezekiel
35:10-15; Jeremiah 49:7-22; Lamentations 4:21f; Psalm 137:7.
Throughout the Old Testament Edom is the object of the prophecy
of bitter judgment. This prophecy had already been fulfilled before
Malachi's time, Malachi 1:3,4. About 300 B.C. Edom was occupied
by the Nabataeans, descendants of Nebajoth, Genesis 25:13, cf.
Isaiah 60:7. Ever since its conquest by the Mohammedans in the
seventh century A.D. the land has been lying wild and waste, as
had been foretold by the prophets, Isaiah 34, Jeremiah 49, and
Ezekiel 35.

The prophet sees the Hero approaching *ḥamūts beghādhīm.*
ḥamūts (from *ḥāmats*), in its formal sense, means strong, sharp,
intense; in the realm of color it takes on the meaning of bright,
rich crimson. The word is often translated as red, or crimson, in
agreement with the LXX. That specific color is mentioned in the
following verse, but here we prefer to retain the basic meaning of
ḥamūts, since the prophet commonly employs first the more general term and then narrows it down in a following explanation. Regarding the epexegetical genitive (*beghādhīm*) following the passive participle or verbal adjective *ḥamūts* in the construct state, cf.
Gr. 116, k, p. 358f and 128, x, p. 418f: shining as to garments.

The demonstrative *zeh*, which at the beginning of the sentence
was enclitic, is now in the third clause treated as the equivalent of
a relative: the one who, he who, Gr. 138, g, p. 446. *hādhūr
bilebhūshō*, splendidly appareled in His garments, repeats the
thought expressed in *ḥamūts beghādhīm*, but with emphasis on
the beauty and stately dignity of the Conqueror. The participle
tsō'eh, bending, bowing (of prisoners in 51:14), here would indicate
the proud, backward bending carriage, as the word is used in the
Arabic. Vitringa's "*huc illuc se motitans*," Delitzsch's "bending to
and fro," and Ewald's "stretching himself to full height" are somewhat too fantastic. Luther's "*einhergeht*" follows Symmachus and
the Vulgate, which read *tsō'ed* instead of *tsō'eh*, a term that describes a solemn, majestic carriage, 2 Samuel 6:13; Judges 5:4;
Psalm 68:8(7). The Hero advances proudly in the fullness of His
strength. His carriage already indicates that the battle has been
fought and won.

The answer to the question regarding the identity of the approaching Hero is not given, as Delitzsch supposes, in a voice that
could be heard afar off. The fact that the speaker continues his
speech immediately after identifying himself shows that his steps
have brought him close to the questioner. He answers: It is I, the

Proclaimer of Salvation, etc. The answer is of great import, since it distinguishes the person of this speaker from all other speakers, identifies and characterizes Him as an individual different from all others. *bitsedhāqāh* cannot therefore mean "according to the rule of truth and right," as Delitzsch supposes, because that could be said of any messenger sent from God. *tsedhāqāh* can here have no other than the specific, pregnant meaning of salvation, the salvation of the covenant, δικαιοσύνη θεοῦ, a sense in which the prophet so often uses this word. The characteristic by which the Lord is distinguished from all gods of the nations is that He speaks in, or of (*be*), this righteousness, that He reveals, proclaims, promises it. Thus, especially, in 45:19-23; 41:22-29; 43:9-12; 44:7f; 45:7f; 46:10; 48:3,5,6,16; 51:4ff; 55:11. The *tsedhāqāh* of this verse is the *yeshu'ath 'elōhēynū* of 52:10; it is the *tsedheq* in which the Lord calls His Servant in 42:6, and Cyrus in 45:13. It is that righteousness which became an objective reality in Zion, and of which chapter 62 treats: *tsidhqāh, yeshu'āthāh* (verse 1), *tsidhqēkh, kebhōdhēkh* (verse 2), through which Zion became a *tehillāh* on the earth (verse 7), and which was to be announced to her, in verse 11, as *yish'ekh*. The very close connection between this chapter and the preceding one, which spoke exclusively and in clearest terms of this righteousness, should make it clear that this chapter uses the term in the same sense. A comparison of verse 5 with 59:16ff establishes beyond any question the certainty that what is here referred to as a help and support of the Lord in carrying out His judgment is, in reference to His people, *tsedhāqāh* and *yeshu'āh, Heilsgerechtigkeit,* righteousness unto salvation.

There remains only the question whether *be* before *tsedhāqāh* makes the righteousness subjective or objective. If *bitsedhāqāh* is to be understood adverbially, then *tsedhāqāh* refers to God's judgment of grace and salvation upon Israel — He who speaks in the faithfulness of His grace and salvation. Or shall it be understood objectively: He who proclaims righteousness and salvation? A decisive answer cannot be supplied by the grammar, since *be* is frequently used to introduce the object of a mental act; cf. Deuteronomy 6:7; 1 Samuel 19:3f; Gr. 119, 1, p. 380. We prefer to understand it in the objective sense.

medhabbēr is not here used in the ordinary sense of "speaking," for that would hardly have indicated some special characteristic of the Lord, and that is clearly here intended. The word is used in its more emphatic, pregnant sense of pronouncing, preaching, revealing, proclaiming. The participial form designates the speaking as

customary, characteristic, distinctive. In *medhabbēr bitsedhāqāh*
the participle has the force of a noun, instead of the verbal sense
of the form in *medhabbēr tsedhāqāh.* Not: One who now and then
speaks righteousness; but: One who is the speaker of righteousness by profession, the Preacher, the Prophet of righteousness.
The phrase has the same meaning as *dōbhēr tsedheq* in 45:19:
Proclaimer of salvation. The phrase is essentially the equivalent
of *mebhassēr,* εὐαγγελιστής, in 41:27, cf. 40:9. For the objective
use of *be* to express greater emphasis, see Gr. 119, q, p. 380f.

In *medhabbēr* the Hero identifies Himself, as in the references
cited above, as the one true Revealer of salvation. Besides Him
there is no Savior, as He has repeatedly asserted and established.
medhabbēr unmistakably characterizes Him as the God of Israel,
the Lord. The second characteristic peculiar to the Hero is that He
is *rabh lehoshi'a,* mighty to save. Both expressions are to be understood in their pregnant sense. *rabh* — altogether great, almighty.
hōshī'a has a broader meaning than simply "to help"; it is used in
the more specific sense of "to accomplish the promised deliverance
and salvation of Israel." *rabh lehōshī'a* is another expression like
mōshi'a, mōshī'ekh, mōshī'ekhā, terms that are used so often in
Isaiah, 43:3,11; 45:15,21; 49:26; 60:16; 63:8. It is like *'abhīr
ya'aqōbh,* Israel's Deliverer and almighty Hero, who unfailingly
accomplishes her temporal and eternal salvation, and besides
whom there is no real Savior. The two expressions supplement
each other: *medhabbēr bitsedhāqāh* is the Hero as Revealer and
Proclaimer of salvation; *rabh lehōshī'a* is the Mighty One who performs the promised salvation.

² מַדּ֫וּעַ אָדֹם לִלְבוּשֶׁ֑ךָ וּבְגָדֶ֖יךָ כְּדֹרֵ֥ךְ בְּגַֽת׃

The Hero's answer clearly revealed that He who was approaching in shining garments, splendidly appareled, irresistibly powerful, was the Savior of Israel, the Mighty One of Jacob. But the
prophet's eyes are still fastened on the stained garments of the
Hero, and so he asks: Whence is the red stain on your garments,
and why is your clothing like that of one who has trodden the
grapes in the wine troughs? For *maddū'a* see 50:2. He seeks the
reason for the red stains. The adjective *'ādhōm* is here used as a
neuter noun, as is indicated by the *le* in *lebhūshekhā. 'ādhōm*
usually signifies a dark red; only once is it used for the bright red
of the cheeks, Song of Songs 5:10. Since the word is here used of
blood, it can only signify a dark red, the color that stains the garments of one who has been treading a winepress. *dōrēkh* is a geni-

tive in meaning, although not in form. Although *gath* is in pause, it has retained its short Pathach. This is not unusual in the case of monosyllables. The comparison with the garments of one who has been treading a winepress, suggests that the clothing of the Hero is not colored a uniform dark red, but is spotted and splashed with red.

פּוּרָה ׀ דָּרַכְתִּי לְבַדִּי וּמֵעַמִּים אֵין־אִישׁ אִתִּי
וְאֶדְרְכֵם בְּאַפִּי וְאֶרְמְסֵם בַּחֲמָתִי
וְיֵז נִצְחָם עַל־בְּגָדַי וְכָל־מַלְבּוּשַׁי אֶגְאָלְתִּי ׃

pūrah (from *pūr*, to break) is just a synonym of *gath*, a winepress or trough. The word seems to have been chosen for euphonic reasons. The Hero adapts His answer to the picture used by the questioner. Yes, indeed, it was a trampling of a winepress that stained My garments with red. *dārakhtī* is a historic perfect. The Hero narrates. He *has* been treading a winepress. The following clauses all explain how His garments became so thoroughly spattered with blood, so stained and soiled. He has had to tread the press alone, without help or support from any direction or from any person. *'ammīm* combines all the peoples of the world into one. *'eyn 'īsh* does not refer to any one nation, but to any single person. *'ittī,* with Me, that is, at My side as a companion in arms. Not one man out of the whole world of nations stood at the side of the Hero. This clause explains and emphasizes *lebhaddī.* The copulative *Waws* with following imperfects, instead of expected *Waw* consecutive, may be explained by the vividness of the narration. The sense is, however, usually consecutive, as in *we'edhrekhēm.* In this clause the emphasis is on *be'appī,* in the next it is on *bahamāthī.* In wrath and hot anger He stamped and trampled (*rāmas*), because he was forced to battle all the peoples of the world alone, see the final words of verse 5. The *Waw* in *we'edhrekhēm* is therefore in its sense a consecutive. The clause that begins with *weyēz* (apoc. impf. Qal of *nāzāh,* to sprinkle) is also consecutive. Because He had been crushing and trampling the nations in His anger, His garments became spattered and soiled with their lifeblood.

In earlier commentaries and dictionaries, *nētsah* was usually explained as a formal concept meaning "glowing," "conspicuous"; consequently: glory; or in reference to time: eternity, a long period. *lamenatstseah,* the superscription of many Psalms, was understood to mean: for the director of the temple music. In more

recent times, scholars derive the word from an Arabic and
Ethiopic root *nātsah* meaning to sprinkle, to spray, which would
lead to the meaning of spray, juice, lifeblood in the noun-form.
This derivation appeals to us because of the preceding related
word *nāzāh*, from which *weyēz* is formed. *'egh'altī* is an Arama-
ism for *high'altī*, a perf. Hiphil of *gā'al*, to soil, 59:3; cf. Gr. 53, p, p.
147. The Qamets is pausal.

4 כִּי יוֹם נָקָם בְּלִבִּי וּשְׁנַת גְּאוּלַי בָּאָה:

Verse 4 supplies the reason for the trampling of the nations as
in a winepress and for the vehemence with which the Hero carries
out His grim work. The speaker goes back into the time before this
momentous act and uses the pluperfect tense. The two clauses are
extraordinarily vivid. "A day of vengeance" instead of our simple
"vengeance"; "was in My mind" instead of "I had in mind." He
speaks in His capacity of *qedhōsh yisrā'el*, who in His zeal for His
people now remorselessly avenges all the injustice that had been
inflicted on them and recompenses a hundredfold, cf. 51:22f; 52:4f;
49:24ff; 59:18. The next clause is also in the pluperfect tense: the
year of My redemption had come. *ge'ulīm* may be construed as a
Qal passive participle of *gā'al* — My redeemed. Ewald, Bredenkamp, and others take the word in that sense. But the LXX understood the word to be an abstract form and translated it with
λύτρωσις. The Peshitta, the Vulgate, Gesenius, Delitzsch, and
Cheyne agree with the LXX. Some more recent scholars have
emended the text to read *gemulīm*, compensation. No matter how
the form is explained, the sense is that which Luther so perfectly
expressed with his *"Das Jahr die Meinen zu erloesen"* — the year
to redeem My own. The *year* of My redeemed, resp. of My redemption, is an allusion to the "Year of Jubilee."

5 וְאַבִּיט וְאֵין עֹזֵר וְאֶשְׁתּוֹמֵם וְאֵין סוֹמֵךְ
וַתּוֹשַׁע לִי זְרֹעִי וַחֲמָתִי הִיא סְמָכָתְנִי:

For comments on a similar anthropomorphic description, see
the remarks on 59:16ff. The lively form of description continues,
and for that reason the copulative *Waws* with the verbs are not to
be changed to the consecutive form. The Narrator explains His
raging anger. When He saw that He was all alone in His battle
with the nations of the world, He looked about Him for help, but
there was none. The terror of battle overcame Him (*'eshtōmēm*),
but there was no one who might have sprung to His assistance.

"Then" — now at last there is a *Waw* consecutive — "must My own arm help Me; and My wrath, it supported Me." The grim rage of battle must guide His arm, remove the terror of conflict, and take the place of any help from without. A number of manuscripts offer *tsidhqāthī* (cf. 59:16) instead of *ḥamāthī*. But that reading does not change matters, because the *ḥēmāh* of the Lord is but the obverse side of His *tsedhāqāh*. But *ḥēmāh* is better suited to this situation, because destruction of the enemies is of primary interest in the description, and the deliverance of His own is secondary.

$$ \text{וְאָב֤וּס עַמִּים֙ בְּאַפִּ֔י וַאֲשַׁכְּרֵ֖ם בַּחֲמָתִ֑י} \quad ^6 $$
$$ \text{וְאוֹרִ֥יד לָאָ֖רֶץ נִצְחָֽם׃} $$

The sentence begins with the *Waw* copula with the imperfect. The first *Waw* is consecutive, or if you wish, descriptive, in meaning: "And so." *būs* is a less robust word than *rāmas*, but stronger than *dārakh*, and its meaning is "to trample under foot." Cf. Zechariah 10:5 where it is used of treading in the mire; Psalms 44:6(5) and 60:14(12); also Isaiah 18:2,7; 22:5. The wrath and anger of the Hero are here also presented as the means of doing battle and as the source of strength and energy. The wrath of the Hero is one aspect of the conflict, the other is the total destruction of the enemy, as the concluding words of the verse once more point out: "I let their lifeblood run into the ground." Instead of *'ashakkerēm*, I made them drunken, some commentators prefer the reading of the Targum and of several codices, *'ashabberēm*, I smashed or shattered them, to complete the parallel with *'ābhūs*. Still, being made drunken by the wrath of the Lord is a genuinely Isaianic thought (51:17,22,23, and elsewhere), which fits very well into the context. Commentators who exaggerate the meaning of *'ābhūs* by translating, "I will grind them into powder," consider "I will make them drunken" to be too weak a parallel. But if *'ābhūs* is rendered normally with "tread into the dust," the climax develops naturally into "made them drunken in My wrath," and put them to death.

With this section (chapters 61, 62, and 63:1-6) the prophet actually reaches the end of his prophecy. Beyond the perfect glorification of Zion and the total destruction of her enemies, there is really nothing new still to be said. What follows in the final Triad (63:7 through chapter 66) is partly confirmation of what has already been said, partly elaboration of preceding thoughts, but for the most part, a description of the consequences of this preaching as to the people and as to the Lord. As chapters 34 and 35 form a conclusion to Isaiah I, so chapters 61 to 63:1-6 form the conclusion of Isaiah II. Chapter 63:1-6 corresponds to chapter 34. Both of these chapters give a final account; they are the history of the end. Chapter 35 and chapters 61 and 62 treat of the final glorification of Zion; chapters 34 and 63:1-6, of the final judgment upon her enemies. There is no mention whatsoever of Babylon in these chapters. Here and in chapters 34 and 35, the scene of the judgment is laid in Edom, and the object of the judgment are all nations. In both sections the judgment is described from the point of view of the Day of Vengeance of the Lord (34:8; 63:4), which all prophets after Joel and Obadiah proclaim. In these chapters it is the Lord Himself who carries out the judgment; in the New Testament it is "by that Man whom He hath ordained," Acts 17:31. The Revelation of St. John describes the same judgment in still another way, chapters 19 and 20.

THIRD TRIAD
Chapters 63:7-66

*The New Order in its Final State:
the Rejection of Israel and
the Adoption of the Gentiles.*

The New Order in its Final State: the Rejection of Israel and the Adoption of the Gentiles.

In a highly dramatic three-act finale, the prophet brings his prophecy of the future kingdom of the Messiah to a close. The promise of the future deliverance and the glorification of Zion has been set forth in great detail and with great frequency in the preceding chapters. In Isaiah 61, 62, and 63:1-6 it was again reviewed in a brilliant portrayal. Now, in these closing discourses, the prophet opens to our view the final results of his preaching. First of all, he shows us, in 63:7 to 64:12, what effect his preaching will have on faithful Israel. He introduces Israel in the form of a pious person offering up a prayer. As one overwhelmed by all the goodness he has received at the hands of the Lord, he sees that Israel's present misery is a consequence of her unfaithfulness to the Lord, and with a bitter and almost despondent cry he for the last time pleads with the Lord that He grant deliverance to His people. Chapters 65 and 66 contain the Lord's definitive answer to this prayer: Israel, being hardened, has been rejected; the Lord will preserve only a remnant. In the new order, all the old promises shall be abundantly fulfilled in this remnant, and the consummation shall be attained (65). Violently demolishing the old, external, ineffectual order, the Lord carries out a speedy judgment of destruction upon the unregenerate and heathenized people, comforts those that remain "as one whom his mother comforteth," and accepts the gentiles, who lead the scattered children of Israel back to Jerusalem from all parts of the world.

First Discourse: Chapters 63:7-64:12

The final, ardent prayer of faithful Israel for grace toward all Israel and for deliverance of the people.

This prayer, proceeding as it does out of the tumult of an anguished heart, does not express itself in the quiet, measured phrases of earlier strophes. A clear division of the prayer into parts is thus made difficult. However, three separate utterances can be distinguished, each of which begins with a quiet description of conditions, rises to an ardent passionate plea, and then more quietly sets forth the reasons for the plea. The first such utterance comprises eleven verses, 7-17, linking the prayer for deliverance (verses 15-17) to a description of the many benefits of God's grace received in times past (verses 7-14). The second utterance, the shortest and most vehement of the three, in verses 18 and 19 describes the present misery, pleads passionately with the Lord (64:1-3) that He intervene with force, and in verse 4 comes to rest in the confident expectation of the Lord's miraculous help. The third utterance contrasts the erstwhile friendliness of the Lord with His present anger over the incurable sinfulness of the people; it pleads fervently that the Lord abate His anger for the sake of the unchangeable covenant between the Lord and Israel, which seems to have been breached by the present desolation of land, city, and temple (verses 8-12).

This section contains many exegetical difficulties, and the text seems to be corrupt in several places. Critical conjecture has made unrestrained use of the opportunity.

First Strophe: 63:7-17: *The many great deeds of grace that the Lord had done in the old days are the ground for the present pleas for mercy and deliverance.*

7 *I will praise the lovingkindness of the Lord, the Lord's glorious deeds.*
   According to all that the Lord has done for us,
   Besides His abundant goodness to the house of Israel,
   Which in His compassion and the fullness of His loving-kindness He showed to them.
8 *And said: For surely they are My people,*
   Children who will not deceive!
   And He became their Savior in all their afflictions.
9 *Not by emissary or angel — with His own countenance He saved them,*

   In His love and compassion He redeemed them,
   Lifted them up and carried them all the days of old.
10 *But they resisted and vexed His Holy Spirit,*
   So that He turned to be their enemy and warred against them.
11 *Then did His people remember the olden days, the days of Moses:*
   Where is He who led them up out of the sea, the Shepherd of His flock?
   Where is He who put His Holy Spirit in their midst?
12 *Who caused the arm of His majesty to go at Moses' right hand,*
   Who split the waters before them,
   To make for Himself a glorious name?
13 *He led them through the depths of waters;*
   Like horses upon the plain, they did not stumble,
14 *Like cattle going into the valley,*
   The Spirit of the Lord led them to rest.
   So did You lead Your people to make for Yourself a glorious name.
15 *Look down from heaven and see,*
   From Your holy, majestic dwelling;
   Where now is Your zeal, and where Your glorious deeds?
   Your yearning pity and Your compassion have been shut off toward me.

16 *But surely, You are our Father!*
   For Abraham knows us not
   And Israel does not acknowledge us;
   You, O Lord, are our Father;
   Our Savior from of old — that is Your name.
17 *Why do You let us stray, O Lord, from Your paths,*
   Why harden our heart, so as not to fear You?
   Return, for Your servants' sake,
   For the sake of the tribes of Your inheritance.

⁷ חַסְדֵי יְהוָה ׀ אַזְכִּיר תְּהִלֹּת יְהוָה
כְּעַל כֹּל אֲשֶׁר־גְּמָלָנוּ יְהוָה וְרַב־טוּב לְבֵית יִשְׂרָאֵל
אֲשֶׁר־גְּמָלָם כְּרַחֲמָיו וּכְרֹב חֲסָדָיו:

It is not necessarily the prophet himself who offers up this prayer, but rather some person whom the prophet imagines to be representative of the believers in Israel. Compare the *'elay* at the end of verse 15. His prayer begins with a short hymn in praise of the *ḥasdēy YHWH.* This form in the construct plural was understood by the LXX, Luther, and others, to represent an abstract attribute, such as grace or goodness. But here, as in most occurrences of the word (cf. Ps. 106:7; Gen. 32:11[10]; Isa. 55:3), the word means acts of loving-kindness, deeds of the Lord's grace, which are the object of *gemālānū* and *gemālām*, and which flow out of the Lord's compassion (*keraḥamāyw*). The plural *ḥasādhāyw*, on the other hand, which is parallel to *raḥamāyw* and with it is governed by the same particle *ke*, is to be understood in the abstract sense, as a synonym of *raḥamāyw:* according to His compassion and the fullness of His grace, cf. Psalm 106:45. Similarly, the *tehillōth* are the concrete glorious deeds of the Lord. The speaker, in his prayer of praise, calls these to remembrance. *ke'al* is a compound preposition: in accordance with what is fitting (cf. 59:18). His hymn of praise is to be in keeping with all the good that the Lord has done for us. In *werabh ṭūbh* the subject matter with which this prayer of praise (*'azkīr*) deals is stated in somewhat different terms. *rabh* might best be understood as a noun in the construct state in the sense of *rōbh*, like *rabh ṭūbhekhā* in Psalm 145:7: the greatness of Your deeds of goodness. The translation "great of goodness" as an adjective attribute of the Lord only confuses the construction of this sentence. *ṭūbh*, however, should not be understood subjectively, as the quality of goodness. That translation leads to an absurdity: "The good quality of the Lord which He showed us according to His mercy." *rabh ṭūbh* is objective and concrete: The abundance of good that He has done to us. The phrase thus corresponds exactly to *ḥasdēy* and *tehillōth* in the first clause and refers back to them. The *le* in *lebhēyth* indicates at once that all this abundance of good has been showered upon Israel. In *keraḥamāyw*, etc. (*ke* corresponds to the more strongly expressive *ke'al* in the second clause), according to His compassion, is given the source out of which the *rabh ṭūbh*, the

639

hasdēy, and the *tehillōth* flowed. The suffix in *gemālām* is plural
because it refers to the collective house of Israel.

The structure of this verse is sufficiently clear as it stands, without the many emendations that have been suggested.

$$\text{וַיֹּאמֶר אַךְ־עַמִּי הֵמָּה בָּנִים לֹא יְשַׁקֵּרוּ}$$
$$\text{וַיְהִי לָהֶם לְמוֹשִׁיעַ :}^{8}$$

The anthropomorphic *wayyō'mer* is consecutive. Out of His compassion and out of the fullness of His grace "He spoke." *'akh* is
here strongly affirmative. In the term *'ammī* lies the reason for
the many proofs of grace shown particularly to the house of Israel.
They were God's *'am* by virtue of His special choice, and they had
been taken up into His special care, so that He must now care for
them in a special way. God's honor is closely associated with
Israel's welfare, cf. Exodus 33:13. *bānīm lō' yeshaqqērū,* children
who will not deceive, contains a new thought. Just as the first
clause makes God's faithfulness toward the people that now are
His the reason for His many proofs of grace, so this second clause
expresses the Lord's trust that they as His children will keep the
faith with Him. And so, for that reason, He did prove Himself to be
their constant Deliverer and helped them, not occasionally, not
now and then, but constantly. Proof of that lies in the *wayehī* with
its participial predicate.

$$\text{בְּכָל־צָרָתָם |}^{9}$$
$$\text{לֹא צָר וּמַלְאַךְ פָּנָיו הוֹשִׁיעָם}$$
$$\text{בְּאַהֲבָתוֹ וּבְחֶמְלָתוֹ הוּא גְאָלָם}$$
$$\text{וַיְנַטְּלֵם וַיְנַשְּׂאֵם כָּל־יְמֵי עוֹלָם :}$$

Our translation does not in this instance follow the Masoretic
text in its arrangement of words as marked by the interpunctuation, or in its substitution of the Qere *lō* (to him, his) for the Kethib
lō' (not). Here the text does not seem to be in order. No matter how
one understands *lō* (*lō'*) *tsar* in connection with *bekhol tsārāthām,*
it always seems forced. The LXX offers the simplest solution. It
connects *bekhol tsārāthām* with *wayehī lāhem lemōshīa'* and
reads: And He became a Savior to them in all their affliction. It retains *lō'* (not), reads *tsīr,* a messenger, in place of *tsar* and arrives
at this very plausible reading:

Καὶ ἐγένετο αὐτοῖς εἰς ϛωτηρίαν ἐκ πάσης

θλίψεως αὐτῶν οὐ πρέσβυς *(tsīr)* οὐδὲ

ἄγγελος, ἀλλ᾽ αὐτὸς ἔσωσεν αὐτοὺς, κτλ.

That is a literal translation, except that *mal'akh* is not read as a construct, but as the absolute with Qamets instead of Patah in the final syllable, and *pānāyw* is made the subject of the following verb and translated with αὐτός . This translation would also require that *hoshī'um* be read for *hoshī'am*. But *panīm* with its modifying suffix could also be construed as an instrumental accusative, and then no change in the form would be needed, Gr. 117, s, p. 367f. Cf. *bepānāyw*, Deuteronomy 4:37. For the meaning of "countenance" in such a connection see 2 Samuel 17:11: "in your own person." The countenance of the Lord is no doubt the gracious presence of God in the physical revelation of the glory of God, as in the pillar of fire and the pillar of cloud that guided Israel in the wilderness. Cf. Exodus 33:14 and 15, and the following verses. All discussion of the possible meaning of the translation "angel of His countenance" is irrelevant, since that expression occurs nowhere else in the Bible. The ultimate meaning of *pānāyw* is, of course, the Christ. The concept "angel of the Lord" must also be treated with care, as will appear when one compares Exodus 33:2 with verse 3 of that chapter.* *be'ahabhāthō ūbhehemlāthō* is best treated as a hendiadys: in His loving compassion, or in His compassionate love. Incidents like those related in Exodus 32 and 33 and Numbers 14 are meant, whereas *wayenattelēm*, He lifted them up, and *wayenasse'em*, He carried them, refer to the daily assistance, care, and protection, cf. Deuteronomy 32:10ff. *yemēy 'olām* are the days of the wandering in the wilderness, to which the prophets and the Psalms so often refer as reminders of the Lord's loving care of His people.

וְהֵ֫מָּה מָר֣וּ וְעִצְּב֗וּ אֶת־ר֣וּחַ קָדְשׁ֑וֹ 10

וַיֵּהָפֵ֥ךְ לָהֶ֛ם לְאוֹיֵ֖ב ה֥וּא נִלְחַם־בָּֽם׃

The initial *we* is adversative. "But they" did not respond to the trust that was placed in them. Luther's translation of *mārū*, "*sie erbitterten und entruesteten*," does not confuse *mārāh* with *mārar*, because *mārar* is always intransitive in the Qal, while *mārāh* is

---

*The Masoretic text can also be translated as it stands: "In all their affliction He was not (their) enemy, but the Angel of His Countenance saved them."

construed as a transitive (cf. Num. 20:24) and can very well be translated with embitter or provoke. The close connection of *mārū* with *we'itstsebhū* by means of *Merkha cum Tiphcha* also suggests the transitive meaning. They provoked and grieved, that is, by grieving the Spirit they provoked, etc. There is, however, nothing to prevent translating the word as an intransitive. The LXX has ἠπεℓϑησαν. Paul seems to have been quoting *'itstsebhū 'eth rūah qodhshō* in Ephesians 4:30: "and grieve not the Holy Spirit."

"God turned to be their enemy" has reference to such occurrences as the worship of the golden calf, Exodus 32:27ff; Taberah, Numbers 11:1,33ff; the fiery serpents, Numbers 21:6; Shittim, Numbers 25; "their carcasses shall fall in the wilderness," Numbers 14 and Deuteronomy 1; and to later defeats suffered at the time of the conquest, under the judges, in David's time, and under the kings, besides other visitations. The *hū'* in this verse refers back to *hū'* in verse 9. The same Lord who otherwise delivered them also turned and warred against them in His own person.

11 וַיִּזְכֹּר יְמֵי־עוֹלָם מֹשֶׁה עַמּוֹ
אַיֵּה הַמַּעֲלֵם מִיָּם אֵת רֹעֵי צֹאנוֹ
אַיֵּה הַשָּׂם בְּקִרְבּוֹ אֶת־רוּחַ קָדְשׁוֹ׃

In verse 11 the text is again uncertain. As the text stands, it can only be translated: Then did His people remember the days of old of Moses. *'ammō* at the end of the clause thus becomes the subject of *wayyizkōr*, and *mōsheh* is a genitive dependent on *yemēy 'ōlam*. The word order emphasizes the object. The Masoretic accentuation *Munach cum Athnach* makes *'ammō* dependent on *mōsheh* and makes the whole phrase the object of *wayyizkōr*. The Vulgate and Luther accept that construction and make the Lord the implied subject of the sentence: And He remembered the days of old, of Moses, of His people. But that does not make good sense, especially in view of the following questions introduced by *'ayyēh*, which are clearly asked by the people. The LXX does not have the words *mōsheh 'ammō*; the Syriac translation and a number of manuscripts have *'abhdō* instead of *'ammō*. But even so the difficulty is not removed, so long as "Lord" is made the subject of *wayyizkōr*. The context requires that the people be made the subject. The meaning that best suits the context is derived from this arrangement: *wayyizkerū* (plural) *yemēy 'ōlam mōsheh 'abhdō*: and they remembered the days of old, of His servant Moses. Most recent scholars translate thus. But an impersonal subject of *wayyizkōr* is also satisfactory: Then one remembered.

'ayyēh introduces the questions that the people asked in times of affliction when they remembered the days of Moses. In "Where is? " lies a complaint that the Lord is no longer so ready to help them out of trouble as He had been in Moses' time. The question also pleads that the Lord intervene now as He once had done. The text of the following clauses is uncertain. The LXX, the Syriac version, Itala, the Dead Sea Scrolls, and a few manuscripts have *hamma'aleh*, without suffix, instead of *hamma'alēm*, "who led up" instead of "who led them up." That reading makes *'eth rō'eh tsō'nō* the object: Who led up out of the sea the shepherd of His flock. Since that makes Moses alone the object of the Lord's leading, some recent scholars have changed *miyyām* into *mimmayim*, out of the water, and made the whole passage refer to the drawing of the infant Moses out of the water of the Nile. But that interpretation has been dragged in by sheer force. Some manuscripts have the plural construct *rō'ey* instead of the singular.* Delitzsch considers this to be the correct reading. The LXX, the Targum, and the *Vetus Latina* have the singular *rō'eh* as does the Bomberg edition of 1525. Since *'eth* is rendered emphatic by the Yethib, Delitzsch insists on the meaning "together with," *una cum*, a very acceptable translation. We prefer to accept *hamma'alēm* without change and to construe *rō'eh tsō'nō* as in apposition to the subject of this verb: Where is He who led them up out of the sea — He, the Shepherd of His flock? It is not necessary to delete *'eth*, since it serves here, as in many other instances, to give special emphasis to the subject, Gr. 117, i, p. 365. If *'eth rō'eh tsō'nō* is construed as the object, and even if *'eth* receives the meaning of together with, the phrase seems to be more or less meaningless; but if the phrase is interpreted as referring to the Lord, who led them up out of the sea, it fits the context perfectly. As the true Shepherd, He led the people whom He had taken into His care up out of the sea. With this construction it is no longer necessary to make the suffix in *beqirbō* refer specifically to Moses. It refers to the people: In its midst, that is, in the midst of the people. It is self-evident that it was into the hearts of Moses and his subordinates that the Lord put His Holy Spirit, cf. Numbers 11:17,25ff; 14:24; 27:18; Deuteronomy 34:9. In them and in all the faithful the Holy Spirit was in the midst of the people.

---

*The Dead Sea Scrolls read: *rō'ey*, as does the Kittel text used in this book. The Hebrew text used by Prof. Pieper has the singular: *rō'eh*.

¹² מוֹלִיךְ֙ לִימִ֣ין מֹשֶׁ֔ה זְר֖וֹעַ תִּפְאַרְתּ֑וֹ
בּ֤וֹקֵעַ מַ֙יִם֙ מִפְּנֵיהֶ֔ם לַעֲשׂ֥וֹת ל֖וֹ שֵׁ֥ם עוֹלָֽם ׃

"He caused the arm of His majesty to go at Moses' right hand,"
means that Moses' right hand, his power, did not stand alone, because the Lord had placed His own almighty power into Moses'
service. A concrete example is the parting of the waters of the Red
Sea (Exod. 14) and this was but one of many such mighty works
with which He helped Moses. Exodus 14 and 15, especially 15:14ff,
explain how He made for Himself a glorious name.

¹³ מוֹלִיכָ֖ם בַּתְּהֹמ֑וֹת כַּסּ֥וּס בַּמִּדְבָּ֖ר לֹ֥א יִכָּשֵֽׁלוּ ׃

The Hiphil participle *mōlīkhām* is treated as a noun with suffix,
whereas *ma'alēm* in verse 11 has a verbal suffix, cf. Gr. 116, g, p.
357f. The translation is therefore: He was their leader in or
through the floods; like horses (*sūs* with the article is generic) in
the plain they did not stumble (*midhbār* is here only a contrasting
term to *tehōmōth*). That is the construction required by the accentuation. If one substitutes for the Athnach in *battehōmōth* a
minor distinctive accent and then translates: "Who led them
through the floods like horses in the plain, they did not stumble,"
that would be substituting *mōlīkhēm* for *mōlīkhām*, and the Athnach would have to be placed in *bammidhbār*. The passage
through the *tehōmōth* most likely does not end with the passage
through the Red Sea, but includes the subsequent crossing of
streams, such as the Jordan. Psalms 106:9 and 77:17(16) do not
prevent that interpretation. Because the passage through many
waters is meant, *mōlīkhām* is treated as a noun. Cf. the passage
quoted from Sellin in Gr. 116, f, p. 357: "Sellin shows that the participle when construed as a *verb* expresses a single and comparatively transitory act, or relates to particular cases, historical facts,
and the like, while the participle treated as a *noun* indicates repeated, enduring, or commonly occurring acts, occupations, and
thoughts." And finally, the LXX rendering of ἐκοπίασαν for *yik-
kāshelū* may be the correct translation, for *kāshal* frequently
means to ᴦrow weary, cf. 40:30.

¹⁴ כַּבְּהֵמָה֙ בַּבִּקְעָ֣ה תֵרֵ֔ד ר֥וּחַ יְהוָ֖ה תְּנִיחֶ֑נּוּ
כֵּ֤ן נִהַ֙גְתָּ֙ עַמְּךָ֔ לַעֲשׂ֥וֹת לְךָ֖ שֵׁ֥ם תִּפְאָֽרֶת ׃

Because of the *kēn* one is tempted to understand the final clause as an apodosis to the first clause with its initial *ka*, and to subordinate *rūaḥ YHWH tenīḥennū* as a relative clause modifying the opening phrase, as Luther did. But *rūaḥ YHWH tenīḥennū*, without a connecting particle, is already the apodosis to the opening clause. The masculine suffix in *tenīḥennū* cannot refer to the feminine *behēmāh*, but must refer to some such concept as *'am.* Therefore: Like cattle that go into the valley the Spirit brought it (the people) to rest. There is no reason why *tenīḥennū* (Hiphil of *nūaḥ*) should be changed to *tanḥennū* (Hiphil of *nāḥāh*), as Proverbs 29:17 demonstrates. The sentence beginning with *kēn nihaghtā* is a summary of God's gracious acts and is the occasion for the following prayer. — See Psalms 78, 105, 106, 107.

> הַבֵּט מִשָּׁמַיִם וּרְאֵה מִזְּבֻל קָדְשְׁךָ וְתִפְאַרְתֶּךָ 15
> אַיֵּה קִנְאָתְךָ וּגְבוּרֹתֶךָ הֲמוֹן מֵעֶיךָ
> וְרַחֲמֶיךָ אֵלַי הִתְאַפָּקוּ :

After describing how in earlier periods of affliction the people in the days of Moses turned to their Deliverer (verses 11 and 12), who had given them rest in the land of Canaan (verses 13 and 14), the prayer now turns to the almighty and merciful God with its appeal for similar help in the present trouble. "Look down from heaven and see." The Lord appears to have withdrawn into heaven, as though no longer willing to have anything to do with His people. The petitioner seeks to move the Lord to act and to intervene in the present trouble. First of all, he entreats the Lord to turn His attention to the desperate situation in which the people were lying. *hibbīṭ* and *rā'āh* are related to each other like a deliberate act and its consequence. May the Lord look down from heaven in order to become aware! The designation of heaven as the holy and glorious dwelling place of the Lord (cf. Gr. 135, n, p. 440, for the significance of the two adjectives) is made clear by the second and third words in the question that follows. Like the question in verse 11, it begins with *'ayyēh. qin'athekhā*, Your zeal, is explained by *qodhshekhā.* The Lord (and His dwelling) is *qādhōsh*, especially in respect to His zeal for His people (cf. 40:25 in connection with *qādhōsh*). In a similar way, *gebhūrōthekhā* (defective plural suffix!), Your mighty deeds, is related to *tiph'artekhā.* The Lord is glorious, as His mighty acts attest. He dwells "on high and holy," 57:15; therefore His zeal and His grace ought to reveal themselves to Israel in acts of deliverance. The following clause tells why that does not happen: "The tumult of Your feelings, and Your compassion have ceased toward me." The LXX translates *hamōn* with πλῆθος, renders *weraḥameykhā* and *mē'eykhā* as genitives, and construes the whole as the object of the clause. It changes *'ēlay hith'appāqū* into *'al nā' tith'appāq (mimmennū)* and arrives at this sense: "Do not withhold from us the abundance of Your compassion and Your mercy!" The *kī* of the next clause fits neatly into this construction. But an acceptable translation is also possible leaving the Masoretic text unchanged.

16 כִּי־אַתָּה אָבִינוּ

כִּי אַבְרָהָם לֹא יְדָעָנוּ וְיִשְׂרָאֵל לֹא יַכִּירָנוּ
אַתָּה יְהוָה אָבִינוּ גֹּאֲלֵנוּ מֵעוֹלָם שְׁמֶךָ׃

kī — kī is like *kī wekī,* for — and. "For You are our Father, and Abraham knows us not, and Israel pays no attention to us." No human being, not even the most revered of them, but the Lord alone is Israel's loving Provider. The designation of Father for God or the Lord is comparatively rare in the Old Testament. The term is frequently used to designate the relation of God as the begetter of His creatures, of man, and of the people of Israel (cf. Jer. 3:4,19), but more commonly of the bond of God's love for His creatures, or of both at the same time. Cf. 9:5(6). In our passage the term "Father" is used in its full sense, whereas in 64:8 it is used in the first sense. Luther's translation of *yedhā'ānū,* "*weiss von uns nicht,*"and of *yakkīrānū,* "*kennet uns nicht,*"is not strong enough. Both terms should be given as intensive a meaning as possible, as in Psalm 142:4f(3f) (*yādha'tā, makkīr*), Deuteronomy 33:9, etc. The terms are here used in contrast to *'ābhīnū* and *gō'alēnū,* which certainly do not refer to Abraham and Israel. Cf. Psalm 146 on the subject. The Qamets instead of Tsere in *yakkīrānū* is pausal. In the last clause, the accentuation (Merkha cum Tiphcha) joins *mē'ōlām* to *gō'alēnū;* therefore, not as Luther has it: "Our Redeemer, from of old that is Your name"; but: "Our Redeemer from of old; that is Your name." In Israel the Lord is known and confessed as God who really helps and delivers from trouble.

17 לָמָּה תַתְעֵנוּ יְהוָה מִדְּרָכֶיךָ תַּקְשִׁיחַ לִבֵּנוּ מִיִּרְאָתֶךָ
שׁוּב לְמַעַן עֲבָדֶיךָ שִׁבְטֵי נַחֲלָתֶךָ׃

Because the name *gō'alēnū* for God was so firmly founded in the history of Israel, and had become a popular designation of the God

of Israel, a name that publicly proclaimed God's readiness to come
to the assistance of His people, the petitioner cannot understand
why He does not act in regard to Israel's present decadent condition. He asks: "Why do You let us err, O Lord, away from Your
ways?" It is just dogmatic prejudice, and it is entirely unnecessary, to explain the Hiphil terms *thath'enu* and *taqshiah* as merely
tolerative. In the mind of the person uttering this prayer, both
terms were conceived as strongly causative, as is evidenced by his
choice of *qashah*, a more vigorous verb, in preference to the common and gentler term *qashah*. In this chapter, as indeed throughout the Old Testament, the doctrine is again and again pronounced, that hardening of the heart, causing it to stray ever
farther from God's ways, is the act of the *Lord* (not of "God");
not, of course, *a priori* in the sense of Calvinistic predestination
(cf. Rom. 11:11), but *ex posteriori*, in the sense of a judgment upon
the persistent despisers of His grace and of His covenant. It is not
God (*elohim*) who hardens the heart, for He is but the Author of
all things in all of nature; but it is the Lord Jehovah, the Lord of
grace who is *qadhosh* (6:3; 40:25), whose grace cannot be violated,
and who hardens those who persistently scoff at His grace (Gal.
6:7). He does exactly what is written here: He causes and brings
into effect that they wander away from His wholesome ways of
grace, He hardens the heart, turns the hearts into blocks of wood
and stone, *miyyir'atho*, away from His fear, so that they can no
longer *fear* and cannot return in childlike confidence to their
heavenly Father and Savior. Thus did Isaiah become the prophet
of the hardening of hearts for incurable Israel, that is, the man
through whose preaching the Lord gave the persistently rebellious
people over to the irrevocable judgment of hardening of the heart,
chapter 6; Romans 11:7ff.

The last line contains an ardent plea to the Lord for a change of
heart toward the hardened people. *shubh* refers first of all to the
emotions. With *lema'an* (which must be repeated before *shibhtey*)
the petitioner, employing the Old Testament way of speaking,
bases his appeal on the covenant relation that existed between the
Lord and Israel as a nation. The divine answer is given in chapter
65; cf. Romans 9:6ff; 11:1ff.

Second Strophe: 63:18-64:4: *Since, in the eyes of men, the
Lord's covenant with His people seems to have been broken, the
prophet pleads that the Lord reveal Himself in fearful acts of
judgment for the rescue of Israel, so that the enemies might recog-*

nize that the Lord is a God who lends His mighty hand to deliver His people.

63:18 *They are in possession of Your people unto the very last remnant,*
     Our enemies trample upon Your sanctuary.

  19 *We are as if You had never ruled over them,*
     As though they had never been called by Your name.

64:1 *Oh, that You would rend the heavens and descend,*
     That the hills might fall down before Your countenance!

  2 *(Might descend) as when fire devours dry twigs.*
     As when fire brings water to boil,
     In order to make known Your name to Your enemies,
     So that the heathen tremble before You,

  3 *When You would do fearful things that we dared not expect!*
     Oh, that You would descend that the hills might be moved before You!

  4 *For, from the beginning it has never been heard, never seen,*
     No eye but Yours has ever seen a God
     Who comes to the help of him who trusts in Him.

לְמִצְעָר יָרְשׁוּ עַם־ קָדְשֶׁךָ צָרֵינוּ בּוֹסְסוּ מִקְדָּשֶׁךָ׃ 18

With a brief description of the misery of the people, the prayer takes a new direction. Whether or not the text of the opening clause is corrupt, cannot be determined. The LXX has τοῦ ἁγίου σου, ἵνα μικρὸν κληρονομήσωμεν τοῦ ὄρους : "in order that we might in a short time come into possession of Your holy mountain," a reading that seems to be based on a text having *nirshāh har* instead of *yāreshū 'am*, and that interprets *lammitsʿar* as an adverb of time. It is difficult to understand why Delitzsch too insists on translating it as an adverb of time, since *mitsʿar* has a concrete, not an abstract, meaning in Genesis 19:20; Job 8:7; 2 Chronicles 24:24. Likewise also *mizʿar* in Isaiah 16:14, which Delitzsch incorrectly cites as an example of the temporal meaning of the word. In 24:6 the word actually takes on a numerical sense; and besides, *le* certainly is not primarily a particle of time, but is used to indicate direction toward something, either in a physical or an ethical sense. We understand the *le* in *lammitsʿar* in the sense of *'adh le*, "Unto the smallest part," including the terminal point, that is, up to and including the last small part, totally. Luther's "*schier gar*" excludes the terminal point, and does not agree with the facts in the case. We would say: "Unto the last remnant they possess Your holy people." This solution is simple, possible, and suitable, and besides makes all emendations of the text unnecessary. *yārash* is, of course, used in the sense of Genesis 22:17;

648

24:60; Deuteronomy 9:1; 11:23, and its subject is readily supplied
by *tsāreynū* in the next clause. The Pilel perfect *bōsesū* and the
perfect in *yāreshū* are not historic perfects, but present perfects:
They have trampled and even now trample Your holy place after
having taken possession of it and having destroyed it, Gr. 106, a, p.
309, and g, p. 311. *miqdāsh* is primarily the temple and its courts,
but the term is broad enough to include the city also.

¹⁹ הָיִ֙ינוּ֙ מֵֽעוֹלָ֔ם לֹֽא־מָשַׁ֣לְתָּ בָּ֔ם לֹֽא־נִקְרָ֥א שִׁמְךָ֖ עֲלֵיהֶ֑ם

mēʿōlām lōʾ, etc. and *lōʾ niqrāʾ*, etc., are condensed expressions,
the predicate of *hāyīnū*. It is necessary to supply the proper particles of comparison and to use the subjunctive mood, thus: "We
have become as though You had never ruled over us, and as
though Your name had never been named over them (us)." For
the meaning of this last phrase, cf. 43:7; Deuteronomy 28:10; 2
Chronicles 7:14; Jeremiah 25:29. We express it with the phrase
"called by someone's name" or "named after someone," in this
case, named *ʿam YHWH*. Cf. verse 8: *ʾakh ʿammī hēmmāh*. With
this complaint the prophet's prayer places the present misery of
Israel in complete contrast to the covenant relation between the
Lord and His people; he, so to speak, casts all God's promises as
unfulfilled at His feet. And still, clinging to those same promises,
he breaks forth in the following supplication.

לוּא־קָרַ֤עְתָּ שָׁמַ֙יִם֙ יָרַ֔דְתָּ מִפָּנֶ֖יךָ הָרִ֥ים נָזֹֽלּוּ׃

The Masoretic division of chapters, which should have begun
chapter 64 at 63:7, has here, for no reason at all, divided verse 19.*
The person uttering this prayer could not break off at 19a and
then after a pause make a fresh start with such a violent expression of emotion as we have in 64:1. The words in 64:1 should be
connected directly with the thought in 63:19a, the beginning of a
strong outburst of emotion that continues through verse 4. *lū'
qāraʿtā shāmayim yāradhtā* has the sound of an explosion: "Oh,
that You would rend the heavens and descend!" Concerning *lū*
(here written with *Aleph*) with the perfect but referring to future
time, cf. Gr. 151, e, p. 477 and 159, l, p. 494. Cf. also 48:18. *lū'* must
be repeated before *mippāneykhā*, and the last clause should not
be treated as consecutive. *nāzōllū* is not a Qal perfect of *nāzal*, to
flow, but a Niphal perfect of *zālal*, to sway, to fall. For *o* instead of

---

*The verses of chapter 64 are numbered according to the English text. In the He-
brew text verse 1 is combined with 63:19.

a in the Niphal, cf. Gr. 67, t, p. 181; and dd, p. 183. The petitioner pleads for a sudden, violent demonstration of the Lord's power for the deliverance of His people and for judgment upon their enemies. His conception of the form and manner of the Lord's self-revelation is majestic and altogether vigorous. Cf. *habbēṭ* in 63:15.

$$ \text{כִּקְדֹּחַ אֵשׁ הֲמָסִים} \quad \text{מַיִם תִּבְעֶה־אֵשׁ} \quad ^1 $$
$$ \text{לְהוֹדִיעַ שִׁמְךָ לְצָרֶיךָ} \quad \text{מִפָּנֶיךָ גּוֹיִם יִרְגָּזוּ׃} $$

yāradhtā must be repeated before *kiqedhōaḥ*. On the infinitive *qedhōaḥ* instead of a finite verb, cf. Gr. 115, h and i, p. 355. *'esh* is the subject, and *hamāsīm*, brushwood, is the object. Before *mayim* the *ke* of *kiqedhōaḥ* must be repeated, and *'asher* is to be supplied before *tibh'eh*, Gr. 155, h, p. 487. The translation is: "As when fire consumes dry brushwood; as when fire causes water to boil." *tibh'eh* is transitive. In the next two clauses the thought of judgment upon the enemies moves into the foreground, but the predominant thought of the prayer is always the burning desire for the deliverance of the people. In the background lies the desire to establish the truth of Israel's confession of the special relation that existed between Israel and the one true God. That relation had been expressed in 63:17b-19. The prayer implores the Lord that He reveal His name to His enemies, so that they may tremble in fear before Him. "The Holy One of Israel," "the Mighty One of Jacob," and similar names involve both God's grace toward Israel and His wrath against His enemies. Cf. remarks on 40:3. The idea of purpose expressed by the infinitive *lehōdhīa'* is continued, without a conjunction, in the finite verb *yirgāzū*, cf. Gr. 114, r, p. 352. On the coordination of the verbs without a conjunction see Gr. 120, d, g, h, p. 386f.

$$ \text{בַּעֲשׂוֹתְךָ נוֹרָאוֹת לֹא נְקַוֶּה} \quad \text{יָרַדְתָּ מִפָּנֶיךָ הָרִים נָזֹלּוּ׃} \quad ^2 $$

This sentence should be treated as an adverbial modifier closely connected with the preceding purpose clause. It is still governed by *lū'* of verse 1. "Oh, that You would descend (verse 1) — as when fire devours (verse 2) — so that they tremble (verse 3) — when You would (subjunctive governed by *lū'*) do fearful things (verse 3)." *nōrā'ōth* is a Niphal fem. plur. participle of *yārē'*, to fear: fearful, terrible things. Something more is meant than those acts of God that send fear into the hearts of all His creatures. The prayer

calls for a visible descent of God from heaven in judgment upon
His enemies, accompanied by such fearful wonders as the rending
asunder of the hills. For this reason *yāradhtā mippāneykhā* of
verse 1 is repeated. *'asher* must be supplied before *lō' neqawweh.*
The *nōrā'ōth* are such phenomena as exceed every human expectation and make a mockery of all human imagination. These are
thoughts that have to do with the end of all things, as in 66:6ff and
15f, and are echoed in the words of the Lord, Luke 23:30; Revelation 6:16f. Cf. Isaiah 2:10-22; Hosea 10:8. — As in verse 1,
lū' must be supplied before *yāradhtā.*

וּמֵעוֹלָם לֹא־שָׁמְעוּ   לֹא הֶאֱזִינוּ   3

עַיִן לֹא־רָאָתָה אֱלֹהִים זוּלָתְךָ   יַעֲשֶׂה לִמְחַכֵּה־לוֹ:

This verse expresses the basis on which the preceding long and
impassioned plea is based, that God stretch forth His mighty arm
against the enemies for the deliverance of His people. The subject
of *lō' shāme'ū,* etc., is really the enemies, although the next clause
'ayin lō' rā'athāh extends the subject and makes it general. The
enemies do not believe in a miraculous intervention of the gods or
of one God in the interests of a certain people. From of old they
have never heard or really observed anything of the kind, nor had
their eyes ever seen such an act of God. Therefore they are secure
and unafraid, and when they do violence to Israel they do not feel
that they need to fear that the God of this people will ever intervene to help them, although their prophets and teachers often
speak of such divine help. But among the gods, God is an exception. He is in fact a God who comes to the rescue of those who wait
upon Him in faith. The prayer implores the Lord that He reveal
Himself in terrible deeds, so that the secure, unbelieving, and
stubborn enemies may become aware that He is a God who helps.
The *ū* at the beginning of this verse must therefore be translated
with "for." The simplest explanation of the function of *'elōhīm* in
the sentence is to construe it as the object of *shāme'ū* and also of
the other two verbs in 4a, while *zūlāthekhā* is an adverbial modifier, "besides You." *'asher* must be supplied before *ya'aseh*: "A
God besides You, who, etc." *'āsāh* has the usual meaning of this
verb, to act, to accomplish, to provide, to carry out. The verb seems
strange here only because it is isolated. But cf. 44:23; 46:4, where
it is used in the same way and sense. Here it is the equivalent of to
intervene, to take action. Paul, in 1 Corinthians 2:9, exactly expresses the meaning of this verse. — For Tsere instead of Segol in
limḥakkēh, see Gr. 75, hh, p. 215.

Third Strophe: 64:5-12: *The Lord's wrath has delivered Israel into the hands of its own sins. The Lord is implored because of His covenant of grace to take to heart the ruin of Israel's glory and to cease His anger.*

5   *You were friendly to those who with joy kept the faith,*
      Who remembered You in Your ways;
      But lo, You — You became angry, so that we sinned;
      Long (were You angry) with them, and how could we have been
        helped?

6   *And so we become altogether as the unclean,*
      And all our righteousness as a defiled garment;
      So did we all fade away like leaves,
      And our guilt bore us away like the wind.

7   *And (now) there is none who calls upon Your name,*
      Who could rouse himself to cling to You;
      For (now) You have hidden Your face from us,
      And delivered us into the power of our sins.

8   *But now, O Lord, You are our Father,*
      We are clay, You are our potter,
      We are all of us the work of Your hand.

9   *O Lord, do not be angry without measure,*
      And do not remember our guilt forever;
      Behold, consider, we beseech You, that we are all Your people!

10 *Your holy cities have become a waste,*
      Zion — it has become a wilderness,
      Jerusalem a desert.

11 *Our holy and glorious house,*
      Where our fathers praised You,
      Has been given up to the burning with fire,
      And all that we delighted in has become a desolation.

12 *O Lord, do You for these things restrain Yourself?*
      Keep silent and afflict us without end?

⁴ פָּגַעְתָּ אֶת־שָׂשׂ וְעֹשֵׂה צֶּדֶק בִּדְרָכֶיךָ יִזְכְּרוּךָ
הֵן־אַתָּה קָצַפְתָּ וַנֶּחֱטָא בָּהֶם עוֹלָם וְנִוָּשֵׁעַ :

    As in 63:7ff the petitioner began his prayer by recalling the former graciousness of the Lord, so here he, so to speak, takes another deep breath, again recalls the Lord's kindness, and launches into the third and last part of his prayer. *pāgha'* means to meet or encounter in a friendly manner, cf. 47:3. Its object, "him who rejoices and performs righteousness," is best construed as a hendiadys: "him who joyfully performs righteousness." *tsedheq* is the righteousness of the covenant, and therefore "performing righteousness" — keeping the faith with the Lord. *'asher* has been omitted before *bidherākhekhā* because there has been a change from the collective singular to the plural. Supplying "walking" to "in Your ways," we have this thought: "Walking in Your ways, they remember Your ways as blessed and give thanks for them." Briefly the thought is, that to His faithful children (cf. 63:8) the Lord has been a true and faithful God. But: "Lo, You — You burst forth in anger." Cf. 54:7 and 8. *hēn 'attāh* sets off *qātsaphtā* as something fearfully out of the ordinary, something that Israel had not at all expected. Had the Lord not concluded a covenant of grace with them! Cf. 63:8 and 9. The consequence of His anger was *wanneḥetā*, "that we sinned."

The commentators might have discovered a solution of the difficulty here if they had permitted this and the following words to remain as they are in the text without attempting emendations that still do not satisfy. It is dogmatic prejudice that prompts the efforts to avoid the fact that Israel's sin is here represented as a consequence of God's wrath. But that fact has already been stated in 63:17. It was the Lord's anger over Israel's unfaithfulness that had permitted them to stray from His ways and hardened their hearts. That is a consistent teaching of divine revelation: *peccatum peccati poena est* — as Luther remarks. The God of grace is indeed a God of great patience, Exodus 34:6; but He is also a holy and zealous God, who does not permit Himself to be mocked. How soon His patience with the man of iniquity will come to an end, lies in His own discretion. Every sin against grace grieves the Holy Spirit and may at any instant call down a decree of final judgment. And then, as a consequence, sin bursts out into activity, sinning with a conscience hardened to all grace. That is what happened in Israel, and that is what this passage says.

wa with the imperfect *neḥetā* following the perfect *qātsaphtā* is clearly consecutive. If anyone objects to the translation: "and so we sinned," he may prefer to follow us in our translation: "*da hatten wir's verwirkt*," "and so we become liable." This latter interpretation is based on Genesis 43:9; 44:32; Leviticus 5:7,11; Habakkuk 2:10; Proverbs 20:2 (cf. the lexicon); but in either translation, the sense remains essentially the same. He who sins just once too often against God's grace is lost; he has forfeited God's grace, and now he *must* sin. According to chapters 1 and 6 of Isaiah, that was the lot of Israel according to the flesh. Isaiah was the prophet of the hardening of hearts, and the tone of this prayer proceeds from the consciousness that this hardening had become a fact in Israel.

It is a despondent prayer, almost void of hope that Israel as a people might be saved; and nowhere does the prayer rise to a certainty of faith that such a salvation would come to the people. It is a resigned, unhappy lament over Israel's sad lot, a *qīnāh* like the Lamentations of Jeremiah, which cannot reconcile itself to Israel's fate.

The next clause, *bāhem 'ōlām weniwwāshēa'*, presents a real difficulty. The difficulty does not lie in *bāhem 'ōlām*, although that phrase has puzzled many a commentator. According to the simplest rules of parallelism, *qātsaphtā* must be repeated before this phrase. *qātsaphtā* is usually followed by *'al* and the person, but here it is construed with *be*: "You were angry against them (change from first to third person) for a long time." The real difficulty lies in *weniwwāshēa'*, literally: "and we were helped," (Niphal imperfect, first plural). Luther's "*Uns wurde aber dennoch geholfen*" does not fit into the context, and his translation would necessitate doing violence to the consecutive *wa* with *nehī* in the next verse. Commentators who do not easily deviate from the Masoretic text have construed *weniwwāshēa'* as a question: and should we have been helped? Delitzsch reverses the position of the two middle consonants and suggests *neshawwēa'* (Piel imperfect first person plural of *shūa'*): "and we cry out," namely, in vain. The change to *weniphsha'* (Niphal of *pāsha'*, to deal faithlessly) would yield the impossible meaning: "and we were treated faithlessly." There are other, even more violent emendations. And so, there is hardly a way out, except to take *weniwwāshēa'* to be a question. Thus we do not deviate from the opening line of thought and can accept the consecutive *wa* before the following *nehī* at its full value.

5 וַנְּהִי כַטָּמֵא כֻּלָּנוּ וּכְבֶגֶד עִדִּים כָּל־צִדְקֹתֵינוּ
וַנָּבֶל כֶּעָלֶה כֻּלָּנוּ וַעֲוֹנֵנוּ כָּרוּחַ יִשָּׂאֻנוּ :

wa in *wannehī* is in line with the *wa* in *wanneheṭā'*. It is a *Waw* consecutive imperfect, and therefore we *must* translate: and so, therefore, consequently we became, or have become. Any translation that does not express this consecutive idea destroys the intended sense. That we, all of us, have become as "unclean" (the cry of the lepers, Lev. 13:45) is together with *neheṭā'* a consequence of the prolonged wrath of the Lord; but its immediate cause is to be found in *neheṭā'* and in the negative answer to the question in *weniwwāshēaʿ*. As a consequence of God's wrath, Israel was thoroughly infected with sin, and like a leper, was being consumed by an incurable disease. As the leper was shunned and loathed by men (Lev. 13), so Israel had become an object of abhorrence to the Lord.

The second clause, "and all our righteousness (intensive plural!) like a menstrual garment," conveys the identical thought in a different picture. The second half of the verse is still governed by a *Waw* consecutive imperfect: "And so we are all like withered leaves." The form *nābhēl* is not derived from *nābhēl* (40:7), nor from *bālāh*, but from *bālal* (Hiphil imperfect, first person plural), although the meaning is derived from the root *nābhēl*, to wither (a so-called metaplasm). The last clause, "and our iniquities bore us away like the wind," carries out the picture of their complete destruction as a people. The article with *rūaḥ* is generic. Although *ʿawōnēnū* is singular in form, the predicate *yissāʾunū* shows that the plural idea is intended, as at the end of verse 7. The masculine form instead of the usual feminine *ʿawōnōthēynū* seems to lend strength to the statement. These two verses, 5 and 6, develop this thought: You were indeed a gracious God toward the faithful people, but You became angry, and so we drifted always deeper into sin. We became completely infected with sin and became an abhorrence in Your eyes. Our iniquity and our guilt carry us away into destruction.

6 וְאֵין־קוֹרֵא בְשִׁמְךָ מִתְעוֹרֵר לְהַחֲזִיק בָּךְ
כִּי־הִסְתַּרְתָּ פָנֶיךָ מִמֶּנּוּ וַתְּמוּגֵנוּ בְּיַד־עֲוֹנֵנוּ׃

Following the account of the reasons for Israel's present unhappy condition, the prayer in verse 7 briefly describes the dull despair that has taken control over all hearts: And there is none who calls on Your name. The participial construction describes an existing and continuing condition. Despairing unbelief has overcome the people. This is, of course, hyperbole because the petitioner is well aware that a faithful remnant still exists. The prayer continues with the participial construction in *mithʿōrēr*, one who rouses himself, that is, one who is capable of rousing himself to a decision. The Hiphil infinitive *haḥazīq* (*ḥāzaq*) expresses both the idea of taking hold and of holding fast, followed by *be* with the object grasped — our "clinging to." The second part of the verse, introduced by *kī*, contains the reason for the statement in the first

655

part: "For You have hidden Your face from us." This is *qātsaphtā* of verse 5 in another form. Thus, even the despair of the people is a consequence of the Lord's anger. He has withdrawn His grace from the people; yes, more, He has delivered us into the hand, that is, into the power of our iniquities, and our guilt works itself out to our total destruction. In form, *temūghenū* is Qal imperfect, second singular masculine, of *mūgh*, to be soft, to sway, to flow. Since the verb occurs only in transitive forms, some explain it as a shortened form of the Polel, *temōgheghēnū*. The oldest translations, the LXX, Targum, and Syriac read *temaggenēnū* (Piel of *māghan*): You have delivered us παρέδωκας (cf. Rom. 1:26,28). *miggēn beyadh* occurs also in Genesis 14:20. Should *temūghēnū*, however, prove to be a transitive Qal form, the meaning would be: Thou hast let us melt away. *beyadh*, into the hand, into the power of, removes all doubt as to the intended meaning of the verb.

וְעַתָּה יְהוָה אָבִינוּ אָתָּה 7
אֲנַחְנוּ הַחֹמֶר וְאַתָּה יֹצְרֵנוּ וּמַעֲשֵׂה יָדְךָ כֻּלָּנוּ:

Following the description of Israel's desperate condition (verse 7), the prayer turns again to intercession. *we'attāh* is most emphatic: and yet, nevertheless, but still (cf. the lexicon on *gam 'at-tāh* under *'attāh*). "Nevertheless You are still our Father." As in 63:16, the petitioner clings fast to the Lord; he appeals to the covenant relation that exists between the Lord and the people. In the very fullest sense, the Lord is Israel's Creator and Father. In Abraham and Jacob He had chosen this people for His own, had accepted and reared it, had guided it miraculously and greatly exalted it, Isaiah 1:2. Whatever stature Israel had attained was the special doing of the Lord in the people's history. In its totality the people was *ma'asēh yādhō*, the work of His hand. On that fact the petition that now follows is based.

אַל־תִּקְצֹף יְהוָה עַד־מְאֹד וְאַל־לָעַד תִּזְכֹּר עָוֹן 8
הֵן הַבֶּט־נָא עַמְּךָ כֻלָּנוּ:

The petition is clothed in modest terms. Not *'adh me'ōdh*, but beyond measure, not forever, so he pleads, may the anger of the Lord continue. *lā'adh*, forever, repeats *'adh me'ōdh* in stronger form.

May the Lord's anger be temporary, not eternal, final! Cf. 54:7,8. May He once again, in His grace, be merciful to Israel!

There now follows, extending almost to the end of this section, a statement of the two bases on which the prayer is based: the covenant relation and Israel's misery and shame. The first of these bases appears in this verse. May the Lord consider that all of Israel is His chosen people, His own people, 63:8! That is one reason why He should cease His anger. The second reason follows in verses 10 and 11.

9 עָרֵי קָדְשְׁךָ הָיוּ מִדְבָּר

צִיּוֹן מִדְבָּר הָיָתָה   יְרוּשָׁלַ͏ִם שְׁמָמָה:

10 בֵּית קָדְשֵׁנוּ וְתִפְאַרְתֵּנוּ   אֲשֶׁר הִלְלוּךָ אֲבֹתֵינוּ

הָיָה לִשְׂרֵפַת אֵשׁ   וְכָל־מַחֲמַדֵּינוּ הָיָה לְחָרְבָּה:

The plural, "Your holy cities," is hardly a reference to the various sections of the city of Jerusalem, although the LXX has πόλις τοῦ ἁγίου σου. Meant are the many other cities of the Holy Land that were destroyed together with Jerusalem. The *one* city is twice referred to by those designations that are most likely to move the Lord's compassion and zeal: Zion, Jerusalem! All, everything lies waste and desolate, cf. Lamentations 1:1ff; 2:1ff. The change from *midhbār* to *shemāmāh* is purely poetic. It should be noted that the cities are called "Your holy cities"; whereas in verse 11 the temple is called "Our holy house." The "Your" is a direct appeal to the Lord's honor, based on such words of the Lord as 42:8; 48:11. The temple is called "our holy and glorious house" because it was the one public house of prayer of the one true God for all of Israel and for all nations of the world (56:7). Only there could be observed the worship desired by the Lord. So long as the temple lay in ruins, the Lord was deprived of the true worship of His people and of the nations. There did our fathers serve You. But we cannot serve You, so long as the temple lies in ruins. The temple is called holy and glorious, because the Holy One of Israel dwelt there in the glory of His grace, not because of any physical splendor of the structure, Psalms 26:8; 132:14. *hāyāh liserēphath 'esh.* Literally: "It has become for the burning of fire," that is, it has fallen a prey to consuming flames. *mahamaddēynū*, a plural of *mahmadh* with suffix (from *hāmadh*, to desire) has been

657

beautifully rendered by Luther as: "*Alles das wir Schoenes hatten*," whatever of beauty we possessed. Again, the reference is not to Jerusalem's palaces and such, but to the places and provisions for worship, to the courts of the temple, the sacrifices, to the great altar of sacrifice, etc., together with the times and seasons of worship, the priests — in short, all that Israel possessed in the way of worship that so greatly excelled the rites of the gentiles. Luther's translation of *hāyāh lehorbāh*, "*ist zuschanden gemacht*," has been put to shame, is strikingly appropriate. Concerning the singular *hāyāh* with *kol*, cf. Gr. 146, c, p. 467.

הַעַל־אֵלֶּה תִתְאַפַּק יְהוָה   תֶּחֱשֶׁה וּתְעַנֵּנוּ עַד־מְאֹד: ¹¹

The prayer closes with the pleading question: "Do You restrain Yourself for these things? Will You continue to be silent and put us altogether to shame?" The form *thith'appaq* is of special significance. *'aphaq* means to be firm; in the Hithpael, to make oneself firm, to steel one's heart. In this instance the meaning is: to subject one's heart to violence, to restrain it with force. The fundamental attitude of the Lord toward Israel is one of goodness, love, compassion, and grace, cf. 49:15f; Exodus 34:6; Jeremiah 31:20. The Lord must forcibly restrain Himself if He is to withhold His grace from Israel. The Lord's heart is affected like that of a father or mother when compelled to close heart and home to an incorrigible child. In closing, the prayer appeals to this infinite compassion, calling upon God by His covenant name, Lord, the name in which God's grace was revealed to Israel. *tehesheh* and *te'annēnu* refer to God's treatment of Israel in a physical sense and look to the future. Can, or will, the Lord silently contemplate Israel's ruin and let it take its course without interrupting it? Can He, or will He, humble, afflict, and dishonor the people finally and completely (*'adh me'ōdh*)?

With these questions the prayer comes to an end. It is a cry of pain that reaches to the gate of heaven. It pleads for the deliverance and restoration of Israel as a nation. It strikes every chord. It places its reliance on the promised grace of the covenant and sets the misery of the people before the Lord's eyes. It hesitates to come to an end. It is filled with firm faith in the Lord's goodness, His fatherly love, and His faithfulness. But even at the close, the prayer has not yet come to the happy certainty that it has been favorably heard. The cry of pain with which it closes still leaves the answer and the question of Israel's acceptance into God's favor dangling. — If the commentators had correctly perceived the tone of the prayer, they would not have erred so widely in their exegesis of the answer that follows in chapter 65.

Second Discourse: Chapter 65

The final rejection of apostate Israel and the preservation of the faithful Remnant for a blessed new order of things.

If plain facts and an unprejudiced mind still have some validity, then it will have to be admitted that in this chapter and the next we have the answer to the prayer in chapter 63. Jewish tradition and the Christian Church have consistently held that view. Luther, Zwingli, and Calvin were followed by Ewald, Delitzsch, Hahn, and some more recent commentators in holding this view. But some of the later commentators (including even Bredenkamp), and especially the modern critics, apodictically reject this view because this chapter does not deal with the chief complaint in the prayer, namely, that Israel had fallen so deeply into sin as a consequence of Jehovah's anger. Furthermore, they argue, verses 3-5 and verse 11 go back to pre-exilic idolatry in Israel. Thus Cheyne in his "Prophecies of Isaiah II." Duhm's "Trito-Isaiah" (chapters 56-66) is assumed to have been written at the time of Ezra and Nehemiah against the Samaritan schism. But sound exegesis refutes these conjectures. This discourse proves throughout to be the answer to the foregoing prayer. It has three parts: verses 1-7, the Lord's answer rejects the complaint; verses 8-16, the preservation of the faithful Remnant in contrast to the incurable mass; verses 17-25, the new glory of those who are saved.

First Strophe: verses 1-7: *The Lord's answer rejecting the complaint.*

1   *I do let Myself be consulted by those who did not require it,*
     I let Myself be found by those who did not seek Me;
     I say: "Here am I; here am I!"
     To a people that had never been named after My name.

2   *I have at all times stretched out My hands toward a rebel-*
      lious people,
    Who walk in a way that is not good, after their own thoughts.

3   *This people constantly provokes Me to My face,*
    Offering sacrifices in gardens and burning incense on tiles.

4   *Who dwell in tombs, and spend the night in caves,*
    Who eat the flesh of swine, and in their vessels have a broth
      of abominations.

5   *Who say (to Me) : Remain where You are!*
    Do not come near me, I am now a holy thing to You!
    They are a smoke in My nostrils, a continually burning flame.

6   *Truly, it is written before Me:*
    I will not be silent: I will recompense,
    Into their bosoms will I repay it,

7   *Your sins and your fathers' sins together, says the Lord;*
    Who burned incense on the mountain and dishonored Me on the hills,
    And first of all, I will measure out their recompense into their bosom.

נִדְרַשְׁתִּי לְלֹוא שָׁאָלוּ נִמְצֵאתִי לְלֹא בִקְשֻׁנִי 1

אָמַרְתִּי הִנֵּנִי הִנֵּנִי אֶל־גֹּוי לֹא־קֹרָא בִשְׁמִי:

lelo' is the same as *la'asher lo'*, Gr. 155, n, p. 488f. *nidhrashtī*
and *nimtsē'thī* are tolerative Niphal forms, Gr. 51, c, p. 137 — to let
oneself be approached, found. What kind of perfects are these? It
is customary to interpret them as historical perfects, like *pērastī*
in verse 2, and to refer them to the people of Israel, who then
naturally become the subject of *shā'alū* and *biqeshunī*. In support
of this interpretation the Pual *qōrā'* in the last clause is changed
into a Qal form, *qārā'*. The translation then is: I have let Myself
be asked — and I have let Myself be found, etc. However, no proof
has yet been discovered to show that this is a necessary interpretation. Nevertheless, Paul has been faulted for understanding verse 1 as being spoken of the gentiles, and verse 2 as in contrast to them. But Paul and the translators of the LXX, who certainly knew Hebrew and whose way of thinking was Hebrew, were
right, and the modern interpreters are wrong. *nidhrashtī* and
nimtsē'thī are not historical perfects; they are gnomic perfects,
which express an action as one of common experience, or even as
proverbial, Gr. 106, k, p. 312. See the examples cited in the
reference to the grammar. It is the Greek gnomic aorist which
Paul and the LXX both use here and then translate *shā'alū* and *bi-*
qeshunī with verbs in the present tense — ἐπερωτῶσιν
ζητοῦσιν . These verbs in the present tense clearly show that

they considered *nidhrashtī* and *nimtsē'thī* to refer to present time: I do let Myself be consulted by those who do not inquire after Me; and I do let Myself be found by those who do not seek after Me. With present tenses in the relative clauses, a historical perfect in the main clause is clearly out of the question, whereas the dependent clauses readily tolerate either a preterite or a present tense: I permit Myself to be found by those who did not seek Me. According to this interpretation, the Lord is uttering the truth that He reveals Himself and lets Himself be found by people who do not search after Him, or have not sought Him, a truth of revelation that is fundamental to the whole Gospel. This is the doctrine of the *free* grace of the Lord, a doctrine that was not discovered by Paul, but which is found everywhere in the Old Testament. Cf. Exodus 33:19. Isaiah especially emphasizes it. Cf. 43:22ff as an example.

It is God's way to reveal Himself to such as have never sought Him out. Had He waited until He had been sought after, there would never have been a revelation of God's grace. It is of this way of the Lord that He is speaking in this passage. In accordance with Deuteronomy 32:21, Paul is entirely consistent with this truth when he makes the application of it to the acceptance of the gentiles and contrasts Israel as a people that had received grace according to the same divine principle but had treated it with contempt and had in consequence been rejected. It is difficult to understand why the exegetes who take *nidhrashtī* and the other perfect verbs to be historical perfects, have failed to see that these perfects are here used in the gnomic sense. Hahn even maintained that these clauses should be understood as questions and be translated: "Is it possible that I should be found by such as do not seek Me?" But the Lord at times even turns away such people as seek Him, Ezekiel 14:3; 20:3, 31! It is self-evident that the clause beginning with *'amartī* must be construed like the first two clauses.

Delitzsch's tendency toward millennialism explains why he charges Paul with misunderstanding this passage as well as Hosea 2:1 (1:10) and 2:25 (23), for it is on these passages that he grounds his expectation of a physical fulfillment of the promises to Israel and a universal conversion of the Jews.

The use of *gōy* instead of *'am* does not necessarily indicate that a gentile nation is meant; but the Masoretic text of the relative clause, *('asher) lō' qōrā' bishemī,* does definitely point to a gentile people. "A people that was not named after My name" (*qōrā'* is a

Pual perfect) cannot be said of Israel, because Israel was the *one* people that was named after the Lord's name, 43:7; Jeremiah 14:9; 15:16. The use of *niqrā'*, a Niphal, in this connection, is by no means proof that the Pual could not have the same meaning, but would have to be rendered "called by the Lord," as in 48:12. The scholars who supplied the vowel signs to the text were themselves Hebrews, and they also had the LXX with its τῷ ἔϑνει οἳ οὐκ ἐκάλεσάν μου τὸ ὄνομα as a guide to guard them, if necessary, from employing un-Hebrew constructions. If they read *qōrā'*, and not *qārā'*, that is proof sufficient that they felt this to be good Hebrew, and that the reference is to gentiles, as both the LXX and Paul understood it. Finally, even the reading of *qārā'* instead of *qōrā'* would not necessarily change the sense or forbid the use of the gnomic tense in the three preceding clauses. Luther, who followed the Vulgate, based his translation on *qārā'* and still did not alter the sense of the passage. He correctly rendered the perfects with present tenses. Unfortunately, he did not do so in translating the aorists in Romans 10.

2 פֵּרַ֧שְׂתִּי יָדַ֛י כָּל־הַיּ֖וֹם אֶל־עַ֣ם סוֹרֵ֑ר

הַהֹלְכִים֙ הַדֶּ֣רֶךְ לֹא־ט֔וֹב אַחַ֖ר מַחְשְׁבֹתֵיהֶֽם׃

With *pērastī*, "I have stretched out," the tense of the verbs changes from the present to the historical perfect. But even here it is possible to employ the present perfect, Gr. 106, g, p. 311 (cf. *pērastī* in Ps. 143:6): for a long time and even now I do still stretch out, etc. Luther's translation can be justified grammatically. But the following adverbial modifiers: throughout the whole day, that is, through all this time without ceasing; toward a rebellious people; the historical details cited in the next verse; and the sins of the fathers referred to in verse 7, all show that *pērastī* pertains to the past. The present is, however, not excluded but is included, as is indicated by the mention of "your transgressions" in addition to those of the fathers. Throughout the day, that is, throughout the entire period of His covenant relation to Israel, He has been stretching out His compassionate, gracious, and helping hands (Matt. 11:28) toward an *'am sōrēr*, a rebellious, headstrong people. That had been Israel's way from Exodus 14:11 on, a characteristic that revealed itself in Elim, Exodus 16:2, at Sinai, Exodus 32:1ff, and again and again up to the end. All were alike rebellious, the lowly and the great, princes and people, Isaiah 1:23; 30:1; Jeremiah 5:23; Hosea 9:15; cf. Isaiah 48:4. This people did not understand obedience; it had to go its own headstrong way; it would rather perish than retreat from its stubbornness. But when disaster was imminent and the knife was at their throats, they cried aloud to God for help. However, as soon as it was again possible to breathe freely, they again walked *'aḥar maḥshe-bhōtheyhem*, after their own ideas. These ideas were always *lō'-ṭōbh*, un-good, evil (Gr. 152, Note 1, p. 478), always leading to disaster. That was characteristic of this people, and that is its character to this day over against Christianity, and nothing changes it. God's election of grace effects a change in the individual, but the rest are hardened, Romans 11:7.

Verses 1 and 2 are an answer in general terms to the foregoing prayer. The prayer was essentially a plea that the Lord might cease His anger and return to the intimate relationship of the covenant, 63:15-17; 64:3,4,7,8(4,5,8,9). It closes with the cry: Will You forever be angry? This is the real point of the prayer, a point that would not have been missed by Cheyne and others if they had been unprejudiced (see the introductory remarks to this chapter). It is true that the prayer did touch on the question of God's foreknowledge and providence. The question is put: *Why* do You let us stray, O Lord, from Your paths, why harden our hearts, so as not to fear You (63:17)? Behold, consider, we beseech You, that we are all Your people (64:8[9])! To that demand in the prayer these two verses supply the answer: Unasked, I approach every people that ever becomes a recipient of My grace (verse 1); but that people is lost to which I have continually stretched out My hand of grace in vain, as I have to this people. This is the Lord's answer to the *Why?* of the prayer, and for this reason He does not grant the prayer's plea. This answer goes back to the ultimate basis on which all things rest, back to the mystery of mysteries: God's majestic will, concerning which He renders an account to no one ("I will be gracious to whom I will be gracious and will show mercy on whom I will show mercy," Exod. 33:19; Rom. 9:15). To this truth there is, however, no Calvinistic counterpart of an *a priori* predestination to damnation, Romans 11:11. God rejects a people that has received grace, but recklessly and scornfully squandered it; but He does not accept instruction from anyone as to when the moment of the hardening of the hearts has arrived. That decision is His; He freely decides when the time for rejection and hardening has arrived (Rom. 9:18), just as He had freely and unasked extended His grace in the first place. Once the decision of hardening had been reached, no prayer can change it. This being the situation in these verbs, it is beyond comprehension that some scholars still say that this chapter does not respond to the foregoing prayer. The adverse criticism and the fragmentation of Isaiah rests on just such assertions. And everyone who does not accept this scientific fraud is called "behind the times."

3 הָעָם הַמַּכְעִיסִים אוֹתִי עַל־פָּנַי תָּמִיד
זֹבְחִים בַּגַּנּוֹת וּמְקַטְּרִים עַל־הַלְּבֵנִים :

4 הַיֹּשְׁבִים בַּקְּבָרִים וּבַנְּצוּרִים יָלִינוּ
הָאֹכְלִים בְּשַׂר הַחֲזִיר וּפְרַק פִּגֻּלִים כְּלֵיהֶם :

5 הָאֹמְרִים קְרַב אֵלֶיךָ אַל־תִּגַּשׁ־בִּי כִּי קְדַשְׁתִּיךָ
אֵלֶּה עָשָׁן בְּאַפִּי אֵשׁ יֹקֶדֶת כָּל־הַיּוֹם:

Verses 3-5 contain a detailed description of the incurable recalcitrancy of the people, which was briefly sketched in verse 2. The recurring participles in these verses are used in their verbal sense, not as nouns. Actions that have been constantly repeated and become customary, are by these participles at the same time designated as occurring in specific cases, cf. Gr. 116, 3, f, note, p. 357. Since they express what is customary, the participles are not to be construed as referring to any specific time. They are actions both of the past and of the present. Thus have they done, and thus they continue to do. The collective *'am* is construed with the plural, since the reference is to individual, not to collective sins. As *'am sōrēr,* etc., in verse 2 pointed back to *mārū* in 63:10, so here *hammakh'īsīm* (*kā'as*) is linked to *we'itstsebhū* in that verse. *kā'as* and *'ātsabh* are synonyms meaning to provoke, to vex, to offend. *'al pānay tāmīdh* is not, as Luther supposed, the predicate. The predicate lies in *hammakh'īsīm;* and *'al pānay* (to My face) is like *tāmīdh,* a separate adverbial modifier. It characterizes the insolence with which the rebellious people provoke the Lord. As for the detailed acts that are now enumerated, they are neither to be ascribed to the fathers alone during pre-exilic times (verse 7), nor are they exclusively idolatrous acts attributed to the exilic and post-exilic generations. Here, as in verse 7, the sins of both generations are placed side by side. The sacrifices in gardens, under every green tree, under oaks and terebinths, have already been censured in 1:29; 57:5ff; Ezekiel 6:13; cf. Hosea 4:13. Compare especially 57:5-7 with this passage. Burning incense on *lebhēnīm,* bricks, which was expressly contrary to Exodus

20:25, certainly refers to the Babylonian time, because the making of bricks was a Babylonian industry, cf. Genesis 11:3. Lodging in graves (hewn into the rocks), spending nights in hidden places, (*netsūrīm,* Qal passive participle of *nātsar)* were practices connected with spiritualism. Such attempts to communicate with the dead through mediums were in those days common practice throughout paganism, cf. Deuteronomy 18:11; Isaiah 8:19; 1 Samuel 28 (Saul at Endor). Israel would have practiced this kind of spiritualism more freely during the exile than at home, because in Babylon the Lord had refused "to be inquired of" by them, Ezekiel 14:3, etc. The eating of swine's flesh, however, had quite likely become more common in Israel in imitation of the Babylonians, or perhaps at an even earlier time in imitation of the Egyptians, among whom the sacrifice of swine was practiced. The context indicates that the reference here is to cultic practices. *pheraq* are broken pieces, chunks. The Qere has *meraq,* a stew. According to Ezekiel 4:14; Leviticus 7:18 and 19:7, *piggul* is Levitically unclean, decaying flesh; the plural is either abstract decay, or concretely, decaying pieces. Our idiom would require *be* before *keleyhem;* but "a brew of abomination are their vessels" is good idiomatic Hebrew, which has a fondness for synecdoche, cf. Jeremiah 24:2.

In verse 5 these hardboiled apostates, who had sunk to the lowest level of the superstitious mystery cults and to the most degrading forms of idolatry, are introduced as speakers. They say *qerabh 'eleykhā,* draw near to Yourself — an idiomatic expression that has no exact counterpart in English. It is something like "Stay where you are, don't come near me, keep to yourself." *qedhashtīkhā,* for I am sacred in respect to you, is an intransitive Qal with accusative suffix. A change to Piel, *qiddashtīkhā,* I make you sacred, I sanctify you (by contact with Me), as in Ezekiel 44:19; 46:20, is not necessary, since the phrase does not stand isolated (cf. Zech. 7:5), Gr. 117, x, p. 369, and besides would be unclear, no matter what person would be thought of as being addressed. Surprisingly, most commentators understand these words of the idolators as being addressed to their brethren who are still clinging to Jehovah. But what could be their interest in warning them? The utterance is rather an expression of the attitude of their hearts toward the Lord, with whom they want nothing more to do, since they deem themselves to have attained to a higher form of worship. This defiant attitude explains the Lord's revulsion as expressed in the words that follow immediately and in close connection: These — with backward reference — are a smoke in My nostrils, a continually burning flame. These words do not say that they are as unbearable to the Lord as are smoke and flame in a man's nostrils. The meaning is to be found in Jeremiah 17:4: by their insolence they have filled the Lord's nostrils with smoke and kindled in His face a constantly burning flame, that is, an unquenchable, consuming wrath, cf. Deuteronomy 32:22; Psalm 18:9(8).

6 הִנֵּה כְתוּבָה לְפָנָי

לֹא אֶחֱשֶׁה כִּי אִם־שִׁלַּמְתִּי וְשִׁלַּמְתִּי עַל־חֵיקָם :

7 עֲוֺנֺתֵיכֶם וַעֲוֺנֺת אֲבוֹתֵיכֶם יַחְדָּו אָמַר יְהֹוָה

אֲשֶׁר קִטְּרוּ עַל־הֶהָרִים וְעַל־הַגְּבָעוֹת חֵרְפוּנִי

וּמַדֹּתִי פְעֻלָּתָם רִאשֹׁנָה עַל ־חֵיקָם :

In verses 6 and 7, with a fresh outburst, the Lord's threat against the idolaters is continued. The words are like an Amen to the preceding utterance. *hinnēh* is strongly affirmative, surely! It is determined and written down before the eyes of the Lord as something that is irrevocable and at the same time unforgettable. (The reference is to the prayer for the cessation of God's anger in the foregoing chapter.) This writing contained the statement that the Lord will not be silent, etc. That is a direct answer to the *teḥesheh* at the end of the prayer. *kī ʾim shillamtī,* without having recompensed. The Lord is not here saying that He will again converse peacefully with these incorrigibles after having repaid them for their evil deeds. He will not be silent; but He will recompense. Maintaining silence and recompensing are represented as direct opposites by *kī ʾim,* but. The *we* before the second *shillamtī* is epexegetical: yes, indeed, I will repay, Gr. 154, Note 1, b, p. 484. *ʾal hēyqām,* usually *ʾel hēyqām,* like the Qere at the end of verse 7, "into their bosom," expresses the thoroughness of the recompense, cf. Jeremiah 32:18; Luke 6:38. "The thing to be repaid follows in verse 7a; it is not governed, however, by *shillamtī,* as the form of the address clearly shows, but by *ʾashallēm* understood, which may be easily supplied" (Delitzsch). But *shillamtī* can be construed as a prophetic perfect, the perfect of certainty, and then the procedure suggested by Delitzsch is not necessary, Gr. 106, n, p. 312f.

In verse 7 the prophet returns to the direct address in the second person, for the sake of greater emphasis. Your iniquities and

667

the iniquities of your fathers together will I recompense, says the Lord. "Says the Lord" adds emphasis. Whether one takes the following *'asher* to be a relative or a conjunction (because) is immaterial; the sense will not be affected. The sins that are mentioned, idol worship on hilltops, worship on all high places devoted to Astarte and Baal, 57:7; Jeremiah 2:20; 3:6; Ezekiel 6:13, were all associated with the most horrible lewdness. These were primarily the sins of the fathers. They had been introduced by Solomon, 1 Kings 11, and were practiced throughout and beyond Josiah's time by both great and lowly. Neither the prophets nor the pious kings were able to curb them. The generations of the exile copied their fathers in their sin, cf. verse 11; and so Exodus 20:5; 34:7, etc., had to be fulfilled. The Lord will repay — the time for recompense had arrived — *mādhadh,* to weigh out, to compensate according to what is due. The *Waw* before *maddōthī* is the *Waw* apodosis. *rī'shōnāh,* first, first of all, should not be stricken, as some suggest, because it places the retribution against the apostates, in time and in order, ahead of the preservation of the faithful which is described in the following verses.

Second Strophe: verses 8-16: *The preservation of the faithful Remnant in contrast to those who are past all cure.*

8 *Thus says the Lord:*
   As when wine is found in the cluster,
   And one says: Destroy it not, for there is a blessing in it;
   So will I do for the sake of My servants,
   That I do not utterly destroy the whole.
9 *Out of Jacob will I bring forth a seed,*
   Out of Judah an heir to My mountains,
   And My chosen one shall possess it,
   And My servants shall dwell there.
10 *And Sharon shall become a pasture for flocks,*
   And the valley of Achor a resting place for cattle,
   For the good of My people who have sought Me.
11 *But you, who forsake the Lord,*
   Who have forgotten My holy hill,
   Who spread a table for Gad
   And pour out mixed wine for Meni —
12 *I will deliver you to the sword,*
   And all of you shall bow yourselves to the slaughter,
   Because you did not answer when I called,
   Would not hear when I spoke,
   And did what was evil in My eyes,
   And chose what was displeasing to Me,

13 *Therefore thus says the Lord Lord:*
   Truly, My servants shall eat, but you shall go hungry,
   Truly, My servants shall drink, but you shall thirst,
   Truly, My servants shall rejoice, but you shall be put to shame,
14 *Truly, My servants shall sing aloud for gladness of heart,*
   But you shall cry out for soreness of heart, and howl in despair.
15 *You shall leave your name for a cursing for My chosen ones,*
   So that the Lord Lord may slay you;
   But to His servants will He give another name.
16 *So that he who blesses himself on earth will bless himself by the*
   God of Truth;
   And he who swears an oath on earth will swear by the God of Truth;
   Because forgotten are the former afflictions,
   And they are hidden from before My eyes.

8 כֹּה ׀ אָמַר יְהוָה   כַּאֲשֶׁר יִמָּצֵא הַתִּירוֹשׁ בָּאֶשְׁכּוֹל

וְאָמַר אַל־תַּשְׁחִיתֵהוּ   כִּי בְרָכָה בּוֹ

כֵּן אֶעֱשֶׂה לְמַעַן עֲבָדַי   לְבִלְתִּי הַשְׁחִית הַכֹּל׃

9 וְהוֹצֵאתִי מִיַּעֲקֹב זֶרַע   וּמִיהוּדָה יוֹרֵשׁ הָרָי

וִירֵשׁוּהָ בְחִירַי   וַעֲבָדַי יִשְׁכְּנוּ־שָׁמָּה׃

First *(rī'shonāh)* the Lord will destroy the apostates, and then He will shower His goodness upon the preserved Remnant. The discourse begins with the usual emphatic statement: Thus says the Lord. The picture of the juice of the grape in the cluster is perhaps correctly interpreted by most commentators as referring to the presence of both good and bad grapes in a cluster, which, for the sake of the good berries, is not cast aside. Budde makes the fantastic suggestion that the reference here is to a wine song that was sung at the time of the vintage to charm the clusters into producing more bountifully. *ka'asher yimmātse'* and the following *we'āmar* ("Just as there will be found and then one says"), would in our idiom be: "Just as one says, when one finds, etc." The article with *tīrosh* and *'eshkōl* is generic. *yimmātse'* suggests that there had been testing and examining before the finding. But one does not test and examine full and ripe grapes; one does examine more closely those that appear to be unripe, imperfect, or overripe. So, the sense is: If the inspection of a cluster reveals that there is *still* good wine juice in it, then one says to himself, etc. In the phrase *kī bherākhāh bō* the addition of the word *still* brings out the sense more clearly.

669

For the sake of the faithful servants remaining in Israel who comprise the blessing of the choice vintage still remaining in the clusters, the Lord will not completely destroy the people, will not root up the wheat with the tares, Matthew 13:29; cf. 1 Kings 19; Romans 9; but He will cause a seed, a scion, to spring forth from Jacob. The perfect *hōtsē'thī* with *Waw* consecutive perfect following the imperfect *'e'eseh* is to be understood as referring to the future. Jacob and Judah are personifications and do not refer to the northern and southern tribes respectively (cf. 46:3). In Isaiah II Jacob is the usual designation for Israel, the southern tribe which was led captive to Babylon. Cf. 40:27; 41:8, 14, 21; 42:24; chapters 43, 44, 45, etc. Chapter 48:1 is decisive for this interpretation; in that passage those who came forth from Judah are called Israel, and are expressly addressed as "house of Jacob." But Judah is here hardly just a poetic variation of the name Jacob, nor is it a more precise designation for the people of the exile. It is rather the name of the tribe out of which a Governor, a Leader of the people, shall arise, cf. Micah 5:1 (2). This seems to be what is intended by the phrase *yōrēsh hārāy*, a possessor, an inheritor of My mountains, and for that reason the singular is used, which is not here intended as a collective in the sense of "seed." The next phrase speaks of possession by the people: "And My chosen ones shall possess it, etc." The feminine singular suffix in *wīrēshūhā* cannot refer to the plural *hārāy*, My mountains, but must refer to the land, *'erets* understood, 57:13. Those who have been preserved of Israel shall return to their homeland and live there securely under a Ruler of their mountains who shall spring forth from the tribe of Judah.

וְהָיָה הַשָּׁרוֹן לִנְוֵה־צֹאן וְעֵמֶק עָכוֹר לְרֵבֶץ בָּקָר ¹⁰
לְעַמִּי אֲשֶׁר דְּרָשׁוּנִי:

The plain of Sharon is the northern half of the Mediterranean plain of Canaan, from Carmel to Joppa. The plain had a breadth of nine to fifteen miles and was famous for its fertility and its profusion of flowers, 35:2. The plain also served as pasture land, 1 Chronicles 27:29. The valley of Achor near Jericho is historically connected with the sin of Achan, Joshua 7:24. It is possible that the valley derived its name from that event (*ākhar*, to trouble, to cause misfortune). This valley, which extended in the direction of the Dead Sea, was not fertile. The plain of Sharon is to be a *nāweh*, a pasture, a meadow for flocks; but the valley of Achor shall be no more than a *rēbhets,* a resting place for cattle, camels, and caravans. The *le* before *'ammī* indicates that these pastures and resting places shall again serve the Lord's faithful as they had in days gone by. These two areas, naturally, are mentioned as representative of all the glorious areas that the Lord will prepare for His people.

11 וְאַתֶּם֙ עֹזְבֵ֣י יְהֹוָ֔ה הַשְּׁכֵחִ֖ים אֶת־הַ֣ר קָדְשִׁ֑י
הַֽעֹרְכִ֤ים לַגַּד֙ שֻׁלְחָ֔ן וְהַֽמְמַלְאִ֖ים לַמְנִ֥י מִמְסָֽךְ׃

12 וּמָנִ֨יתִי אֶתְכֶ֜ם לַחֶ֗רֶב וְכֻלְּכֶם֙ לַטֶּ֣בַח תִּכְרָ֔עוּ
יַ֤עַן קָרָ֨אתִי֙ וְלֹ֣א עֲנִיתֶ֔ם דִּבַּ֖רְתִּי וְלֹ֣א שְׁמַעְתֶּ֑ם
וַתַּעֲשׂ֤וּ הָרַע֙ בְּעֵינַ֔י וּבַֽאֲשֶׁ֥ר לֹֽא־חָפַ֖צְתִּי בְּחַרְתֶּֽם׃

With *we'attem,* but you, attention is again directed to the apostates. They are so called because they had forsaken the Lord and forgotten His holy mountain (Zion, the place of the temple, where the Lord dwelt and was worshiped) and despising Him had turned to the worship of strange gods. Delitzsch, in his commentary on 65:11, discusses the idol names Gad and Meni. Nothing very definite is known about the gods represented by these names. The names are Hebrew, not Babylonian. Gad (from *gādhadh,* to apportion) means good fortune, and was the name of one of the sons of Jacob and of the tribe that he founded. It was also the name of a well-known prophet of David's time, 1 Samuel 22:5; 2 Samuel 24:11. Since Gad also appears in the names of cities, Baal Gad in northern Canaan and Migdal Gad in Judah (Josh. 11:17; 15:37), it might well have been the name of a Canaanite god.

menī (from *mānāh,* to count, to portion out) is wholly unknown. If Gad and Baal Gad are gods of good fortune, then Meni could well have been a goddess of good fortune. So, it is possible that these idols are to be identified with Baal and Astarte, the sun-god and the moon-goddess, or Jupiter and Venus. In Babylon the exiles gave themselves over to the worship of idols, some of which they had brought along from home; others of which they borrowed from the Babylonians and gave them Hebrew names. Setting a table for Gad and pouring out mixed, or spiced, wine for Meni identify this form of idolatry as connected with *lectisternia,* festivals at which images of gods were laid out on cushions while food and wine were placed before them. To such mean and wretched idolatry had Israel fallen. In verse 12 the

Lord announces retribution for this gross apostasy. The $\bar{u}$ before
manūthī is the *Waw* of the apodosis. There is a play on words here
with the name Meni. The Lord will devote them to the sword, that
is, to death, to the extreme of misfortune, instead of the good fortune sought by the worship of Gad. They will have to bow to the
slaughter-block instead of over the table spread for
Gad. Regarding the paratactic arrangement of phrases in the
following, cf. Gr. 150, m, p. 476, and 50:2; 58:3. Cf. also Proverbs
1:24. The closing words are a development of *sōrēr*, verse 2.

13 לָכֵן כֹּה־אָמַר ׀ אֲדֹנָי יְהֹוִה
הִנֵּה עֲבָדַי ׀ יֹאכֵלוּ וְאַתֶּם תִּרְעָבוּ
הִנֵּה עֲבָדַי יִשְׁתּוּ וְאַתֶּם תִּצְמָאוּ
הִנֵּה עֲבָדַי יִשְׂמָחוּ וְאַתֶּם תֵּבֹשׁוּ׃
14 הִנֵּה עֲבָדַי יָרֹנּוּ מִטּוּב לֵב
וְאַתֶּם תִּצְעֲקוּ מִכְּאֵב לֵב וּמִשֵּׁבֶר רוּחַ תְּיֵלִילוּ׃
15 וְהִנַּחְתֶּם שִׁמְכֶם לִשְׁבוּעָה לִבְחִירַי וֶהֱמִיתְךָ אֲדֹנָי יְהֹוִה
וְלַעֲבָדָיו יִקְרָא שֵׁם אַחֵר׃
16 אֲשֶׁר הַמִּתְבָּרֵךְ בָּאָרֶץ יִתְבָּרֵךְ בֵּאלֹהֵי אָמֵן
וְהַנִּשְׁבָּע בָּאָרֶץ יִשָּׁבַע בֵּאלֹהֵי אָמֵן
כִּי נִשְׁכְּחוּ הַצָּרוֹת הָרִאשֹׁנוֹת וְכִי נִסְתְּרוּ מֵעֵינָי׃

kōh 'āmar is reinforced by *lākhēn*, therefore; and now that the
Lord's threatening words are drawing to a close, Adonai is added
to *YHWH* for still more emphasis. In six contrasting statements
the happy lot of the faithful and the unhappy lot of the godless are
set off against each other in vivid poetic terms. The pictures are
all taken from ordinary life, but they express in physical terms the
spiritual glory of the newly ordered church, which is the subject of
the section beginning at verse 17. *hinnēh* has the force of a particle of affirmation; the language throughout expresses strong feeling. *ṭūbh lēbh* in verse 14 is gladness, happiness of heart; *ke'ēbh
lēbh* is the opposite, soreness and heaviness of heart. *shēbher
rūaḥ*, brokenness of spirit and courage, is despair. Concerning the
uncontracted form *teyēlīlū* for *tēylīlū* (imperfect Hiphil of *yālal*, to
howl) cf. Gr. 70 c, 2, p. 193. Concerning *hinnaḥtem* (from *hinnīaḥ*),
as distinguished from *hēnīaḥ*, both imperfect Hiphil of *nūaḥ*, cf.

the lexicon and Gr. 72, ee, p. 201. *hēnīah* means to cause to rest (cf. 63:14), while *hinnīah* means to set down, to lay down, to confer. *shebhū'ah,* an oath, here has the meaning of a curse. "You shall bestow your name as a curse, as an imprecation, upon My elect." The common explanation of this statement, namely, that the name of the rejected people shall be employed by the elect as a *means* of cursing others, is far wide of the mark. That explanation immediately raises the question whether the oath-formula is contained in *wehemīthekhā,* which cannot be the case, because of the *we* with the perfect. An imperfect would be required, as in Genesis 48:20; Ruth 4:11f. That explanation also makes identification of the singular suffix *khā* in *wehemīthekhā* very difficult. Not as a means to be used in cursing someone else, but as the object of an imprecation, the rejected will impart their name to the elect. They will not bequeath it, as a bequest from the dead, for death does not come until *hemīthekhā* in the following clause. The meaning is that when the elect recall the name of the apostate and idolatrous part of the people, they will call down a curse on that name. As a result of this curse, which does not just dissolve into the air, but is heard by the Lord, He, the Lord of all, will slay them (*hēmīth*) as the final act of retribution. The last clause of verse 15, *wela'abhādhāyw,* etc., again is in strong contrast to the first clause.

Now that the name of the apostate idolaters has become the object of a curse, the elect no longer can or want to call themselves by that name, but the Lord will Himself give them another name. The difficulty is thus resolved. The negative critics, however, since they do not accept such a solution, escape the difficulty by asserting with the greatest assurance that the clause "and the Lord Jehovah will slay you," together with all of verse 16, is a marginal gloss that somehow found its way into the body of the text. Verse 16 describes the effect of the fulfillment of the curse on the inner attitude and the outer life of the remaining faithful people. If someone now blesses himself, he will do so in the name of the God of Truth; and whoever swears an oath will swear by the God of Truth, that is, in the name of the God who faithfully fulfills all His promises to those who fear Him, and who duly carries out every threat, now and through all time to come, cf. 2 Corinthians 1:20; Revelation 3:14. Now that Elohim Jehovah, the almighty and faithful God, has in accordance with His covenant fulfilled all His promises and carried out His threats of retribution, the faith of the believers is perfect and no longer dis-

673

turbed by the doubts that had formerly been raised by repeated affliction. Those afflictions are now forgotten (*nishkeḥū*), not only by the believers, but they are hidden from the eyes of the Lord Himself, cf. Revelation 21:4. *'asher* at the beginning of verse 16 is a consecutive conjunction, so that, Gr. 166, b, p. 505. Is *nishbā'* in the second clause perhaps to be understood in the specific sense of curse, like *shebhū'āh* in verse 15? The contrasting idea in *hithbārēkh* suggests the possibility. But the word also fits well into the context in its usual sense of to swear an oath.

Verses 15c and 16 serve as an introduction to the following strophe, which treats of the establishment of a new order of things.

Third Strophe: verses 17-25: *The new heaven and the new earth.*

17 *For behold, I will create a new heaven and a new earth,*
    And the first shall no longer be remembered, and shall
        not be brought to mind;
18 *But rejoice and exult forever in what I shall create;*
    For behold, I create Jerusalem for a rejoicing and her
        people for a joy,
19 *I Myself will rejoice because of Jerusalem and exult*
        over My people;
    No more shall the sound of weeping be heard in her nor
        the voice of crying.
20 *No more shall there be a sucking child of only a*
        few days,
    Nor an old man who does not complete his days,
    For the young man shall die a hundred years old,
    And the sinner, as the son of a hundred years, shall
        be cursed.
21 *They shall build houses and inhabit them,*
    Plant vineyards and eat their fruit.
22 *They shall not build, and another inhabit,*
    Nor plant so that others eat;
    For like the days of the trees are the days of
        My people
    And my elect shall consume the fruit of the work
        of their hands.
23 *They shall not toil in vain*
    Nor bring forth children for sudden destruction;
    For seed of the blessed of the Lord are they,
    And their offspring — they remain with them.
24 *And it shall come to pass that before they call,*
        I will answer;
    While they are yet speaking, I will hear.

25 *The wolf and the lamb shall feed together,*
And the lion shall eat straw like the ox;
And even the serpent, whose bread is dust —
They shall not hurt nor destroy
In all My holy mountain, says the Lord.

17 כִּי־הִנְנִי בוֹרֵא שָׁמַיִם חֲדָשִׁים וְאֶרֶץ חֲדָשָׁה
וְלֹא תִזָּכַרְנָה הָרִאשֹׁנוֹת וְלֹא תַעֲלֶינָה עַל־לֵב:

18 כִּי־אִם־שִׂישׂוּ וְגִילוּ עֲדֵי־עַד אֲשֶׁר אֲנִי בוֹרֵא
כִּי הִנְנִי בוֹרֵא אֶת־יְרוּשָׁלַם גִּילָה וְעַמָּהּ מָשׂוֹשׂ:

19 וְגַלְתִּי בִירוּשָׁלַם וְשַׂשְׂתִּי בְעַמִּי
וְלֹא־יִשָּׁמַע בָּהּ עוֹד קוֹל בְּכִי וְקוֹל זְעָקָה:

The new heaven and the new earth, as in Genesis 1:1, are a unit, even though each word has its own attribute. It is a new world, a new creation, viewed physically from above and from beneath. The whole is a graphic designation of the new order of things which the Lord will institute. However, as is generally true of the prophecy of the future kingdom of God, time and eternity, New Testament glory and heavenly glory are not sharply distinguished. Moreover, the details of the description are so obviously such as are perceptible by the senses, that it is clear that these are not to be considered and interpreted individually, but purely as impressive elements of the general picture. The following passages should be compared: Isaiah 11; 25:6ff; 26:15ff; 35; Hosea 2:14ff; Micah 4 (Isaiah 2); Zephaniah 3:14ff; 2 Peter 3:13f; Revelation 21. The one great thought that everywhere shines through brightly is the banishment of all evil and sorrow, after the godless have been destroyed, cf. verse 15.

hāri'shōnōth refers to heaven and earth; the reference is not the same here as in verse 16. *'ālāh 'al lēbh,* to be brought to mind, to be recalled to memory. Cf. the lexicon under *lēbh.* In verse 18 there is a shift to the imperative form of the verbs. This is the imperative of assurance, Gr. 110, c, p. 324. Before *'asher, 'al* must be understood. The concrete meaning of *'asher 'anī borē'* is contained in the next clause. The Lord will create Jerusalem anew as a rejoicing and her people as an exultation. Abstract, impersonal terms are used to designate the people of Jerusalem, like *tehillāh* in 62:7. In the church of the future there shall be only joy and rejoicing.

In connection with the words in verse 19: "I Myself will rejoice because of Jerusalem and will exult over My people," Budde makes the following remark: "These two clauses might well be a mistaken interpretation of the two preceding ones; and the first two clauses of verse 18 are also expendable." That is a sample of modern scientific criticism. But see Zephaniah 3:17, where almost the identical words are used. Cf. Deuteronomy 30:9. Does not a spirit of joy on the part of the Lord over the consummation of Jerusalem pervade the entire Scripture of both Testaments, the prophets, Isaiah I and II, through chapter 62, and the Epistle to the Ephesians? In connection with the final clause of verse 19, cf. 25:8; 35:10; Revelation 7:17; 21:4. The features of the church mentioned in these verses of chapter 65 have all been features of the church in eternity, of the absolute perfection of the church, features that do indeed pertain *suo modo* to the church also in this time of grace, *kī nishkehū hatstsārōth hārī'shōnōth,* verse 16, "for the former things are passed away — behold, I make all things new."

לֹא־יִהְיֶ֨ה מִשָּׁ֜ם ע֤וֹד ע֣וּל יָמִים֙ 20

וְזָקֵ֔ן אֲשֶׁ֥ר לֹֽא־יְמַלֵּ֖א אֶת־יָמָ֑יו

כִּ֣י הַנַּ֗עַר בֶּן־מֵאָ֤ה שָׁנָה֙ יָמ֔וּת וְהַ֣חוֹטֶ֔א בֶּן־מֵאָ֥ה שָׁנָ֖ה

יְקֻלָּֽל׃

וּבָנ֥וּ בָתִּ֖ים וְיָשָׁ֑בוּ וְנָטְע֣וּ כְרָמִ֔ים וְאָכְל֖וּ פִּרְיָֽם׃ 21

Without further ado the description turns to concrete details of the temporal New Testament kingdom of the Messiah. *mishshām* is hardly to be translated "from there." *yihyeh* does not fit with that translation, and *wezāqēn* still less. *min,* in this case, serves only to emphasize the adverb "there" as in the LXX ἐκεῖ : "There shall no longer be *there.*" For *yāmīm* in the sense of some days, a few days, cf. Gr. 139, h, p. 449. See also Genesis 24:55 and other passages. The thought is: A sucking child that lives only a few days, etc. Whether in the case of the old man who lives out his days (*yāmīm*), the extreme term of 1000 years is assumed, an age that even the antediluvian fathers only approached, cannot be determined. Nothing is said about that. It is interesting that Josephus in his *Antiquities* has a notice that Manetho, Berosus, Mochus, Hestiaeus, Jerome the Egyptian, Hesiod, Hekataeus, Hellanikus, Akusilaus, Ephorus, and Nikolaus all make mention of the tradition that the age of man at the beginning was 1000 years. Hesiod mentions it in his "Εργα καὶ 'Ημέραι; there are no writings of the other authors extant.

"For the young man (generic singular) will die as a son of 100 years," that is, at the age of 100 (cf. Gr. 128, v, p. 418 and Gen. 5), the meaning being that one who dies at the age of 100 will still be thought of as one who died in his youth. There is much disagreement about the last clause in this verse. The text of the LXX does not agree with that of the Masora, which reads literally: "and the transgressor, as a son of 100 years, shall be cursed." (*hōṭe'*, Qal participle of *hāṭā'*, has segol instead of tsere, after the pattern of the *Lamed-He* verbs, Gr. 75, oo, p. 216). It is too ingenious a translation to render *hōṭe'* with "not attain," to cross out *ben*, and to render the Pual *yequllāl* with "shall be considered cursed." But to declare the whole verse to be an interpolation, or to scoff at it as Duhm does, displays no ingenuity at all. The Scripture of the Old Testament looks upon premature death, in contrast with the long life of the godly man, as a special punishment visited upon the ungodly, cf. Job 15:32; 22:16; 24:19, 24; 27:14; Psalms 55:24(23); 102:25(24). The literal sense of these words is, that a sinner who would otherwise die in middle age or in early youth, will now live to be 100 before the punishing hand of God ends his life. God's patience with sinners and the ungodly, even in the still imperfect order of things, will be doubled, tripled, be tenfold what it had been, yes, will be endlessly increased, cf. Romans 2:4; 9:22; 15:5; 2 Peter 3:9,15. One of the chief differences between the economy of the Old Testament and that of the New Testament is the almost total suspension of the sudden and immediate intervention of the God of grace against believers who fall into sin and commit crime, against nations and generations laden with guilt and stained with blood, and a world that is steadily growing more blasphemous and godless. This passage, verses 20-25, deals with the future of God's people in the New Testament, not with the eternal and perfect church in heaven. The church in eternity was pictured in verses 17-19.

22 לֹא יִבְנוּ וְאַחֵר יֵשֵׁב לֹא יִטְּעוּ וְאַחֵר יֹאכֵל
כִּי־כִימֵי הָעֵץ יְמֵי עַמִּי וּמַעֲשֵׂה יְדֵיהֶם יְבַלּוּ בְחִירָי:
23 לֹא יִיגְעוּ לָרִיק וְלֹא יֵלְדוּ לַבֶּהָלָה
כִּי זֶרַע בְּרוּכֵי יְהוָה הֵמָּה וְצֶאֱצָאֵיהֶם אִתָּם:

Verses 21 and 22 and the first clause of verse 23 are essentially identical with 62:8,9. *'aḥēr*, another, in verse 22, who shall not inhabit what they built, etc., here says abstractly what 62:8,9 express in the concrete terms "enemies" and "children of strangers." What is new here, is the reason given: Like the lifetime of a tree, such as the long-lived cedars, oaks, and terebinths, will the lifetime of My people be, that is, of the individual members of My people; and since they will remain in possession for a long time, undisturbed by outsiders, they will be able to enjoy and consume what the labor of their own hands produced. *yebhallū* is Piel of *bālāh*. "They shall not labor in vain" (verse 23), sums up in negative form the positive that was expressed in verses 21 and 22a and emphasizes it. They are secure in possession of the fruits of their labor. *yīghe'ū* is a Qal imperfect of *yāgha'*. They shall not toil in vain; nor shall they beget children only to have them die an early death. (Sin has also corrupted the blessings of wedlock. Even today the rate of infant mortality ranges up to 150 or more per thousand in some underdeveloped countries. So far as this life in concerned, these infants were born in vain.) That shall change, because they, the parents, are a seed of the blessed of the Lord (partitive genitive), Gr. 128, i, p. 416, that is, they are begotten of the Lord and are a new and blessed generation, and shall themselves beget children for long and effective life in the world.

The expression *wetse'etsā'eyhem 'ittām*, "and their offspring with them," is explained by some commentators as a second subject, in apposition to *hēmmāh*. Job 21:8 cannot be cited against this understanding of the phrase, because *liphnēyhem* and *le'eynēyhem* in that passage surely are not the same as *'ittām* here. The fact that *hēmmāh* is at the end of one clause and is followed immediately by *wetse'etsā'eyhem* supports this explanation, as does also the sense of the passage: They do not beget children for an untimely death, because they themselves as well as their offspring with them are a generation blessed of the Lord. *'ittām* can very well have this local meaning. Isaiah often uses *'eth* in referring to place, for example, in 66:10: *'eth yerushālayim, 'ittāh*. He even uses it of the quarrel of one person *with* another, *'ittī*, Isaiah 50:8. However, no objection can be raised to construing the clause as an independent sentence: "And their offspring are with them," that is, will remain with them in contrast to being begotten for an early, sudden death — a fitting conclusion to these two verses, cf. 61:9.

24 וְהָיָה טֶרֶם־יִקְרָאוּ וַאֲנִי אֶעֱנֶה עוֹד הֵם מְדַבְּרִים וַאֲנִי אֶשְׁמָע׃

25 זְאֵב וְטָלֶה יִרְעוּ כְאֶחָד וְאַרְיֵה כַּבָּקָר יֹאכַל־תֶּבֶן
וְנָחָשׁ עָפָר לַחְמוֹ
לֹא־יָרֵעוּ וְלֹא־יַשְׁחִיתוּ בְּכָל־הַר קָדְשִׁי אָמַר יְהוָה׃

Concerning *terem,* not yet, with the future, cf. Gr. 107, c, p. 314f. They have *not yet* called, and I answer. *wa* before *'anī* is the *Waw* of the apodosis. *medhabberīm:* While they are still speaking. The prayers of New Testament children are acceptable to the Lord, and He answers them. These words express the heartfelt readiness of the Lord to hear all prayers and to answer them with His help. Cf. 30:19; 58:9, and the New Testament promises of the Lord Himself, Luke 11:5-13; John 14:13f; 15:7; 16:23f, etc. In bold strokes, verse 25 portrays the peace of the New Testament kingdom of God on earth. Compare Isaiah 9:1-7; 11:6-9; 35:9; Hosea 2:18; Ezekiel 34:23ff; Job 5:23. There will be peace among the animals and between man and the beasts, as before the Fall. The last half of the verse expresses the same thought in a somewhat more abstract form. In passages such as this, the prophet always has the ideal before his eyes. Being a poet, he gives his imagination free rein; he writes for people with childlike feelings, whose thoughts express themselves in vivid concrete terms; and finally, the prophet does not always make a distinction between the kingdom of God in the New Testament and the eternal kingdom of glory. Those who keep these facts in mind will not call these descriptions false, or ridicule them as crude, unspiritual flights of imagination, or be deluded into seeing in these pictures a basis for the nonsensical doctrine of an earthly millennium. They will rather see in these words a vivid portrayal of the spiritual peace of the kingdom of the Messiah, presented in the symbolism of peace in nature and in the animal kingdom. Interpretation already goes too far when it professes to see in the lion a picture of evil men, and in the lamb a picture of good men. Following that line of thought, is the ox then to symbolize men of strong character, and the serpent men of subtle minds? What we have here is identical with the "peace on earth for men in whom God is well pleased" in the hymn of the angels above Bethlehem, with the only difference that here the thought appears clothed in a childlike form that glorifies the externals.

To sum up: verse 17 conceives the eternal kingdom of God and the New Testament kingdom as an entirely new creation. Verses

18 and 19 may be understood literally if one thinks of Jerusalem as the name for God's people. Perfect peace, no more tears! That characterizes the kingdom of grace here on earth and also in heaven, even though here below much affliction still presses forth many a tear. Verses 17-20 speak chiefly of the perfect kingdom of eternity; verses 20-25 have predominantly to do with the still imperfect kingdom of the Messiah in the New Testament. These are all concrete pictures representing spiritual conditions. They make use of various aspects of natural life to symbolize the divine power and the true imperishable spiritual gifts with which the Holy Spirit endows the believers. Verse 24 refers solely to the New Testament era; verse 25 describes "Peace on Earth."

Comment on a few points of grammar may be in place here. *ke'eḥādh,* like *one,* is the same as *yaḥdāyw,* together. The remark about the serpent may mean that the serpent, once used by Satan as his instrument of evil to seduce our first parents, will have to continue to bear the curse, although like other beasts, the serpent too will be harmless. The grammatical subject of *yārē'ū* (from *rā'a',* with double *Ayin*) and of *yashḥīthū* (both Hiphil forms) is the beasts now grown tame and gentle. The holy hill of the Lord (*har qodhshī*) is the temple hill on which the house of the Lord stood. The term perhaps is broad enough in meaning to include the whole city of Zion and the Holy Land. But this too is a picture of the church. — The strophe began with *hinenī* to command attention; it concludes with *'āmar YHWH* as with a confirming Amen.

Third Discourse: Chapter 66

The end of the old Congregation and the beginning of the new Church.

In chapter 65 we had the beginning of the answer to the prayer contained in chapter 64. Chapter 66 contains a continuation of that answer and its conclusion. The warnings directed against the rebellious people, and the promises given in chapter 65 to the faithful Remnant, are here being brought to fulfillment in the description of the judgment of the Lord. Accompanied by a mighty tumult in the city and the temple, the judgment is carried out that puts an end to the Old Testament congregation and gives birth to a new church, verses 6-9. What precedes in verses 1-5 is a recapitulation of the conditions that were the cause of this judgment. God's anger over the total spiritual decadence of the rebellious people was no longer to be checked, and His mercy toward His own was no longer to be withheld. In verses 10-14 there is a description of the blessedness of the new congregation that has been saved from judgment. This blessed condition of the faithful and the fate of the condemned both reveal the "hand of the Lord." The last section, verses 15-24, describes how the judgment upon the Jews who were defiled by their own abominations has led the gentile world to acknowledge the glory of the Lord and to be incorporated into the new church through the ministrations of the Jews of the Diaspora and those who had been saved in Israel. The chapter has many connections, in vocabulary and in factual references, with what has gone before. The chapter may be divided as follows: verses 1-4; 5-9; 10-14; 15-24 (or 15-19, 20-24).

First Strophe: verses 1-4: *This people has become an abomination that can no longer be borne by the Lord, even though they
make a show of being willing to build Him a new temple.*

1 *Thus says the Lord: Heaven is My throne,*
   And the earth My footstool!
   What manner of house is it that you would build for Me?
   And where, then, is the place of My rest?
2 *For all of these things My hand did make,*
   And so did all this come into being, says the Lord.
   Yet, for this man do I have regard: who is humble
      and of contrite spirit,
   And who trembles at My Word.
3 *He (among you) who slaughters an ox is (before Me)*
      as one who kills a man,
   He who sacrifices a sheep, as one who kills a dog,
   He who brings an oblation, as one who offers swine's blood,
   He who burns incense, as one who worships an idol.
   As they have chosen their own ways,
   And as their souls delight in their abominations,
4 *So will I choose what brings them misfortune,*
   And what they dread, that will I let come to pass,
   For when I called, there was none who answered;
   I spoke and none would listen,
   Yes, they did what was evil in My eyes,
   And what displeased Me, that did they choose.

כֹּה אָמַר יְהוָה 1

הַשָּׁמַיִם כִּסְאִי וְהָאָרֶץ הֲדֹם רַגְלָי

אֵי־זֶה בַיִת אֲשֶׁר תִּבְנוּ־לִי וְאֵי־זֶה מָקוֹם מְנוּחָתִי:

וְאֶת־כָּל־אֵלֶּה יָדִי עָשָׂתָה וַיִּהְיוּ כָל־אֵלֶּה נְאֻם־יְהוָה 2

וְאֶל־זֶה אַבִּיט אֶל־עָנִי וּנְכֵה־רוּחַ וְחָרֵד עַל־דְּבָרִי:

With the familiar forceful affirmation, *kōh ʾamar YHWH,* the
Lord introduces the final discourse. Only in the opening words
does He address the apostates directly; afterward the rejected people are mentioned only in the third person. The highly impressive
opening phrases occur several times elsewhere in Scripture: Matthew 5:34f; 23:22; Acts 7:48ff; Psalms 11:4; 93:2; 103:19. The
words are so plain and simple that no exposition is needed. Compare the application of this truth in Psalm 139 and Jeremiah
23:23f. The two questions that follow are directed to the apostates
("What manner of house is it that you would build for Me? And
where, then, is the place of My rest? "). The obvious answer brings

out the same truth that Paul voiced in his sermon to the Athenians (Acts 17:24). Stephen also cited it in his defense against the "stiff-necked and uncircumcised in hearts and ears" (Acts 7:48f) when they accused him of speaking blasphemous words against the "holy place" (Acts 6:13): The most High does not live in temples made with hands, even though it be the temple of Solomon (Acts 7:47f). The Lord desires neither a temple nor temple worship of those who "do always resist the Holy Ghost: as your fathers did, so do you" (verse 51). God did, indeed, Himself order the building of a temple, and He also instituted temple worship, but only a person who does not understand these words at all or is devoid of spiritual understanding will see a contradiction between that fact and the repeated prophetic visions of Isaiah and other prophets of a future new temple (56:7; 66:20; cf. Matt. 21:13). It is wholly unnecessary and is nowhere justified to interpret these words as being directed against an assumed plan of the exiles to build a temple in Babylon; or against a plan of the Samaritans under Ezra/Nehemiah to build a temple, as Cheyne and Duhm supposed. If any historical situation is to be assumed, then let it be the one recorded in Ezra 3, Haggai 1, and Zechariah 1, when the returned exiles concerned themselves with building the temple commanded by the Lord, although the mass of the people had not experienced any spiritual renewal. But in this discourse there is no explicit reference to a historical situation, and the distinctive quality of the prophecy is entirely the same as that of the rest of Isaiah II.

This is the prophet who, about 700 years before Christ, prophesied the fall of Jerusalem, the destruction of the temple, and the deportation of the people to Babylon; but who also prophesied the return of the exiles to their homeland, who envisioned a new glory for the people, a restoration of land, city, and temple, new grace and a new spirit based on a future expiation of their sin by the vicarious self-sacrifice of the Servant of the Lord. This is the same prophet who by inspiration of the Holy Spirit knows that only a small, truly spiritual remnant will be preserved through the exile, while the mass of the people will remain incorrigible and hardened in their unbelief. Inspired by the Holy Ghost, this prophet sees the people settled again in their old home, but still unregenerate, going through the motions of restoring the temple, the temple worship, and the worship of God, but persisting in their worse than heathen spirit, and yet in a gross carnal spirit asserting for themselves the prerogatives that under God's covenant pertained only to the true Israel.

Against this spirit — situation, if you will — the punitive portion of the conclusion of Isaiah II, namely, chapters 65 and 66, including 66:1, is directed. He whose throne is the heavens and whose footstool, the earth, neither needs nor desires a temple or temple worship of those who in stubbornness of spirit have lost all respect for God's Word and who delight in following only their own ways (verse 3). The spiritual character of Jewry as it developed after the exile, especially in Pharisaism and Sadduceeism, more and more conforms to this picture, as Stephen so plainly demonstrated to the people of his time.

The interrogative particle *'ey* with the demonstrative *zeh* converts the demonstrative into an interrogative: which? what manner of? Cf. 50:1. It could be translated *Where?* without an appreciable change in meaning. The passages cited in the lexicon in support of that meaning are, however, not convincing: 1 Samuel 9:18; Isaiah 50:1; Jeremiah 6:16; Job 28:12,20, cf. Gr. 137, a, p. 443. *menūḥathī,* My rest, is in apposition to *māqōm* (absolute state), not *meqōm* (construct state), but with no difference in meaning. For *menūḥathī* in the sense of temple, cf. Psalm 132:8,14; 1 Chronicles 28:2. *kol 'elleh* in verse 2 refers to all of creation, heaven and earth, as mentioned in verse 1. *wayihyū* is a reminder of *wayehī,* repeated several times in Genesis 1. Duhm interprets *kol 'elleh* as referring to the newly established cultus, temple, and congregation, and *'el zeh* to the afflicted but now obedient congregation, in contrast to an opposition temple planned by the Samaritans. He looks with a kind of pity on those who refer these words to the creation. That is scientific criticism! This verse is, in meaning, a duplicate of Psalm 50:9ff. The Lord desires, not a temple, or sacrifices, or any external forms of worship, but a repentant heart that believes and trusts in Him and clings to Him. This was clearly proclaimed in the very first commandment given on Sinai, Exodus 20:3. This is the true nature of religion in both Testaments, 1 Samuel 15:22; 16:7; Psalms 34:19(18); 51:18f(16f); Matthew 5:3; Isaiah 57:15. This is a fundamental truth that Israel always forgot, and that all the world, including the Christians, keeps on forgetting. As time goes on, the inner spiritual nature of the institution of the church also tends to externalize and to turn to dead orthodoxy and to observance of forms. — The *w* before *'el zeh* is adversative. Its effect, standing apart, as it does, at the beginning, is to emphasize this truth: Such a one it is, to whom I look, that is, upon whom I look with favor. In connection with *'anī* and *nekhēh rūaḥ,* see 41:17; 54:11; 61:1; 57:15. For synonyms of *ḥaredh*, to tremble, cf. Psalm 119:120,161. The very next verse, Psalm 119:162, shows that pure delight in God's word is not inconsistent with trembling in awe of it.

³ שׁוֹחֵ֣ט הַשּׁ֣וֹר מַכֵּה־אִ֗ישׁ זוֹבֵ֤חַ הַשֶּׂה֙ עֹרֵ֣ף כֶּ֔לֶב
מַעֲלֵ֤ה מִנְחָה֙ דַּם־חֲזִ֔יר מַזְכִּ֥יר לְבֹנָ֖ה מְבָ֣רֵֽךְ אָ֑וֶן
גַּם־הֵ֗מָּה בָּֽחֲרוּ֙ בְּדַרְכֵיהֶ֔ם וּבְשִׁקּֽוּצֵיהֶ֖ם נַפְשָׁ֥ם חָפֵֽצָה:
⁴ גַּם־אֲנִ֞י אֶבְחַ֣ר בְּתַעֲלֻלֵיהֶ֗ם וּמְגֽוּרֹתָם֙ אָבִ֣יא לָהֶ֔ם
יַ֤עַן קָרָ֨אתִי֙ וְאֵ֣ין עוֹנֶ֔ה דִּבַּ֖רְתִּי וְלֹ֣א שָׁמֵ֑עוּ
וַיַּעֲשׂ֤וּ הָרַע֙ בְּעֵינַ֔י וּבַאֲשֶׁ֛ר לֹֽא־חָפַ֖צְתִּי בָּחָֽרוּ:

In our translation of the first line of verse 3, we have indicated by parentheses how the various clauses of this verse are to be understood. Although the unregenerate mass of the people were ready to build a new temple, they were still of a stubborn and unbroken spirit and were arrant despisers of God's Word; therefore their worship and their sacrifices were in His judgment objects of loathing and disgust. The various sacrifices that are attributed to them were abominations in His eyes like those mentioned in the predicates. He who slaughters (a contemptuous word for offering) an ox (generic article) is before God as great an abomination as one who murders a man. He who offers a sheep offends the Lord as though he offered up a dog, an unclean animal. *'oreph* is another contemptuous expression, meaning to wring the neck. He who brings an oblation is before the Lord as one who offers up the blood of swine, a stench in His nostrils, all the more so since even the flesh of swine was forbidden food. He who burns incense is as one who worships before an idol. In short, the Lord abhors the sacrifices and the worship of these apostates, who so thoroughly despise His Word. Here we find repeated in essence the contents of verses 10-15 of the first chapter of Isaiah I. The end of the second part of the book returns to the beginning of the first part: This people is an unbearable abomination to the Lord, even in its highest forms of worship.

In regard to the participles without articles in subjects and predicates, cf. Gr. 126, i, p. 406. *ḥemmah* in the last clause of verse

3 is the grammatical subject (not the predicate, as Luther has it) and stands in contrast to *'anī* in verse 4. *gam* is coordinate in *gam hēmmāh* — *gam 'anī*, "as they — so I." The *be* with *darkhēyhem* is the sign of the object after *bāḥar*; therefore, not: They have chosen *in* their ways; but: As they have chosen their ways. *bāḥarū* is a present perfect. They have chosen their ways once and for all and now walk in them. The perfect in *hāphētsāh* expresses an accomplished and existing fact, Gr. 106, g, p. 311. This clause is a concrete expression of the preceding abstract statement. These are their ways: They delight in those things that are an abomination to the Lord. Pagan idols and idol worship are meant, 65:3ff,11; 66:17. *ta'alūlēyhem*, no doubt, are torments, torture. *'ālal* means to plague maliciously, to torment. It is perhaps in this sense that the word is used alongside *na'ar* in Isaiah 3:4, "boys and malicious persons." Here, however, the word must have a passive meaning: what is maliciously done, torments. In any case, the word is synonymous with *megūrōth*, that which one dreads, Proverbs 10:24. Even as they have chosen for themselves that which is an abomination to the Lord, so will He choose and bring upon them what causes horror and torment. This is retribution, 65:6,7,12-15. The grounds given in the following verses duplicate those given in 65:12; cf. 50:2.

Second Strophe: verses 5-9: *Zion in travail: the end of the old and the beginning of the new Church.*

5   *Hear the Word of the Lord, you who tremble at His Word:*
    Your own brethren, who hate you,
    Who thrust you aside for My name's sake, say:
    Let the Lord glorify Himself, so that we may see your joy! —
    They shall be put to shame.
6   *Hark! A tumult in the city! In the temple* — *Hark!*
    Hark! The Lord is dealing out retribution to His enemies!
7   *Before she is in labor, she gives birth,*
    Before the birth pangs come, she has brought a son into the world.
8   *Who has ever heard, ever seen, the like of this?*
    Does a land ever travail in a single day?
    And is a nation ever born at a single stroke —
    So that Zion labored and bore her children at once?
9   *Shall I bring the mother to birth and not let her deliver?*
    Or am I one who lets her deliver and then shuts up the womb?
    Says your God.

שִׁמְעוּ֙ דְּבַר־יְהֹוָ֔ה הַחֲרֵדִ֖ים אֶל־דְּבָר֑וֹ 5

אָמְרוּ֩ אֲחֵיכֶ֨ם שֹׂנְאֵיכֶ֜ם מְנַדֵּיכֶ֗ם לְמַ֤עַן שְׁמִי֙

יִכְבַּ֣ד יְהֹוָ֔ה וְנִרְאֶ֥ה בְשִׂמְחַתְכֶ֖ם וְהֵ֥ם יֵבֹֽשׁוּ׃

The Lord's words addressed to the renegades are at an end, and
from now on they are mentioned only incidentally, in the third
person. The Lord now turns exclusively to His elect. For the scorn
and derision heaped on them by their own godless brethren after
the flesh, the Lord comforts them with the proclamation of the imminent catastrophe which will come unexpectedly and destroy the
godless, but impart to the elect the long-awaited glory. As in the
closing words of verse 2, the elect are referred to as such who
tremble at His Word. Their brethren, that is, people of their own
nation (according to Duhm these are not the brethren but the
Samaritans who want to build an opposition temple!), the apostates, are characterized as people who hate the elect and thrust
them away, cf. Luke 6:22: "who separate you from their company," and John 16:2: "put you out of their synagogs," John 9:22;
12:42. *menaddēykhem* (Piel participle of *nādhāh*, to thrust out) is
accented with a Rebia, which separates this word from the following and compels the joining of *lema'an shemī* with *yikhbadh
YHWH*. The only explanation for that strange combination is that
the scholars who placed the accents had a text that read *shemō* instead of *shemī*. According to our text, *lema'an shemī* is an adverbial modifier of *sōne'eykhem* and *menaddēykhem*: "who hate you
and thrust you out for My name's sake." The grammatical object
of *'amerū* is the clause *yikhbadh YHWH wenir'eh besimḥathkhem*.
After becoming enemies of the Lord, they also become the enemies
of those who belong to the Lord and confess Him, cf. Matthew 24:9.
The worst enemies of the church are those who have broken away
from it. They want to have nothing more to do with the church and
its members, even outwardly. They now delight in heaping scorn
and ridicule on it. Their words reflect their feeling of security and
their defiance of God. *yikhbadh*, "let it be glorious," means "let
Him display His glory!" The Lord is being challenged to reveal
Himself by some miraculous punishment on them, His enemies, if
He is the true God, so that His worshipers might have something
to rejoice over. The Lord will, in very truth, glorify Himself in dealing with these insolent scoffers. They shall be put to shame.
yēbhōshū is in direct contrast to *yikhbadh*. They shall surely experience what they have called down upon themselves. What the
Lord will do is set forth in verses 6-9.

687

6 קוֹל שָׁאוֹן מֵעִיר קוֹל מֵהֵיכָל
קוֹל יְהוָה מְשַׁלֵּם גְּמוּל לְאֹיְבָיו׃

7 בְּטֶרֶם תָּחִיל יָלָדָה
בְּטֶרֶם יָבוֹא חֵבֶל לָהּ וְהִמְלִיטָה זָכָר׃

8 מִי־שָׁמַע כָּזֹאת מִי רָאָה כָּאֵלֶּה
הֲיוּחַל אֶרֶץ בְּיוֹם אֶחָד אִם־יִוָּלֵד גּוֹי פַּעַם אֶחָת
כִּי־חָלָה גַּם־יָלְדָה צִיּוֹן אֶת־בָּנֶיהָ׃

9 הַאֲנִי אַשְׁבִּיר וְלֹא אוֹלִיד יֹאמַר יְהוָה
אִם־אֲנִי הַמּוֹלִיד וְעָצַרְתִּי אָמַר אֱלֹהָיִךְ׃

qōl, repeated three times in verse 6, is an interjection (Gr. 146, b,p.467), as in 40:3 and 6. The thought of this last chapter, in fact, takes up and extends the thoughts contained in chapter 40, the beginning of Isaiah II. Now the glory of the Lord (*yikhbadh*, verse 5) that was proclaimed in chapter 40 is being revealed to friend and foe. The flesh is revealed as grass, and the Word of the Lord as enduring forever. The crisis, the judgment, has come. The speaker hears the sound of a mighty tumult coming to him from the city and the temple. Where we would speak of a tumult *in* the city and the temple, the Hebrew speaks of a tumult *from* the city, just as he says *miqqedem*, from the east, where we say eastward, or to the east and *miyyām*, from the west, for our westward. So, here, *shā'ōn mē'īr*, a tumult from the city, not *in* the city. The explanation of the tumult appears in a brief sentence: It is the Lord wreaking (participle!) vengeance on His enemies. This is that great day of vengeance and retribution of the Lord, the Year of Deliverance of His own, 35:4; 42:13ff; 49:25f; 52:10; 59:17ff; 63:4.

In the New Testament, judgment is always pictured as proceeding from the heavenly dwelling of the Lord. In our passage it issues from His earthly dwelling, the place from which His grace is bestowed. This is the Holy One of Israel: Holy! Holy! Holy! First, endless grace, then endless vengeance upon those who despise His grace. In this judgment the old is destroyed; but Zion itself escapes destruction. Zion experiences a birth out of which a new thing goes forth. Zion is understood as subject of verse 7. Both clauses in the verse have essentially the same meaning. *ḥûl*, which usually has the same meaning as *yaladh*, is here clearly distinguished from *yaladh*, and means to writhe in birth pains, to travail. The second clause circumscribes *taḥil* with *yabho' ḥebhel lah*, a travail comes to her. *himlitah* (*malaṭ*, to escape) is indicative of the meaning of the passage: She has permitted to escape, to slip away. So also the end of verse 8: Zion has given birth to her children at the first sign of travail. The birth pains have hardly begun when the birth is accomplished. Verse 8 declares that to be an unheard-of thing. Since the curse of Genesis 3:16, all birth on earth causes the mother great pain. "I will *greatly* multiply thy sorrow and thy conception." This curse of pain applies also wherever new life is to arise out of old and corrupt conditions, and it is true also of the external church and wherever the downfall of the old takes place. The old dies slowly and painfully. People, and that includes church people, cling tenaciously to the old and traditional, by virtue of a natural *vis inertiae*. They strenuously resist innovation and change. A new birth is preceded by noise and tumult, by discord and strife. The judgment consists in destruction of the old and the overthrow of all hostile powers. But the new which is to be born was in reality there, even before the first *sha'on*. In this case the new thing is the righteous seed and the new life of faith. It was conceived in silence and it developed quietly; but at the collapse of the old, the period of travail comes and with the first sign of birth pains the new is born complete and vigorous. That is what is portrayed here, and that is the history of the church. Zion travails and at the same moment gives birth. That is how the great change took place at the time of Christ; so was it also in the Reformation, and so will it be till the Day of Judgment. This is contrary to the usual course of nature ("Who ever heard, who ever saw such a thing? "). It is something very great that is here being spoken of. An entire land, a great people, is to be born (*yuḥal*, a Hophal form, is the intensive passive); such a thing is not accomplished in a day, or at one stroke. But in the church, in the kingdom of God, it is so accomplished. The church is not subject to the common course of nature, but is under the special government of God, under "rules" and "regulations" formulated by the Holy Spirit and hidden from the eyes of the wise and prudent of this world.

Most commentators understand *baneyha*, her children, to refer to the mass of the exiles, who are here being pictured as suddenly returning homeward and repopulating their city and land. But that explanation requires that Babylon be made the source of this discourse and that it be addressed to the exiles still living there.

Nor does this interpretation agree with verse 3, where the sacrifices are described as being offered in Jerusalem; still less does it agree with verses 6-8 where the admonition to Hark! Hark! locates both the judgment and the new birth in Jerusalem. A purely rationalistic explanation of the discourse would understand verse 1 as being addressed to the people who are again living in their own land and city, and verses 6-8 likewise. In that case, Jerusalem would already have experienced a rebirth in the return of her children and would still have to await a second, much greater, return of the scattered children of Israel from all over the world. We consider both opinions to be mistaken. These two final chapters, as indeed all of Parts II and III of Isaiah II (chapters 49-66), are oriented toward the New Testament and proclaim the downfall of the incorrigible Old Testament people according to the flesh, together with all the external Old Testament forms, and in their place, the birth of a New Testament people and economy. The discourses adopt the point of view of the people who have returned from Babylon to live again in their own land (verses 1,6-8), but the terms and pictures employed are so general that not one word in the text compels us to interpret these prophecies as referring to the history of the exile. We refer the reader to our introductory remarks to Part II, chapters 49-57. Isaiah envisions Christ the Messiah and the church of the New Testament and of eternity, although in describing the church he uses terms that originate in the exile. So too in the present passage. This passage describes the judgment upon the Old Testament church that has become useless, and the birth of the church of the New Testament.

Luther missed the point of verse 9. The three Hiphil forms are strictly causative. "Should I cause the new birth to break through the womb and still not permit it to be born — am I one who does not permit actual birth? " The object of these actions is not the Lord Himself, nor "others," but Zion, which has just been described as being born. Both parts of the verse say the same thing: The Lord does not stop at half-measures. The illustration must have been a familiar one in Israel as the words of Hezekiah show, 37:15-20. If the Lord should leave Zion in the state now assumed to have become reality, then all His labor heretofore expended upon Israel would have been in vain. The last clause says that the Lord is not one who at the last moment of a birth still hinders its completion. The Lord carries to completion every work that He has begun. Out of old Israel there shall arise a new and glorious, and finally, a spiritually perfect Israel.

Third Strophe: verses 10-14: *The new happiness of the delivered congregation.*

10 *Be glad with Jerusalem,*
    Rejoice over her, all you who love her,
    Exult loudly with her, all you who mourned for her,
11 *So that you may suck to your fill at the breast of her comfort,*
    That you may drink and refresh yourselves at her bountiful glory.
12 *For thus says the Lord:*
    Behold, I — I direct peace to her like a river,
    And the glory of the heathen like a torrent, and you shall drink;
    You shall be carried on the hip,
    And shall be fondled on the knees.
13 *Like a man whom his mother comforts, so will I comfort you,*
    Yes, through Jerusalem shall you be comforted.
14 *And when you see it, your heart will rejoice,*
    And your limbs will flourish like the green grass;
    And the mighty hand of the Lord shall be revealed to His servants,
    And He will cause His enemies to feel His vengeance.

שִׂמְחוּ אֶת־יְרוּשָׁלַ͏ִם וְגִילוּ בָהּ כָּל־אֹהֲבֶיהָ ¹⁰
שִׂישׂוּ אִתָּהּ מָשׂושׂ כָּל־הַמִּתְאַבְּלִים עָלֶיהָ׃
לְמַעַן תִּינְקוּ וּשְׂבַעְתֶּם מִשֹּׁד תַּנְחֻמֶיהָ ¹¹
לְמַעַן תָּמֹצּוּ וְהִתְעַנַּגְתֶּם מִזִּיז כְּבוֹדָהּ׃

These verses are addressed to persons who are envisioned as having survived the crisis and now await the new glory. They are called Zion's lovers (*'ōhabhīm*), who had mourned (Hithpael participle) over Zion's earlier misery. All those who mourned over her are meant, 61:2,3; cf. 29:19. They are now to rejoice *with* Jerusalem, be glad *with* her, exult *over* her as her children. Jerusalem is pictured as their mother. *sīsū māsōs* is an example of the internal accusative (Gr. 117,p,p.366), emphasizing the thought. *lema'an* at the beginning of verse 11, means so that, in order that. Here, as always, it is a particle of purpose. The love for Zion and the mourning over her are really prerequisites for, and the means to, the joy that *lema'an* promises; it is faith with its immediate effect on the emotions. No one who remains indifferent to the lot of the church can rejoice in her spiritual treasures. We have translated suck and be satisfied (imperfect with consecutive perfect) as a hendiadys. "The breast of her comforts" refers to Him who is the source and dispenser of her comforts, Psalm 94:19; Job 15:11; Isaiah 57:18. *zīz kebhōdhāh* is a circumscription of "breast of her comforts." Little

691

is known of the meaning of *zīz*.* Some explain it as being related to the Arabic and Assyrian word for nipple, teat, or udder. Others derive it from a verb *zūz* found in Syriac and New Hebrew, meaning to move back and forth, to be shaken. *tāmōtstsū* is a Qal imperfect of *mātsats*, an alternate form of *mātsāh* (51:17), meaning to suck eagerly. It occurs only here. *hith'annaghtem* is a more emphatic synonym of *sebha'tem* — to satisfy oneself, to be refreshed.

כִּי־כֹה ׀ אָמַר יְהֹוָה 12

הִנְנִי נֹטֶה־אֵלֶיהָ כְּנָהָר שָׁלוֹם

וּכְנַחַל שׁוֹטֵף כְּבוֹד גּוֹיִם

וִינַקְתֶּם עַל־צַד תִּנָּשֵׂאוּ וְעַל־בִּרְכַּיִם תְּשָׁעֳשָׁעוּ :

כְּאִישׁ אֲשֶׁר אִמּוֹ תְּנַחֲמֶנּוּ כֵּן אָנֹכִי אֲנַחֶמְכֶם וּבִירוּשָׁלַ͏ִם 13

וּרְאִיתֶם וְשָׂשׂ לִבְּכֶם וְעַצְמוֹתֵיכֶם כַּדֶּשֶׁא תִפְרַחְנָה [תְּנַחֶמוּ : 14

וְנוֹדְעָה יַד־יְהֹוָה אֶת־עֲבָדָיו וְזָעַם אֶת־אֹיְבָיו :

Verse 12 names the *tanḥumīm* (comforts) and the *kābhōdh*, in which the lovers of the church shall rejoice. The Lord is their source and guaranty. He will overwhelm the church with peace and with the glory of the gentiles. These are well-known concepts. For the gift of peace, cf. 9:7; 48:18; 52:7; 53:5; 54:13; 57:19; 60:17. This word represents all spiritual help and salvation. 60:5ff and 61:6 tell us what is meant by the glory of the gentiles. This is not their material goods, but their power, their gifts of intellect, and in general, all the best of what they possess. The church of the New Testament shall possess spiritual, material, and moral treasures in abundance. The pictures used here are of great poetic beauty. The Lord will direct (*nōteh*, a participle indicating continuance of the action) peace to the church like a mighty river, so that she shall be overwhelmed (cf. 48:18), and He will bestow earthly gifts upon her as a rushing stream that overflows its banks. *kenaḥal shōteph* is a weaker picture than *nōteh kenāhār*. *wīnaqtem*, "and you shall drink" stands grammatically isolated. The picture of carrying a child on the side or hip is a familiar one, cf. 60:4. *tesho'oshā'ū* is a Polpal form of *shā'a'*, to rock, to dandle, cf. Gr. 55, f, p. 152f. It is hardly the converted gentiles who are pictured as

---

*The word occurs only here in this sense. In Psalm 50:11 and 80:14 it is found in the combination *zīz sādhay*, "beasts of the field."

dandling Zion's children on their knees, as most commentators have supposed. In 60:4 it is the Jewish Diaspora that is being carried back to Jerusalem in this fashion, but that situation no longer applies here. The next verse, which carries on the thought of verse 12, indicates that it is the Lord Himself who fondles the children. The Lord will take into His arms the children who had been so miserable and oppressed. He will dandle them on His knees and comfort them as a mother comforts a man. The grief of a grown man (* īsh*) is the deepest and heaviest that we know. There is no comfort more heartfelt than that bestowed by a mother on her son. Her son, even though grown to manhood, is still closer to the mother's heart than to the heart of father, brother, or sister. *bīrūshālayim*, through Jerusalem, says that the glory of the church is both substance and means of the divine comfort, even as Jerusalem's misery had been the cause of the mourning of her children.

rā'ah in verse 14 has the more generalized meaning of perceive, as in 44:16. The coordination of *re'ithem* and *sās* is, in our idiom, expressed by subordination of one verb to the other: When you perceive that, then your heart will rejoice. The "sprouting" of the limbs is not, as Duhm opines, a tasteless expression; it is both suitable and Scriptural. Sorrow is said to cause the bones to waste away. Psalm 32:3f; Psalm 38; cf. 22:16ff(15ff). Joy and gladness are said to make the bones that God has broken rejoice, Psalm 51:10(8). But Duhm often ruins the beauty of the language of Scripture by his fundamental contempt both of Scripture and of the mental capacity of its authors, particularly that of the Trito-Isaiah whom he himself invented, and of the capacity of the imaginary redactors of the text. His choice of words sometimes seems intentionally disdainful. — *wenōdhe'ah*, a Niphal consecutive perfect, is not to be translated "become recognized," but "be known" or recognized. It is really a *futurum exactum*, Gr. 106, g, p. 311, and o, p. 313, because verse 14 actually begins with a conditional clause. *zā'am*, to which the same remark applies, is not to be translated "He will punish," for the punishment has already been ordered (verse 6), but "He will carry out the punishment." *'eth* is the sign of the accusative; before *'abhādhāyw* it is a preposition. Today no one believes that God can be so stern. (Ps. 90:11); but the day will come when the power of His anger will be revealed, even as on that same day the fullness of God's goodness will also be revealed, 1 Corinthians 13:12.

Fourth Strophe: verses 15-24:   *The Gospel goes over to the gentile world.*

15 *For behold, the Lord will come in fire,*
    And like the stormwind are His chariots,
    To pay out His wrath in fury
    And His rebuke in flames of fire.

16 *For the Lord will judge with fire,*
    And all flesh with His sword,
    And great will be the multitude of the slain of the Lord.

17 *Behold, they who sanctify and purify themselves for the gardens,*
    Following someone in the midst,
    Who eat the flesh of swine and of unclean things and mice,
    Together shall they be carried away, says the Lord.

18 *Yes, their thoughts and their words — it shall come to pass*
    That I will gather together all nations and tongues,
    And they shall come and see My glory.

19 *And I will do a wonderful thing among them;*
    And such of them as escape will I send to the nations:
    To Tarshish, Phul, and Lud, the archers,
    To Tubal, Javan, and the distant isles,
    Who had never heard My name
    And have never perceived My glory —
    And to the nations they shall proclaim My glory.

20 *And out of all nations they shall bring your brethren,*
    For an offering to the Lord —
    On horses, chariots, litters, mules, and camels
    To Jerusalem, to My holy mountain, says the Lord,
    Even as the children of Israel bring the sacrifice
    In clean vessels to the house of the Lord;

21 *And of them will I make some to be priests and Levites,*
    Says the Lord.

22 *For, even as the new heaven and the new earth that I create*
    Continue before Me, says the Lord,
    So shall your seed and your name continue.

23 *And it shall come to pass from new moon to new moon*
    And from Sabbath to Sabbath,
    All flesh shall come to worship before Me, says the Lord.

24 *And if they go out, they shall gaze on*
    The dead bodies of those that fell before Me;
    For their worm shall not die
    Nor their fire be quenched,
    And they shall be an abhorrence to all flesh.

15 כִּי־הִנֵּה יְהוָה בָּאֵשׁ יָבוֹא וְכַסּוּפָה מַרְכְּבֹתָיו
לְהָשִׁיב בְּחֵמָה אַפּוֹ וְגַעֲרָתוֹ בְּלַהֲבֵי־אֵשׁ:
16 כִּי בָאֵשׁ יְהוָה נִשְׁפָּט וּבְחַרְבּוֹ אֶת־כָּל־בָּשָׂר וְרַבּוּ חַלְלֵי יְהוָה:
17 הַמִּתְקַדְּשִׁים וְהַמִּטַּהֲרִים אֶל־הַגַּנּוֹת אַחַר אַחַד בַּתָּוֶךְ
אֹכְלֵי בְּשַׂר הַחֲזִיר וְהַשֶּׁקֶץ וְהָעַכְבָּר
יַחְדָּו יָסֻפוּ נְאֻם־יְהוָה:

At verse 15 the prophet begins to bring his prophecy to a conclusion. This is an extensive and very impressive section, in which he once more sums up the two chief parts of his prophecy: God's judgment upon those who rebelled against His grace, and the final glorification of the faithful remnant. But this strophe, like all the others, has its individual character. Here it is the sending out of the Gospel into the gentile world (verses 15-19), and the astounding conclusion depicting the eternal punishment of the condemned. Verse 15 recalls verse 6. There the judgment upon the enemies was briefly mentioned in explanation of the tumult proceeding from the city and the temple. Here we are told who is the cause of that tumult. It is the Lord, who comes with fire, His chariots thundering like a violent storm. The picture is in part taken from the battlefield, cf. Jeremiah 4:13 and Nahum 2:3ff (2ff), in part from a tempest in which the Lord walks upon the wings of the wind, Psalm 104:3f. In history the Lord also appeared in fire and spoke out of fire and clouds, Deuteronomy 4 and 5, etc., cf. Psalm 18:8ff (7ff). Psalm 50:2f also speaks of the revelation of God in fire and tempest originating in Zion. The picture of the fiery chariot of the Lord which thunders along like a stormwind appears in its completest form in Ezekiel 1:4ff, especially in verses 13 and 27. Isaiah also employs the picture in 29:6 and 30:27,30. Peter (Acts 2:19,20) is indebted to Joel for the picture. The New Testament consistently teaches the coming of the Lord to judgment in and with fire; whereas the image of the chariot and the whirlwind is no longer prominent. Cf. 2 Thessalonians 1:8; 2 Peter 3:7,10,12; Luke 21:25ff. The myriads of God's chariots in Psalm 68:18(17) (Ezek. 1:24; Isa. 21:9, one angel) guided by angels, in the New Testament become just angels (Matt. 25:31). The picture portends the fearful destructive judgment of the wrath of God. It is the final judgment over the old Jerusalem and all flesh, including also the world of the infidel (verse 16), as the last half of this verse says in plain terms.

No predicate follows *wekhassūphāh markebhōthāyw. yābhō'* has been suggested as predicate, but it is more likely that the simple copula "are" is to be supplied. The following clause of purpose, *lehāshībh*, etc., explains the purpose of the Lord's coming in fire and storm. The hour of retribution has come. The translation of *lehāshībh behēmāh 'appō* with "to quiet His wrath in fire" is possible, but it lacks the support of other passages. The translation "to wreak vengeance" is, however, made certain by Deuteronomy 32:41. *hēmāh* is here the wrathful execution of God's judgment. *ge'ārāh,* a threat or rebuke by word or deed, will be carried out in consuming flames of fire, cf. Psalm 50:3; 2 Thessalonians 1:8.

Verse 16 once more lays emphasis on fire as the means of executing God's judgment and adds the figure of the sword. The sword (65:12) is a symbol of retributive, death-dealing power. Here this power goes into action, and the result is a multitude of slain (*hālal,* to pierce). It should not be overlooked that in the first clause of verse 16 *nishpāt,* Niphal of *shāphat,* is the word for judging. The word is, however, not used in the sense of pronouncing judgment, but rather in the sense of disputing and arguing with the purpose of obtaining justice. With fire and sword and consuming power the Lord establishes the rightness of His cause against the rebels.

Verse 17 furnishes the justification for this violent action. It is the idolatry and the abhorrent heathen practice adopted by the rebels of eating the flesh of swine and other forbidden unclean animals. The verse echoes 65:3ff. The participles *hammithqaddeshīm* (who sanctify themselves) and *hammittaharīm* (who purify themselves) perhaps refer to frequent washings and may be an explanation of *qedhashtūkhā* in 65:5. This sanctifying and cleansing is done for the idols under the direction of someone in the midst who serves as priest and leader and directs the required ceremonies. But no amount of zealous idol worship can save them. Leaders and followers alike shall be carried away by the storm of God's wrath.

18 וְאָנֹכִי מַעֲשֵׂיהֶם וּמַחְשְׁבֹתֵיהֶם בָּאָה לְקַבֵּץ אֶת־כָּל־הַגּוֹיִם וְהַלְּשֹׁנוֹת וּבָאוּ וְרָאוּ אֶת־כְּבוֹדִי׃ 19 וְשַׂמְתִּי בָהֶם אוֹת וְשִׁלַּחְתִּי מֵהֶם פְּלֵיטִים אֶל־הַגּוֹיִם תַּרְשִׁישׁ פּוּל וְלוּד מֹשְׁכֵי קֶשֶׁת תֻּבַל וְיָוָן הָאִיִּים הָרְחֹקִים אֲשֶׁר לֹא־שָׁמְעוּ אֶת־שִׁמְעִי וְלֹא־רָאוּ אֶת־כְּבוֹדִי וְהִגִּידוּ אֶת־ כְּבוֹדִי בַּגּוֹיִם׃

Verse 18 is not as difficult as the commentators seem to have thought it to be. The construction of the verse is unusual, but still not wholly obscure. It should be noted, first of all, that *we'ānōkhī* is to be connected with *bā'āh leqabbēts*, etc. This is a variation from the usual phrase, *hinnēh yāmīm bā'īm weqibbatstī* (39:6; Jer. 7:32; 9:24[25], etc.). Therefore: "And as for Me, it comes to gather together," that is, "As for Me, the time is come that I shall gather together, etc." *ma'asēyhem ūmahshebhōtheyhem* is an adverbial accusative describing a condition or circumstance, Gr. 118, 5, m, p. 374. "I shall gather together the nations and the tongues" (*gōyim* relates to descent, *leshōnōth* to language — concepts that do not always cover each other). The result then is: "As for Me, regarding their deeds and their thoughts, the time is coming for gathering together the nations and the tongues, and they shall come and see My glory." (The *Waw* consecutive perfect occurs often in this chapter, Gr. 112,4,5,p.334,336.) They shall see My glory, because it will be revealed to them by My rebuke of their deeds and their thoughts. The thought that God reveals His glory before all the world by His goodness to Israel and by His vengeance upon His enemies and the godless is expressed repeatedly in Isaiah (52:5,6,10; 49:26; 60:9; 64:2f). It is the underlying purpose of all that He does, 42:8; 48:11. The last clause is not at all to be understood as a pronouncement of judgment upon the assembled gentile nations. They have been gathered together for the one purpose: to see the glory of the Lord revealed through His terrible judgment upon the rebellious members of His own chosen people. This revelation of God's glory is to be understood in the sense of Romans 11:21ff, as a preparation for, and a means of, spreading throughout their lands the Gospel that is to convert them. This purpose is the subject of the next verse.

The meaning of verse 19 depends largely upon the answers given to two questions. What does *'ōth* mean? Is it a sign, or is it a wonder? And secondly, who are the *hem* in *bāhem*, upon whom the Lord will place a mark, or in the other case, among whom He will do a wonder? *'ōth* is a mark, but it is also the word for sign or wonder. *sīm 'ōth* may mean "to set a mark on" (Gen. 4:15) or "to work a sign or wonder" (Ps. 78:43). But *sīm 'ōth be*, so far as we are aware, occurs only in Exodus 10:2 and Psalm 78:43, in the sense of working signs and wonders among or upon people; whereas "to set a mark upon" in Genesis 4:15 is *sīm 'ōth le*. It therefore would seem necessary to give preference to the latter meaning. The prefix *bā* in *bāhem* may be rendered "upon" or "among" them, but the latter meaning seems to fit better into the context. And I will do among them a wonder and send — not *ōthām* "them," since that does not express the intended thought — but *mēhem* "some from among them" (*min partitivum*) as *peleytīm*, refugees, to the nations, to Tarshish, etc. And they shall (or: in order that they) proclaim My glory among the nations. Out of the total number of the assembled tongues and nations, through whose punishment God's glory will be revealed, God will rescue some from the judgment and preserve them as refugees. This is the *'ōth*, the wonder that He will work. A notable wonder indeed! Only by a miracle wrought by God could they escape the judgment. But more than that is meant. These refugees, who were to be messengers of the Gospel among the nations, had been given over to judgment, to slaughter, to fire and sword as rebels (65:12; 66:16). The miracle of *conversion* therefore had to be wrought upon them in the midst of judgment. That is the *'ōth*, the wonder.

The inescapable conclusion is, therefore, that the *hem* in *bāhem* are not the assembled gentiles but the *hem* in *ma'aseyhem* and *maḥshebhōtheyhem*, that is, the Jews who had been delivered to judgment. They, and not the nations that had been but incidentally introduced, are the subject of the discourse from verse 15 to the present point. In the interest of clarity it must, however, be noted that the formal object from verse 15 on is not restricted to apostate Israel, but includes *kol bāsār*, all flesh, verse 16. It is true that those who were remanded to judgment in verse 16 are described as guilty of the same practices as the rebellious Jews in 65:3ff; 66:3; but those practices were characteristically gentile abominations. Consequently, the mention of them implies that the gentile nations also are being consigned to the threatened judgment, by virtue of the all-inclusive *kol bāsār*. But the gentiles are to come to a recognition of the glory of God through the judgment, does that not show that they are actually under the judgment and experience it? That cannot be denied; nor can that conclusion be evaded by the device of making *kol bāsār* refer to the Jewish people only. *kol bāsār*, without special modifiers, never refers to the Jewish people alone. The phrase has the same meaning as *kol haggōyim wehalleshōnōth*. Matthew 25:32, "before Him shall be gathered all nations," sounds like a direct quotation of these words. We have here a prophetic vision of the final judgment of all nations, of all flesh, with a special judgment of the Jewish nation, as in Matthew 24. In spite of that, or perhaps better, for that very reason, the refugees who escape the judgment and become messengers of the Gospel to the gentiles, cannot themselves be escaped gentiles. In the final judgment there are none who escape; much less could such then be sent as messengers of the Gospel to the gentiles. And it is certainly unlikely that the prophet would quote the Lord as saying that He intended to send *gentiles* who had escaped to serve as messengers to other gentiles. The mention of the gentiles presupposes that those who are sent to them are not themselves gentiles, but Jews who have escaped the judgment upon the Jews. Clearly, the persons here spoken of as refugees are Jews who have been going along with the mass of their people, either in Pharisaic blindness or in the abominations mentioned in 65:3ff and 16f as characteristic types of pagan idolatry. They at first appear as bitter enemies of their believing brethren of the Old or of the New Testament (65:5). But then, by a special wonder wrought on their hearts by the Lord, they are converted and become believers, whose spirit burns with zeal because of the grace they have received. From the Lord they now also receive the special call to preach the Gospel to the gentiles, and each according to his circumstances carries out that commission. In short, this is a prophetic reference to Paul and other missionaries of his kind.

Of the different nations mentioned, Tarshish is well known (cf. the comment on 60:9). Pul, or Phul, does not occur elsewhere. It is not mentioned in Genesis 10. The LXX reads Φούδ , which may be correct. *phūt* (*pūt*) occurs in Jeremiah 46:9 along with *kūsh* and the inhabitants of *lūdh,* and also in Ezekiel 27:10 and 30:5. According to Genesis 10:13, the *lūdhīm* are descendants of *mitsrayim*; hence it may be concluded that Kush and Lud were located in North Africa. Jeremiah describes the Ludim as men who handled the bow, and in Egyptian inscriptions the people of Phut are similarly described. The enumeration of the nations then turns from the most westerly land then known to the northern lands. Tubal, Genesis 10:2; Ezekiel 27:13; 32:26; 38:2,3; 39:1 (named with Javan and Meshech) is the tribe of the Tibarenes on the Black Sea; Javan is a name for the Ionians, a name that seems to include all Greeks, or at least the people who inhabited the coastal lands of Asia Minor. The distant isles refer to the dwellers on the islands farther to the west in the Mediterranean Sea and on its coasts. Geographically this prophecy was fulfilled exactly, although the progress of the Gospel among the nations did not follow the order here given, which begins with the nations farthest west and then completes the circuit of the sea. Of all nations of the world, those of the west and the north were the chief recipients of the Gospel message.

²⁰ וְהֵבִ֣יאוּ אֶת־כָּל־אֲחֵיכֶ֣ם מִכָּל־הַגּוֹיִ֣ם ׀ מִנְחָ֣ה ׀ לַיהֹוָ֡ה בַּסּוּסִ֣ים וּבָרֶ֡כֶב וּבַצַּבִּים֩ וּבַפְּרָדִ֨ים וּבַכִּרְכָּר֜וֹת עַ֣ל הַ֧ר קָדְשִׁ֛י יְרוּשָׁלַ֖͏ִם אָמַ֣ר יְהֹוָ֑ה כַּאֲשֶׁ֣ר יָבִ֣יאוּ בְנֵי֩ יִשְׂרָאֵ֨ל אֶת־הַמִּנְחָ֜ה בִּכְלִ֥י טָה֖וֹר בֵּ֥ית יְהֹוָֽה׃

The subject of *hēbhī'u* is not, as one might suppose, those who escaped judgment and became heralds of the glory of God (verse 19), but the *gōyim* who are mentioned at the end of verse 19. In exactly the same manner, the suffix of *thōla'tām* in the second clause of verse 24 refers to the persons designated as *pōshe'ım* in the preceding object clause. In Isaiah II the gathering of the Jewish Diaspora is consistently ascribed to the gentiles, cf. 43:5ff; 49:22; 60:4,9. That it must be the *gōyim* who gather in the Jews of the Diaspora is made evident by the subject (*benēy yisrā'el*) of the last clause of this verse. There we read: *ka'asher yābhī'u benēy yisrā'el*, etc., "even as the children of Israel bring an offering," etc. The act of the children of Israel bringing an offering is exactly parallel with the act of those in the opening clause who bring "your brethren" as an offering. Consequently the subject of *hēbhī'u* at the beginning of the verse must be gentiles, non-Israelites. In the phrase, "your brethren from among all nations," the brethren are in contrast to the gentiles, the Jews of the Diaspora. The gentiles will bring these "brethren" to Jerusalem as a *minhāh*, an offering for the Lord. The terms used here, and their connection, must be carefully defined, if the correct sense is to be preserved. The *minhāh* is not an offering brought in expiation of a sin. A *minhāh* is a gift brought to or for the Lord. This gift consisted of the most precious things that God created for the nurture of man and for the preservation of his body and life — food, grains, olive oil, incense, or wine as a drink-offering. The gift was brought as an offering to God for a "sweet-smelling savor." The purpose of the gift was to give thankful expression of recognition of the great truth that all good and perfect gifts are from above, from the Lord. With this gift the giver declared that everything that he was and everything that he possessed belonged to the Lord and that he devoted himself and all that was his to the Lord's service. In that sense this passage is to be understood. The gentiles are bringing together the Jewish Diaspora out of all the world as an acceptable *minḥah* to the Lord. That implies that these gentiles have been converted. The preaching among those gentiles (*baggōyim*) by the messengers of the Gospel who had escaped the judgment accomplished this. Their *minḥah* is a sweet smelling savor to the Lord.

The *minḥah* is brought *'al har qodhshī*, "to My holy mountain," the place chosen by the Lord for offerings. *yerūshalayim* is usually construed as an *accusativus loci* : to Jerusalem, cf. Gr. 118, d, p. 373 and 90, c, p. 250. Others prefer to treat it as an apposition to *har qodhshī*, Gr. 131, f, p. 425. The name Jerusalem then localizes and defines *har qodhshī*. But *har qodhshī* is not in need of any closer definition. In fact, it is by itself more definite than Jerusalem. Therefore, not: "To My holy mountain Jerusalem," but: "To My holy mountain, to Jerusalem." With this translation one still expects transposition of the two phrases, like Luther's *"gen Jerusalem, zu meinem heiligen Berge,"* because the latter phrase is the more precise of the two.

As means of transportation, horses, chariots (collective singular), litters, mules, and *kirkārōth* are named. The feminine form of *kirkārōth* leads to the assumption that female camels are meant. These are dromedaries. The Hebrew name describes the swaying, rolling movement of the hump when these animals walk or run (*kirkār*, a reduplication of the root of *kārar*, *kārāh*, and *kūr*, to be round, hollow, to scoop out). The word occurs only here. It is not likely that *tsabbīm* are litters that are carried by servants (*mittāh*, Song of Songs 3:7; *'appiryōn*, 3:9), but are probably identical with the *'eghlōth tsābh* of Numbers 7:3, low covered wagons used for traveling. Whether these particular means of travel were chosen from the point of view of comfort or of speed cannot be decided. The *kol* before *'aḥeykhem* points to the correct interpretation: all possible means.

The final clause compares the *minḥah* of the gentiles with the *minḥah* of the children of Israel. The offerings of meal, except for those brought by certain special classes of persons, were, according to Leviticus 2, of five kinds. Whatever the kind of offering that was brought, a part of it was laid on the altar to be burned, as a sweet savor unto the Lord, Leviticus 2:2,9,16. All the rest was set aside for the priests and for the temple service, and it was *qōdhesh qodhāshīm, sanctissimum*. For this reason alone it had to be brought to the Lord's house in clean vessels. But it is not just the means of transportation that are compared to the "clean vessels." Those means are in themselves neither clean nor unclean. It is the converted gentiles themselves who, together with their means of transportation, all unclean in themselves, are now clean by reason of faith. The believing gentiles, with their offerings, are now as acceptable to the Lord as Israel with its offerings.

$$\text{21 וְגַם־מֵהֶם אֶקַּח לַכֹּהֲנִים לַלְוִיִּם אָמַר יְהוָה:}$$

Verse 21 adds an important element to the state of grace in which the gentiles now stand. Not only is their offering now a "sweet savor unto the Lord," but they themselves are elevated to the honorable position of special servants in the temple as priests and Levites who bring their offerings before the Lord. The *we* before *gam* does not confirm what precedes, but is a simple copula: *and* also. *gam* does not necessarily affect the word that immediately follows, but extends to the whole of the following sentence, Gr. 153, p. 483. The thought is not: "And even from among *them*, the converted gentiles, as in contrast to the Israelites, will I take priests and Levites." There has so far been no mention of Israelite priests and Levites. *gam* refers not just to *mēhem*, but to the entire sentence: And even will I take priests and Levites from among them. It was unthinkable to every Jew that the gentiles could bring an acceptable *minḥāh* to the Lord's sanctuary, as stated in verse 20. (Cf. 56:6,7.) To that statement there is now added a plus, confirmed by *'āmar YHWH*, that the Lord will admit them to the high privilege of serving before Him as priests and Levites, a thought that was repugnant to the Jews. Cf. 61:5,6. Our passage is to be understood as an amplification, not as a contradiction of 61:5f; cf. Zechariah 14:16-21. Yes, when the new order is instituted, there will not only be signs and wonders (*'ōth*, verse 19), but wholly new and unheard-of things. The Lord will welcome the offerings of the gentiles; He will let the gentiles lead the entire spiritual Jewish Diaspora to the church; and He will make them, the unclean gentiles, even to be His priests and Levites. Cf. 1 Peter 2:5,9; Revelation 1:6; 5:10.

It is very unusual that the article appears in both *lakkōhanīm* and *lalewīyyim*. One would have expected both words to be written without any article at all. Most manuscripts, among them the most reliable ones, and all the ancient versions, are reported to have the article in both words. Some manuscripts and the LXX do not have the article. Delitzsch says that the articles presuppose the existence of priests and Levites and translates: "And I will add some of them to the priests and to the Levites." But no examples of that kind of construction can be found to support his translation. *la* (*le* with the article) would have to be translated, not "to the priests," but "for the priests," or "in the service of the priests." But all of that is not necessary here. *lāqaḥ la* for *lāqaḥ le* is as likely to occur as *hāyāh la* for *hāyāh le* in Isaiah 29:17; 32:15. The LXX translation ἱερεῖς καὶ Λευίτας is correct. Luther, following Jerome, has the same translation. *lakkōhanīm* and *lalewīyyim* are, moreover, not to be taken in the sense of Deuteronomy 18, as "Levitical priests." As Delitzsch correctly remarks that idea would be expressed by *lakkōhanīm halewīyyim* (cf. Deut. 18:1). The asyndetic arrangement "to priests, to Levites" makes both terms, the narrower and the broader, rank alike. The Levite was chosen for temple service ahead of all other Israelites — that is the point that is emphasized here. Delitzsch and Cheyne support their rendition of "add some of them to the priests and to the Levites" with reference to the great number of priests that will be made necessary by the addition in the New Testament of the great number of the gentiles. But there is nothing of that in the text. The point is that the gentiles will be raised to equal standing with Israel before the Lord.

22 כִּי כַאֲשֶׁר הַשָּׁמַיִם הַחֲדָשִׁים וְהָאָרֶץ הַחֲדָשָׁה אֲשֶׁר אֲנִי עֹשֶׂה עֹמְדִים לְפָנַי נְאֻם־יְהוָה כֵּן יַעֲמֹד זַרְעֲכֶם וְשִׁמְכֶם:

In verse 22 the basis is given for everything that appears in verses 19-21. That section stands in sharp contrast to verses 15-18. Verses 15-18 described the judgment upon the rebels; 19-21 described the rescue of some of them, who then were sent to the gentiles, who were converted and brought their *minḥāh* as an acceptable offering to the Lord, and finally were exalted to equal status with Israel. All of that is substantiated by verse 22. "For as the new heaven and the new earth, which I am about to create (*ʿōseh*, a participle), stand forever before Me, says the Lord, so will your seed and your name also stand." These words are addressed to those who are mentioned in verses 5 and 10-14; to the believers, the remnant of Israel, 65:8,9; the inhabitants of the new creation, 65:17ff. All of these, here again designated as the new heaven and the new earth, will endure forever (*ʿadhēy ʿadh*, 65:18). Equally enduring shall be the seed (the generation) and the name (the memory), and the honor of the inhabitants of the new creation. The purpose of the judgment upon Israel was not that Israel should forever be destroyed and cease to be. From the very beginning God had planned an eternal Israel, one made up first of all of

Jews, but then also of gentiles, a true, spiritual Israel. Only that Israel which was an Israel "after the flesh" and irredeemable was devoted to destruction, as indeed everything that is only "flesh" (verse 16) is so devoted. For this reason some were rescued from the judgment, and the gentiles were made acceptable to become a πλήρωμα to fill out the ἥττημα of the Jews, Romans 11:12ff.

וְהָיָה מִדֵּי־חֹדֶשׁ בְּחָדְשׁוֹ וּמִדֵּי שַׁבָּת בְּשַׁבַּתּוֹ 23

יָבוֹא כָל־בָּשָׂר לְהִשְׁתַּחֲוֹת לְפָנַי אָמַר יְהוָה:

Verse 23 describes the blessed occupation of those who are citizens of the new kingdom of God. The emphatic *wehāyāh* should be connected directly with *yābhō' khol bāsār*. "All flesh," the subject of the sentence, will be correctly understood only if one bears in mind that the new kingdom of God is not divided into two kingdoms, the one temporal and imperfect, the other eternal and perfect. Everything that is said here pertains to the one kingdom. "All flesh" in this connection is all flesh in the new kingdom of God, that is, all inhabitants of the new heaven and the new earth, who are considered as living in a state of perfection. There is no longer any other kind of flesh than this. Flesh in the derogatory sense is pictured as having been judged with rebellious Israel and eradicated (verses 15 and 16). Now "all flesh" of the new order is a purified flesh, which approaches the worship of God in piety and holiness. The act of worship is characteristic of the faithful in the old and imperfect order as well as in the new, perfect order. But the modifying phrases accompanying the act of worship, "new moon after new moon and Sabbath after Sabbath," are chosen from a temporal point of view from the life of the Old Testament and the dispensation of the Law. The language of the Old Testament, particularly the language of prophecy, must move within the restraining bounds of Old Testament life if it is to be understood at all. Such restrictive terms as month and Sabbath are but pictures of the spiritual and eternal things. New Testament prophecy operates within the same restraining bounds, although with somewhat more freedom, cf. the Revelation of St. John. These descriptive terms are intended to express the freedom that characterizes the new worship. They stress the controlling spirit of truth with which the worship is endued, and its unceasing continuance, in contrast to Old Testament worship, which was prescribed by law and legalistically observed. Worship in the economy of the New Testament is indeed still not perfect but the time of perfection is coming.

Much that is arbitrary or irrelevant has been written about *middēy* (construct of *min day*) *ḥodhesh beḥodhshō* and *shabbāth beshabbattō.* But the interpretation does not call for any great ingenuity. *day* expresses what is complete, due, sufficient, abundant, cf. 40:16. *middēy ḥodhesh* then means "from the completeness of the month." The suffix in *ḥodhshō* is pregnant or emphatic, unto its, that is, unto its own, or the next month. Thus: "From the fullness or completeness of a month unto the next or following month," similar to our phrase, "from one month to the next," from month to month, that is, every month and every Sabbath. Cf. *middēy shānāh beshānāh* (1 Sam. 7:16; Zech. 14:16), from year to year.

24 וְיָצְאוּ וְרָאוּ בְּפִגְרֵי הָאֲנָשִׁים הַפֹּשְׁעִים בִּי
כִּי תוֹלַעְתָּם לֹא תָמוּת וְאִשָּׁם לֹא תִכְבֶּה
וְהָיוּ דֵרָאוֹן לְכָל־בָּשָׂר׃

The two perfects introduced by *we* are consecutive perfects, and they follow *yābhō'* in verse 23. At the same time they are also frequentative and are related to each other as protasis and apodosis: And whenever they go forth, they shall see, cf. Gr. 112, kk, p. 337. Their going forth has reference to *lephānay*, cf. verse 23. They go forth from My face, from before Me, that is from the temple. In the temple they are in communion with God through their worship, and there they receive His blessing. But when they go forth from the temple, they see the terrible fate of the rebels who have been under the judgment of God. When they go forth from the temple and Jerusalem (these two have already been designated a unit in verse 20), they come upon *ge' hinnōm*, the valley of wailing and groaning, which lay to the east and south of the temple mount. *tōpheth* also lay in the same area, and here it was that, since the time of Ahaz, children were slaughtered and burned as a sacrifice to Moloch, 2 Chronicles 28:3; 33:6; Jeremiah 7:31f; 19:6. Since very ancient times, filth and carcasses were burned in this valley in fires that were kept constantly burning, and hence the valley was a place of abhorrence for all Jerusalemites. The carcasses of the multitudes slain by the Lord (verse 16) are represented as being cast upon a heap in this valley, gnawed by the worm of decay and burned in the flames of an unquenchable fire. Those who go forth outside the city from before the face of the Lord see these bodies and their gaze rests upon them (*rā'āh be*). These are the carcasses of those known to the beholders as *pōshe'im*, here desig-

705

nated as *hā'anāshīm happōshe'īm* for the sake of emphasis. With this expression, which the prophet here uses for the second time, he brings his book to a close with its beginning, where he wrote *wehem pāshe'u bhī* (chapter 1:2).

It is entirely correct that the beholders are described as gazing with satisfaction upon the decaying and burning carcasses. If Duhm and the unbelievers scoff at the idea, what of it? Let them scoff. God's judgments on earth, like the World War, seem unspeakably horrible to natural man. But they are God's judgments, and they are meant to serve the salvation of His own. And as God Himself, in spite of all His gracious compassion, carries out His judgments with divine benevolence, so also the believers view them with satisfaction. The Christian gives his Yea and Amen to the unimaginably horrible torments of hell, because God has so ordered them and has Himself revealed them, although human nature revolts against the thought of eternal torment.

The description is given in pictures peculiar to the Old Testament. The contrasting fates of the saved and the condemned, of the blessed and the damned, are represented as continuing into eternity. The subject of *thōla'tām* (cf. remarks on the subject of *hēbhī'u,* verse 20) is the apostates. Their worm is the worm of decomposition, 14:11; 41:14; Job 17:14, etc. The worm does not die, they decompose eternally, their death does not cease. Their fire, that is, their torment (Matt. 13:42, etc.), will never be quenched. Yes, eternal torment — the Gospel teaches it. And they shall be a *dhērā'ōn,* an abomination and abhorrence for all flesh, for all blessed and holy flesh, whose blessedness will in no wise be diminished by the fate of those who perish.

And so, Isaiah closes his book. To this day it is offensive to the Jews, as it is to all unbelievers, including the unbelieving exegetes, such as Duhm. They avenge themselves on Isaiah by scoffing and blaspheming, as they do upon all Gospel. But it is the Lord Himself who summed up the Gospel and proclaimed it to all the world in the familiar words: "He that believeth and is baptized shall be saved; but he that believeth not shall be damned," Mark 16:16. — Isaiah preached nothing else, and it remains God's truth till the Day of Judgment.